Dido's Daughters

Literacy, Gender, and Empire
in Early Modern England and France

MARGARET W. FERGUSON

The University of Chicago Press
Chicago and London

Margaret W. Ferguson is professor of English and comparative literature at the University of California, Davis. She is the author of *Trials of Desire: Renaissance Defenses of Poetry* and has co-edited several collections of essays, an anthology of poetry, and a critical edition of Elizabeth Cary's *Tragedy of Mariam.*

The University of Chicago Press, Chicago 60637
The University of Chicago Press, Ltd., London
© 2003 by The University of Chicago
All rights reserved. Published 2003
Printed in the United States of America

12 11 10 09 08 07 06 05 04 03   1 2 3 4 5

ISBN: 0-226-24311-7 (cloth)
ISBN: 0-226-24312-5 (paper)

The University of Chicago Press gratefully acknowledges the generous support of the John Simon Guggenheim Memorial Foundation toward the publication of this book.

Library of Congress Cataloging-in-Publication Data

Ferguson, Margaret W., 1948–
    Dido's daughters : literacy, gender, and empire in early modern England and France / Margaret W. Ferguson
    p. cm.
Includes bibliographical references and index.
ISBN 0-226-24311-7 (cloth : alk. paper) — ISBN 0-226-24312-5 (pbk. : alk. paper)
    1. European literature—Women authors—History and criticism. 2. Literature, Modern—History and criticism. 3. French literature—Women authors—History and criticism. 4. English literature—Women authors—History and criticism. 5. Women—Education—England—History. 6. Women—Education—France—History. I. Title.

PN471 .F45 2003
809'.89287'0904—dc21

2003004087

For David
"With thee conversing I forget all time."

Contents

Illustrations

Acknowledgments

As is fitting for a book centrally concerned with questions about how writers construct and lose themselves in journeys across spaces and times—and between shifting terrains of oral and written discourse—these acknowledgments will inevitably be incomplete. The early stages of my research were supported by fellowships from the National Endowment for the Humanities and the John Simon Guggenheim Memorial Foundation. The Humanities Center of the Australian National University, under the generous leadership of Ian Donaldson, gave me an office and much collegiality during my first summer of reading Aphra Behn. I received substantial gifts of time from the University of Colorado, in the form of a Faculty Fellowship, and from Columbia University, in the form of leaves facilitated by two able chairs of English, Steven Marcus and David Damrosch. I thank them warmly. I also thank my chair at the University of California, Davis, Linda Morris; the director of the Davis Humanities Institute, Georges Van Den Abbeele; and the members of a Humanities Institute seminar at Davis (2001) and of a History of the Book seminar at Stanford (2001) for valuable comments on late versions of my work. Earlier audiences, too numerous to list here, enriched my thinking with many questions and counterarguments. Thanks also to Charles Middleton, former dean of arts and sciences at the University of Colorado, now president of Roosevelt University, and Elizabeth Langland, dean of arts and letters at the University of California, Davis, for materially enabling my research. I am grateful to the staffs of the libraries of Yale and Columbia Universities, and of the Universities of Colorado and California (both the Berkeley and Davis campuses), for acts of kindness far above the call of duty. Highly literate staff members at the New York Public, Newberry, and Huntington Libraries provided me with valuable advice. I owe particular debts of gratitude to Paul Saenger and Paul Gehl, of the Newberry Library. I am also extremely grateful to my editor at the University of Chicago Press, Alan Thomas; and to others at the press without whose patience and expert help this book would not have seen the light of day: Renate Gokl, Randolph Petilos, and Christine Schwab. As manuscript editor, Lys Ann Shore gave substantive advice of very high quality.

Earlier versions of some parts of this book have appeared elsewhere. Material from chapter 5 appeared in "Recreating the Rules of the Game: Marguerite de Navarre's *Heptaméron*," in *Creative Imitation: New Essays on Renaissance Literature in Honor of Thomas M. Greene,* edited by David Quint et al. (Binghamton, N.Y.: Medieval and Renaissance Texts and Studies, 1992), 153–89, copyright Arizona Board of Regents for Arizona State University. Some of the material in chapter 6 appeared in "Running On with Almost Public Voice," in *Tradition and the Talents of Women,* edited by Florence Howe (Urbana: University of Illinois Press, 1991), 37–67, copyright 1991 by Board of Trustees of the University of Illinois, used with permission of the University of Illinois Press; and in "Transmuting Othello: Aphra Behn's *Oroonoko,*" in *Cross Cultural Performances: Differences in Women's Re-Visions of Shakespeare,* edited by Marianne Novy (Urbana: University of Illinois Press, 1993), 15–49, copyright 1993 by Board of Trustees of the University of Illinois, used with permission of the University of Illinois Press. Some of the material in chapter 7 appeared in "News from the New World: Miscegenous Romance in Aphra Behn's *Oroonoko* and *The Widow Ranter,*" in *The Production of English Renaissance Culture,* edited by David Lee Miller, Sharon O'Dair, and Harold Weber (Ithaca: Cornell University Press, 1994), 151–89, copyright © 1994 by Cornell University, used by permission of the publisher, Cornell University Press; and in "Juggling the Categories of Race, Class, and Gender," in *Women, "Race," and Writing in the Early Modern Period,* edited by Margo Hendricks and Patricia Parker (New York: Routledge, 1994), 225–39, used by permission of the publisher. My thanks to the publishers for their permission to reuse these materials.

Throughout the years of this book's making, my students have given me a treasure of ideas and encouragement. Some of the students to whom I'm most indebted worked as my research assistants: Dan Cook, Pam Erens, Onnaca Heron, Jenny Hill, Molly Hillard, Katie Kalpin, Yvette Kisor, Bill Knight, Andrew Majeske, Judith Rose, Yumna Siddiqi, Elliott Trice, and Laura Wilson. Other former students, many of whom are now teachers, offered gifts of information, brilliant papers, acute questions, and critical readings of parts of my manuscript that I tried out in the classroom. I'm particularly grateful to Bianca Calabresi, Sarah Cusk, David Glimp, Heidi Brayman Hackel, Jennifer Hellwarth, Claire Kinney, Sara Morrison, Rhonda Sanford, Deborah Uman, Molly Whalen, and Liz Wiesen. I owe special thanks to Eve Sanders for years of intelligent help that culminated in a critical reading of my entire manuscript. I also warmly thank my teachers; they will see their marks in this book well beyond what the notes and bibliography say about them. To Harold Bloom, John Freccero, Thomas Greene, Geoffrey Hartman, Judith Herz, and Neil Herz I owe special debts; each of these teacher-scholars shaped my cultural literacy in ways I am only now beginning to grasp.

In addition to my students and teachers, others among my friends have contributed significant threads to this book's text; some dear friends (they will know who they are) have helped especially by unraveling my weaker threads. For help of many different kinds, and with regret that I don't have space to say more about each gift-giver, I am grateful to Katherine Acheson, John Archer, David Bartholomae, Elaine Beilin, Caroline Bowden, Seeta Chaganti, Mary Cregan, David Cressy, Katherine Eggert, Claire Farago, Joan Ferrante, Catherine Gallagher, Lowell Gallagher, Eileen Gillooly, Jonathan Goldberg, Nan Goodman, Margreta de Grazia, Margaret Hannay, Elizabeth Hanson, Jonathan Hart, Ralph Hexter, J. Michael Holquist, Jim Holstun, Clark Hulse, Alessa Johns, Ann Rosalind Jones, Constance Jordan, Peggy Knapp, Mary Ellen Lamb, Seth Lerer, Zachary Lesser, Kate Lilley, Joe Loewenstein, Julia Lupton, Nadia Margolis, David Lee Miller, Janis Butler Molm, Lise Nolan, Marianne Novy, Mary Nyquist, Sharon O'Dair, Stephen Orgel, Barbara Packer, Jill Phillips, Maureen Quilligan, David Quint, Régine Reynolds, Jeffrey Robinson, Peter Rudnytsky, Maria Ruegg, David Sacks, Winfried Schleiner, James Shapiro, Meredith Skura, Patricia Meyer Spacks, Gary Spear, Peter Stallybrass, Jennifer Summit, Charlotte Sussman, Thomas Tanselle, Ted Tayler, Betty Travitsky, Nancy Vickers, Ray Waddington, Wendy Wall, Claire Waters, Valerie Wayne, Harold Webber, Barry Weller, R L Widmann, Charles Wilcox, Charity Cannon Willard, Diana de Armas Wilson, Nancy Wright, Georgiana Ziegler, and Steven Zwicker.

Edward Said's work has indelibly marked my thinking on empire; his friendship has been a sustaining pleasure. Jean Howard talked me through much of the book and showed me how to rethink key parts of the argument. Frances Dolan, Carla Freccero, Richard Halpern, Ralph Hexter, Julia Levine, Heather James, Colin MacCabe, Marjorie McIntosh, Marijane Osborne, Albert Rabil, Elizabeth Robertson, and Mary Poovey read large sections of the book and gave rich comments. I am grateful for their help, and the book is much the better for it, too. Jennifer Wicke significantly influenced my thinking about feminist theory; I thank her for that and for her supportive friendship. Rachel Jacoff has educated me on Dante and on all things Italian since we began our friendship in New Haven years ago. David Kastan replied generously to innumerable cries for help with facts and fictions. This book is often in dialogue with John Guillory's work on cultural capital; conversations with John since our graduate-school days have enriched my life. Karen Newman read the entire manuscript and helped me shorten as well as sharpen it. Mary Beth Rose also read the entire manuscript and commented on it incisively. Her suggestions were full of learning and wit, as were the many phone conversations in which she lifted me from the Slough of Despond. I have been fortunate in my pre-print readers; they have made this a better book than it was. They are not, of course, responsible for the remaining mistakes.

My mother, Mary Anne Ferguson, also read the whole manuscript—in several versions—with critical acuity and great tact; I thank her, with love. I am grateful too for the many gifts, intellectual, emotional, and material, given me by my sister and brother, Jean and Stephen Carr, both experts in literacy. I am also deeply grateful for the support of my sister and brother, Lucy and Phil Tenenbaum; of my parents-in-law, Christiane and Charles Simpson; and of my daughters, Susanna, Marianne, and Christina. The history of these three children's births—and of their subsequent questions, jokes, and fibs—sediments several of the stories told in this book. My daughter Susanna deserves special thanks for helping me with notes and bibliography at a late stage of production. I also received valuable help during the book's endgame from Margie Towery, Betsy Blumenthal, Brynne Gray, and Laura Maestrelli. For her sustaining friendship and many gifts of time during the last six years of the book's writing, I thank Anna Marie Tucker-Schwab.

It's utterly conventional, and yet, to me, completely amazing, that I can end this opening gesture of saying incomplete thanks by naming David Simpson. He didn't type any of my pages, but he read them all and rewrote more of them than I can count. Without further words (on this page, at least), I dedicate this book to him.

Prologue

hic templum Iunoni ingens Sidonia Dido/condebat, donis opulentum et numine di-
vae. [Here Sidonian (Phoenician) Dido was founding a mighty temple to Juno, rich in
gifts and the presence of the goddess.]

VERGIL, Aeneid

Dido is not often associated with literacy, but in many stories she is both a victim and a perpetrator of lies.[1] Her skills as a speaker who shapes truth to fit
political and economic needs are closely linked to her strengths as the leg-
endary founder and ruler of Carthage. Whether Dido killed herself after listening to and being abandoned by the future founder of Rome, as Vergil maintains in the *Aeneid,* or whether, as an earlier tradition claims, she never met
Aeneas at all, her city became Rome's major economic and political rival after
her (disputed) death; it was subsequently destroyed and then, during the reign
of Vergil's imperial patron Augustus, rebuilt as a colony dedicated to the Roman goddess Juno. Dido's fate as a maker, receiver, and subject of narrative
turns out to be intricately tied up with debates about the history and legitimacy of the Roman empire. For this reason, and also because she became a focus for enduring debate about history and fiction, about licit and illicit sexual
behavior, about masculine and feminine social roles, and about the dangers of
speaking and listening to strangers, she is an apt guide into the theoretical and
historical territories explored in this book about literacy, gender, and empire.
The plural entities signaled by those three words constitute a site of historical
struggle in which the stakes are at once ideological, economic, political, and
erotic. I approach this reconstructed site as if it were a stage with changing
scenes. History is represented and explored here but also, necessarily, selected
and altered; figures gendered male and female sometimes play separate roles
but at other times blend or exchange them, often during fights for dominance
that almost always continue beyond a given protagonist's death.

   Because Dido is the only character in Vergil's epic to die in a way that somehow deceives not only humans but the gods—one of whom, Venus, has cruelly deceived Dido—she opens a space for my inquiry into a topic that is not
a recoverable set of facts but rather a set of shifting relations that are constitutively shaped in the very process of being interpreted. Dying "neither in the

course of fate [*nam quia nec fato*], nor by a death she had earned [in battle]"
(*Aeneid,* 4.696), Dido manages to escape Fate—however briefly—by dying
before her appointed time (*ante diem*) (697). She does so by committing suicide with Aeneas's sword, having led her nurse and her sister into believing she
was about to perform a ritual (perhaps a ritual sacrifice) for the Roman god
Jupiter who has, along with Venus, played cruelly with Dido's life. For a moment—one decried by her sister Anna as a moment of fraud—Dido surprises
the gods and many of Vergil's readers as well. In that moment of surprise,
supremely painful for Dido herself (her death is delayed because the gods have
not prepared for it), she becomes a brilliant emblem for a human departure
from a foreordained historical narrative. Although her fate is, of course, being
manipulated by Vergil, in ways that later writers will challenge as well as admire, the poet himself seems to grant to this one character at this one moment
an agency that creates a kind of rift in the poem's ideological fabric. The rift is
a mystery the poem leaves unexplained. Dido comes at the threshold of this
book because the multiple versions of her story challenge the notion that history had to happen the way it did, or that it did happen the way any single textual or nontextual source of information suggests that it happened. Dido's stories thus dramatize the existence of competing histories in what counts (for
some) as the cultural literacy of the West.

Alphabetic literacy plays a significant role in many scholarly narratives
about how an arguably modern world emerged from the era known as the
Middle Ages.[2] For some scholars, literacy costars with print and Protestantism
in a narrative of human progress toward enlightenment and toward increasingly representational rather than authoritarian forms of government.[3] For
others, literacy (or rather, a type of alphabetic literacy mistakenly equated with
literacy per se) plays a tyrant's part in the story of modern Western imperialism conceived as beginning in 1492.[4] For yet other scholars, literacy, usually
conjoined with numeracy, plays an ambiguous, Hamlet-like role in a drama
conceived less as a Whiggish comedy of progress than as a problem play with
tragic overtones. Members of all three groups engage in arguments about
literacy as a cause of new modes of abstract "spatialized" cognition, of apprehension of time, and of human interaction in a "bourgeois public sphere"
itself construed (and debated) as part of larger narratives about the development of nation states, of capitalism, and, more specifically, of a form of
capitalism we may just now be defining as an epoch with a beginning and an
end: what Benedict Anderson calls "print capitalism."[5]

Students of modernization have seldom attended to the ways in which literacy has historically been marked by ideologies of gender and by distinctly

gendered practices of language use. There is, however, important work on the gendering of education in early modern Europe; there is also an important branch of "history of the book" scholarship devoted to the content of medieval and early modern women's reading, as well as a newer branch of scholarship exploring various historically contingent and gendered "practices" of reading.[6] Feminist literary scholars, moreover, have done a great deal during the last two decades to find, edit, and interpret manuscript and printed writings by women while also expanding our understanding of women's reading. Modern feminist scholars in the anglophone tradition, however, have tended not to consider literacy itself as an object of theoretical inquiry. This situation is beginning to change through the work of scholars such as Eve Rachele Sanders, Linda Timmermans, Frances E. Dolan, and others who are exploring significant intersections between specific aspects of literacy and ideologies of gender.[7] Even those who have been taking gender into significant account as they illuminate specific historical processes of reading, writing, education, identity formation, and publication have tended to define literacy itself in a familiar way, as a set of skills construed as the ability to read and write in one vernacular language. Issues of gender and social class intervene, with important consequences, in the replication and distribution of literate skills, but the definition of literacy in terms of (unevenly) accessible skills in reading and writing is still widely assumed as a base for historiographical inquiry into the topic.

This pragmatic view of literacy is useful, even educationally compelling, in certain contexts. It is widely accepted not only by feminist critics implicitly protesting the unequal distribution of literacy in present and past Western societies but also by social historians of the early modern period; one recent historian remarks, indeed, that a version of this definition of literacy emerged (or, I would say, reemerged) during the early modern era.[8] This view of literacy is inadequate, however, for a mode of analysis that seeks to understand life-worlds different from our own and also to allow for ways in which those worlds might *not* necessarily have developed into modern societies as we in the West conceive them. Assumptions about the nature and value of literacy, deeply ingrained, of course, in members of the academic subculture, are among the hardest to interrogate, whether we are looking at past societies or at present ones in the developing world (think about the teleological assumptions underpinning the term *developing*). This book attempts to brush against the grain by arguing for a skeptical analysis of literacy as a shifting and plural phenomenon.[9] *Literacy* in my usage almost always connotes "literacies" and points to a social relation that has interpersonal, intercultural, international, and interlingual dimensions.[10] Instead of asking, "What is literacy?" we might ask, rather, "What counts as literacy for whom, and under what particular circumstances?" These questions draw on but do not stop with John Guillory's suggestion that we define literacy as the answers to the following questions: "Who reads? What do they read? How do they read? In what social and institutional circumstances? Who writes? In what social and institutional circumstances? For whom?" (Guillory, *Cultural Capital*, 18).[11] The answers to these questions will never be fully accessible to empirical research.

A definition of literacy that takes the form of questions rather than propositions is an important step toward seeing literacy as a site of contest. Another step is to supplement Guillory's definition with other questions that open the site of contest to questions of speech and of communication broadly construed.[12] Who has disputed a given definition of literacy? And who might have done so in ways we have to work hard to imagine in order to notice traces of them in the Western historical record? These latter questions destabilize definitions that implicitly assume that "good" literacy entails mastery of reading and writing in a single national or standardized language.

I argue that the idea of a uniform national language has a long and socially fraught history that, when studied, invites us to complicate our ideas about what it means to be literate in one's national language. Such languages, sometimes called "prestige dialects" by modern sociolinguists, have historical roots in competing ideas about the value and nature of languages, as well as about the social standing of those who teach languages to the young. Competing ideas about language are closely interwoven with competing ideas about female and male natures and their respective qualities: instability, for instance, is associated with "mother" tongues, such as English and Yiddish, whereas stability is ascribed to "paternal" tongues, such as Latin and Hebrew.[13] Modern debates about standardized languages often proceed as if speech and writing were distinct objects of study (and of instruction). I suggest, in contrast, that we should study standardization, a key facet of modernization, as a field of ongoing social contest in which various, often hierarchizing, ideas about speech and writing have significant social consequences.[14] So do debates about what counts as an appropriate language practice for a person of a certain social standing and related debates about what counts as foreign or alien in linguistic domains. Linguists estimate that between ten thousand and forty thousand new words entered English between the fifteenth and the seventeenth centuries; these were words "borrowed" (or stolen) from many languages. A similar lexical expansion occurred in France, though on a smaller scale. The process was hotly debated by clerkly writers, with some arguing against the new imports as tainted goods, while others advocated the enrichment of the native tongue. Many learned coinages introduced during this period did not have a long life; they are thus part of an arena of linguistic practice and reflection in which what was contingently defined as "outlandish" could fade from view as if the fading were a natural rather than a cultural process. To take a famous example of a writer who would undoubtedly be attacked today as a flagrant user of abstruse jargon, Shakespeare himself is credited with no fewer than seventeen hundred neologisms, including compounds. Of these, many became part of what linguists like to call the "common core" of a language (e.g., *amazement, negotiate, pedant*); many others, however (e.g., *dispropertied* and *superdainty*), did not, for reasons scholars continue to debate.[15] What enters or does not enter a given language over time is an enormously complex question, whether we consider time as the arc of history or as the time of an individual life, with the potent variable of schooling shaping the issue of what language one acquires and how many "hard usuall" words one can recognize, much less use. That paradoxical phrase "hard usuall," from the title page of an early English dictionary addressed to women readers, is one to which I return in chapter 2 (see fig. 2 below).

In those societies in which literacy counts at all as a marker of distinction—and thanks to the modernizing process, this means virtually all societies today—it solicits analysis as what John Guillory and Pierre Bourdieu have influentially defined as "symbolic" or "cultural" capital.[16] In the geotemporal period under scrutiny here—England and France between 1400 and 1690, when capitalism itself was an emergent rather than a dominant socioeconomic system—the concept of cultural capital cannot fully explain the ways in which literacy works as a site of social contest. Some in the population did not value literacy as we do, although some did—and these latter tend, for obvious reasons, to be those whom modern scholars cite. This point underscores my belief, shared with Guillory, that current debates about the literary canon and hence about "cultural literacy" are too often blind to problems of exclusion that occur at the level of access to the educational institutions that purport to provide students with the tools of literacy. Nonetheless, I do not wish to use a phrase like "access to literacy," as Guillory sometimes does in his argument, because it seems to me to concede too much to the (dominant) modern notion of literacy as a technology that one can acquire (buy) through schooling. Sometimes, and for some influential groups, literacy *is* just that; but sometimes it is not.

If you accept my premise that literacy is a site of social contest in the present and was so also—differently but consequentially—in the European past, you can see why the English word *literacy,* derived from the Latin *littera,* "letter," is a term shot through with historical ironies and signs of struggle. As we find ourselves daily invited to contemplate our own historical moment as a process of (uneven) transition from Gutenberg's galaxy to Bill Gates's, we may be in an increasingly good position to learn from looking back to a time when oral, manuscript, and print cultures overlapped and often competed. Looking back, we can note, for instance, that forms of literacy associated with the new technology of printing—new to Europe, at least—were often gendered masculine as well as marked (in England but not in France) with a lower-class stigma.[17] Forms of literacy and their attendant technologies have a long history of being differentially distributed across lines of gender, as well as across other lines with both empirical and ideological features (those between social classes, for instance, or nations, or speakers of different languages and dialects). If you are interested in why and with what consequences more boys than girls are learning computer languages in some parts of the world today, this book will provide you with some scaffolding for answers.

The book has two parts, of three and four chapters respectively. Part 1 focuses mainly on problems of defining and valuing literacy in the late medieval and early modern polities I analyze as imperial nations. Chapter 1 analyzes past and present definitions of literacy and the debates about its social value often embedded in those definitions; this chapter also considers questions of evidence. Chapter 2 studies the interlocking histories of French and English, in relation to Latin, as linguistic matrices for competing types of gendered literacy. Chapter 3 focuses on ideologies of "imperial nationalism" as a second-order matrix for gendered theories of literacy and for gendered educational practices. Part 2 consists of case studies of four women writers, two born in French territories (Christine de Pizan [d. 1417] and Marguerite de Navarre [d. 1549]) and two in English territories (Elizabeth Cary [d. 1639] and Aphra Behn [d. 1689]). None of these women offers us the kind of rich archive of evidence about historical reading practices that scholars have been fruitfully exploring in the wake of Lisa Jardine and Anthony Grafton's important work on Gabriel Harvey's annotations in the margin of his copy of Livy.[18] But very few early modern women, even those who evidently owned a number of manuscripts and books, left holograph records of their reading thoughts, and this is not surprising given that ideologies of gender tended to silence women not only as public speakers but also as the kind of readers who record thoughts on book pages.[19] Lacking the empirical archive that marginalia considered as "reading diaries" provide, we nonetheless have from each of these women a significant body of writing that testifies to active and sometimes highly unconventional ways of reading, including reflections on the politics and ontology of different methods of communication and interpretive communities.

While I recognize the apparent asymmetry of focusing on two French writers who wrote in the fifteenth and sixteenth centuries, and two English writers who wrote in the early and late seventeenth century, respectively, I believe that these four figures have enough in common, even as they differ, to qualify as exemplary cases in my revisionary history.[20] The writers studied in part 2, like other educated European women who could have been fruitfully studied as well, resemble Dido in the sense that they act on what they perceive as past wrongs by successfully seizing properties and prerogatives normatively defined as male.[21] These properties include specific male-authored texts (the *Decameron*, for instance, and the Bible), as well as discursive domains associated with competitions between men. These domains include epic and lyric poetry, historiography, theology, and travel writing. I argue that in the context of changing and competing ideas about gendered literacy in imperial political contexts, a type of masculine author figure produced by specific educational and publication practices was increasingly available to women as a role to be played or, in an alternative but equally significant metaphor, as a property to be stolen.

This study's central argument is that literacy is a social phenomenon surrounded and often constituted by interesting lies, as well as by highly interested constructions of evidence on the part of writers from various historical eras including our own. Texts by educated women writers—the writers whom I group under the rubric of "Dido's daughters"—provide ample and sometimes surprising supports for studying the history of literacy in close conjunction with the history of lying and hence with the history of those texts and institutional practices we study under and in the name of literature.

Let me illustrate this point with reference to the last of the writers in my grouping, the woman of letters whose name, perhaps a nom de plume, is Aphra Behn. According to John Dryden, Behn "understood not Latin," but she nonetheless contributed to a volume that Dryden compiled containing English versions of Ovid's *Heroides*, poetic letters ostensibly written by famous women to the lovers who had abandoned them. Ovid's *Epistles, Translated by Several Hands*, was published in 1680, and included Behn's "paraphrase" of Oenone's letter to Paris. The volume was aimed at readers who needed a translation to understand Ovid's appropriation of ancient female voices; questions about what we would now term "intellectual property" clearly intermingle with questions about why a book of translations from the Latin would not only include but boldly advertise the presence, among its "several Hands," of one conspicuously marked as female.[22] Dryden singles out Behn not only as a contributor from the "Fair Sex" who doesn't know Latin but also as one whose ignorance somehow challenges—puts to shame—the knowledge possessed by those (men) who do know the ancient language: "I was desir'd to say that the Authour who is of the Fair Sex, understood not Latine. But if she does not, I am afraid she has given us occasion to be asham'd who do."[23]

Dryden also calls attention to Behn as one whose translation strays further than the others' do from the original "Authors Sence"; whereas the men's translations take "some little Latitude" in their deviation from the original text, Behn's poem illustrates a type of translation Dryden classifies as "imitation" and describes as "assum[ing] the liberty not only to vary from the words & sense; but to forsake them both as he [sic] sees occasion." Dryden's choice of the verb *forsake* implies a witty parallel between Ovid's original text, forsaken at will by the female translator, and the abandoned women whom Ovid portrays as speakers and as writers of letters in the *Heroides*. Developing Dryden's suggestion in her highly self-reflective practice of free translation, Behn adds to Ovid's text a scene in which Oenone compares herself to an abandoned sheep: "Like me forsaken, like me forlorn," she exclaims.[24] Behn's additions (and there are many, for her poem is more than twice as long as Ovid's) give Ovid's poem new cultural resonances. Her version of his Trojan nymph Oenone fleetingly resembles Christianity's male hero on the cross, for instance, when she compares herself to a forsaken sheep (see Matt. 46:27).[25] And Behn's female speaker/writer also comes to resemble Vergil's Dido. Behn describes Oenone gliding "like a Ghost" through a "Grove" in a simile that does not occur in Ovid's text; the image ironically recalls Vergil's famous portrait of Dido's shade in the underworld, "embowered in a myrtle grove" (*Aeneid*, 6.442) and furiously silent in the face of Aeneas's lame efforts to excuse himself for abandoning her.[26]

In the textual landscape exemplified by Behn's work for Dryden's book, distinctions between translation, imitation, and original creation are often conspicuously blurred.[27] So are distinctions between male and female voices. Gender identity here becomes both a theme and a rhetorical construction, no less mobile than the phenomenon of translation itself. A perception of the cultural and ontological mobility of translation seems, indeed, to underlie the malleable notions of gender that attach to translation in the late medieval and early modern eras. Site and object of debates about political, religious, and erotic faithfulness, translation was famously defined as a "femall" mode of discourse by Montaigne's English translator John Florio in 1603; but that gender designation, perhaps tailored to flatter the six noblewomen to whom Florio dedicated his (Montaigne's) book in three different prefaces, should be read as one move in a discursive game in which writers could cross-dress to suit different occasions and readers (Florio, "Epistle Dedicatorie" to *The Essayes of Montaigne*, xv). In another preface (to his Italian-English dictionary, the *Worlde of Words* of 1598), Florio countered the Italian proverb, "*Le parole sono femine & i fatti sono maschy*, Wordes they are women, and deeds they are men," by announcing that "wordes and deeds with me are all one gender."[28] In the textual terrain exemplified by Behn's and Florio's works of translation, gender identity like literacy is a phenomenon that may be counterfeited.

I invoke Dryden's way of making a truth-claim about a woman writer's relation to Latin to dramatize the difficulty of taking statements about literacy literally. Desires—for fame, money, and sexual dominance, among others—swirl around in Dryden's preface and color what we see both of the male reporter and of the historical female subject whose degree and kind of literacy, as a reader and as a writer, is at issue. Such desires play a constitutive role in forming the archive about literacy. Why did Behn "desire" Dryden to publicize to the readers of a multi-authored book that one contributor "understood not Latine"? The formulation invites the reader's curiosity: we wonder if Behn may in truth have known more Latin than she instructed Dryden to ascribe to her; we wonder, too, if Dryden and Behn were somehow colluding in this jointly produced statement about a seemingly incredible feat of female literacy that puts men to shame. Above all, the formulation invites the reader to ask what it means to "understand" or possess a language and its literary products, especially a language such as Latin, which even in our own day has considerable cultural capital.[29] In Behn's time, Latin had significant, although not uncontested, cultural prestige and was notoriously possessed (in some fashion) by more men than women because Latin was taught in grammar schools that excluded women on principle, even if there were some exceptions in practice. Behn strikingly illustrates how a female writer and reader positions herself in complex agonistic relation to Latin and the kind of education it connotes. She makes her female gender conspicuously part of her literate persona as a woman competing on and for territory held by men. She thus at once enters and remains marginal to a literary and linguistic domain that she herself helps to define. This, I contend, is the domain of cultural literacy.

Behn's case as a translator of Ovid shows that an alleged lack of a certain kind of literacy may be a cultural and even an economic asset. Both Dryden and Behn, it appears, were using the project of Englishing Ovid's love letters to attract readers whose attitude toward Latin and its literary treasures might include a complex emotional mix of scorn, shame, and desire. The readership of a vernacular *Heroides* would have included some people who knew Ovid through Golding's translation of the racy *Metamorphoses* and Shakespeare's

uses of Ovid on the stage. Women might have been prominent among potential readers; Ovid was repeatedly named in conduct books, educational treatises, and theological discourses as a prime example of what women should
not read, lest reading endanger their chastity.[30] By assuming the masculine role
of "imitator" empowered to forsake her source, but also by mingling her English "female" voice with that of Ovid's nymph, Behn appeals to different readers while raising questions about gender, property, and economies of desire
that are highly pertinent to any analysis of the ways in which cultural literacy—often presupposing "basic" literacy in a standard language other than
one's first tongue—works as a site of social performance.

Behn the translator of Latin illustrates my argument for approaching the
topic of literacy with considerable skepticism about the evidence any single
party to the contest presents in support of his or her views. Statements about
one's own or someone else's literacy seem often to work like statements about
one's own or someone else's sexual experience. One may downplay as well as
exaggerate degrees and kinds of literate knowledge, depending on what one
hopes to gain from one's interlocutors or audience. Behn's statement about
her grasp of Latin is mediated through Dryden's pen and also through his own
desire, as compiler and preface writer, to sell his book to female and non-
grammar-school-educated male readers. Such readers might be intrigued by
the reference to a female translator who "understands not Latin" but nonetheless brings some, perhaps unfaithful, facsimile of its literary products to English readers. Behn's (reported) claim about her lack of Latin underscores my
claim that what counts as literacy is not only something we need to interpret
with reference to specific cultural and rhetorical contexts, but also something
that can be, and often has been, feigned. In early modern English, *to feign* can
mean "to counterfeit" as well as "to desire."

Gender identities are one of the things writers feign. Christine de Pizan
tells the reader in her *Mutacion de Fortune* that after being widowed and being
forced to write for a living, she "became male." "Je ne ment pas" [I do not lie],
she adds.[31] Like many other women writers, de Pizan represents her entry into
literary activity as a masculine performance. She also publicly reflects on (and
sometimes exploits) her female gender, as when she anticipates Behn by suggesting that Latin is a masculine domain (see chapter 4). In the domain of letters, facts about one's body and education may be fictionalized as the occasion
demands. The concept of gendered literacies as I use it in this book encompasses a set of practices by persons highly aware that they must write with or
against readers' expectations about gender roles; it also includes discursive
prescriptions and institutional rules working to divide literate practices into
male and female kinds. I am particularly concerned with modes of literacy dis-

cursively defined as "female" and, by an important ideological extension, as "imperfect"—a term often used in early modern medical discourses to define the female in relation to the male.[32] "Imperfect" literacies are partial according to different standards of full or true literacy. While partial forms of literacy are of great interest to me and to other modern scholars, I do not assume that modern, apparently ideologically neutral ideas of partial literacy are altogether distinguishable from late medieval and early modern ideologies defining certain literacies as appropriate for "imperfect" social subjects.[33] I argue that a professional class of clerks and educators, mostly consisting of men, played a key role during the early modern era in shaping historically novel and distinctly self- or "group"-interested notions of partial literacy. Defined with respect to ideas about Latinity, "mother" tongues, the social purposes of education, and norms of behavior appropriate to persons of different genders and social status, ideologies of partial literacy are a major focus of my study. When I describe modes of literacy as partial, female, or "imperfectly" male, I point to cultural constructions that affected the agency of many historical subjects of various social ranks. Women, I suspect, were disproportionately affected, but I have no statistical proof of this (I suggest later, indeed, that statistics about literacies are rarely a solid ground for an argument). My shifting ways of naming the aspects of gendered literacy I am analyzing may seem untidy, but I am attempting to avoid reifying my main subjects/objects of inquiry, while also respecting that they had and have material existences beyond the discursive realm.[34]

Concepts of gendered literacy, sometimes functioning as censoring ideologies, influenced practices, which, in turn, influenced how concepts of literacy were articulated, and to whom. The attempt to reconstruct aspects of this dialectic begins in and returns frequently to the problem of missing evidence, gaps in the historical record that are not just accidental but constitutive of the topic of literacy. Recognizing these gaps allows us to conceive of the past in terms of potentialities, roads not taken, as well as actualities—roads taken, for a variety of reasons, and with various costs as well as benefits for some social groups but not for others. That we can know only traces or parts of what we infer to have been the empirical contours of women's literacy (in terms of individual skills or of demographic extension thereof) adds to the epistemological complexity of the topic. It requires study of cultural theories and practices that shed light not only on historical women's practices of reading and writing but also on their opportunities for communication broadly understood. These include speaking, an important form of publication in the late medieval/early modern period as it is now.[35] They also include hearing others read; dictating words to scribes; and, in general, conveying thoughts to vari-

ous kinds of audiences through various media.[36] Although literacy is often
conceptually opposed to orality or, in some schemas, is seen as its natural historical successor, my study is concerned with both the material and the metaphorical connections among speaking, writing, reading, and communicating
in other ways as well—through embroidered images, for instance, or through
remaining silent when others expect one to speak.

A consequence of pursuing a dialectical and skeptical argument about the
relation between concepts and historical practices of gendered literacy is recognizing that "commonsense" (modern) definitions of literacy as the ability
both to read and to write in one language may blind us to the ways in which
literacy worked as a field of serious cultural conflict—only partially recoverable through the inherently problematic archive of written documents—during the centuries studied in this book. This era, which spans the common divide between the Middle Ages and the Renaissance (or early modern period),
saw a gradual shift not only from feudal to (increasingly) capitalist social formations, but also from a European society dominated by clerical literacy in
Latin and centered in Rome to a society increasingly parceled and marked by
lay (but still mainly elite) literacies in vernaculars associated with those entities later to be named nation-states.[37]

A focus on changes in the cultural domain of literacy allows us to see
important continuities in the rationales for territorial expansion given by different elites at different historical moments stretching from the ancient Roman empire through its medieval "Holy" successor and the late medieval/
early modern monarchies studied here, to the "nations" that Benedict Anderson and others have seen coming into historical view only in the late
eighteenth century.[38] In chapter 3, I attempt to clarify some of the historical
overlaps between ideas of the "nation" and ideas of "empire." By focusing
throughout on French-English rivalries that emerged over several centuries—
rivalries over language and over possession of territories on both sides of the
Atlantic—I attempt to show how different the old story of the rise of the vernaculars looks when we reread it as part of a contest between political entities
with imperial aspirations articulated, and sometimes critiqued, by members
of an emergent group of persons educated to serve the monarchy. The group
was predominantly male, but some historical women worked on its margins
and contributed gender-inflected perspectives to the project of representing
and justifying imperial nations.

At a time when many groups categorized as "other" were almost completely excluded from alphabetic literacy, European women writers straddle
in an exemplary way the ideological boundary between the "inside" and the
"outside" of a social group being newly defined as a nation-state. Until access

to European literacies for groups such as Amerindians and Africans expanded and changed, relatively privileged European women writers offer one of the few paths we have to the question of how people responded to being classified as illiterate or subliterate in an imperial context.[39] There are other paths that could and should be further explored, especially those offered by the growing body of evidence garnered in recent decades from manuscript as well as printed sources about how some nonelite European women (or men writing under women's names or anonymously) understood types of literacy as signs of social distinction.[40] My study contributes indirectly to research on women who had little or no formal schooling by calling attention to traces of sociolinguistic struggles for authority within the archive comprising educated women's writing.

This book seeks to disrupt the still-dominant scholarly consensus that neither historical women nor cultural theories about gender difference had much to do with the changes in literacy that have been seen as causes—or effects—of the modernizing process. Drawing on scholarship in several disciplines, I attempt to build conceptual bridges between two relatively new areas of interdisciplinary and international research: feminist inquiry, chiefly by historians and literary scholars, into late medieval and early modern ideas about gender, including those articulated by historical women; and the burgeoning field of literacy studies, which has developed since World War II with contributions from anthropologists, sociolinguists, psychologists, historians (particularly historians of the book and historians of education), and English composition theorists.[41] The last-mentioned group has much to teach colleagues in literary studies, who do not, as a rule, teach writing and grammar to secondary- and tertiary-level students whose literacy has been, for some years, in a state of perceived crisis.

My chief focus is on the Atlantic monarchies of France and England during the late medieval and early modern eras. No discussion of gender, literacy, and empire in these two polities can proceed, however, without some attention to developments that occurred in other countries and times; what counts as "another country" is indeed one of the questions my book examines, as do many of the multilingual writers I study. In the course of this book I refer to texts that were produced and events that occurred in Italy, Germany, Spain, the Low Countries, and elsewhere in the world.[42] Conceptualizations of non-European Others, including a Dido associated with the "luxurious" East, emerge in constant tension with changing perceptions of what and where Europe is. Some of my arguments about the gendering of literacy in two northern Atlantic monarchies will, I hope, have implications for cultural historians who focus on other political entities in other times and places.

I also hope to contribute to the growing body of work on gender and nationalism by a more sustained effort than has yet been made to analyze gendered theories and practices of literacy within the context of late medieval and early modern nation-building—and, in particular, with attention to the efforts on the part of a literate class to legitimate, but sometimes also to reshape and critique, those nations and their imperial ambitions.[43] I see these clerkly discourses as important for understanding not only the national borders reproduced in much modern scholarship but also the vexed border between the Middle Ages and what followed it—a period associated with modernity, regardless of whether it is named "Renaissance" or "early modern." As early as the fourteenth century, the Middle Ages were being constructed as a "premodernity" associated, in some still-influential schema, with femininity, lack of individuation, and oral, as opposed to written, modes of discourse. In some formulations of the period distinction, moreover, the so-called Middle Ages, sandwiched by definition between a valued classical era and a valued modernity both associated with "reason," were negatively associated with the non-Western—something defined as a potential threat to Greco-Roman culture. The sixteenth-century art historian Giorgio Vasari epitomizes this tendency when he contrasts "la buona maniera greca antica" [the good antique Greek style] with a style he attributes to the "Grecchi vecchi e non antichi" [the Greeks who belonged to the past but not to antiquity], which is to say, the *oriental* Greeks, or "Byzantines."[44] The Middle Ages, as a past that is "old" but not "antique," often serve as a repository for ideas about what is "not" the true modernity of the West. In this way, the Middle Ages resemble Dido's Carthage—a place where Vergil's Aeneas stops but does not stay.

Interrogating various scholarly accounts of the Renaissance or early modern period as the origin of the modern era, I attempt to write a history not of a world we have lost (in Peter Laslett's well-known phrase), but rather of a world we have arguably inherited—but only in part, and often by dubious means that were shaped and rationalized by specific groups and individual agents. The metaphor of contestable inheritance is central to my study and shapes my invocation of Dido as a muse. I also invoke Marx as a muse for this revisionist history. His scattered and often ambiguous discussions of the period he calls the "transition" from feudalism to capitalism have given rise to significant debates among modern historians and cultural theorists.[45] For my purposes, the details of these debates are less important than their starting point in Marx's effort to conceptualize a notion of historical transition that is not a linear progression. In this effort, he deploys a significant metaphor drawn from the realm of literary, specifically of dramatic, production: "Das Vorspiel der Umwalzung, welche die Grundlage der kapitalistischen Produktionsweise schuf, ereignet im letzten des 15. und den ersten Dezennien des 16. Jahrhunderts," he writes, in a sentence that one of his modern English translators renders as follows: "The prelude to the revolution that laid the foundation of the capitalist mode of production was played out in the last third of the fifteenth century and the first few decades of the sixteenth."[46] The German word *Vorspiel* signals something that comes before the drama—the prelude or prologue. The dramatic metaphor may color our interpretation of what Marx means by *Umwalzung* (upheaval)—something less definitionally assertive than "revolution." The metaphor of a prologue to a historical drama whose plot and even genre are not fully known informs my vision of the fifteenth through the seventeenth centuries as something that deviates slightly but significantly from what is usually denoted either by the word *Renaissance* or by the apparently less honorific but still teleologically charged term *early modern.*[47]

The concept of a prologue to modernity allows me some purchase on the problems of (overdetermined) causality and of retrospective history-writing encountered by any student of (western European) literacy. I draw on those aspects of Marx's work and recent interpretations of it that help us analyze past socioeconomic formations, without arguing that any single element *necessitates* a certain historical development.[48] My own project aims at once to demystify culturally dominant forms of genetic theorizing and to provide parts of a new narrative that does not claim that what literacy became, for "us," is what it was destined to be. I seek to steer a narrative path between a historicism which says that one can and should interpret the past without imposing on it one's present views and a presentism which says one can and should read the past *only* from the concerns and perspectives of one's present moment. As Walter Benjamin articulated this idea of a middle path, the historian's task is to "grasp the constellation which his own era has formed with an earlier one."[49] His metaphor of the "constellation" asks us to chart our place in relation to the multiple stars of the past—stars that make up a group recognizable to the observer educated about the existence of the known constellations—and to respect the peculiar features and "placements" of past moments relative to each other as well as to our present moment. (The present is imagined as one star in a constellation, not as the sun of a planetary system.)

Because many Renaissance educators saw themselves as the heirs of Rome, and as the revivers and rescuers of its Latin language, the history this book narrates about gendered theories and practices of literacy in the late medieval and early modern era(s) is inextricably linked to the long-contested story of

Rome's cultural legacy. Not all strands in that complex legacy originated in Rome, but most were transmitted to later generations by means of texts written in Latin. This is true even of those strands formed in parts of the ancient Mediterranean basin (Israel, for instance, or Carthage, in North Africa) that were, at certain historical moments, bitterly opposed to Roman values and/or to Rome's imperial dominion. As soon as we think about Latin as a critical instrument for cultural transmission broadly understood—a political, economic, and linguistic phenomenon that medieval and Renaissance scholars called the *translatio studii et imperii*—we are invited (though many have refused the invitation) to think about asymmetries of gender and class in the spheres of education and, more generally, of language use. Latin was taught, for complicated and institutionally significant reasons, to more boys than girls during the medieval and early modern eras, and it was taught more to rich boys in urban centers than to poor ones in provincial or colonial locales.

Few will disagree that a person's gender, social status, and region of birth affected, and continue to affect, his or her access to the cultural legacy of Rome. My study creates lenses through which to look anew—and in some ways askance—at cultural changes in the domains of language and communicative media that have often been described in terms of a transition from Latin to vernacular languages, and from predominantly clerical to increasingly lay educators. This perceived transition from clerical to lay literacy, discussed by Erich Auerbach and by many feminist scholars as an enabling condition for women's increasing participation in the cultural activities of reading and writing during the early modern era, is more complex, and has more counterintuitive dimensions than many cultural historians have allowed. My study cautions, for instance, against equating the "vernacular" too easily with the notion of a "mother tongue." A woman's lack of Latin could and often did go hand in hand with a certain perceived "illiteracy" in English. This is because "English" was a language beginning to be standardized, in part through school exercises involving English-Latin translation. It was not a language most people living in England knew in a way that indicated mastery or "true" literacy as defined by an emergent class of educators and writers. People lacking a proper grammar-school education could be mocked, then, as *illiterate* in a language we might call the "Latinate vernacular." This phrase names a form of English substantively marked, in syntax and diction, by the training of many elite speakers and writers of English, who relearned this language, as it were, when they were learning Latin in the grammar school. At issue are not only privileged uses and users of language, but also what counts as valuable knowledge in a given language. The historical process whereby different kinds of truth-claims were articulated and competed for authority has recently been the object of much scholarly discussion; in this book I call attention to some of the ways in which ideologies of gender served to distinguish valuable language uses—and genres of discourse—from ones deemed less valuable or less authoritative.

In a telling scene in *The Rivals* (1773), Sheridan's Mrs. Malaprop interrupts Lydia's thought process to exclaim, "You thought, Miss! I don't know any business you have to think at all; thought does not become a young woman. But the point we would request of you is, that you will promise to forget this fellow—to illiterate him, I say, quite from your memory."[50] Mrs. Malaprop's comic use of *illiterate* for *obliterate* illustrates an important strand in my argument: illiteracy, particularly of the kind that old and lower-class women exemplify in the literature of the late medieval and early modern eras, is part of a larger story about cultural remembering and forgetting. Mrs. Malaprop, like her older sister-in-speech Mistress Quickly, "often mistakes an abstract Latinate term for a like-sounding familiar and concrete one." Writing about Mistress Quickly in the phrase just quoted, Margreta de Grazia wittily remarks how Shakespeare's female character hears "'incarnate' as carnation (*Henry V,* 2.3.29) and charges Falstaff with being a 'honeysuckle' instead of a homicidal villain (*2 Henry IV,* 2.1.44)"; de Grazia's most telling example, for my purposes, occurs when Mistress Quickly hears the metalinguistic word *nouns*—a word known only to those who study language as a formal (and usually a foreign) system—as "wounds" (*Merry Wives,* 4.1.20).[51] This joke, with its allusion to the experience of physical pain well known to schoolboys studying grammar in Shakespeare's time, would have been funniest, I surmise, to the literate males in Shakespeare's audience. The example of Shakespeare's Mistress Quickly reminds us that those who were exploring what the "national" vernacular could do against Latin were transforming their native tongues (named "dialects" in the 1570s, as Paula Blank has shown) according to a linguistic ideal that went under many names in early modern French and English texts (e.g., "the King's English," "le bon français"). Sometimes denoting an ideal of speech and sometimes an ideal of "correct" writing, most of the names are obviously ideological fictions (e.g., "common English"), although modern critics sometimes write as if these names referred directly to a sociolinguistic reality. I argue that these various and fascinating ways of describing a language desired by clerks do point to significant, if unevenly distributed, changes in the domains of language use and education, but the names also work to mask the fact that there was no single mother tongue that mothers and nurses could have taught to their toddlers everywhere in the lands claimed by French and English monarchs.[52] The speech of those felt to lack literacy, defined as correct usage, was increasingly becoming the material for literate culture to study (in antiquarian projects) and to mock. The latter activity helped create defensive fictions on the part of those deemed illiterate, and the mocking worked also to solidify the mocker's identity as a member of a social group distinguished by its possession of (a type of) literacy. In a seventeenth-century collection of jests, Nicholas Le Strange offers a telling example of such a mode of social distinction: he names a female source, "my mother," for the following joke: "An illiterate Dunce should have read, we have meate sufficient for your selves and Provender for your Asses, and he Read, we have meate sufficient for your selves, and Peradventure for your Asses."[53]

This book dramatizes the importance of Rome and its dominant language to any historical study of why and with what consequences literacy in Europe came to be a set of phenomena to which, and to the understanding of which, gender difference matters—as do other modalities of social difference for which gender sometimes stands in, with problematic consequences. Such ideological substitutions are important for any study of social relations and language uses within imperial territories. How are such territories defined? Acknowledging the existence of important socioeconomic distinctions among types of empire and of imperialism, and acknowledging also the existence of much scholarship debating the nature of those distinctions, I take as a point of definitional departure Rupert Emerson's claim that "imperial" conditions are those arising "from the domination of one people by another."[54] I immediately qualify his definition, however, by remarking that my study repeatedly questions the notion of "one people." Without denying that some individuals felt themselves, often passionately, to be members of a single people—whether defined by ethnic, nationalistic, and/or religious criteria— and without denying that some discursive and visual representations of groups and individuals as one are critically important to conceptions of empire and to its much debated relation to capitalism, I want to stress that my use of the word *empire* signals a site of contested meaning rather than an empirical phenomenon whose precise features are specifiable. I examine statements about empire made by late medieval and early modern writers themselves, in conjunction with discussions by modern scholars. I am interested, however, not only in discursive representations of empire but also in the social conditions to which these representations imperfectly point. We can increase our understanding of those social conditions if we attend to historical women's heretofore little-studied discourses about past, present, and future empires. *Empire,* in this book's argument, like *literacy,* is a signifier that points to sets of questions rather than to answers. Empirical facts are part of the signified I seek to illuminate, but they are not the whole of it. I am especially interested in late medieval and early modern instances of what Mary Louise Pratt terms "contact zones" in *Imperial Eyes*, her study of post-Renaissance travel writing; I also draw on the concept of "internal colonies" developed by Lenin, Gramsci, and some more recent students of imperial forms of nationalism.[55]

Let me return now to Dido as a figure for the complexities of countering empire from within its sphere of literate influence, the sphere made by many texts that shaped historiographical narrative in support of Rome's claim to dominion without temporal or spatial end (*imperium sine fine*) (*Aeneid*, 1.279). My epigraph from the most culturally prestigious of such texts is meant to underscore the difficulty as well as the possibility of tracing and evaluating alternative stories. Dido's case shows that some alternative versions of an imperial story, even those that quite aggressively challenge an influential writer's claims to truth, may work to extend the empire's ideological dominion over its subjects—including those who live in later regimes that adapt aspects of that empire's regulatory vision.

The alternative Dido is not a unified or coherent phenomenon; she consists in certain writers' claims about dates, events, and names that differ strikingly from those made in Vergil's story; she also arises from subtle textual effects of allusion, elision, emphasis, and figuration. In both major versions of her history, she is a Phoenician princess who flees her native land after her husband Acerbus (Sychaeus in Vergil's story) is killed by her greedy brother Pygmalion, the king of Tyre. She takes her brother's treasure, movable property she feels she rightly owns through inheritance from her husband, and becomes an exile. Eventually, she founds Carthage as a prototypical colony whose name is the Greek rendering of the Phoenician for "New Town." She builds her city on land appropriated from a Libyan king (Iarbas or Hierbas) who later becomes her suitor. At this point, the traditions diverge significantly.

In the apparently older one, which surfaces first in fragments of a Greek history from the third century B.C.E. and which extends through Latin histories known to Vergil's contemporaries, through Christian patristic writings, through texts by Petrarch, Boccaccio, and others into the early modern era and beyond, Dido builds her city without ever encountering a wandering Trojan named Aeneas; indeed, as Ralph Hexter observes, traditional chronologies of Troy's fall and the founding of Carthage and Rome preclude such a meeting ("Sidonian Dido," 338). The heroine of this tradition, usually named Elissa, remains faithful to the memory of her dead husband and kills herself on a flaming pyre rather than marry Iarbas. In some versions, he threatens war if she does not marry him; in other versions, her own subjects demand that she take him as a husband.[56] In the other major tradition, which may not have originated with Vergil in all details but which was early on associated with his artistic power to make readers prefer fiction to history, Dido interrupts the

labor of building her city's walls to give hospitality and eventually love to a
stranger bearing an account of Troy's fall. Manipulated by quarreling gods
and maddened by a passion causally and figuratively related to her passion for
Aeneas's narrative, this unchaste Dido kills herself after being abandoned by
Aeneas.[57]

Medieval and early modern writers inherited not only two competing narrative traditions about Dido but also a tradition of commentary holding that
a great poet whose epic became a centerpiece of boys' education across Europe
had lied about an exemplary queen.[58] The Vergilian lie, as Christopher Baswell
has elegantly demonstrated, includes a significant curtailment of Dido's own
agency as a clever liar appropriating land for her colonizing project through a
stratagem having to do with a bull's hide.[59] In her *Book of the City of Ladies*
(1405) Christine de Pizan makes the bull's hide story a centerpiece of an allegorical reading of Dido that draws on elements of both the Vergilian and non-
Vergilian traditions to explore Dido's double role as colonizer and as victim of
another's colonizing mission. De Pizan's version of Dido seems to be the first
to make Dido's spoken manipulation of her tyrant brother and her African
host into an allegory for imperial writing—although one could argue that
Vergil's marginalization of Dido's agency as producer rather than recipient of
discourse implies just such an analogy.[60] Vergil indeed seems to stage a covert
competition with the Carthaginian queen by showing her quality of cleverness
at work chiefly in the stratagems she devises—and pays dearly for—in order
to die "before her time." De Pizan takes up the gauntlet Vergil throws down by
exploiting various aspects of Dido's textual remains to recreate her as a hybrid
figure for the female writer/reader's self-elected role as the builder of a city of
ladies on a "field of letters" occupied mainly by men. Among the masculine
authorities who, in de Pizan's view, promulgate erroneous views about history,
society, and female nature are not only Vergil but also St. Paul, whose epistles
to various audiences in a nascent Christian empire created a "stumbling
block" to later Christian women's efforts to communicate their ideas about religion and other matters through various forms of publication.[61]

De Pizan alludes to Dido in many works but focuses in the *City of Ladies*
on the challenge Dido poses to certain masculinist aspects of Rome's cultural
legacy. Among these, de Pizan includes various Roman tyrants' efforts to suppress Christianity in the centuries before Augustine's *City of God* represented
Rome as the quintessential city of sinful man. Adding a new element to the "alternative" Dido tradition as she found it, misogynistically inflected, in Boccaccio's *De claris mulieribus* (*Concerning Famous Women*), de Pizan presents
Dido as an imperial figure who not only lies to gain land but also "institutes"
laws and thereby founds a code of judgment that persists over time whether in

oral or written form. For de Pizan, "founding" laws seems to be the fundamental act of the literate governor; her definition of literacy includes the ability to speak both as a queen and as an evangelizing martyr who resists others'
tyranny. Thus de Pizan uses her own literacy to enter an ongoing contest over
Dido's cultural meanings and over the meaning of history itself.

De Pizan reinvents Dido as a cultural mother for the woman writer aspiring to appropriate textual territory for political purposes. The reinvention is
not a simple thing to assess, either from a psychoanalytic or from a historical
perspective, and many ironies inhere in my own attempt to read Dido as a maternal figure, of sorts, in an imperial cultural matrix. One of the most salient
ironies is that modern scholars have identified elements in the historical Dido-
materials, especially in the descriptions of her ritual suicide by burning, that
point to her connection with religious practices of child sacrifice regarded as
barbarous by the West. This practice was "central to the Carthaginians' sense
of themselves and of their enemies' [especially the Romans'] sense of Otherness," James Davidson remarks ("Domesticating Dido," 72). The gendered line
of Otherness that my own narrative traces often shows symbolic mothers and
daughters operating in morally shady territories, against as well as in alliance
with each other, in ways that dramatize competitions among languages, generations, and systems of value.

The name *Dido* is defined by de Pizan as a synonym for "virago" (manly
woman), but has been explained by modern scholars as probably derived from
an African word for "wanderer."[62] Dido's name stands at the threshold of this
book as a proper noun with multiple meanings that point to disputes about
various forms of property—the dead husband's or living brother's "treasure,"
the African king's land, the woman's sexual being. At once outside and inside
the cultural domain of Rome, Dido is an apt emblem for the divided perspectives on empire, and on property more generally, offered by the female writers
analyzed here as "Dido's daughters." These writers inherit from her a divided
perspective on Rome and on the laws of marriage and inheritance: such laws
rarely give equal rights to men and women. Some parts or versions of Dido's
story offer critiques of Roman imperial ideology no less sharp than her famous
snubbing of Aeneas when she meets but refuses to speak to him in Vergil's underworld. As Ralph Hexter explains, the epithet *Sidonian*, used to describe
Dido in the passage quoted in my epigraph, carried connotations of wealth for
Vergil's first readers; early commentators suggest that *Sidonian* in the Vergilian
context signified a constellation of ideas very similar to that which European
conquerors of America would later cite as part of the effort to legitimate the
conquest of new lands and the fabulous wealth those lands were thought
to hold. *Sidonian* signifies "'luxurious,' 'excessively pleasure-loving,' 'effemi-

nate'" (Hexter, "Sidonian Dido," 356). If Vergil gives us a Dido who stands in for what Romans perceived as Other and hence saw as ripe for conquest in the name of (Western) civilization, it is not surprising that later writers associate Dido with qualities of blackness, savagery, and duplicity that are important to emergent discourses of race. In the influential translation of the *Aeneid* begun by Thomas Phaer and completed (in 1573) by Thomas Twyne, for instance, Dido is described as the Moorish Queen of "Moores, that have of dooble toong the name." "Moorishness," however, does not necessarily connote a quality legible on the body's surface; the preface to this translation describes Carthaginians as "white Moors in Affrike."[63] The ideological connections between Dido, black and white Moors, and duplicitous tongues prove important for early modern writers exploring complex nodes of social difference in which one category can often substitute for another. For Elizabeth Cary and Aphra Behn as well as for Shakespeare, Dido's various stories provide a rich resource for exploring how her qualities of imputed otherness may migrate to (or infect) the men who come within her sphere of verbal and erotic power. The conceptual category of "Dido's daughters" can therefore include historical and fictional men who lose (or threaten) ideals of masculinity associated with Rome's long cultural imperium. Among these male figures are Shakespeare's Mark Antony and Othello, for instance, as well as Cary's King Herod and Behn's African prince Oroonoko; behind such characters are not only aspects of Dido and Aeneas but also aspects of Dido's "other" suitor, Iarbas.[64]

The "Sidonian Dido" whom Vergil depicts as building a temple to Juno has yet another resonance for my study. Why should a Phoenician queen build a temple to a Roman goddess rather than to the Semitic goddess Tannit? As Hexter asks, "Are the Punic peoples so lacking in their own history that they must adopt Rome's?" ("Sidonian Dido," 356). Vergil's epithet "Sidonian" (Phoenician), used in a line that shows Dido building a temple to Juno, dramatizes the difficulty later readers have had in imagining Dido as something truly other than an "outsider who wants *entrée* into Roman history and culture" (ibid.). It is hard to counter Vergil's version of Dido—and of her desires—because we lack the kind of evidence that historians and literary critics most commonly rely on in efforts at cultural reconstruction. "Even today," Hexter remarks, "the details of the Phoenician pantheon and its cultic history are not easily recuperated. They are reconstructed largely by triangulating archeological evidence and the literary testimonies of other peoples, since we possess few Phoenician and no Carthaginian literary, that is narrative or mythological, texts" (ibid., 347).

Because Dido comes to us from a culture that has left few historical records in the form of alphabetic texts, her story dramatizes problems having to do with literate culture's representations of modes of being perceived both as female (or effeminate) and as illiterate in the sense of lacking in what the dominant culture defines as necessary knowledge. From the fourteenth century at least, Adam Fox has argued, the phrase "'old wives' tale' was synonymous with tale-telling"; and by the sixteenth century in England, "old wives' tale" connoted "any story, tradition, or belief which was thought to be inconsequential or false" (*Oral and Literate Culture,* 175). The gendering of literacy that occurred, I claim, in the early modern era contributes to broad cultural debates about what constitutes "truthful" discourse and whose truth-claims will command belief. A contest among different truths in different languages marks the history of Dido as it unrolls across time and space. She is important for a study of literacy, however, because her figure poses questions not only about interpreters' roles in making history but also about how (or whether) we deal with gaps in the written record. Dido is among other things a famous name that points to such gaps, to things that fame forgot. From which African tongue did her "nickname" come? In what language did the Phoenician Dido speak to the Libyan prince Iarbas before she was made to speak in Vergil's Latin or (earlier) in the Greek of Timaeus of Taormina? And in what kind of perhaps non-alphabetical signs might she have "instituted" those laws which Christine de Pizan sees as critical to the woman's envisioned roles as governor and cultural authority? Can we project any "truth" against which some stable definition of Dido's lies—and the lies against her—could be measured? Dido oversees my effort to contribute to a new history of literacy that at least partially remembers forms of literacy other than our own, forms that are paradoxical (to most of us) because they entail thinking of literacy beyond the English word's literal rootedness in the Latin word *littera.*

Positioned by their experience of gender to be particularly attentive to questions about social distinctions and struggle for domination, the writers I study in part 2 stand metaphorically, as Dido/Elissa does, inside and outside a once and future empire. Also like Dido/Elissa, these writers play with and against the audience's expectations about proper feminine behavior. Each thus becomes a virago, a woman acting (in both senses of that word) like a man. These writers participate in a widespread early modern interrogation of gender roles: do such roles originate in God-given (and Fall-inflected) "nature," in language conventions, or, perhaps, in the clothes one chooses to wear or the pen one chooses to wield? Like the hero and heroine of the anonymous pamphlets *Hic Mulier* and *Haec Vir* (1620; fig. 1), the women writers studied in this book dramatize the ways in which rules of gender, like rules of grammar,

HIC MVLIER:

OR,

The Man-Woman:

Being a Medicine to cure the Coltiſh Diſea

the Staggers in the *Maſculine-Feminine*

of our Times.

· Expreſt in a briefe Declamation.

Non omnes poſſumus omnes.

Miſtris, will you be trim'd or truſſ'd ?

FIGURE 1

Title pages from two anonymously authored pamphlets about cross-dressing and gender confusion,
Hic Mulier and *Haec Vir* (1620). (*Hic Mulier* photo courtesy of The Newberry Library, Chicago.
Haec Vir reproduced by permission of The Huntington Library, San Marino, California, RB 61257)

HÆC-VIR:
OR
The Womanish-Man:

Being an Anſwere to a late Booke intituled
Hic-Mulier.

Expreſt in a briefe Dialogue betweene *Hæc-*
Vir the Womaniſh-Man, and *Hic-Mulier* the
Man-Woman.

London printed for *I. T.* and are to be ſold at Chriſt Church gate. 1620.

can be bent. Like the cutting of the woman's hair shown in the woodcut frontispiece of *Hic Mulier,* the bending of rules has costs. These too are explored here, not only with respect to writers socially defined as female but also with respect to the male writers these women so often imitate, debate, and threaten.[65] The clerkly traditions of writing that I analyze show competing notions of masculinity as well as of femininity at work and impinging in significant ways on definitions of literacy in imperial nations.

My exemplary writers participate in and benefit from a literate culture that valued secular fame despite the problems in doing so if one wrote (as three of my four case-study authors did) in the service of some version of Christianity. All four of these writers offer searching commentaries, in writing manifestly aimed at future as well as contemporary readers, on women acting in two apparently contradictory roles: as oppressed subjects of imperial regimes and as rulers, or potential (that is, self-imagined) rulers, of new worlds. I argue that there is a dialectical relation between the role of perceived victimhood and that of imagined ruler; I further argue that the sometimes disconcerting shifts between the two roles often depend on ideas about property, theft, and the cultural relativity of legal systems—all ideas deeply implicated in historical debates about, and efforts to legitimize, imperial behaviors on the part of individual early modern monarchs and their evolving states.

My exploration of women writers' fantasies of imperial rule overlaps in significant ways with Catherine Gallagher's influential thesis that "Toryism and feminism converge because the ideology of absolute monarchy provides, in particular historical situations, a transition to an ideology of the absolute self" ("Embracing the Absolute," 25). Her argument has considerable explanatory power, I believe, especially for writers like Margaret Cavendish and Aphra Behn who explicitly embrace royalist metaphors in their representations of female political (and literary) authority. Looking at women writers' imperial fantasies (which include fantasies of subjection and self-sacrifice) from a more international and longer historical perspective than Gallagher adopts, however, I also attempt to supplement her causal narrative. I consider, for instance, how literate women drew on and adapted humanist ideologies of fame for their imperial self-representations; I also explore the myriad ways in which they drew on—and sometimes heretically reformulated—key religious doctrines from both Catholic and Protestant sources. My readings lead me to attribute to women writers' fantasies of empire a more politically critical or at least ambivalent strain than Gallagher finds; the verbal fantasies I study criticize aspects of "absolutist" political ideologies—and their attendant theological rhetorics—in significant ways. The writers analyzed here appropriate discursive territory claimed by others (male and female) in order to guide their imagined audiences to new (or, more precisely, partially new) social visions, including a re-visioning of hierarchies based on gender.

Attempting to legitimate their own ambitions and discursive behavior, the educated women writers studied in this book (and I touch on many others besides the four named in the chapters of part 2) create authorial personae that both register and challenge their societies' ways of distinguishing between proper feminine and proper masculine behavior, especially in the sphere of language. Their education itself, however, and the constraints of the emerging system of publication for a metropolitan audience, limit the scope of any critique such women might make, as well as the language in which they might make it. These four women writers shed light on the complex processes by which Europeans sought to legitimate emergent nation-states as the heirs of the Roman empire. The legitimation of empire, as I construe it here, is not a monolithic enterprise; it includes much mystification but also some moments of serious ethical and epistemological critique. Building their own definitions of female literacy on the definitions they inherited from various sources, some well known, some almost buried in—or by—the archive, these women writers penned representations of empire worthy of attention, and requiring considerable labors of decoding; representing empire is not a safe business. As the figurative heirs of Dido, the women writers studied here invite us to ponder the paradoxes and limits of any representation of empire made in European vernacular languages whose grammars were derived from Latin and were formulated—and deployed—by men and women of letters schooled in the history of Rome. Although European women were less likely than men to have been deeply marked by the educational institutions that transmitted one of Rome's major legacies—the idea, as the bishop of Avila put it in 1492, that language is an instrument of empire—women who could write well enough to enter the historical record in a language valued by the makers of the archive communicate to us from within the imperial pale limned by the bishop.

The bishop of Avila's well-known statement is part of a complex effort to justify a novel cultural object—a grammar of a vernacular language.[66] A major task of the following chapters is to analyze the competing cultural meanings of such a book as it was seen by its author and by its differently positioned potential readers. Among these were women who acted like men by writing as well as reading texts in various languages. In so doing, they used language to legitimate ideologies of empire, while also offering alternative visions of worlds in which property is more justly apportioned than it was in the world they inherited. In the following chapters, we will often see literacy equated with many different kinds of property: land; movable objects; daughters and wives claimed by fathers and husbands; Africans made into American slaves by "lying" English Christians. The metaphorical equations are important, but they are also reductive. This book argues that literacy, historically speaking, is something far more complex and unbounded than most modern concepts of property allow.

~ PART ONE ~

Theoretical and Historical Considerations

Competing Concepts of Literacy in Imperial Contexts
Definitions, Debates, Interpretive Models

Complicating and "problematizing" are the characteristic activity of the academy, which takes things that ostensibly, from the commonsense point of view, seem simple and uncontroversial—a literary classic, a war, an election, an epidemic, a comic strip— and shows that they are . . . less stable and self-evident than we thought.
GERALD GRAFF, *Beyond the Culture Wars*

A key hypothesis of this chapter is that literacy becomes an urgent definitional and political problem, a concept around which debates arise, in geo-temporal contexts we can describe as imperial according to the general criteria discussed in my prologue. It is when empires are rising or falling—and hence producing numerous discourses of legitimation—that competing definitions and practices of literacy most strikingly appear in the historical record. These conditions obtain, of course, throughout the modern period broadly construed (1400–2000). Whether predominantly pursuing colonizing or decolonizing policies, imperial states engage in similar projects of rationalization, political control, and disciplining of subjects. Regimes of education and literacy are central to such projects. Although in later chapters I am primarily interested in emergent empires, here I attempt to explore some of the ways in which our views of early modern empires and their literacies are not only shaped (as they must inevitably be) by our own historical position but also deformed (in ways they needn't continue to be) by inadequate reflection on some of the investments in empire that we, as modern writers and readers, share (in part) with some of our educated forebears.

As a modern academic emphasis with roots in sociology, psychology, anthropology, linguistics, the history of education, literary studies, and philosophy, literacy studies arose in North American and Western European universities after World War II.[1] In those years the United States was assuming new imperial powers (arguably to conduct a form of colonization that gave novel importance to the domains of culture and communication), while the United Kingdom and France were engaging in processes of imperial withdrawal and disaggregation. Given this context for the emergence of literacy studies as a heterogeneous and international (albeit mainly a First World) academic area (not quite unified enough to be a field), it is not surprising that one of the few modern scholars who has attempted to survey the discursive area as a whole, Harvey Graff, has concluded that almost all of the scholars working on literacy from the 1950s to the present, both in older areas such as anthropology and cognitive psychology and in newer areas such as the history of the book, have "labored under the spectre and shadows of modernization theories with their strong assumptions of literacy's role, powers, and provenance" (*Literacy Myth*, xvi). This means that much of the scholarship on literacy produced in modern universities—and such scholarship is the main focus of this chapter's inquiry—has had the expansion and/or the decline of empire as a major condition of production.

The symmetry of the contemporary (post-1945) attention to a "crisis" in literacy with the differently institutionalized but similarly urgent dramatization of literacy in the early modern period speaks for another condition shared by early- and late-modern imperial states: they are never stable entities, never secured forever; on the contrary, they require a constant effort to create what is supposed to be already there by disciplining both the internal and the peripheral components of their populations—both an "us" and a "them" (who may, with education, become [like] us). This claim helps to explain certain similarities in the structures of arguments about literacy made by scholars in the early modern era and scholars writing yesterday and today. Among the latter group, moreover, similarities of argument exist beneath what appear to be highly divergent political views. We will see such similarities occurring along a spectrum from regarding modernization as an admirable advance in civilization (that word being a historically significant synonym for "culture") to regarding it as a social process immensely destructive of cultures in the plural, anthropological sense of the term—the social entities we call "indigenous" or "local" or "popular" cultures depending on our disciplinary formation.[2] In the last decade, scholars whose research depends on the past or present existence of such entities have become more likely than their predecessors in the 1950s and 1960s were to see European alphabetic literacy as a tool of hegemony (understood as manufactured consent) or of overt domination in colonizing projects, such as that which the Spanish undertook in sixteenth-century New Spain.[3]

Walter D. Mignolo has studied a set of early modern Spanish writings about the vernacular language that may be regarded as ur-texts for many modern debates about the ontology of literacy and its social effects. In *The Darker Side of the Renaissance*, Mignolo analyzes, among other foundational works on Western literacy, the *Gramática de la lengua castellana* by Elio Antonio de Nebrija, composed in 1492; a treatise on orthography that Nebrija published in

1517; and Bernardo de Aldrete's treatise on the origins of Castilian (*Orígenes de la lengua castellana*) of 1606.[4] The first of these texts is the subject of the well-known anecdote to which I alluded at the end of my prologue: Nebrija's carefully constructed reminder to Queen Isabella of a verbal exchange in which his own voice was replaced by the more authoritative voice of a bishop. Addressing the queen now in a written and printed prologue, and using his familiarity with her to enhance his prestige with other readers, Nebrija describes the moment when he presented a draft of his grammar to the queen and she asked him "what end such a grammar could possibly serve": "Upon this, the Bishop of Avila interrupted to answer in my stead. What he said was this: 'Soon Your Majesty will have placed her yoke upon many barbarians who speak outlandish tongues. By this, your victory, these people shall stand in a new need; the need for the laws the victor owes to the vanquished, and the need for the language we shall bring with us.' My grammar shall serve to impart them the Castilian tongue, as we have used grammar to teach Latin to our young."[5] Nebrija articulates a view not only of the social function of alphabetic letters but also of their superiority to images for conveying ideas; both theories emerge in the context of his analysis of the Spanish New World as a sphere where there are, in his apparently innocuous phrase, "many different voices."[6] Controlling those differences turns out to be a key aim of Nebrija's theory of language. The grammarian's belief in the superiority of the alphabetic letter over other writing systems he regards as pictographic, Mignolo suggests, was a function of desire not to "represent" the voice faithfully in writing but rather to "tame" the voice seen as an unruly generator of variation (*Darker Side of the Renaissance*, 43, 319). Unlike theorists in the tradition identified and critiqued by Jacques Derrida—the "phonocentric" tradition that understands writing as an imitation of speech—Nebrija belongs to a graphocentric tradition that has roots in classical and medieval clerkly views of Latin.[7] Avatars of this tradition are no less important than phonocentric thinkers for understanding ideologies of ethnocentricity critical to the emergence of modern empires and to modern debates about literacy. If, as Derrida argued in an essay of 1966, "ethnology could have been born as a science only at the moment when a de-centering had come about: at the moment when European culture . . . had been *dislocated*, driven from its locus, and forced to stop considering itself as the culture of reference," then we can begin to see the significance of Nebrija's grammar—and its justificatory preface—in the long history of modernization as a legitimating discourse for empire.[8] Nebrija articulates his theory of the superiority of the alphabetic letter to other modes of writing just when an educational ideology, developed in relation to small groups of children learning Latin under the institutional umbrella of the Roman Catholic Church, was being adapted

to rationalize types of vernacular language instruction needed by monarchical states for potentially large groups of subjects. These groups included not
only children but also those adults perceived as in some sense like them—"imperfectly" developed at present but perhaps (and here is the political rub) with
the potential to become like educated men in the future. Within that "perhaps" and those analogies lurk many early modern perceptions of literacy
as a double-edged sword, a commodity or a power (conceptions differ) that
may be abused to foment disorder as well as used to cement or extend it.[9] Barbarians and women were often caught within the web of thought that viewed
literacy as a tool of social control that could under certain circumstances be
turned against the rulers and hence needed constant regulation.

The early modern graphocentric tradition epitomized in Nebrija's grammar of Castilian has modern heirs in influential histories of writing, such as
that of I. J. Gelb, which was first published in 1953. Gelb does not construe
writing as an imitation of speech but does see alphabetic writing as something more conceptually advanced than ancient Indian petroglyphs or the
more recent "pictographic" letters sent between North American Indians
consigned to reservations. "Such pictures do not represent writing," Gelb insists, "because they do not form part of a conventional system of signs and can
be understood only by the man who drew them or by his family and close
friends who had heard of the event" (*Study of Writing*, 27). Belying the latter
contention in his own interpretations of numerous "primitive" pictures by Indian men (and even one by an Indian woman to her lover), Gelb makes his argument elegantly and dogmatically circular by insisting that Native American
picture-writing is not a "conventional system of signs" because it *originates* in
mimesis even if the signs *look* highly stylized: "There is no doubt in my mind
that such geometric designs do not represent abstract forms but are the result
of a schematic development from real pictures."[10]

Gelb's words, like Nebrija's, should be read as products of a long tradition of Eurocentric thinking that associates the Latin alphabetic letter with
the values of cultural literacy understood as a mark of—and a capacity
for—(Western) civilization itself. Although Claude Lévi-Strauss belongs to
a phonocentric rather than a graphocentric branch of this tradition, it is the
conceptual struggle for and about a European (or European–North American) center that matters to my argument, and it is that struggle which Lévi-
Strauss's famous essay "The Writing Lesson" from 1955 will help us to examine in some detail later in this chapter. His essay offers a cogent and quite
complex statement of what has subsequently become known as the "Great
Divide" (or "Great Leap") theory of literacy, one of the two major positions
at stake in postwar debates on the topic. Although that theory, dominant in

the 1960s and 1970s, has often been critiqued in recent years (most extensively by Brian Street in a series of works beginning with his 1984 study *Literacy in Theory and Practice*), it continues to exert considerable pressure on historical studies of literacy as well as on popular notions of education. Its key assumptions are that literacy is a transcultural set of technologies for reading and writing, and that those who possess these technologies think differently—in a fundamental way—from those who do not. Street attacks members of this school for considering literacy to be an ideologically neutral technology and for thus, often unwittingly, serving as apologists for modernization considered as a form of Western imperialism. Street draws on Derrida's authority to advocate an alternative model of literacy as a culturally "embedded" and hence highly variable set of theories and practices of communication. Street makes particular use of the famous but difficult concept of "arche-writing" that Derrida introduced in *De la grammatologie,* in a chapter mounting a detailed critique of Lévi-Strauss's "Writing Lesson." Using Derrida's concept of arche-writing to set forth a relativistic argument that every culture has its own specific forms of literacy, Street, like others who translate Derrida for their own polemical purposes, sometimes simplifies his position on questions of epistemology and ethnocentrism. Because Lévi-Strauss and Derrida dramatize a strong version of the debate between what might be called an essentialist and a relativist view of literacy, I rehearse their positions in some detail later in this chapter.

My return to a French debate on literacy from the 1950s and 1960s is one of the several efforts this chapter makes at bridge-building—at translations, that is, across times and spaces and languages. Drawing connections between modern debates about literacy and scholarship on medieval and early modern literacy is one of those efforts; another consists in enlivening, perhaps even extending, conversations between those who do literacy studies in various academic sites and those who do literary studies, especially but not only literary theory, in North America, the United Kingdom, and France. *Literacy* does not appear in Frank Lentricchia and Thomas McLaughlin's well-known handbook *Critical Terms for Literary Study.* Although there are some well-known literary critics who have made literacy a central part of their object of inquiry in recent years, most literary theorists (as opposed to the group that has come to be known in the United States as composition theorists) have remained marginal to the development of literacy studies as a field.[11] This is partly caused, I believe, by the widening institutional divide between those who teach literature and literary criticism at the college level, either in English or in foreign language departments, and those who teach allegedly more basic literacy skills in composition courses and in those language courses focusing on grammar and conversation—the prerequisites, as they are called, to the study of literature by students who commit to it through the institutional choice of a major. There is a growing body of critical commentary on this stratification in language and literature branches of the humanities.[12] This stratification is often dramatized by the existence of differently remunerated teaching staffs for the language and the literature sectors of departments with words like *English, German,* and *Romance Studies* on their Web pages.

My call in this chapter and throughout this book for opening—and revisiting—lines of communication between the institutionally separated spheres of literacy and literary studies sets the stage for my contention that the gendered ideology of "imperfect" literacy cannot be effectively analyzed in any of its historical instances (including that which I hypothesize as existing in our own North American educational context) unless skills of critical reading, often considered the preserve of advanced literature students and their graduate and faculty teachers, are more fully deployed than they have been on the questions of language, evidence, and symbolic violence at the heart of modern debates about literacy. This is not to privilege literature—much less a notion of "literary language"—as something that can rescue or improve literacy studies; it is, however, to say that habits of attention and, above all, of skepticism—habits that can be fostered in any part of the educational institution but that are sometimes associated, often disapprovingly, with the domain of deconstructive theory—are in my (not disinterested) view critical to remedying a situation of divorce that is arguably having unhealthy repercussions.

Literacy and/as Literature

Literacy and *literature* intertwine so tightly . . . that the latter has never ceased to imply both the ability to read and the condition of being well read—and thereby to convey the sense of *polite learning* through the arts of grammar and rhetoric.

TRINH T. MINH-HA, *Woman, Native, Other*

Occasionally an academic book exerts influence far beyond the academy. One such is E. D. Hirsch's *Cultural Literacy: What Every American Needs to Know* (1988). It has authorized, for instance, the production of ingenious educational devices for a market of anxious parents: flashcard sets of useful facts designed for children as young as kindergarten and increasing in alleged difficulty for each grade level. The production of flashcards also reinscribes one of the traditionally reductionist ideas of what "literacy" is: something made of simple, portable items of information. The flashcards teaching cultural literacy are fascinating symptoms of a widespread feeling that the public schools are somehow not doing their job, and that literary critics, especially those who explore deconstructive theory in abstruse jargon, are doing nothing useful to remedy the situation. "Facts" such as the "functional illiteracy" of 20 percent of adults in the United States are bruited about, and an "international literacy crisis," as Harvey Graff dryly remarks, is "proclaimed for the late twentieth century" and for the early twenty-first as well.[13] Statements about the crisis come from the left as well as from the right: "Twenty-five million American adults cannot read the poison warnings on a can of pesticide, a letter from their child's teacher, or the front page of a daily paper," Jonathan Kozol states in *Illiterate America* (4). One may well agree with Kozol's general argument, in this and other books, that unequal distribution of wealth is blighting American society and undermining its democratic claims to educate the young, but one should nonetheless, I suggest, question Kozol's use of a literacy/illiteracy dyad to carry his larger political critique. What potentially mystifying work is that binary opposition doing, especially when it appears, as it so frequently does, bolstered by the authority of statistics? How do we know—how does Kozol know—how many Americans can't read the label on a pesticide can?[14] Where, in other words, do the numbers come from?

The crisis of literacy is regularly linked (although not by Kozol) to the failure of educators to teach good English either in primary and secondary schools or in the college-level courses known as "freshman English." I refer here to an ideological construction of what *should* be accomplished in such courses; this is quite different from what is actually now being done in many courses, where the emphasis is on critical thinking and the processes of writing rather than on correction of student errors in grammar.[15] The relation between pedagogical practice, legitimating theories produced in academic settings, and the more amorphous set of perceptions about teaching to which I allude is complex; but those perceptions lie at the horizons of my argument, and I hope ultimately to shed some light on them—which is not the same thing as altering them—by looking critically at aspects of the long if tense marriage that used to exist (in languages with large inheritances from Latin) between ideas of literacy and ideas of literature.

"Originally," writes Donald Kelley, "'literature' (*literatura*) was the Latin for the Greek alphabet and the term *grammatice,* as Polydor Vergil and other humanists noted; but even in classical times it displayed expansionist tendencies. 'Springing from a tiny fountainhead,' Quintilian wrote, 'it has gathered strength from the historians and critics [*historicorum criticorumque*] and has swollen to the dimensions of a brimming river.'" Since then, "'it has usurped practically all the departments of knowledge'" ("Writing Cultural History," 357). "Literature," in this now quaint-seeming philological vision, has an imperialist history and no single referent, since its "original" meaning (in the Greco-Roman tradition) is to signifiers, alphabetic letters. Even though other scholars present different (and less certain) genealogies for the Latin word, Kelley's definitional argument is interesting in part for its multilingual presentation: literature, he writes, is "*bonae literae, belles-lettres*" (ibid., 355).[16] His specialist readers are presumed to know these phrases ("good letters, beautiful letters"), and thus the scholars' own discourse illustrates the connection between cultural literacy and an education in a literary curriculum ambiguously reliant, for centuries, on translations, but nonetheless purporting to concern elements in a Western cultural unit whose members in principle communicate freely across national borders. This is the course of study known informally as "Greats" at Oxford and, more formally, as "Literae Humaniorum." Kelley focuses attention on a definitional tradition that has classical roots but a Renaissance humanist reincarnation, French Enlightenment ratifications, and some continuing institutional life in Oxbridge and in the "core" curriculum humanities courses at, for example, Columbia University and St. Johns College. The original rationales for and continuing existence of such courses support Guillory's argument that "the 'West' is a real political-economic entity, even though its cultural homogeneity lags far behind the unity of its politico-economic system. The image of that cultural unity remains . . . [an] ideological support for the real unity of the West in its imperial relations with the Third World" (*Cultural Capital,* 355n. 64). Such courses, however, may be more marginal than central to social reproductive processes in modern Western societies today, as scholars such as Guillory and David Bartholomae have recently argued from quite different critical angles of vision.

Bartholomae has shown that, as early as the 1930s in the United States, some adult literacy programs were excluding "literature," in the sense of "imaginative writing," from the types of materials deemed best suited for literacy instruction, construed as "basic" instruction in one linguistic code.[17] The same tactic is visible in one of the earliest books aimed at teaching adults to read a vernacular language, Giovanni Antonio Tagliente's *Libro maistrevole* (Venice, 1524). Bypassing the short religious texts common in vernacular primers for children and completely uninterested in the Latin literary models stressed in humanist grammar schools, Tagliente starts his students off with lists of mercantile phrases and proceeds to models of business letters.[18] This example suggests that the history of commercial literacies has a certain autonomy, although it clearly also should be studied in relation to the history of literacies grounded in literary curricula and, for centuries, tied to instruction in Latin both in Protestant and in Catholic (especially Jesuit) secondary schools.

"The historical function of the literary curriculum," Guillory argues, is "no longer crucially important for the social order" (*Cultural Capital*, 263). He provocatively defines that function as "to produce at the lower levels of the educational system a practice of Standard English, and at the higher levels a more refined bourgeois language, a 'literary' English" (ibid.). I share Guillory's interest in the relation between literature reified as a body of texts and education in a national "standard" language; I argue, however, that both in the early modern era and today, the ideology of a national standard language has been closely linked to ideological disputes about the value (and indeed the nature) of multilingualism. I do not think we can generalize about a decline in the social utility of literary curricula—as pedagogically instantiated in U.S. departments of foreign languages as well as in departments of English—until we incorporate questions about multilingualism directly into our analyses of the contemporary humanities system in general and, in particular, the hierarchical linguistic situation Guillory himself analyzes with reference to sociolinguistic theorizations of "diglossia" (for a discussion of this term, see below). Changes in the social function of the literary curriculum have many causes; the one I focus on here supplements Guillory's analysis by emphasizing historical precedents for an ideological contest that appears, today, in the distinction between instruction in literature and instruction in what counts, in the American university context, as more basic subject matter: writing a language correctly and, in foreign language curricula, speaking it correctly, too. The hierarchical relation between different kinds of multilingualism—one of which, I argue, has masqueraded historically as a national or common English—is highly unstable.

If defining "literature" in relation to literacy is a precondition for sharpening the terms of our contemporary arguments about the current functions of literature and language instruction in the American academy and in the society at large, we can profitably start by revisiting Raymond Williams's statement (from 1976) about the deceptive simplicity of the "conventional contemporary meaning" of *literature* (*Keywords*, 183). Williams counters that impression of simplicity by noting that until the nineteenth century, *literature* and *literacy* were used interchangeably to denote both the condition of being well-read and an ability to read (and/or write) alphabetic letters with some degree of competence (ibid., 184). *Literature* came to refer to a given literary work or production only at the end of the eighteenth century; and its first appearances in its common modern sense of "literary production as a whole" occur in the early nineteenth century, at about the same time as the French noun *littérature* acquired this same meaning.[19] Only fairly recently, then, has *literature* become semantically separated from *literacy* in English usage. In the second edition of Johnson's *Dictionary* (1755), the only meanings given for *literature* are "learning" and "skill in letters." If you were *literate,* in the England of Ben Jonson or Samuel Johnson, you had *literature,* conceived as a kind of thing or possession rather than as an activity of interpretation and writing. This conception still lurks, I believe, in modern notions of cultural literacy and in the structure of some secondary- and college-level courses that attempt to give students an acquaintance with a multilingual tradition in ten or thirteen weeks.

The *Oxford English Dictionary* offers examples of *illiteracy* going back to 1660, nearly two hundred years before this dictionary's first examples of *literacy* as a noun; the compilers opine that the latter term was created because the former needed an "antithesis." But the wonderful word *illiterature,* glossed as "illiteracy," occurs as early as 1592, and the adjectival *illiterate* (also spelled "illiturate"), denoting "ignorant of letters or literature," is first cited for 1556, in a passage attacking judges. In his *Dictionarie of the French and English Tongues* (1611), Cotgrave defines *Illeteré/ée* as "illiterate, unlearned, ignorant." The notion of "illiteracy" as a mark of low social status bleeds quietly into English from Latin clerical culture; one can hardly tell when the concept or the word become properly English. *Litteratus* in classical Latin, however, had one meaning not carried over into early modern English: although it did have the familiar meaning of "liberally educated" or "well read," it could also mean—when applied to a person of servant or slave status—branded, marked with an owner's letters (*litterae* or *literae*: the number of t's varies both in Latin texts and in vernacular citations of them, giving the word and its cognates, notably *litteratus/literatus,* an interesting material instability).

I will have more to say later about the problems of hierarchical social relations lurking in ancient Greek, Latin, and early modern vernacular terms for literacy and its opposite. For the moment, I want to note that literature provides an important if untrustworthy site of evidence about the subjectivity of persons defined, by others, as lacking in the qualities with which literacy is associated. When the illiterate subject is represented in letters, he or she is almost always an occasion for shared humor between a writer and a reader who is presumed to be more literate than the character figured as illiterate: Mrs. Malaprop, for instance, or Shakespeare's Mistress Quickly, or his low-ranking men like Dogberry and the "mechanicals" of *A Midsummer Night's Dream.* Even those literary texts that attempt to represent the illiterate's perspective sympathetically are constrained in their efforts by the conventions of the standard language: the dialectal speech often attributed to foreigners, provincials, and/or illiterates (the groups intermingle in many canonical representations) cannot but seem, to any reader who has made it through secondary school, the speech of someone who is badly educated, substandard, rather than "differently" educated. Certain modern academic disciplines, notably anthropology, social history, linguistics, and folklore studies, have attempted to represent the "illiterate" person's perspective more neutrally than most texts do that are now classified as literary; but the investigator who writes nonetheless always translates, to some degree or another, the (alleged) words of the nonwriter (who may or may not also be a nonreader). And translation is never ideologically innocent; indeed, translation, not only between languages and cultures but also between media, has long been recognized by literary theorists and anthropologists as a locus of conceptual and practical problems pertaining to notions of the individual and his/her property.[20]

In Romance languages descended from Latin the concepts of basic and cultural literacy are terminologically more distinct than they are in English: French has *alphabétisation* to denote the process of acquiring one's letters and *être cultivé* to denote a state of cultural literacy; both major meanings of the Latin *illitteratus,* however, seem to have migrated into French, Spanish, and Italian forms (the French *illettré* we have already seen; the Italian cousin is *illetterato*; the Spanish, *iletrado* or *iliterato*). German and Dutch also tend to distinguish between notions of basic and cultural literacy. One learns to spell (*buchstabieren,* from the interestingly typographical German term for "letter," *der Buchstabe*), and one thus acquires knowledge or skill (*Kenntnis* or *Fähigkeit*) in reading and writing (compare the Dutch phrase for "literate," *het lezen en schrijven*). If a German person is culturally literate, he or she has *Bildung,* and might therefore know to call an illiterate person *analphabet,* from the Greek. Dutch uses the plural noun *geletterden* (lettered ones) to describe the group that educated English people sometimes call "literati." There is a tendency for Latin and Greek terms related to literacy to migrate into modern European usages; sometimes this happens in ways that reveal anxieties among the educated classes about their own and others' cultural literacy. German usage includes the foreign word (*Fremdwort*) *Literat,* and this, according to Herbert Grundmann, has been used since the nineteenth century as a "shameword" (*Schimpfwort*) denoting a condition of foolish pomposity (Grundmann, "*Litteratus-illitteratus,*" 1–2). Ideologies of national identity impinge in strange ways on ideologies of a "Western" cultural literacy rooted in Latin, as we will see later in some early modern French and English instances of debates about importing foreign terms into an allegedly pure linguistic entity. The modern German spelling works, in any case, to naturalize the book as a repository of cultural value, although the codex form of writing is a fairly recent (perhaps now an endangered) phenomenon. The English term *literacy,* in contrast, naturalizes the alphabetic letter in ways that are highly problematic for a multicultural theorization of literacy.[21]

Because theories and practices we associate with Renaissance humanism have so powerfully shaped what most educated people in modern Western states have come to recognize and value as literacy, I am necessarily concerned as much with the stories scholars tell about literacy—in various sites, at various times—as I am with what we can reconstruct about empirical practices associated with literacy. To say this is not to minimize the task of describing those practices as precisely as we can, given the lacunae in the evidence, but it is important to acknowledge that the present study is an effort of cultural interpretation. As such it relies, albeit often skeptically, on secondary as well as primary sources, and even calls that distinction into question by emphasizing the ways in which "primary" textual materials are themselves, in many cases, edited, censored, and/or "translated" phenomena—in other words, *not* primary in any ontological sense. In any case, the archives, for students of literacy in its various relations to modes of discourse that came to count as "literature," are not simply there for excavating. As we will see in chapter 3, writers like Rabelais, Spenser, and Shakespeare promiscuously mixed foreign with (allegedly) native words; in so doing, they contributed to lively and still ongoing contests about distinctions among a national language, an "ancient" national tongue, a foreign tongue, and a dialect. Although modern literary critics often suggest that writers who have become canonical helped to create our national standard languages, such writers were frequently perceived by their contemporaries as writing "outlandishly," threatening the "common dialect" or, more accurately, those who felt their linguistic status endangered by not knowing someone else's words. Certain verbal practices, it seems, may make certain people feel illiterate; if the illiterate person has a relatively high rather than a relatively low social rank, an experience of illiteracy may result in the denunciation or even the censorship of a certain literate practice. For this reason among others, literary critics need to put literacy—but only under erasure, not like a flashcard—into our pedagogical and scholarly discourses about literary terms and, more generally, into the ways we define our field. Are literacy studies outside the domain of literary studies, or internal colonies, or both at once? We can perhaps gain a broader perspective on this question of boundaries and (stratified) academic domains if we look at some of the modern debates generated by literacy scholars located in various academic sites and concerned with oral and literate cultures all over the world at many different times. These include the cultures that exist in the paradoxical construction identified by Johannes Fabian in *Of Time and the Other: How Anthropology Makes Its Object* (1983): cultures that Western academics view as premodern even though they exist contemporaneously with our modernity.

Debates about Literacy, Modernization, and Ethnocentrism

I turn now to explore modern literacy debates through the lens provided by the Lévi-Strauss/Derrida debate about writing, mentioned above, which has been discussed in many critical contexts.[22] Because it forcefully delineates the range of conceptual options on literacy that I will be exploring throughout this study, however, and because its implications and even many of its terms have arguably been misunderstood or forgotten by later commentators—not to mention by literacy theorists who engage with some of the same difficult issues without having read the French debate, even in translation—I think it is important to rehearse it here. Both Lévi-Strauss and Derrida have some surprising and little-remarked perceptions about the relation between gender and language; further, Derrida's reading of Lévi-Strauss's text models modes of interpretation, self-reflexivity, and skepticism that I seek to encourage in the literacy debate at large, both in its contemporary and in its historiographical instances.

The chapter in *Tristes Tropiques* (1955) entitled "The Writing Lesson" ("Leçon d'écriture") is from the start also a discussion of reading; the triple pun in the word *leçon* ("lesson," "reading," and "sound" [*le son*]) opens the question of who reads, who takes instruction from the writing in question. The narrative extends and interrogates a line of anthropological thinking that led Lévi-Strauss, in 1954, to change the title of the "lecture course he gave at the Parisian Ecole Pratique des Hautes Etudes" from "Religions des peuples non-civilisées" to "Religions comparées des peuples sans écriture."[23] He justifies this change in a passage that stresses his desire to counter the ideology of evolutionary progress, which so often underpins the distinction in the social sciences between "primitive" and "civilized" peoples. Acknowledging the problem of depicting others in terms of a privative concept (*without* writing or *non*-civilized), Lévi-Strauss maintains that his new title is superior because it is more ideologically neutral than the original one. To describe a people as being "without writing," Lévi-Strauss insists, "is a statement of fact which does not imply a value judgment."[24] He appears to elaborate this point in *Tristes Tropiques,* but does so, I believe, with an ironic twist: the divide exists, but the drive toward modernity attributed to literate minds, with the special cognitive abilities that Lévi-Strauss (like other Great Divide theorists) ascribes to such minds, turns out to have greater ethical, political, and professional costs than the first-person narrator imagined. The "lesson" is directed at his own ignorance as well as at the (different) kind of ignorance he ascribes to those people "without writing" whom he is studying. In describing that second kind of ignorance, he offers a succinct statement of the Great Divide thesis: "After eliminating all other criteria which have been put forward to distinguish between barbarism and civilization, it is tempting to retain this one at least: there are peoples with, or without, writing; the former are able to store up their past achievements and to move with ever increasing rapidity to the goal they have set themselves, whereas the latter, being incapable of remembering the past beyond the narrow margin of individual memory, seem bound to remain imprisoned in a fluctuating history which will always lack both a beginning and any lasting awareness of an aim" (391; Fr., 317). Compare this vision of the Nambikwara Indians of 1950s Brazil with Eric Havelock's vision of the preliterate Greek peoples inhabiting ancient Athens, and you will see the structural parallels that exist between the theory of modernization informing an American classicist's view of illiteracy and that of a French anthropologist. Writing in 1963, Havelock argues that literacy, defined as the ability to produce and decode works in the Greek alphabet, fosters human capacities for objectivity, goal-directed thinking, and abstraction—qualities that Havelock finds in Plato's writings and that he contrasts with the qualities of mind possessed (he claims) by those preliterate Greeks who acquired their education through listening to oral-formulaic poems such as Homer's. Ignoring Plato's own arguments in the *Phaedrus* that writing harms the powers of memory, Havelock provocatively insists on the cultural significance of a change in modes of education in fifth-century Athens, as a system of learning through oral imitation gave way (at least for a small group of male citizens) to one based on dialectical debate and on texts written in alphabetic letters.[25]

In more recent publications, Havelock has continued to maintain the Great Divide thesis as he articulated it in the *Preface to Plato*.[26] And another, even better known proponent of this thesis, Walter Ong, has also continued to elaborate his early position that "writing restructures thought," even as he has argued that others are interpreting him reductively.[27] Lévi-Strauss shares with Havelock, Ong, and others trained in a variety of disciplines a fundamental belief that there are critical cognitive differences between members of oral cultures and members of literate ones, both then and now. Ong's work has been enormously influential, not only on anglophone academic discourses but also on the policies of development agencies funded by governments and international bodies.[28] Basing his distinctions between orality and literacy on an ontological contrast between sound, as something that only exists in its departing, and written marks, which "fix" impressions in a way sound cannot, Ong posits a series of contrasts between oral and literate cultures and—by a somewhat problematic extension—modes of individual consciousness as well. He characterizes the "oral" or "verbomotor" culture as formulaic, con-

servative, "agonistically toned," empathetic, homeostatic, situational, and reliant upon memorization. The literate world, in contrast, is characterized by
"context free language," "autonomous discourse," and "analytical" thought.[29]

It is worth reiterating that proponents of this theory hold widely different
views of the cultural value of the qualities they associate with the literate mind.
Perhaps because he is writing as France is undergoing decolonization and perhaps also because his fieldwork gives him a sense of the costs of modernization
("tristes tropiques") uncontemplated by many U.S. scholars writing in the
1960s, Lévi-Strauss provides an unusually dark or minor-key early version of
the Great Divide thesis and one that not only is allied to existentialist analyses
of modern alienation but also anticipates postmodernist analyses of the culturally leveling effects of globalization. Although Lévi-Strauss offers an oddly
traditional and chaste image of the instrument of such leveling—pen and paper, not Coca Cola bottles—his perspective on intercultural exchange is sufficiently complex and ironic that it invites us to notice ambivalences in other
Great Divide discourses. Ong, for example, suggests not only that literacy is
critical to human progress, individual and social, but also that it poses an apparent if not finally real threat to a sense of community.[30] "Oral cultures today," he writes, "value their oral traditions and agonize over the loss of those
traditions, but I have never encountered an oral culture that does not want to
achieve literacy as soon as possible. Some individuals do of course resist literacy, but they are mostly soon lost sight of" (*Orality and Literacy*, 175). "Resisting literacy" is presented here as both irrational and impossible; this is a
displaced and quite conservative political argument rooted in a theological
concept of history as providence. Ong exposes something important about
many versions of the Great Divide theory: they read like slightly secularized
narratives about the Fall of Man, whether the Fall is seen as fundamentally *felix* (liberating) or as a confirmation of the eternal and unchangeable division
between the elect and the damned. Ong's ambivalence about the human costs
of literacy and the modernizing process whose telos is the West is unaccom-
panied by any meditation on political agency, whether that of the scholar or
that of the "illiterate" person (in our midst or elsewhere). The question of
agency tends, however, to resurface in the sometimes murky waters of the
modern literacy debates; both Lévi-Strauss and Derrida have some light to
shed on this question.

Lévi-Strauss not only registers the problem of the (literate) observer's relation to the (presumed illiterate) person or culture, but dramatizes the relation
as involving hierarchies of power and methodologically significant potentials
for mixings, hybridizations, of features (and peoples) deemed oral and literate. But Lévi-Strauss's allegiance to a Rousseauistic tradition of idealizing

speech and, with it, an image of primitive society prevents him, as Derrida shows, from following some of the logical implications of his own story.[31] Having described himself as "tempted" to retain the distinction between "people with writing" and "people without writing" as the last viable means an ethical anthropologist has of distinguishing between barbarism and civilization (*Tristes Tropiques*, 391; Fr., 317), he succumbs to the temptation in an exemplary way through a romantic inversion of the notions of "civilized" and "barbarous"—an inversion that has forerunners in Montaigne's "Des cannibales" and in Rousseau's writings as well. The inversion seems politically liberal when contrasted with previous anthropological statements (e.g., Lévy-Bruhl's, from early in the twentieth century) about the "inferiority" of "mental function" to be observed among primitive peoples.[32] Nonetheless, an inversion of a hierarchy of value is not a thorough-going critique of its terms, as Derrida argues in his response to Lévi-Strauss, the chapter of *Of Grammatology* called "The Violence of the Letter: From Lévi-Strauss to Rousseau." Nor is the anthropologist's rhetorical mixture of self-accusation and self-exoneration a satisfactory response, in Derrida's view, to the enormously complex questions of knowledge and agency that arise in the paradigmatic situation of intercultural confrontation that Lévi-Strauss represents in his chapter. That narrative, Derrida states, is part of "the anthropological war, the essential confrontation that opens communication between peoples and cultures, even when that communication is not practiced under the banner of colonial or missionary oppression" (*Grammatology*, 107; Fr., 157). In this scene of battle, Lévi-Strauss depicts himself as being the bearer—but only an unwitting one—of an instrument of civilization that turns out to have barbarous rather than enlightening effects on the Native "others" (*Tristes Tropiques*, 389; Fr., 317). Derrida reads the chapter as belonging to the genre of the confession, the *mea culpa* made with Rousseauistic bad faith because the anthropologist "assumes entire responsibility for a violation that satisfied him" (*Grammatology*, 114; Fr., 167). Derrida, in contrast, will argue for a smaller degree of responsibility for and a greater degree of dissatisfaction with a (redefined) violation.

The Nambikwara writing lesson occurs, or rather, its social effects first become visible, after a "hazardous" journey to a meeting of disparate Indian groups—a meeting the anthropologist himself has requested, from a "reluctant" chief, in order to pursue the scientific goals of demographic measurement. The Western observer has already begun to alter the subjects/objects of his investigation, but he discovers just how far he has gone only when he sees the chief intervening in a ritual exchange of gifts by pretending to read a paper covered with "wavy horizontal lines" that he himself, it turns out, has written, or rather, has drawn in imitation of the anthropologist's behavior when making field notes. Lévi-Strauss, like Shelley's Frankenstein, is shocked by his own creation. Unlike the other Indians who have playfully imitated the anthropologist's writing on pieces of paper he gave out, the chief "had further ambitions"; indeed, he "was the only one who had grasped the purpose of writing" as Lévi-Strauss represents himself, through this incident, coming to understand or measure it (the object of measurement has shifted from native to Western civilization and its discontents). The chief uses his feigned ability to read and write to "astonish his companions, to convince them that he was acting as an intermediary agent for the exchange of goods, that he was in alliance with the white man and shared his secrets" (*Tristes Tropiques*, 389; Fr., 315). The chief, in short, uses writing without really understanding it for a "sociological rather than an intellectual purpose" (390; Fr., 317). Through writing, he seeks to increase his authority and introduces into his society heretofore unknown stratifications, dissensions, and deceit. The anthropologist is deeply troubled by the incident, and during a bout of insomnia the following night he reflects on the paradox that writing has "vastly increased man's ability to preserve knowledge" and yet has also, in practice, worked more for "the exploitation of human beings than [for] their enlightenment" (391–92; Fr., 317–18). Lévi-Strauss doesn't exempt his own writing from this generalization, which therefore takes the form of an interesting modern variant of the Cretan liar paradox: "all Cretans are liars; I am a Cretan." "The primary function of written communication is to facilitate slavery," Lévi Strauss states; he then gives the Cretan liar's clause, which unsettles the initial truth-claim even as it calls attention to the possibility that Lévi-Strauss's present discourse is a tool that both serves and conceals an exploitative political power: "the use of writing for disinterested purposes, and as a source of intellectual and aesthetic pleasure, is a secondary result, and more often than not it may even be turned into a means of strengthening, justifying, or concealing the other" (393; Fr., 318).

Lévi-Strauss seems to present the Western scientist as playing an initially unwitting (innocent?) Satan to the Nambikwara chief's Eve. The story recalls various New World narratives that show Europeans coming to Native Americans like Greeks bearing false gifts to the Trojans—or like Vergil's Aeneas coming to make use of Dido's hospitality and leaving her as a victim of the imperial project sponsored by Jupiter and Venus (but not by Juno, who wants to rewrite the story to make a tragedy-in-the-making into a comedy ending in intercultural marriage).[33] Penetrating the walls of an apparently innocent primitive culture, the modern European brings a gift of literacy that contains a dangerous temptation to (new) desires for power over others. Leaving the meeting where the traditional gift exchange was subverted by the self-aggrandizing chief, who had been somehow corrupted by the experience of watching the anthropologist write, Lévi-Strauss loses his way and finds himself "alone in the bush." The immediate cause of his sudden loss of his social place—between natives and Europeans but a member of neither group—is his mule, but the mule's problem and mode of traveling symbolize problems in Lévi-Strauss's own relation to history and to language. The mule, he writes, "had ulcers in its mouth which were causing it pain. It either rushed impatiently ahead or came to a sudden stop. The two of us fell out" (389; Fr., 315). The mule moves through time and space no less joltingly than the anthropologist does, and the mule seems to be bearing a punishment that literalizes the guilt of his rider for having somehow done harm to a native people's hitherto innocent domain of orality.

Reading Lévi-Strauss's intricate story with sustained attention, Derrida diagnoses it as dramatizing a fundamental misconception about the innocence, naturalness, and "self-presence" of oral language. Derrida arguably neglects one detail in the narrative that suggests Lévi-Strauss's ambivalent awareness that the long history of imperialism has already darkened the (imputed) innocence of the Indians.[34] Still, there is ample evidence in the story to support Derrida's charge that it generally illustrates the metaphysical tendency he names "phonologism," the privileging of speech over writing (*Grammatology*, 102; Fr., 151).[35] He sees this metaphysical idealization of voice (as Presence, as the Divine Word, as a transcendental "center") functioning as a key element in a line of thinking about "oral" cultures that runs from Rousseau to Lévi-Strauss (and beyond on both ends).[36] Attacking the authorizing model of phonetic writing as a profoundly ethnocentric notion, Derrida also interrogates ideas about the alphabet that have informed many anthropological discourses, until very recently, and many articulations of the Great Divide theory of literacy as well. The first of these premises is that the Greco-Roman alphabet "was invented only once" (around 1500 B.C.E.).[37] Second, every true alphabet in the world derives directly or indirectly from the original Semitic one.[38] Third, knowledge of alphabetic writing enables rational, abstract modes of thought impossible either in oral cultures of the sort we have seen Havelock describing in ancient Greece or in those cultures that employ notational systems allegedly more primitive, more "pictographic," less "efficient," less "intelligent," than the alphabet.[39] Derrida insists, in contrast, that the epistemological, ontological, and politico-ethical qualities that Lévi-Strauss associates with (alphabetic) writing inhere rather in the structure of language itself—a structure conceived as challenging the distinction between signifier and signified and also the distinction (rearticulated by Saussure) between language as a system and language as an instance (*langue* vs. *parole*). For Derrida, the "structure" of language cannot ever be fully grasped because it includes usage—a historical domain both of speech and writing (*Grammatology*, 108; Fr., 158). In this structure, "difference" and "violence" are there from the start, in those features of language Derrida associates with a hypothesized primal expropriation of subjectivity (as "self-presence") through the workings of human language. The structure of language, in Spivak's apt gloss, "is always already inhabited by the trace," the sign "of a perennial alterity" (*Grammatology*, xxxix). This is the complex of notions that Derrida names "archi-écriture" ("arche-writing") and clearly defines—with epistemological consequences not always appreciated by his critics—as a priori concepts (*Grammatology*, 108; Fr., 158–59).

Derrida's universalizing argument is carefully phrased; his use of a metaphysical a priori does not mean he is uninterested in empirical issues or in the materiality of history, and his use of the term *écriture* to describe something posited as a "general" phenomenon, common to all cultures, should not too easily be dismissed (as we will see Ong doing) as a form of ethnocentric blindness equivalent to those he critiques in the phonocentric tradition. The Derridean proposition that most forcefully challenges the Great Divide theory of literacy goes as follows: "If writing is no longer understood in the narrow sense of linear and phonetic notation, it should be possible to say that all societies capable of producing, that is to say of obliterating, their proper names, and of bringing classificatory difference into play, practice writing in general. No reality or concept would therefore correspond to the expression 'society without writing'" (*Grammatology*, 109; Fr., 161). I draw two conclusions from this statement. On the one hand, Derrida offers what seems to me a highly credible universal in his insistence that any imagined speech is always preceded (logically, not temporally) by a capacity for "writing in general," understood as "bringing classificatory difference into play." This generalization seems preferable both on logical and empirical grounds to the Great Divide theory in its strong or positive form. The strong form of the Great Divide theory, which holds that alphabetic literacy causes or is a necessary precondition for scientific, "objective" thinking of a kind unknown to nonliterate peoples, cannot be proven empirically and tends, in many discursive situations, to lead to circular reasoning.[40] Granting the strength of Derrida's claim of a capacity for "general writing" in all cultures, however, does not mean that we need to assume that his discourse escapes the problems of ethnocentricity with which he is concerned. Some critics have objected to his use of the metaphor of writing itself, as a form of ethnocentrism; this line of objection seems to me to have little critical force. A more pertinent critique—and one less fully anticipated by Derrida than the writing-metaphor objections—might interrogate his apparent privileging of the proper name in his hypotheses about "arche-writing." Might not this emphasis replicate identity concerns that are specifically Western and modern?

Derrida readily admits, indeed insists, that the language and hence the angles of vision with which he attempts to critique Western metaphysical traditions are "not alien" to the history of those traditions: "we cannot utter a single destructive proposition which has not already slipped into the form, the logic, and the implicit postulations of precisely what it seeks to contest" ("Structure, Sign, and Play," 250). He also insists—rightly, I believe—that there is no purely ethical position from which to critique what one perceives as instances of ethnocentric discourse. This does not mean, however, that one should slacken one's critical attention to such instances as they occur either in one's own or others' thinking. Derrida's formulation of this point seems to me important both for how we understand his critique of Lévi-Strauss and for how we read those who have joined the modern literacy debates as readers of the initial phase of the Derrida/Lévi-Strauss debate. Commenting on the philosophical project that came to be known as "deconstruction" in the United States, Derrida writes in a paper first published in an oral form (presumably from a written but not yet printed script) in Baltimore (that is, in a foreign, New World place, to an international audience) that "the critique of ethnocentrism—the very condition of ethnology" is "systematically and historically contemporaneous with the destruction of the history of metaphysics" ("Structure, Sign, and Play," 252).[41] Thus Derrida associates his own deconstructive project with a critique informing, indeed enabling, that science of ethnology he elsewhere describes as arising in the Renaissance, at the moment of Europe's "decentering" through its encounter with the New World. Ethnology, he writes, is "primarily a European science employing traditional concepts, however much it may struggle against them":

> Consequently, whether he wants to or not—and this does not depend on a decision on his part—the ethnologist accepts into his discourse the premises of ethnocentrism at the very moment when he is employed in denouncing them. This necessity is irreducible; it is not a historical contingency. . . . But if nobody can escape this necessity, and if no one is therefore responsible for giving in to it . . . this does not mean that all the ways of giving in to it are of an equal pertinence. The quality and the fecundity of a discourse are perhaps measured by the critical rigor with which this relationship to the history of metaphysics and to inherited concepts is thought. . . . A problem of *economy* and *strategy*. ("Structure, Sign, and Play," 252, emphasis in original)

Derrida argues, then, for making distinctions among ethnocentric discourses not from a grand position of ethical purity available (he claims) to none of us in the West, but rather from the more modest position of assessing "economies and strategies" of discourse. He illustrates this idea when he shows that Lévi-Strauss's image of Nambikwara society as one "without writing" depends on the suppression of evidence that Lévi-Strauss himself gives elsewhere in his text—evidence about the graphic designs, or *ierkariukedjutu,* incised by the Nambikwara on their gourds and other objects, for instance, and also evidence about the complexities of Nambikwara *speech* insofar as the anthropologist has begun to understand its conventions.[42] Derrida calls attention to an amazing scene where the anthropologist himself plays the role of the student acquiring forbidden knowledge of linguistic secrets and hence of speech as a complex domain of "difference" in Nambikwara society. This scene, which Howard Bloch perspicuously calls "a lesson in speaking" (*Etymologies and Genealogies,* 6), occurs just two chapters before the more famous story of the writing lesson. In the earlier chapter Lévi-Strauss describes himself penetrating to a knowledge of Nambikwara culture that had heretofore been closed to him because of a taboo on proper names. Watching children play one day, the anthropologist suddenly becomes implicated in the scene of play when a little girl runs to him "for protection"; the play turns serious when she begins to whisper a "great secret" in his ear. "As I did not understand I had to ask her to repeat it over and over again" (*Tristes Tropiques,* 365; Fr., 294). It turns out that she is telling her somewhat dim interlocutor-pupil the name of her enemy—breaking the taboo to gain an advantage in a scene of social struggle. Soon thereafter another little girl, the adversary of the first, "tried in her turn to tell me what seemed to be another secret." Eventually, Lévi-Strauss acquires the adults' secret names as well as those of the transgressive children; then his information "dried up," and the girls presumably were punished, although he doesn't mention their punishment as a consequence of his intervention in an alien culture. He does, however, use an old trope that genders the (Western) self as male and the Other as female. The chapter about the little girls begins with a description of the local landscape as literally marked by a line of communication among cultures, a telegraph wire held up by poles creating a kind of surreal writing that Lévi-Strauss reads as a sign of "man's former presence and of the futility [*vanité*] of his efforts" (355; Fr., 286). This marking, which as Derrida observes anticipates the "wavy lines" of the chief's feigned writing, also marks the landscape itself; once "virgin," it still threatens consciousness: "Completely virgin landscapes [*paysages complètement vierges*] have a monotony which deprives their wildness of any significant value. They withhold themselves from man" (354; Fr., 286).

Lévi-Strauss's text offers no simple moral for the student of literacy as a locus of social struggle within and between what counts as cultures. His text

does tell us that native girls use speech—and in this case, speech about language—for just the "sociological" purposes he later sees and laments in the
actions of the chief, who uses a (superficial) understanding of writing for his
own political purposes and thus exposes the true nature of writing to the observing European teacher—who is also a pupil. Both these chapters of *Tristes
Tropiques* represent complex scenes of education; in both, I would suggest, the
politics of gender are significant but by no means easily legible. Derrida sees
this facet of the scenes of cultural encounter, but only, as it were, in passing,
just as he sees, and theoretically allows for, other bits of evidence in the cultural scene he is scrupulously describing, analyzing, and finally using for his
own professional (sociological and intellectual) purposes. "Let us note," he
writes, deploying the device of the parenthesis, the marking of something as
supplemental to the main topic of the sentence, "that we speak here of an act
of war and that there is much to say about the fact that it is little girls who open
themselves to this game and these hostilities" (*Grammatology*, 111; Fr., 164). Let
me attempt now to reflect on that parenthesis and other aspects of the Lévi-
Strauss/Derrida debate that have particular bearing on the arguments about
gender, literacy, and empire in later chapters of this book.

Further Lessons from the Lévi-Strauss/Derrida Debate
on Literacy and Modernization

An agonistic rhetoric is one of the legacies of Renaissance schools, and indeed
of the classical rhetorical and pedagogical traditions in which boys learned,
with their grammar, to argue *in utramque partem,* on both sides of the question, while at the same time learning to act as if one side were the clear win-
ner.[43] This is the tradition that Walter Ong and Eric Havelock conflate with
alphabetic literacy per se, and which Lévi-Strauss does as well when he associates deceit with (Western) writing. The little Brazilian girls represented in his
book of course complicate that idea, and so does he, by choosing to represent
them at all. Philosophical premises do not always govern all of the evidence
about culture that a given text may provide, which is why I contend that deconstructive reading practices are at least as important as polemical formulations of theoretical positions in our efforts to understand literacy as a locus for
social struggle then and now, there and here.

The first lesson I draw from the Lévi-Strauss/Derrida debate as a paradigmatic instance of the contrasting views of Great Divide and "culturalist" approaches to literacy is that the epistemological problems of ethnocentrism are
central and inescapable whenever we undertake to analyze literacy in cultures
distant from our own in time and/or in space. These problems may, moreover,

be equally inescapable for discussions of literacy in what counts as our "own" cultures; we presume likeness among human minds in order to communicate, and some linguists (Chomsky, for instance) hypothesize a universal "deep structure" of grammar, but the presumption of similarity cannot be empirically proven, as skeptical philosophers from Montaigne through Wittgenstein have emphasized. It would therefore be useful to think hard and in fairly detailed ways about how to enact a skeptical view of literacy and literacies. How do we strike an epistemological and rhetorical balance—in terms of a strategy and an economy, as Derrida puts it—between unwittingly projecting our culture's (dominant) notions of literacy onto the evidence we can collect from other cultures, and assuming (naïvely) that we can locate, much less describe, modes of literacy that might count as "arche-writing" when such modes are utterly alien to our own categories of thought about writing, reading, speaking, communicating through bodily gesture, and, of course, lying? There is no simple answer to this question; it leads, in Derridean terms, to an *aporia,* a space of doubt without a pathway to transcendental truth. Posing the question and attempting rigorously to distinguish among different varieties of ethnocentric discourse are nonetheless within our scope as interpretive agents. These mental actions may help us avoid unskeptical versions either of the Great Divide theory or of the culturalist model that Brian Street advocates, in a way that draws on Derrida's authority but not on his difficult (and hence easily forgotten) argument about our own embeddedness in a system of language that has a long history.

While arguing in useful ways against what I have called the positive form of the Great Divide theory—"literate people do think differently from nonliterate ones"—some proponents of a culturalist view of literacy have tended not to be sufficiently skeptical about their own findings and methods.[44] On the one hand, they are quite right to insist that we do not know that literate people (all) think differently from (all) nonliterate people, because we do not know if what we define as literacy is a social variable that has the kind of universalizing weight that most Great Divide theorists presume. On the other hand, we do not know that some people who are nonliterate as we (variously) define that condition do *not* think differently than we do; nor can we say for sure whether literacy is a significant cause of that difference. Brian Street proclaims, for instance (in a refutation of Ong), that "all people have conventions for formalizing, distancing, analyzing, separating, holding some things constant" (*Social Literacies,* 157). But how can Street know that his view of "all people" is true, any more than Ong can know that "writing restructures thought" in all circumstances? Writing may restructure, or at least alter, thought processes in some social situations; but since we have no way of assessing this claim independently of many variables—including, in anthropological situations, the presence of the writing observer—the strong or positive form of the claims made by Street, as a representative of the British "culturalist" school of literacy theorists, and by Ong, as a representative of the U.S. Great Divide school, both invite skepticism. It is easy to dismiss Ong's views as politically conservative, but the universalizing moment in Street's liberal, relativistic theory may also have conservative effects: his formulation might well turn a student's or researcher's attention away from possible evidence that some people do not have the "conventions" Street defines in the last analysis as a function of human nature. Derrida too makes a version of this move—but he does so, as we have seen, with a small but significant difference, using a hypothetical formulation that leaves some room for difference, for counterevidence to be thought at the far edge of the mind.

A second and related lesson to be drawn from the foregoing partial mapping of the territory of literacy studies through the lens of the Lévi-Strauss/Derrida debate is that one cannot simply pay lip service to the methodological problem presented by one's own historical, and in many cases professional, investment in a particular view of literacy. If, as Derrida demonstrates, Lévi-Strauss misrepresents the ample evidence that the Nambikwara were not a pastorally "oral" tribe before his visit to them, the misrepresentation derives logically from an ideological "set" that has been, until recently, very important to most Western academic anthropologists' professional identities and to their sense of their *authority.* If the cultures studied by anthropologists or historians are not isolatable as "wholes" with special, unique, features discernible by means of the scholar's trained eye; and if, moreover, the historian's or anthropologist's cultural objects of study "are always already writing themselves," as James Clifford puts it, echoing Derrida, then "the special status of the fieldworker-scholar who 'brings the culture into writing' is undercut" ("On Ethnographic Allegory," 118). An over- or at the least a mis-estimate of the difference between one's own language uses and those of the persons (subjects/objects) one studies is likely, it seems, if one is an anthropologist; indeed, Lévi-Strauss himself suggests how important it is, professionally speaking, for him to have an "oral" people as an object of study and at the same time to depreciate his own "literate" culture as imperialist in a way that is common to a significant minority of modern scholars. Despite his insistence that the designation *nonliterate* implies no value judgment, we see that Lévi-Strauss values societies "without writing" for professional (as well as other) reasons: "Better than our traditions, whose transformation accelerates with the ever increasing mass of knowledge accumulated in books, these traditions [nonliterate ones] lend themselves to an experimental research which requires a relative stability in its object."[45] Anthropologists, and their increasingly close academic cousins, literary scholars who practice New Historicism or cultural poetics or feminist cultural criticism, need to acknowledge the more than merely theoretical possibility of this kind of professional bias so as to anticipate and as far as possible compensate for such an "effect of the observer" on the very constitution of the object studied—the phenomenon that Heisenberg's Uncertainty Principle famously dramatizes in the field of subatomic physics.[46]

A third lesson is this: the force of Derrida's argument for "arche-writing"— the challenges it poses to think, if not outside, at least on the margins of our inherited conceptual boxes—has only intermittently been registered in anglophone discourses on literacy. Going back to Derrida reading Lévi-Strauss is thus, to my mind, a way of looking to possible lines of future inquiry focused on literacies of the past as well as of the present and even the future. Some of Derrida's recent readers have appreciated the innovative aspects of his theorizations of literacy, but some, it seems to me, have critiqued him in reductive ways. Among the first group of readers is Elizabeth Boone, who cites the utopian "exergue" of Derrida's *Of Grammatology* to argue for the importance of going beyond Western notions of writing that connect it either with speech or with the medium of the printed book. A student of ancient American systems of notation who is also interested in how we "envision information" in scientific discourses and electronic media, Boone quotes Derrida's statement that "beyond theoretical mathematics, the development of the practical methods of information retrieval extends the possibilities of the 'message' vastly, to the point where it is no longer the 'written' translation of a language."[47] Derrida goes on in the same passage to imagine a new "science of writing," grammatology, that "runs the risk of never being established as such and with that name"; as a potentially nameless phenomenon, it carries the writer's vision of a science (as knowledge) that goes beyond "all technical and epistemological obstacles as well as all the theological and metaphysical impediments that have limited it hitherto" (*Grammatology*, 4; Fr., 13).

On the basis of this passage and many others that put his own use of terms such as *écriture* and even *grammatologie* under erasure, I would argue that it is reductive to accuse Derrida of ethnocentric violence because he uses such terms to envision modes of human communication that predate—or postdate—the Western time/space/reach of what he defines as "logocentrism." Walter Ong makes just such an accusation when he describes grammatology as "the most text-bound of all ideologies."[48] Lévi-Strauss makes a similar objection when, in *Mythologiques,* he contrasts the "palpable cultural wealth of native America with the self-enclosing sterility of a certain western philosophy."[49] Gordon Brotherston himself—like other recent scholars, including Walter Mignolo and Jonathan Goldberg—articulates a softened version of this objection. I take it seriously, but I also want to state again that Derrida fully anticipates it as an epistemological and rhetorical problem—one that he addresses more carefully, I believe, than do many of his recent critics. Consider this example. After discussing the evidence that Lévi-Strauss suppresses concerning Nambikwara notations as diagrams "describing, explaining, writing, a genealogy and a social structure," Derrida states that "here one passes from arche-writing to writing in the colloquial sense [*écriture au sens commun*]. This passage, whose difficulty I do not wish to underestimate, is not a passage from speech to writing; it operates within writing in general" (*Grammatology*, 124–25; Fr., 182). The phrasing seems designed to remind us of how hard it is to think of a word like *writing* in other than its Western common senses, here defined as profoundly ideological. Since nothing in Derrida's text seems to devalue empirical contributions to our knowledge of other systems of notation, it may be a sign of this particular intellectual's cultural prestige (especially in a U.S. context) that so many scholars actually working on Native American artifacts both cite Derrida as a liberating influence and evince a wish that he had somehow confirmed or authorized their own research agendas. Brotherston, for instance, complains that Derrida's apparent lack of interest in "the particular social and political functions of script" has led him to misunderstand the relation between the Middle American Aztec and Mayan scripts; a lack of attention (construed as a lack of esteem) has, in general, led Derrida "to concern himself more with . . . [the] ideological force [of "script aversion"] within his and our tradition than with any other reality it may have effectively displaced" ("Towards a Grammatology of America," 202). I doubt the justice of this conclusion, just as I doubt Walter Mignolo's critique when he charges that Derrida "is working within an evolutionary concept of writing" because the first section of *De la grammatologie* is entitled "L'Ecriture avant la lettre" ("Writing before the Letter" or "Writing before Writing").[50] As the word plays in this title phrase suggest, Derrida constantly interrogates evolutionary models. To read *avant* simply as denoting "before" in a temporal rather than a logical sense is a misreading of the sort we can identify even in a theoretical universe lacking absolute truths. I see no evidence that Derrida believes (as Mignolo infers from the phrase "avant la lettre") that "once the letter was invented, alternative forms of writing lost importance" (*Darker Side of the Renaissance*, 318). Mignolo errs in finding in Derrida's text any assertion about the "importance" of Mignolo's own research interests. Derrida seems to me fully in accord with those who seek "other realities" in nonalphabetic scripts. But Derrida's analyses of our structures of thought and language provide no confirmation of the idea that shifting one's evidentiary field from European writings to pre-Columbian knots and other material traces of nonalphabetic signifying systems will help us in the difficult passage from writing in a "narrow" sense to writing in the "general" sense. Our best hope is to shuttle back and forth as rigorously as possible, testing conclusions as we go, between the hypothetical pole signaled by "arche-writing" and the various evidentiary fields about writing in the "narrow" senses (plural) that we are constantly constructing—and, one hopes, expanding as well.

The debate on literacy partially but powerfully figured in Derrida's and Lévi-Strauss's texts has, I believe, considerable critical import for scholars working on ancient, medieval, and early modern literacies, whether in European or American contexts. Street's culturalist version of Derrida's model does not call attention to the ways in which definitions and practices of literacy might be *contested* within a given cultural unit, but the Derridean concept of an originary difference and violence in human language provides a horizon for any inquiry, including this one, that seeks to understand how literacy works within as well as among what we deem to be cultural units. Even as Derrida's concept of "difference" remains critical to my analysis, however, I wish to leave open the possibility that this Western philosophical concept may sometimes work to distract our attention from modalities of difference other than the linguistic. I follow Derrida, then, in believing that one should stop using the dyad writing/nonwriting (or literacy/illiteracy) to make a heuristic division between "them" and "us," ignoring all the different kinds and degrees of literacy—products of various subcultures and also of demographic hybridizations—that have existed in most societies, including those of early modern Europe and our own. I do not assume (nor, I think, does Derrida) that because all societies may have some kind of "arche-writing," it follows that no historically significant transitions have occurred from some types of socially valued (and/or compelled) literacies to others. And the former, especially if they involve esoteric or exoteric *oral* practices, may well be *defined* as "illiteracy" by socially influential persons or groups.

My effort to define a model that learns from and draws on elements in both the Derridean and the Lévi-Straussian discourses on writing (and practices of textual and cultural reading) requires considerable vigilance against a problem that I see (albeit only rarely) in Derrida's rhetorical practice and that appears often in the discursive practices of many scholars attempting the difficult passage Derrida identifies between empirical research on culturally specific modes of literacy and generalizations about them. Derrida himself sometimes moves from a priori propositions to other apodictic generalizations in a way that allows the rhetoric of certainty suitable to the former (according at least to the protocols of a certain literate philosophical tradition) to bleed into statements about evidentiary fields that cannot, by definition, be mastered by the individual, culturally situated researcher. One example occurs in a paragraph of *De la grammatologie* leading up to the statement about "not underestimating" the difficulty of the passage from writing in the "colloquial" (i.e., the Western commonsensical) meaning and writing in the "general" (nondoxical but still potentially ethnocentric) meaning Derrida has ascribed to it. "It is now known [*on sait maintenant*]," he states, "thanks to unquestionable and abundant information, that the birth of writing (in the colloquial sense) was nearly everywhere and most often linked to genealogical anxiety" (*Grammatology*, 124; Fr., 182). Such a formulation invites us to ask: to whom is this so generally and impersonally known? And for what purposes is it being proffered—uneasily ("nearly everywhere," "most often")—as a cross-cultural truth? Such formulations distinguish not between those with writing and those without writing, but rather between groups with different, and differently valued, kinds of knowledge. Professional scholars may be particularly blind to the moments when they make such distinctions in their own scholarly rhetoric (in texts or in the oral/textual scene of the classroom). I suggest, however, that we need to attend to such moments because they are often where groups are divided into fully and partially literate social beings; and this division may have existential and political consequences we scholar-teachers cannot readily see.

Which brings me to the last lesson I will draw here from Derrida's and Lévi-Strauss's writing lessons, interpreted as complex statements about Western traditions of reading, writing, and speaking. I remarked earlier that Lévi-Strauss dramatizes himself playing a role like that of Satan to Milton's Eve. The chief who at once abuses the anthropologist's playful gift and attempts to usurp his role as secret-bearer is clearly portrayed as being at once a very good and a very bad student. The modern Brazilian chief belongs, indeed, to the company of "imperfect" literates I have mentioned before. He is gendered female and inferior because he has, like Milton's Eve, only a "superficial" knowledge of what the male scientist brings. The scientist turns out to be like Adam as well as like Satan—a man deeply dependent on the figure who is at once like and unlike him, and whose desires he fails to read until it's too late. The anthropologist's wife, described in "The Writing Lesson" as the first to be infected by a belated or secondary version of a venereal disease the Westerners brought to America long ago, seems allegorically related both to the Nambikwara chief and to those young girls who turn the tables on Lévi-Strauss by becoming the bearers of illicit information. What is structurally similar between the girls and the chief (and perhaps the wife?) is that the professional anthropologist needs them, depends on them for his living even as he defines them as different—and differently literate—than he is. The hierarchy of superior/inferior is labile; part of the educator's task is to stabilize it, and part of my task here is to look again at the evidence of instability that the written record provides—partly because some of that record was produced by women and, as Lévi-Strauss acknowledges, by girls who transgressed their culture's most sacred rules of language.

The French anthropologist Marc de Civrieux describes a non-Western scene of language use that interestingly frames Lévi-Strauss's description of the transgressive Nambikwara girls while also supporting Derrida's argument for difference, including gender difference, as a focus for cross-cultural study—even if we cannot deduce from such study a principle of knowledge hierarchies as a universal norm, any more than we can deduce from the known evidence about languages (constantly changing, constantly being changed by the observer) that there is such a thing as universal grammar. By the same token, of course, we cannot deduce that there is *not* such a thing. We are necessarily, not accidentally, in a state of partial knowledge, it seems, about cross-cultural literacy/illiteracy (literacies/illiteracies). Nonetheless, we can learn something from unfamiliar examples, such as the one Civrieux supplies: "The *Watunna* is in its essence a secret teaching restricted to the circle of men who undergo the initiations of the *Wanwanna* festivals. But there is another, popular *Watunna* which belongs to everyone regardless of sex or age, and this is the *Watunna* told in everyday language."[51] This example dramatizes that hierarchies of language use overlap with hierarchies based on gender and age, in non-European contexts as well as in European societies, where hierarchies of language use have often been associated (as they are in Lévi-Strauss) with some members of the group possessing, and others lacking, a kind of power linked to a specific language (or linguistic skill). Starting from the assumption that there was and is a broad social field in which distinctions between men and women are filtered through and enforced by differences in people's relations to language, I argue that we need a clearer understanding of how ideologies of gender have intersected with ideologies of literacy in social situations where certain powers are associated with a certain language. With that clearer understanding may perhaps come some sharper perspective on tensions between "high" and "low" languages—often gendered male and female—in our contemporary world, both in Western and in non-Western societies, and in the accelerating (if politically asymmetrical) transactions among them. In 1959 Charles Ferguson (no relation) introduced the term *diglossia* to describe

a "relatively stable language situation in which, in addition to the primary dialects of the language . . . there is a very divergent, highly codified (often grammatically more complex) superposed variety, the vehicle of a large and respected body of written literature, either of an earlier period or in another
speech community, which is learned largely by formal education" ("Diglossia," 435). For Ferguson, this hierarchical situation was fully accepted as culturally legitimate by a people assumed to be homogeneous, and the "high" and
"low" language uses were complementary, not a source of conflict or competition. More recent students of the concept of diglossia, however, notably the
Israeli scholar Joshua Fishman, have paid increasing attention to the "disruption of diglossia at the national level" and to the conflicts that arise, for individuals and groups, when one language or variety of language displaces another.[52] A major link between the late medieval/early modern eras in European
territories and our own modernity might indeed be the existence of diglossic
situations with high incidences of disruption. A historical disruption that has
often been seen as a beneficent change was the so-called rise of the vernacular
tongues and the consequent challenge to the long-standing and geographically widespread diglossic situation in which, to put it briefly, Latin ruled.
What happened when that rule began visibly to crumble? The answer is complex, and may well entail paying new attention to the pockets of resistance that
existed in the imperium of medieval Latin. But the old answer, in the form
given by Erich Auerbach, is still a valuable place to begin retelling the modernization story with an eye on gender, diglossia, and definitions of literacy related to old and new conceptions of "literature."

According to Auerbach, the "essential structural difference between the
Middle Ages and the Renaissance" is that the former era lacked a "cultivated
public," a "sizable minority of educated persons" capable of "deriving cultivated pleasure from literature" and of "expressing a culture rooted in their actual living conditions" (*Literary Language and Its Public*, 241). It is a remarkable, if implicit, statement against the institution of the Roman Catholic
Church, for one could argue that the clergy constituted precisely such a "minority of educated persons" and did both enjoy and create works that are now
classified as literary. (How in any case can Auerbach know that the monks and
priests did *not* enjoy a "literature" "rooted in their actual living conditions"?)
Auerbach's secular bias, which he shares with those early humanists who described the Catholic Middle Ages as a period of darkness following the enlightenment of classical antiquity, emerges most strikingly in his subsequent
remark that "only when the mother tongue had once again become the true
vehicle of culture" could such a social group emerge—a class he calls a "cultivated public" and sees, distinctly, as including women and slaves as well as

high-status men. For Auerbach, the "pleasures" of literature seem to go hand in hand with some democratization of cultural capital and with heterosexual intercourse of various sorts: "At this time," he writes, discussing the centuries of the Roman empire, "the educated public included women, and these were not all members of high society; there were also the *puellae* of the elegies," the "girls" whom Propertius and Ovid imagined as among the audience for their erotic poetry (*Literary Language and Its Public*, 241).

Auerbach surely displays a certain professional bias in seeing a shift in *language use* as the essential distinction between two periods; moreover, he arguably implies a misleading equality for women in his descriptions of both the Roman empire and the Renaissance return to using the "mother tongue" (this "return," as I argue in chapter 2, involved an important clerkly transformation of European vernaculars). Nonetheless, the basic shift in language practices that he stresses—implicitly at the expense of the clergy and the nonvernacular Latin, spoken and written, of the medieval Church—was indeed momentous for many European peoples and for American and African peoples of the kind Nebrija envisioned as language students in the prologue to his Castilian grammar. What Auerbach sees as a positive historical change toward modernity in that "other world" of premodern Europe was beneficial for some social subjects, including many noblewomen who became "arbiters of lay piety" and, in some cases, patrons and even unacknowledged coauthors of texts later deemed literary.[53] But the benefits of the change Auerbach posits should not blind us to the costs it entailed for many (we cannot begin to say how many) premodern subjects.

Pre-/Early Modern Literacies: Questions of Definition and Evidence

I have proposed that cultural historians of medieval and early modern Europe are working mostly from hybrid versions of the two main positions in the modern literacy debates, the positions I have associated with, on the one hand, the Great Divide theorists, who see literacy as a specific set of skills engendering specific (but transcultural) mental effects in individuals and in groups, and, on the other hand, the "culturalists," who see literacy as a socially embedded and highly variable set of meaning-making activities that, as hypothesized in the Derridean notion of "arche-writing," are not necessarily tied to the alphabetic letter but are definitely tied—once they become objects of study to someone not from that culture—to the epistemological problems of the so-called observer effect. Sometimes the imprint of the Great Divide perspective is heavy in work on early modern literacy and education: "literacy," Lawrence Stone stated in 1977, is "probably a necessary precondition for introspection" (*Family, Sex, and Marriage,* 226). The imprint of the Great Divide theory is also visible, I suggest, in the tendency of many students of historical literacy to claim that literacy (associated with progress) has been steadily increasing (with a few setbacks such as the Dark Ages in Europe) since Athens' days of glory. Vast overestimates, or at least very vague estimates, of the proportion of a given population that could read and/or write abound in the literature, though they have been bracingly (and controversially) challenged by recent scholars such as David Cressy (for Tudor-Stuart England) and William Harris (for ancient Greece and Rome).[54] The task of measurement (whether for individuals or across populations) depends on the task of defining literacy, and that is where some of the most interesting problems in the hybrid theoretical models emerge. Keith Thomas, for instance, in a pioneering article that did much to disaggregate literacy as an object of study for students of early modern England, nonetheless writes of "full literacy" (or the condition of being "wholly literate"), as if that phenomenon were self-evidently the ability to read and write alphabetic texts (at what level he does not specify). In the course of discriminating—valuably and, for modern readers, counterintuitively—between the ability to decipher black-letter (Gothic) typefaces and the ability to read roman letters, Thomas slides from a statement about a hypothesized early modern reader to the following (easily falsifiable) generalization about his own contemporaries: "After all, everyone today can read a sixteenth-century book, but only a tiny minority can read an original sixteenth-century letter" ("Meaning of Literacy," 100).

The difficult passage noted by Derrida, from a priori statements to generalizations about constructed fields of empirical evidence, turns out to be something few scholars of literacy negotiate without slips, whether they are writing from a Great Divide perspective or from a culturally relativist perspective, or from a mixture of the two. My own exposition does not escape the rhetorical and epistemological problems I observe in others, but I hope, in the following brief discussion of some medieval, early modern, and modern definitions of literacy, to begin to illustrate a skeptical theoretical perspective on literacy as both a dynamic and a contested phenomenon.

Issues of epistemological relativity and cultural contest appear in some of our earliest alphabetic records about literacy. In a study of "ancient literacy" focusing (only) on Greece and Rome, William Harris observes that a "a very large number of Greek papyrus documents, almost all from Egypt, mention the literacy of one or more of those participating in the recorded transaction."[55] He reserves what is to me his most interesting point for a footnote, however, where he adds that "it is sometimes possible, and very occasionally it is likely, that the person referred to as illiterate was illiterate *in Greek* but literate in Egyptian" (*Ancient Literacy*, 141n. 124). The example dramatizes that literacy is never defined in a cultural vacuum; these days, even anthropologists are finding that there are no purely oral societies, for the native you studied five years ago may be reading, even laughing at, your book when you next visit his or her remote island. In the often tense contact zones of the ancient Mediterranean world, it is not surprising to find our records about literacy marked by epistemological uncertainties of the sort Harris relegates to his footnote. Such uncertainties are a problem, as we will see, if one's aim is to measure literacy across a population. For the moment, let us remark that there is already a problem of different cultures—or of differently cultured people—as soon as one notices that literacy is almost always defined as part of a dyad.[56] The Greek word *agrammatos* and the Latin *illitteratus*, Harris remarks, "seem to veer between the meanings 'uncultured' and 'incapable of reading and [/or?] writing.' Even the expression *litteras (ne)scire*, 'not to know letters,' may refer to lack of culture rather than to illiteracy in the narrow sense."[57] The modern English word *literate* oscillates, as we have seen, in just the way Harris describes for its Greek and (classical) Latin ancestors. The meaning of the Latin term and its cognate forms is always dependent on context; hence, for us, it is always the product of an act of reading over, under, and around that form of spurious certainty that dictionaries often give to the unwary.

If the modern English word *literate* shares with its classical Greek and Latin counterparts a tendency to oscillate between different meanings (one of which cannot be construed, I believe, as any more "literal" than another), our word has also inherited a set of meanings not known to the ancient Romans but enormously important for the millennium usually known as the Middle Ages. During this era and in many parts of the territory spiritually ruled by the Roman Catholic Church, the dominant (but not for that reason self-evident or uncontested) meaning of *litteratus* had to do not only with having, or appearing to have, some knowledge of Latin but also with being a member of a priestly caste. During this era, Michael Clanchy has remarked, Europe was dominated not by the priestly elite who monopolized writing "but by warriors with a non-literate sense of values"; the remarkable transformation of the classical Roman dyad *litteratus/illitteratus* into the medieval Christian dyad *clericus/laicus* was in part, Clanchy suggests, the result of a cultural battle for authority and power waged (from a defensive position) by the Church and its priests (*From Memory to Written Record*, 178). A certain theory and practice of literacy served, then, to make and maintain key social distinctions between the clergy and the laity. These theories and practices have been ably explored in recent years by medievalists who are pursuing a culturalist agenda of the sort Brian Street recommends to modern ethnographers. The problem for cultural historians attempting to recover what the members of medieval culture(s) understood literacy to be is that the native informants are mainly *litterati* writing from within the Church, although documents by heretics provide valuable glimpses into oppositional literacies.[58] Roger Chartier makes a similar point when he suggests that "historians have accepted as a definition of popular religion the one that the clergy themselves made," a definition linking popular with superstitious ("Culture as Appropriation," 230). The problems raised by the clerkly perspective on nonclerkly instances of literate behavior are dramatized by the example of St. Godric of Norfolk. Godric, born around 1065 to peasant parents, worked to become a merchant and eventually, around the age of forty, after combining business with religion by traveling to many far-flung shrines, learned the Psalms from a large psalter given him by a kinsman (Clanchy, *From Memory to Written Record*, 190). Soon thereafter, Godric "tenaciously applied his memory to 'hearing, reading and chanting,'" imitating boys at St. Mary's church in Durham who were "learning the first elements of letters." Thus self-educated, Godric was derided by the devil as a "stinking old peasant," according to his biographer, Reginald, who himself described Godric as "*laicus, illitteratus* and *idiota.*"[59] I am less persuaded than Clanchy that such a statement was written "without malice." It was, in any case, written by an observer who assumes his superiority to the person seeking to acquire some of the skills—and hence the social prerogatives—of literacy.

Reginald's chain of synonyms becomes even more interesting when we note that underlying the apparent circularity of many medieval definitions of *litteratus* as *clericus* is documentary evidence suggesting that the mastery or knowledge that clerics associated with literacy in Latin did not necessarily pertain at all to activities of writing or reading. To give just one example, when Pope Paschal III came to France in 1107, he met Abbot Guibert de Nogent and spoke to him—as the abbot himself relates in *De vita sua*—"non materno sermone, sed literis" ("not in maternal speech but in literate speech" or, less literally, "in Latin"). The claim to literacy here is not to a writerly mastery of letters but to a command of spoken Latin.[60] The claim, of course, comes to us only via a written record evidently penned by the abbot himself; but the statement nonetheless counters the modern assumption that literacy and writing are virtually synonymous. The medieval phrase *ars dictaminis*, denoting one of the three main branches of rhetoric, indicates that the physical act of writing was normally, rather than exceptionally, separated from the art of composing a text. One *dictated* one's words to a scribe, and whether one actually possessed the skill of alphabetic inscription often cannot be inferred from the remaining evidence about *litterati*.[61] In some cases, the term *litteratus* is clearly used to describe a mastery of Latin that does not involve skills either in deciphering or in reproducing alphabetic letters. M. B. Parkes describes Count Baldwin II of Guines, whose clerks read to him from his great library and who was esteemed (by clerks like those he employed) as highly *litteratus,* though he could neither read nor write for himself.[62]

"The clergy," John Boswell argues, "were by and large the only literate class during the [European] Middle Ages."[63] Much recent scholarship has been devoted to showing that some types of literacy and numeracy were in truth possessed not only by members of the praying estate but also by laypersons— in the terms of medieval estate theory, those who fought or governed (the aristocracy) and those who labored (the peasantry). I shall have more to say later about the literacies of the laity and the ways they are construed (often as "partial") by modern scholars. For the moment, I want to underscore the significance of Boswell's nuanced generalization for a study of literacy as a site of social contest. Boswell points our attention toward the Roman Catholic Church as an institution within whose sphere of influence literacy was both influentially defined and largely practiced for many centuries. The Church played a major role in gendering the field of literacy during the European Middle Ages; the influence of that gendering was felt, even in Reformed countries, long after the Middle Ages merged into the early modern era. Women as a group had less institutional access to what a powerful elite in their society defined as literacy than men did, simply because women were barred, on the authority of Saint Paul, from officiating in the Roman Catholic Church. Women "could not take the sacrament of the priestly order (*ordinatio*)"; hence women could enter the religious class only by taking the veil (Shahar, *Fourth Estate,* 1–2). Because many nunneries required girls to bring some sort of dowry with them, more high-status women than commoners entered the "regular" clergy, which starts to be distinguished from the "secular" clergy, or priestly hierarchy, in the twelfth century.[64] Men of various classes entered the clerical estate in significantly greater numbers than women did, and men of different social backgrounds had a greater chance of becoming *litteratus,* in the sense defined and regulated by the Church, than women did.

The cultural significance of this claim—and despite the gaps in demographic evidence, few historians would dispute it—will be elaborated in my discussion in chapter 2 of how the masculinist, even misogynous, attitudes of a predominantly male priesthood affected discourses about languages and language use. The absence of women from the Catholic priesthood that officiated at masses and administered the sacrament of communion (an absence that persists, of course, to this day) arguably exerts a subtle ideological pressure not only on medieval and early modern clerkly conceptions about literacy and language, but also on modern scholars who observe and explain that

distant culture. In some recent studies of medieval literacy, scholars write
women out of the picture simply by pronouncing so authoritatively on medieval culture that it becomes difficult to think about groups including women
who might have contested—in practice and/or in theory—the definitions of
literacy made visible by institutions such as the Church and the monarchical
court. Michael Clanchy has contributed enormously to our knowledge of late
medieval literacies in England by showing the importance of written records
not only among the lay nobility but also in peasant culture (for land convey-
ances, for instance). He nonetheless illustrates how easy it is to occlude gender
ideology as part of his object of study when he writes that "by the twelfth century *clericus* meant *litteratus, laicus* meant *illiteratus*" (*From Memory to Written Record*, 178). Meant *for whom*? Perhaps the definition with its normatively
masculine forms was accepted by that fraction of nuns who read and wrote in
Latin, but would it have been accepted by the "notable number of [Jewish]
women" whom Clanchy himself describes earlier as "literate in Hebrew" and
often, because of their business transactions with Christians, knowledgeable
as well in Latin, French, and English (ibid., 156)? Clanchy also describes medieval commentators who explicitly remark absurdities in uses of the synonyms just mentioned; Philip of Harvengt complains, for instance, in a text
dating from the 1180s, that "if anyone is comparing a knight who is *litteratus*
with a priest who is ignorant, he will exclaim with confidence and affirm with
an oath that the knight is a better *clericus* than the priest" (ibid., 178). Clanchy
interprets this passage as showing that "a learned knight would be called a *clericus*," and hence that "a person described as *clericus* in a document was not
necessarily a member of the clergy" (ibid., 178–79). That seems quite possible,
but if a contemporary is capable of mocking the usage, then why claim that
clericus "means" *litteratus* in this century? This may seem a trivial matter of
phrasing, but we need to be particularly careful about generalizations when
the topic is literacy. We should not assume that we know what the term *litteratus* means when we encounter it in a pre-eighteenth-century document; the
definition can only emerge (and then provisionally) from a labor of interpretation that will necessarily challenge the severely historicist position Clanchy
adopts when he insists that "medieval ideas of literacy were so different from
those of today that some modern questions are meaningless" (ibid., 182). Such
a statement assumes that the modern scholar knows the totality of medieval
culture well enough to pronounce on the complete irrelevance of "some modern questions" to the cultural object of study. The rhetorical effect of such a
statement is to discourage questions, and to do so from a position of authority closely akin to that which Michel Foucault critiques in the practitioners of
what he calls "total history" and which he describes as the mistaken idea that

"between all the events of a well-defined spatio-temporal area . . . it must be possible to establish a system of homogeneous relations" (*Archaeology of Knowledge*, 3). Clanchy's statement calls into question, against itself, all assurances about what literacy was and about which questions can be assumed to be askable.

Having suggested that the medieval association of literacy with Latinity was a dominant and highly influential phenomenon but not, even in its heyday, an uncontested one, I shall now consider some late medieval practices of literacy that escaped the dominant clerical ideology and that therefore offer an important context for understanding the momentous change that made literacy as knowledge (or feigned knowledge) of Latin a residual rather than dominant cultural meaning. Emergent meanings included the idea of literacy as an individual's competence in both reading and writing a vernacular language—the dominant meaning of the term today. I do not, however, believe that this meaning was dominant or even widely known in the sixteenth century. I would therefore qualify the description of the process of historical change given by Adam Fox: "In the high Middle Ages the term 'literatus' had denoted a cleric, or else someone 'scholarly' or 'learned' in the classics; 'illiteratus,' meanwhile, generally meant either a layman or someone without knowledge of ancient authors. All of these senses lingered throughout the early modern period. . . . But by the end of the fourteenth century the modern usages, denoting *basic ability to read and write in the vernacular,* were becoming widespread. In the sixteenth century they were normal" (*Oral and Literate Culture*, 46, my emphasis). Fox offers no evidence at all for the claim that a conception of literacy in this modern sense was "becoming widespread" by the end of the fourteenth century. Nor does he consider the possibility that some version of this definition existed before the Middle Ages, although William Harris finds just this idea of literacy—as competence in both reading and writing—in a passage by Tertullian (*Ancient Literacy,* 302). What interests me most in Fox's argument, however, is that his illustrations don't actually support the claim that literacy was normally seen as the ability to *both* read and write by the sixteenth century. He gives two examples to support the thesis. One example, from a late Elizabethan chorographical work, describes witnesses being able to sign title deeds "if they were literate"; the other, from Shakespeare's *Two Gentlemen of Verona*, refers to a "clownish servant" as an "illiterate loiterer" when "it is thought that he '[can] not read' a 'paper'" (Fox, *Oral and Literate Culture,* 46–47). The separation of a writing "illiteracy" from that involving failure to read is significant because reading and writing skills were not taught together in most early modern elementary schools. This is a key point, with ramifications I will continue to explore in this chapter. In contrast to most modern Western children, who learn to make letters before they can read whole sentences, early modern children (and adults) in both French and English sites, in houses and in primary schools, learned to read religious texts— and recite catechisms—long before they learned to write, if they learned the latter skill at all. Many children, especially girls and lower-class boys, did not stay in school long enough to embark on writing instruction, which required a much greater expenditure of money than reading a hornbook did.[65] Moreover, there is considerable evidence that in some early modern primary schools, curricula were differentiated in ways that reflected official views that girls should learn to read and sew, but not to write and do sums.[66] Fox is certainly right that an important change occurred in the cultural sphere of literacy between the medieval and early modern periods, but his description of the change and his way of adducing evidence for it arguably show an ideology of modernization at work on literacy as an object of scholarly study. No one writing from a modern academic institutional site can altogether escape the distorting effects of that powerful ideology, but one can go back to the always mediated evidentiary field and shake it up a bit—as I now hope to do—in order to allow dissenting, and sometimes perplexing, traces to cloud the picture of how and for whom historical changes occurred, and in what they consisted. New questions and knowledges may emerge from muddying the waters.

Many people in late medieval and early Renaissance Europe seem not to have considered either reading or writing as valuable skills necessary for their ways of living. Though written documents in various languages were increasingly important for many aspects of social life in English and French territories from the eleventh through the seventeenth centuries, access to written documents for most people, ranging from nobles to peasants, usually depended on hearing texts read and/or commissioning clerks to write them, without being able to read or write themselves. And such dependence on written texts, stressed by historians concerned with the social functions of literacy, coexisted, if uneasily, with widely held attitudes of scorn for clerks and their skills. Some aristocrats regarded the ability to write as a derogation of noble estate (the pen is lowlier than the sword).[67] Commoners too seem often to have viewed the ability to write as a debit—even an ethical blemish—rather than as an asset. This view is refracted—albeit within a complex ideological agenda—in Shakespeare's 2 Henry VI. In that play, Jack Cade interrogates a captured clerk with the question, "Dost thou use to write thy name, or hast thou a mark to thyself like an honest plain-dealing man?" The clerk's acknowledgment of his ability to write his name prompts Cade and his followers to hang the offender "with his pen and inkhorn about his neck."[68]

The historical Jack Cade, in striking contrast to Shakespeare's, had the ability to use pen and ink to write petitions. Specifically, Cade used his vernacular literacy to lead an uprising in 1450. He is represented by chronicler Edward Hall—in a text available to Shakespeare—as a "younge man of . . . pregnant wit" whose advisers were "scholemasters" and "teachers."[69] Shakespeare rewrites history to make Jack Cade resemble rebels in an earlier uprising, the Peasants' Revolt of 1381. Shakespeare thus arguably participates in a clerkly revision of history that extends over centuries to create an ideological distance between "illiterate" rebels and those who use their skills of writing to preserve social order. One can certainly see this clerkly tradition at work on the Peasants' Revolt: historians from the fifteenth-century chronicler Thomas Walsingham to G. M. Trevelyan in the early twentieth century have seen the rebels' "hostility to writing" in 1381 as (in Trevelyan's words), "the most universal feature of the Rising."[70] Walsingham, indeed, was so horrified by the burning of documents and "butchery" of clerks that he "subsumed the murder of various officials under the broader hostility to writing," as Susan Crane remarks in her study of competing ideas of literacy in this scene of social and economic struggle.[71] Such a "subsumption" is a significant ideological distortion, for it turns a symptom of economic discontent that seems particularly threatening to clerks into a major cause and also the most salient "feature" of the Peasants' Revolt. There is no doubt that documents were spectacularly destroyed in the 1381 uprising, but as Steven Justice shows in his brilliant book *Writing and Rebellion*, the rebels also preserved old documents if it suited their interests to do so; the point was to show "that the documents were available, subject to public deliberation, and disposable" (70). Justice reads the rising as a complex protest against the "stupefyingly unjust" system under which the poor lived and worked (ibid., 156). The rural poor certainly expressed hostility toward the clergy and the nobles, but the hostility had much more to do with the clergy and the gentry's wealth than with their literacy per se.[72] The tradition of historiographical writing in which Shakespeare arguably participates represents ignorant peasants as murderously hostile to literate men; this tradition has obscured but not totally destroyed the evidence that some of the rebels themselves possessed and used vernacular literacy as an instrument of insurgency. Justice's research counters the picture Crane presents when she argues that "the rebels remain outside representation in that they do not represent themselves for the written record" ("Writing Lesson," 201), although the novelty of Justice's research—which was conducted only in the late twentieth century— confirms Crane's perception of a long-durational "image" or ideology of the lower class as completely illiterate and, hence, as irrational (ibid.). The alleged irrationality of lower-class people and of women in general was, of course, a good reason, in the eyes of some literate persons, for withholding education altogether from those deemed incapable of using it except to threaten the social order. This ideological logic underpins the paradoxical situation analyzed by Frances E. Dolan in "Reading, Writing, and Other Crimes." This is the situation in which witchcraft cases could be, and were, bolstered both by accusations of literacy and by accusations of illiteracy.[73]

A site of fluctuating moral, theological, and political evaluations in late medieval and early modern England and France, literacy is also a site of contestation under the law—and in its multiple records. As Dolan remarks, under English common law, "an offender's literacy might enable him both to perpetrate speech crimes and to seek pardon (and avoid execution) for certain felonies" ("Reading, Writing, and Other Crimes," 145). But the offender's gender mattered too. English men but not women could "avoid execution for certain offenses by means of a legal fiction linking them to the clergy. In the Middle Ages, clerics had the right to be tried in ecclesiastical rather than royal courts for certain offenses. Proving that they were clerics by demonstrating their ability to read Latin, they could escape punishment in secular courts. In practice, this came to mean that those men who could read could achieve formal pardon and escape hanging" for various capital crimes (ibid.). By the early seventeenth century, the loophole had been narrowed for laymen (one could no longer claim benefit of clergy for murder and rape, for instance), but it was still widely used, as Cynthia Herrup's research on Sussex court records has shown.[74] The high number of successful pleas suggests that judges employed "flexible definitions of 'literacy'" (Dolan, "Reading, Writing, and Other Crimes," 145). It also seems likely that some male felons used their memories and strong feigning talents rather than their alphabetic decoding skills to substantiate their claims to be clerics. Since a common proof of clerical status was the ability to read Psalm 51, verse 1, the wonderfully named "neck verse," a man's memory might suffice to make him literate in the eyes of the law. So might his noble rank; as Eve Sanders remarks, Edward VI's first Parliament "allowed peers to plead benefit of clergy in regard to criminal offenses even if they could not read, and protected them, if convicted, from the penalty of being branded" (*Gender and Literacy*, 17).

Benefit of clergy is clearly a legal fiction that gave more benefits to some social subjects than to others, and feminist scholars have rightly noted the asymmetries between this loophole and the "plea of the belly" available to those female felons in England who could demonstrate or plausibly feign pregnancy to a judge and a jury of matrons.[75] Over several centuries of English history, a woman's literacy meant less in the eyes of the law than did her potential for maternity. But this conclusion, drawn by a number of recent scholars, needs to be correlated with further discussion about what it means that

King James's Parliament promulgated a law in 1622 extending the right to claim benefit of clergy to women convicted of stealing less than ten shillings' worth of goods because "so many women do suffer death for small causes."[76] One can interpret this law as a paltry exception to the larger rule allowing men but not women to claim material benefits from their literacy, but one may also interpret it as a record of its makers' perception of some significant change occurring in the field of literacy and in the society at large. The lawmakers evidently saw that increasing numbers of poor women possessed some kind of vernacular literacy—enough to make it plausible to extend to them a benefit already being applied to non-Latin-speaking Protestant men. Moreover, the lawmakers may have observed that such women and their kin were capable of fomenting social unrest at a gross miscarriage of justice, one named as such by many writers including Thomas More in the (Latin) *Utopia* of 1516. To execute someone for stealing a loaf of bread may have seemed excessive to at least some among James's literate lawmakers.

As the complex example of benefit of clergy suggests, many representations of literacy show strains in the clerical ideology defining literacy as the preserve of men knowledgeable in Latin. It is difficult to generalize about degrees of skill in vernacular reading and/or writing in late medieval and early modern England and France; members of different social classes, performing vastly different kinds of verbal actions from biblical glossing to economic accounting to the composition and consumption of racy pamphlets, romances, and sonnets, ascribed significantly different meanings to their dealings with written signs.[77] Moreover, many of these dealings were aurally and pictorially mediated, giving rise to numerous forms of literacy in different and mixed media. Historians have done much of late to increase our understanding of these different kinds of literacy, but when they are referred to as "partial literacies," we can see the imprint of the Great Divide theory that associates full or true literacy with alphabetic reading and writing. Some scholars, however, have begun to explore the ways in which late medieval documents are designed for users with different literacies that are not necessarily structured hierarchically. In chapter 4 we will see Christine de Pizan and Marguerite Porete imagining auditors as well as readers of their works; Porete polemically argues that the "unlearned" constitute a better audience for God's Word than clerks do. And for de Pizan, those with some ability to read French but not Latin offer the writer a culturally novel opportunity to revise classical myths she regards as misogynistic.[78] Bella Millett has discussed twelfth- and thirteenth-century manuscripts evidently designed both for analphabetic but visually literate listeners and for readers with different kinds and degrees of linguistic knowledge. The St. Albans Psalter, prepared for a well-born lady named Christina of

Markgate, opens with forty full-page miniatures depicting scenes from the Life of Christ. The text also includes the oldest surviving copy of the Old French *chanson* of St. Alexis, as well as an extract from a letter of Gregory "defending the use of pictures as a means of instructing the illiterate" and given both in the original Latin and in a French translation. The manuscript also includes the Latin Psalter, which "could have been used by anyone (including Christina) with a basic training in literacy," and a "lengthy untranslated Latin gloss on the first Psalm" (Millett, "English Recluses and the Development of Vernacular Literature," 91–92). Such cultural productions, with hybrid media as well as different imagined audiences, became more common in the high Middle Ages as more nonclerical subjects—members of the aristocracy and some commoners—evidently acquired skills in listening to or reading vernacular texts and in grasping texts in relation to visual representations. The mixed-media document aimed at readers with different kinds of knowledge and power persists into the early modern period and is clearly important for literary critics interested in how writers devise strategies for avoiding censorship. Techniques of allegorical encoding work to create what we might call deniability effects while also soliciting attention from readers who share the writer's religious or political goals. With the rise of vernacular literacies and the concomitant production of vernacular translations of the Bible, the clergy as a group began to lose their cultural hold on definitions and practices of literacy. The process was uneven; although she was the king's sister, Marguerite de Navarre was censored by Sorbonne theologians for a practice of literacy that offended official readers because it entailed the use of marginal citations from an early vernacular bible (see chapter 5).

We can view the phenomenon of multiple literacies in medieval and early modern England and France in the frame provided by two propositions accepted, if not uniformly interpreted, by all historians of literacy I have read: (1) the majority of the population of Europe between the fourth and the eighteenth centuries was unable to read or write alphabetically in any language; (2) the civilization in Europe in these centuries was, in Franz Baüml's phrase, "a literate civilization" in the sense that knowledge "indispensable" to the culture was transmitted in writing.[79] Accepting these two, only apparently paradoxical propositions does not require us to agree with Baüml's exact formulation of the latter point, written in a familiar authoritative-generalizing mode: "*the* knowledge indispensable to the functioning of medieval society was transmitted in writing: the Bible and its exegesis, statutory laws, and documents of all kinds" ("Varieties and Consequences," 237, my emphasis). My argument emends such a statement to say that *some* knowledges indispensable to some people were transmitted in writing, and that such knowledges were increasingly, if unevenly, of kinds amenable to being transmitted in numerical and vernacular language forms. Thus the society gradually became less dependent on a priestly caste unified by its knowledge of Latin and committed to a type of knowledge associated with that sacred language—a version of the situation scholars have called "scribal literacy."[80] Instead of distinguishing broadly between "preliterate" and "literate" societies, as historians and anthropologists sometimes do without examining the teleological assumptions in the former phrase, and instead of describing entire societies on the grounds that they possess "craftsman's literacy" as opposed to "mass literacy," I suggest that we construct our narrative of historical change on more finely calibrated analyses of how in a given society different kinds of knowledge, transmitted in different forms, gain and lose prestige in part through changes in institutions, economic structures, and governments, but in part also through struggles over cultural meaning carried out in various sites with various kinds of traces.[81]

An emphasis on literacy as a site of social contest, of complex negotiations (including deceptive ones) among those who produce signs, those who receive them, and/or those who attempt to govern or limit the boundaries of what may be produced, interpreted, and even thought, leads to a revised version of the stories many literary scholars tell about the rise of vernacular literacy as a key feature (and sometimes a cause) of the transition from medieval to early modern social formations. My emphasis on contest also invites some revision of the stories recent historians have been telling about medieval, early modern, and modern understandings of literacy. Dissenting from Adam Fox's explicit, and many other historians' implicit, assumption that a notion of literacy as the (basic) ability both to read and write in the vernacular became somehow dominant ("widespread") in a Renaissance era associated with the rise of nation-states and various challenges, political and theological, to the hegemony of the Roman Catholic Church, I readily grant that this conception of literacy was one among several meanings emergent on several cultural stages. But I dispute the assumption that this conception of literacy counted as "full" literacy for educated men in anything like the way it does for modern scholars. Indeed, we shall see educated men referring to those who can read, and perhaps even write, in one vernacular language as "unskilled" in letters. To analyze the ideologies of literacy emerging from and within the long clerical association of literacy with Latinity (or with a diglossic structure in which the "native" tongue is deemed lower than a foreign one), we must suspend some modern assumptions as far as we can. Above all, we must be skeptical about our desire to define literacy in ways that lend themselves to the task of measuring literacy across populations.

It is clear that estimates about literacy as a demographically measurable phenomenon vary enormously depending on how the skills in question are defined. Many scholars have tended to see literacy gradually increasing—these are the literacy "optimists," as William Harris calls them, and they have usually defined literacy as the ability to read alphabetically.[82] This definition underpins statements such as the following, printed in the *New Pelican Guide to English Literature* (1982) and quoted in Clanchy's essay on the role of mothers in teaching reading in the Middle Ages: "Probably more than half the population could read, though not necessarily also write, by 1500 [in England]."[83] The problem, of course, as David Kastan once remarked, is that reading leaves no traces of its occurrence.[84] Historians of reading thus frequently turn, willy-nilly, into historians of writing; in so doing, they often find themselves contemplating material obstacles to knowledge.[85] Marginalia, for instance, those fascinating traces of past readers' often informal reactions to a text, do not remain in the archives in anything like the numbers in which we can infer such notations to have been produced because the trade in rare books evolved in a way that privileged "virgin" margins to messily scribbled-on ones—unless, of course, the scribblers were famous.[86]

Some modern historians, dismayed by the paucity of evidence for measuring literacy defined as reading ability, have resorted instead to the "signature method" of measuring literacy. This method takes a written trace—a proper name—as a sign from which one can allegedly infer reading abilities across a certain population. Using this method of defining and measuring literacy, David Cressy has concluded that there was "70% illiteracy among men and 90% among women at the time of the [English] civil war" (*Literacy and the Social Order*, 176). Elsewhere in the same study, he restates the estimate for "illiterate" women in a passage that curiously, as Frances Dolan has remarked, seems to hold women—and especially mothers—"accountable for their low levels of literacy." "The truth is that most mothers were useless for the transmission of literacy because most of them were themselves unable to write. Some could read who could not write, but even these could hardly have taken their children much beyond the ABC. Close to 90% of the women in seventeenth-century England could not even write their names, so few of them could have made satisfactory teachers."[87] If one is trying to measure literacy through writing, one may be less tolerant of mothers and the differentiated kinds of knowledge they often practiced and passed on than if one is studying literacy as a function of the history of reading. Illustrating the latter approach, Clanchy analyzes medieval mothers who "initiate" children into culturally valuable kinds of religious knowledge that are not necessarily located in Latin or even in vernacular letters; he examines domestic pedagogical sites dependent as much on visual images and oral recitation as on texts in codex form ("Learning to Read," 34–37).

One conclusion to draw from the difference between Cressy's and Clanchy's views of mothers as educators is that students of literacy in medieval and early modern contexts must beware of making truth-claims based on the modern assumption that the phenomenon naturally includes both reading and writing. In the cultures under scrutiny, reading and writing behaviors were separated in significant ideological ways: many statements about the value of reading that Cressy and others cite as evidence of attitudes about literacy do not imply a positive attitude—or any attitude at all—about education in writing.[88] Reading and writing operations were also separated, as I have noted, in the methods, stages, and materials of primary education. Unless we disaggregate our modern conception of literacy, we cannot interpret a cultural situation in which a person who could read a broadsheet ballad might never learn to write, and one who could sign her or his name might very well not be able to read the document in question.

If, as Clanchy suggests, a mother could initiate a child into a community's sacred knowledge without possessing much Latin or even competence in alphabetic letters, such a woman could also initiate children into less sanctified domains of knowledge. As a cultural figure, she always carried the potential to teach illicit materials and/or to teach matters of doctrine in heretical ways. Early modern humanist educators, inheritors of the clerical priestly caste, often saw mothers and nurses as pedagogical rivals to male teachers; the threat was that such women might not merely serve as passive conduits to knowledge (on the Catholic model, denigrated by Protestants, of the Virgin teaching Christ or of Anne, the Virgin's mother, teaching her daughter); they might, rather, intervene in and even reshape domains of knowledge.[89] Hence, as we will see in chapter 2, many early modern educators sought either to instruct mothers in their duties or to remove children, especially male children, from the mother and especially from the lowly wet-nurse's sphere of influence, often associated with orality and with unregulated ("superstitious") genres of discourse. The threat for the modern historian is different but perhaps not unrelated: because more women than men lacked the alphabetic (and doctrinal) literacies taught in late medieval and early modern schools, what mothers and nurses taught is less amenable to being measured statistically than what men taught (some) children, mostly boys, in schools.

It is not surprising that a historian who seeks to measure literacy rates in an alien culture of the past would construe the teacher's role as the transmission of (alphabetic) literacy; other kinds of knowledge transmitted by various teachers, including female speakers of vernacular tongues, are missing from Cressy's picture. Without denying that his and others' attempts to measure early modern literacy have enriched our knowledge of social practices pertaining to reading and writing, I think we need to be clear that such measurement attempts originate in and return a set of modern concerns (and modernizing ideologies) that are discernible, but only in an emergent and problematic way, among some elites in the culture under scrutiny. Thomas More famously declared, in the context of a conservative theological argument denying that reading the Scriptures was important for salvation, that "far more than four parts of all the whole divided into ten could never read English yet."[90] Cressy interprets this remark, which he quotes from More's *Apologye* of 1533, as "suggesting that possibly up to 60% of the population could read," and he goes on to dispute such a statistic (*Literacy and the Social Order,* 44). But More's statement, which Richard Altick rightly calls "obscure," should not, in my view, even be approached as a statistical proposition in the modern sense (*English Common Reader,* 15–16). The discursive regime of statistics began only in the 1690s, though it certainly had some bureaucratic precursors in English and French governmental practices of identifying and collecting social data, mainly for purposes of taxation and for more amorphous projects (a group to which More's arguably belongs) of assessing and controlling opinions on political and religious matters important to the state.[91] Statistical statements, it seems, must therefore be subjected to interpretive pressure. What territories, for instance, are included in More's "whole"? What does he mean by "English"? How can his statement be correlated with other fragmentary and enigmatic statements about demographic "facts" that have remained in the written record, such as the observation made by Stephen Gardiner, bishop of Winchester, in 1547 that "not the hundredth part of the realme" could read (Altick, *English Common Reader,* 16)? Were More and Gardiner, two religious authorities from opposite sides of what became a Great Divide in faith, seeing entirely different "realms" of English readers? And what was Edmund Burke seeing when, in 1790, he "is said to have estimated that there were 80,000 readers in all of England"? This number, as Paul Hunter remarks, is seductive because "except for retrospective estimates—based on signatures in documents, on what modern demographers call 'back projection,' or on analogy and intuition—it is the only numerical 'figure' we have for eighteenth-century literacy in England, Wales, or Scotland" (*Before Novels,* 62–63). Hunter notes, however, that Burke's number has been disputed from the beginning, partly because it is so "shockingly low." If Burke is right, and if we take More's statement about percentages at face value—that is, if we take it as belonging to a genre of statements about demographic facts—fewer people could read in the England of 1790 than in the England of 1533 (Burke's estimate attributes reading abilities to about 1.3 percent of the approximately 6 million people in England at the time of the American Revolution). There are, in short, some serious problems at the heart of the modern scholarly business of determining statistics about early modern literacy; we might do well to step back from the business altogether and ask why we are pursuing it when the evidence is so enormously rich in variables and poor in credible truth-claims.

Statistics on early modern literacy are unreliable partly because the criterion of signatures is biased against women of various ranks as well as against many poor men who lacked access to the kinds of property transactions that provide our chief secular archive of signed documents in England before 1642.[92] In that year, the "Protestation Returns," a set of documents demonstrating allegiance to the Commonwealth Government and signed, in principle at least, by all adult males, created "the only seventeenth century evidence" about literacy (I would say, about minimal writing ability) that provides a cross-section from all over England; scholars who have studied the Protestation Returns conclude that there was a "signature-literacy rate of 30 percent for men and 10 percent for women."[93] For France there is no similar census-type of evidence until signing the *acte de mariage* became compulsory, for both men and women, in 1676. Nonetheless, François Furet and Jacques Ozouf, the two major historians of early modern French literacy, agree with Cressy that signatures provide "un bon baromètre de l'alphabétisation."[94] Other scholars, however, among them Margaret Spufford, Alain Derville, and Keith Thomas, have mounted serious critiques of historians' reliance on the signature method of measuring (and defining) literacy.[95] The method is arguably useless for studies focusing on women and nonelite groups because so many social factors other than a simple inability (or disinclination) to sign one's name play such a large role in determining the absence of such signatures from the historical record. As Franz Baüml has remarked, "the problem is not the employment of a signature as one of several criteria, or as possibly conclusive evidence for literacy, but the reliance on its *absence* or *substitute* [e.g., the X mark] as necessarily an indicator of illiteracy. For the act of signing (or not signing) by writing one's name below a given text is a . . . socially conditioned message, quite apart from the name which is, or is not, written by the hand of its bearer" ("Varieties and Consequences," 240–41). Moreover, the widespread use of seals in the place of "authentic" signatures by kings, chancellors, and even peasants (such as the widow Emma who contracted with the abbot of Gloucester in 1230 to "perform ploughing and other duties") suggests the difficulty of inferring "illiteracy" from an *absence* of a written signature.[96] Possession of a seal, as Clanchy remarks, "implied that its owner could read his own name, as well as being prepared to authenticate documents with the impress of his 'signature'" (*From Memory to Written Record*, 35). But possession and use of a seal does not tell us anything certain about whether a person could write—her own name or anything else.

The separation I have stressed previously between reading and writing skills in early modern societies—a separation assumed in some contemporary discourses and embedded in educational practices—poses a major problem for historians seeking to measure rates of literacy, though many scholars downplay the problem by arguing that the ability to sign is a fairly reliable "intermediate indicator between ability to read and ability to write, the number of people able to sign being fewer than those able to read, but more than those able to write."[97] The idea of a signature as a reliable if "intermediate" indicator looks considerably more dubious, however, when one carefully considers how gender and status asymmetries in the population that had access to formal education impinge on efforts to measure literacy across a broad social spectrum. The measurement problem becomes even thornier, in my opinion, when we recall that reading was taught *before* writing in many early modern English and French primary schools. The divide between literacy as the ability to receive instruction and literacy as the ability both to receive and to produce discourses and mathematical accounts is at the heart of the clerkly ideology of "partial" or imperfect literacy that I have mentioned before and will analyze in some detail in chapter 2. For the moment, I want to reiterate the need for skepticism about statistics such as Cressy's; these show women as a socially undifferentiated group at the bottom of a reconstructed hierarchy that indicates "how well the ranking based on [men's] literacy agreed with the ordering by status and esteem, and also the degree to which literacy was commensurate with alternative rankings by occupation and wealth" (Cressy, *Literacy and the Social Order*, 118).

Because of the problems inherent in the signature method of measuring literacy, some scholars have concluded that there is "absolutely no way of knowing how many women below the level of the gentry in England learnt to read" (Spufford, *Small Books*, 35). Feminist scholars such as Suzanne Hull and Caroline Lucas, who have inferred literacy rates not from written signatures but from the evidence provided by numbers of printed books dedicated to noblewomen and/or explicitly addressed to women, arrive at a considerably higher estimate of the number of English women readers than Cressy does.[98] Ironically, Cressy turned to the signature method in the first place because of his frustration with "indirect" types of evidence, most of which are "contaminated by the bias and interest" of human recorders (*Literacy and the Social Order*, 45) and all of which converge to support a "broad, vague, and uncontroversial" picture of "an increasingly literate population in the late sixteenth and early seventeenth centuries" (ibid., 53). Faced with such a predictable picture, we might pause to ask not how we can measure literacy better but why we moderns are so eager to quantify literacy in the first place. The prestige our society accords to scientific numbers lies behind this scholarly drive to measurement; so, I suspect, do unexamined ideologies of modernization that make contemporary societies' literacy rates into key indicators for decisions about allocating money for development. In any case, too heavy an emphasis on measuring literacy may be preventing us from asking other questions—and from exploring the kinds of evidence, new and old, that different questions might bring into play. Building on Cressy's valuable work while also interrogating its reliance on signatures, scholars have recently been expanding the archive of materials about literacy (through a focus on marginal annotations, for instance). Scholars have also recontextualized and hence reinterpreted documents long known to specialists but also not known, as Steven Justice argues for the set of enigmatic vernacular letters he rereads in *Writing and Rebellion*.[99]

It is fascinating to consider what our educated precursors meant when they wrote about literacy numbers—when, for instance, Giovanni Villani states that there were "from eight to ten thousand boys and girls learning to read" in Florence in the late 1330s. However, we must analyze such statements as if we were ethnographers attempting to understand an alien culture rather than as historians adducing them as evidence in a familiar modern quest for historical fact.[100] If ever greater accuracy is the hermeneutic goal of the numbers game, it seems doomed to failure. I don't think we are ever going to be able to say with any degree of certainty how many people could read and/or write in late medieval and early modern European societies; we lack reliable ways of measuring (what counts as) "basic literacy" rates in our own society. One reason for this is that so long as literacy is bound up with questions of social status, people are going to misrepresent or "produce" their kinds and degrees of this form of cultural capital. We cannot say for sure when people began to feel shame about being considered "illiterate," but anyone trained in psychoanalytic methods of interpretation can surmise that the process was well under way by the time Shakespeare represented poor people being willing to kill a clerk because he was (in some sense) literate. Historians have long recognized problems in determining rates of literacy on the basis of "unverified self-assessment," and some have worried about generalizations based on signatures because signatures don't emerge from a social vacuum; signing a marriage register, for instance, may be a highly charged act if one knows one's spouse cannot sign.[101] I can see why historians and sociologists do not want to allow questions of lying and shame to muddy the waters of the statistical enterprise, but I think Cressy is drawing much too neat a line between pre- and early modern behaviors and modern ones when he asserts that "the op- probrium attached to making a mark" was "so slight or nonexistent [before the eighteenth century] that learning a signature for its own sake must have been uncommon. There were no advantages in pretending to be literate when one was not; a signature had none of the power of a neck-verse" ("Levels of Illiteracy in England," 106). How can this claim be credible for a society in which, as Cressy himself elsewhere asserts, "exhortations to pious writing were by no means unusual" (*Literacy and the Social Order*, 6) and, for some subjects, in some economic and/or political contexts, the ability to write (to communi- cate, for instance, with others at a distance who might share one's views) might be just as important as the ability to read?

To ask such questions is to highlight the epistemological as well as histori- cal gaps between modern "commonsense" understandings of literacy and the set of phenomena that come under the rubric of early modern literacy. Recent scholars pursuing a culturalist approach have begun to explore those gaps in several ways, one of which involves examining the variety of forms in which alphabetic signs composing non-Latin writings appeared in early modern Europe. There were many different typefaces and scripts circulating in En- gland, as Keith Thomas remarks; indeed many commoners would have found it easier to read texts printed in "black-letter" type than in roman type; and some people who could have read a printed text would have found one in a Chancery hand illegible.[102] Despite the modern assumption that if one knows how to read, one can read any "basic" text and can, moreover, teach oneself to write, the journeys from one kind of reading to another, and from any reading to any writing, seem to have been full of complex stages and obstacles for early modern women as well as for many men in the provinces, the colonies, and the lower ranks of society.

Even when men and women had some degree of skill in alphabetic writing, a significant evidentiary problem remains for the modern scholar because such subjects might have good reasons for disguising their possession of writing skills. One significant mode of disguise was writing anonymously or pseudonymously. Because of the "stigma of print" that existed in England (though not, it seems, in France), some well-born English men and women chose to write pseudonymously, as also did persons interested in articulating censorable religious and/or political ideas. The existence of such works, which interrogate modern notions of authorship as ownership of one's text, may spur us to broaden the evidentiary field for literacy to include a wide range of doubtful, multiple, or partial forms of text production and social interaction. Seeing authorship as a spectrum of activities, some of them sites of sharp historical debate about cultural values and also about property rights and gender roles, is a precondition for studying literacies of the late medieval and early modern periods.

Such an expanded conception of authorship would include translation in its area of investigation. Translation allows us to study instances of writing as revisionary readings of precursor texts. Moreover, as I argued in the prologue, translation is a key site for reflecting on (and counterfeiting) literacy, gender, and kinds and degrees of political and religious faith. The boundary between interpretation and primary text becomes as blurry as that between author and translator for the cultural historian interested in literacy as a scene of social contest. Marguerite de Navarre dramatizes group debates about sacred and secular narratives in her *Heptaméron*; there, a Bible reading (a *leçon*, with the same ambiguities activated by Lévi-Strauss's use of that term in *Tristes Tropiques*) issues from an authoritative older woman in a mixed-gendered aristocratic gathering and prompts other interlocutors to disagree sharply, while they also engage in courtly banter. Such scenes of mixed reading and speech, leading some characters to write their thoughts down before the next day's session, also occur in Castiglione's *Courtier* (1516). Such scenes belong to a tradition of cultural practice we can only partly reconstruct, since the oral component is filtered through the writing either of contemporaries or of modern scholars such as Erich Auerbach. He makes images of noblewomen leading vernacular reading sessions (and thus inspiring or becoming patrons of writers he imagines only as male) critical to his vision of the transition between the Middle Ages and the Renaissance (*Literary Language and Its Public*, 204).

I am arguing, then, that the consolations of any "direct," "uncontaminated" evidence about early modern literacies are simply not available to us. Recent scholars of medieval and early modern European cultures have done a great deal (though much still remains to do) toward the project of reconceiving the evidentiary field for research on gendered literacies. Scholars have been exploring what Cressy calls "indirect" evidence about literacy, ranging from records about wills, book production, book ownership, and school curricula, through letters, literary works (especially prefaces addressing female readers), and inventories in notarial archives, to court records and opinions bearing on reading and writing in legal statutes. The fuzziness of the information available from such sources need not, however, be a cause for lament; on the contrary, it can be seen as an asset to a model of cultural interpretation that interrogates scholarly claims to epistemological certainty or closure. These claims may say as much about our institutions of knowledge production and their hierarchies as about some putative objects of knowledge and the possibility of objectivity itself.[103] In any case, historical information about literacy dramatizes the relation between disciplinary routines in the early modern period and those that continue to condition the ways in which they are described or produced in the post-1945 configuration of empire—a configuration that is always different from and similar to past configurations to a degree we can never hope to specify exactly but that may nonetheless become more visible through labors of comparative analysis.

In chapter 2 I look in more historical detail at the intertwined linguistic matrices of the territories claimed by French and British monarchs during an era characterized, for the historian of literacy, by the intensity of the competitions among languages, and in particular by a situation that the French educator René Balibar has termed *colinguisme*.[104] This situation, a variant of the modern ones Joshua Fishman describes as "destabilized" multilingual or "diglossic" situations, arises in Europe when Latin, regional vernaculars, and theories and practices of "illustrious" or "official" vernaculars exist in a structural relation of competition and mutual definition.[105] From these linguistic matrices, associated with different kinds of language education, various literacies emerged and were often then deployed to redefine the linguistic matrices. In the French and English territories with which I am particularly concerned, the question of language is enormously complex, partly because versions of both nations' languages were used for centuries on both sides of the body known as La Manche or the English Channel, and on British islands in that channel, Jersey, Guernsey, and Sark, where "Anglo-Norman-French" languages (some call them dialects) are still spoken today, though only rarely to strangers.[106] There are, in short, more provincial language practices on earth than most metropolitan scholars allow.

Sociolinguistic Matrices for Early Modern Literacies
Paternal Latin, Mother Tongues, and Illustrious Vernaculars

Language and literacy are two distinct entities, and . . . the second term is a shorthand
description for a determinate set of relations that we have to language, relations that
arose under, and were conditioned by, concrete historical circumstances.
VLAD GODZICH, "The Culture of Illiteracy"

The distinction between speech and writing is useful for classifying the problems that the
rising sun of the New World and the twilight of medieval Christianity would reveal to an
intelligentsia.
MICHEL DE CERTEAU, *The Writing of History*

Only when the making of the "nation," an entirely abstract group based on law, creates
new usages and functions does it become indispensable to forge a *standard* language.
PIERRE BOURDIEU, *Language and Symbolic Power*

Many historians and sociolinguists concur in linking early efforts to promote
"standard" vernacular languages with the emergence of nationalist ideologies
accompanying or at least enabling the emergence of the nation-state in Europe.[1] There is less consensus, however, about what the word *standard* means
when applied to past or present language uses, whether in speech or writing.
There is, as I have noted, a long history of debate about standard or standardized language (the latter phrase evokes something mysteriously agentless, as
does the kindred notion of "received pronunciation"). Although I will not, after this sentence, put quotation marks around "standard" or many of the other
terms that modern as well as early modern writers have used to denote the
phenomenon under discussion, I will assume that words such as *standard, national, uniform, pure,* and *proper,* when applied to proper names for languages
such as English, French, or Italian, point to an arena of ongoing inquiry and
debate rather than to a set of empirically specifiable features of either spoken
or written practice.

Many modern scholars do, to be sure, understand standardization in language as a self-evident notion, a reference both to a set of facts about language
and to a phenomenon that is valuable to the economic and educational mis-
sions of modern societies. Other theorists, however, constituting an increasingly visible minority coming from several academic disciplines, hold with

Raymond Williams that a standard language occurs when "a selected (in English, class-based) usage becomes authoritative," providing a model of "correctness, which, widely backed by educational institutions," works to "convict a majority of native speakers . . . of speaking their own language 'incorrectly.'"[2] Williams further argues that in many discursive contexts—those, for instance, defining dialects as "subordinate" versions of a "singular" national language—the standard becomes a metaphysical fiction defining language as "existing in other than its actual variations" (*Keywords,* 106).

In what follows, I explore a field of textual evidence, including a clerkly tradition of idealist thinking about Latin and several English writers' ambivalent statements about French, that works to complicate both the minority and the majority modern views of standard languages. I am not a neutral arbiter between these positions. On the contrary, I maintain that the minority view has much more to offer the feminist cultural historian than the majority view does; at the same time, however, I follow Colin MacCabe in believing that the minority modernist view on standardization articulated by Williams and others has tended to privilege speech over writing (for politically understandable but no longer analytically useful reasons) and has thus neglected to analyze the imbrication of (the idea of) a national standard in what MacCabe calls a "heterogeneous system of language-practice"—and, I would add, of language theories (*Eloquence of the Vulgar,* 64). In the historical terrain explored here, theories about languages shape practices, and vice versa. I also stress that debates about the relative value of different languages—Latin versus a "mother tongue," for instance, but also English versus French and "northern" languages versus southern ones—impinge on the history of the idea of a national standard just as strongly, though in different ways, as do debates about the relative value of speech versus writing as objects of scholarly inquiry.

The question of when, and how, written standards impinged on oral language uses is exceedingly complex—more so, in part because of the evidentiary weight of the written record, than scholars of medieval and early modern cultures sometimes allow. Joseph B. Trahern writes, for instance, in his introduction to a collection of essays entitled *Standardizing English,* that "Middle English standards . . . differ sharply from [our] modern conception [of a standard language] . . . in that they exist, and existed, *only* in the written mode, for standardisation in spoken English belongs to a much later period" (3). By a "much later period," Trahern seems to mean the eighteenth century; like many scholars focusing on early written documents, however, he excludes from his field of inquiry evidence pertaining to how ideologies about proper speech were disseminated through written texts. A history of standardization as a heterogeneous set of discourses in which ideas about speech and writing influenced practices in both domains, and vice versa, must relinquish neatly linear dating schemes. At the same time it must deploy a highly skeptical attitude toward evidence pertaining to relations between prescriptive texts and actual social practices in populations divided by gender, social status, religion, and many other factors influencing how people use languages and—equally important, from my perspective—how people feel that language use works as a mark of social difference. Texts discussed in this chapter and the next suggest, in any case, that prescriptive statements about speech, emanating from members of a clerkly class dependent on writing (and teaching) for a living, made ideas about standard speech a culturally significant phenomenon in England and France long before the eighteenth century.

Early modern concepts of a standard language, as I've suggested, come under many names and have many ideological filiations. I focus here chiefly on those that lead us back to late medieval discourses about the superiority of Latin, as a timeless, stable, and masculine language, over vernaculars figured as variable and feminine.[3] Deriving even some of their terms for a vernacular ideal of language from Cicero's authoritative example (the ideal speech should be pure, for instance, as Cicero proclaimed in *De oratore*), early modern educators and men of letters used such words as *proper, right, common, usual,* and *received* to describe an idea of language also denoted by the phrase "the King's English."[4] This last phrase points almost comically to the discrepancy between an emergent idea of language as the property of the crown and the actual linguistic practices of various monarchs: think for instance of the highly regional style in orthography and (Scots) diction of James I; his spoken English would hardly have exemplified the ideal of proper speech articulated by some of his contemporaries. A similarly heterogeneous cluster of adjectives, among them *bon, propre,* and *naturelle,* points to an emergent ideal of good style in French.[5] Any attempt to trace the embedded (and sometimes contradictory) historical meanings of these terms—consider, for example, the clashing ideological fictions in "King's English" and "common English"—undermines common modern assumptions about standard languages as natural adjuncts (causes and effects) of the modernizing process, with its emphasis on the efficiencies of standardization in various social spheres.

The clerkly discourses examined in this chapter and the next at once refract and seek to manage changes in the sphere of language. These discourses also, I contend, contributed substantially to making French and English into prestige dialects that were, like Latin, *not* accessible to a great many historical subjects. These people, because of their gender, their class status, and/or their geographical distance from the places where the new, national vernaculars were chiefly taught and modeled, found themselves in the odd situation of not knowing what some of their countrymen referred to as their mother tongue. False mothers were multiplying, it seems, as were bastard speakers of the language(s) of the land. Whether or not such speakers acquired alphabetic literacy, they mostly lacked access to forms of the written language culturally marked as worthy of reproduction through manuscript copying and, later, print.

To put such historical subjects more fully into the picture of the history of literacy than has usually been the case, my story begins when England became a "conquest" of that part of France (the Roman empire's Gallia) known as Normandy.[6] The Norman Conquest decisively shaped the way in which the English nation-state emerged. According to Anthony Smith, the Normans illustrate how an "aristocratic *ethnie*" (or ethnic community) can use "bureaucratic incorporation" of "subject ethnies" to lay the foundation for a "unitary" state.[7] The Norman Conquest, which made English territories a part of an evolving political entity we now call France, also proved decisive for the development of a national language and a nation-state on the French side of the Channel. French, moreover, played a key role in the development of gendered concepts of literacy and of language, as we will see.

During the late medieval and early modern eras in both French and English territories, an old language of empire, Latin, which had been adopted by the transnational institution of the Roman Catholic Church, was gradually replaced, in many spheres of social life, by other languages that were "imperial" in at least two senses. First, such languages were chiefly developed by clerks working for monarchies seeking to expand their territories and powers. Second, such languages, both in practice and in theory, were modeled on Latin, or, more precisely, on an ideal of *Latinitas* encompassing both the grammatical and the rhetorical features denoted in a phrase like *bonae litterae*; this ideal is illustrated in well-known humanist texts such as Erasmus's *Ciceronianus, or, A Dialogue on the Best Style of Speaking* (1528). Clearly conflating elements of what modern scholars consider both "basic" and "cultural" literacy, the ideal of *Latinitas* was conceived by Roman rhetoricians and by their Renaissance heirs as a "correct" linguistic practice, one free from "barbarisms," "solecisms," and "corruptions." This ideal had qualities easily transferred from the language itself to language users. Those defined as "barbarians" spoke a barbarous Latin and lacked "literature." By the sixteenth century in England, the social realm of "not-literature" encompassed what John Colet, dean of St. Paul's grammar school, called "blotterature," the product of a person unable to form good letters with his pen as well as, in a more figurative sense, a book "below the standards of polite learning."[8] In his *English School-Maister* of 1596, Edmund Coote uses the adjective *unskilfull* to describe those he is addressing as potential teachers of elementary schools and whom he distinguishes from the "learneder sort." His comment is interesting because he is directing his instruction to "men and women of trades (as Taylors, Weavers, Shop-keepers, Seamsters, and such other)" (A3r)—that is, persons who are clearly highly skilled in their trade but are nonetheless defined by the educator as unskilled. Coote's formulation points to the emergent conception of imperfect or partial literacy, which I have discussed earlier. This conception is something different from, but nonetheless related to, the dominant medieval definition of literacy as mastery of Latin; this type of literacy for the "unskillful" should not be equated with the emergent modern definition of literacy as basic competence in the reading and writing of one vernacular language. It is a partial or imperfect kind of literacy for people defined chiefly as readers, not writers, by educated men creating texts in a grammaticized vernacular. As such, this ideological construction stresses a relative or relational literacy that emerges from a vision of reader-consumers adumbrated by writers deeply attached to an old idea of Latinity but also invested—for economic, political, and theological reasons—in reaching an audience that lacks more than a smattering of Latin, that has considerable competence in deciphering alphabetic letters in the vernacular, and that needs, above all, to be persuaded that it would benefit from (further) education in the form of a book. This clerkly construction is visible (in a typically negative formulation) in Edmund Rive's statement of 1618: "it is impossible for an English person thoroughly to understand his own language, to speake or write it rightly, without the skill of Latine"; it has a venerable and international history, as Paul Grendler suggests in his study of Renaissance Italian education.[9] An early and influential articulation of this view appears in Dante's decision to write his Christian epic for an audience *volgari e non litterati*.[10] The phrase refers, I contend, to readers (or auditors) who can understand a text written in (a version of) Italian but who are "not lettered" because they lack Latin.

When Dante writes in a version of Italian, he addresses urban readers (and perhaps auditors) who are most likely members of Dante's own middling class and his social superiors (MacCabe, *Eloquence of the Vulgar*, 148). Members of this audience, which might potentially include women and other social inferiors as well, have as a defining characteristic that the writer who himself knows Latin sees these *volgari* as literate enough to be educated, drawn in some way to a cause in which the writer's own interests are engaged. Defining an educable or partially literate audience, Dante also influentially defined a vernacular language that is in need of being made more "illustrious" than it currently is: language, like the "vulgar" reader, becomes a site to be improved by the educator's labor. Dante, I argue, plays a key role in the historical emergence of a new concept of literacy and language, and a readership that included women and nonclerical men. This complex of ideas goes hand in hand with Dante's call for a "unified" Italy, a monarchy to be modeled on (an idea of) the Roman empire.

The complex of ideas about language, literacy, readers, and the state is a metropolitan cultural product by virtue of its references to language standards formulated by ancient Romans and by virtue also of its dissemination chiefly in urban and courtly centers, such as Rome, Florence, Paris, and London.[11] Ideas about the best language—to be spoken and written by the best people but to be recognized, as superior, by other people too, including those who wish to rise socially through education—are yoked, but not in any natural fashion, with emergent ideas about what constitutes the center of a state, social and geographical. According to this emergent set of discourses, which corresponds in ways we cannot easily specify to actual historical practices, a certain kind of literacy or literature is by definition unavailable to those who speak only—and only speak—provincial tongues. Before such tongues were defined as "provincial" with reference to an early modern concept of an imperial center, they were defined as "diverse" by Latin-speaking clerks whose descriptions of linguistic diversity frequently come with expressions of desire to correct a lamentable situation. I see those medieval clerkly discourses as a significant matrix for contested concepts of early modern literacy.

Diverse Tongues

> Our langage now used varyeth ferre from that whiche was used and spoken whan I was borne. For we englysshemen ben borne under the domynacyon of the mone . . . [Like the moon], that comyn englysshe that is spoken in one shyre varyeth from a nother. In so much that . . . a mercer cam in to an hows and axed for mete, and specyally he axyd after eggys. And the goode wyf answerede, that she coude speke no frenshe. And the merchaunt ws anygry for he also coulde speke no frenshe, but wolde have hadde egges; and she understode him not.
>
> CAXTON, preface to his translation of Vergil's *Eneydos*

For Caxton, as for many before and after him in the clerkly tradition, diversity of language is an impediment to a project of nation-building that sees England as an heir of Rome. The egg-selling "goode wyf" referred to in my epigraph is a comic and lower-class version of Vergil's Dido insofar as she figures a certain resistance to Caxton's project, a man of letters' version, we might say, of Aeneas's epic labor. The example of the woman impeding trade reminds us that in precapitalist Europe, most men and women spoke regional languages disseminated within and between the political entities we now call nations. Even modern European peoples still speak such languages, and they do so

more often than most tourists or educators realize; now, however, an un-
counted (uncountable?) number of regional language speakers are bilingual
and thus can disguise their uses of nonnational native tongues. But perhaps
degrees of such bilingualism existed in more instances than we know of in medieval Europe, too; it's hard to know, and that is part of my argument against
simplified versions (and evaluations) of the modernizing story. Both medieval
and early modern *litterati* discuss the phenomenon of great linguistic diversity, and they usually define it negatively, through a contrast with an ideal of
linguistic stability and unity. The contrast is not infrequently gendered, as it is
in the passage from Caxton's prologue. Caxton depicts a comic scenario of
misunderstanding but implies a serious problem for England and Englishmen. The problem has both political and economic dimensions, as Caxton
suggests. The lower-status woman in his prologue serves as an emblem for the
variability of the "mother tongue" itself and for the emasculated condition
which that variability seems, in Caxton's view, to foster. Englishmen, who are
now "under the domynacyon of the mone," can remedy their situation by a
patient, heroic, and Aeneas-like *labor* on the part of literate men like himself—
a labor that includes "enriching" English through translation of foreign works
and also stabilizing the language by various means including, for Caxton, the
technology of print itself.

The instability Caxton saw and sought to correct is dramatized by a
fourteenth-century Cambridge manuscript that, according to its scribe, was
"translate oute of northarn tonge into sutherne that it schulde the bettir be
vnderstondyn of men that be of the selve countrie."[12] The scribe points to the
chasm between "northern" and "southern" languages that existed both in English and in French writers' perceptions of their lands as geographical entities
possessing some kind of unity—or ideas thereof derived from descriptions
of Roman Gaul or Britain—beneath linguistic diversity. Though the "north/
south" linguistic split developed in strikingly different ways in late medieval
France and England, clerks in both countries worked at the behest of aristocratic patrons not only to define such a split but also to assimilate it to an ideologically charged dichotomy between metropolitan and provincial modes of
language use. In so doing, clerks participated in a process well known to medievalists but obscured in courses and texts that stress a "history of the English
language" consisting of a linear development from "old English" to "Middle
English" to "modern English." If, however, the four major dialects usually considered under the rubric of Old English were replaced, as W. F. Bolton writes,
by "five in Middle English, with an emergent sixth in the London region, an
amalgam of the characteristics of East Midlands with some of those of the
South Eastern and a few of South Western," that process of replacement, like
the subsequent "rise" of the so-called standard versions of English, did not

simply happen by nature ("Early History of English," 293). Nor did Francien, the name given by nineteenth-century scholars to the language of the Parisian region, become the dominant language of France by even such a bleak natural process as the Darwinian survival of the fittest. On the contrary, according to Bernard Cerquiglini, scholars oversimplify matters considerably when they attribute an originary and positive quality to a dialect they identify as one historically spoken in the Ile de France region.[13] Cerquiglini makes a persuasive case for Francien being a clerkly—and interregional—written language that came to predominate, in the Ile de France region, only after the thirteenth century and only after literary and bureaucratic writing began to affect the speech of the elite. Although many sixteenth-century humanist educators liked to compare languages to plants, some stronger, some weaker than others and all in need of "cultivation," such organic analogies are highly misleading.

In the territory the Romans called Britannicae Insulae—and which they thus unified linguistically as part and parcel of an imperial colonizing project—there were, of course, more languages even than those which historians of English usually describe as "dialects" (I will return to that vexed word). One fourteenth-century English manuscript, perhaps by Lydgate, attributes the linguistic "confusion" of England to England's having been five times invaded by strangers (including the Romans) who "each time had changed the language."[14] In the territory that became France there were also many languages. They were used on both sides of the great divide between the southern and northern language groups known as the *langue(s) d'oc* and *langue(s) d'oïl*.[15] Words from the former are preserved in legal deeds from the eleventh century, and by the beginning of the twelfth the vernacular literary movement of the troubadours had begun. The *langue d'oc* developed during the next two centuries in complex relation to the development of heretical religious movements opposed not only to the doctrines of the Church but to its institutional language. Philippe Wolff tells the story of two "Cathari" from Toulouse presenting Church officials with a statement in Occitan in 1178; the officials, who had been sent to combat heresy, invited the Cathar representatives to speak Latin "so as to be better understood," but the two men "professed to know none, and the discussion had to be continued in *langue d'oc*" (*Western Languages,* 151).

In addition to the multiple local languages spoken in various territories claimed by English and French monarchs during the late medieval era, some people spoke a "craft" or "guild" language—usually a language that varied from a regional one more in lexical than in syntactic features, as modern professional languages do also, often thereby incurring the charge of being "jargon." That negatively charged word, appropriated into English from French in the fourteenth century, once meant, in both tongues, an inarticulate sound, as in birds' warbling; by the seventeenth century, however, some educated English men of letters were using it to describe a "barbarous, rude, or debased language" and, in particular, a "hybrid" or mixed language (*OED*). The new meaning itself participates in a process of "debasing" that occurred over many centuries but did so, I contend, in a more contested (and less conclusive) way than many modern scholars suggest. Sometimes our own professional habits of discourse prevent us from attending to the evidence of conflict in the field of language use. These habits may result in an oversimplifying of the stories of modernization we tell—even when we are telling them critically. Two examples may serve to illustrate this point. One is provided by Pierre Bourdieu when he states categorically that between the fifteenth and seventeenth centuries, the term *patois* (defined in *OED* as an "English" word, derived from French, meaning "illiterate dialect") "ceased to mean 'incomprehensible speech' and began to refer to 'corrupted' and coarse speech, such as that of the common or 'vulgar' people" (*Language and Symbolic Power*, 47). Such a statement comes, epistemologically, from outside and above the domain of historical oral usage—a domain of "diverse tongues" that we cannot directly know, but which nonetheless has left many traces in the written record of meanings for the word *patois* other than the two Bourdieu gives to describe a change he takes as definitively symptomatic of the modernizing process. Brunetto Latini explains in a text written around 1267 that he speaks in the French "patois" rather than the Italian one because the former is "plus delitable et plus commune a toutes gens."[16] Here we see that the term may well have been used when issues of language comprehension and language choice were at stake—but not all uses or users would have seen the "patois" from the outside and therefore judged it "incomprehensible" during the early period Bourdieu hypothesizes (following some recent French lexicographers); nor does it seem likely to me that the early positive or neutral meanings of the word (*en sa patois*, meaning *à sa façon*, "in his or her way") would have disappeared by the seventeenth century.[17] In other words, Bourdieu may correctly point to a significant drift or trend—but the evidence is partial and the matter entails so much speculation about people's perspectives on their own and others' languages (and their own versus others' social standing) that one risks reinforcing or even extending a repressive social process when one makes such authoritative pronouncements about modernization based on linguistic evidence that is not, by definition, representative of how a fractured population spoke or even wrote.

My second example comes from a book mentioned earlier, Adam Fox's history of orality and literacy in England. He states that "the [English] term 'dialect' emerged in the last quarter of the sixteenth century to refer to those subordinate varieties of the vernacular which did not conform to 'pure,' 'common,' or 'usual' English" (*Oral and Literate Culture,* 57). Fox cites Paula Blank as an authority for this view about the meaning of *dialect,* but some of Blank's evidence directly counters Fox's apodictic statement. The evidence doesn't even come from the speech of some lowly peasant as refracted in a literate person's text; rather, it comes from a figure both produced by and parodic of the scholarly tradition, that "E. K." who annotated Spenser's *Shepheardes Calendar.* In his preface to that work (1579), E. K. insists that the poet's habit of using "old words" should not be so indulged that "the commen Dialecte and manner of speaking" be "corrupted" by the practice.[18] As Blank demonstrates, *dialect* in English initially signified simply a "manner of speaking." The word was used in positive ways before it became associated with a "subordinated" form of a (standard) language. Although the *OED* cites that second meaning as arising contemporaneously with the first (in the 1570s), none of the examples the *OED* gives for the second meaning occurring before 1794 actually supports the definition. On the contrary, the examples (e.g., "certaine Hebrew dialectes," "the Aolic dialect") suggest that the English word here signifies a non-English manner of speaking. Both Fox and the compilers of the "D" section of the *OED* seem unable to grasp the evidence that *dialect* could initially be used to signify a "common" language that was indeed sometimes contrasted (albeit ironically, as in E. K.'s preface) to the "outlandish" languages used (and invented) by scholars and poets. The various meanings of *dialect* in English, Blank shows, emerge in a changing and contentious field of discourse where descriptions of language use always need to be interpreted with reference to the writer's social location and rhetorical/ideological aims. The first dictionary definition of *dialect,* indeed—John Bullokar's in *An English Expositor* (1616)—presents it simply as a "difference of language" (Blank, *Broken English,* 7). In this usage, *dialect* names a relation to or a perception of language rather than an essence. Bullokar does associate dialectal difference with difference "of Place," but without making any comments about the superiority of some places to others. In many early modern texts, however, *dialect* does work polemically (though not always predictably) in discursive efforts to discriminate valued language uses—and users—from ones that the writer or his employer wants to devalue. Some of the early battles in which *dialect* plays a role point ahead to the modern sociolinguist's joke: "What's the difference between a language and a dialect? The former has an army and a navy."[19] Some early uses of *dialect,* however, denote difference in ways we find hard to imagine. The meanings Bourdieu and Fox attribute to *patois* and *dialect* respectively (and it is interesting that the words become synonyms in modern French dictionaries like the *Petit Larousse*) did emerge and did become dominant—but not without opposition. The traces of these opposing voices solicit our attention, along with the ways in which they were represented and, as part of that process, defined as appropriate objects for punishment by Church and state authorities.

Heretical religious sects, criminals, and scholars were all, at one time or another, characterized as having a dangerous "difference" of language; it is often hard, especially in the cases of heretics and criminals, to discern what the vilified language practice consisted in. Scholars have fared better because they had more control of the written record, more recourse against censoring powers. Nonetheless, the parallels are instructive—and remain so, since modern attacks on scholarly jargon, almost always directed against humanists rather than scientists, often accuse the users of the jargon in question of a kind of criminal or heretical stance with regard to the national body politic. The Lollards were repeatedly accused of having a "distinctive language" in which peculiarities of vocabulary were yoked to specific features of preaching style and—by extension—to dangerous aspects of Lollard doctrine (Hudson, "Lollard Sect Vocabulary?" 16). The Lollards were perceived as thieves of Christ's true legacy, as held by the Church. Secular thieves were also accused of using their distinctive languages against the social order. Paula Blank shows that the "original English-English dictionaries" were glossaries of "cant," a language allegedly invented by its users to dupe others (*Broken English*, 18). Significantly, the criminals' "cant" is a "jargon," in the emergent sense of that word—a "hybrid" language that challenges the idea of national borders as well as of state authority. In his *Description of England* (1577), William Harrison describes beggars and thieves as having "devised" a language that "none but themselves are able to understand"; they name it "canting," he reports, but others call it "pedlers' French." "The first deviser thereof was hanged by the neck, a just reward" (cited in Blank, *Broken English*, 18). A mixture of French and "invented" words, the criminals' language as Harrison describes it sounds amazingly like the instances of hybrid language use both invented and parodied by Rabelais—or by English writers like Spenser, Shakespeare, and Nashe, all of whom coined new words with abandon while also mocking clerkly jargons. Blank explores the connection between the work of thieves and the work of men of letters in her chapter "Thieves of Language" (*Broken English*, 33–68). I do so in later chapters of this book discussing women writers who reflected on and sought to justify modes of verbal imitation and invention (as "counterfeiting" of new words, for instance) that look very like theft. The idea of a professional language—of thieves or of *litterati*—opens an important window onto the modernizing process as a set of interlocked socioeconomic and ideological changes. Clerks often served the monarchy, but they also created spaces for opposition. Sometimes the opposition was merely of the loyal variety in its long-term effects, but sometimes it worked—and might continue to work—unpredictably. Such, I think, is the exemplary value of the early "glossaries" of criminal cants, dialects, or jargons, which we know (very partially) through writings of those who at once deplored these languages and were fascinated by them, perhaps because in some ways the criminal cants held up a mirror to more respectable varieties of English and French that were also increasingly hybrid and full of neologisms drawn from around the world. If London criminals spoke "pedlers' French," they did so in order to profit, though in unsanctioned ways, from an expanding system of trade. There were, Blank tells us, official efforts to censor their use of a "secret" language, this "venomous and disgusting ulcer of our nation" that one sixteenth-century observer characterized as "no proper dialect but a cant jargon."[20] What is the difference between "proper dialect" and "cant jargon"? The latter, it seems, became the object of monarchical censorship—as, in the same century, did the dialects/languages of Welsh and Gaelic. The censorship of criminal jargon took the fascinating form of indictments making it illegal to use precisely those terms which the "glossaries" of cant explained to readers of a vernacular language. Such readers thus became included in the circle of those who could be punished for designating "certain criminals such as dicers, carders, or vagrants by terms that identified their true means of gaining a living"; the rationale for the punishment was that "these terms, many of them cant words, referred to 'occupations' forbidden by the state."[21] Here is a telling example of clerkly glossers and state authorities ostensibly both working to devalue and suppress criminal language and livelihood, but the efforts at suppression, fantastically justified by one glosser as aimed at rendering the cant-language "obsolete" through exposing it to view, had the effect of at least preserving some traces of this diverse linguistic practice and the illicit behaviors it enabled.

The French word *argot* initially signified the peculiar speech of criminals, but the word came in time, like *jargon*, to refer to any professional language. Thieves, men of letters, members of Parisian craft guilds—all were perceived by others to have a "difference of language," although only the men of letters exhibited the difference chiefly in writings that eventually became part of the discourses constituting the proper language of France. In the centuries before that language was codified, however, as *le français national*, work-based languages or dialects formed part of the situation of "diverse tongues" I am exploring here. This was never quite the situation of decentered, "free and democratized language," the "intense interorientation of dialects within [the] vernacular," famously hypothesized by M. M. Bakhtin—but Bakhtin was himself writing from a situation of intense state censorship and understandably saw the "linguistic revolutions of the Renaissance" in a highly utopian light.[22] In later chapters I explore specific instances of censorship directed against uses of language deemed heterodox and dangerous by Church and monarchical authorities on both sides of the Channel, and on both sides of the usual divide between medieval and Renaissance periods.

We need to know more about the situation of linguistic diversity existing, as it were, "beneath" the arch of Latin deployed in the Church, in courts served by many clerks, and, after the twelfth century, in the universities. The "particularism of the medieval polity," Vlad Godzich remarks, its division "into entities of considerable political, social, economic, and even legal autonomy bound up with each other by bonds of feudal allegiance, is accompanied by considerable linguistic diversity that does not stop at the borders of each of these entities" ("Culture of Illiteracy," 30). We also need to know more about the ways in which a situation of linguistic diversity often seen as "medieval" may have persisted into the Renaissance beneath the arch of our own ideas about the emergence of national vernaculars, the clerkly filter through which we inevitably see this situation of oral and literate diversity. The clerkly tradition repeatedly *regrets* vernacular diversity and interprets it through the biblical story of the Tower of Babel. That story, unlike the New Testament story of the Pentecost, sees linguistic multiplicity as the result of a pride-driven Fall into confusion and division.[23] Looking at the matter from a different angle, however, we can see "diversity of tongues" and multiplicity of media—oral, written, and, eventually, printed—as the components of a complex imperial culture that changed over time, but not in a way that simply supports the idea of an epochal shift from "oral" to "literate" societies, much less from oral to literate "mentalities." The societies in question were more various, across times as well as spaces, than such generalizations suggest, even when the generalizations are granted some causal force in shaping history.

If we think carefully about how modes of communication are figured in late medieval and early modern texts, we will notice many moments where resistance to an authority-claiming written discourse (including that of the Bible) is figured as female and oral. In *Pantagruel* (1532), for instance, Rabelais has an anonymous female voice interrupt the narrator to express incredulity at the narrator's account "of the origin and antiquity of the great Pantagruel." "Avez vous bien le tout entendu? . . . Car, si ne le croiez, non foys je, fist elle" [Have you thoroughly understood all this? . . . For if you do not believe it— "Indeed I don't" said she].[24] Here, the female interlocutor not only stands in for a skeptical reader or auditor (evidently unafraid of the narrator's truncated threat to the "unbelieving"), but also arguably conjures up—for Rabelais's contemporary readers and auditors—scenes of heterosexual conversation where women spoke up from positions of (at least assumed) authority. One can, of course, read such a moment as a misogynist erasure of the female (reduced to a nameless *elle*) and as a comic, homosocial allusion to the topos of the "unruly" woman, but that is perhaps to grant too much authority to the

textual tradition, too little to the oral/aural scenario the book at once represents and transforms.

The image of the skeptical or resistant female occurs often enough in late
medieval and early modern texts to complicate any notion that women as a
group were substantially silenced either by their illiteracy or by normative ideologies of femininity. Signs of skepticism or, more broadly, of *deviation* from
what some Renaissance scholars still conjure up (usually in passing) as a homogeneous medieval Catholic culture may be easier to notice and assess if we
consider medieval linguistic diversity as a phenomenon that persisted, in
some ways, beyond the end of the feudal era and that requires new research
agendas and paradigms. Lee Patterson has cogently critiqued the notion of a
homogeneous "Age of Faith" in which individuals are imagined as protected
from "the self-consciousness that tormented Petrarch and that reached its fulfillment in Shakespeare" ("On the Margin," 98). Attention to representations
of medieval women's voices—heretical and devout and sometimes devoutly
heretical—can help us complicate the images of "medieval man" produced by
various students of Renaissance men's achievements, from Jacob Burckhardt
to Joel Fineman to Francis Barker. Attention to the complex linguistic situation in which a writer like Marie de France produced her versions of "Breton"
lays in England, for instance, may help us better understand linguistic hybrid-
ity as a key component of early modern literacy. I turn now to consider some
of the ways in which the event known as the Norman Conquest shaped the linguistic fields upon which later contests over literacy took place.

Sociolinguistic Consequences of the Conquest:
French and Latin Tongues in English Sites

Writing in 1617, Fynes Moryson sees the Norman Conquest of England as a
repetition—not without benefit to the conquered—of the Roman colonization of England in the fifth century: "as the wise Romans . . . enlarged their
conquests, so they did spread their language with their laws, and the divine
service all in the Latin tongue, and by rewards and preferments invited men to
speak it, [so] . . . also the Normans in England brought in the use of the French
tongue in our Common Law."[25] In this idealized vision of history, the Roman
empire gently blends into the Holy Roman empire (military Latin seamlessly
becoming the Latin of "the divine service"); these Latin dominions of language and culture are followed by a Norman invasion that brings "common
law" without, evidently, drastically affecting the "common language" of English in which Moryson writes—and which, indeed, he is here imagining as a
wholly suitable language for a new empire. His formulation, which brilliantly
conflates the idea of "uniting" minds under imperial rule with a call to "alien-

ate" subjects from their local languages (he is writing specifically to chastise the Irish, who have so far failed to learn English), presents the Normans less as the bringers of what other Renaissance writers saw as a dreadful "yoke" stifling Saxon liberty than as a precursor of, and model for, England's own assumption of an imperial mantle. He offers a comforting version of the *translatio imperii* theory, according to which there is no competition for imperial dominion but rather an inexorable westward movement of power from one empire to its successor.[26] Moryson implies that Protestant England will simply replace the ancient Romans, the medieval Church, and the Normans as colonizer of new territories. Maturing into empire from former colony, England will extend its cultural sway as if Spanish and Dutch—much less contemporary French—contenders for imperial power did not exist. Moryson belongs to the long clerkly tradition that articulates and transmits the idea of an imperial language to which others are naturally "subordinate," in the phrase used by the second *OED* definition of *dialect*. The idea persists even when there is disagreement, sometimes only implicit, about which language shall occupy the imperial position. Roger Bacon used the term *idiomata* to refer to lesser modes of speech (contrasted with greater ones) in his thirteenth-century *Greek Grammar*.[27] There is a striking contrast between this theory, which I explore in greater detail below, and the historical situation of a confusing competition among languages that in truth obtained after 1066 in England. So striking is the contrast that we may think of the clerkly theory as constituting, in part, a defensive reaction to the facts.

During the decades after the Norman conquest, Anglo-Saxon—one name both for a literary language and for a "language of record" used for government and economic transactions in a certain, small part of England—was rather quickly replaced by Latin as a language of record.[28] In the following centuries, Latin gradually came to compete, as a more widely deployed written language in England than Anglo-Saxon had been, with a form of written French and also, eventually, with a form of written English fostered by the court and in particular by the institution of the Chancery. Michael Clanchy tells part of this complex story, for England, in *From Memory to Written Record: 1066–1307*; Brian Stock tells a somewhat parallel story for French territories in *The Implications of Literacy*. The Norman conquest of England is a decisive event in both these important works of modern scholarship; the Norman kingdom, which extended into Italian as well as into English lands, served as a "bridge" for a gradual social change from government via the monarch's spoken word (aided by written texts "set down to recall the contents of royal commandments made orally") to government increasingly reliant on scribal or clerkly activity (Stock, *Implications of Literacy*, 16).

Clanchy argues that the Norman innovation of using Latin rather than

Anglo-Saxon as the language of royal writs played an important role in changing the *structure* as well as the extent of the "partial" literacies characteristic
both of Anglo-Saxon and of Norman England. Though the evidence is problematic—among other reasons, because the Normans may have destroyed
many Anglo-Saxon documents—there are many indications that William the
Conqueror and his Latin-writing clerks strengthened the government bureaucracy at the same time that they increased the use of written documents
for government purposes (especially for taxation and for transferring property from English to Norman hands). Scholars disagree about the extent of lay
literacy in pre-Norman Britain, but Clanchy seems justified in doubting "that
England was governed by a bureaucracy using documents in its routine procedures before 1066" (*From Memory to Written Record*, 17).

Clanchy warns against inferring from his emphasis on 1066 that "the Normans had greater expertise in writing than the Anglo-Saxons" (*From Memory
to Written Record*, 12). On the contrary, "the Normans before 1066 had not
shown such a consistent interest as the Anglo-Saxons in recording their history and institutions in literate forms."[29] Moreover, the Anglo-Saxon tradition
of writing may even have "shown the Normans the usefulness of writing," as
one English scribe, Orderic Vitalis, claims when he remarks that his fellow
monks of Saint-Evroul in Normandy "shrank from bending their minds to the
task of composing or writing down their traditions. So in the end I, who came
here from the remote parts of Mercia as a ten-year-old boy [in 1085, without
any knowledge of Anglo-Norman,] have endeavored to commit to writing an
account of the deeds of the Normans for Normans to read" (cited in ibid., 12–
13, 168). This story obliquely reminds us that lurking beneath the evolutionary
model of history implied by Clanchy's title (and implied also in Brian Stock's
view of the Normans as a "bridge" culture for the spread of administrative
forms of literacy) are stories of *competitions* among language uses and among
language users from different geographical regions. English women as a group
arguably lost ground in one of these competitions because their access to religious education in Latin decreased even as Latin was becoming newly important for nonreligious uses in Anglo-Norman society. William closed many
monasteries and convents, including some of the "double monasteries" governed by learned nuns.[30]

Generalizations about women's language uses in this era are, of course,
very difficult to make, partly because it is hard to describe the linguistic situation in early Norman England. There are major gaps in the evidence concerning not only speech practices but also the authors, the copyists, and the provenance of manuscripts. These evidentiary problems are enhanced by confusing
and arguably anachronistic uses of the adjectives *French* and *English* in modern scholarly writing. For example, consider Clanchy's statement that the

"earliest and best manuscript (dating from the 1140's perhaps) of the *Chanson de Roland* is English, although it is probably not indigenous as its language is predominantly Francien" (*From Memory to Written Record*, 168). This seems to mean that a scribe born in the Ile-de-France region copied the *Chanson* while living in England; the adjective *English* thus defines an idea of textual property in terms of a manuscript's place of production rather than its scribe's first language and/or place of origin. By this line of reasoning many early texts that seem to have been "originally" written in some form of French could be regarded as "English": Marie de France's *Lais,* for instance, described by one recent scholar as written in "French" with "scattered occurrences" of English words and English place names, might well be considered "English" because the poems were evidently composed in England for an Anglo-Norman audience, though the first-person authorial persona describes herself in the epilogue to the fables as being "of France" ("Marie ai num, si suis de France").[31] Some scholars have interpreted this latter statement to mean that Marie was born in the Ile-de-France region, but others argue that she was of Norman birth and used a "literary" dialect that probably differed considerably from common Norman speech.

Women's relations to literacy (or, more precisely, to what counted as literacy) in both English and French territories were profoundly affected by the way in which prestige dialects of the vernacular arose in complex relation to Latin as the language both of the Holy Roman empire and of the earlier Roman empire that had once included Britain and France.[32] In England, moreover, the social differentiation of literacy was particularly affected by the historical developments that made Norman French, for several centuries, an official language of England—particularly in law—along with Latin. From the conquest through the seventeenth century and beyond, ideologies of gender impinged on discourses (and educational practices) pertaining to French and Latin. Kathleen Lambley's important if now little-known work (from 1920) on the teaching of French in Tudor-Stuart England, with sections surveying earlier centuries as well, presents rich evidence that English women were enjoined to learn French—and eventually, "Parisian" as opposed to provincial forms of French—through an instructional medium (the "conversational" handbook) that bypassed not only the (male) institution of the grammar school but also its constitutive emphasis on Latin language learning through a formal study of grammar.[33]

The role of French in the history of the English language, and in the history of ideologies of language and language instruction, is a key result of the conquest, for students of early modern literacy and empire. In the later Middle Ages French came to be associated, in England, with the genre of romance (often dealing with the *matière de Bretagne,* the mythical history of Britain) and with "idle" readers, members of the upper social strata and often female.[34] Pre-dating and eventually paralleling the development of (Norman) French as a "language of record" is the development of courtly dialects for works that may be broadly classified as literary insofar as they aimed at pleasurable instruction for elite audiences in both Norman and Ile-de-France locales. A tradition of critiquing such texts began quite early with Latin-writing clerks, such as Wal-ter Map; he chastised the "trifling mummers" who celebrated Frankish heroes like Charlemagne "in vulgar rhymes" (cited in Clanchy, *From Memory to Writ-ten Record*, 157). Though Norman French was the language of a brutal male conqueror and, for many decades, of aristocratic warriors who seldom fol-lowed the codes of chivalry adumbrated in French metrical romances, Map's comment suggests that versions of French, including Provençal, were also as-sociated with a certain "triflingness" and "sweetness" that made them unsuit-able for serious masculine matters among the clerks of Norman England. En-glish writers do not explicitly associate the French language with aristocratic effeminacy (to my knowledge) until the sixteenth century.[35] From the twelfth century on, however, they do associate the French language (or a version thereof), with sexuality and upper-class bodies, with romance and with a cer-tain seductive superficiality that we might call "fashion."

Unlike Latin grammars, didactic treatises produced in England during the thirteenth and fourteenth centuries and aimed at teaching the French lan-guage frequently were addressed to women, conflated mothers and children as subjects of instruction, and devoted an early lesson to words for the parts of the body.[36] Such language lessons have different connotations when they are directed by male clerks to adult female readers or auditors than when directed at children (typically figured as young boys). In the late thirteenth-century manuscript entitled *Le Treytyz qe mounsire Guater de Bibelesworthe fist a ma dame Dyonisie de Mounchensy pur aprise de langwage*, for instance, the author announces "primes en Fraunceys ly devez dire/Coment soun cors deyt de-scrivere" [first in French you must tell him (or her) how to describe his (or her) body].[37] Such lessons from the didactic treatises aimed at women who might hear as well as read them reverberated in the popular imagination throughout the early modern era, as I will argue in chapter 3, in discussing the scene in which Shakespeare's King Henry V briefly becomes a "pupil" of French while mastering a French lady and her country.

Such vernacular language lessons, whether offered through didactic hand-books or in the parodic form of Shakespeare's drama, clearly draw on differ-ent cultural ideas about language, literacy, sexuality, and gender than do the traditional Latin grammar book lessons aimed at boys. Knowledge of French becomes, indeed, ambiguously entwined with ideologies of gender and of sta-tus from an early point in postconquest English history. John or Jehan Barton, in his *Donait françois* of 1400, explains (in French) that English people need to know French so that they "may enjoy intercourse [*entrecommuner*] with their neighbours, the good folk of the kingdom of France; that they may better understand the laws of England, of which a great many are still written in French," and also because "beaucoup de bones choses sont misez en François." Last but not least, Barton notes, English speakers need to learn French because ladies and gentlemen usually write to each other in Romance: "toutes les sires et dames en mesme roiaume d'Engleterre volentiers s'entrescrivent en romance."[38] Tropes imbuing French with a particular *kind* of foreignness are part of the cultural stock of what became a prestige or metropolitan dialect of English during the late medieval and early modern eras. Although that dialect did not, in truth, possess the uniformity that modern linguists attribute to a standard, nor was it capable of reproduction throughout the realm through a system of national schooling, it did emerge as a cultural force that inhered, I suspect, as much in the dissemination of discourses about its (ideal) features or orthography and pronunciation as in its actual use by any given set of elite speakers or writers. It emerged, as did a metropolitan dialect of France, as an ideological fiction with some (hard to specify) historical instantiations and effects; the latter become easier to analyze in later centuries when systems of national schooling are established. One theorist who has studied the French version of such a system, Renée Balibar, provides us with a useful theoretical frame for thinking about multilingual matrices for historical contests focused on education and literacy. Through the lens provided by her notion of *colinguisme* as a structured relation of competition among "official" languages, I want now to look more closely at a certain history of three mixed and yet competing languages—French, English, and Latin—by which early modern ideas about literacy, gender, and empire were definitively marked.

Colinguisme and the Clerks

Many of the forms of modern written English originated as the conscious or unconscious choices of a handful of men in a strategic position at the moment of the creation of the official language.

JOHN FISHER, as quoted by one of his students

Colinguisme, as Balibar defines it, denotes "the association of certain state languages within an apparatus of languages in which they find their legitimacy and their working material" [l'association de certaines langues d'Etat dans un appareil de langues où elles trouvent leur légitimité et leur matière à exercices].[39] Balibar initially develops her argument through a discussion of the first document written (or so scholars have maintained) in French: the Oaths of Strasbourg of 842. Her governing assumption, which not all historians will be inclined to accept, is that something we can fairly consider "languages" of (a) state come into being considerably earlier than most historians think the French state itself did. I read her revisionary account of the Oaths of Strasbourg, a foundational story in French schools and wider culture, as supplementing rather than displacing the traditional story that sees the French nation-state emerging, as a bureaucratic entity with centralizing and imperial ambitions, only in the sixteenth century; her account also supplements the traditional story historians of literacy tell about the "scribal" renaissance of the eleventh and twelfth centuries.[40]

A prestige dialect of French, which would form the basis for the later language she calls "le français national et international," came into being with the oaths and continues to function (though with changes in lexicon and syntax) within a network where the language is "officially and grammatically associated with its ancient language (Latin, itself tied to Greek) and with its associate languages [langues partenaires]."[41] These latter may differ at different historical moments. Balibar's intricate analysis of the Oaths of Strasbourg, which were designed to cement the union between two grandsons of Charlemagne, Louis the German and Charles the Bald, demonstrates that the clerks who wrote the serments effectively created two new vernacular written languages, Roman French and Germanic, out of a welter of oral practices that have been occluded in historical accounts, which assume that the clerks merely recorded the oaths in two major languages actually spoken by the two armies involved in the "union."[42] Consolidating their own power and that of the kings, the clerks "reversed the translating operation which, until then, they had performed only from the written Latin text into various oral vulgarized versions, and produced two written texts [of the oaths] in two tongues derived from oral languages, in such a way that each one of those texts might be rendered with rigorous accuracy in the other and in Latin." Thus were created "two state languages, each as valid as Latin for use in diplomatic recording and yet distinct from each other as signs of two different territories" (Balibar, "National Language, Education, Literature," 134). Thus colinguisme was working, already in the ninth century, to link Germanic and French territories, and their various dialects, in a relation of structural mutual dependence and equally structural antagonism.

The Norman Conquest sets the stage for the development of colinguisme among French, Latin, and an official form of written English in territories claimed (often simultaneously) by English and French monarchs.[43] I consider that linguistic relation central to the transition from feudal to capitalist societies. However we understand that set of historical changes, we cannot afford to simplify the narrative of transformation by neglecting the different impacts of change on different groups—sometimes competing groups—within the diglossic, triglossic, or "colingual" societies we are analyzing. Although Balibar offers no historical commentary on the history of *colinguisme* in France between the Oaths of Strasbourg and the French Revolution, her definition of the phenomenon as a "theoretical practice associated with political thinking," and hence a practice to be distinguished from "bilinguism [and] plurilinguism," illuminates many facets of language use and ideology in French and English territories—indeed, between these territories—from the eleventh through the seventeenth centuries ("National Language, Education, Literature," 127). She helps us set certain language "events" within a broad context of French/English political rivalry, for instance, while also stressing that the rivalry itself was at once enabled by and productive of linguistic events to which we should attend. Increasing our appreciation of the structural connections between English and French as "national" languages, Balibar invites us to see beyond the nationalism of some modern French historians who dismiss the first extant French grammar, the *Donait françois*, because it was written by a foreigner for foreigners.[44] She similarly invites us to think in new ways about the first full grammar of English, produced in 1580 by one Jacques Bellot; this book was written for French Huguenot immigrants to England at a time when English, "according to Bellot's contemporary John Florio, was 'worth nothing past Dover.'"[45]

English scholars who sought to remedy that problem of perceived cultural provinciality repeatedly looked to France as well as to the classical authors for help in making English more metropolitan, and, by the same token, more appropriate as an instrument for a possible empire. In his *Excellencie of the English Tongue* (c. 1596–99, first published in the second edition of William Camden's *Remaines Concerning Britain*, 1614), Richard Carew stated his desire to seek out "with what Commendations I may attire our English language, as Stephanus hath done for the French and divers others for theirs" (37). Carew is evidently referring here to the French Protestant Robert Estienne's important efforts to enrich French through compiling his *Dictionarium seu Latinae linguae thesaurus* in 1531; in its first two editions this book contained numerous French equivalents for Latin words and phrases. In 1538 Estienne published an abridged version of the dictionary, the *Dictionarium Latinogallicum*, for young French students of Latin.[46] The "official" dimension of his efforts—not lost on an English competitor-admirer like Carew—appears in a royal edict of 1539, which consolidated "similar though less comprehensive royal edicts of the past fifty years" by stating that "thenceforth, in the exercise of justice, all judgments and other procedures were to be pronounced, recorded, and delivered to the parties in French only" (Wooldridge, "Birth of French Lexicography," 178).

If, as Balibar argues persuasively with respect to eighteenth- and nineteenth-century education, the institution of *literature* cannot be dissociated from the practices of written language recognized and taught by the state, the early modern era is critical to understanding the historically vexed relation between what counts as literature and what has been defined as the national language in the territories ruled by French and English monarchs ("National Language, Education, Literature," 145). "French language and literature," Balibar notes, "exist only in relation to English language and literature, within their respective historical apparatuses" (ibid., 147). There is, however, an important asymmetry that has already been reflected in my discussion: in the centuries after the Norman conquest of the English kingdoms, versions of the French language, including that taught at "Stratford atte Bowe," were a substantially more pervasive cultural force in the territories on the English side of the Channel than versions of English were on the French side.[47] Nonetheless, the linguistic agency of many subjects on both sides of the Channel was arguably diminished or at least devalued, its potential lost, by the emerging distinctions between metropolitan and provincial language uses and by the increasingly important roles played by male clerks in societies that were increasingly "administered" on the model of the ancient Roman empire.[48]

Clanchy's work on England helps us concretize Balibar's theory of *colinguisme* and at the same time enriches our understanding of the sociolinguistic matrices for contested and gendered ideas of literacy. He remarks, for instance, that "contact with England, with its long tradition of non-Latin literature, may have helped to develop French as a written language"; he also notes that "very little written French exists of any sort, other than Occitan, before the twelfth century" (*From Memory to Written Record,* 168). One may query the implicit teleology of this argument, which suggests that the development of "French" couldn't have proceeded had Occitan continued to be the main branch of the written language; it is nonetheless true, so far as we know, that the language of the Ile-de-France region was seldom used for writing before 1100, and in texts which scholars cite as early instances of "Old French," the Francien elements are often hypothesized as existing "behind" regional contaminations introduced by later scribes living in Provence or in England. To the eyes of a nonspecialist, some of these scholarly assertions look like an ideological back-formation with linguistic-nationalist inflections. Whatever "French" was as a written language, the forms in which its early history comes to us are often marked by the "insular graphies" of England, as one modern historian of the French language wonderfully calls them.[49] And whatever "English" was in the centuries immediately following the conquest, its *declining* status as a written language was due in large part to the preference, among William's clerks, for Latin and French, and to their power to enforce their preferences on the written record. By so doing, they alienated some groups, including many women, from that record with consequences we can barely surmise but which we should not therefore deem unimportant. The notion of *colinguisme* helps us construct a critical perspective on the history of clerkly language use—and clerkly discourses on the nature of language—during the centuries when prestige forms of the vernacular were assuming new cultural functions. I look now at three overlapping but not identical facets of that cultural process: (1) the emergence, in discursive sites ranging from thirteenth-century Latin grammar books to sixteenth-century English courtly poems, of powerfully gendered figures of the vernacular; (2) the increasing use of a "regulated" metropolitan vernacular for literary and bureaucratic purposes in French and English territories; and (3) the developing concern, among *litterati* trained in humanist schools, to "illustrate" the vernacular so it could compete with Latin and Greek (and other European vernaculars) as a language fit for "noble" literary expression. The second and third of these movements have been the subject of much scholarly discussion, but their implications for a history of early modern literacy have not yet been carefully explored. My aim here is to begin that task by yoking some strands of the history of the national languages to a strand in clerkly discourses that reveals the metaphor of the "mother tongue" to be not just a metaphor.

Figuring, Regulating, and Illustrating the Mother Tongues

[V]ulgarem locutionem asserimus, quam sine omni regula nutricem imitantes accipimus. Est et inde alia locutio secundaria nobis, quam Romani grammaticam vocaverunt. [By the vulgar tongue I mean that which we learn without any rule, in imitating our nurse. From this we have another, secondary language, which the Romans called grammar.]

DANTE, *De vulgari eloquentia*

The first four dictionaries of the English language were explicitly aimed at explaining "hard words" to female readers, as Juliet Fleming has recently shown.[50] The first of these dictionaries, Robert Cawdrey's quadrilingual *Table Alphabeticall* of 1604, promised in its long title that its "hard usuall English wordes, borrowed from the Hebrew, Greeke, Latine, or French," had been rendered into "plaine English words, gathered for the benefit and helpe of Ladies, Gentlewomen, or any other unskilfull persons" (fig. 2). Echoing the description of an unskilled group of (educable) readers we saw earlier in

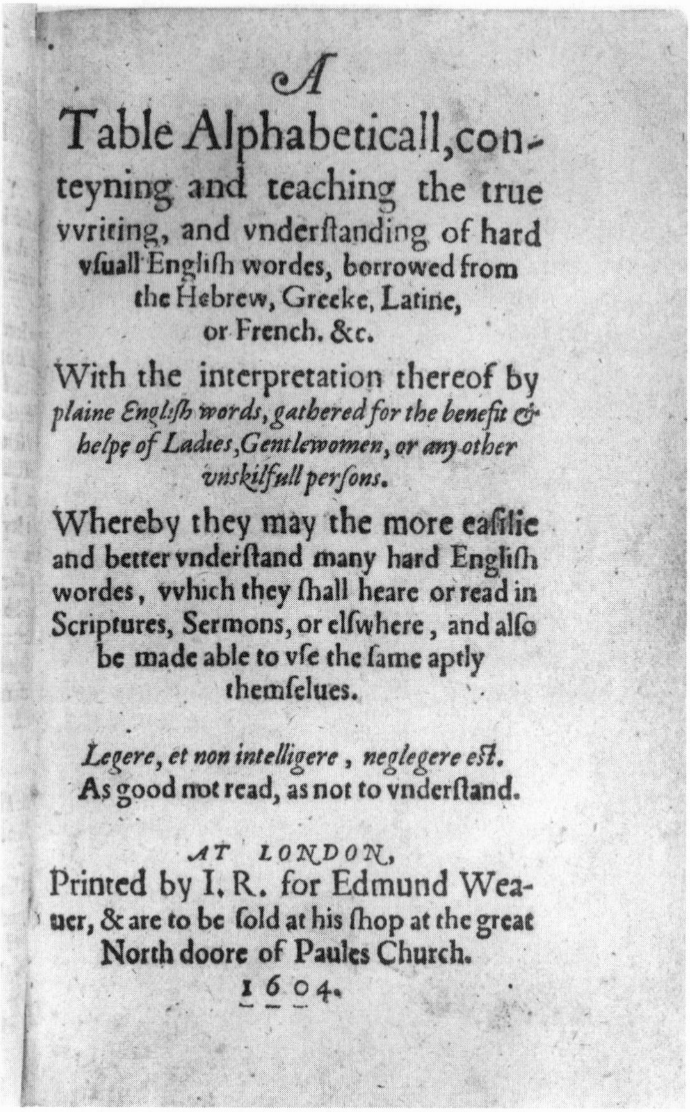

A

Table Alphabeticall, con-
teyning and teaching the true
vvriting, and vnderſtanding of hard
vſuall Engliſh wordes, borrowed from
the Hebrew, Greeke, Latine,
or French. &c.

With the interpretation thereof by
plaine Engliſh words, gathered for the benefit &
helpe of Ladies, Gentlewomen, or any other
unskilfull perſons.

Whereby they may the more eaſilie
and better vnderſtand many hard Engliſh
wordes, vvhich they ſhall heare or read in
Scriptures, Sermons, or elſwhere, and alſo
be made able to vſe the ſame aptly
themſelues.

Legere, et non intelligere , neglegere eſt.
As good not read, as not to vnderſtand.

AT LONDON,
Printed by I. R. for Edmund Wea-
uer, & are to be ſold at his ſhop at the great
North doore of Paules Church.
1604.

FIGURE 2

Title page from Robert Cawdrey's early dictionary, *A Table Alphabeticall* (1604), addressed to
"Ladies, Gentlewomen, or any other unskilfull persons." (Reproduced courtesy of
The Bodleian Library, University of Oxford, Mal 754[2], neg. pr. 939)

Coote's *English School-Maister,* Cawdrey redefines as pupils in need of in-struction a group of female readers who, as we saw in chapter 1, had long con-stituted some portion of the audience for vernacular literary and religious writings in both French and English. Ladies, like the mother tongue, were of-ten constructed as in need of improvement through conduct books or edu-cational treatises. How do clerkly discourses about the vernacular refract the pressures that historical women of different ranks exerted on men's ideas about the vernacular language? As a set of ideas and as a set of (partially lost) practices, the vernacular is most definitely not a homogeneous phenomenon, any more than women are a single social group, but both the vernacular and women were often constructed as singular entities when they were discursively coupled.

Gendered ideologies of the vernacular worked to alienate a significant part of the female (and lower-class or regionally "peripheral" male) population from a metropolitan language that was playing different social roles than Latin in the Middle Ages or the West-Saxon literary and administrative language in preconquest England. The development of gendered ideologies of the vernac-ular, especially but not only through the three clerkly movements I analyze here, had significant consequences for early modern theories and practices of education that stressed the value of "uniformity."

The humanist investment in "uniformity" was critically shaped by a tradi-tion of writing and thinking about the nature of Latin that flowed under the well-known polemical divide between humanist and scholastic concepts (and uses) of Latin. In twelfth- and thirteenth-century texts on grammar written in French and English territories, as Serge Lusignan has shown, Latin is repeat-edly contrasted to the vernacular(s) on one (or more) of three grounds: its mode of learning, its origin, and its mode of signifying (*Parler vulgairement,* 42). Vernacular languages, which are initially learned orally—that is, by a mode of imitation not mediated by texts—and in household sites, were repeatedly associated in late medieval and early modern texts with feminine language uses and genres, as well as with mothers and nurses wrongly exercis-ing pedagogical authority. Moreover, humanist educators often objected to the "elementary" education children received in the vernacular under the au-thority, too often, of women and badly educated (poor) men.[51] The vernacu-lar, and sites of vernacular education, were associated with ideas of the female, while Latin, taught by men whether in aristocratic households or Church or grammar schools, was associated with ideas of the male.

The gendered opposition that subtends the contrast between Latin—used as a synonym for *grammar* in some medieval texts—and the "mother tongues" is obvious when the contrast is drawn in terms of *mode d'appren-*

tissage and conceived in terms of opposed social spaces associated with orality, on the one hand, and, on the other, with writing and learning by "rules."
Learning through imitation is important in both educational domains, but
the authority of the model to be imitated differs and is subject to debate. A less
visible but in my view equally important ideology of gender informs the other
two major grounds of contrast discussed by Lusignan. Vernacular words were
seen as deriving from a realm of social *convention* associated with individual
pleasure and caprice, whereas Latin words derive "directly from Greek and indirectly from Hebrew and from the language of God, from whence comes their
[alleged quality of] unity" (*Parler vulgairement,* 42). This line of argument,
which Lusignan rightly links with the common topos of the Tower of Babel,
defines and values Latin as "one" in contrast to the "diversity" of the vernacular languages. Latin, of course, did change, "both in respect to its development
into Vulgar Latin and thence the Romance languages, and in respect to Latin
as the spoken medium of the Church and the Universities."[52] Humanist attacks
on scholastic uses of Latin clearly challenge the contrast between Latin and the
vernaculars when the contrast rests on the unity/multiplicity dyad. Nonetheless, both Renaissance and medieval clerks gave a positive, even a reverential
valence to what Tim Machan has aptly called the "necritude" of Latin ("Editing, Orality," 230). The clerks impute to Latin qualities of fixity, authority, and
power by equating Latin with its grammar, its *langue,* in the Saussurian opposition between *langue* as "system" and *parole* as "individual instance." Medieval clerks arguably anticipate this modern ideological distinction, which in
both its Saussurian and its Chomskian versions has had much to do with the
marginalization of the "sociality" of language in the development of the modern academic discipline of linguistics.[53] Privileging *langue* over a realm of *parole* defined as ephemeral, the modern Saussurian linguist, like the medieval
clerk, diverts scholarly attention from the realm in which women's language
uses chiefly occurred—and to which modern sociolinguists, rejecting the
Saussurian construction of *langue* as the chief object of study, have recently
granted new cultural capital. In so doing, they participate in that redefinition
of historical inquiry which takes "inequalities in the appropriation of common materials or practices" as a major object of study.[54]

   Roger Bacon's *Greek Grammar* of the thirteenth century provides a particularly interesting formulation of the distinction between the "one" (Latin)
and the "many" (vernacular dialects) by defining the former as a "substance"
to be discerned in the usage of clerks and all other literate persons, while the
latter, by virtue of their contrast with the philosophically and theologically
charged notion of *substancia,* are implicitly defined as like the Aristotelian "attributes" of Absolute Being. Bacon thus neatly occludes the fact that *some*

vernaculars (languages he classifies as "teutonic," for instance) were *not* descended from Latin, unlike French, and hence are not properly described by the *substancia* metaphor, which makes subordinate languages ontologically dependent on Latin. Linguistic "substance" thus, with elegant circularity, becomes a quasi-divine and all-encompassing phenomenon revealed only in the usage of the "literate," the clerisy comprising those who know Latin; variability is ejected, by definition, from the *idea* of Latin:

> For in that Latin language which is one, there are many idioms. But their substance consists in that language in which clerks and literate persons communicate. Idioms are many according to the number of nations using that language. Therefore it is pronounced and written differently by Italians, and differently by Hispanics, and differently by Gauls, and by Germans, and by English people et cetera.

> [In lingua enim latina que vna est, sunt multa idiomata. Substancia enim ipsius lingue consistit in hijs in quibus communicant clerici et literati omnes. Idiomata vero sunt multa secundum multitudinem nacionum vtencium hac lingua. Quia aliter in multis pronunciant et scribunt ytalici, et aliter hyspani, et aliter gallici, et aliter teutonici et aliter anglici et ceteri.][55]

Clerkly arguments for Latin as "one" versus the vernacular as "many" also frequently define Hebrew as the *forme matricielle* of the two other learned or "sacred" languages, Latin and Greek. Lusignan's phrase invites a point he doesn't make—namely, that this theory of language implicitly privileges a foreign and learned verbal "matrix" over the native or mother tongue. Building on this line of speculation, some late medieval theorists of language like Henry de Crissy insist that the conventional mode of signification, which Aristotle and Roger Bacon regarded as characteristic of language in general, is truly typical only of vernacular languages; Latin words, in contrast, signify in an "almost ontological" way for such Christian theorists (Lusignan, *Parler vulgairement*, 42–43). The notion of a divine ground (and origin) of Latin signification contributes not a little, Lusignan speculates, to the exalted idea of grammar we find in many late medieval treatises; the synonymy of grammar and Latin, noted above, contributes in turn to an idea we find in works from Giles de Rome's *De regimine principum* of 1285 to Joachim du Bellay's *Deffense et illustration de la langue françoyse* of 1549 and Richard Mulcaster's *Elementarie* of 1582: that Latin is more "complete and perfect" than any vulgar tongue, a better instrument for expressing "the nature of things, the customs of men, the course of the stars and all of that which [men] wish to discuss."[56] This line of thinking about Latin goes back to William the Conqueror's clerks, for whom, writes Clanchy, Latin was not only the revered language of the Church fathers but also "the indispensable language of lordship and management" (*From Memory to Written Record*, 168). This change in the dominant written language from West Saxon to Latin did not mean that royal writs "ceased to be proclaimed in English in the county court, but only that a text in Anglo-Saxon was no longer provided" (ibid., 165). For most people in England, however, the difference would have mattered little; Anglo-Saxon texts, when read aloud, would have sounded to most listeners in most parts of England "almost as foreign and archaic" as Latin (ibid.).

Important as theories and practices of Latin are to the history of medieval literacy, both contemporary and modern scholars sometimes grant Latin so large a role that they simplify the colingual situation that existed in England after the conquest and that contributed decisively to the eventual shape that a national English was to take. There is ample evidence that Norman French was the chief spoken language of the court and much of the aristocracy for several centuries after the conquest, though the dominance of any form of French is roundly denied by many modern English historians, arguably fighting nationalist battles in a way that is quite anachronistic for studies of a geo-temporal domain that some historians have called the Norman Channel state. Clanchy and others insist that the common people never stopped speaking English (or, I would counter, the versions thereof that some observers thought no less "foreign" than French). And some modern scholars so dislike the notion that Norman French was spoken in aristocratic circles that they misrepresent the evidence. In a book called *The Triumph of English*, for instance, Basil Cottle seems to be writing against the Norman linguistic yoke when he states that "Henry V had so little French that he could not even woo in it, as Shakespeare makes clear" (22). Cottle prefers Shakespeare's version of history to that given by most of Henry's modern biographers, who tell us that Henry's mother—who almost certainly spoke French but perhaps spoke English as well—died when he was eight; that he had an English nurse, Joan Warwyn, to whom he later granted an annuity; and that he spent time in his early teens at the court of his royal French-speaking uncle Richard II.[57] He undoubtedly learned French well, even if it wasn't his primary tongue, and he used French and Latin for his official correspondence until August 1417. At that point, according to Christopher Allmand, Henry made a deliberate and politic shift from a version of French to a version of English in letters addressed to his taxpaying subjects and particularly designed for London merchants. Having landed in France on his second expedition to acquire lands he and his royal forebears regarded as rightfully theirs, he suddenly commenced writing to his English subjects in their own tongue. "English," Allmand notes, "would be the language calculated to have the most effect in securing active military assistance or the provisions required to feed an army active on French soil" (*Henry V,* 422). The case of Henry V suggests the need for reading with considerable skepticism the modern, and indeed early modern, accounts of the colingual situation in late medieval England; there is much that we simply don't know—and that some historians don't seem to mind not knowing—about how people in England spoke in domestic spaces, whether they were kings and queens or commoners.

The relation between spoken and written language practice in England after 1066 is exceedingly complex, and Clanchy has done a great deal both to recognize and to untangle some of that complexity. He states, for instance, that "medieval vernacular literary texts often reflect oral diction" (*From Memory to Written Record,* 160). This hypothesis is supported, according to Machan, by "repeated references to a listening audience" in the metrical romances, and by their employment of "formulaic diction" ("Editing, Orality," 236). In contrast to literary texts that give us at least some glimpses of oral practices, business documents, according to Clanchy, constitute an evidentiary arena in which

> not only the style and register but even the language itself might change in the process of transforming the spoken into the written word. A statement made in court in English or French, for example, might be written down in Latin, or conversely a Latin charter might be read out in English or French. . . . The fact that a statement is recorded in a certain language does not mean that it was originally made in that language. . . . A royal message to a sheriff in the thirteenth century might have been spoken by the king in French, written out in Latin, and then read to the recipient in English. Although this conjecture cannot be conclusively proved, because only the language of record survives, some explicit evidence of such interchangeability of languages begins to appear by the end of the thirteenth century. (*From Memory to Written Record,* 160)

Members of the clerkly class would have been the chief masters of that "interchangeability," and hence they both create and deform much of what we know of the linguistic practices "behind" the structure of "official" *colinguisme* Clanchy describes here. Even in Clanchy's own careful formulation, one sees the traces of clerical hypostatizations that obscure the fact that *English* and *French* are terms for multiple spoken and, at a particular historical moment, equally multiple written language practices. It is hard to appreciate the multiplicity of those practices without feeling out of control of one's evidentiary field, which may be why a tone of exasperation so often colors both modern and early modern accounts of a sociolinguistic state of affairs felt by *litterati* to be somehow "alien" to the state of affairs they know. In medieval scriptoria, for instance, there was, according to one modern scholar, "some regard for consistency and communicative efficiency, and consequently, a notion of correctness in orthography within limited localities. However, when a work was copied outside the area of its origin, new habits of spelling were imposed, so that works may be in effect translated from one dialect to another, sometimes with great diligence, but more often resulting in a mixed language lacking all consistency. The resulting variety of language within texts is matched by the variety in the practice of individual scribes, among whom consistency in spelling co-existed with wild inconsistency."[58] Because the value of consistency has become self-evident in modern industrial and postindustrial states, it seems to be hard for scholars not to view orthographic inconsistency as a metaphysical lack. This idea has a long history: it is evident already in Roger Bacon's view that one who uses *idioma* merits ridicule. The idea appears much later in Smollett's comic representation of Winifred Jenkins in *Humphrey Clinker* (1771). Her status as a provincial female "sarvant" (she is Welsh) is graphically dramatized by her nonstandard speech depicted in nonstandard spelling: she writes *no* for "know," for instance, *vrong* for "wrong" (*Humphrey Clinker*, 66). Writing or speaking in *idioma* marks one as low on a hierarchy of value created largely by clerks but gradually disseminated and deployed in ways that have made most of us forget just how unnatural it is for consistency of spelling to work as a marker of social worth or individual intelligence. Bacon's reference to a *purum Gallicum* suggests that already by the thirteenth century an ideal of unity and consistency embodied in Latin was being extended, by a few *litterati*, to concepts of the vernacular.[59]

Even in the twelfth century some clerks were beginning to think of the vernacular as an appropriate language for official documents—or at least for first drafts thereof. Clanchy cites evidence that a version of French was being used to draft official documents in the 1170s (*From Memory to Written Record*, 169). And as I noted earlier, varieties of Norman French were certainly used for literary purposes on both sides of the Channel for some decades before French became a respectable language for official documents. By the fourteenth century, however, "writs, charters, petitions, memoranda and lawyers' textbooks were increasingly written in French, though Latin also continued" (ibid., 162). J. D. Burnley observes, with a touch of nationalistic chagrin, that "throughout the thirteenth and fourteenth centuries England did indeed possess a standard written language, but paradoxically that language was a form of French."[60] Burnley describes the situation in fourteenth-century England as one of *diglossia*, "in which the superordinate language bore no dialectal relation to the demotic, and the latter was of little interest to literate people" ("Sources of Standardisation," 35). But Burnley's traditional (dyadic) concept of diglossia is inadequate to describe the highly unstable colingual situation in England,

where *two* culturally prestigious "foreign" languages were operating in conjunction with multiple vernacular dialects.[61] Even before English emerged
during the late fourteenth and fifteenth centuries as an official language, it was
placed in competition with French and Latin in clerical discourses. "The relative dignity and status of the three principal languages (Latin, French and English) was a favorite subject of debate" among clerks in the late twelfth century,
Clanchy remarks, and he cites among other examples Abbot Samson's statement that a new prior of Bury St. Edmunds could eschew Latin and its orna-
ments to preach "in French or better still in English."[62] This clerical tradition
tends to get lost in modern histories of standardized English that take Locke's
Essay Concerning Human Understanding (1690) or Swift's "Proposal for Correcting, Improving, and Ascertaining the English Tongue" (1712) as starting
points for discussion.[63]

Texts were written in versions of English even in the century after the conquest; scribes at monasteries like Canterbury fought a rear-guard action to
preserve Anglo-Saxon, while poems and chronicles began to appear in forms
of what we call Middle English. Still, most scholars date the emergence of anything like a standard written English only to the fifteenth century, when the
Lollards briefly developed a highly consistent written style and when the royal
government of Henry V began to develop the set of relatively uniform writing practices that were known as "signet" and "chancery" styles.[64] Malcolm
Richardson gives a detailed account of this history in "Henry V, the English
Chancery, and Chancery English," building on John Hurt Fisher's study
"Chancery and the Emergence of Standard Written English in the Fifteenth
Century." The so-called signet (royal) and chancery styles were practiced only
by male writers working at Westminster and in London; the Chancery was located at the Westminster Court, but its record-keeping centers were on or near
Chancery Lane, in the City. The one hundred and twenty-odd clerks who
worked in the Chancery's elaborate (and well-overseen) hierarchy had a significant effect on other groups of clerks who lived in close proximity to each
other in London, among them those who worked for the Privy Seal Office, the
Court of the King's Bench, the Court of Common Pleas, and the Exchequer, as
well as clerks studying law at the Inns of Court (some of whom may have
learned writing skills from fellow lodgers who worked in Chancery).[65] The
Chancery clerks, Fisher has shown, were not native speakers of the "London
dialect" because they came mostly from the East Midlands; their local speech
patterns clearly affected their guild-determined efforts to regularize their orthography, and hence it is too simple to say that the London dialect (actually
there were several) became the standard for English.

The amalgam of clerkly language practices that constituted the beginnings of standard English, according to recent scholarly accounts, shows clear traces of the clerks' training in both Latin and French styles of writing.[66] But any discussion of French influences on English is complicated by the fact that clerks were distinguishing between Norman French and a pure French as early as the twelfth century. Burnley cites Alanus, a twelfth-century commentator on the *Ad Herennium,* marvelously illustrating the concept of *Latinitas* with a vernacular example: "thus Gallicum is said to be pure when Normanisms do not intrude" ("Sources of Standardisation," 35). By the mid-thirteenth century, "French of the Paris area was well on the road to becoming a standard," Burnley argues, before rephrasing his point in a way that better respects the state of the evidence: the French of Paris "was at least being forcefully promoted as such" (ibid., 32). Because language standards exist at the level of ideology before (and arguably after) they are thought by historians actually to have come into existence, the historiography of standardization is fraught with problems. Burnley acknowledges some of them and hints rhetorically at others. He initially defines a standard language—with traces of the Platonic metaphysics we have seen Roger Bacon deploying and Raymond Williams deploring—as "a form of language—that is of its phonology, morphology, syntax, and lexis—which is superordinate to geographically variant forms, and realised in both spoken and written modes, and in the latter by a consistent orthography" (ibid., 23). But even this concept of a "superordinate" dialect has to be modified for the medieval period, he notes, because standards existed "*only* in the written mode," and with degrees of orthographic consistency that very seldom had any noticeable influence on writing practices beyond specific royal centers. I am arguing, however, that *ideologies* of standard languages existed for speech as well as for writing and are equally important for the cultural historian, if much harder to relate to changes in the realm of language practices. And such ideologies are often formulated by means of translations from one cultural domain to another, in which the first is accorded more prestige than the second. A telling example of such cultural translation occurs when English humanists such as John Florio cite Cicero's praise of his mother-in-law's speech to illustrate his contention that "it is easier for women to keep the old pronunciation unspoiled, as they do not converse with a number of people." Florio—perhaps because he is addressing noblewomen from whom he hopes to obtain patronage—offers a construction of women's speech that contrasts sharply with the view of (lower-class) women's speech as "unclean," which I cited earlier from Elyot's *Boke Named the Governour.*[67] Views of gendered speech are strongly inflected by views of social status in the several traditions of clerical writing examined in this book.

The hypothesized speaking and extant writing of Norman-French and/or of Norman English complicate the standard histories of French and English as standard languages. Sometimes scholars of the English language simply deny that the term *Anglo-Norman* denotes a "real" language: it was not a "vernacular, in a dictionary's sense of being the language or dialect of the country, because 'Anglo-Normandy' never existed as one homogeneous country and it ceased altogether with King John's loss of Normandy in 1204," writes Clanchy, for instance (*From Memory to Written Record*, 167). If we put political pressure on Clanchy's imaginary dictionary's identification of a real vernacular with a "homogeneous" country, however, we can see that Anglo-Norman was as real (or unreal) a language as English or French was during a period that extended well beyond an Anglo-French king's loss of Normandy in 1204.

By at least the fifteenth century the French that was a "partner" language for metropolitan written English was beginning to influence the rhetorical styles of literary as well as legal and economic writings in English, as Burnley argues in his study of "curial" or "clergial" prose styles. These styles were shaped, in particular, by several works by Christine de Pizan that were translated in the fifteenth century and sometimes printed by Caxton.[68] As we will see in chapter 4, de Pizan uses various techniques, including "doublet" phrases in which one word is more Latinate than the other, to address readers and auditors with different kinds of language knowledge and hence different literacies. De Pizan, in contrast to her English translators, is explicitly concerned with women in her audience who lack Latin but may have some knowledge of vernacular letters.

Despite the claims of many scholars that an Ile-de-France regional dialect was emerging as a proto-national tongue from the eleventh century onward, it seems more accurate to suggest, following Balibar and Cerquiglini, that a form of *françois*—the medieval term for a language forged and disseminated, in writing, by a clerkly class—was appropriated for official uses by the Capetian dynasty when the monarchy settled in the Ile-de-France in the eleventh century (Cerquiglini, *Naissance du français,* 118). Although Cerquiglini may polemically overstate the dominance of an "interregional" clerkly language for this early period—he fails to mention Anglo-Norman, although another group of clerks was using this language in the eleventh and twelfth centuries— the language of the Parisian court would certainly play a key role in the process Ferdinand Brunot refers to, with a certain nationalist energy, as "l'émancipation du français."[69] The "emancipation" he has in mind is from Latin, and by telling the story that way, he contributes to ideologies of imperial nationalism. What tends to get lost, in traditional stories of how *le francien* (seen as a language natural to France's capital region) gradually superseded Latin, is any awareness, even in the form of questions, of the multiple histories of those who spoke but didn't write forms of French—or of those who wrote in French languages different from that used by the *langue d'oil* clerks. Insofar as modern historians of the language adopt the perspective as well as the metaphors of early humanist scholars—especially the metaphors of a competition among "noble" languages, which transfer to the realm of clerkly labor the glamour of aristocratic warfare—standard histories of the standardization of language work to distract attention from the messier, often quieter, ways in which certain languages or linguistic practices disappear, or at least disappear from areas of culture considered important. We need, therefore, to pay attention to ideologies of gender and status if we are to appreciate late medieval and early modern writing about language as a social field that pitted "good" versions of several different languages against "bad" or "corrupt" versions.[70] These latter versions were associated with lower-status men and with women of various ranks who were by implication in need of male clerkly instruction. Standardized, centralized, or metropolitan "prestige dialects" thus arise not only in colingual relation to other official (and foreign) languages, as Balibar argues, but also through socially consequential gestures of degrading various languages and language users. I turn now to some texts by "literary" authors who contribute to these processes not as the authorities they have since become (in publishing and educational sites) but rather as participants in a complex cultural battle to define an imperial or metropolitan vernacular. In this battle, what is "barbarous" or "corrupt" is often gendered female and ideologically devalued. But the male/female opposition, like that between metropolitan and barbarian, proves too simple: something remains for the feminist student of literacy, some puzzle inviting us to look again at the language of the text(s).

Gendering and Illustrating the Vernacular

> And gladly wolde he lerne and gladly teche.
> CHAUCER, on the Clerk, "General Prologue" to the *Canterbury Tales*

The regulation and "illustration" of the vernacular language may not strike modern readers as an exciting field of cultural debate, either in its early modern or in its modern instances. I argue here, however, that this field is part of the larger cultural arena in which struggles over ideas about human bodies intersected with contests over men's and women's "nature" and (correlatively) their proper roles in society. Many discourses about the vernacular, in several genres, display the powerful fantasy anatomized by Janet Adelman: the fantasy of being at once invulnerable to and capable of escaping from a "maternal matrix." The matrix Adelman is exploring (with specific reference to *Macbeth*) is constituted by the mother's body, whereas the matrix I am exploring here is the one associated with the mother tongue, the language of babble (Babel) before it becomes a potential medium for reason. Some of the passionate protests men make against the bodily matrix, I contend, they also make against the linguistic one. An earl who wanted to use witchcraft to kill James VI of Scotland thought it possible, as Adelman explains, "that the seed of man and woman might be brought to perfection otherwise than by the matrix of the woman."[71] Early modern educators like Richard Mulcaster, writing about "how to reduce our English tung to som certain rule, for writing and reading, for words and speaking," imagine education as a matrix that can both replace and somehow incorporate that of the mother tongue; as part of this process, Mulcaster would drastically decrease the authority of mothers, nurses, and female teachers. He sees education as a passage or escape from an original state of linguistic "filth" and "barbarism" to a state of "refinement" and "uniformity."[72]

Early modern scholars invite us to see an apparently pedantic interest in uniformity of spelling as but one facet of a larger historical concern for "purity" or "cleanness" in bloodlines and behavior, including verbal behavior. This latter concern draws inspiration from many cultural sources, among them classical rhetoricians and their warnings against "corruption," "solecism," and "barbarism." Chaucer offers two concise examples of gender ideologies intersecting with ideologies of the vernacular focusing on the problem of corruption. In the "General Prologue" of the *Canterbury Tales,* Chaucer famously depicts a prioress, Madame Eglentyne. Her pretensions to elegance are suggested by her title and name; the narrator pricks those pretensions (some critics say gently; I disagree) by writing: "Frenssh she spak ful faire and fetisly, / After the scole of Stratford atte Bowe."[73] The cultural perception of a difference between the French of Paris and provincial (English) versions becomes a major rationale for the subgenre of didactic discourse I mentioned at the beginning of this chapter, the French-language treatises for English speakers including (and often directed toward) middling- and upper-class women. Chaucer's miniature portrait of Madame Eglentyne points to a class of partially literate women aspiring to increase their social status through possession of French and failing—in the eyes of more fully literate clerks—by falling on the wrong side of a metropolitan/provincial border.

Chaucer again links a female character with an impure "provincial" mode of speech in the "Man of Lawes Tale," a narrative based on a folk tale included in an Anglo-Norman chronicle written around 1335 by Nicholas Trivet. Chaucer describes the long-suffering heroine Custance, daughter of the Roman emperor, arriving on the coast of Northumberland after a harrowing voyage; in this depiction of a divided sixth-century Britain where all the Christians have fled to Wales (*Works*, 68, line 544), the name "Northumberland" seems to signify extreme barbarism and provinciality. Cast by the waves "fer in North-humberlond," Custance meets a local "man of law" and communicates with him not "en Sassoneys" (in Saxon), as Trivet had specified,[74] but rather in what Chaucer interestingly describes as "a maner Latyn corrupt" (*Works*, 67, line 519). In his note on this passage, the editor F. N. Robinson remarks Chaucer's "unusual" concern for historical detail in his description of late Roman Britain. John Burrow has argued that Chaucer had some access to a "tradition concerning the 'corruption' of Latin," a tradition possibly based on Isidore of Seville's theory of four historical stages of the Latin language ("Priscus" [early or pure], "Latinus," "Romanus," and "Mixtus").[75] This last stage, which Isidore associates with the postimperial era, is characterized by "barbarisms" and "solecisms" corrupting (*corrumpens*) the "integrity" of the Latin. Burrow's argument for Chaucer's knowledge of Isidore's "historical decline" theory of Latin—which contrasts with theories that stress the timeless perfection of Latin as a grammatical system—is persuasive, but Burrow does not ask why a heroine who is the daughter of an emperor of Rome should be described as speaking "corrupt" Latin to a Northumberland constable. Did she perhaps forget her metropolitan Latin in her long years of wandering and trial? Or did she deliberately descend from her native *hochsprache* into a corrupt form of Latin in order to communicate with the provincial constable? Or did an ideological association of females and "corrupt" speech create a logical gap between Chaucer's description of his heroine's high birth and upbringing in the capital of the empire and his description of her speech in England? No answer to these questions is available, but given that Chaucer seems deliberately to have altered his source on this detail of Custance's language, adding the notion of "corrupt," we should entertain the idea that Chaucer was sending some sort of signal to his contemporary audience, or perhaps specifically to the segment of that audience composed of clerks (including "Men of Lawe"), when he depicts a woman of nearly unbelievable moral virtue speaking a "corrupt" Latin.

These Chaucerian ladies remind us once again that the matrix of non-official, mostly oral language uses out of which *colinguisme* arose is known to us only through the filter of clerkly literacy and its persistent concern for purity in both texts and women. Corruption of the text by scribal copying, J. D. Burnley observes, "was a well recognized phenomenon in medieval commentary," and this "notion of corruption is extendable to the language also."[76] Indeed the *OED* entry on *corrupt* suggests that the word's predominant uses in this era related to texts rather than to human bodies or souls. Some male authors' concerns for women's purity are clearly driven by a potent mixture of ideologies of language and ideologies of gender. "The opposition between purity and corruption as states of the language," Burnley adds, can be traced back at least to Giraldus Cambrensis, who "in the 1190's, in his *Description of Wales*, considered the language of Devon to represent the purest English. The remainder of the country, he thought, had had its linguistic resources corrupted by contact with Danes and Norwegians" ("Sources of Standardisation," 33). In Osbern Bokenham's *Mappula Angliae* of around 1440, we find a similar idea from a different regional perspective: "In Bokenham's view the barbarians who have corrupted English are now the Scots, but French too has played its part. An attempt by ordinary people to master French . . . has meant that 'by processe of tyme barbariʒid thei in bothyn and spekyne neythyr good ffrensch nor good Englyssh'" (ibid.).

For many French and English humanist writers the vernacular—homogenized in order to be contrasted to Latin—was inherently "impure" and gendered female. The process of ideological degradation Bourdieu illustrates with the example of *patois*, discussed above, had a gendered dimension that he and other historians of national languages mostly overlook. Yet the characterization of mother tongues as objects to be improved went hand in hand, eventually, with institutional practices that entailed complex forms of mental colonization. Precisely because there *was* no single vernacular, a new one had to be fashioned on the model of Latin and through a "primary" practical education that occurred for many centuries in Latin, and later in a form of French that might have been more alien to many children in French territories than Latin was because children would at least have heard Latin in church. As late as 1905, according to Furet and Ozouf, a manual of elementary French subtitled *Le français par l'image* was published for "the children in our patois-speaking provinces . . . [for] the young natives in our colonies, as well as for children learning French abroad" (*Reading and Writing*, 283). Since French, like English, was fashioned at important moments in its history by members of the class Roger Bacon names *clerici et literati*, we should not read uncritically those histories of the language offered by humanists (and their modern philological heirs) concerned with nationalist competitions in which specific vernaculars can be compared with each other and with the *literary* languages of ancient Greece and Rome. This is not to say such stories had no significant effects: they clearly did. But they are not the only stories history offers us.

The vernacular language should thus be seen, however counterintuitively, as a kind of ideological back-formation, a product of political and economic as well as professional-intellectual interests tied to the emergent phenomena we now call nation-states. Not surprisingly, the notion of "the vernacular" or "vulgar" or "mother" tongue was often reified, as a unified entity, in the complex rhetoric of praise and blame bestowed upon vernacular language uses by educated male writers (educated, that is, in Latin and sometimes in Greek). In du Bellay's *Deffense et illustration de la langue françoyse* (1549), for instance, the vernacular is both exalted (as a *potentially* great literary language) and anatomized as an object in need of reform: du Bellay describes the French language as blighted by the "ulcer and corrupted flesh" of bad poetry; for the sake of "la santé de nostre Langue," someone must "cauterize" the diseased flesh (179). The metaphor, with its implicit justification of the male humanist writer's "work" as a kind of verbal surgery capable of healing a (feminized) language, can be usefully compared to what John Skelton has a female character named Margery awkwardly say in *The Boke of Philip Sparrow*:

> Oure language is so rustye
> So cankered and so ful
> Of frowades and so dul
> That if I wold apply
> To write ornatly
> I wot not where to finde
> Termes to serve my mynde.[77]

The vernacular as construed here is not only distinctly feminine but is also somehow both too old (rusty) and too young to work properly as an instrument of educated men's intercourse with other men, including the dead of classical Greece and Rome.

The vernacular language, when conceived as natural, may be valued positively (as in Cicero's influential meditation on his mother-in-law's "pure" if primitive speech) or negatively; in either case, it becomes ideologically available, like a colonial territory, for cultivating activities on the part of men of letters. Thus ideologies of the vernacular, often gendered, may be analyzed as part of a larger ideological matrix in which *litterati* define and justify the necessity of their social roles. Because most *litterati* were men defining their somewhat eccentric masculinities (as in the notion of a *noblesse de robe* contrasted with a *noblesse d'épée*) against various cultural challenges, it is not surprising to find male clerks in late medieval and early modern contexts dusting off old prescriptions against female public authority—Saint Paul's dicta against women's teaching and preaching, for instance—and using them for new ideological purposes. And it is also not surprising to find women writers entering the domain of public letters with arguments that gender identity— like language itself—is a conventional rather than a natural phenomenon. The figuring of the mother tongue as a thing in need of cultivating and, in some cases, of purging or chastising, had different effects on differently positioned historical subjects, both male and female. We can find in the written record many traces of men and women internalizing negative images of themselves that are clearly yoked to negative images of their ways of speaking—traces of "nature" that they cannot remove through the kinds of education afforded them. Thomas Madryn, for example, a Welsh captain serving the Earl of Essex, was recorded in 1598 making an apology to the earl for "speaking false English."[78] An English observer in a border town writes that one Welsh inhabitant could not speak English "without any corruption from his mother-tongue, which doth commonly infect our country, so that they cannot speak English but that they be discovered by their vicious pronunciation or idiotisms" (one of those "idiotisms" was the tendency to use *she* and *her* as "all purpose pronouns").[79]

Provincial and female users of the vernacular, like their languages, are figured as in need of discipline because of that "waveringe" quality remarked by Caxton in his preface to his English *Aeneid*. James and Lesley Milroy identify the "complaint" as the chief vehicle for clerkly discussions of the "standard" language between the eighteenth century and the present; we can see that tradition of complaint, focused on the idea of the vernacular, beginning earlier (*Authority in Language*, chap. 2). The Scotsman Gawin Douglas, in the preface to his translation of the *Aeneid* of 1553, uses even harsher terms to chastise his native tongue; describing the barbarous lewdness and "penurite" of his Scots version of English "besyde Latin," he follows Caxton in implicitly defining his epic labor as a transplanting of Latin's greatness onto English linguistic soil (cited in Jones, *Triumph of the English Language*, 16). The perception of a present *absence* (or, in Sidney's phrase for Stella, an "absent presence") at the center of the humanist project of language improvement—which was also a project of language unification and regulation—leads Roger Ascham, among others, to write as if male Latin and Greek "Authors," themselves authorized by the Christian God, were to be the legitimate guardians of a newly refashioned mother tongue. According to this strand of gendered figuration in humanist writing, the English teacher or educator is a kind of farmer "grafting" a superior plant onto the native stock. "Therefore," writes Ascham, "wise fathers" will "weed" their children from "ill things" in language, "grafting" into them the knowledge of those two languages that Ascham—rather oddly failing to mention Hebrew—sees God providentially designating as the "trew Paterne of Eloquence"; no examples of such eloquence, he adds, exist "in any other mother tong."[80] The vernacular language is, in this figuration, not only a fictitious unity but also a docile feminized subject, ripe and even grateful for being beautified by a skilled male hand: as Richard Pynson remarks, in the preface to his 1526 edition of *The Canterbury Tales*, the author is he who "by his labour / embelyshed / ornated / and made fayre our englysshe" (cited in Jones, *Triumph of the English Language*, 26).

This figuration of the vernacular as a female subject to be improved by the hand of the male writer is structurally related to the perception of the vernacular as impure, discussed above. For the mother tongue, like the mother, preexists the individual male writer, and if he defines himself as an "illustrator" of the native tongue, sooner or later he is likely to reflect that other men have been there before him. The lady is not a virgin. Indeed the mother tongue, I contend, is often allegorically limned as a cruel, teasing, and sullied woman, a corrupted version of the Petrarchan lady who is a figure for the Petrarchan poetic text. Laura's name punningly plays on *l'aura* (the breeze of inspiration) and the *laure* (laurels) the poet hopes to receive for his writing.[81] It is no accident, I believe, that one of Petrarch's best Renaissance readers, the poet credited for first "Englishing" Petrarch's vernacular love sonnet, provides us with an oblique but important figuration of the vernacular as precisely a fallen lady.

Thomas Wyatt's "Who So List to Hount" has often been read as a topical allegory about the poet's illicit love for Anne Boleyn, who belongs to another, more powerful man (Caesar/Henry VIII), but the poem can also be read as alluding both to Wyatt's experience as an ambassador and to his concern with cultural translation.[82] Among its many unstable meanings, it offers a reflection, distinctly marked by masculinist ideologies of language, on the poet's task as a *belated translator* of Petrarch's vernacular into a tongue widely regarded as less elegant than the Italian. Reading the poem as a metapoetical allegory allows us to enrich rather than exclude the topical readings, and it also allows us to see, in an emblematic way, how the *idea* of the feminized vernacular is at once a cause and an effect of a colingual situation of competition that now extends to include Italian as well as French among the *partenaire* languages.[83] In this colingual situation, moreover, the male English author occupies two positions his culture defines as "imperfectly masculine"—which is to say, feminine, according to the influential although not hegemonic "one sex" model of gender much discussed by recent critics and the (contested) basis, as explained in my prologue, for this book's hypotheses about an enduring ideology of "imperfect" literacy.[84] Metapoetically, Wyatt as scribe is a "handmaiden" to Petrarch because he is translating Petrarch's poem, and within the drama of the text, the "I" is emasculated by being one of those hunters who "comes always behind" and who is forbidden possession of the hind by the (written) word of a Father, whether political or theological:

> Who so list to hount, I knowe where is an hynde.
> But as for me, helas, I may no more:

The vayne travaill hath weried me so sore.
I ame of theim that farthest commeth behinde;
Yet may I by no meanes my weried mynde
Drawe from the Diere: but as she fleeth afore
Faynting I folowe. I leve of therefore,
Sins in a nett I seke to hold the wynde.
Who list her hount, I put him owte of dowbte,
As well as I may spend his tyme in vain:
And graven with Diamonds, in letters plain
There is written her faier neck rounde abowte:
Noli me tangere, for Cesars I ame.
And wylde for to hold, though I seme tame.[85]

This poem personifies the vernacular language not only through the punning "deer" but also, and in striking contrast to Petrarch's original (*Canzoniere,* 190), as a prostitute, passed from the hand of one male writer to another in an increasingly used condition.[86] The speaker's envious bitterness, initially directed at the lady "hynde," is, however, dramatically and complexly redirected by the "wild irony," as Stephen Foley calls it, of the final couplet (*Sir Thomas Wyatt,* 98). The first part of line 13 alludes to a famous biblical text, John 20:17, which recounts Christ's words to the fallen woman Mary Magdalene—words that Petrarch had given in Italian ("Nessun mi tócchi").[87] By translating the words of Christ not into English ("touch me not") but "back" into the original Latin of the Roman Catholic Bible, Wyatt's poem suddenly sanctifies the lady (restoring what she possessed all along in Petrarch's emblematic allegorical poem), while mounting a subtle critique of both the English male speaker and of his "earthly" master, Henry VIII, who was at just this time engaged in denying the authority of Christ's papal representative in order to pursue what many in England felt to be distinctly vulgar desires for a tainted woman.[88] The implicit contrast between the king and the heavenly "Caesar" is underscored and ironized—the latter in a way that could have protected the poet against a hostile royal reading of the poem—by the tension between the biblical subtext of the line and its secular counterpart. While the Bible, in Tyndale's translation, has Christ say "Touch me not; for I am not yet ascended to my Father," the Petrarchan line was and still is commonly glossed with reference to words inscribed on the collars of the classical, non-Christian emperor's deer: "Noli me tangere quia Caesaris sum."[89]

Is Wyatt bowing submissively ("like a woman") to his king's prerogatives over royal "property"—women, deer, and the English language itself (called the King's English by some contemporaries, as we have seen)? Or is Wyatt using creative translation to comment critically both on the English language and on England's willful Caesar, who is arguably *not* behaving in a way that makes him worthy of representing God's will on earth or serving as the poet's master?[90] True obedience, Christ suggests in John 20:17, entails preserving oneself as the pure "property" of the Father, although there has been much debate about just what conception of property is at work in this passage.[91] But the Bible itself, as many of Wyatt's countrymen realized full well in the decades following Henry's divorce from Katherine of Aragon and from the Roman Church, offers ambiguous advice about the proper disposition of both spiritual and temporal property. Wyatt's poem alludes to this question through its second biblical echo. According to the gospels of Luke and Matthew, when the scribes and chief priests seeking to "lay hold" of Christ asked him whether it was lawful "to give tribute unto Caesar," Christ showed them a coin with Caesar's image on it and said, in words better known than is their rather complex narrative context, "Render unto Caesar the things that be Caesar's; and unto God the things that be God's" (Luke 20:25; Matt. 22:21). Here, as with the "noli me tangere" passage, there is disagreement about what Christ's words mean.[92] Christ does not directly answer the chief priests' question about "lawfulness" of tribute, nor does he say how one discriminates between God's property and Caesar's. The problem became even more thorny in cultures where one allegorical name for God was Caesar, and where kings like Henry VIII claimed to be divinely appointed to "represent" God. Through the figure of the coin—translated as "penny" in the King James Version—the problem of representation, the "king's real or his stamped face," as Donne would put it, becomes paramount, and reminds us of the Hebrew God's reiterated distaste for "graven images." The image of the coin also dramatizes the poet's subversive power to counterfeit royal and theological images. The old Romance-language pun on translators as traitors (*traduttore/traditore*) reminds us, moreover, that the opposition which both early modern clerks and modern feminists often draw between males who assume authorial (verbally productive) roles and females who are expected to be "chaste, silent, and obedient"— readers or consumers of others' words rather than producers of cultural documents—slides into some more complex, more unstably triangular structure when both men and women occupy the role of translator. In figuring the vernacular itself or the vernacular text as feminine, the male author repeatedly risks losing his own stereotypical gender bearings in his linguistic matrix.[93]

The interpretive alternatives suggested by Wyatt's translation of Petrarch—and particularly of the line in which Wyatt renders Petrarch's Italian not into the King's English but into St. Jerome's Latin—offer a rich illustration of Balibar's theory of *colinguisme* as a matrix for the emergence of what counts as a modern national language and the literary texts that are anthologized and taught—as Wyatt's poem is—as illustrations of how that language developed. The third edition of the *Norton Anthology of Poetry* prints a modernized version of the Egerton manuscript copy of Wyatt's poem but does not mention that it is a translation of an Italian poem, nor do the editors give a biblical citation for Wyatt's "noli me tangere" line, though the note does mention Anne Boleyn and Henry VIII.[94]

Wyatt's poem, like many other texts from the early sixteenth century that also playfully or seriously allegorize a metapoetical quest for the "eloquent vernacular" as a quest for a version of Petrarch's Laura—she who already in Petrarch figured the male poet's own ambition—suggests the need to supplement Bourdieu's argument that a significant shift in the meaning of *patois* occurred during the early modern era. The supplement (in all the ambiguous senses of that term) is that ideologies of gender, and particularly the idea of the female as a "property" of men, play a much more significant part than Bourdieu and others have seen in a broad set of discourses on the qualities of the vulgar or mother tongue. Subtending the pervasive idea that the vernacular is like female "nature," an entity in need either of protection from foreign contamination and/or of improvement—sometimes by "borrowing" words from other tongues, sometimes by being ruled through grammar, sometimes by retrieving "old" words from the past—is the idea that educated men should devise artful ways to cultivate the vernacular as if it were a colonial territory. Our "Mother tonge," says E. K. in his preface to Spenser's *Shepheardes Calender,* "hath long time ben counted most bare and barrein."[95] Many Renaissance men, Spenser included, undertook to improve the vernacular (sometimes by restoring her to an allegedly more ancient or pure nature); in so doing, they contributed to a historical process of occlusion that has left us with less information than some of us now desire about how versions of English and French worked as cultural matrices in their "unimproved" states. We must therefore look for traces of what lies beside and behind, as well as within, what Dante famously named "the eloquent vulgar tongue" in the treatise he wrote between 1301 and 1306.[96] Standing—as one of John Freccero's students memorably put it, "with one foot in the Middle Ages and the other pointing to the rising sun of the Renaissance"—and offering an influential argument for the idea of a single national language superior to the babble of multiple mother tongues, Dante draws together many of the themes discussed in this chapter as well as in the next, on imperial nationalism as a matrix for early modern literacies.

Unfinished in Dante's lifetime, *De vulgari eloquentia* was read in manuscript by Trissino and others concerned with "la questione della lingua"; the treatise was first printed in Paris, in its Latin original, in 1577.[97] Its central notion of an "eloquent" vernacular contributed to the construction of that set

of theories about language, with corresponding practices, which we associate
with Renaissance humanism but which I am viewing here as the product of a
masculinized scribal culture that worked across Europe for many centuries
and produced ideas of linguistic unity profoundly important for ideologies of
national unity.[98] Dante wrote his treatise to promote a vision of a unified Italy
that would not begin to be realized, even as an official fiction, until the nineteenth century—a time when, perhaps not coincidentally, the idea of an Italian Renaissance would also take on many of the features it continues to have
in modern Western societies and school curricula.[99] One historian estimates
that in 1861, just a year after Burckhardt's *Civilization of the Renaissance in Italy*
was published, "not more than 2 to 3% of the Italian population would have
understood Italian."[100]

Dante presents his "eloquent vernacular" as the fit linguistic vehicle for a
distinctly *imperial* Italy. The eloquent vernacular belongs to no single region
of Italy, not even Tuscany; rather, it unites what is best from each "native" dialect, and thus produces a higher, more powerful, entity. Dante describes it as
"cardinal, courtly, and curial," and explains the middle adjective (*aulicus*) in
clearly political terms:

> The reason we call it courtly is as follows: if we Italians had a court it would
> be an imperial one; and if a court is a common home of all the realm, and an
> august ruler of all parts of the realm, it would be fitting that whatever is of such
> a character as to be common to all parts without being peculiar to any should
> frequent this court and dwell there: nor is there any other abode worthy of so
> great an inmate.
>
> [Quia vero aulicum nominamus, illud causa est, quod, si aulam nos Ytali
> haberemus, palatinum foret. Nam si aula totius regni comunis est domus et
> omnium regni partium gubernatrix augusta, quicquid tale est ut omnibus sit
> comune nec proprium ulli, conveniens est ut in ea conversetur et habitet; nec
> aliquod aliud habitaculum tanto dignum est habitante.] (*De vulgari eloquen-
> tia*, 1.18.2, pp. 150–52)

Dante's theory anticipates a tendency to conflate the ideas of *nation* and *empire* in many later discussions of an "illustrious" vernacular language, discussions that dramatize the violence done to the provinces—and to languages
and language speakers defined as provincial or regional or colonial—in the
process of nation-building that has traditionally been seen as heralding the
end of feudalism in many Western European countries. Dante, indeed, articulates a theory of the "illustrious vernacular" through a highly elaborated and
socially resonant set of *discriminations* between "good" and "bad" types of
language. Dante's method for constructing an "illustrious" language for his

imagined *patria*, a unified Italy, is shot through, and in an exemplary way, with ideologies of gender. The illustrious language, described explicitly as a "paternal" language made for "noble" men, involves an explicit devaluation, region by region, of the various mother tongues of Italy, the "native" languages that Dante examines and finds inadequate to his purposes. His illustrated prescriptions for an illustrious language, the product of his fantastic clerkly learning and imagination, are so flagrantly, even deliriously, ideological that they provide a fine perspective on a field in which grammar and biology are, as it were, at the extremes of a social spectrum, each exerting pressures on what the other is thought to be "by nature."

Dante articulates his vision of the "illustrious," "eloquent," "cardinal," "curial," and "courtly" vernacular, after showing that it belongs to no single region of Italy, through the central metaphor of the sieve (*cribrum*).[101] The "sifting" Dante prescribes and performs entails distinguishing not only among genres, forms, and words, but also among persons. For Dante, the illustrious language, "just like our behavior in other matters and our dress, demands men of like quality to its own . . . who excel in genius and knowledge" [exigit ergo istud sibi consimiles viros, quaemadmodum alii nostri mores et habitus. . . . excellentes ingenio et scientia querit] (2.1.5–6, pp. 164–66). The illustrious language is not only "suited" for a certain kind of man, but is also compared to a "father" in its authority and composed, Dante explicitly insists, of "manly words" (*virilia*), as contrasted to "childish" words (like the names children use, in their native dialects, for their mothers and fathers) and to "feminine" ones.[102]

By "feminine" words Dante does not simply mean words grammatically feminine in gender. In the category of *muliebra* he places words he considers excessively "soft," in terms of both semantics and sound, it seems: *dolciada* and *placevole* are his examples (2.7.4, p. 228). Within the preferred category of *virilia*, he also makes discriminations that have strong social resonances, with reference not only to hierarchies of gender but also to those of class. Dividing "manly" words into the categories of *silvestria* and *urbana*, he subdivides each of these categories into "good" and "bad" kinds of diction. Good "urban" words are "combed out" (*pexa*) and "shaggy" (*irsuta*), whereas bad "urban" words are "glossy" (*lubrica*) and "rumpled" (*reburra*). Examples of these last two (bad) categories are, respectively, the words *femina* and *corpo* (2.7.4, p. 228). The illustrations remind us that the feminine was often equated with the corporeal in hierarchies of value such as Neoplatonism, which placed the masculine and the spiritual above the feminine and the corporeal. The illustrations also help explain why manuals for *vernacular* language instruction, in contrast to Latin and Greek grammars, were frequently addressed to

women, and even ventriloquized women's voices, as the male authors performed their assumed pedagogical task of teaching "elementary" things to an
audience defined as capable of partial or imperfect literacy. This clerkly construction often conveys an ideological view of certain readers and language
users as closer to the realm of the body—and sometimes, the realm of artisanal labor as well—than are those who learn Latin through the methods of
imitating great authors and engaging in the common grammar school practice of double translation. In a treatise written during the reign of England's
Henry V, for instance, the author explains that he has entitled his work *Femina* because "as women teach infants the maternal speech, so this book will
seek to teach young peoples in the speech and rhetoric of Gaul" [sicut femina
docet infantem loqui maternam, sic docet iste liber iuvenes rethorice loqui
Gallicum prout infra patebit].[103] The treatise brilliantly illustrates the historical process I have been exploring in this chapter and will continue to study in
the next: a process whereby a male-authored book takes the place of a female
teacher who used oral means of instruction. Through the clerkly vision and
practice embodied in the book, the woman changes from a producer and con-
veyer of knowledge about a mother tongue to a recipient of instruction, a
pupil who needs an educator's help with what the dictionary-maker Cawdrey
called "hard usuall wordes."

Through its descriptions of types of diction "unsuitable" for the illustrious vernacular, Dante's treatise offers a useful historical perspective on the
discursive genre mentioned earlier in this chapter, the genre to which the linguistically hybrid treatise *Femina* belongs. With chapter headings in simple
Latin, the bulk of the treatise consists of rhyming couplets in a French full
of "provincialisms"—that is, phrases drawn from Norman, Picard, Walloon,
and other regional tongues—followed by full translations in a version of English.[104] At the bottom of the page, notes give "pseudo-English equivalents of
the sounds of words written otherwise in the text" (Lambley, *Teaching and
Cultivation*, 28). Dante's treatise is also a linguistically hybrid text through its
inclusion of written words transcribing what Dante defines as different (good,
bad) styles of vernacular speech; his treatise provides a complex rationale for
his decision to write his epic in Italian. His imagined ideal reader was to be the
master of a vernacular already somehow improved and possessing the cultural
capital of Latin. "[B]ut remain, reader, on your bench," Dante writes in *Paradiso*; Armando Petrucci cites this line as evidence for his view that Dante
imagined "the codices that would contain the *Commedia* as books not different from those in Latin that he and other intellectuals of the time habitually
read at desks: parchment, of large format, written in formal 'littera textualis'"
(*Writers and Readers*, 189–90).

Dante's fantasy of authorial control was not realized, in part because many of his actual readers did not speak or understand *volgare* as an equivalent to Latin; "the earliest and principal manuscript diffusion of the *Commedia,*" Petrucci observes, occurred not through large-format "study" books aimed at intellectuals but rather through "codices executed in chancery or mercantile minuscule, manuscripts of rough manufacture and for private use" (*Writers and Readers,* 190). In his *De vulgari eloquentia,* Dante at once registers and attempts to manage anxieties about the existence of women and merchant readers who lack Latin, study benches, and a desire for imposing "desk books." In calling for an improved vernacular, Dante's treatise points to an emergent clerkly investment in addressing but also controlling readers who were "like women" in that they lacked full literacy, defined as command of the paternal language; defective with respect to clerks, as women in general were held (by Aristotelians) to be defective with respect to men, such readers were both threatening and desirable as subjects ripe for instruction.

Dante's treatise also offers a useful historical perspective on the ideal—now often taken as a fact—of a unified national language. The notion of grammar is a cornerstone for that ideal's emergence and operation in early modern Europe and in many of the places where Europeans traveled. Once one's vernacular has a grammar, it is more like Latin than like the spoken *idioma* used by those who are *illitterati* in a historically new sense illustrated by Shakespeare's Mistress Quickly: ignorant of their "own" language (as taught in grammar schools) rather than simply ignorant of Latin. In imbuing not only his prescriptions but also his examples with hierarchical social meanings, Dante may be seen, then, as an illustrious father of a key intellectual enterprise of the Renaissance, the enterprise undertaken by humanist intellectuals of constructing their vernaculars as tongues suitable for "illustrious men" and capable of competing manfully against other national/imperial languages as well as against the great ancient tongues of Latin and Greek. Such humanist competitions, like the status and gender-inflected literacies they helped to create, were both enabled by and embedded in a set of ideologies I have explored here as a second-order matrix for early modern literacies. The story of the sociolinguistic matrix begun in this chapter will perforce continue, with some odd twists and turns, in my next chapter's discussion of imperial/nationalist discourses produced by literate men in the fifteenth and sixteenth centuries. Those men played an important role in both shaping and disseminating three intersecting ideological webs: one focused on gender, one on literacy, one on the defining of monarchies as imperial nations. These intersections were influentially described—and illustrated linguistically—by members of what I have been analyzing as an emergent clerkly class or class fraction, a group including theologians, educators, translators, and authors of conduct books, who contributed in all sorts of ways to what Norbert Elias has famously, if ironically, called "the civilizing process."

That process is one whereby aristocratic male aggression was "restrained," in Elias's view, or, as Jonathan Goldberg has persuasively argued, *redirected* in various ways, some of which were less visible (especially in the metropoles) than were such older (and increasingly prohibited) rituals as dueling.[105] Goldberg indeed argues specifically for a redirection of aristocratic (I would add, clerkly) violence onto colonial sites. His point can be correlated with my final argument in this chapter. Clerkly ideologies helped prepare the way, I've suggested, for the development of national vernaculars in France and England; these ideologies also prepared European observers of New World societies to see what was new through lenses colored by old ideologies of gender. Although Europeans who represented Native American men—and eventually African slaves as well—sometimes attributed to them a kind of hypermasculinity, that sexual mythology usually testifies to a desire to render those "other" men impotent, unthreatening, "like a woman," which is to say, in psychoanalytic terms, a castrated man, and, in the terms provided by early modern medical authorities, an "imperfect" male.[106] Cultural difference, such a conceptually and psychologically difficult phenomenon for European explorers and colonists, seems often to have been construed, and rendered less unsettling, by reference to a more familiar (hierarchical) opposition: that between the sexes. Indeed, as I argue in more detail in chapter 7, European ideologies of gender—articulated by European writers of both sexes—shaped the colonizers' earliest perceptions of the American landscape and also of its languages and social structures. As Native Americans became material for European literature (in its broadest sense), the idea of gender difference was overlaid—sometimes in surprising ways—on the idea of cultural difference. A striking example occurs in César de Rochefort's "natural and moral history" of the Antilles, first published in Rotterdam in 1658 with "un Vocabulaire Caribe" and soon thereafter translated into Dutch and English. In chapter 10 of this work, which comes after a chapter on "ornament" and before one on "customs," de Rochefort takes up the issue of the native language of the people he has observed.[107] There are, he reports, two languages rather than one, and these overlap in an interesting way: "[T]he men have many expressions which are theirs [*qui leur sont propres*], and these the women understand well, but never pronounce. And the women also have words and sentences [*des mots & des phrases*] which the men don't use at all, lest they be mocked [*à moins que de se faire moquer*]. From this the situation arises that in a good part of their conversation [*leur entretien*], one would say that the women have a different language than the men do" (*Histoire naturelle*, 449, my translation).

De Rochefort explains that his dictionary of Caribbean words will illustrate these different languages, and he partly delivers on his promise: for some nouns (but not for all, nor for any verbs, adjectives, or other parts of speech in his list) he gives forms both for "H[ommes]" and for "F[emmes]." The selection seems oddly arbitrary: *mon frere ainé*, "my older brother," translates (in the European's version of the Caribs' language, which includes transcription, of course, into the Roman alphabet) as "H. *hanbin.* F. *Niboukayem.*" But later in this section of the "Vocabulaire," entitled "Parenté & Alliance," de Rochefort gives just one translation for "Le Cousin non marié à la Cousine, *Yapataganum.*" Either there is no "female" term for this relation—and for some relations, the male and female nouns are indeed the same, according to de Rochefort—or the European observer has not had an occasion to hear the women talking about this particular kind of unmarried cousin. In either case, the ethnographic record is at once marked, strikingly, by the observer's perception of the existence of gendered languages and also rendered enigmatic, since we are left with many, indeed the majority, of the terms in the dictionary given only in the "male" version.

The Carib language, in this construction, is thus Other to de Rochefort's French, but the Carib women's language is even *more* different, it seems, than that of the men. This second degree of otherness is explained as the result of a history that oddly parallels that of the European conquest of the Americas. Once, according to the "savages of Dominica," the Antillean islands were occupied by the Arawak "Nation," but then the Caribs came and destroyed that nation "entirely"—except for the women whom the Caribs married, "to populate the country." Those survivors, a logically confusing supplement to a nation "entirely" destroyed, "conserved their language, teaching it to their daughters, and accustoming them [the girls] to speak as they [the women] did." And this "practice" has continued to the present, de Rochefort states, before going on to contain the radical implications of this "history" by assimilating it to European practices of educating boys in Latin—or in an "illustrious vernacular"—which is not the language of the mothers and sisters of the country. Here is how his narrative of the "two languages" ends: "But the boys, although they well understand the speech of their Mothers and sisters, nonetheless follow their Fathers and their brothers, and fashion themselves by their language [*se faconnent à leur Langage*, which could also be translated "attach themselves to their language"], from the age of five or six." The story itself "fashions" or attaches the Caribbean peoples to the Europeans' customs and language by making the boys somehow choose to enter a masculinized linguistic sphere once they reach the age of five or six—shortly before the age when European boys of the middling and upper classes often began their formal schooling either in Latin, the *sermo patrius,* or in one of those "illustrious" vernaculars we have seen Dante distinguishing from a "soft" speech associated with women and small children. As John of Trevisa put it in a translation of 1382 reprinted by Caxton a century later, boys of seven should be "put and sette to lore vnder tutours and compelled to fonge [i.e., undergo] lore and chastisinge."[108]

In an intriguing coda to his little story of gendered languages, de Rochefort notes that in order to "confirm" his story of the dual language system's "origins," someone has alleged that there is some conformity between the language of the Arawaks of the Continent (Terre Ferme) and that of the female Caribs on the islands. An "allegation" of some conformity is perhaps not an altogether reliable argument even in the author's eyes, but he does suggest, in his conclusion, that the doubleness of language that he has thus far been describing with apparent objectivity is not a morally neutral phenomenon. "But it should be remarked," he writes, "that the Caribes of the Continent, men and women both, speak the same language, not having corrupted their natural language by marriages with strange women" (*Histoire naturelle*, 450, my translation).

The "other" other language, here, is finally revealed to be a "corrupting" force, an alien presence in the body politic. Although the young boys seem to turn voluntarily away from this source of potential corruption, and although the women are ritually restrained from tainting the preserve of the men's language (they "understand" it well, but don't ever "pronounce" it), de Rochefort's story nonetheless leaves the reader with a strong sense that the Carib women are alien to their own "Nation" and have something of the flavor of dangerous Amazons in their apparently assimilated "Arawak" natures. Their choice to pass their language on from one female generation to another—into the present—makes them, in any case, bearers of the history of a defeated people and potential allies with the contemporary continental Arawaks who might possibly harbor hopes of revenge despite the common European construction of the Arawaks as the "gentle" natives, in contrast to the violent Caribs.[109] The "mixed" Arawak-Carib women with their ambiguously same but different language seem, in the end, to bear for de Rochefort a warning against mixing too closely with the natives, through intercourse with females.[110]

The "crisis of the aristocracy" analyzed by Lawrence Stone and many others involved a traumatic process of education for men. The late feudal aristocracy, as Perry Anderson observes, gradually had to shed "military exercise of private violence, social patterns of vassal loyalty, economic habits of hereditary insouciance, political rights of representative autonomy, and cultural attributes of unlettered ignorance. It had to learn the new avocations of a disciplined officer, a literate functionary, a polished courtier, and a more or less prudent estate owner."[111] Many male aristocrats, in other words, had to learn skills that had previously belonged chiefly to the clerics—and indeed many impecunious aristocrats joined educated commoners in the partially secular clerisy I've mentioned before as a *noblesse de robe*.[112] A monarch like Queen Elizabeth, cited by Roger Ascham as a prize pupil in acquisition of Latin and Greek culture, not only participated as a "virago" or man-woman in this group, but also helped to shape it by policies of channeling the nobleman's "martial training and disposition in service to the crown."[113] Monarchs of early modern states were not only educated and served, but also in some cases subtly influenced, by the socially mixed group I am analyzing under the rubric of *litterati*. Among this group were women like Marguerite de Navarre, sister of the king of France, who used her pen in various attempts to influence royal policies. Such women challenged normative ideas of proper feminine behavior as well as the emergent idea of female literacy I have been sketching here: the reception rather than the production of educative materials.

From that group of intellectuals who constituted a new "writing class" developing during this era, scholars in the humanities have inherited that notion of the Renaissance as a rebirth, a notion that carries with it a powerful masculinist ideology. This includes, as one of its many strands, the idea that *biological* mothers, and the mother tongues of the vernacular, are less culturally valuable than intellectual fathers and the ancient languages of Hebrew, Greek, and Latin, languages often figured as paternal, as more unified and enduring than the vernaculars, and, in some cases, as directly descended from the Word of God the Father. Pico's famous *Oration on the Dignity of Man* can serve as a vivid final example of this tendency, a sort of coda to Dante's *De vulgari eloquentia* and de Rochefort's narrative of a language "corrupted" by the existence of a female speech somehow both within and outside the space of *la langue*. Pico's text offers a humanist retelling of the Genesis Creation story, a retelling that dramatizes Adam's "fluid" ontology while altogether occluding Eve's role either in the Creation or in the Fall (the Fall, in fact, doesn't exist as a unique historical event in Pico's high humanist and highly Pelagian fable). Pico, like many other members of the clerkly writing class, often either erased or depreciated women in the course of defining (and giving cultural value to) language practices passed not from mother to child but from male teacher and writer to male—or in some rare cases female—students and readers. Female students, however, although an increasingly important audience for *litterati* serving the state or (in Dante's case) the idea of one, were absolutely excluded from the church councils and universities in which early notions of what counts as a nation were debated. It is to those demographically masculine cultural sites that I now turn, having attempted in this chapter to supplement the story that Stone, Elias, and others have told about an emergent class of men of letters. I have looked here at some of the ways in which members of that class formulated and redeployed ideologies of gender in connection with ideologies of language. In the next chapter, I consider how ideologies of imperial nationhood join with ideologies of national languages as a key social matrix for early modern literacy.

Discourses of Imperial Nationalism
as Matrices for Early Modern Literacies

I would have the weakest woman [*mulierculae*] read the Gospels and the Epistles of Saint Paul . . . I would have those words translated into all [vulgar] languages [*vulgi linguam*], so that not only Scots and Irishmen, but Turks and Saracens might read them.

ERASMUS, preface to his edition of the New Testament (1516)

So meny people longages and tongues.

JOHN OF TREVISA, translation of Ranulph Higden's *Polychronicon* (1387)

[U]n preux, un conquerent, un pretendent et aspirant à l'empire univers ne peut tousjours avoir ses aizes. [A mighty man, a conqueror, a claimant and aspirant to universal empire cannot always idle at his ease.]

FRANÇOIS RABELAIS, *Gargantua* (1534)

And who in time knowes whither we may vent
The treasure of our tongue, to what strange shores
This gaine of our best glory shal be sent
T'inrich vnknowing Nations with our stores?
What worlds in th'yet vnformed Occident
May come refin'd with th'accents that are ours?

SAMUEL DANIEL, *Musophilus, Containing a generall defence of all learning* (1599)

I argued in chapter 2 for the importance of situating early modern theories and practices of gendered literacy within a history of complex and competitive relations among languages—relations that do not fit neatly within modern disciplinary categories of periodization or of "national" histories. In this chapter, I extend that argument to consider early discourses of nationalism as a second-order matrix for gendered theories and practices of literacy. Nations, nationality, and nationalism are much debated phenomena, with questions of definition often tied to questions about dating.[1] I enter this large scene of scholarly inquiry in order to present and analyze evidence that supports, but also perhaps complicates, two of Benedict Anderson's important arguments about nations as "imagined communities." One is that print-capitalism enabled the historical emergence of a distinctly "modern" nation-state, however we define that paradoxical phenomenon; the second is that print-capitalism itself was dialectically related to epochal changes in language use that had economic, political, and social causes—and consequences.[2]

The evidence discussed here and in later chapters of this book strongly supports Anderson's thesis that capitalism would likely have remained a phenomenon of "petty proportions" had it not been preceded and accompanied by changes in the domain of language use (*Imagined Communities*, 43). More specifically, Anderson posits the emergence of "administrative vernaculars," followed by different, and increasingly standardized, "print languages," as critical to the rise of capitalism in the West. Capitalism, to put the matter simply, both needed and helped to produce the creation of "print languages" that were "capable of dissemination through the market" (ibid., 44). Such languages, far fewer in number than the regional idiolects of medieval Europe but of course more numerous than the "sacred" languages that go under the name of Latin, were, in Anderson's view, more important to the process of socioeconomic transition than classical Marxist theory allows. Changes in language use, especially those spurred by Protestantism, "created unified fields of exchange and communication below Latin and above the spoken vernaculars"; this helped "lay the basis for national consciousness" while at the same time contributing to the (uneven) demise of the "imagined community" of the feudal era, the medieval Christian community Anderson sees as "held together" by religious belief and, in particular, by people's belief in the "unique sacredness of their languages" and scripts (ibid., 44, 13).

Anderson's view of the Christian Middle Ages is debatable on several counts.[3] So, I believe, is the tendency to technological determinism sometimes apparent in his discussion of print-capitalism. Nonetheless, he makes an enormous contribution to our understanding of history by seeking to remedy the neglect of the "anomaly" of the nation-form in classical Marxist theory (*Imagined Communities*, 3). He rightly stresses the importance of mechanically reproducible languages to those forms of nationalism that grow out of and contribute to capitalism. I suggest, however, that preprint clerkly ideologies about the value of "illustrious" vernaculars and teachable (hence socially reproducible) languages contributed—before and then in conjunction with Protestantism, Counter-Reformation Catholicism, and print technologies—to the complex set of historical changes Anderson analyzes. I do not wish to overestimate the role of intellectuals in the emergence of new language practices and values; Anderson is surely right to emphasize the gradual, uneven, and partly "fatal" or haphazard dimensions of the changes that occurred over several centuries as Latin gave way to vernacular "languages of power" (ibid., 45). No one can know just how to evaluate the causal force of the educational discourses and practices (as well as monarchical policies on language use) produced over time by an international group of literati. Nonetheless, it seems to me important to complicate Anderson's story insofar as it shows a typically modernist tendency (one we have also seen in the Great Divide literacy theorists) to define a premodern period in terms of "unselfconscious" processes of change in the linguistic domain, while attributing agency and "selfconsciousness" to those who formulated linguistic policies for nineteenth- and twentieth-century dynastic nations.[4] The story outlined in the previous chapter and in this one also complicates Anderson's story—along with some told by recent historians of early modern England/Britain—by suggesting that the paradoxes of imperial nationalism are present from the time when capitalism and nationalism begin their complex alliance.[5]

I am most interested in the paradox that makes the nation at once a "bounded" and an "unbounded" entity. Anderson stresses the former quality early in his book: the nation, he declares in his introductory definition, is "inherently limited," and "no nation imagines itself coterminous with mankind" (*Imagined Communities*, 6). These assertions can be questioned on historical grounds. Both Protestants and Catholics in sixteenth-century England could evidently imagine a nation not "inherently limited" and, indeed, potentially extending to all mankind; for some Protestants, as Claire McEachern has shown, the existence of many nations, languages, and religions was uneasily interpreted with reference to the biblical story of the Tower of Babel (*Poetics of English Nationhood*, 113–16). The idea of *redeeming* an originary, prideful fall into diversity of belief and language arguably underlies the visions of an expanding English empire discussed later in this chapter. In any case, ideas of national boundedness have often existed in paradoxical relation to ideas about an unbounded religious or patriotic mandate (Gregerson, "Colonials Write the Nation," 169). Anderson himself turns with increasing urgency (but always in discussions of later periods) to formulations that attempt to capture the paradoxical ties that bind national to imperial entities. He describes nineteenth-century "official nationalisms," for instance, working to legitimate the act of "stretching the short tight skin of the nation over the gigantic body of empire" (*Imagined Communities*, 86). In another striking metaphor, he writes about "the inventive legerdemain" that was "required to permit the empire to appear attractive in national drag."[6] To see how such metaphors might apply to late medieval and early modern articulations of nationalism, we need to be skeptical about those parts of Anderson's argument which rely on a theory of history as moving from an "unselfconscious" (medieval, Christian) phase to a "selfconscious" (modern, secular) one. Such a view of history—and Anderson himself often challenges it—may distort the historical evidence about the complex relations among "administrative vernaculars," "metropolitan" dialects shaped by educated elites, and "print languages." Moreover, such a view of history is too linear to accommodate the strange temporality of nations as putative unities that are also pluralities served—and partly defined—by literati interested in contests for dominion between various rulers and their legitimating images. For many of these rulers, there is no clear line between sacred and secular realms, or between the past and the present.

To study the discourses of imperial nationalism as a matrix for gendered theories and practices of literacy invites us to see conceptions of national unity, with their associated ideological calls for a "uniform" language, in dialectical relation to theories as well as practices that stress diversity within (and of necessity, on the borders of) the entities emerging as "empire-states." I take that phrase from Perry Anderson, who uses it to describe a geopolitical entity first called "Britain" by the Romans.[7] Scholars of early modern France and England have recently been studying aspects of this dialectic, some stressing ideologies and historical practices contributing to unification, others stressing resistances to it, as Paula Blank does in her important work on "broken English" in the early modern era.[8] My main contribution to this lively field of scholarly debate—beyond my local effort to provide a context for assessing arguments about nations and language use advanced by the writers studied in part 2 of this book—derives from my emphasis on the long-standing rivalry between France and England; I see this rivalry repeatedly shaping descriptions of two monarchies' historical emergence as separate (but yoked) nation-states.

In an influential book on nationalism, Liah Greenfeld argues for taking England—in contrast to France—as the first true "nation" in history. She readily acknowledges that not all the people of England were actually included in the nation, so defined, in the first century of its existence—the sixteenth, in her account.[9] But she spends little time on such people because the teleological drive of her argument prevents those excluded from the nation from being considered historically significant. It also causes her so fully to identify with monarchical efforts to impose unity of language on an existent multiplicity that she describes the French crown's "linguistic policy" as "not forceful enough" in compelling all citizens to use French (*Nationalism*, 99). Greenfeld's view of the "unified" nation as the key element in the modernizing process leads her, at times, to some remarkable generalizations about culture and, implicitly, some untenable assumptions about the modern sociologist's ability to master an evidentiary field. "Cultural creativity in this period [that of sixteenth-century England] was almost invariably—and exclusively—motivated by patriotism," Greenfeld writes (*Nationalism*, 43). I think that we don't know enough about nonelite women or, indeed, about most people in early modern England even to begin to support such a thesis about motivations for "cultural creativity" among England's various subjects.

We can, however, safely surmise that one's gender, along with one's social status and one's place of birth, had some effect on whether or not one felt anything like "patriotism" or even knew about that (evolving) concept's existence during the late medieval and early modern eras.[10] Nira Yuval-Davis and Floya Anthias have rightly stressed in their study of women and the twentieth-century nation-state that "there is no unitary category of women which can be unproblematically conceived as the focus of ethnic, national or state policies and discourses." It is also true that many women are affected, though differently, by the tendency for females to be constructed as "signifiers of ethnic/national differences—as a focus and symbol in ideological discourses used in the construction, reproduction and transformation of ethnic/national categories" (Yuval-Davis and Anthias, eds., *Woman-Nation-State,* 7). It is not surprising, given the association of feminine qualities with those of various groups felt to be somehow outsiders and dangers to the body politic, that women and ideas about them do not fit neatly into ideas about nations as social wholes or unities. And it is also not surprising that some elite women of the transitional period exhibit attitudes of skepticism toward emergent ideologies of patriotism. *Patria,* signifying both a heavenly and an earthly "fatherland" (from the Latin word for "father" and imported by Carolingian clerks to describe a "Frankish empire"), was in any event a disputed notion in the Renaissance.[11] In 1550 an anonymous critic attacked Joachim du Bellay for using the word *patrie* instead of the more traditional *pays* on the grounds that the new-coined word was an "Italian corruption." Fearing to "disfigure" Latin, "ancient" French poets eschewed such words and "were content with what was properly their own."[12] Marguerite de Navarre, competing with Boccaccio and with some of her own French contemporaries for verbal properties pertaining to women and their claims to interpret God's word, used the phrase *celeste patrie* in a text published in 1558 (see chapter 5); she did so in a way that interrogates some French writers' views of their language and their nation. That entity, like the vernacular itself, was often personified as female. The gendered metaphors sometimes point to social tensions and anxieties; the "mother" tongue becomes a tenuously held property endangered by foreign invaders. Jean de Montreuil, in a paradoxical gesture of praising French in a Latin treatise, claims that the former language is superior to English, German, and other European tongues because of its *pureté,* its imperviousness to foreign influences.[13] But Montreuil's ideas about his own mother tongue, like his ideas about what he hypostatizes as English and German, are clearly a clerkly idealization superimposed on a messy situation where borders among tongues are permeable. Early modern translators, including those who participated in the late medieval traditions of translation as a form of exegesis, both practiced and advocated a process of "importing" foreign terms into versions of French in order to enrich its lexicon; the same process was occurring, with some *litterati* lamenting and others praising it, in versions of written English.[14]

If, as I have been arguing, there was no such thing as a pure and uniform mother tongue, the feminine personifications of the concept arguably attest to the anxiety that many *litterati* felt about a situation of linguistic variety. We have seen Dante attempting to master such a situation by the notion of a male-created "illustrious" vernacular, a "son of Latin," as it were. France may be addressed as "mère des arts" in a famous sonnet of du Bellay's *Regrets,* but that aristocratic poet and defender of an "illustrious" French—or rather, of a potential for French to become as illustrious as Latin, Italian, and Greek—reveals the dark side of his encomium when he paradoxically defends the French language by calling for the violent removal of the "corrupted flesh" of the vernacular he had inherited from medieval writers.[15] The question of the mother tongue, as we saw in chapter 2, becomes complexly intertwined with questions about gender and property for many *litterati* trained in more than one language and hence capable of *comparing* them. Nationalist ideologies were nurtured in the apparently arcane discursive arena of debates about the history, ontology, and future of vernacular languages as these were perceived by men trained to think bilingually through the humanist pedagogical method of double translation. In the mid-seventeenth century, John Hare approves of borrowing words from the "learned" (i.e., ancient) languages but inveighs, with more passion than logic, against neologisms drawn from the French; advocating a "purging" of "all words and terms" of Norman and French "descent," he praises a "Saxon"-based English that could be understood by any English person without the help of a dictionary, "which now is requisite to him that will rightly understand or speak even usual English."[16] Hare's call for a pure English defined, illogically, as a language that would be Saxon in essence but could nonetheless include borrowings from Latin and Greek, though definitely not from French, should be read as a passionate but incoherent response to a situation of enormous linguistic change. As Paula Blank notes in her important chapter on the ideological and economic debates surrounding the practice of "neologism" construed as "theft," between 1500 and 1659 as many as twenty-five thousand new words may have entered the English language—although many of these words remained unknown to speakers like Mistress Quickly and some may have been "invented" by the very men—the lexicographers—to whom modern scholars go for statistics on changes in the language.[17]

Modern ideas about cultural literacy, and about its significance in an emergent system of social distinction, owe more than has been previously acknowledged, I contend, to late medieval and early modern discussions of the vernacular both as a hypostatized language allegedly held in "common" by inhabitants of the monarchy and as an "inadequate" language—often figured

as female—in need of cultivation.[18] In this chapter I continue to draw on Balibar's concept of *colinguisme* as a situation of structured competition in which
conflicts center on "the power of translation" (Balibar, "National Language,
Education, Literature," 127). In the case of France and England, the competition was never simply between two nation-states, even when long-term disputes like the Hundred Years War make it seem as if it were. Relations to other
European *partenaire* states were always at stake; and so, I maintain, were relations between vernacular and ancient languages. Although the "universalism"
of empire is often contrasted to the particularism said to be typical of centralized nations, many recent scholars of early modern England have seen the two
types of states to be related.[19] Jodi Mikalachki, for instance, argues in *The
Legacy of Boadicea* that "some larger concept of empire, some larger external
order within which the nation both pays tribute and rebels, is endemic to the
articulation of nationalism" (11). I argue that at some points in that long process of "articulation," what counts as a nation becomes so intertwined with
what counts as an empire that the two terms (and various other ones including *kingdom, commonwealth, pays, patrie,* and *country*) become linked in a
complex international history in which imperial fantasies—sometimes related to new educational emphases, such as a geography curriculum at Oxford
and Cambridge developed in the late sixteenth century—gestated in consequential ways.[20] Although England's American empire did not yet exist in
the sixteenth and early seventeenth centuries (it was an "empire nowhere,"
as Jeffrey Knapp points out), that doesn't mean that the English monarchy
doesn't merit the title of "empire" in the following sense given by the *OED*:
"an extensive territory (esp. an aggregate of many separate states) under the
sway of an emperor or supreme ruler; also, an aggregate of subject territories
ruled over by a sovereign state."[21] One may say that sixteenth-century Wales
was not a "state," but it was certainly one of the "subject territories" that English kings sought to rule, as we will see French kings seeking control of an
"internal colony" such as Navarre. Some of these monarchs, and their literate
servants, articulated their ambitions with explicit attention to the model of
ancient Rome.[22] For such monarchs and *litterati, imperium* could arguably
denote an extensive territorial possession as well as an attribute of kingship.

This claim is important because many scholars believe, with Nicholas
Canny, that "the word 'empire,' which was particularly favoured by Henry
VIII" after his breach with Rome, "called to mind the relative isolation of England through the centuries rather than its dominion over foreign territories."[23] This view—often expressed with positivist certainty about what words
mean and to whom—derives, it seems, from G. R. Elton's argument that when
the English Parliament officially stated in an Act of Appeals of 1533 that "[t]his

realme of England is an Impire," the proposition heralds the "modern" state because it breaks in two significant ways with the meaning Elton identifies as the predominant medieval one: *empire* denoting the type of power and authority possessed, in temporal matters, by an *imperator* or ruler.[24] The first new meaning of the term (the "modern" meaning, according to Elton) lies in its use to signify "sovereignty in spiritual matters" as well as temporal ones; the second new meaning is the denoting of "a political unit, a self-governing state free from 'the authority of any foreign potentates' . . . a sovereign national state."[25] The *OED* confirms Elton's claim by citing the 1533 Act of Appeals as the first (and sole) example for the seventh meaning of *empire*: "a country of which the sovereign owes no allegiance to any foreign superior." Without disputing that this is one significant meaning for *empire* in the context under discussion, I want to suggest that the word also called to mind other meanings, including a modern one Elton doesn't mention—the meaning of vast and increasing dominions that Miles Coverdale implies when, in translating the second book of Chronicles (36:20) in 1535, he describes the dominion possessed by the ancient Persians as an "empyre," thus changing the word Tyndale had used in this passage ("kingdom"). This change arguably alludes to the English awareness of imperial ambitions in modern as well as ancient Eastern states. Henry VIII's rival Francis saw the Ottoman ruler Süleyman the Magnificent as a major player on the European political stage; Süleyman, reported Francis, "detests the emperor [Charles V] and his title of *Caesar*, he, the Turk, causing himself to be called *Caesar*."[26]

In 1533 Henry VIII was already the ruler of a kingdom that could be considered an "empire" in an ancient as well as incipiently modern sense of that word—*imperium* as an "aggregate of many separate states." This is the meaning the *OED* gives for the word as used in a chronicle history of England written around 1330: "Adelard of Westsex was kyng of the Empire." Other usages of the term in this sense—which is ignored by Elton's story of a dyadic shift from a "medieval" to a "modern" meaning—appear in texts written in English both before and after the act of 1533. The *OED* cites, among others, Shakespeare's in *Antony and Cleopatra*: "Let the wide Arch of the rang'd Empire fall" (1.1.34); and any English person who knew enough French and Latin to comprehend Rabelais's extraordinary blending of learned and popular lexicons could have read the passage cited in the epigraph to this chapter, a passage from a book published just a year after the English Parliament's Act of Appeals. In this passage from *Gargantua*, Rabelais offers an extended vernacular imitation of two ancient texts mocking imperial ambitions, Lucian's dialogue "The Ship, or the Wishes" and Plutarch's "Life of Pyrrhus." Rabelais describes with comic geographical detail the desires for "universal empire" (*empire univers*) held by a foolishly ambitious king named Picrochole ("bitter choler"). Picrochole, whose vanity is fed by irresponsible courtier-counselors well read in classical and Renaissance literature about voyages to foreign lands, is led to imagine that he will be able to conquer "England, Ireland, and Scotland" among many other parts of the globe. Invited by his greedy counselors to model himself on emperors like Alexander of Macedon and Augustus Caesar, Rabelais's Picrochole is clearly indebted to the critiques of the imperial and war-mongering ambitions of actual European monarchs, including Henry VIII, articulated by humanist scholars like Erasmus and More.

More resigned his position of lord chancellor a year before the Act of Appeals proclaimed England an empire. Two years later, he was executed for treasonously opposing Henry's claim that England should have a separate "head" from that of the "one body" of Christendom ruled, in spiritual matters, by the pope. More's history as a royal servant, and Rabelais's description of a war-mongering king whose very first mock-epic "conquests" involve conquering neighboring regions of France—regions which he does not distinguish from countries like Spain and England—dramatize the complexity of one of the main questions addressed in this chapter: What is an empire or a nation in transitional-era England or France, if we take into account, in our definitions, the views of those who may dispute the monarch's definition? Among those are some members of the literate class-fragment, men and women who may seem in hindsight merely members of a loyal opposition, but who may nonetheless have held and risked punishment for genuinely unorthodox views; much depends on how, in retrospect, we define what was orthodox or dominant in a culture.

There is, I believe, considerable evidence that some early modern writers and rulers desired their realms to become "empires" in the primary sense given by the *OED*: "supreme and extensive political dominion," "absolute sway." *Empire* denotes the kind of dominion the Roman emperors had enjoyed and that Spanish monarchs seemed to be intent on acquiring, at least in English eyes, in the late 1580s. The history of such terms as *nation, kingdom, commonwealth, pays, patrie,* and *empire* is very complicated; my aim here is not to sort out that history, a task that has been undertaken by many others.[27] Rather, I explore a discursive area in which overlapping concepts of political and economic dominion were significantly yoked to debates about national languages in ways that help us understand the contributions of a literate class not only to the formation of imperial nations, but also to a history of such nations that notices dissonant voices in various sociolects. This discursive territory provides counterevidence to scholarly accounts like that of Ernest Gellner, who believes that it is anachronistic to posit either "nations" or "nationalism" as existing before the industrial age in Europe.

Gellner argues that nations emerge only when literacy extends from an elite clerisy to a general population; literacy is "universalized," in his view, only when agrarian societies give way to industrial ones in the late eighteenth century (*Nations and Nationalism*, 17–18). He describes this historical process as a "gelding" that occurs, as he puts it—clearly envisioning both his own audience and the "general population" as composed solely of men—"when every man Jack amongst us is a Mamluk *de Robe*, putting the obligations to his calling above the claims of kinship" (ibid., 18). "Gelding" is a set of strategies deployed by a central state to counter the danger to the state posed by men's links to kinship groups—links that compete, as Plato argued, with male citizens' (and especially military officers') duties to serve the state (ibid., 15). Gellner's book illustrates a tendency evident in much writing on nations and nationhood, including studies that argue for earlier forms of "nationhood" than Gellner allows. The tendency is to associate nationhood and its accompanying ideology, nationalism, with mass literacy and/or with its written products, while treating literacy as an uncontested and presumptively male domain.

Underlying this tendency is one I've mentioned before: to take late medieval and early modern clerkly authors at their word when they write of the vernacular as a single phenomenon in ways that both anticipate and help create the modern nation-state. In arguing that that phenomenon—as a still-debated set of practices, institutions, and ideologies—was anticipated by clerks writing during the Hundred Years War, I do not wish simply to play the scholarly game of trumping others by locating new moments for the birth of something like "the nation." Cases can be plausibly made for many such births, and that is part of my point. In looking at an early crucible for (ideas of) nationhood, I want to stress the futility of looking for one birth-moment, even of the sort Benedict Anderson offers when he writes, before no fewer than three chapters devoted to multiple "prologues" of nationalism (with the intriguing titles "Cultural Roots," "Origins of National Consciousness," and "Pioneers"), that the modern form of nationalism made its "appearance . . . toward the end of the eighteenth century" (*Imagined Communities*, 12). Anderson, however, complicates his own gesture toward defining a single moment for the emergence of the modern nation when he writes about the three paradoxes that have often "perplexed, not to say irritated," theorists of nationalism. These are, "1) The objective modernity of nations to the historian's eye vs. their subjective antiquity in the eyes of nationalists. 2) The formal universality of nationality as a socio-cultural concept—in the modern world everyone can, should, will 'have' a nationality, as he or she 'has' a gender—vs. the irremediable particularity of its concrete manifestations, such that, by definition, 'Greek' nationality is *sui generis*. 3) The 'political' power of nationalisms vs. their philosophical poverty and even incoherence" (ibid., 5).

Without denying that something new and materially significant happened to nations both in the eighteenth and in the sixteenth centuries, I suggest that Anderson's own descriptions of the paradoxes of nationalism can provide a useful entrée into the clerkly debates prompted by the Hundred Years War (1337–1453). Among the *litterati* who debated the question of what is a nation at the turn of the fifteenth century was Christine de Pizan, whose contributions to the discourse of the imperial nation I analyze in chapter 4. The terms in which she considered the question—with some heterodoxies colored by her gender—were initially developed in the writings of men whose attitude toward the great split in the papacy known as the Schism led them to question both papal and monarchical authority in subtle ways. Their writings blurred the boundary between temporal and religious realms and between clerical and lay audiences; though some of the writings were in Latin and thus legible only to fellow clerks, others were in a version of French, reflecting the clerks' situation as servants of a nation being defined, in part, by its status as at war with another entity claiming nationhood on both secular and theological grounds.

Clerkly Ideas of Nationhood at the Church Council of Constance (1417) and in Other Wartime Contexts

In 1417—the very year in which the historical Henry V was deciding, as noted in chapter 2, to write official letters to potential tax-paying subjects in a version of English rather than in a version of French or Latin—there occurred a debate in which the word *natio* is at issue. Earlier medieval texts had used that term to designate notions of "clan, tribe, province, or kingdom" in contexts pertaining to groups made up of merchants and/or university students and their teachers.[28] The clerical debate of 1417 recounts an argument that occurred at the Council of Constance over the "right of one people to rank as a nation" in that international assembly with both secular and ecclesiastical "representatives" of various Catholic territories. That context is the historical conflict within Catholic Europe reflected by and resulting from the heated battle among cardinals and kings about who was the rightful pope.[29] The return of the papacy to Rome after its sojourn in Avignon had created a metropolitan center of control that irritated many secular authorities, and they were increasingly disposed to challenge Rome's power: "national governments, and lesser principalities, demanded their own influence over any such decision [between rival claimants to papal power], as a means of control over their own clerical subjects" (Crowder, *Unity, Heresy and Reform,* 2). With the disputes over the papal succession, there began a "division of Europe, ecclesiastical and secular, which proved agonizing to resolve" (ibid.) and which profoundly shaped the political and theological terms in which later divisions of the Church were framed, including the divisions known as the Protestant Reformation.

The Schism posed particularly grave problems for priestly intellectuals, "who were continually required to reexamine their ideas about the source of authority in the Church," and who eventually played major roles in the five remarkable "general councils" held during the fifteenth century to resolve the crisis of authority. Jean Gerson, the chancellor of the University of Paris and a key player in the debates about women's heresy and literacy I explore in chapter 4, illustrates the struggle that many fairly conservative *litterati* underwent as a consequence of the Schism. Gerson came reluctantly to believe that a general council was both a necessary and a legitimate counterauthority to that of a "heretical pope" (Crowder, *Unity, Heresy and Reform*, 3). Gerson's teacher Pierre d'Ailly wrote a memorandum to the cardinals in 1409 articulating arguments in favor of a general council, even if that council was not summoned or attended by the pope. Drawing on Aristotle's notion of *epieikeia*, a forerunner of the early modern "equity law" that "gave the overriding purpose of a law greater importance than the strict letter," and drawing also on elements of the canon law that countered notions of unlimited papal monarchy, d'Ailly articulated the position that "the good of the whole body of the Church rather than of its head alone was paramount."[30] Many of the elements of later Protestant critiques of papal authority may be found in d'Ailly's memorandum—along with elements of later (and earlier) arguments against the absolute power of secular monarchs.[31] Paradoxically, however, d'Ailly's arguments against supreme papal power paved the way for the great achievement of the Council of Constance (1414–18): the restoration of the Church to obedience to one pope and hence the reaffirmation of papal monarchy (Crowder, *Unity, Heresy and Reform*, 4–5). Even more paradoxically, in the complex contest of ideas about papal and secular monarchy, d'Ailly and the ambassadors of Charles VI engaged in a bitter dispute with representatives of the Duke of Burgundy about the theory of "legitimate" tyrannicide—a theory that is critical to Christine de Pizan's writings both about French kings and about the female saints she depicts as fighting tyrants (ancient Roman patriarchs who look rather like modern French ones).

Questions about legitimate sovereignty were intricately yoked to those debated at the Council of Constance about what should constitute a proper "nation." On the authority of practices developed in earlier Church councils, and perhaps influenced by concepts of nations as corporate bodies in the universities, "nations" at Constance based their claim to a political voice "not on the number or status of the members present" but rather on "the power and importance of the land whence they came" (Loomis, "Nationality at the

Council of Constance," 515, 512). But those claims were also based on conflict-ing textual authorities about how Catholic Christendom was to be geograph-ically divided.[32] The term *nation*, first used in an ecclesiastical institutional context (so far as we know) in 1274, came to designate both the representers (delegates to a Church council) and the represented people (ibid., 510, 513). This argument directly counters Greenfeld's neatly linear semantic history of *nation* in which she distinguishes conciliar theories and usages of *nation* from the truly modern theories and usages (which, in her view, first and uniquely appear in sixteenth-century England—but not in France until the eighteenth century) on the grounds that in conciliar uses of the term, *natio* refers only to an "elite," not to the (idea of the) "people" that Greenfeld takes as the essence of modern nationalism.[33]

At Constance, England was one of the four nations deemed to have the standing necessary to vote as a unit in sessions of the council as a whole. The others were France, Italy, and Germany. Spain, which had once been a nation at Church councils, was initially absent from Constance because Spain had given its allegiance to a papal claimant unrecognized by the council. In 1415 d'Ailly had argued for allowing university clerics and representatives of princes, both clerical and lay, to vote as members of the council's nations, and he had thus helped to weaken those bishops and abbots who supported papal prerogatives. In 1416, however, worried by the English victory at Agincourt (1415), and by Henry V's treaty of alliance with the German emperor Sigis-mond (1416), d'Ailly attacked the "national system" he had once supported; in particular, he attacked England's right to national status, citing a papal bull that had long ago divided the territory known as the Roman "obedience" into four parts: "the first comprising France, Navarre, and Majorca; the second Germany, England, Hungary, Poland . . . etc.; the third, the Spanish king-doms; and the fourth, Italy, Sicily, Sardinia [etc.]" (Loomis, "Nationality at the Council of Constance," 516). Since a small delegation from Aragon had just ar-rived at the council, claiming its rightful place as a nation, d'Ailly argued that England should cede its place to Spain (ibid., 517). In support of this view, this clerical opponent of absolute papal power supported his monarch's interest by citing another papal bull depicting England as a small and unimportant province of the Church. By the ruling in question, "all England constituted just one thirty-sixth of the Roman obedience." Loomis paraphrases the re-mainder of the interestingly numerical argument d'Ailly mounts against En-gland in his *De ecclesiastica potestate*: "How absurd to permit [England] to play the part of one fourth or even, after Spain was admitted as a nation, of one fifth! If she were to continue as a separate nation, all the great nations of the council should be divided into smaller nations, each equivalent to England and each with a vote. Otherwise the ancient canonical method of voting in councils by individuals should be restored" (ibid.). The "national system" employed by the Church administration had gotten out of hand and hence could be attacked as a historically contingent phenomenon, unauthorized by authoritative papal texts.[34] D'Ailly's views caused great umbrage among the English, and numerous, almost comical incidents of national jockeying for prestige occurred in the next year, my own favorite being the dispute between the English and the Aragonese about exactly where their respective seals were to be placed on a routine document.[35] Eventually, a French royal proctor sought permission to read a paper setting forth the views of his party. This proctor, Jean Campan, was shouted down, but he succeeded in getting his statement entered into the written record of the council.[36] Then Thomas Polton, one of the council's official notaries, delivered—again for the Latin written record— an English answer to the French argument on nationhood. Polton indignantly countered Campan's several reasons for maintaining that England was not really a *natio principalis,* but only a *natio particularis.*[37] Historians interpret the latter phrase as the equivalent of the political *regna,* or kingdom (Allmand, *Henry V,* 417; Genêt, "English Nationalism," 65). *Natio principalis,* equivalent to what Campan seems to have meant when he referred to "Gallia" as one of the *nationes generales,* is an altogether trickier concept.[38] Historians translate it as "principal nation," and some have explained it as a "medieval," as opposed to a "modern," notion of "nation."[39] I would argue, however, that Polton's and Campan's ideas of a "general" or "principal" nation draw not only on medieval theories, which made "political diversity within a wider political and cultural unit" a chief criterion of ecclesiastical nationhood, but also on classical theories—and examples—of empires where peoples speaking one language ruled those who spoke other languages. Within the context of the medieval ecclesiastical institution, linguistic diversity was a minor issue; all the delegates from all "principal" or "particular" nations were clerics, and all spoke Latin. Writers like d'Ailly, Campan, and Polton, however, were attempting to manage secular as well as religious conflicts within the framework of an ecclesiastical council, and traces of older, more secular ideas about political units, and their relation to non-Latin-speaking subjects, appear in all of the documents in the *natio* dispute at Constance. If we consider *empire,* either in its medieval or in its classical form, a possible synonym for *principal nation,* we will be more skeptical than Allmand and Loomis are about Polton's argument concerning the role of language in constituting a *natio principalis.* Loomis and Allmand (the latter, it is worth recalling here, writing a well-respected modern biography of Henry V) read Polton as articulating a view held by certain sixteenth-century clerks and monarchs, as well as by many modern scholars—namely, that a nation consists of people who speak the same language.[40] Polton does allude to that view, but he does so in a way that suggests that it was by no means hegemonic. Indeed, he grapples with the problem of certain peoples' reluctance to belong to a given nation, the language of which is *not* theirs, by arguing that a given people's disinclination to be part of the English "nation" and to obey the English king has no bearing on whether their territory in truth belongs to England.[41] Although he introduces his discussion of language with a statement that seems to support the common modern view of one nation, one language, Polton begins to turn a problem of diversity into a claim of strength (Allmand, *Henry V,* 417–18). England, he writes, is comparable to France in everything "necessary to being a nation with an authentic voice . . . whether the nation is understood as a people [*gens*], distinct from another by blood relationship [*cognationem*] and association [*collectionem*] or by difference of language [*diversitatem linguarum*],—which is the chief and surest proof of being a nation, and its very essence, either by divine or human law." His phrase *diversitatem linguarum* might well be translated by the Chaucerian phrase "diversity of language" rather than by "difference" of language (Crowder's translation) or, as Loomis suggests, by "peculiarity" of language.[42] *Difference* and *peculiarity* support a modern nationalistic reading of Polton's position, whereas what he (or his scribe) actually wrote shows two different views of the nation competing with each other in the same text. The second, less commonsensical view wins out in Polton's passage, though it loses credibility (and even existence!) in the writings of modern commentators.

Polton begins by turning the comparability of the French and English nations into a contrast, to the detriment of the country possessing (or so Polton maintains) just "one vernacular which is wholly or in part understandable in every part of the nation" (Crowder, *Unity, Heresy and Reform,* 121). *That* nation is France. In the "famous English or British nation," however, "there are five languages, one of which does not understand another. These are English . . . Welsh, Irish, Gascon and Cornish. It could be claimed with every right that there should be representation for as many nations as there are distinct languages. By an even stronger right [however] ought they, as a principal nation, to represent a fourth or fifth part of the papal obedience in a general council and elsewhere" (ibid.). As my interpolated *however* suggests, the logic of this passage is slippery. If one reads it carefully, and with attention to the clue initially given with the ambiguous earlier phrase *diversitatem linguarum,* one can see Polton arguing that England has a *better* claim than France to be a *natio principalis* precisely because England (or Britain) has a greater diversity of languages than France (or Gaul). While such diversity of tongues might "with every right" constitute an argument for granting "particular nation" status to all the different regions Polton mentions—and that he had earlier described as not always doing "what the king of England tells them to do"—a "greater right" makes them rightly part of the English/British nation. In the rhetorical move subordinating "every right" to a "greater right," we can see an imperial ideology emerging—still fragile, but elegant in the utter arbitrariness of the logical/ideological equation "diversity of languages = principal nation." The beauty of Polton's formulation, from my perspective, is that it reveals the fictionality of the alternative, and historically more popular, equation: one nation = one language. Indeed we can observe Polton falsifying the French situation in order to make his own polemical pro-English point; not only was there not a single language of France at any point during the late medieval era, there was also a significant strand in French clerkly writing that articulated, for France, precisely the argument Polton was using for England: the argument that France was superior to England because that "petit royaume" "n'a qu'une seule langue."[43]

The strand of nationalist argument I have been examining—the imperial-nationalist strand—has no moral superiority to the "one language" strand, and indeed the two are dialectically related as discourses of political legitimation. We need to be aware of both strands, however, to understand the contested social arena in which early modern nations and their differential types of literacy emerged. Polton's view of England as an internally divided but nonetheless important "nation" points ahead to political and economic attempts to manage those divisions during the Tudor and Stuart regimes. Because, as Paula Blank has noted, "there were no linguistic academies established in early modern England, no state institutions working" to "regulate" the language, it is tempting to view the linguistic richness of Elizabethan literature as a kind of Bakhtinian scene of freedom and revel.[44] We need to resist that temptation—and the comforting view of the Anglo-American tradition it subtends (especially the view of that tradition as inherently opposed to the petty "rules" of academies such as those later instituted in France, Italy, and Spain)—if we are to read the story of modernization with an eye to its costs to others as well as its benefits to us.

Recalling that many people in early modern monarchical territories did not speak or write the prestige dialect used in the court and (by some people) in the capital city, we can appreciate the importance of vernacular texts written by Latin-speaking clerks to an audience clearly conceived as literate enough to receive education about why they should define themselves as members of a given nation. In these documents one can see the emergent definition of "partial" literacy that I discussed in chapter 2. This is literacy defined not as mastery of Latin but rather as a capacity to receive instruction in the vernacular—an inferior language for "imperfect" people, but a language nonetheless being modeled on Latin and intermittently seen as useful for na-

tional administrative and propaganda purposes. Such a literacy entails submissive reception of discourse, but not the production of alternative narratives; hence it is appropriate for subjects of nascent empires.

Such literacy was both presumed to exist and encouraged (as an ideological goal) by French and English royal clerks attempting to garner popular support for their monarchical combatant in the Hundred Years War. P. S. Lewis
argues that writers addressing a lay audience, specifically including those
who don't understand Latin ("qui point n'entendent Latin"), worked to create
some kind of unity of attitude toward their monarchs' dynastic dispute among
skeptical members of the populations on both sides of the Channel.[45] The
French propagandists were particularly concerned to sway "regional" waver-
ers, those inhabiting "internal colonies."[46] The French cause was not warmly
embraced in Guyenne, for instance, and many Norman aristocrats as well as
commoners evidently thought that living under an English king would be no
worse (or better) than living under a French one (Lewis, "War Propaganda and
Historiography," 7). From the beginning of the war princely lords of certain
French territories—Artois, for instance, and Alençon—had been "eager to
point out to the king of England the claims he might have in France" (ibid., 8).
Writers on both sides of the dispute worried, as if it were Holy Scripture, the
obscure and contradictory textual tradition pertaining to the Salic Law and
its (alleged) famous clause that, according to one manuscript gloss, "excludes
and totally forecloses women from the power of succeeding to the crown of
France" [exclut et forclot femmes de tout en tout de povoir succeder à la
couronne de France].[47]

Fewer early English efforts to appeal to (and create) nationalist sentiment
survive than French ones; perhaps, Lewis speculates, fewer were written. In
1461, however, one author wrote a "breve treatise" in order "to bringe the
people oute of doute than han nat herd of the cronycles and of the lineal de-
scennse unto the crownes of Englande, of Fraunce . . . and unto the duchie of
Normandie sith it was first conquest and made" (cited in Lewis, "War Propaganda and Historiography," 15). Such treatises, addressed in both French and
English to subjects who might not have "heard of" the chronicle justifications
of aristocratic land claims, were eagerly exhumed and printed in the late sixteenth and early seventeenth centuries.[48] In those years, England and France
were not officially at war; nonetheless, their old love/hate relationship, fueled
by new developments such as England's loss of Calais in 1558, the St. Bartholomew's Day massacre of French Protestants in 1572, and Queen Elizabeth's prolonged flirtation with the idea of marrying the Duke of Alençon in
the 1580s, produced an ongoing cultural narrative with chapters in both languages but more, it seems, in English than in French during the late sixteenth
and early seventeenth centuries.[49]

This asymmetry perhaps testifies to the interest, on the part of some English *litterati,* in avenging the old wound of the Norman Conquest. Kathleen Lambley cites petitions made to Henry VIII against the continued use of French in England, especially at court, "'as thereby ys testified our subjectyon to the Normannys'" (*Teaching and Cultivation,* 22). If one seeks to undo the humiliating sexual, military, and linguistic legacies of the Conquest, the story of England's heroic king Henry V offers rich resources.[50] In his own time, he did a great deal to help promote French nationalist sentiments through his "scourging" of France prior to his famous victory at Agincourt (1415).[51] Late in the sixteenth century, however, through the pen of a playwright who drew on but drastically altered aspects of English history (as reported by chronicles and other texts) that did not suit his purposes, this king emerges as a complex hero of imperial nationalism. In the course of the play, a duke with the same noble name as Elizabeth's suitor is mentioned (although he is not among the *dramatis personae*) as the gentleman from whom Henry took the glove he later gives to the soldier Williams as a token of disguised royal honor (4.8.26); Bartholomew's Day is also mentioned in a way that wittily translates its offense to England into a counter-story about French subjection to English power. Burgundy (in the Folio text) fawningly consents to Henry's possession of a French princess's maiden body—with or without her consent—by comparing the royal French lady in question, Katherine, to a fly "at Bartholomew-tide, blind" and willing to "endure handling, which before they would not abide looking on" (5.2.285–87). Editors usually gloss "Bartholomew-tide" simply as a reference to a hot part of summer when insects grow sluggish (St. Bartholomew's Day is August 24). Like Jonathan Baldo, however, I think that few in Shakespeare's first audiences—whether Catholic or Protestant—would have heard the phrase "Bartholomew-tide" without remembering the massacre of Huguenots that occurred on this saint's day in 1572 (Baldo, "Wars of Memory in *Henry V,*" 142–43). The topical allusion gives ironic resonance to Shakespeare's way of degrading a French princess. As many critics have noted, Katherine is treated as a spoil of war, her body likened to the "maiden" cities such as Harfleur that Henry has raped in the course of his progress to the marriage he hopes will secure his victory over the land.[52] The loss of Calais is symbolically undone in the play's complex restaging of history to make Englishmen, not Normans, into conquerors.

A Late Sixteenth-Century Translation of a Fifteenth-Century Hero

In contrast to the historical Henry V, Shakespeare's king does not speak good French (although he appears to understand it well enough). He also does not have to contend with "anti-Lancastrian rebellions and Lollard activity" at home; nor does he have to resort to cruel stratagems when he goes abroad to fight the French.[53] He wins a definitive military and matrimonial victory in Shakespeare's play, although in history (as Shakespeare's own final Chorus suggests, looking "ahead" at the end to the Henry VI plays) the victory was incomplete, for the king died—father of a sickly son—before France was securely "made one" with England. In Shakespeare's revisionary history, moreover, Henry's Irish, Welsh, and Scottish captains quarrel with each other but can speak to and be clearly understood by the king who claimed in his wild youth to be able to "speak with any tinker in his own language" (*Henry IV*, 2.4.19). Jamy, the representative of Scotland in Shakespeare's *Henry V*, is loyal to England, though his historical counterpart would very likely have been among the Scottish troops sent to help the dauphin fight the English (Allmand, *Henry V*, 128). Shakespeare's stage Scotsman speaks in a "northen" dialect but not one with any of the specifically Scots orthographic features (representing "Scots" pronunciation) that one finds (for instance) in King James's treatise on Scots poetics, included in his published *Essayes* of 1584 (Blank, *Broken English*, 159). Shakespeare's Scotsman, Paula Blank speculates, contributes to that project of "anglicizing" Scotland and its language that King James would himself pursue (while making an interesting and paradoxical exception for Scots *literature*) once he came to the English throne. "It sal be vary gud, gud feith, gud captens bath," Jamy says, in one of the play's many examples of linguistic nationalism at work (*Henry V*, 3.3.43).[54]

Shakespeare's *Henry V* has produced an unusually rich body of critical literature debating how to assess the character of the king (epic hero or a Machiavellian schemer?) and, more recently, how to assess the ideological work the play performs for or against the Tudor (and, proleptically, the Stuart) state.[55] Critics are notoriously divided on whether the play serves to promote a new national unity or to expose it (subversively) as a costly fiction. No one doubts, however, that the play is a powerful document of nationalist ideology which deploys representations of language, along with representations of a peculiarly "English" masculinity, for political ends. The ends are what is contested; my brief contribution to the scene of debate involves suggesting that the play speaks to, and draws from, an emergent imperial nationalism that relies on at least two fictions of legitimation. These, I contend, are apparently contradictory. One adumbrates the (to us) familiar ideal of national and linguistic unity; the other, an ideal of England as a new Roman empire in which the (male) ruler controls his subjects despite (or because) the peoples are divided among themselves and speak many different tongues. This second ideal is important to examine, I think, and not only because it harks back to the debate about *natio* we have analyzed with reference to a Church council that occurred during the historical Henry V's reign. It also provides a historical precedent for a kind of nationalism that Anderson and others have seen emerging only recently ("nations can now be imagined without linguistic communality," he writes [*Imagined Communities*, 135]). Now, yes, but also, I am suggesting, at certain points in the past. Not all species of nation—now or in the past—have required "mass" literacy in a single national language supported by print technology, although some definitions of *nation* (Gellner's, for example) seem to presuppose just this connection between (a certain) literacy and the emergence of the nation. I am arguing, however, that nationalist ideologies, like those of Protestantism, may officially promote literacy for all subjects of the polity, while in actuality the nations in question not only tolerate but benefit from multiple language uses and highly stratified forms of literacy.

Ideas of the nation as a linguistically plural, even divided, entity were available as an ideological resource in the sixteenth century—a resource potentially as valuable as the fiction of national unity and the desideratum of one language. Both these views of the nation relied on an unstable relationship (in theory and in practice) between the King's English and English as a "common" tongue. Describing Shakespeare's *Henry V* as a paradoxical linguistic space in which "polyvocality" prevails without the mutual incomprehension that typically characterizes the fall into Babel, Claire McEachern remarks that controlled "faction" may in some circumstances be preferable to the leveling of social distinction implicit in the idea of a common, transparent language. "For if everyone were to speak the King's English," she asks, "would it still belong to the King?" (*Poetics of English Nationhood*, 120).

Let me reply to that question with another that admits of no clear answer: "What is my nation? Who talks of my nation," the Irish captain MacMorris testily exclaims in response to what he hears as an insult from the Welsh Fluellen (*Henry V*, 3.2.124). The Irishman's question has usually been interpreted as an expression of *Irish* patriotism, a resistance to the project of "British" absorption of provincial nations as colonies. Several recent critics have argued, however, that MacMorris feels his race or nation is being unfairly distinguished from the English nation. Philip Edwards paraphrases MacMorris's question as "Who are you, a Welshman, to talk of the Irish as though they were a separate nation from you? I belong in this family as much as you do."[56] Such ambiguity is part and parcel of the way the play works to imply a national unity within diversity; "alien" voices from three frequently rebellious parts of the monarchy are represented as comprehensible—at least to the king and to the audience—and are thus symbolically subjected to English rule, being "purged," according to Steven Mullaney, of all that is "base and gross."[57] In a well-known study of the play's "production and containment of subversion and disorder," Stephen Greenblatt compares Shakespeare's practices of allowing "alien voices" into his text's discursive space with those displayed by

Thomas Hariot in his *Brief and True Account of the New Found Land of Virginia*; for Greenblatt, the recording of other voices may create a "sense of instability" in the text (or in the reader?), but that sense is soon contained, for it is only "momentary."[58] But what is the moment the critic has in mind? Different audiences and readers, differently situated, might take different meanings from textual examples such as Fluellen's mispronunciation of the letter *b* as *p* when comparing the king to a conquering classical hero.[59] Fluellen here voices a perspective on the king's imperial ambitions that is familiar from many humanist critiques of the war-lust of monarchs like Henry VIII.

Such a perspective might well have been gratifying to the financially prudent, foreign-war-resisting monarch on the throne when *Henry V* was first performed, the "gracious empress" mentioned by the Chorus that opens Act 5 in the Folio text. Questions about whether the play promotes or undermines the unity and power of the English/British monarchy may well be off-target, as Katherine Eggert suggests, if they fail to consider how it mattered—to Shakespeare and to his various audiences, not only in 1599 but later—that the English monarchy was ruled for more than forty years by a queen who claimed a king's powers.[60] A notion of "otherness" implicitly associated with female rule and explicitly associated with femininity, with effeminization, and with France, has received much attention from recent critics of *Henry V.* Building on their insights, I suggest that the "imperial" model of nationalism works most visibly (for overdetermined reasons) in the two scenes that dramatize an English conquest of France in terms of a French queen's subjection to the King's English as well as to his sexual and dynastic "will." The English lesson scene of Act 3, scene 2, in which an "old gentlewoman" named Alice plays the role of inept teacher to her mistress, the princess Katherine, effects a complex ritual humiliation of females and of the French nation. Forced to prepare for her arranged marriage by submitting to a bawdy lesson dealing with words for body parts (and, in English puns, with sexual activities like buggery and prostitution), Katherine is divested of her rank.[61] As Helen Ostovich observes, the princess enduring her language lesson becomes like one of "the daughters of Harfleur," a woman trapped in a walled city being invaded by enemy soldiers "in a context of coarse physicality" ("Teach You Our Princess English?" 153). The princess is embarrassed by having to (mis)pronounce English words (*foot* and *count*) that have sexual meanings in French improper for a lady to invoke. The analogy between Katherine's own sexual fate and that of the French land is reinforced, Katherine Eggert suggests, by the fact that some of the words the princess learns (*hand,* for example, and *chin*) echo terms the play itself uses elsewhere to describe Henry's military conquest (*hand,* for instance, "recalls the 'bloody hand' and 'foul hand' of English soldiery with which Henry has just threatened Harfleur [3.2.12, 34]"). Even the princess's mistakes (e.g., *mails* for *nails*) assimilate her education in language to Henry's military project (Eggert, *Showing Like a Queen*, 87–88). Eggert is right that Katherine's English lesson is more militarily inflected than the usual "naming games" one plays with a child; I suggest, however, that part of Shakespeare's joke rests on the linguistic staging of language-learning scenes—both this one and the climactic "wooing" scene of 5.2—that parody one of the long-enduring cultural legacies of the Norman Conquest: the tradition of pedagogical discourse exemplified in a treatise like *Femina*. That tradition, briefly examined in chapter 2, had already become a subject for farce; in a popular Elizabethan production entitled *Jack Drum's Entertainment*, "the comic Frenchman" is a "grossly lascivious foreigner with a ludicrous accent" who "repeatedly seeks out . . . Englishwomen to whom he may teach French" (Ostovich, "Teach You Our Princess English?" 195). Revising and capitalizing on this anti-French cultural vein, Shakespeare offers his audience and readers a French princess speaking her connection with a conquered land through such words as *count*. Here she activates the *cunt/country* pun commonly used "in diatribes against Elizabeth, Mary Queen of Scots, or the institution of queenship itself" (Eggert, "Nostalgia and the Not Yet Late Queen," 548n. 27).

Ideologies of nationhood, language, and gender are tightly knotted in Shakespeare's *Henry V*, and nowhere more so than in its final scene. Here, the king poses as a "plain speaking" Englishman seeking union with a lovely French lass: "And, Kate, when France is mine and I am yours, then yours is France, and you are mine" (5.2.180–82). Reducing the princess to "Kate"— with its pun on *cates* as foods—allies the king with Petrucchio (*The Taming of the Shrew*) and other Shakespearean figures of the masculine educator.[62] Speaking of union, however, Henry (like others in the tradition of literate educators this book examines) arguably looks for inspiration to Roman imperial practices. He momentarily assumes the subordinate role of a language-learner in a foreign place, resembling the Aeneas who praises Dido's beauty when he first enters her walled city of Carthage: "Fair Catherine, and most fair,/Will you vouchsafe to teach a soldier terms/Such as will enter at a lady's ear,/And plead his love-suit to her gentle heart?" (5.2.98–101). Leaving the question open whether he would like to learn French or the language of courtly love (the two may in his view be synonymous), Henry quickly assumes the dominating role of teacher, a role that Katherine herself pliantly, and in line with Pauline and humanist theories about women's unsuitability for pedagogical authority, declines: "Your majesty shall mock at me. I cannot speak your England" (102–3). Her former female teacher, meanwhile, the "old gentlewoman" now made younger when the flattering king addresses her as "fair one" (117), is demoted to the odd role of a translator who is not really needed by the principal parties to the exchange.

The exchange is both linguistic and economic, as it was in an earlier scene of French/English verbal mingling (4.4), which showed Pistol communicating (with the help of a relatively powerless "Boy" translator, Falstaff's page) with the French soldier whose "gorge" Pistol plans to cut until he learns that the gentleman captive has money to offer for his life. To Pistol, French is no more or less foreign than an English regional tongue, as he shows when he hilariously assumes that the King's self-identifying phrase "Harry le roi" makes him "of Cornish crew" (4.1.51). In this regard resembling the lowly and coarse Pistol, Shakespeare's King Harry seems hardly to care whether the French tongue is truly "other" to an English one or not. It matters no more to his plan than Katherine's brief expressions of resistance to his construction of their present and future relationship matter to the outcome of their conversation: no matter what she says, she ends by submitting to his kiss, although she insists that it is against her country's customs. Here we see that her transformation from Henry's ostensible teacher to his pupil also entails her transformation from possessing some cultural autonomy to being a colonial subject whose "customs" must be set aside to suit the conqueror's will. "Teach you our princess English?" Burgundy asks, as he enters with Katherine's father upon the scene of the kiss (5.2.261–62).

Henry demonstrates in this final scene that the imperial ruler can function perfectly well in a situation where his new subject does not speak the master tongue any better than he speaks hers. Her political abjection is symbolized by her gender, giving ironic force to Henry's invitation that she express consent to a *fait accompli*: "Put off your maiden blushes, avouch the thoughts of your heart with the looks of an empress, take me by the hand and say, 'Harry of England, I am thine'—which word thou shalt no sooner bless mine ear withal, but I will tell thee aloud, 'England is thine, Ireland is thine, France is thine, and Henry Plantagenet is thine'" (5.2.218–23). But by mentioning Ireland and calling Katherine his "empress," Henry introduces some complexities of historical memory into his scene of triumphant comic wooing. His words here recall the speech with which the Chorus opens Act 5. The speech is read by most editors and critics as alluding (with complex and proliferating ironies) to Robert Devereux, the second Earl of Essex, at the moment when he triumphantly left England to quell Tyrone's Irish rebellion in 1599: Essex failed miserably in his campaign and was imprisoned by his queen for deserting his post in Ireland. He subsequently rebelled against her authority, did not receive the popular support in London for which he had hoped, and was tried and executed for treason in February 1601.[63]

How London doth pour out her citizens.
The Mayor and all his brethren, in best sort,

Like to the senators of th'antique Rome,
With the plebeians swarming at their heels,
Go forth to fetch their conqu'ring Caesar in—
As, by a lower but high-loving likelihood,
Were now the general of our gracious Empress—
As in good time he may—from Ireland coming . . .

(5.0.24–31)

The Chorus compares Essex here not only to a fifteenth-century king who defeated the French at Agincourt but also to an unspecified "conqu'ring Caesar" welcomed home to Rome by both senators and plebeians. The lines—and their absence from the quarto of 1600—have been the subject of much critical discussion. I invoke them here to make one final point about Shakespeare's *Henry V* as a document of imperial nationalism. The Chorus blithely limns a regime with not one but two potential rulers: the "general" is Elizabeth's servant, but insofar as he is "like" King Henry, or a Roman conqueror, he is a ruler in his own right and, by the rules of Roman and English gender hierarchy, the superior to all females. The play delicately alludes to a potential and gendered contest for the leader's prerogatives in its final scene as well, in a passage where Henry attempts to speak French and, in so doing, breaks a rule of grammar. His mistake occurs just after he poses a question about his dynastic future that neither history nor the princess answers affirmatively: "Shall not thou and I . . . compound a boy, half-French, half-English, that shall go to Constantinople and take the Turk by the beard? Shall we not? What says thou, my fair flower-de-luce" (5.2.193–97). Receiving from her only the unsatisfactory statement, "I do not know dat," Henry tries more extravagant flattery: "How answer you, *la plus belle Catherine du monde, mon très chère et divine déesse*?" The king's French, Katherine responds, is "faux," and indeed it is: he has used a masculine possessive pronoun with the feminine noun, *déesse*. Many editors do not gloss the mistake at all; Gary Taylor notes, however, that it is "probably deliberate," an illustration of the idea of "false French," rather than a compositor's error (*Henry V,* 274). Commentators in general have paid less attention to Henry's broken French than to Katherine's broken English. Reading Henry's mistake in conjunction with the Chorus's speech likening Henry both to Essex and to a "conquering Roman," however, we can surmise that the error alludes to other kinds of falsity—political, erotic, imperial—even as it demonstrates Henry's "false French." His mistake implies that he thinks all substantives that belong to him must follow his gender, as it were, rather than possibly having a different one. His mistake thus beautifully encapsulates the analogy he has previously drawn between his own use of French and a dependent, newly married wife (5.2.170–73).[64] French hanging from the king's tongue like a wife around her husband's neck is his to use as he pleases. But he is not altogether in control of the language's meanings; nor is he altogether in control of his bride or of their now merged nations' future. The ironies of history hinted at in the Chorus's speech—Ireland repeatedly rejected English efforts to subdue it, as France did after Agincourt; Essex, once Elizabeth's favorite and even a possible husband for her, fell quickly from glory to financial and political bankruptcy—reverberate also in the play's final scene. Henry's address to Katherine as "la plus belle . . . du monde, mon . . . déesse" recalls several moments in Vergil's imperial epic. One is when the hero, shipwrecked on the foreign shores of Carthage, first recognizes his mother: "O dea certe," he exclaims (*Aeneid,* 1.328), in a famous phrase Shakespeare translates for Ferdinand's first vision of Miranda in the new world of *The Tempest* ("most sure the goddess" [1.2.425]). Vergil's Venus then describes the human female who wields the scepter in this new place ("imperium Dido . . . regit" [1.340]), and Aeneas, eager to see this female leader ("dux femina facti" [364]), eventually finds her among other "wondrous sights" (494). She is a queen whose beauty apparently surpasses that of Venus herself: "regina . . . forma pulcherrima Dido," writes Vergil. If one hears this line behind Henry's address to his "plus belle Catherine du monde, mon . . . déesse," this Kate becomes a figurative daughter of Dido, a *divina virago* who looks ahead to Queen Elizabeth.[65]

Unlike Aeneas and the Earl of Essex, Shakespeare's Henry makes his Dido his wife and thus seems to secure his imperial line through a blood union with a female "other." The outcome seems precisely what Juno had hoped Aeneas would gain by marrying Dido and thus preventing a war between people of different "races." In this regard, Shakespeare's epic play seems uncannily to anticipate aspects of James's monarchical policy: his self-presentation as a Roman ruler and his theory of a British "union" that would merge bloodlines rather than spilling blood in "civil" wars. As Paula Blank observes, James "repeatedly invoked 'nature' as the grounds for uniting England and Scotland, arguing that the union of the kingdoms had already been effected in his body or person": "I desire a perfect Union of Lawes and persons, and such Naturalizing as may make one body of both Kingdomes under mee your King." The Union, James proclaimed in his first speech to the English Parliament, is "made in my blood."[66]

I have been describing Shakespeare's play as a document of imperialist nationalism that draws on two different but dialectically related visions of the imperial nation. I want now to suggest that both strands of national-imperial legitimation compete, in ways that Shakespeare's play sometimes registers, with the narratives provided by history—here invoked as something different from, though known through, historiography. Shakespeare's play gestures toward history when Katherine refuses to join Henry in his fantasy about a son who would continue his journey of epic conquest all the way to Constantinople; the play also perhaps gestures toward a history known to some in Shakespeare's audiences when the mistaken phrase "mon déesse" points (as I have suggested) back to the virago Dido and forward to a (chaste) Elizabeth. Katherine Eggert has brilliantly argued that Shakespeare's play seals its ideological "refusal of female rule" by suppressing a genealogical fact reported by Holinshed in his chronicles as well as by other writers: Katherine of France lived on after Henry V's early death—and after the birth of their sickly son Henry VI—to marry a second time and through this marriage to "become the great-great-grandmother of Elizabeth Tudor" (*Showing Like a Queen*, 96). If, however, Elizabeth's image shimmers through Henry's false French invocation of a goddess who turns out to be only temporarily "his"—and if Elizabeth appears, as it were, in a grammar error occurring right after Katherine has obliquely undermined Henry's hopes for an epic future carried through the male line—perhaps history has a good laugh at Henry's expense. It's not the last laugh, by any means, but it helps explain why the play continues to provoke debate about what exactly it means to "support" or "resist" a dominant ideology. The readers and spectators of the play remain uncertain (and in this they resemble the epic hero and the historical author) about the final outcome, in the play's terms, the "issue," of the linguistic and political contests it dramatizes.

Making and Mystifying Others

I have sought to recontextualize aspects of Shakespeare's play about Henry's "famous victories" by viewing it as participating in an enduring cultural enterprise of producing social unions and distinctions. I turn now to a wider look at that enterprise of making others through language games involving ridicule and analogy. During the late medieval and early modern eras, a language called English was frequently defined as more valuable than other languages, including French, Welsh, Gaelic, and Scots, each of which existed ambiguously both inside and outside England's shifting borders. French was, of course, the language of English law for centuries, and some of its terms remain in use today.[67] Such languages were often perceived as threats like invading armies. In July 1400, for instance, Henry Percy, justiciar of Chester, wrote in the prince's name—and in Latin—to summon archers to resist the Scots who proposed "to make war against the language and people of England" [ad linguam et gentem eiusdem regni debellandum]. An anonymous text in the records of the earldom of Chester, dated 1407, decries the intention of the Welsh "to destroy the English tongue as far as they can and turn it into the Welsh tongue" [et ad linguam Anglicanam pro posse suorum destruendam et in linguam Wellensicam convertendam].[68] Juliet Fleming discusses a rich body of evidence portraying French as a devious, cunning, *lingua mulierum*.[69] That phrase comes from Peter Erondells's instructional treatise of 1605, *The French Garden: for English Ladyes and Gentlewomen to walke in*; like many other treatises ostensibly aimed at teaching French as a desirable accomplishment for privileged women, the text displays marked ambivalence both toward women and toward French. French is "delicate, but over nice as a woman, scarce daring to open her lippes for feare of marring her countenance," opines Richard Carew around 1596, in his *Excellencie of the English Tongue* (43). Some years earlier, when Queen Elizabeth was contemplating marriage to the Duke of Alençon, John Stubbes passionately warned her against French licentiousness and effeminacy, both qualities evident in a language marked by "hissing and lisping."[70] Stubbes here neatly anticipates a Swedish writer who maintained in 1683 that Eve was tempted in French.[71]

English characterizations of French during the fifteenth and particularly the sixteenth centuries, like English characterizations of other regional languages that are at once "foreign" and objects of dynastic, and eventually more broadly nationalist/imperialist, desires, exhibit a strange paradox: the language is seen both as effeminate and as hypermasculine, with true English masculinity emerging ideologically, through a sexualized rhetorical grid, as a "middle of the road" phenomenon. Ann Jones and Peter Stallybrass have analyzed the ways in which the Irish language and people were construed in some sixteenth-century English texts both as effeminate (in the common Renaissance sense denoting men "contaminated" by women) and as barbarically aggressive; the Irish were alleged to be an innately warlike people (like their reputed ancestors, the Scythians) who could only be "managed"—as certain English writers like Spenser argued—through a policy of military subjugation.[72] Moreover, within a set of "kindred" languages marked, in English eyes, as both "foreign" and potentially English (that is, convertible to or properly replaceable by the King's English), substitutions could be easily made, at least in the realm of discourse, because such languages shared the paradoxical (and labile) quality of being "abnormal" with respect to a norm associated with English masculinity. Whether the abnormality took the form of too little masculinity (effeminacy) or too much (barbaric aggressivity), writers could use the *structure* of language polemic to allude to Ireland or Wales when they wrote of France, and vice versa. Shakespeare's comparison of Henry V to Essex, discussed above, should be read in this context of French/

Irish analogies. Similarly, as Jonathan Baldo has argued, Shakespeare's depictions of Owen Glendower's rebellion in the *Henry IV* plays would have invited a contemporary audience to see connections between the "Great Irish Revolt" of the 1590s and the revolt of the Welsh under Owain Glyn Dŵr in the early 1400s ("Wars of Memory in *Henry V*," 146). The "equivalencies" among different regional languages impinge, then, on the metaphorical genderings (and hence hierarchies) of languages in the early modern era; moreover, the representation of "foreign" languages as female and effeminate colored the cultural reception of actual women's speech and writing even as long-standing ideologies about female verbal production (transgressive from the beginning, according to Genesis) shaped perceptions of language difference. Those differences, like the ones between the male and the female, needed constant rearticulation, lest they collapse.

English nationalist ideology as it developed between the reign of Henry V and its representation by Shakespeare raises the ancient imperial question about how to distinguish between a "civil" war and one against foreigners. In his brilliant study of epic and empire, David Quint observes that Vergil's representation of the Battle of Actium on Aeneas's shield prompts just that question—at least for those who know enough about Augustus's battle against Antony and his Egyptian lover Cleopatra to know that the historical battle "was, in fact, the climax of a civil war, Roman against Roman," rather than the battle between unified, masculine Romans and disunified, feminized Others depicted in Vergil's poem (*Epic and Empire*, 23). Depicting one's enemies as Other—in "race" or gender—is a valuable defensive strategy when the actual differences one is contending with are multiple, confusing, contested. Derogatory images of vernacular tongues—and their speakers—occur in many texts produced during the late medieval and early modern eras; writers working in courtly sites evidently transferred to nonmetropolitan vernaculars ideas that Latin-writing clerks had expressed about the vernacular in general. Diversity in *idioma*, Roger Bacon had insisted, leads to social ridicule; J. D. Burnley cites the French fabliau of the *Dous anglois de l'anel* in which "the defective French of two Englishmen leads to misadventure when they confuse the pronunciation of the word for 'lamb' with that for 'ass.'"[73] This tale also stigmatizes the language of Auvergne, however, suggesting that the narrative works rather as an ideological assertion of "*francien* against provincial forms of French" than of "Gallic chauvinism" (Burnley, "Sources of Standardisation," 32). The English heroine of the fourteenth-century romance *Jehan et Blonde* is criticized for her accent, as is the historical poet Conon de Béthune; born in Picardy, he was attacked for having "not been born at Pontoise," in the Ile-de-France region (ibid.). Metropolitan perspectives are strong and long-lived. Even Serge Lusignan, a modern Canadian scholar highly sensitive to the politics of language, relies on an interesting but fraught decision to define a linguistic *domaine français* that includes England but not Provence: "par domaine français nous entendons l'aire geographique des parlers d'oil" (*Parler vulgairement,* 12). Lusignan's decision not to consider *langues d'oc* as part of his book's topic reflects a view of French historically conditioned by the institution of the royal court. He justifies his decision to exclude the *parlers d'oc* from his study of the vernacular on the grounds that they "constitute another language whose singularity and wealth of cultural experience are worthy of a separate study" [constituent une autre langue dont la singularité et la richesse de l'expérience culturelle devrait donner lieu à une étude autonome] (ibid.). That may well be so—but the problems as well as the benefits of such "autonomy" lurk in the statement.

The location of Paris meant that southern France epitomized a certain idea of stubborn (and often heretical) provincialism; the location of England's capital, in contrast, rendered huge parts of northern England (and all of Scotland) provincial. Already in the twelfth century William of Malmesbury, a southerner (d. c. 1143), was mocking the language of the Northumbrians in words that the translator John of Trevisa, another southerner, renders into a form of English barely legible to modern readers in his version of a chronicle by the northerner Ranulph Higden.[74] The language of York, to a man from Cornwall like Trevisa, is no less alien ("scharp, slytting, and frotyng, and vnschape," as he puts it) than the language of Calais, and it is therefore no surprise to find pitched territorial battles for control of the linguistic realm occurring among English clerks as early as the fourteenth century. In the "Reeve's Tale," as I mentioned in chapter 2, Chaucer gives two Cambridge undergraduates "a variety of language which has northern features in it, and we are clearly supposed to see this difference as significant."[75] That members of the clerkly class recognized and in some cases objected to Chaucer's denigration of a northern speech is suggested by the fact that scribes copying the *Canterbury Tales* after the appearance of the Haenwrt manuscript ("the oldest and most authoritative manuscript of the poem," according to N. F. Blake) handled this part of the text in two quite different ways. Some scribes replaced northern forms by southern ones, evidently to defuse the parody; others, however, *added* northern forms, devising orthographic representations of northern speech patterns in ways that defined the latter as laughably "provincial" (Blake, "Standardising Shakespeare's Non-standard Language," 59). Thus the clerks continued the cultural game (or battle, depending on one's regional perspective) that Chaucer had begun.

The anonymous resistance of a few clerical copyists of a "canonical" literary work written (so the textbooks tell us) in what was destined to become the "London dialect" and hence the conduit for the development from medieval

to modern English, reminds us that the process known as standardization occurred over many centuries and with many pockets of resistance, some continuing. Bourdieu is partly right when he says that "the process of linguistic
unification went hand in hand with the process of constructing the monarchical state" (*Language and Symbolic Power,* 46). But such a formulation presents unity—of state and language—as an achieved fact or social product
rather than as a set of prescriptions and practices that have historically been
challenged by various groups and by many linguistic practices, including
some that left traces in the written record even when they occurred outside the
spheres of influence of the court or the school.

One famous articulation of the idea of a spoken standard in English focuses on the court rather than the school as the chief site where modeling of
good speech occurs. This is George Puttenham's recommendation (in his *Arte
of English Poesie* of 1589) that readers should take as their model the "usuall
speach of the Court" and that of the area within sixty miles of London, which
would include the London-Oxford-Cambridge triangle.[76] But Puttenham
complicates his prescription by acknowledging that even the English of the
metropolis and its key institutions is somehow the product of historical "mixings" of different peoples and languages. Trying to define both spoken and
written English as a language comparable to ancient Latin and Greek, Puttenham writes:

> [W]hen I say language, I meane the speach wherein the poet or maker writeth
> be it Greek or Latine, or as our case is the vulgar English, and when it is pecu-
> liar unto a contrey it is called the mother speach of that people; the Greekes
> terme it *Idioma*: so is ours at this day the Norman English. Before the Conquest
> of the Normans, it was the Anglesaxon, and before that the British, which as
> some will, is at this day, the Walsh, or as others affirme, the Cornish: I for my
> part thinke neither of them both, as they be now spoken and p[r]onounced . . .
> [Y]e shall therefore take the usuall speach of the Court, and that of London and
> the shires lying about London within lx. myles, and not much above. (*Arte of
> English Poesie,* 156–57)

The *idioma* of England is a *hybrid* phenomenon, and Puttenham's nationalist agenda prevents him from using Roger Bacon's notion of a superordinate
"substance" of Latin to counter the perception of historical change in the
realm of language and the problems such change poses for any notion of
"ownership" or "propriety" (both are aspects of what is "peculiar" to a "con-
trey") in the realm of language. Puttenham describes some possible challenges
to the metropolitan standard even as he insists on its necessity. Having identified the "mother speach" of his country as "the Norman English," he gives a

miniature historical narrative that stretches into the present and a possible future before such a future is censored by the writer's expression of judgment:
("I for my part . . ."). In admitting that some unnamed persons believe that a
non-Norman version of the vernacular has survived centuries of postconquest
history and is still discernible in a provincial language such as Welsh or
Cornish, Puttenham hints at the idea that the vernacular is a political and
historically contingent phenomenon rather than anything so natural as the
metaphor of the mother tongue implies. But Puttenham uses the diversity
of local opinions about the history of a non-Norman English to support his
dismissal of the Cornish and Welsh languages as well as their users' (competing) claims to being more truly English, or British, than those whose language
is, in Puttenham's phrase, "the usuall speach of the Court." Before he prescribes a metropolitan and aristocratic language for his literate audience,
however, Puttenham gives us a glimpse of those nonmetropolitan women
and men who might disagree with his perspective on the various languages;
there are, he backhandedly admits, several claimants to the throne occupied
by what he calls a "mother speach."

Puttenham's well-known statement about a national language should be
read in the context of the English monarchy's long-standing efforts to create,
in Nicholas Canny's phrase, a "composite dominion" consisting of "the three
kingdoms of England, Scotland, and Ireland, and the principality of Wales."
This dominion would not be officially proclaimed until the Union of the
Crowns in 1603, when James I of England (formerly James VI of Scotland)
used the "mythical name" of "Britain" or "Great Britain" to persuade his "diverse subjects" to "shift their loyalties from their local communities" to the
new political entity that had been created (Canny, introduction to *Origins of
Empire*, 1). Ideas about unifying England's diverse peoples had been circulating, however, for many years before James proclaimed his union and before
Elizabeth demanded the appearance of submission to the Church of England
with her Parliament's statutory Act of Uniformity in 1559. That act repealed
Mary Tudor's abrogation of two statutes on uniformity of the religious service
passed during Edward's Protestant reign. In the first of these (1549) Parliament
established the authority of Cranmer's new Book of Common Prayer, replacing diverse "uses" of service with one service in the vernacular language to be
used "throughout England and in Wales, at Calais and the marches of the
same."[77] The act includes a fascinating exception, however: educated men may
be exempted from following the "uniform" vernacular service and, by implication, the uniformity of belief the service in the mother tongue was aimed at
securing. Any man "that understandeth the Greek, Latin and Hebrew tongue,
or other strange tongue," may say his prayers "privately" in such tongues;

moreover, in the enclaves of Oxford and Cambridge, any services except the Holy Communion may be done "in Greek, Latin or Hebrew" (Elton, ed., *Tudor Constitution*, 405).

Uniformity of (vernacular) language and religious thought was clearly regarded as more critical for some subjects than for others. Variety can be more easily tolerated among the privileged, who have other ties that bind them to the crown. This point complicates the common idea that Protestantism and its handmaid, print, promoted a sense of English nationalism as well as the use of the English tongue among a populace hypostatized as a "people." Consider, for example, the set of well-known restrictions that Henry VIII placed on Bible reading in English. Having allowed the so-called Great Bible (based on Tyndale's translation) to be printed in 1540 with a new preface stressing the book's openness to "all manner of persons, men, women, young, old, learned, unlearned," the king swiftly backtracked by means of the 1543 Act for the Advancement of True Religion and for the Abolishment of the Contrary.[78] The act drew distinctions among readers along lines of rank, occupation, and (somewhat confusingly) gender: Bible reading in English was completely forbidden to "woomen or artificers, prentises journeymen serving men of the degrees of yeomen or undre, husbandmen and laborers." At the other end of the spectrum, the act granted complete freedom to "Everye noble man and gentleman" to read the Bible himself or to have it read aloud to anyone in the household.[79] "It took only one member of the nobility to authorize free access to Scripture," Gilmont comments ("Protestant Reformations," 221). This statement is not quite accurate, however, since the act created a separate category for noble *women* and for middling-class readers; such persons "maie read to themselves alone and not to others any [books] of the Byble." This middle category, in which noble women are separated out from the group of "woomen" associated with men and boys of the yeoman's rank and below, is constituted for those subjects capable of what I call imperfect or "partial" literacy. They were seen—by the king, members of Parliament, and the men of letters who drafted the act—as having competence to read but not the competence or authority to guide others in their interpretations. They could, in other words, consume the Bible but not generate opinions about it in a public even so small as a household reading group.

Authorities more fervently Protestant in their own beliefs than King Henry shared his doubts about the social reception of vernacular Scripture; Martin Luther beat a dramatic retreat, after the Peasants' War, from his early view "that every Christian [should] study for himself the . . . pure Word of God"; the later Luther wrote two catechisms and insisted that they should become "the layman's Bible" because they contained "the whole of what every Christian must know of Christian doctrine."[80] Although some radical Protestant sects continued to promote the reformers' ideal of the priesthood of all believers, many Protestant theologians came to positions on reading and interpretation no less conservative than those held by Catholic opponents of vernacular translation—and not all Catholics did oppose such translation, as the example of Marguerite de Navarre suggests. Ideologies of literacy shaped by the needs of the clerkly class persist across the Catholic/Protestant divide in Europe—and across the lines many historians use to distinguish the medieval and the early modern eras.

There is a significant gap between ideological promotions of the mother tongue for certain specific uses and what we can know about how much anything resembling English was actually used in the territories claimed by English monarchs either in religious contexts or in others. The Book of Common Prayer was prescribed for everyone, but the rhetoric of Edward's second Act of Uniformity (1552) suggests that many were "willfully and damnably" refusing "to come to their parish churches" for services in the mother tongue. In Elizabeth's 1559 act, the specific financial penalties for such nonconformity are spelled out; the stiff fines for recusancy are a major reason why historians have found more recusants among the nobility than among other social strata in England (see chapter 6). Elizabeth's act also spells out the right of the state to punish anyone who in "interludes, plays, songs, rhymes, or by other open words," declares "anything in the derogation, depraving or despising" of the Book of Common Prayer (Elton, ed., *Tudor Constitution*, 412). The reiteration of such demands for uniformity in religious thought and in discourse about it indicates how difficult it was to enforce them; Edward's second act admits that "a great number of people in divers parts of this realm" are "living either without knowledge or without due fear of God"—or rather, without due "fear" of the monarchy's power to enforce its interpretation of God's Word (ibid., 406).

Even before Henry's break with the Church of Rome impelled him to pass his own parliamentary statute "abolishing diversity in opinions" (1539), English kings and their educated clerks had been formulating rules about the dominion of an English language in non-English-speaking parts of the monarchy—specifically, Ireland—as early as the mid-fourteenth century.[81] And by 1540 John Palsgrave argued in his preface to a translation dedicated to Henry VIII that too much linguistic diversity even among the clerkly class (those coming to universities to be trained as priests) was impeding the king's educational and administrative aims; Palsgrave hoped his own book would contribute to remedying the problem he identified, and would do so by making English "uniforme throughe out all your graces domynions."[82] Palsgrave here anticipates the view articulated by Richard Mulcaster, the headmaster of the Merchant Taylors' School in London. Mulcaster calls for "uniformity" in English spelling in his *Elementarie* of 1582; in the same text, he yokes his program for improving English through bringing "foreign" words into the language to an imagined future when England—now "no Empire"—may become one, even as English becomes an ever richer language and thus more like Latin. At present, he says, the English tongue "is of small reatch, it stretcheth no further than this Iland of ours, naie not there over," but Mulcaster looks again and again toward a day when the "reatch" of England—and of its educated men—will increase (*First Part of the Elementarie,* 271). Like Caxton in the preface to Vergil's *Eneydos,* Puttenham seems to associate the powers of print and education with a newly "masculinized" England. He enjoins his countrymen to an Aeneas-like "labor" in the field of eloquence; they should compete with Demosthenes and Cicero, and make Protestant England the heir of ancient Rome. "And why not indede co[m]parable unto them in all points through out for his naturall tung? Our brains can bring furth, our co[n]ceits will bear life: our tungs be not tyed, and our labor is our own" (ibid., 272).

Mulcaster anticipates a line in English educational discourse that envisions English as a "universal" language of an empire in which many people's minds, as Fynes Moryson puts it, are "unite[d] or alienate[d]" in a "community of language" such as that achieved by the Romans and after them, by the Normans.[83] In this view, elaborated by Alexander Gill, "there is no more suitable language than English" to serve "to unify the speech of all peoples in one universal vocabulary."[84] In contrast to Moryson's vision of the Roman colonists going out into the world to "spread" their language and their laws, Mulcaster imagines all parts of the world coming into England, as it were, through a process of linguistic incorporation of the alien into a unified island-whole. This process entails "borrowing" foreign words and anglicizing their spelling; with great ideological finesse, Mulcaster coins a new name for such incorporation—"enfranchisement." He also proposes to pursue his goal of unity by reforming the "matter and manner of teaching"; for "*uniformitie* in *teaching*" creates "dispatch" or efficiency in learning, as he puts it in his *Positions Concerning the Training Up of Children* (1581).[85]

Mulcaster's call for uniformity in teaching methods is, I believe, ideologically akin to the insistence on "exact replication" of a model that Jonathan Goldberg has analyzed in treatises by sixteenth- and seventeenth-century English writing masters.[86] Advocating uniformity in language and education as a tool of nation-building, Mulcaster also calls for increasing uniformity in the class of educators by decreasing differences of gender and training. He laments that elementary education, at present, is left to the "meanest, and therefore to the worst" (*Positions,* 232). To remedy this situation, Mulcaster urges that more men be "allured" to the job by higher pay and by the establishment of a "seminarie for excellent maisters" within the university (ibid., 232, 235). Decrying part-time teachers, many of whom would have been female, Mulcaster argues that "likeness in abilitie" among teachers will promote the "honour of the countrey" (ibid., 261).[87] The goal of uniformity thus extends beyond the realm of language to the language teachers working in public institutions. On the question of private tutors, Mulcaster is a bit less strict, granting that for girls' education, teachers of "their owne sex were fittest in some respectes"; nonetheless, he concludes, assuming the male gender of his readers, "ours frame them [i.e., girls] best, and with good regard to some circumstances will bring them up excellently well" (ibid., 184).

The current "diversity" of language uses in England, like the demographic diversity signaled, for Mulcaster, by the presence of diversely trained teachers, is an impediment to the imperial future Mulcaster imagines for his country. His vision echoes Erasmus's call for educational reform in the *De pueris instituendis* (1529). Erasmus seeks to purge even the earliest education of boys from the corrupting influences of women teachers and the genres of oral discourse associated with lower-class females. He denounces women for wasting boys' time with "ridiculous riddles, stories of dreams, of ghosts, witches, fairies, demons . . . useless lies from vulgar histories [*inutilium mendaciorum ex vulgaribus historiis*]."[88] Women's influence should, he implies, be radically curtailed, both in the nursery and in the primary school classroom.[89] He makes a partial exception for upper-class mothers in *Puerpera* (1526), his treatise advocating breast-feeding. In this text, published in England twice in 1606 and again in 1626 under the title *The New Mother,* Erasmus tells well-born women that St. Paul blames them "if their children degenerate from godly courses."[90] He recruits mothers, as Valerie Wayne observes, for the "ideological maintenance" of their children, but he attempts at the same time to regulate their influence; the new mother is encouraged to contribute to her son's development "not by teaching him his letters, which was his father's responsibility, but by nursing him and thereby giving him a healthy body and a virtuous soul."[91]

The nation limned in letters, Spenser's well-known vision of "a kingdom of our own language," is a relational concept best grasped within the international framework wherein ideas of corporate identity were developing in various overlapping institutional spheres populated mostly by male clerks.[92] Different as these various spheres were, almost everyone who belonged to one, or who debated the meaning of nationhood, had left his or her *natio* in the root sense of a birthplace to come to a metropolis. In so doing, members of late medieval and early modern nations lost that condition of monolingualism that has often been seen as a hallmark of provincialism and, in some anthropological theories, of the "primitive" or "savage" mind. Anticipating such views of monolingualism, Roger Bacon attacks as "idiots" those peoples (*gens*) who know only their own idiom or native tongue and are hence ignorant of the language of others: "Et idiota qui est contentus sua proprietate loquendi, nesciens proprietates sermonis aliorum."[93] Any attempt to look behind such a clerkly ideology must avoid two epistemological fallacies: one is simply to assume that such a condition of monolingualism really existed for most nonliterate Europeans during the Middle Ages.[94] The other is to assume the nonexistence of language practices quite different from those of modern educated people. The latter practices are permeated by mostly unconscious uses of that strange form of bilingualism created by learning one's "own" language through a terminology of grammar instruction derived from Latin and Greek—a terminology that continues, in however truncated a form, to shape modern anglophone and francophone schoolchildren's awareness that they are speaking, or spelling, "incorrectly." Warning us against the first assumption are recent anthropological studies showing that "illiterate" (analphabetic) peoples can have extraordinary multilingual competencies in cultures where *hierarchies* of language evidently do not obtain in any of the ways we have come to recognize from the study of European history; the Vaupes Indians of the Amazon basin, for instance, still speak fluently "at least three languages, many speak four or five, and some understand as many as ten."[95] Warning us against both assumptions are many feminist and New (as well as old) Historicist arguments against projection of modern (First World) assumptions onto peoples of other cultures. Such projection can never be altogether avoided, but its effects can be analyzed and partly offset if we recall, as we are reading works defined as literary, that such texts at once preserve and efface verbal practices culturally defined as nonliterary and as nonliterate. In this work of preservation and effacement of an "other" realm of language use, the texts analyzed in part 2 of this book are like translations; indeed, many of the texts to which I now turn, by educated women writing in metropolitan dialects, are actively engaged in the process known as *translatio studii et imperii*, the translation of cultures and empires.

PART TWO

Literacy in Action and in Fantasy
Case Studies

Interlude

[W]hether that women may not at al discourse in learning, for men lay in their claim
to be sole possessioners of knowledge, or whether they [women] may in some maner
that is by limitation or appointment in some kinde of learning, my perswasion hath
bene thus, that it is all one for a woman to pen a story, as for a man to addresse his story
to a woman.

MARGARET TYLER, preface to her translation of Diego de Ortúñez de Calahorra,
Mirrour of Princely Deedes and Knighthood (1578)

Contests about the cultural category of "women" are critical to the stories
about gender, literacy, and empire I tell in part 2 of my book. I introduce it with
a text by a woman who may well have been a servant in a great house because
I am interested in the ways in which women's literacies—as performed in
communal as well as individual forms of reading, writing, speaking, weaving,
and sewing—show servants sometimes addressing mistresses and even taking
their places through literate practices that revise social hierarchies both in fantasy and (sometimes) in fact.[1] Margaret Tyler serves here as a kind of place
marker, calling for further scholarly attention to writers who gendered themselves female for the public record and who used their vernacular literacies explicitly to seek change in the existing distribution of real and symbolic capital.
The latter includes the quality named "freedom" by a group that signed itself
"the Maydens of London" in a document of 1567, a "Letter" addressed "to the
vertuous Matrones & Mistresses of the same [London], in defense of their
lawfull Libertie."

The women studied in the next four chapters—one born to the high
French aristocracy; one married to an English gentleman, later a viscount, who
needed her (middling-class) dowry; one the daughter of a court physician/
astrologer who depended on aristocratic patronage for her living; and one
who portrayed herself as well born even though she probably was the daughter of a wet-nurse—are all deeply engaged with the aristocracy (and ideas of
aristocratic nature and culture) in their writings. Nonetheless, each of these
women wrote extensively about indignities experienced by servants (in Behn's
case, the servants are unjustly enslaved African aristocrats), and each used her
literacy, if only intermittently, to explore subordinated people's longings for
expanded social freedoms. These women writers also, however, used their

literacies to legitimize their nations' ambitions for various kinds of territorial expansion, which often entailed a decrease in subjects' liberties. There are no simple ways of describing the ideological and political effects of the literate performances studied here. But these women share—beneath their many ideological differences—a strong desire to reject the Pauline strictures against women's public authority that I mentioned at the outset of this book; they therefore also challenge the emergent bifurcation of the field of literacy into reception and production, the former associated with "imperfect" subjects who need instruction, the latter with verbal *copia,* with masculinity, and with the mastery of languages. I have defined the mastery of languages as an ideal of full literacy against which notions of partial and often feminized literacies were constructed. This included the contrasting but yoked images of the obediently chaste reader of devotional literature and the disobediently lustful reader of romance, and changed over time, as Mary Ellen Lamb has argued, in response to pressures from the book market.[2] Beneath the changes runs a remarkably consistent refrain, however, from male authors of conduct books aimed at female readers—a set of authors attempting to negotiate the paradoxes I have discussed in previous chapters in relation to the emergent concept of partially literate subjects. These paradoxes, stemming from a professional relationship mediated by exigencies of state and religious institutions, are those encountered by *litterati* dependent on readers who are educable, but not so educable that they will become counterfeiters or usurpers of the clerks' cultural prerogatives, including biblical interpretation. These paradoxes underlie Juan Luis Vives's extension of St. Paul's prescriptions against female preachers to include female teachers and "rulers" of schools, in his *Instruction of a Christen Woman* (Latin, 1523, translated c. 1529). Addressing his book to Queen Katherine of Aragon and her daughter Mary, Vives argues passionately for a female educational regime dedicated to the preservation of chastity in the maid, the wife, and the widow. In support of this ruling idea, Vives derives from St. Paul's command that "you shall nat speke in congregatyon and gatherynge of people" the following interpretation: "this . . . meaneth that you shall not medle with matters of realmes or cities[;] your owne house is a cite great inough for you."[3] For Vives, females should not assume positions of authority even in their own (royal or common) houses, much less in spaces outside them, such as schools, churches, cities, or realms.

How the future Queen Mary felt about Vives's treatise we don't know, but she could have found a counterstatement to many of its political positions on women, although not to its high premium on chastity, had she read Christine de Pizan's *Cité des dames* either in French or in the English translation printed in 1521 (see chapter 4). De Pizan creates her own trio of female goddess figures to bypass St. Paul's authority on matters pertaining to women assuming male roles of teaching, preaching, and ruling. More than two centuries later, however, on the English side of the Channel, a man of letters named Richard Allestree was using St. Paul in a manner very similar to that of Vives. In his *Ladies Calling* of 1673, Allestree reinterprets St. Paul in order to persuade "gifted women of our Age" not to use their gifts so actively that they fail to remember that they need help from precisely the kind of instructional manual Allestree is writing. The apostle, Allestree states,

> espressly enjoins Women to keep silence in the Church, where he affirms it a shame for them to speak: and tho this seems only restrain'd to the Ecclesiastical Assemblies, yet even so it reaches home to the gifted women of our age, who take upon them to be Teachers; whereas he allowed them not to speak in the Church. . . . The Apostle seems to ground the Phrase, [let women learn in silence (1 Tim. 2:11)] not only on the inferiority of the woman in regard to the creation and first sin . . . but also on the presumtion that they needed instruction; towards which, silence has alwaies bin reckoned an indispensible qualification. . . . If som women of our age think they have outgon that novice state the Apostle supposes, and want no teaching; I must crave leave to believe, they want that very first principle which should set them to learn, viz, the knowledg of their own ignorance.[4]

The frontispiece to Allestree's treatise illustrates the historical persistence of the ideological construction I have termed imperfect or partial literacy: the concept of a feminized subject whose status as a reader but not a writer makes her subject to instruction, especially religious instruction as conveyed and controlled by a class of clerks (or intellectuals) that retains imaginary roots in the Latin-speaking priesthood long after the Catholic church has been officially exiled from Protestant England (fig. 3). Allestree's frontispiece also shows how easily a cultural image of an obedient, partially literate reader may acquire different meanings for some reader-viewers whose powers of interpretation serve the desires Allestree is attempting to suppress with St. Paul's help. The woman with the book in her left hand appears to be dutifully receiving wisdom from the divine crown above her and from a visually parallel image of authority, the part of the scroll (resembling a girdle or belt?) containing the book's title. The instruction the woman has received from above has apparently had the useful effect of making her scorn the signs of worldly ambition, which are scattered at her feet. Yet the image may also be read as dramatizing the way in which "gifted women" of the early modern age could and did rebel against St. Paul's—and Allestree's—authority. The woman is evidently intended to represent obedient reading, but intention does not govern effect. The picture itself calls attention to the question of the woman's desires, her fantasies, the realm of thought invoked by her enigmatic smile and her

gaze, which focuses neither on the crown nor on the book but on a space beyond the picture-frame. The educated women studied here, all fluent in the
language of irony, all adept at reinterpreting authoritative texts to serve new
purposes, could well have seen the woman represented on Allestree's frontispiece as someone just about to stand up and reach for the crown above her.
The crown's meaning would be open for interpretation.

As Tyler's example indicates, women addressing a public audience in imperial contexts developed various rhetorical strategies for avoiding censure
while contesting dominant concepts of both literacy and gender.[5] Tyler, for instance, while seeming to grant to men the sphere of "learned" discourse they
have claimed for themselves, suggests that a different set of gender rules operates in the sphere of vernacular story-writing. Seeking to anticipate and dis-
arm male critics who might bar women from that discursive terrain also, she
presents her own act of "penning" a story as being on an ontological continuum ("all one") not only with men's story-writing for women but, by implication, with men's expectations that women will read the stories men "address" to women. A potentially transgressive act of writing is represented as
both "one" with and as slyly subservient to a man's decision to address his
words to female readers. Reading is thus allied to writing, in this construction
of female literacy, rather than separated from it; and the distinction between
the genders is also undermined.

Although we know little about Tyler's biography, we do know that her
translation of Ortuñez's romance achieved enough cultural currency in England to be singled out as an example of the dangerously frivolous kind of
reading a servant girl might engage in with her mistress.[6] Satirizing a scene of
female reading as a scene of licentious sexuality, a passage in Sir Thomas Overbury's *Characters* (c. 1613) describes a "chambermaid" with enough education
to serve as a "she secretary" being "so carried away with the Mirror of Knighthood she is many times resolved to run out of herself, and become a lady-
errant. If she catch a clap, she divides it . . . equally between the master and the
servingman."[7] Well educated, although perhaps lower born than most of the
women studied in later chapters of this book, Tyler resembles those women in
feeling obliged both to define and to justify her act of writing with reference to
men's claims to cultural dominion—and to the dominant ideology of gendered literacy already discussed: the ideology of female literacy as dutiful or
devotional reading rather than as writing or interpretation aimed at a public
audience and at future fame. As challengers to assumed or customary claims
in the domain of culture—and well aware that daughters and married women
were defined by a wide range of early modern jurists as lacking legal capacity
in property disputes—the women writers studied here show considerable

interest in debates about how different legal systems serve (or fail to serve) the ideal of justice.[8] Christine de Pizan, indeed, writes from the practical experience of pursuing property claims, as a young widow, in a Parisian court; Marguerite de Navarre exposes contradictions between secular and ecclesiastical laws concerning marriage; Elizabeth Cary probes the asymmetries of gender in biblical and (by implication) English laws of divorce; and Aphra Behn poses questions about a lack of authority and property rights experienced both by white English women (at home and in the American colonies) and by Africans brought to America as slaves. Thematic inquiries into the legality of certain property claims in both domestic and imperial-national settings occur in all the works studied in the following chapters; these inquiries about what constitutes legitimate property are frequently the locus where ideas about female literacy intersect with ideas about empires.

Like Tyler, the writers studied in the following chapters were mistresses of more than one language. Engaging in acts of covert and overt translation, they interrogated various boundaries thought to exist between peoples, including emergent boundaries between nation-states. Such boundaries were viewed, by some of these women's contemporaries and readers, as necessary for the maintenance of proper social order. Always risking offending such readers, and sometimes risking censure from their own "courts of conscience," too, these women writers were deeply engaged with contemporary disputes among groups who spoke different languages and sometimes held wildly differing theological and political opinions.[9] Christine de Pizan, daughter of an Italian man of letters who served the French court of Charles V, had a son who served in an aristocratic household in England during the Hundred Years War. Marguerite de Navarre, sister of the king of France, was married to a man who sought to govern a kingdom claimed both by France and by Spain. Elizabeth Cary learned many languages in her youth (including Transylvanian) and at several points in her life credited France, and the French language, with more authority than Protestant England and its tongue(s); she also displeased her Protestant husband by attempting (with disastrous results recorded by one of her Catholic daughters) to improve the lot of poor people in England's Irish colony. Aphra Behn, who had been "reproached," she claims, for being an "American," knew enough Dutch to work as a spy in the Netherlands; she translated several works from French into English and was sufficiently interested in the language of African slaves transported to England's colony of Surinam to reproduce several Indian and African words in her narrative. As a latter-day Dido refashioning and lying to an African prince who resembles the ancient Iarbas, Behn provides a Janus-faced ending for this study of literacy, gender, and empire.

An Empire of Her Own
Literacy as Appropriation in Christine de Pizan's
Livre de la Cité des Dames

> They cut off my voice
> So I grew two voices
> In two different tongues . . .
> ALICIA PARTNOY, "Song of the Exiled"

> Friend, to whom God and Nature have conceded the gift of a love of study far beyond the
> common lot of woman, prepare parchment, quill, and ink, and write the words issuing
> from my breast; for I wish to reveal everything to you . . . I was burned, destroyed, and
> reduced to ashes . . . through cruel Fortune . . . Yet . . . [now I] appear young, new, fresh,
> flourishing, and beautiful [although] more than a thousand years have already passed
> since my birth.
> CHRISTINE DE PIZAN, *Lavision-Christine*

Like all the various Didos represented in ancient texts, Christine de Pizan emigrated from her native land to a new one and there, as a widow, sought to
build a city. Hers was a city of words built on a "field of letters" (*champ d'écriture*) with many materials appropriated from others.[1] Dido, indeed, as I noted
in the prologue, is one of the figures de Pizan refashions for her own writerly
purposes in the *Livre de la cité des dames* of 1405. Here Dido becomes a key allegorical figure for the female writer attempting to establish her authority in a
milieu where she was doubly an alien. A native of Venice who was transplanted
to Paris as a small child, when her father came to serve Charles V of France as
astrologer and court physician, de Pizan herself became a female clerk—what
she called a *clergesce*—in a society where almost all clerks were men.[2] Forced
to work to support her young family after her husband's death—and after a
traumatic failure to win a legal suit for property she believed she was owed—
she used her multilingual skills in reading and writing to address various audiences, including aristocratic patrons with differing geopolitical allegiances;
many of her patrons were from French territories, but some were from England, Italy, and the Low Countries.[3] In shaping her words for different audiences, she constructed various writerly personae to legitimate her authority.[4]

This chapter focuses on the ways in which de Pizan shaped those personae to articulate a complex vision of empire that included prominent roles for female scribes, prophets, evangelists, and governors. This vision of empire encompasses, first, a concern with a "universal" or world monarchy. The passage cited in my epigraph, from an autobiographical poem written in the same year as the *Cité des dames*, alludes to each of these roles in a complex drama of self-legitimization: de Pizan pictures herself being called to a scribal vocation with religious dimensions by a crowned woman representing France and named Libera ("the free one").[5] A vision of empire with a transplanted female ruler at its center—a ruler served (but also inspired and created) by a female scribe—is central to de Pizan's work and constitutes a revisionary appropriation of the old theory of *translatio imperii et studii,* the "westering" of empire and culture.[6] The second component of de Pizan's vision of empire is her emphasis on the ethically slippery virtue of prudence as an instrument women as well as men can use for "conquest and governance." Third, there is a deep interest in the issues of censorship and self-censorship in imperial regimes, and, finally, an equally deep concern with legitimate and illegitimate appropriations of real and symbolic property. De Pizan's vision of empire is formulated differently, sometimes contradictorily, in texts in both prose and verse designed for different audiences. In these texts, strands of imperial-nationalist discourse intersect with strands of Christian utopian thought and also with strands of discourse that might be called "prudentially" feminist. In the *Cité des dames* de Pizan sets out to reappropriate, for the good of her sex, her adopted country, and her Church, an idea of female "nature" that had been misrepresented by male authors from the beginnings of time to the present. This is a grand feminist project, innovative in its scope but rooted, as Natalie Zemon Davis has observed, in the old tradition of writing about "women worthies."[7] De Pizan makes ideologically significant revisions of her most important source in this tradition, Boccaccio's *De claris mulieribus*; in so doing, she creates quite a different moral perspective than Boccaccio's text offers on historical and mythical women who challenge normative ideals of femininity. Her prudential feminism, as I have called it, has a darker side, however—one that has received little critical attention. I refer here to her epistemologically and ethically complex relation to previous *female* writers—particularly French mystics of the recent past—whose work she arguably both appropriates and suppresses in her portraits of female saints suffering oppression and defying male authorities in ancient Rome. Approaching the *Cité* as a document of empire, we can see that de Pizan's representations of female saints using their verbal skills to extend the frontiers of Christ's dominion work ideologically both to create and to mystify significant analogies between certain women in the Roman imperium, on the one hand, and, on the other, women from the recent past (and perhaps even from de Pizan's present) who challenged the authority of French cultural authorities linked to the Church, the court, and the University of Paris. The names of these women, and their contributions to the culture of the territories named France, are less fully preserved in the historical archive than de Pizan's own words are. Indeed, her words help to create this situation even as they expose it—partially—for critique.

By calling attention to problems in de Pizan's ways of imitating and citing women whose modes of literacy differ from hers, I shall show how her female literacy works in exemplary fashion to illuminate problems pertaining to the transmission—and suppression—of different cultural voices in an imperial context. The empire limned in de Pizan's works is an imagined polity that harks back not only to Rome but also to its cultural opponents, St. Augustine's City of God and Dido's Carthage. Representing herself as guided by three female goddesses (fig. 4, *left*) and as imitating Dido in the enterprise of building a new city (fig. 4, *right*), de Pizan creates an unprecedented portrait of a woman of letters assuming ambitions and modes of authority commonly reserved for men. De Pizan's empire of letters is built on and out of fragments of others' books, but it also refracts historical struggles and oral discourses we can only partially reconstruct. This chapter contributes to that labor of rebuilding.

Contexts for Reading the *Cité* as a Document of Empire

Like many of her male contemporaries, de Pizan articulated her views about France's present and (ideal) future through active readings of history, especially the history of ancient Rome depicted (differently) by Vergil and other classical *auctores*. Admiration for the imperial phase of Roman history was particularly strong in France during the period of proliferating factionalism in the aristocracy after the death of Charles V. The dynastic battles of the Hundred Years War were going on, and the Church was suffering the crisis of governorship known as the Great Schism. In 1395 Charles VI of France ordered all poets and balladeers to forgo mention of the Schism. It was nonetheless present in the minds, and probably in the conversations and private correspondence, of many members of the French learned elite, including its anomalously female member.[8] Observing a world without a clear secular or religious leader, and dependent on patrons scattered around Europe, de Pizan dreamed of a powerful ruler who could "pacify" the whole world. Her dream stressed peace rather than war, although not, I think, with quite the unwavering pacifist sentiments ascribed to her by Berenice Carroll. While this modern feminist critic rightly calls attention to de Pizan's differences from some male authorities

FIGURE 4
Manuscript illumination of Christine de Pizan in her study with her goddesses (*left*)
and building the City of Ladies as Dido built Carthage (*right*).
(Reproduced by permission of The British Library, Harley 4431, fol. 290)

whose schemes for a universal monarchy centered in France included calls for violent military action, the "impassioned condemnation[s]" of the evils of war that Carroll finds in some of de Pizan's writings—her "Epistre à Isabeau" (1405), for example, or her *Lamentation sur les maux de France* (1410), or her *Livre de la Paix* (1412)—need to be read in conjunction with the more ideologically mixed statements about war as a means to dominion made in other of de Pizan's works.[9]

In the *Livre du corps de policie* (*The Book of the Body Politic*), for instance, begun at the Duke of Burgundy's request in 1404 for the young dauphin Louis of Guyenne (the one so unflatteringly depicted by Shakespeare in *Henry V*), de Pizan sought to educate the prince in the duties of being the "head" of the body politic; at the same time she sought to inspire aristocratic readers—the "arms and hands" of the state—to exhibit military prowess similar to that displayed by exemplary Roman and French precursors.[10] De Pizan expressed an ideal of *la France* based on the image of the Roman empire—which extended its domination by its rulers' "virtues" as well as by strength of arms.[11] This image underlies her association of "prudence" with "conquest," her reiterated cautions against civil war, her various contributions to contemporary legal debates about what constitutes a "just war," and her admiration for Charles V's and later Joan of Arc's military feats, including their victories over England.[12] In the *Livre du corps de policie* she develops the metaphor of the king as absolute "head" of state from John of Salisbury but explicitly rejects his (Aristotelian) belief in the legitimacy of resistance to tyrants.[13]

Her refusal to support a theory legitimizing resistance to tyrants in a text of 1404 may seem odd to modern anglophone readers who remember the striking scene in part 3 of the *Cité des dames* where St. Christine resists a tyrant quite violently—by blinding him with a piece of her tongue (*Cité*, 239; Fr., 3:1009). One of my aims in this brief discussion of contexts for interpreting the *Cité* as a document of empire is to suggest how difficult it is to infer de Pizan's political views from any single formulation in any one of the more than thirty works she penned over the course of a long and extremely unusual career as a female clerk.[14] Granting, of course, that she may have changed her mind about large questions such as the legitimacy of force and of tyrannicide, I wish to stress that her survival as a professional writer, at a time when most male clerks had institutional support of a kind she lacked, required her to develop unusual skills in reading her (potential) audience—and in adjusting her words in accordance with what her reading dictated about the contemporary social text. To label her as a woman who held "radical" or "conservative" political views (by modern standards) is arguably to simplify the question of what her literacy was and how it worked. Much more historicizing research needs to be

done, I suspect, before we will be able to describe her views on such interrelated subjects as war, monarchical forms of government, resistance to tyranny,
and women's proper social roles. Her vision of empire emerges, in any case,
obliquely, and is intricately linked to her efforts to legitimate herself as a literate agent in a highly factionalized political milieu.

   We can see her intertwining self-legitimation with the legitimation of (a vision of) empire in her poetic "dream vision" of 1402–3, the autobiographical
Livre du chemin de long estude. Echoing a passage from Dante's *Inferno* in her
title, she narrates her adventures during a "universal voyage."[15] She is guided
by the Cumaean Sybil as Dante was guided on his *Commedia* voyage by Vergil,
and she arrives at the Court of Reason where four queens, Wisdom, Nobility,
Chivalry, and Wealth, are debating precisely the question of who should be the
"absolute" monarch of a proposed world empire that would remedy the faults
of the present world. Unable to agree, they decide to refer the question to a
princely court in France; the Sibyl proposes de Pizan as their messenger to this
court.[16] When she arrives back on earth, de Pizan turns out to have taken detailed *written notes* on the oral debate about absolute empire that occurred at
the Court of Reason. She thus advertises her own notarial skills to potential
patrons and, in so doing, anticipates the role she plays when she "records"
speeches given by the three female authorities who help her build her City of
Ladies. The relation between female scribe and female ruler is complex and
highly labile throughout de Pizan's oeuvre; the relation receives its fullest
statement, I think, in the *Cité*—a text not written, so far as we know, for any
specific patron and therefore arguably freer than others to conduct utopian
speculations that implicitly challenge aspects of the current social order.[17]

   There is no question that de Pizan goes further in the *Cité* than she had in
previous writings to associate the quality of "prudence" with women's incursion, either as writer or as ruler, into a cultural territory doxically reserved for
men. In *Lavision-Christine,* de Pizan praises her dead husband for being the
kind of clerkly servant of state whose pen promotes "wise and prudent conquest and government" (*sage et prudent conqueste et gouvernement*).[18] In the
same passage, she associates her husband's virtuous prudence with his ambition to "mount on high" (*monter en hault*). She thus legitimates his potentially
culpable ambition as prudence and sets the stage for her own exercise of this
virtue as a widow. Justifying her writing, she describes it as an activity she is
forced to pursue because she is alone and must occupy the man's role of
provider. Etienne's death, which she describes as following shortly upon that
of her beloved if extravagant father, required her to support her mother, a
dowerless niece, and "iii enfanz petiz et de grant mainage" [three small children with large upkeep].[19] The discussion of a widow's appropriation of her

husband's quality of ambitious prudence in *Lavision* foreshadows the portrait of Dido in the *Cité*, while also harking back to de Pizan's treatment of prudence in her hagiographic biography of the king whom her father came to France to serve. In two early chapters of her *Livre des fais et bonnes meurs du sage roy Charles V* (c. 1404), she elaborates on St. Thomas Aquinas's definition of prudence, from his commentary on Aristotle's *Metaphysics,* as something that comes, like rhetoric, from the "practical" part of the soul and that focuses on "workable things" (*choses ouvrables*).[20] And in her *Epistre d'Othéa* (1399–1400), she personifies prudence as a newly named goddess, Othea.[21] Her work as a female clerk—a *femme escripse* as she calls it in *Lavision,* in a phrase that can signify both a "writing woman" and a "written" one—required her to transgress the cultural rule that women should remain in a private sphere.[22] She repeatedly sought to legitimate that transgression, invoking necessity and defining prudence as a virtue women could appropriate from men for purposes some men would deplore.

Appropriation as Theme and Tactic in the *Cité des dames*

Le Livre de la cité des dames is written in a clerkly variant of a courtly, metropolitan dialect. Its diction and style are shaped by the bureaucratic writing practices developed by clerks of the Curia (the papal court) and adapted by servants of the French monarchy. De Pizan's style reflects her reading in a variety of genres and languages; she has a penchant for neologisms, and she adapts the clerical habit of using doublets in ways that seem aimed not only at fellow clerks but also at female readers of the vernacular. Her version of a *style curiale* or *style clergiale* was later imitated in other European countries, both in Latin and, eventually, in vernacular documents: de Pizan's own writing became an influence on fifteenth-century English prose through the translation of several of her works and their early printing by Caxton.[23] The *style clergiale* was particularly associated with the institution of the royal chancery in both France and England; the chief features of the style, as exhibited in de Pizan's prose as well as that of many of her male contemporaries and followers, are "formulaic expressions, terms of reference (*dessusdit, le dit, cette dit*), introductory phrases, Latinate words, elaborate explanations, legal phrases, synonyms . . . (particularly doublets [e.g., "to have and to hold"]), reliance on the passive voice, and a grave, ceremonious tone. . . . Writers preferred the long sentence drawn out by the use of subordinate clauses, especially relatives. Clauses progress in chains, one being embedded in another" (Bornstein, "French Influence," 370–71).

The "doublet," although often decried by modern teachers as a feature of a prolix style (mere "filler," as one of my own professors put it), deserves a careful look, for de Pizan uses it deftly as a tool for cultural translation aimed at audiences whose members differed in gender as well as in their knowledge of Latin. For those readers or auditors who were *illiterate* in the dominant clerkly sense of being unable to read Latin, de Pizan's doublets proffer the "enrichment" of synonyms, one usually more Latinate than the other.[24] De Pizan's knowledge of Latin and of more than one vernacular makes her a perfect teacher for the kind of woman Shakespeare mocks in his portrait of Mistress Quickly. Such women, as I have argued, had an "imperfect" or partial literacy in the eyes of many educated men. While potentially educating such women by broadening their lexicon, de Pizan's style also serves as a potential weapon of self-defense against the learned men in her audience. If one term in a doublet carries a subversive connotation, allay your reader's unease with another. Conceptual *alternatives* can be slipped into the discursive arena under the guise of synonyms; the rhetorical elaboration of an "official" style can become a method of prudential writing aimed at different audiences.[25] If a book is described, for instance, as "fait et compilé" by de Pizan (*Livre des fais et bonnes meurs,* ed. Solente, 1:1), do we read the verbs as describing one activity or two? In that area of ambiguity—between the terms of the doublet, as it were—many questions about de Pizan's writerly authority reside without demanding an immediate answer.

De Pizan begins to establish her authority as the writer of the *Cité* by means of a prudent ruse: she depicts herself humbly obeying others in authority—three goddesses named Rayson, Droitture, and Justice—in the activity of building a city of ladies. Assuming a role of scribe to royal (specifically, queenly) authority similar to the role she had already limned in the *Chemin de long estude* and in *Lavision-Christine,* de Pizan records in writing ostensibly oral conversations between herself and the goddesses. In part 1, with the aid of Rayson, the female scribe lays the metaphorical foundations for the city by recounting stories of various pagan women. One of the most important of these foundational stories (and I am here considering all of part 1 as foundational to the city/empire) is Dido's.

Through the Dido story, as well as through her general allegorical strategy of at once creating and hiding her authority in the represented "voices" of her goddesses, de Pizan engages in a textual version of the culturally ambiguous act epitomized in Vergil's use of the verb *condebat* to describe Dido's building of her temple to Juno. Laden with ironies, the verb appears both at the very beginning of the *Aeneid,* to describe the building of the city of Rome ("dum conderet urbem," line 5) and, near the epic's end, to describe Aeneas's act of burying his sword in Turnus's breast (12.950).[26] One builds, as Ralph Hexter observes, by hiding the origins of the physical or cultural structure. The first part of de Pizan's book, figuring the pagan women who are the foundation stones for her city's walls, entails a censoring or burying of certain narratives about women's evil; the burying symbolically kills, or at least suppresses, the narrator's expressed fear that women lack important virtues and the power to accomplish great things. In response to a question de Pizan poses about "where Prudence is found in the natural sensibility of women" (*Cité*, 86; Fr., 2:761), Rayson tells a very partial version of Dido's story, one that omits the best known feature of the best known version—namely, Dido's tragic love for Aeneas.[27] For learned readers, the omission would have been striking; for readers or auditors lacking acquaintance with Vergil's text (whether in Latin or in Italian or French manuscript translations that would not, of course, have circulated widely), the omission would not have existed as such: instead, the story would have seemed newly built. Although the story occurs after the ones clearly representing the "stones" of the city in de Pizan's allegorical scheme, the thematic importance of Dido's city-building leads me to consider the first version of her story as a foundational text for de Pizan's book. Appropriately, Rayson's version stresses the similarities between the builder of the book entitled *Cité des dames* and the ancient heroine whose building of the city of Carthage threatened Roman cultural and political hegemony. Through her initial rendition of Dido's story, and through her return to Dido in the different context of part 2, where the muse is not Rayson but Droitture (Rectitude or Law), de Pizan poses questions about whether the *Cité* itself is an illicit theft or, on the contrary, a justifiable appropriation of metaphorical territories and textual treasures.

Such treasures are associated with the Latin language itself in a segment of *Lavision* that is highly germane to the extended inquiry in the *Cité* into the question of culture as a patrimony. De Pizan portrays herself acquiring some modes and an unspecified amount of that patrimony only when she "returns" to a life of solitude after her work as a wife and mother is nearly over. Solitude, she writes, is what "naturally pleases her," and from this condition, often seen as unnatural for women, she received a gift of memory. Paradoxically, the memory is of being in company and of receiving from oral communication nuggets of Latin treasure that she then stored up in her memory but subsequently lost (in part). De Pizan constructs a drama of memory in which Latin plays a major but somewhat enigmatic role: "there came back to me from earlier days memorized passages of Latin and the languages [*parleurs*] of the noble sciences—various sententiae and polished rhetoric that I had heard in the past when my dear, dead husband and father had been alive, even though because of my folly, I retained little of what I had heard from them."[28] De Pizan here presents Latin and its wisdom—as expressed probably in examples of ancient oratory ("speeches" seems a better translation of *parleurs* than "languages")—as a treasure she acquired through listening to dear men who authorized the gift. The mention of their death, however, makes Latin now, in the present of the writing moment, into something that de Pizan has inherited from those who would be controlling her (as their property) were they still alive. What she once gained through listening has been partly lost through her "folly" (a self-deprecating and patently false description of what she has already revealed to be her fulfillment of maternal duties), but some goods remain—and more might be acquired through reading, which is what the *Cité des dames* shows de Pizan doing when she is alone in her study. Reading is how one listens to the dead. I therefore don't agree with those critics who assume that de Pizan could not read Latin because there is evidence in the *Cité des dames* that she knew a French translation of one of her major Latin sources, Boccaccio's *De claris mulieribus*.[29] Like many educated people today, de Pizan may well have known enough Latin to read it with the help of a translation. She leaves obscure the relation between dutiful listening, memory, and the active labor of reading, but the passage suggests, as does her portrait of Dido in the *Cité des dames,* that widows don't protect and enlarge their property only by listening to men.

De Pizan's goddess Rayson is a product of various acts of reading and translating; she is polemically dissimilar to the character named Reason in the *Romance of the Rose,* but she recalls Dante's guides Vergil and Beatrice, and also Boethius's consoling interlocutor, Lady Philosophy. Rayson initially portrays Dido as a virtuous appropriator of her brother's treasure. The true ownership of the treasure is in doubt, because the treasure first belonged to Dido's husband, whom de Pizan names "Acerbe Ciceon ou Ciceus" (*Cité,* 96; Fr., 2:769), following Boccaccio who combines traditions by giving the husband two names (*Famous Women,* ed. Brown, 166–67). Dido's brother Pygmalion, Rayson explains, was "evil, cruel, and extraordinarily greedy"; he killed Sychaeus to get hold of the treasure, but Sychaeus, following his wife's advice, had hidden the treasure in a secret place. The detail of the wife's advice, which points to the woman's power to govern a man, is absent in Boccaccio's text and in the anonymous French translation, *Des cleres femmes* of 1401.[30] Although devastated with grief for her husband's death, Dido, according to Rayson, is reasonable enough to fear that her brother will suspect her of having hidden his treasure. Dido decides, prudently, to flee, taking the treasure with her.

De Pizan's story stresses general moral questions about the legitimacy of stealing already-stolen goods, while also alluding, I think, to contemporary French debates, in legal and other discursive arenas, about widows' inheritances of their husbands' goods and, more generally, about women's ability to own and transmit property at all. Having herself inherited her husband's debts but not those properties to which she felt she was rightly entitled—and which she unsuccessfully attempted to win in court—de Pizan brings considerable autobiographical investment to the problems of female inheritance encountered by the "widow Dido" (as Shakespeare memorably called her in *The Tempest*).[31]

De Pizan just hints at a question about the morality of Dido's actions in a passage describing them as illustrations of what Richards's English translation calls "clever[ness]"; de Pizan's text, here following the 1401 *Cleres femmes,* uses the less morally neutral term of *malice.*[32] The ambiguous ethical status of Dido's behavior toward her brother has considerable allegorical importance; both here and elsewhere in the book, de Pizan treats sister-brother relations (and competitions for property) as a mirror reflecting the ambiguities of her writerly relations to the male "clercs et autres," as she calls them, whose books expressing hostile views of women cast the author into depression in the opening scene of her book (*Cité,* 3; Fr., 2:618). Among those clerks, I would suggest, is Boccaccio. He dedicated his *De claris mulieribus* to Andrea Acciaiuoli of Florence, but he exhibits considerable ambivalence toward her and toward other female readers, real and imagined. And female readers from de Pizan through Boccaccio's recent translator Virginia Brown have commented on the ambivalence. Brown finds his dedication so tactless that she wonders whether Boccaccio actually expected Acciaiuoli to read the Latin text (*Famous Women,* xiv–xv). Marilyn Desmond discusses various instances where Boccaccio's narrator preemptively corrects the "untutored" responses he anticipates from female readers (*Reading Dido,* 66). Susan Noakes offers a fascinating analysis of Boccaccio's recurring image of a female reader with the power to "dismember" the male author; she sees such a reader as part of Boccaccio's developing view of the "author-reader relation as one of struggle" (*Timely Reading,* 96). De Pizan never criticizes Boccaccio directly, but she does effectively dismember his portraits of famous women. She omits, for example, his emphasis on the clever Dido ultimately tricked by men—the *principes* of Carthage—into an unwanted choice between marriage to Iarbas or suicide.[33]

De Pizan's allegorical parallel between herself and Dido as sisters who steal justifiably from their brothers is the product of many textual details; one is the description of Dido's ruse of deceiving her brother by substituting "heavy things of no value" (*choses pesans de nulle vallue*) for the treasure he expected to reappropriate after she fled from Phoenicia.[34] Knowing that he "would have her followed as soon as he knew of her departure," Dido, in Richards's translation, "had large trunks, coffers, and bundles secretly filled with heavy, worthless objects, as though these were her treasure, so that by turning these trunks and bundles over to her brother's envoys, they would let her go and not impede her voyage."[35] I suspect a pun on *malles* here ("trunks" or "males"), as I suspect a bawdy pun on *pierres,* equivalent to that on the English *stones;* there is certainly an echo, in the phrase "choses pesans de nulle vallue," of de Pizan's opening description of the clerk Matheolus's book as being "de nulle autorité" ("of no authority" [*Cité,* 3; Fr., 2:617]). The joke deepens when we recall that de Pizan had picked Matheolus's book in a mistaken quest for something "light," something that would provide relief from the "pesanteur des sentences de divers aucteurs" (in Richards's translation, "weighty opinions of various authors" [*Cité,* 3; Fr., 2:616]). Dido's "malice," like that of de Pizan, appears to consist partly in the pleasures of gaining revenge on bad brothers; how better to do so than to substitute "light" things, appropriate to men's view of women's wits, for the "heavy" treasures, sexual and otherwise, that men value?

Later in the Dido narrative of part 1, de Pizan begins to provide moral justification for prudent women's "malice," which includes the ability and willingness to lie. When Dido's brother angrily sends envoys to Africa demanding the treasure back, she proffers a didactic fiction: "She told all his envoys," de Pizan writes, "that the treasure had been perfectly intact when she had given it up to be taken to her brother and that it could be that those who had received it had stolen it and replaced it with counterfeits, or that, by chance, because of the sin committed by the king in having her husband murdered, the gods had not wanted him to enjoy her husband's treasure and so had transmuted it" (*Cité,* 94–95; Fr., 2:774). By obliquely likening her own writing to the acts of beneficent theft and lying performed by Dido, de Pizan counters those who define female literacy as a sinful foray into a masculine domain of culture.

My hypothesis that Dido's actions toward Pygmalion shadow de Pizan's toward clerkly brothers in general and Boccaccio in particular finds further support in her version of the story of Cornificia, which precedes Dido's tale and comes, as Quilligan shrewdly notes, at a point "of extreme architectural (and structural) juncture" in part 1. Cornificia appears just when the narrative moves from the section allegorically describing the city's foundation—composed of stories about heroic female warriors—to the section describing the city's walls, which are constructed by stories about women who are "textual adepts"—that is, renowned for inventing alphabets and other things that enable cultural production (Quilligan, *Allegory of Female Authority,* 96).

Cornificia, de Pizan writes,

was sent to school by her parents along with her brother Cornificius when they were both children, thanks to deception and trickery. This little girl so devoted herself to study and with such marvelous intelligence that she began to savor the sweet taste of knowledge acquired through study. Nor was it easy to take her away from this joy to which she more and more applied herself, neglecting all other feminine activities. . . . [S]he wanted to hear and know about every branch of learning, which she then mastered so thoroughly that she surpassed her brother, who was also a very great poet, and excelled in every field of learning. Knowledge was not enough for her unless she could put her mind to work and her pen to paper in the compilation of several very famous books. These works, as well as her poems, were much prized during the time of St. Gregory and he himself mentions them. The Italian, Boccaccio, who was a great poet, discusses this fact in his work and at the same time praises this woman: "O most great honor for a woman who abandoned all feminine activities and applied and devoted her mind to the study of the greatest scholars!" (*Cité*, 64–65; Fr., 2:723–24)

There is, significantly, no agent in de Pizan's sentence who could be held responsible for the "deception and trickery" (*de trufferie et de ruse*) that allow Cornificia to gain an education along with her brother. In a detail that performatively enacts the competitive process she is describing, de Pizan insists that Cornificia "surpassed" her brother (whether in learning or as a "great poet" or both is left ambiguous). In Boccaccio's text and its 1401 French translation, the girl achieves the extraordinary status of being "equal" to her brother.[36] Neither Boccaccio's Latin version nor the 1401 *Cleres femmes* mentions the girl's education at all, much less its acquisition through means that recall Dido's morally dubious tactics for extending her property. Boccaccio attributes Cornificia's poetic abilities simply to her having been "nourished by the Castalian spring" (*Famous Women*, 352–53). He uses her, typically, as a negative example with which to reproach modern women for their "slothfulness" and lack of confidence.[37] "Let slothful women be ashamed," Boccaccio (and his French translator) exclaim, in a rhetorical move that Constance Jordan describes as "a *concessio*, a refutation of its apparent thesis" about the "glory" of women—or rather, of pagan women only, for Boccaccio explicitly limits his concept of female *claritas* (excellence and fame) to examples drawn from pagan antiquity.[38] In contrast to Boccaccio, de Pizan includes Christian women—past and contemporary—in her *Cité des dames*; in general, she uses Boccaccio's authority to give a message that differs from his and his French translator's in both tone and content. While he repeatedly reveals his doubt about whether contemporary women can emulate the chastity he praises in some pagan women, he also shows doubt about whether modern Italian women *should* emulate the "manly" virtues that allowed (some) pagan women to act in the public domain. De Pizan, in contrast, constructs examples designed to draw contemporary female readers away from feelings of despair about their "nature," even as she leaves prudently vague the political implications of encouraging "Every-woman" to desire knowledge and an opportunity to compete with men, as Cornificia does.

Citing her "author" with apparent reverence, but in truth citing a Boccaccio who has been transformed to serve as proof for a new idea, de Pizan's own female figure of authority, Rayson, uses her own version of Dido's "deceit and trickery" in handling—and competing with—her source: "As further proof of what I am telling you," she says to the writer playing the role of humble pupil, "Boccaccio also talks about the attitude of women who despise themselves and their own minds and who, as though they were born in the mountains totally ignorant of virtue and honor, turn disconsolate. God has given them such beautiful minds to apply themselves, if they want to, in any of the fields where glorious and excellent men are active. My dear daughter, you can see how this author Boccaccio testifies to what I have told you and how he praises and approves learning in women" (*Cité,* 65; Fr., 2:724–25). Rayson uses the ironic figure of *antiphrasis,* which she had described in her opening lesson on how the woman writer should counter misogynist poets. Such poets, Rayson observed, often "mean the contrary of what their words openly say," and hence "one can interpret them according to the grammatical figure of *antiphrasis,* which means, as you know, that if you call something bad, in fact, it is good, and also vice versa. Thus I advise you to profit from their works and to interpret them in [a profitable way, whatever they intended], in those passages where they attack women" (*Cité,* 7; Fr., 2:624).[39]

Although de Pizan borrows from the *De claris mulieribus* throughout part 1, Boccaccio is first cited as an *auctor* in the Cornificia story. The naming of the source at just this moment seems to me significant because it is here that de Pizan begins allegorically to define her complex relation to Boccaccio as a "brother" Italian and poet. Adding to Boccaccio's story the idea that a well-educated female author-figure not only equals but "surpasses" her brother, de Pizan invites any reader who has access to Boccaccio's text, in the Latin or the French versions, to enter into a subtle textual and interpretive game of competition, a game that construes the relation between female writer and male precursor not within the familiar trope of daughter/father, but rather as a sibling rivalry in which *both* authors are readers—and also compilers—of historical materials from prior sources. The goal of the game may be intended to be a moral lesson for de Pizan's readers (of both sexes), but the means consist of amoral rhetorical tropings or turnings on, and from, a prior text.[40]

Eager that her reader not miss the point, de Pizan mentions Boccaccio again in her next story, about the Roman woman Proba; this story does not follow Cornificia's in Boccaccio's text. Although Proba might seem to exemplify "a kind of composition that pays great respect to the auctores," de Pizan stresses a certain imperialist violence at the heart of Proba's practices of reading and writing (Quilligan, *Allegory of Female Authority*, 96). As Rayson explains, Proba used Vergil's poetry—to which Boccaccio says that she was "devoted"—to formulate a set of truths entirely foreign to Vergil's historical or imaginative world.[41] Eager to accomplish her own aims, Proba "ran" (*couroit*) through Vergil's verses:

> [I]n one part she would take several entire verses unchanged and in another borrow small snatches of verse and, through marvelous craftsmanship and conceptual subtlety, she was able to construct entire lines of orderly verse. She would put small pieces together, coupling and joining them, all the while respecting the metrical rules, art and measure in the individual feet, as well as the conjoining of verses, and without making any mistakes she arranged her verses so masterfully that no man could do better. In this way, starting from the creation of the world, she composed the opening of her book, and following all the stories of the Old and New Testament she came as far as the sending of the Holy Spirit to the Apostles, adapting Vergil's works to fit all this in so orderly a way that someone who only knew this work would have thought that Vergil had been both a prophet and evangelist. For these reasons, Boccaccio himself says that this woman merits great recognition and praise. (*Cité*, 66; Fr., 2:726–27)

Although Boccaccio does not share de Pizan's view that "no man could do better" than Proba, he does acknowledge that Proba did something remarkable to Vergil, something that might potentially deceive a reader who is not *expertissimus*—that is, fully literate in the way Boccaccio himself is. "So expertly did she place whole lines together and combine fragments . . . that no one except a real connoisseur could detect the sutures [*compages*] . . . so neatly was it done that a person unacquainted with this work [literally, method of composition] would easily believe Vergil to have been both prophet and evangelist [*huius compositi ignarus homo prophetam pariter et evangelistam facile credat fuisse Virgilium*]" (*Famous Women*, Story 97, 412–13). Boccaccio thus tells his own reader, including Christine de Pizan, that Proba has effectively *counterfeited* her male-authored source so that an "ignorant" reader—an adjective that may mean both "ignorant" in general and "unfamiliar with this particular work's devices"—will think that Vergil somehow intended to express a Christian message, as God's divinely inspired prophets and evangelists did according to Christian theories of figural interpretation. In other words, Proba so transformed Vergil's text that his actual "intention," whatever it was, disappears from cultural view—just as Rayson recommended in her discussion of the female interpreter's license to use antiphrasis to read misogynist

poets "profitably" whatever their intention may have been.[42] Vergil's pagan letters become, in Proba's hand, a vehicle for expressing the "spirit" of Judeo-
Christian Scripture—or rather the spirit as Proba understands it, for why
should she *rewrite* sacred Scripture in Vergil's words if that Scripture were perfectly adequate in its "original" verbal form? In effect, Proba becomes a figure
for de Pizan herself as cultural translator: Proba marries Vergil's texts with
those of the Bible and thereby produces something quite new and strange.

   Constance Jordan interprets Boccaccio's description of Proba as showing
his adherence (here, though not everywhere in the *De claris mulieribus*) to an
Aristotelian conception of woman's proper nature as "conserving what her
husband has invented or acquired" rather than engaging in original creation.
"Proba's poetic function," in Jordan's view, "is limited to re-presenting what
male poets have written and does not extend to changing the canon" ("Boccaccio's In-famous Women," 30). The idea that Proba's *Cento* could deceive an
"ignorant" reader suggests to me, however, that Boccaccio appreciates, even if
he is somewhat anxious about, the cultural implications of Proba's kind of
"composition." It is a type of composition that in some respects resembles
what Boccaccio himself does not only in the *De claris mulieribus* but also in
works like the *Genealogy of the Pagan Gods,* where he collects "fragments" of
others' works and attempts, as the physician Aesculapius did with the torn
body of Hippolytus, to make them "whole" again, so that an "ignorant" reader
might not realize that they had existed differently in a different cultural context.[43] We may read Boccaccio's rendition of Proba's story in the light of his
own worries about how "ignorant" readers will understand his project of collecting "such fragments of the ancient wreck as God willed" (Osgood, *Boccaccio on Poetry,* 15). In doing so, we can see that Boccaccio may be using Proba
to explore the general problem of the relation between pagan and Christian
cultures—and also the viability of his attempted solution in the *De claris
mulieribus,* which is simply to decline to draw his exemplars from Christian
(and hence contemporary) women, on the grounds that a "higher law" than
the classical ideal of "glory" governs the behavior of Christian women. Proba,
as Quilligan notes, is a Christian, and hence her presence in his book "breaks
[Boccaccio's] own rule" of exclusion (*Allegory of Female Authority,* 98). Does
her story's presence signal a certain anxiety about the propriety of his general
project—as he had signaled his anxiety about compiling stories of the "ancient wreck" by imagining "impious" readers tearing his book "limb from
limb," in a kind of nightmare reversal of his metaphor for his own act of collecting as giving life to a fragmented body?[44]

   De Pizan clearly chooses not to follow Boccaccio's authority on the question of the propriety of telling pagan women's stories along with those of

Christian women.[45] Her portrait of Proba "appropriating" Vergil's verses as a vehicle for a universal Christian message works both to announce and to justify her own procedures with regard to Boccaccio's book. As Richards justly notes, "Proba's treatment of Virgil exemplifies in part de Pizan's relationship to Boccaccio, whom she rewrites and Christianizes" (*Cité*, 262n). De Pizan not only implicitly criticizes Boccaccio for failing to treat Christian women; she also implicitly criticizes him for failing to do to his pagan source material what Proba and de Pizan do to theirs. She thus rides rough-shod over the anxious and delicate sense of cultural *difference* that some early humanists, including Boccaccio, sometimes articulate. Boccaccio may justly be accused of misogyny by feminist critics, but such accusations should not blind us to the cultural imperialism inherent in de Pizan's feminist and Christian agendas. Such cultural imperialism was, of course, licensed by a long tradition of using pagan writings for Christian purposes—"stealing Egyptian gold" for Israelite use, as Augustine explained and justified the practice in his *De doctrina Christiana*.[46] And there was in addition the interpretive tradition, movingly dramatized by Dante, of seeing Vergil as a "prophet" of Christianity who did not live to see his vision fulfilled. Nonetheless, we need to appreciate the violent elements in de Pizan's praise of, and identification with, a figure like Proba, to begin to understand the complex and unconventional relation between de Pizan's revisions of Boccaccio and her revisions of the Bible. Like Proba, who was both "devoted" to her classical *auctor* and an eager promoter of the Scripture, de Pizan uses her skills of literacy to effect a shocking and highly original marriage between pagan and scriptural sources. She does so, I shall argue, by interrogating and eventually re-creating the very idea of an authoritative "source."

Appropriating the (Idea of the) Source

In the long section of part 1 devoted to female originators—Carmentis the inventor of the Roman alphabet and system of Laws, Minerva who "invented a shorthand Greek script" as well as the technique of making armor, Ceres, "the first to discover cultivation and to invent the necessary tools," among other examples—Rayson remarks on the "massive ingratitude" of the men who deride women's knowledge and their usefulness to the world, saying they are good only for "bearing children and sewing" (*Cité*, 73, 75, 77; Fr., 2:739, 743, 746). Such men, she adds, "are like people who live off the goods of others without knowing their source and without thanking anyone" [sont comme ceulx qui vivent des biens et ne scevent dont ilz viennent, ne graces n'en rendent a nulluy] (*Cité*, 77; Fr., 2:747). With a self-reflexive ambition that seems positively

Miltonic, de Pizan sets out in her book to "correct" such ingratitude toward women as figures of the source, both in their roles as mothers and in their roles of cultural creators. De Pizan begins the revision of one major source-text of her culture, the Bible, by taking Proba as her model—a textual figure whom she herself has (re)created. Through Proba—whose innovative powers are partly hidden in the way her story is related—de Pizan proceeds with the task of explaining and justifying a highly complex rewriting of scriptural history— and, implicitly, the other histories, past and present, which Scripture is made to authorize during an era when "religion," as Fredric Jameson remarks in an essay on Milton, "is the master-code in which issues are conceived and de-bated" ("Religion and Ideology," 37). Neatly evading the crucial question posed by the story of Proba—whether Scripture is in any significant way *altered* when it is "retold" in the words of a pagan author (whose very language, of course, differs from those of the original texts)—de Pizan adapts secular au-thors' words to her purposes as Proba is said to have adapted Vergil's. Also like Proba, de Pizan starts "with the creation." The problem of female nature, she clearly perceives, begins with Genesis, and more particularly, with that book's portrait of a female creator who produces Evil even before she is allowed her subordinate and, after the Fall, painful reproductive role.

Appropriately enough, de Pizan begins to rewrite Eve's story at the begin-ning of her book, where she substitutes a narrative about her own reading of a clerkly book filled with ideas apparently authorized by God's Word in Genesis for the version of Eve's story with which Boccaccio had begun *De claris mulieribus.* That story—like Proba's, an exception to his general rule against mixing narratives from pagan and (Judeo-)Christian traditions—character-istically begins by praising its subject, Eve, glorious "mother of us all" and a woman "cloaked in a radiance unknown to us" (*Famous Women,* 14–15). With massive authorization from tradition, Boccaccio ends his portrait, as is his wont, by making Eve a negative example of women's "fame": "With a woman's fickleness [*levitate feminea*]," he writes—not raising the Miltonic question of whether the Creator had perhaps erred in *making* a defective female nature— "Eve believed him [Satan] more than was good for her or for us; foolishly, she thought that she was about to rise to greater heights" (*Famous Women,* 16–17).

Instead of telling us all about Eve, de Pizan tells us a less familiar story about her own experience of reading what clerks have written about women. She dramatizes the need for a revised version of the biblical creation narrative by a veiled threat: the woman who *believes* the misogynistic doctrines set forth by clerks like Matheolus, as de Pizan herself did, will find herself perilously close to *disbelieving* a central Catholic doctrine that Augustine had vigorously asserted against Manichean dualism: that God's Creation was fundamentally good. Critics have not to my knowledge given sufficient attention to the serious theological problem de Pizan raises when she suggests, in her opening scene, that the words of misogynist authorities—words she likens to a "deafening fountain" (*fontaine resourdant*, which Richards translates as "gushing fountain" [*Cité*, 4; Fr., 2:619])—have led her into a state of sin in which she is becoming deaf to God's Word.[47] Far from refreshing, the divine Source, imaged classically in the fountain, is hurtful, engendering a sinful reaction in de Pizan. Its first symptom is a "stupor," according to Richards's translation; the French word is *etargie* (lethargy) and is often related to *acedia*—the cardinal sin of hopelessness seen by some medieval theologians as the source of a "daughter" sin, despair. With what is arguably a strategic prudence, de Pizan frames her passionate lament questioning God's purposes in creating her a woman and in creating woman at all with acknowledgments that the lament springs from a sinning mind: the word *etargie* introduces the lament, which closes with a phrase defining the speaker as having been "in . . . folly" (*en fouleur*). The long intervening passage, much of which is an apostrophe to God, voices doubt in his creative project: "I wondered how such a worthy artisan could have deigned to make such an abominable work, which, from what they say, is the vessel as well as the refuge and abode of every evil and vice" (*Cité*, 5; Fr., 2:620–21). It also cajoles, even challenges the Deity to acknowledge an improved version of his originary purpose:

> Oh, God, how can this be? For unless I stray from my faith, I must never doubt that Your infinite wisdom and most perfect goodness ever created anything which was not good. Did You yourself not create woman in a very special way and since that time did You not give her all those inclinations which it pleased You for her to have? And how could it be that You could go wrong in anything?

> [Ha! Dieux, comment puet cecy estre? Car se je ne erre en la foye, je ne doy mye doubter que ton inffinnie sapience et tres parfaitte bonté ait riens fait que tout ne soit bon? Ne fourmas tu toy meismes tres singulierement femme, et des lors luy donnas toutes telles inclinacions qu'il te plaisoit qu'elle eust? Et comment pourroit ce estre que tu y eusses en riens failly?] (*Cité*, 5; Fr., 2:620–21)

In the book that follows this initial scene of reading, de Pizan creates—out of bits and pieces of innumerable prior texts originally in many languages—a redeemed image of womankind; in so doing, she implicitly saves herself from the sin of "straying from [her] faith" by offering her readers, herself, and her God a new version of many parts of Scripture that are alienating for Christian women. She avoids the appearance of insubordination or heretical leanings by offering her revised versions of both sacred and secular texts as if these versions were the *true* originals authorized by her three female guides: what God and some of his authorial sons had intended, but had (as it were) forgotten and/or allowed to be misunderstood.

We can begin to appreciate the potentially heretical and censorable aspect of de Pizan's revisionary project by looking briefly at a passage in part 1 that constitutes a significant counterpoint to the author's lament in the prologue. In the later passage, too, de Pizan is concerned to refute Matheolus and the tradition he forcefully, even comically, represents when, in an imagined dialogue with God, he tells the deity not to bother with women's salvation at all because "reason" clearly shows ("par raison apperte") that women lack souls in the first place. Moreover, all reasonable beings (men) see that women caused "our" fall ("nostre perte") and "your death," that is, the death Christ paid to save men but not (in Matheolus's view) women.[48] De Pizan's personification of a female Reason refutes Matheolus's pseudo-logic, which would lead, if women readers believed it, to despair in one of its technical theological senses—loss of faith in the possibility of one's salvation. Adducing the example of the Samaritan woman and offering a counterexample to Matheolus's device of engaging in direct dialogue with God, de Pizan's Rayson not only criticizes Matheolus's view of Eve but offers a redeemed version of the opening scene where de Pizan articulated potentially heretical laments about Creation (or the official story thereof) to an apparently unresponding God. Here, Rayson presents a woman alienated by an accident of birth from the Judeo-Christian faith ("a sinner who did not even live under Your Law") engaging in eloquent conversation with a God (as Christ) who not only treats her as a respected being but shows an interest in her soul that many modern clerks and even bishops lack. The passage shows de Pizan effectively *displacing* anger at God onto men who are showing themselves unworthy shepherds of half their flock:

> with great eloquence, the Samaritan woman spoke well on her own behalf when she went to the well to draw water and met Jesus Christ sitting there completely exhausted. O blessed Godhead conjoined to this worthy body! How could You allow Your holy mouth to speak at such length for the sake of this little bit of a woman and a sinner who did not even live under Your Law? You truly demonstrated that You did not in the least disdain the pious sex of women. God, how often would our contemporary pontiffs deign to discuss anything with some simple little woman, let alone her own salvation? (*Cité*, 30; Fr., 2:662)

The relationship between the Samaritan woman and Christ—an idealized relation of dialogic mutuality—has an Old Testament analogue that de Pizan treats with great subtlety and through which she begins to educate her reader in the techniques of interpreting her own book *as if* it were a legitimate version of or supplement to Scripture. After her prologue lamenting God's creation of woman and what male authors have made of it, and after introducing her three allegorical ladies as "fountains" of wisdom (a metaphor that sets the ladies in clear opposition to the "deafening fountain" constituted by the misogynist traditions), de Pizan has Rayson "clear the ground" of "bad stones" through a series of arguments against authorities who espouse the idea of women's natural inferiority. The first extended illustration Rayson offers is the story of Nicaula (Nicolle). This portrait is not the first "stone" in de Pizan's own city— that allegorical role is given to the notoriously "incestuous" queen Semiramis.[49] But this story does constitute de Pizan's first extended borrowing from Boccaccio's *De claris mulieribus*, and Nicaula shares with de Pizan's autobiographical "frame story" the structural role of replacing Boccaccio's first portrait, that of Eve. Not surprisingly, Nicaula is in many respects a figure for the author of the *Cité des dames* herself.

De Pizan's first example is richly hybrid with respect to her own textual sources: described by Boccaccio (though *not* accorded the role of legal innovator that de Pizan gives her), Nicaula is also mentioned in both the Old and New Testaments (though under a different name), in several Church Fathers' writings, and in a thirteenth-century text by Jacobus de Voragine called *The Golden Legend* (*Legenda aurea*). Nicaula (again under another name) also appears in innumerable church sculptures and manuscript illustrations. If Rayson begins the "illustrative" part of her argument with a woman whose fame—unlike Eve's—will be no more obvious to the modern reader than it was, we may surmise, to the original audience of the *Cité des dames,* the narrative technique inaugurates de Pizan's important strategy of revising history for literate members of her audience while re-creating it for those not schooled in certain cultural traditions. She pursues this double aim, with its potentially different effects on audiences of different cultural literacies, by frequently withholding key information about the figures she is describing. Such information would have been commonsensical or *doxical* to learned readers but quite possibly new—or no more authoritative than de Pizan's own "information" is—to unlearned readers, including, of course, many women who might have heard the book read aloud. We have seen this technique in the Dido portrait, which defers any allusion to the Vergilian story of "Dido in love" to part 2, while even there presenting Dido in a more favorable light than Vergil sheds on her in his epic. De Pizan deploys this technique of narrative fragmenting and defamiliarizing (for the learned) even more shockingly with Medea, who is presented in part 1 only as woman of enormous beauty and learning. In part 2, where the more culturally familiar image of Medea in love occurs—albeit with new inflections—right after the "Vergilian" Dido enters the text, de Pizan omits all mention of Medea's infamous murder of her children by Jason. De Pizan first uses this narrative and hermeneutic technique with the figure of Nicaula. This figure's more familiar identity is revealed only in part 2. Boccaccio mentions both the names of this "Empress"—the second one quite casually—in a single narrative entitled "Nicaula, Queen of Ethiopia" (*Famous Women*, Story 43, 180–83). De Pizan, in contrast, distributes the story and its meanings in two textual spaces. The technique requires a different kind of mental work from the reader or listener than does Boccaccio's technique of self-contained vignettes. For clerks schooled in the tradition of biblical exegesis, de Pizan's writerly technique would entail the rather shocking idea that a vernacular text by a woman requires interpretation according to hermeneutic principles commonly applied (by clerks) to Scripture. In Nicaula's case, the technique results in something that closely resembles the movement from the "shadowy types" of the Old Testament to the truth ascribed, by a long tradition of Christian readers, to the New Testament.

Nicaula first appears not only "in the place of" Boccaccio's Eve, but also as part of Rayson's complex, even apparently contradictory response to de Pizan's question of "why women are not in the seats of legal counsel"—that is, why they do not serve in law courts. Rayson's initial answer to this question seems, as Maureen Quilligan remarks, "a very conservative defense" of a "conventional division of sexual labor" (*Allegory of Female Authority*, 66): "As to this particular question, dear friend, one could just as well ask why God did not ordain that men fulfill the offices of women, and women the offices of men. So I must answer this question by saying that just as a wise and well ordered lord organizes his domain so that one servant accomplishes one task and another servant another task, and that what the one does the other does not do, God has similarly ordained man and woman to serve him in different offices" (*Cité*, 31; Fr., 2:665). Only when Rayson ends the "sermonlike" part of her discourse and turns to the illustration or exemplum does one realize that Rayson's apparently question-dampening statement, "one could just as well ask why God did not ordain that men fulfill the offices of women, and women the offices of men," has not really laid to rest the question. Why *did* God ordain a strict sexual division of labor if, as Rayson maintains, women are no less capable than men of understanding and practicing the law (*Cité*, 32; Fr., 2:666)? Quilligan explains de Pizan's "regressive tactic"—which justifies the exclusion of women from a domain that de Pizan herself had entered as a widow suing for her property rights—by suggesting that de Pizan is in truth defending "difference" in a way that "authorizes a peculiarly female set of potencies that provide for reciprocity with men" (*Allegory of Female Authority*, 66). Those "potencies," Quilligan intriguingly argues—to explain why

Rayson goes on to give examples of women who *govern* with "great prudence"—involve an ideology of a distinctly "feminine" knowledge as "far beyond whatever had an origin in the written" (ibid., 67). Rayson does promise
to tell stories of great women philosophers who have "mastered fields far more
complicated, subtle, and lofty than written laws and man-made institutions"
[apprises de trop plus soubtilles sciences et plus haultes que ne sont lois es-
criptes et establissemens d'ommes] (*Cité*, 32; Fr., 2:667). For the moment,
however, Rayson gives examples of women who *do* have a "natural" capacity
for "politics and government," and who did participate fully—indeed constitutively—in the legal realm from which Rayson has just excluded women on
the grounds of a "natural" (divinely ordained) division of labor. There is a
contradiction here, which I think resists resolution in terms of Quilligan's
notion of an "oral" modality of distinctly feminine wisdom, although such a
concept is indeed sometimes adumbrated in the *Cité des dames*. De Pizan's
own status as a writing woman, like her personal experience in the contemporary legal domain, impinges in odd ways on her handling of many questions
concerning both orality and women's "nature." In the section introducing the
Nicaula story, a contradiction about women's relation to "the law" is exfoliated
rather than resolved by Rayson's invocation of a figure who occupies a peculiarly marginal position with respect to the kinds of "laws," written or oral, associated with the authority of the Judeo-Christian God. Nicaula, like the
Samaritan woman, is "inside" the scriptural tradition in the sense that she is
mentioned in the Bible, but she is "outside the law" in the sense that she is a
gentile.[50] Nicaula is also outside the law in a different sense, one that I take to
be critical to de Pizan's theory of literacy as entailing a complex (and manipu-
lable) relation between the letter and the spirit of scriptural authority. Nicaula
is outside the letter of the Bible, but she is nonetheless within the text—or,
more precisely, within one woman's reading of the text—because she appears
there under another name. Nicaula's story contributes to the general process
of interrogating the legitimacy of the law that Quilligan sees occurring in part
1, in preparation for the appearance of de Pizan's figure of Droitture in part 2.
The example of Nicaula serves, I think, to question the legitimacy of Judeo-
Christian laws, whether in written or oral form. The example does so partly
through describing Nicaula as a woman who not only was the first to live "according to laws and coordinated policy" but who also *instituted* those very laws
("elle meismes institua loys tres droitturieres pour gouverner son puepple"
[*Cité*, 32; Fr., 2:667]). *To institute* is a verb that eludes the dichotomy of "writ-
ten/oral"; as an instituter, Nicaula possessed and succeeded in transmitting a
socially authoritative Word. This Word, I argue, implicitly rivals the dominion
of established "law" both religious and secular.

Introducing Nicaula and other "great women rulers who have lived in past times," Rayson not only shows that women have a "natural sense for politics and government," but also implies the illogic and arbitrariness of the ostensibly divinely ordained status quo by citing an example clearly charged with autobiographical reference: even some contemporary women, she says, especially widows, have managed "all their affairs following the deaths of their husbands" in ways that demonstrate that "a woman with a mind is fit for all tasks" [femme qui a entendement est couvenable en toutes choses] (*Cité*, 32; Fr., 2:666). If this is Rayson's "truth," then the sexual division of labor ostensibly rooted in God's authority seems quite unreasonable; as I read it, the story of Nicaula interrogates political and theological orders based on any division of labor that bars women from the sphere of law-making and governing—in other words, from the sphere of *justice* so crucial to de Pizan's vision of queens who would rule their imperial city-states as Dido ruled hers, "gloriously in peace" (*Cité*, 188; Fr., 3:929).

Named in the story's title only as "l'empereris Nicolle," de Pizan's empress "was the first," Rayson explains, "to live according to laws and coordinated policies, and she destroyed and abolished the crude customs found in the territories over which she was lord and reformed the rude manners of the savage Ethiopians" (*Cité*, 32; Fr., 2:666–67). In this story about a woman given narrative priority not because she was chronologically the first-born of her sex—albeit logically and temporally secondary to Adam—but rather because she performed "originary" civilizing deeds, de Pizan cannily whets the reader's curiosity to know more about this remarkable lady; the story ends by giving readers of the Bible some clues about the lady's "real" identity, if not (yet) her second and more famous name. De Pizan's narrative technique is deliberately provocative, and it works, as I've suggested, to invite both learned and unlearned readers to practice a biblical style of reading typologically. De Pizan's part 2 reveals Nicaula to be none other than the Queen of Sheba.[51] "What more shall I tell you about this lady?" asks Rayson teasingly in the inaugural portrait of part 1:

> "She was so wise and so capable a ruler that even the Holy Scriptures speak of her great virtue. She herself instituted laws of far-reaching justice for governing her people. She enjoyed great nobility and vast wealth—almost as much as all the men who have ever lived. She was profoundly learned in the Scriptures and all fields of knowledge, and she had so lofty a heart that she did not deign to marry, nor did she desire that any man be at her side."

> ["Que te diroye de ceste dame? Elle fu tant saige et de tant grant gouvernement que meismes la sainte Escripture parle de sa grant vertu. Elle meismes institua loys tres droitturieres pour gouverner son peupple. Elle habonda de grant no-

blesce et combleté de richesces presque autant que tous les hommes qui
oncques furent. Elle fu parfonde et experte es escriptures et sciences, et tant
ot hault couraige que marier ne se daigna, ne voulst que homme se acostast
a elle."] (*Cité*, 33; Fr., 2:667–68)

Nicaula reappears early in part 2, part of a section on women prophets related by the muse-authority of this new part of the *Cité des dames,* Droitture
("Rectitude," as Richards translates her name, but the French emphasizes the
institution of the law more than this English translation does [*Cité*, 105–6; Fr.,
2:796–98]). Ironically, given Rayson's closing statement about Nicaula's independence, the figure whom Droitture (re-)introduces as "la royne Saba" was
almost always portrayed at the side of King Solomon in late medieval sculptures and book illustrations.[52] Drawing on the story of Sheba's visit to
Solomon in 2 Chron. 9:1–12 and also on Jesus' mention, in his sermon against
the Pharisees, of a "Queen of the South" who "shall rise up in the judgment
with this generation, and shall condemn it; for she came from the uttermost
parts of the earth to hear the wisdom of Solomon" (Matt. 12:39–43; compare
Luke 11:29–32), Christian exegetes began to offer a typological interpretation
of the Queen of Sheba and Solomon from the early fifth century C.E. In the
view of Prudentius (c. 400 C.E.), Solomon is a type of Christ and Sheba a type
of the gentiles who come from afar to worship him.[53] A slightly different interpretation comes from Isidore of Seville in the seventh century; for him, the
Queen of Sheba is a type of the Church, and hence allied with other types of
the community of believers, such as the Virgin Mary.[54] Writing in confirmation of Isidore's interpretation in the early ninth century, Hrabanus Maurus
drew on Josephus's *Antiquities of the Jews* to give the Queen of Sheba the name
"Nikaule" and the crown of Ethiopia.[55] Most significantly, for my reading of de
Pizan's complex use of Nicaula-Sheba, is a later medieval exegetical tradition
that was widely known in de Pizan's time but for which, as Paul F. Watson observes, there is "barely a shred of biblical evidence" ("Queen of Sheba in Christian Tradition," 121). This extrascriptural identity allies Nicaula/Sheba not
only with the idea of an "instituted" set of written laws but also with the idea
of oral female prophecy; Nicaula/Sheba thus becomes a pivotal figure in de
Pizan's exploration of women's relation to powerful words whether spoken or
written. In the influential work called the *Legend of the True Cross,* which was
redacted in many texts but most notably in Jacobus de Voragine's *Legenda aurea,* we find a story about the Queen of Sheba that is absent from Boccaccio's
narrative but clearly important to de Pizan's revision of Boccaccio's as well as
the Old Testament's general views of women. The Queen of Sheba, according
to the *Legenda aurea,* relates that when "Adam lay dying, his son Seth travelled

to the Garden of Eden to buy a few drops of oil from the Tree of Mercy. The Archangel Michael gave Seth instead a branch of the Tree of Knowledge of Good and Evil, telling him that on the day when this tree would bear fruit, Adam would be made whole" (quoted in Silberman, "Queen of Sheba in Jewish Tradition," 67). When Seth returned, he found Adam dead and "planted the branch of the Tree over his father's grave." Centuries later, the tree having grown mightily, Solomon tried to use it for building the Temple. His workmen, however, discovered that it was sometimes too short, sometimes too long, for whatever they needed. In the words of the *Legenda aurea*, the workmen then "became impatient and threw it [the recalcitrant tree] across a pond to serve as a bridge. And when the Queen of Sheba came to test Solomon with hard questions, she had occasion to cross the pond, and she saw in spirit that the Saviour of the world would one day hang upon this tree. She therefore refused to put her foot on it, but knelt instead to adore it . . . Solomon had the tree taken away and ordered it to be buried in the earth" (quoted in ibid., 122). This wood (of course) was later dug up and used to make the True Cross; still later it was rediscovered by Helen, the mother of Constantine.[56]

In contrast to Boccaccio's account, which emphasizes the Queen of Sheba's experience of awe in the face of Solomon's wise responses to the "difficult questions" she poses, the *Legenda aurea* provides de Pizan with an image of the queen as a pedagogical authority in her own right, a chosen vessel for prophetic wisdom about the True Cross which even Solomon does not possess and which—at least in de Pizan's version—he does not properly appreciate.[57] Her queen, unlike Boccaccio's, "tested" (*esprouva*) Solomon with her questions—like a schoolmistress—and was impressed not by *him* but rather by knowledge that is pointedly described as being "a special gift from God" rather than a product of man's wit ("non par engin humain Salomon avoit si grant sagesce, mais par especial don de Dieu" [*Cité*, 105; Fr., 2:796]). After telling how the queen bestowed many rich gifts upon Solomon, de Pizan's Droitture mentions that "several writings" (*aucunes escriptures*) discuss this woman's "wisdom and prophecies." An example—absent in Boccaccio and in the 1401 translation—describes the queen walking with Solomon when she suddenly sees a board lying across a mud puddle. She stops to worship it, saying, "This board, now held in such great contempt and set under foot, will, when the time comes, be honored above all other pieces of wood in the world and adorned with precious gems from the treasures of princes. And he who will destroy the law of the Jews will die on the wood of this plank" (*Cité*, 106; Fr., 2:797). The prophecy, like the piece of wood itself, is scorned by all who hear it. Since de Pizan, unlike Jacobus de Voragine, explicitly has the queen walking with Solomon when she discovers and explains the piece of wood, and since she omits the detail in the *Legenda aurea* describing him burying the tree in response to the queen's words, it seems clear that de Pizan's allegory places the queen, the unrecognized "True Cross" symbolizing Christ, and the female author herself—maker of "aucunes escriptures" that blur the line between sacred and secular writing—in a category that both alludes to and "corrects" the most famous pagan figure of female prophecy: Cassandra.[58] Like Cassandra, Sheba, Christ, and by implication de Pizan—as well as some of her female "Christ figures" like Griselda—are unappreciated and in some cases even reviled by contemporary audiences, some figured as powerful rulers, judges, or tyrannical husbands—for instance, Solomon, Pontius Pilate, or the cruel husband of Griselda, who behaves toward his wife as God does toward his servant Job. Unlike Cassandra, de Pizan's figures of "unappreciated wisdom" *ultimately* do receive recognition and approbation for their insights and virtue; they are carriers or "translators" of a truth that must await the future for full unveiling.[59] In the Nicaula-Sheba stories of the *Cité des dames*—in the "typological" implication of their narrative separation and unfolding, as well as in their complex intertextual revisions—we can begin to see de Pizan identifying herself with her name-brother Christ while writing a book that in some extraordinary ways claims to supplement, or even supplant, the Bible.

Nicaula/Sheba's relation to Solomon—a relation that begins with intellectual "testing," and is followed by gift-giving and an attempt to instruct the man in "prophetic" wisdom—becomes, in de Pizan's hands, a brilliant alternative to Eve's relation to Adam and, more generally, to the subordinate relation to men prescribed for Eve's daughters in most texts by Adam's sons. De Pizan's Nicaula/Sheba governs with "wonderful prudence" a territory she inherits from men but also transforms, or rather, "reforms." The territory ruled by Nicaula/Sheba, de Pizan observes, was "not just a small land" but "the kingdom of Arabia, Ethiopia, Egypt, and the island of Meroe (which is very long and wide and filled with all kinds of goods)." Like the historical Elizabeth Tudor, de Pizan's Sheba "[has no] desire that any man be at her side" [ne voulst que homme se acostast a elle] (*Cité*, 33; Fr., 2:668). She occupies the primary narrative position that Boccaccio and the Bible give to Eve because she begins de Pizan's revisionary story about female author-figures who rule "rich" empires on their own rather than as consorts of men. In part 3, which relates how the "high roofs" of the city were completed and which "noble ladies were chosen to reside in the great palaces," de Pizan reveals what has previously been only intimated: women who build empires need no (mortal) "men at their side" because such women find (or create) independent authority in the idea that they are wives, daughters, or sisters of Christ (*Cité*, 217; Fr., 3:974). He is de Pizan's emblem of a truly enlightened male, a superhuman male capable of hearing and immediately valuing and heeding virtuous women's words. To set the stage for a discussion of the spiritual empire limned in part 3, I want to discuss the problem of censorship as de Pizan introduces it—in connection with a pagan woman named Leaena—in part 2, the part of the textual city presided over by Droitture.

This muse figure, whose name alludes to the institution of the Law as well as to abstract ideas of "rectitude," describes a Greek woman named Leaena ("Leonce" in the French) who bites "her own tongue off with her teeth in front of the judge so that he would have no chance of making her talk using torture" (*Cité*, 184; Fr., 3:923). Immediately after this story, which foreshadows that of the writer's name-saint in part 3, the narrator poses a question. Why, she wonders, have so many ladies "who were both extremely wise and literate [*lettrees*] and who could compose and dictate their beautiful books in such a fair style, suffered so long without protesting against the horrors charged by different men when they [literate women] knew that these men were greatly mistaken" (*Cité*, 184–85; Fr., 3:924)?

Censorship and self-censorship, of the violent sort just described in Leaena's story, would seem to be a major answer to de Pizan's question, for the narrative structure implies a strong analogy between female speech and writing. But Droitture's response to the character's question, perhaps *enacting* an aspect of how the threat of censorship works in and on this very text, offers another, more "positive" explanation for literate women's silence on the topic of women's oppression. "My dear friend," says Droitture, "you can see from what has been said . . . how all the ladies whose outstanding virtues I told you about above occupied their minds in various specialized works [*oeuvres differanciees l'une de l'autre*] and not at all in any one activity. The composition of this work [*ceste oeuvre à bastir*] has been reserved for you and not for them, for their works have been written to benefit people of clear understanding and true discernment, without their having written any other work on the subject" (*Cité*, 185; Fr., 2:924). In other words, some unnamed agent (God? Fortune?) has "reserved" (*reservé*) this work of making a synthetic defense of women for de Pizan alone, even though previous women had both the literate skills and the knowledge of oppression necessary to undertake it.

The explanation is enigmatic both conceptually and linguistically, as a comparison of Richards's translation with the original French (or rather, with one manuscript version thereof) suggests. The French explanatory clause for why the work of defending women is "reserved" for de Pizan alone goes as follows: "car par leurs oeuvres estoyent assez les femmes louees aux gens de bon entendement et de consideracion vraye sans ce que autre escrip elles en feissent" (3:924). Richards's translation renders the writer/audience relation in terms of the former's *intent* to "benefit" an elite audience, whereas the French (as I construe it) presents the author/audience relation in terms of how the audience *responded* to the author's work: by *praising* it, and therefore (some-how) rendering further writing unnecessary. The tortuous sentence signals a problem in de Pizan's view of a female writer's relation to her audience and—perhaps—in her sense of her own authority to undertake the task of defend-ing women, and their right to public voice, *as if* other women hadn't done that before her. Following Richards's translation, one could interpret her as locat-ing her *difference* from other women writers in her desire to address a "mixed" audience rather than one composed solely of "people of clear understanding and true discernment." Looking not only at the French text but also at the gaps or silences signaled by the difficulty of translating the passage, however, I would suggest that de Pizan has not resolved the problem of her (imagined) audience any more than some of her female precursors did.

The Leaena story in part 2, as Kevin Brownlee has astutely suggested, al-ludes to Ovid's story of Philomela (the classical prototype for the violently censored woman).[60] The story also, I contend, foreshadows that of the author's namesake in part 3—a story in which a woman named Christine willingly un-dergoes a torture that involves her tongue being cut off "at the root," and in which the author, who avoids the ultimate fate of bodily mutilation and mar-tyrdom, is singled out by name for a symbolic baptism that constitutes her election and legitimation, in the eyes of a heavenly judge if not of earthly ones, as a writer. The social fact of censorship, which had silenced women in French territories who sought to use their tongues or their pens to teach large au-diences, underlies and shapes de Pizan's "prudent" qualities as a writer and in particular, I argue, her clever ways of addressing herself to an audience com-plexly divided. The divisions ran along lines of gender and social status, but also along a spectrum running from Latinate literacy to an "oral/aural" ver-nacular literacy that would have enabled some people who did not read Latin to *hear* de Pizan's book read aloud in its hybrid French larded with doublets yoking Latinate words with more familiar terms. If, as I am surmising, her book was designed for readers and listeners with widely varying types of lin-guistic competence, some members of her real and/or imagined audience might have taken her revisionary version of world history as an "original" and true one.

Christ's Sisters:
Building a Spiritual Empire through Women's Word(s)

I myself have given Him [Jesus] to you, as to the Virgin.
GOD'S WORDS TO NA PROUS BONETA, as reported in the record of her
confession to the Inquisition before her death by burning (1325)

By the grace of our Lord, this creature [the author] had written into heart the holy life
that Jesus Christ had led on earth. . . . She had put sweet Jesus Christ so firmly into her
heart that it sometimes seemed to her that He was present and that He held a closed book
in His hand in order to teach from it. . . . When she was not expecting it, it seemed to her
that the book opened itself. . . . The inside of this book was like a beautiful mirror. . . . In
this book appeared a delightful place, so large that the entire world seems small by comparison. . . . On the second clasp was written: *"Mirabilis Deus in sanctis suis,* God is marvelous in His saints."

MARGUERITE D'OINGT, *Miroir*

Ceste Ame, dit Amour, est dame des Vertuz, fille de Deite, seur de Sapience, et espouse
d'Amour. [This soul, called Love, is mistress of the Virtues, daughter of the Deity, sister
of Wisdom and wife of Love.]

MARGUERITE PORETE, *Le Mirouer des simples ames*

The final part of de Pizan's *Cité des dames* is governed, metaphorically speaking, by the goddess-muse figure named Justice. She "populates" the walled
City of Ladies with Christian saints, and in so doing, she dramatizes the paradox at the heart of de Pizan's architectural metaphor. The city is like a convent, girdled by walls designed to protect female chastity and honor the City's
queen, the Virgin Mary. But this is also a city that harbors female evangelists
and, in the hidden foundation stones, amoral queens, Amazonian warriors,
and other figures from pagan history. The city is enclosed and looks from one
perspective like a prison protecting society's norms of female behavior; in the
city's buried foundations and in its metaphorical towers, however, appear
women with powerful ambitions to establish or extend their dominions. In
story after story narrated by Justice in part 3, a girl or woman defies secular
male authorities, including biological fathers, to embrace Christ and often
to preach his message to a wide audience. Correcting Boccaccio by including
among "famous" women those who died for Christ, de Pizan turns to Vincent of Beauvais—whom she explicitly names as her source at the beginning
of the story of her namesake Christine—for model saints' lives. She also turns
(again) to Dante. The tripartite structure of her book clearly allies her third
section with his *Paradiso,* and Maureen Quilligan has persuasively argued for
a more specific (and revisionary) allusion to canto 15 of *Paradiso*—Dante's
encounter with his martyred great-grandfather Cacciaguida—in de Pizan's
central story of her martyred patron saint, Christine.[61] I shall suggest, however, that de Pizan's third part is also indebted—though in a necessarily occluded way that poses many problems for scholarly argumentation—to various female religious figures of the late Middle Ages who inhabit a shadowy
territory with respect to what the Catholic Church regarded, at any given
point, as heresy. Such figures include the three whose words are quoted in my

epigraphs. In the case of Na Prous Boneta, who was *illitterata* in the sense that she did not know Latin, the words come to us only in the mediated and translated form of a Latin court document (which, however, leaves some phrases in the original Provençal).[62] Marguerite d'Oingt (d. 1310), a more privileged lady than Na Prous, came from an ancient Lyonnais family.[63] Her words come to us in Franco-Provençal, via a manuscript copied soon after her death that still exists in Grenoble.[64] Marguerite d'Oingt was prioress of a Carthusian convent near modern Poleteins and died on the "right" side of the heresy/orthodoxy line—after submitting her account of her visions in the *Miroir* to a spiritual adviser, who in turn submitted them to an official church body (the "Chapter General") for approval in 1294. Both she and Marguerite Porete meditated on female spiritual heroism in ways that contribute substantially to our understanding of the *heterodoxy* that historically underlies various efforts to distinguish the orthodox from the heretical.[65] Porete died at the stake in the same year that d'Oingt died "in the Church."

If we read de Pizan's narratives about female saints in the context of what historians can reconstruct about religious thinkers associated with the so-called movement of the free spirit, certain aspects of an ideology we might call imperial utopianism come into sharper focus than they have in most critical discussions of part 3 of the *Cité des dames*. For example, consider the peculiar temporality of the city, as both a "preparation" for the Christian heaven and as a possible alternative to the Church Fathers' ideas about heaven, which included the remarkable notion of a "celestial gynaeceum" that would perpetuate the monastic division of the sexes in the afterlife.[66] Relevant here are the widely disseminated (if variously interpreted) ideas of Joachim da Fiore.[67] Some of Joachim's later interpreters—Peter John Olivi, followed by Na Prous Boneta, for instance—prophesied that the whole Church system "was to be superseded" in a new age of the Holy Spirit.[68] Na Prous Boneta herself crossed the line into heresy partly because she saw herself not only as the herald of a new, "third" age that would be realized on earth; she believed that she was in some ways the Holy Spirit, "and that people can be saved only if they believe in her."[69] Some of Joachim's heirs believed, moreover, that their souls, even while attached to their bodies, were "liberated from the earthly condition and made 'glorious,'" transmuted in such a way that they were "citizens in the city of the pure spirit."[70] I propose that de Pizan's third part draws on strands of apocalyptic thinking that emerged from a cultural territory where the difference between orthodoxy and heresy was not by any means fixed, where gender as well as class often played a role in the determination of heresy, and where the boundaries of orthodoxy were repeatedly tested by women with varying degrees and types of literacy. In part 3 of the *Cité des dames,* de Pizan describes a utopian city ruled by Christ's beloved mother, the Virgin Mary. This city may well draw on an orthodox but now little-known set of ideas about a "celestial gynaeceum," but de Pizan's city also, I believe, bears significant resemblance to the spaces imagined and prophesied by female preachers of the free spirit like Na Prous Boneta, Marguerite Porete, and Marguerite d'Oingt, who saw in Christ's "book-mirror" a "delightful place larger than the world."

The *proselytizing* drive of de Pizan's saints, their desire to spread Christ's word to large audiences, invites us to connect the apparently antithetical spatial images of a walled city and an expanding empire.[71] Classical as well as Renaissance empires began in and with a powerful metropolis, but de Pizan's stress on the separation of the city from surrounding dangers—through the image of the walls—may deflect the reader's attention from the ways in which her city works as an empire *in nuce* through the relation of its inhabitants' histories as "converters of the pagan" and through the ambiguously utopian quality of their "present" temporality. Through her stress on women's powers of teaching—against the wishes of fathers, judges, and king/tyrants—de Pizan adumbrates an ideology of empire as the expansion of (virtuous) women's cultural power.

Their desire both to remain virgins and actively to teach spiritual "truths" invariably brings the women of part 3 into repeated conflict with earthly judges and the legal systems they interpret and enforce. As R. Howard Bloch observes, with reference to the thirteenth-century hagiography of Christine of Markyate, the saint's refusal to marry "represents an abrogation of the feudal familial right to 'husband' its offspring so as to ensure both the continuity of the genealogical line and of the ancestral fief" (*Etymologies and Genealogies,* 181). In the tripartite structure of de Pizan's book, with its Dantesque movement from infernal to purgatorial to paradisal spaces, the muse of Justice replaces the muse of Law, but purgatorial tortures continue to be reenacted in the final part of the text. De Pizan's saints are hardly unique in being punished for their stubborn faith by being tortured and eventually killed. They are unusual, however, in the degree to which their punishments are yoked to their verbal aggressivity—and in the author's stress on the Deity's approval of his female saints' speech acts. De Pizan's image of a "city" into which the martyred women are received ambiguously supplements her thematic insistence that her saints' defiance of earthly authority was authorized and gratefully received by God. Her third part thus elaborates an idea she had already explored in her various revisions of Boccaccio's portraits of pagan women: "virtue" is a contested quality, and she who is excoriated by some—as Christ was—may be (justly) revered by others, in the present or (more likely) the future. Although much recent criticism of the *Cité des dames* has focused on the problems for modern feminist readers posed by the apparently sado-masochistic dimensions of de Pizan's portraits of female saints being mutilated in horrifying ways before dying for (their version of) Christ, the portraits acquire another dimension of meaning when the book is read as a document of competing empires, historical and imagined.[72]

The historical analogues to de Pizan's apparently "orthodox" saints' stories dramatize the presence, in the territory known as France, of violently competing perspectives on crucial issues and personages. That the very existence of such competing perspectives has been obscured by many narrative accounts of a hypostatized "medieval Age of Faith" is itself a testimony to the power of what one might fairly call an imperial style of history writing. De Pizan at once contributes to the hegemony of that style and—very partially—exposes some of its ideological mechanisms. We can see the latter operations, however, only when we read her text in the light of the near-contemporary cultural subtext provided by the parallels between her "orthodox" saints, living mostly in the time of the *Roman* empire and defying *pagan* authority, and the *vitae* and in some cases the writings of historical religious women living in French imperial territories and defying ostensibly Christian authorities—the kind of authorities whose behavior was seen as hugely "unchristian" by brethren of the free spirit like Na Prous Boneta. She compared the Church's approval of a mass burning of lepers in 1321–22 to Herod's slaughter of the innocents.[73]

Because some of the historical women who saw themselves as prophets or vessels of the Holy Spirit lacked the skills of alphabetic literacy, and because many of them were judged heretical by church authorities, the history of the reception of their words is full of gaps.[74] I cannot state that de Pizan knew the Latin text of Na Prous Boneta's confession—dictated to a court notary in Provençal in 1325 and read back to her for her "confirmation"—but I surmise that de Pizan knew, by oral report or by reading, words spoken by women who were *like* Na Prous Boneta in many respects but chiefly because they claimed *direct* rather than mediated access to the "holy spirit" and because they defied male "judges" in order to preach their views to an audience. The followers of Na Prous Boneta and some of the readers of Marguerite Porete defied the Church's official judgment of these women by viewing them as martyrs rather than heretics. Na Prous Boneta was herself a follower of one Peter John Olivi, who died at peace with the Church in 1297 but whose apocalyptic theology, influenced by the widely disseminated views of Joachim da Fiore on a new "third age" of history, was full of tenets later deemed heretical by officers of the Inquisition. Joachim himself had the ambiguous fate of being "in the Church" at his death in 1202 but being the author of works subsequently condemned by the same institution.[75] As Joachim's case demonstrates, one's body could be

orthodox at the time of one's death, even as one's "soul"—especially in the
worldly "afterlife" provided by the technology of writing—was deemed dangerously heretical. The line between heresy and orthodoxy, even in the same
human subject, was thin, shifting, and in important ways dependent on power
struggles among the perspectives of different groups and individuals.

In her history of the movement of the free spirit, Romana Guarnieri mentions the well-known *vitae* of many late medieval religious women who were
not deemed heretical but who certainly defied St. Paul's strictures against
women assuming pedagogical authority—figures such as Marie of Oignies
(1177–1213), Cristina "the Miraculous" (1150–1224), Ivetta (1157–1228), Lut-
garda of Tongres (1182–1246), Giuliana of Mont Cornillon (1193–1258), and
Heilwig Bloemardinne (d. c. 1336), among others.[76] The last-named, a mystical visionary who lived in Brussels, is reported to have written many works,
now lost, "in which she treated the spirit of liberty identified by her."[77] According to a text by Henricus Pomerius, a contemporary of de Pizan, Bloemardinne was venerated by her many disciples—among them many aristocrats,
including Duchess Marie d'Evreux—as an *inventrix* of a new doctrine. There
is no evidence, so far as I know, about whether or not de Pizan knew of
Bloemardinne, but we have seen evidence of de Pizan's fascination with female
"inventors" and leaders. It is an open question whether her silence about near-
contemporary examples of female spiritual leaders betokens ignorance of
their existence, disapproval of their theological ideas, and/or a prudent alle-
gorizing technique that entails a deliberate "suppression" of recent history
while also providing—for certain readers at least—narrative details that invite and even foment potentially subversive ideas about what constitutes
heroic female behavior in the near as well as the distant past, in French as well
as in Roman imperial territories.

The hypothesis that de Pizan was simply ignorant of the writings (and reported acts and words) of recent French female mystics seems less likely to me
than the other two hypotheses, especially when we consider the case of Marguerite Porete. There is strong evidence that one of the male authorities with
whom de Pizan was most closely connected in Paris, Jean Gerson, knew Porete's *Mirouer des simples ames,* for in his commentary on Mark 1:4, written in
November–December 1401 and entitled "De distinctione verarum revela-
tionum a falsis," Gerson mentions a little book composed with "almost incredible subtlety" by a woman called Maria de Valenciennes [libello incredi-
bili pene subtilitate ab una foemina composito, quae Maria de Valenciennes
dicebatur].[78] On the basis of his subsequent description of the book's theological argument, Guarnieri concludes that his "Maria de Valenciennes" was
none other than Marguerite Porete, who was burned with her book in her na-

tive city of Valenciennes sometime between 1296 and 1306.[79] Guarnieri does
not mention, however, that Gerson uses this *libellus* composed by a woman in
a section of his argument devoted to women's particular susceptibility to "false
revelations" and to the danger of lay spiritual movements ("Beghardi et
Beghardae") in which men and women live together (rather than in the safer
sex-segregated spaces of monasteries and convents) and frequently fall into
prideful confusions about what constitutes "divine" love and what constitutes
"dilectione vitiosa" ("corrupt delight") (Gerson, *Oeuvres,* 3:51). Gerson is quite
exercised about "mere women" (*muliericulas*) who assume they have the
wisdom and authority to write about divine love, without suspecting that
they are in truth inspired by the devil; such women with their "famous revelations" tempt others into insanity—the "delirium" exhibited, for instance,
by a woman who was convinced that she was Christ with his ability "to fly
through the air."[80] It is thus in the context of a severe if epistemologically tricky
critique of women who have "unauthorized" visions of *identification* with
the Deity, and who attempt to communicate these visions in ways that fan
"vehement" passions that are easy to find but difficult to regulate ("facilior in-
venitur et regi difficilior"), that Gerson mentions Porete's "almost unbeliev-
ably subtle" book. I do not know whether de Pizan read either Porete's or Gerson's manuscripts (the latter, as a "magistral" work, was widely distributed),
but she was certainly in direct contact with Gerson in 1401–2, and many of the
female figures in the *Cité des dames,* especially but not only the saints of part 3,
claim a spiritual authority similar to that which Gerson mocks and rather anx-
iously decries in the paragraphs including the mention of a woman's "subtle"
book. De Pizan's Justice states, "I am in God and God is in me, and we are as
one and the same" [Je suis en dieu et dieu est en moy, et sommes comme une
meismes chose] (*Cité,* 14; Fr., 2:635); this figure certainly sounds like Porete's
Soul, who is described by her sister Amour as being altogether "like the Deity,
because she [the Soul] is transformed into God, by whom she has held her
true form" [semblable a la Deite, car elle est muee en Dieu . . . par quoy elle
a sa vraye forme detenue] (*Mirouer,* ed. Guarnieri, 551, my translation).
These female authorities are fashioned to offer forceful rebuttals to the Pauline view that women are logically and temporally secondary creatures in God's
Creation.

    In Gerson's view, however, women repeat Eve's initial error when they
think they have direct access to God's love, without the governing mediation
of a male priest. Porete, to whom Gerson refers as "Maria," is not speaking
(writing) for God but rather for passions generated in the phallic "swelling"
(*tumiditas*) of her own mind. Gerson deflates this "incredibly subtle" woman's
pretensions in a way that might well have interested the female clerk who

would later depict herself receiving enlightenment from three female authorities who present themselves as "daughters of God" who also are "one" with
him. De Pizan acknowledges the possibility that they might bear (or be) "false
revelations" when she writes of her fear "that some phantom [*aucune fantome*]
had come to tempt me"; "filled with great fright," she "made the Sign of the
Cross on her forehead" before embarking on her conversation with Rayson
and her "splendid" sisters (*Cité*, 6; Fr., 2:622). The female "compositor" of the
Cité des dames evidently occupies the same spiritually dangerous territory
that Gerson limns, and attempts to control, in his discussion of Maria de Valenciennes's "confusion" about types of love and the dangers of fantasy—the
same subjects he discussed in the famous turn-of-the-century quarrel about
the *Romance of the Rose* in which he entered on de Pizan's side, although for
reasons quite different from her desire to refute Jean de Meun's "slander" of
women.[81] Gerson cites Vergil to underscore his point about Maria's "subtle"
book: remember, he tells his male addressee, that passage from the *Eclogues*
(8.108) that goes "An qui amant, ipsi sibi somnia fingunt" [Or do lovers fashion their own dreams?]. The quoted line, which closes Vergil's poem, comes
after the speaker has seen a miraculous omen whose meaning and validity he
feels compelled to interrogate: "Credimus," he asks ("Can we believe it?"), and
then follows the line Gerson quotes.[82]

Gerson's fascinating judgment of Porete's text (and I accept Guarnieri's argument that what he read *was* a version of Porete's text) is riddled with ironies
when one realizes that he is commenting on a book that in certain ways refutes
Jean de Meun's immensely popular ideas about the relation of "reason" and
"love" no less firmly than de Pizan refuted those ideas, both in the documents
of the "quarrel" from 1401–2 and in her later *Cité des dames*. Borrowing heavily from the allegorical vocabulary of the *Romance of the Rose,* as Don Eric
Levine has noted, Porete depicts Raison as a *servant*—and sometimes comically obtuse interlocutor—of a character named Amour and identified with
divine rather than earthly love.[83] Though Porete's theological ideas and style
are very different from de Pizan's, there are intriguing points of convergence
between the *Mirouer* and the *Cité des dames*. Both vernacular texts explicitly
and sometimes exclusively address an audience of women: "Hee, dames nient
cognues, dit l'Ame qui ce livre fist escrire," writes Porete, for instance, with
charming directness [Hey, unknown ladies, said the Soul who caused this book
to be written] (*Mirouer,* ed. Guarnieri, 614, my translation). Both texts depict
various allegorical characters, including those of Raison and Justice, in conversation with a female author-figure (the "Ame" in Marguerite).[84] Both texts
attempt to "correct" an immensely popular male-authored text, which itself,
as David Hult notes, was rife with precisely the kind of philosophical "errors"
associated with the male clerical tradition centered in the university—a site of

clerical activity that was not infrequently at odds with the institution of the Church.[85] Both de Pizan and Porete take aim not only at Jean de Meun but at the male clerical tradition he represents, although de Pizan's aim is to expose clerkly errors about female nature, while Porete's stated aim (in her prefatory poem) is to show that "Love and Faith" are the "Ladies of the House" and are greater than Reason—or at least than the "Raison" revered (pridefully, she suggests) by "Theologiens ne aultres clers" (*Mirouer,* ed. Guarnieri, 520).

Gerson, the chancellor of the University of Paris, plays an intriguing if still only partly excavated role in a cultural debate about sexuality, women, and what constitutes "orthodoxy"—a debate in which Marguerite Porete and de Pizan both participate in ways that also remain to be more fully analyzed than I can do here. Knowing only the tip of the iceberg about the social, theological, and political implications of the "quarrel" about the *Romance of the Rose* in which Gerson sides with de Pizan against the defenders of Jean de Meun, I nonetheless venture to suggest that his comment on the "almost incredible subtlety" of Maria de Valenciennes's book merits further research in the context of the status of the *Romance of the Rose* as a nodal point in the complex history of heresies—or, more precisely, charges of heretical "error"—in the far-from-unified polity of early modern France.

Ironically enough, one of Gerson's institutional predecessors, a master of theology at the Sorbonne named Godfrey de Fontaines, had given official approval to Porete's book when she initially submitted it to him and to two other authorities, as she tells us in her preface.[86] Godfrey was highly impressed by Porete's learning and found the book "ymaad of a spirit so strong and so kuttynge," that there "ben but fewe such or noone," according to a fifteenth-century English translation of his words (cited from Doiron, ed., "Marguerite Porete," 250). Unusual theological ideas readily crossed the English Channel during the Hundred Years War, even if the words expressing those ideas were written in French by a female writer. Precisely because Porete's book was so powerful and unusual, however, Godfrey warned that it should be read by few. One of the other judges to whom Porete sent her book shared this opinion (Sanders, "*Auctor* and *Auctoritas,*" 2). We can infer that she disregarded such warnings from the subsequent order, issued by the bishop of Cambrai, that the *Mirouer* be burned in Valenciennes. At that time she was again instructed not to circulate her book, and again she defied episcopal authority as well as the dictum of St. Paul: "I suffer not a woman to teach, nor to usurp authority over the man, but to be in silence" (1 Tim. 2:12). Between 1306 and 1308, a new bishop of Cambria, Philip of Marigny, "took Porete into custody . . . on charges of having sent her book to Bishop John of Châlons-sur-Marne and of having circulated it among the simple people" (Sanders, "*Auctor* and *Auctoritas,*" 2). Her gender and desires to reach a wide audience seem to have played at least as great a role in her ultimate fate as her theological opinions; in her trial of 1310 in Paris, a commission of canon lawyers told Porete, "In you [is] such rebelliousness and stubborness, [that] we bring sentence of greater excommunication." Finding her book "injurious," full of "heresy and errors," the commission recommended to the secular authorities that she be mutilated and burned, along with her book; "all privately owned copies of *The Mirror*," moreover, were to be "submitted to authorities within a month on pain of excommunication."[87] Many owners of copies of the book evidently followed Porete's example in disobeying orders, for the book continued to circulate and was soon translated into Latin, Spanish, and English.[88] Marguerite de Navarre clearly had access to a French copy of Porete's book when she wrote her *Miroir de l'âme pécheresse*—a work condemned by the Sorbonne in 1531 and soon thereafter by Calvin in his tract against the Libertines. The poem would later be translated into English by the young Elizabeth Tudor.[89]

That Porete's "injurious" ideas were officially censored but not fully suppressed (Guarnieri located one early manuscript copy of Porete's book in the library of a religious house that does not want to be known as the owner of a book deemed heretical) acquires a certain symbolic resonance—especially for readers of de Pizan's *Cité des dames*—when we note that according to one fourteenth-century writer, Jean d'Outremeuse, Porete "translated the divine Scripture, in which translation she erred greatly in articles of faith" [translatat la divine Escripture, en queile translation mult elle errat es artycles de la foid] (Guarnieri, "Il Movimento," 412, my translation). Porete offers an intriguing historical analogue to de Pizan's Proba, who as we recall "translated" Holy Scripture into the words of Vergil. Noticing that the documents of Porete's trial do not mention her as a translator of Scripture, Guarnieri astutely suggests that the activity in question was not translation in a literal sense, as one editor has assumed, but rather translation in the figurative sense of *trapasso*, a "going beyond." I agree with this interpretation, although I would add that any "literal" translation also always "goes beyond" the text and hence betrays or supplants it—as the old dictum *traduttore/traditore* suggests. Guarnieri supports her reading by citing a passage in the continuation of *Les Grandes chroniques de la France* that describes Porete as a *beguine clergesse* (ibid.).

This is the only instance of the term *clergesse* I have found prior to de Pizan's use of the word in the *Cité des dames* (71; Fr., 2:735). Given de Pizan's thematic concern with female originators and inventors, it is ironic that one modern critic claims that de Pizan herself coined the term *clergesce* for her portrait of Carmentis, inventor of letters and a figure of the female writer as originator par excellence.[90] De Pizan praises this woman not only for first instituting *written* laws in her country but also for inventing the Latin alphabet and syntax—that is, a grammaticized language of empire (*Cité*, 71–72; Fr.,

2:735–36). In de Pizan's narrative, Carmentis symbolically harnesses both the oral and written powers of song (*carmen*) for the good of the state. Perhaps, in de Pizan's utopian world, Carmentis would have drafted and interpreted the laws of her polity in a way that would have spared a woman like Porete from the laws of Church and crown in de Pizan's France. In the *Cité,* and especially in the portraits of *clergesce* figures like Proba and Carmentis, the historical figure of Porete is at once (re-)created and hidden.

Porete's text—like de Pizan's written in a courtly, metropolitan dialect that has "clerkly" features—exists in the archive, but few among today's culturally literate know it. A "waking" dream vision with roots in the genre of the allegorical *débat* or *consolatio,* and also indebted to Dante's *Commedia,* Porete's book adapts the popular medieval genre of the *miroir* to autobiographical uses specifically inflected for a female writer.[91] Porete follows Marguerite d'Oingt and other mystical writers in referring to herself in the third rather than the first person.[92] Nonetheless, a self-portrait emerges from her dialogue that raises epistemological and social questions similar, in some important respects, to those raised by the saints de Pizan represents in part 3 of the *Cité des dames* and by the historical/mythical heroine de Pizan later eulogized in her *Ditié de Jehanne d'Arc* (1429). Porete's figure of a female soul—described in her prologue as "l'Ame touchee de dieu"—belongs to a socially problematic group of women who hear voices that they claim come directly from God. That is why Jean Gerson found Porete and her book worthy of attack.

The same medieval chronicler who calls Porete a *beguine clergesse,* and thus, I suggest, marks her as a key unnamed precursor for de Pizan herself, tells us of a historical woman who "went beyond and transcended divine Scripture" [avait trespassee et transcendee l'escripture devine].[93] Although that very phrase might well be applied to de Pizan's Proba and to the author of the *Cité des dames* herself, de Pizan "went beyond" and "trespassed upon" Scripture in ways more prudent, it seems, more acceptable to what her powerful contemporaries considered reasonable, than those used by Porete or by some of the saints represented in de Pizan's text. There is nonetheless a striking connection between de Pizan's use of her pen to attack men's "false" writings and the saint whom she represents as literally smashing her father's valuable idols and then giving the fragments to the poor for new uses—a detail mentioned neither in Christine's named source for the tale, Vincent of Beauvais's *Speculum historiale,* nor in another of her Latin source-texts for part 3, Jacobus de Voragine's *Legenda aurea.* That detail does appear, however, in a thirteenth-century poem of vernacular hagiography by Gautier de Coinci.[94]

A *bricoleuse* whose methods of compilation serve a highly original allegorical vision, de Pizan arguably alludes to her own writing practices through the image of a saint reusing fragments of cultural "idols" for new and morally beneficent purposes. This detail allies de Pizan's St. Christine with her brother Christ, as does the passage describing her miraculous ability to walk on water—a miracle mentioned neither by Vincent of Beauvais nor by de Coinci (*Cité*, 236; Fr., 2:1004).[95] In another fascinating portrait of the saint as rebellious daughter (and figure of the female author), de Pizan's St. Euphrosyna flees from her father to avoid being married off, enters a monastery where she dresses as a man and takes the hard-to-pronounce name of "Smaragdus," and refuses to disclose her identity when her father visits her many years later. Only after her death does the father learn the truth: the dead monk "held something written in his hand which no one could remove" except the father, who took the paper "and read within [*lut dedans*] how she was his daughter and that no one should touch her body to bury her except for him" (*Cité*, 245; Fr., 2:1017–18). Both St. Christine and St. Euphrosyna/Smaragdus, one through powerful speech that converts huge audiences, one through a written text read posthumously by a single man (and subsequently by de Pizan's readers), allegorize the female author as someone who imitates Christ and his Word—with all its mysterious power—while remaining strangely "outside the laws" of various figures of the father.

Part 3 of the *Cité des dames* presents the now-completed city itself as walled refuge for virtuous women threatened not only by the "foolish love" and lies of men but also, I suggest, by secular and theological laws that threaten to censor women who would speak or write a certain kind of Christian message. St. Christine's father assumes the role of judge and tortures his daughter horribly for her refusal to obey his rules about religious belief and practice; when he dies, his place is taken by a new judge named Dyon, who, after also torturing the girl, is replaced by yet a third judge, Julian, who orders that Christine's tongue be cut out because "she unceasingly pronounced the name of Jesus Christ" (*Cité*, 239; Fr., 2:1008). This is a nightmarish scene of censorship, but St. Christine miraculously transcends the censorer: "She spat this cut-off piece of her tongue into the tyrant's face [*celle cracha le coupon de sa langue au visaige du tyrant*], putting out one of his eyes. She then said to him, speaking as clearly as ever, 'Tyrant, what does it profit you to have my tongue cut out so that it cannot bless God, when my soul will bless him forever while yours languishes forever in eternal damnation? And because you did not heed my words, my tongue has blinded you, with good reason'" (*Cité*, 239–40; Fr., 2:1009). The figure of the paternal tyrant, significantly conflated with that of the judge, is confounded in an astonishing variant on an Oedipal punishment.

Not only passively resisting but actively avenging herself on an earthly father figure, de Pizan's St. Christine fulfills the potential for aggressive "malice" that we saw in de Pizan's portrait of Dido in part 1. As Dido looks like a lying thief of treasure to her (wicked) brother, so St. Christine seems—from the perspective of Urban and her other earthly judges—a dangerous "sorceress." Sometimes covertly—by intertextual revision—sometimes explicitly, the book repeatedly registers the existence of antithetical ethical judgments on most of its female heroines. A notable exception to this rule is the Virgin Mary, the "Queen" of the City of Ladies. The Virgin, however, is not represented as a speaker or allegorized as a writer; hence, she is exempt, as it were, from the complex economy of trial and punishment that centers on women's words, and for which economy the life of Christ himself, as crucified preacher and teacher, serves as a primary model. He was reviled; he was revered, and by increasing numbers after his death. In attempting to tip the balance toward the reverential pole of the ancient opposition reported by others, de Pizan arguably sought to extend Christ's empire; she sought at the same time to extend the territory occupied by word-wielding women, whether prophets relying mainly on oral transmission or writers relying on what Aphra Behn would call the female pen. This latter group includes the author who bore Christ's name in her own. Unlike Milton, she left no written record of spiritual wrestling with the possibility that self-love lurked like a snake in an authorial identification with Christ.

De Pizan's ambiguous and sometimes contradictory vision of a Christian-Amazonian community has as its institutional analogue not only the convent—the enclosed architectural space into which women can withdraw from the world—but also the city that aspires to grow into an empire. Remember Dido, to whom de Pizan obliquely likens her own fiction-making activity in the *Cité des dames*. Through that analogy, she boldly counters those who define female literacy as a sinful foray into a masculine domain of culture. In the Dido portrait, and in several other passages that use the motif of the sister stealing literal or metaphorical riches from her brother—Cornificia, for instance, and possibly even St. Christine—the book offers a strikingly unconventional and amoral perspective on female literacy. This perspective anticipates one described in Trinh T. Minh-ha's *Woman, Native, Other*. She recounts a story about how Lady Murasaki picked up Chinese by eavesdropping on her brother's lessons but was careful to conceal her knowledge. Pretending she could not understand a single character of this language, she wrote only in Japanese. "It was, indeed, less of an encroachment upon male privilege to write in the *native* language, which learned men of eleventh-century Japan considered to be vulgar (therefore a language suitable for a woman or a commoner)" (*Woman, Native, Other*, 19). Trinh sees Lady Murasaki as resembling Madame Lafayette in seventeenth-century France, who "studied Latin in secret (therefore stole culture) . . . whose maiden name was de La Vergne, [and who therefore] was associated with Lavernia, the Roman goddess of theft" (ibid.).

In their meditations on literate women as thieves of cultural treasure, de Pizan and Trinh seem to join rhetorical forces in celebrating and legitimating powerful women who steal from powerful men. In truth, however, both authors leave us with a more complex ethical and epistemological perspective on the question of female literacies and their cultural workings. For both authors place us in a disturbingly relativist landscape where privileged ladies who justifiably steal cultural goods from their male peers also steal, rather less justifiably, from those who are poorer than they are in cultural capital. De Pizan's unusual access to aristocratic patrons and to a language of learned allegory unavailable to a less "lettered" (and less prudent) woman like Na Prous Boneta invites us to see the parallel between de Pizan's act of writing and the act of cultural foundation performed by her character Dido.

Dido, we recall, exercises her prudent "malice" not only on her wicked brother but also on the original inhabitants of the African site upon which she wants to build her city. In a passage that eerily anticipates—by some eighty years—passages in Columbus's early letters describing the native Arawak Indians' gentle willingness to become colonial subjects, de Pizan describes how the inhabitants of Africa came to look, in wonder, at Dido's ship when it lands.

> After the people saw the lady and realized that her followers were men of peace, they brought them many provisions. And the lady spoke to them graciously and told them that, because of the good she had heard recounted about their country, they had come to live there, provided that the natives were agreed, who thereupon indicated their willingness. Pretending that she did not wish to make a very large settlement on foreign land, the lady asked them to sell her only as much land on the beach which a cowhide [*cuir de beuf*] would enclose. . . . This request was granted to her, and once the conditions of the sale were drawn up and sworn between them, the lady then demonstrated her cleverness [*scavoir*] and prudence: she took out a cowhide and cut it into the thinnest possible strips and then connected them together in a kind of belt, which she spread out on the ground around the port and which enclosed a marvelously large piece of land. The sellers were very surprised at this and amazed by the ruse and cleverness [*scens*] of this woman, but, nevertheless, they had to keep their part of the bargain. (*Cité*, 93–94; Fr., 2:773)

De Pizan's version of this story adds a fascinating image to the many earlier versions that had been written down before her, some of them subversively, as Christopher Baswell has shown, in the margins of copies of Vergil's own epic. Vergil renders the story in an enigmatic two lines that almost completely obscure Dido's agency as a leader with imperial ambitions; Vergilian annotators, copyists, and others in the pedagogical tradition stretching from late antiquity through the Middle Ages and beyond merged their accounts, paradoxically, with those by redactors of the non-Vergilian Dido in telling this story of the bull's hide (*byrsa*, in Vergil's text) in a way that stresses Dido's cleverness.[96] But none of the earlier redactors, to my knowledge, compares the cut-up bull's hide (interestingly regendered as a cow's hide in Richards's translation) to a belt. The image is ripe with meaning in the context of de Pizan's concluding images of female saints from whose chaste (closed) bodies issue boldly evangelizing words. In allying Dido's city-building ruse to the image of a chastity belt deployed to mark off territory appropriated from others, de Pizan offers a brilliantly feminized emblem for one of the central paradoxes of imperial nationalism as it will later operate in Protestant England. There, on a sea-girdled island often imaged as Queen Elizabeth's virgin body, Protestant intellectuals formulated visions of imperial expansion justified as a spreading of religious truth. In chapter 3, we saw such visions adumbrated in Shakespeare's *Henry V* and in Mulcaster's hopes for expanding the "reach" of England through the teaching of a (uniform) version of its language. Linda Gregerson explains the ideological project of English imperial nationalism in terms of a "foundational" tension "between a bounded community of fixed parameters and an expansionary community of unbounded mandate"; this tension increases exponentially, she adds, "when the community identifies itself, a priori or after the fact, as one of faith" ("Colonials Write the Nation," 169). Writing for a heterodox imagined community of faith at once within and outside the wider temporal and spatial domain of Catholicism, de Pizan gives us a Dido whose ruse of "belting" someone else's land looks retroactively prophetic, not only with respect to later historical instances of imperial nationalist ideology at work but also with respect to de Pizan's own carefully structured book: Dido's belted city-space becomes a "type" of the City of Ladies and the book that represents (and builds) it. In part 3 of that book, ruled by Lady Justice, the city is revealed to house virgins bearing an imperially expanding but revised version of Christ's Word.

De Pizan and the narrator of part 1, Rayson, seem to have nothing but admiration for Dido's cleverness, but the narrative of a nascent female foundation built on the dispossession of cultural "others" prompts me to return to the question of de Pizan's silence about female precursors, such as Na Prous Boneta and Marguerite Porete. The striking linkage of violent female self-censorship with the question of female precursors in part 2, and the return to the Philomela image of the tongueless woman in the St. Christine story of part 3, suggest an interpretation that supplements the ones sketched earlier in this chapter. Might de Pizan be "shadowing forth" the stories of unorthodox near-contemporaries in the stories of orthodox saints she borrows (ostentatiously) from clerics such as Vincent of Beauvais? I have argued that she deliberately

adapts typological methods of interpretation to her own dispersed presentation of certain narratives; might it not follow that she is at once veiling and
foreshadowing a "truth" too dangerous to speak in the present time through
her narratives of female saints and their dismembered bodies?

That seems to me a possible way of interpreting de Pizan's relation to certain female precursors who used their verbal powers in less prudent ways than
de Pizan did. At the same time, however, we must consider the possibility that
de Pizan's prophetic typology works not only to preserve but also to suppress
her heretical female precursors. However passionately her book defends an
abstract ideal of female virtue, it does so by appropriating and arguably "ac-
culturating"—for socially powerful readers—words spoken or written by historical women who had been more overtly critical than de Pizan was of the
quality of justice available in the "earthly empire" of France.

It is an irony of history that de Pizan's *Cité des dames* first appeared in print
in England, the great rival of French national-imperial designs. Her book was
translated into English over a century after it initially appeared in French—
and much later than many other of de Pizan's texts had been Englished,
printed, and shaped, as Jennifer Summit has persuasively argued, for gentlemen readers, or rather, for a "new breed of courtiers" seeking advancement
(*Lost Property*, 97). Published by Henry Pepwell, presented to the Earl of Kent
in Pepwell's preface, and there specifically said to be "by" Bryan Ansley, the
translator who was, in Pepwell's words, "Yoman of the seller / with the eight
kynge Henry," the book clearly appears as an object circulating "between
men."[97] Summit shows that Pepwell follows other male English appropriators
of de Pizan's work when, in his prologue to *The Boke of the Cyte of Ladyes*, he
renders the female author "marginal to the lines of masculine textual exchange
deemed central to the book's production" (*Lost Property*, 95); his prologue sit-
uates de Pizan's text in a "community that binds patron, translator, and
printer" beneath the "sheltering figure of the king." Summit's argument for a
striking revision of the book's "story of genesis" in its English version—a revision that includes an appropriation of the figure of the "prudent" woman
writer as an enabling model for laymen taking on new administrative roles in
the Tudor court—makes a valuable contribution to new research into de
Pizan's English reception.[98]

I want to supplement Summit's argument by offering a different answer
than she does to the question of why the English translation of the *Cité des
dames*, unlike de Pizan's other works, appeared just at the moment when, as
Summit notes, both Henry VIII and Pepwell's patron the Earl of Kent were undergoing a crisis of "biosocial reproduction."[99] At a moment when Henry was
"deeply concerned about his own reproductive troubles and lack of a legitimate heir," did Ansley and his publisher Pepwell perhaps desire to educate the

king and to be rewarded by him for bringing to England a book about the powers and virtues of female rulers (Summit, *Lost Property,* 99–100)? If so, there is no evidence that Henry actually read the book Ansley translated. Henry was famously more ready to crown his illegitimate son Fitzroy than his legitimate daughters. After Fitzroy's death, Parliament restored Mary and Elizabeth to the succession but not to legitimate status, and Henry's final will of 1547 preserved the ambiguity by allowing "our daughters Mary and Elizabeth" rights to "the sayd imperial Crowne" after the death of Edward and of any male heirs either he or Henry might have. Henry conspicuously described Edward—and only Edward—as "lawfully begotten."[100]

While showing how de Pizan's book was appropriated by and for English men, Summit and other scholars have unearthed new evidence that English women may have known, or known of, de Pizan's book about a city ruled by female saints with pagan queens in its foundation stones. On the tantalizingly incomplete evidentiary ground of records about the existence of tapestries that are now lost, for instance, Susan Groag Bell has argued that English women connected with the Tudor and Stuart courts may well have been able to view scenes from de Pizan's *Cité des dames* published in a visual rather than a textual medium.[101] We have no evidence of male or female readers' comments on copies of Ansley's translation, but Cristina Malcolmson has recently discussed evidence that manuscript copies of the original French text—with the question of the female writer's authority unmediated by an English printer—were available in sixteenth- and seventeenth-century England. She argues that educated women connected with the court could have read the *Cité des dames* in manuscript; among these possible readers would have been Margaret Cavendish, who may, with her husband, have owned the important Harley manuscript collection of de Pizan's work in the mid-seventeenth century (Malcolmson, "Christine de Pizan's *City of Ladies*"). Though we cannot be certain that Elizabeth Tudor herself knew the *Cité des dames,* this royal woman whose example informs so many seventeenth-century women writers' fantasies about female-ruled empires (including Margaret Cavendish's *New Blazing World* of 1667) certainly read a text by a later French woman writer named Marguerite de Navarre. A writer who was also a queen—albeit a married one—de Navarre had known, and had probably been served by, Elizabeth's mother Anne Boleyn.[102] At age eleven Elizabeth made the translation, mentioned earlier, of de Navarre's 1,700-line *Miroir.* This text is clearly indebted to a reading of Porete's *Mirouer des simples ames* and may also reflect a knowledge of de Pizan's *Cité des dames.*[103]

The connections among texts by Marguerite Porete, Marguerite de Navarre, Christine de Pizan, and Elizabeth Tudor are fascinating and shadowy. I cannot trace them here in either their empirical or their thematic dimensions, but I do want to suggest, in conclusion to this chapter and anticipation of the next, that potentially heretical ideas about religion and women's social roles, including queenship, seem to be closely interwoven into the English/French nexus sketched here. In this French/English connection, we can glimpse some but not all of the ways in which multilingual women with alphabetic literacy sought, through writing and no doubt through conversations as well, to educate some portion of a once and future audience about what queens, or potential queens, might do to reform the world. In this effort at reformation, theological and secular aims are intricately knotted, as they were in the nascent empire that Marguerite de Navarre saw her brother Francis attempting to enlarge in the late 1530s. In a piece of history de Navarre recreates in her *Heptaméron,* Francis filled some French ships bound for Canada with convicts and charged their captains to increase the dominion of the Catholic Church. His sister, dubious about this rationale for empire-building, sought to reflect critically and in a courtly metropolitan language on what true reformation, led by women, might look like at home and abroad. Among her readers was her daughter Jeanne d'Albret, who bitterly protested her status as a pawn in games of dynastic marriage played by her father, her uncle the king, and her mother. However, Jeanne was educated to be a queen, and she did exercise independent ruling power after her mother's death. She did so most significantly after the death of her second husband, Antoine de Bourbon, in 1562; entering the widowed state so imaginatively explored by Christine de Pizan, Jeanne signed herself "Reigne" and converted publicly to Calvinism, which she established, not without opposition from some of her subjects, as the official religion of Navarre in 1563.[104] In a letter of 1555, written six years after Marguerite de Navarre's death and three years before her *Heptaméron* was first printed, Jeanne d'Albret described her mother as "hesitating" between "the two religions" and as prevented from following Jeanne's own path of decision by powerful men, the husband who "slapped her right cheek and forbade her sharply to meddle in matters of doctrine" when he found her praying with Protestant ministers, and the brother who ordered her "not to get new doctrines in her head, so that from then on she confined herself to amusing stories."[105] Those *romans jovials* are not so light—nor such a turn from "matters of doctrine"—as Jeanne d'Albret's written words say they are. But dissimulation and the "deceits" of allegorical indirection were techniques that Jeanne d'Albret would have learned well from her mother's oral and written words, or from the words de Pizan wrote about queens such as Dido and Sheba.

Making the World Anew
Female Literacy as Reformation and Translation
in Marguerite de Navarre's *Heptaméron*

Theologiens ne aultres clers
Point n'en aurez l'entendement
Tant aiez les engins clers
Se n'y procedez humblement
Et que Amour et Foy ensement
Vous facent surmonter Raison,
Qui dames sont de la maison. . . .

Theologians and other clerks
you will not have the [necessary] understanding
no matter how clear your minds are,
if you don't proceed humbly[;]
and if Love and Faith together,
who are ladies of the house,
don't make you rise above Reason. . . .
MARGUERITE PORETE, prefatory poem addressed to
the reader in *Le Mirouer des simples ames*

Gracious Far-Near! Oh she who names you thus
Described you better, so it seemed to me,
Than many a learned man whose days were spent
In study of his books; I marveled then
How that could be—a lowly maiden's mind
So wondrously endowed with heavenly grace!
. . . For of His goodness he makes like Himself
The unworthy vessel where through grace He dwells. . . .
The spirit made me master of my books,
Who was their slave. . . .
MARGUERITE DE NAVARRE, *Les Prisons*

Like Christine de Pizan, Marguerite de Navarre appropriates both oral and written materials to construct an imperialist ideological project of her own—one that repeatedly stresses the need to restrain men's political and sexual ambitions.[1] Also like de Pizan, de Navarre at once opens and mystifies lines of communication among women across generational and class lines. In particular, de Navarre uses the figure of the wandering female religious person, or beguine, to decenter and implicitly critique a vision of empire advanced by the French monarchy and by the men of letters who served de Navarre's brother François I and his successor, Henri II. Drawing on the rhetoric of the Protestant Reformation to legitimize her vision of a Christian empire in which literate women play authoritative, indeed potentially governing, roles, de Navarre, like de Pizan, looks for inspiration to the subversive late medieval (and defiantly Catholic) example of Marguerite Porete. De Navarre's choice to recreate aspects of Porete's literary and historical example for new political and theological uses is crucial, I shall argue, to the revisionary project of imperial mapping I ascribe to the author—or, more precisely, to the writer, compiler, translator, and internal persona—of the book named *L'Heptaméron* after de Navarre's death.

De Navarre remained a practicing Catholic throughout her life, but like her mother, Louise de Savoie, and her daughter, Jeanne d'Albret, de Navarre was closely aligned with the Reformist movement in France. She translated Luther's 1518 commentary on the Lord's Prayer and was associated with the so-called Spiritual Libertines; during her life, she traveled quite far from various male authorities' views of orthodoxy in both her printed and manuscript writings.[2] Her first printed book of three long poems (1531) included the *Miroir de l'âme pécheresse,* modeled on Porete's *Mirouer,* as well as a passionate "Oraison" to Jesus Christ that begins with a free French translation of the Salve Regina, the Latin prayer to the Virgin Mary.[3] This volume offended Calvin as well as the Faculty of Theology at the Sorbonne; Calvin attacked the book as antinomian in his treatise *Against the Fantastic Sect of the Libertines,* and the Sorbonne theologians put it on the Index of prohibited books for a brief time in 1533, when its popularity among readers had been signaled by three new printings.[4] The first edition of the book contained numerous marginal passages from Jacques Lefèvre d'Etaples's French translation of the Bible; these may have upset the guardians of Catholic orthodoxy as much as or more than the book's theological statement.[5] The volume certainly emerged (and re-emerged) in the tense context of Reformist opposition to those Catholics who, in Lefèvre d'Etaples's words, "do not want the simple folk to see and read the gospel of God in their own language"; one of the 1533 printings of the *Miroir* included the printer's praise of new signs he was using—marks such as the apostrophe, the acute accent, and the cedilla—to make "the French language clearer, and easier to understand" for new readers of God's word.[6]

Like Porete's *Mirouer,* which was glossed and read as orthodox in England although it was condemned as heretical in France, de Navarre's first book shows how easily certain ways of producing and reproducing texts could "dilute the border between orthodoxy and unorthodoxy."[7] Political pressures

affected the border too; the prohibition against de Navarre's *Miroir* volume
was quickly withdrawn after her brother the king intervened. In the intellectually anarchic but socially stratified world of early modern religious dispute,
many evangelical reformers did not wish to leave the Church they sought to
cleanse.[8] In this setting, the denounced *Miroir* evidently said something of sufficient interest to metropolitan readers of various social positions and religious beliefs that it was reprinted seven times before 1539 (de Navarre, *Prisons*,
ed. Dale, ix). In 1544 the eleven-year-old Elizabeth Tudor wrote out an English
translation of the text to present to her new stepmother, Catherine Parr; four
years later the Protestant polemicist and nationalist scholar John Bale, for
complexly intertwined political and religious reasons, decided to capitalize on
Elizabeth's translation by having a copy of it printed in Wesel (a city in what
became Germany), with a prefatory letter and a conclusion by Bale himself.
Travel—across geographical spaces, times, languages, media, and socially constructed barriers between faiths—is central to my argument about de Navarre's literacy as an instrument of reform. I read one very short and seldom
analyzed story of the *Heptaméron* as a parable that illuminates significant aspects of de Navarre's theory and practice of literacy; the story does so by means
of a Bible-reading heroine who resembles de Navarre herself in certain ways.[9]
The heroine also recalls aspects of de Navarre's historical mother and daughter. Finally, she figures forth a Christianized version of Dido the wanderer and
a radically reformed, one might fairly say ascetic, version of Dido the empire-
builder. Dido the wanderer becomes Porete the beguine in de Navarre's unusual vision of empire. And the memory of Porete's death by fire—like Dido's
for a radically different love-object—arguably exerts considerable pressure on
de Navarre's project of extending France's empire for the sake of a God conspicuously served by women.

The heroine of the story in question, number 67 in the order of tales given
by the most authoritative manuscript of the work, is an unnamed woman
(more on her contested "historical" name later), allegedly from an artisanal
background that turns out also to be criminal. She embarks on a journey to
Canada led by Jean François de la Rocque, Sieur de Roberval. The journey is
interrupted, for her, by an experience of exile on an Atlantic island. The causes
of the exile are contested by several sixteenth-century writers, as we will see. In
de Navarre's version, the first to be published and evidently a deliberate revision of an oral narrative known to many members of her courtly circle, the
heroine, herself innocent, chooses to accompany her criminal husband to the
island after he has committed a treasonous act against Roberval. The wife actively uses her powers of speech to change Roberval's judgment of the case; she
persuades him to banish the husband to an island rather than executing him.

During the course of the tale, de Navarre's heroine changes status from virtuous wife of a criminal to virtuous widow first surviving alone on the island, then earning her own living through intellectual labor back in France. On the island, she becomes a kind of female Robinson Crusoe, though without a Friday.[10] She does, however, have a New Testament, and with its help—and that of a lion-killing "arquebus" she takes from her husband after his death—she ekes out a meager life from the island's harsh nature.[11] She is eventually rescued by seamen from one of Roberval's vessels. God causes the ship to sail by the island so that the woman's great virtue should not be "hidden" forever from the eyes of men; publishing her virtue, and through it, God's "glory," is evidently a major motive for de Navarre's revisionary act of storytelling. The seamen who rescue the heroine become corroborating witnesses, it seems, for a history they would have found "beyond belief" (*incroiable*) had they not learned through this woman's example of God's miraculous ways of nourishing his true servants.[12] Back in France, in the port city of La Rochelle—which is not necessarily the woman's original home—she finds a new way of living through her literacy. De Navarre defines "true" literacy, as Porete does, not simply as technical skills of reading and writing, but rather as the workings of God's spirit through the words (written but also oral) of his servants, especially his women. The women are figured as eager learners as well as teachers; at the end of Story 67, before the tale itself becomes an occasion for debate among the *Heptaméron*'s company, the heroine becomes a teacher to whom the ladies of La Rochelle send their daughters "to learn to read and write" (*Heptaméron,* 504; Fr., 394). Presumably, these daughters learn more than just basic literacy from this humble woman who has already demonstrated her authority as a minister to her husband and as a critical reader of Scripture. These daughters, I suggest, point to the multilayered and mixed-gender readers of the *Heptaméron* itself, persons who could learn, if they would, from de Navarre's own pedagogical practice of literacy.

De Navarre's Bible-reading colonist-castaway is, I argue, a significant figure for the female writer of the *Heptaméron* intervening in a field of emergent imperial discourse and doing so as a critical reader of other texts including the Bible. The heroine of Story 67 highlights the ways in which de Navarre modeled her authorial persona on the example of a female writer whose own allegorical heroine, the Amye, is apostrophized as "Gentil Loing Près" in de Navarre's *Prisons* (see the epigraph to this chapter). This poetic work was composed in the last years of de Navarre's life and was not printed until 1896, when Abel Lefranc discovered a copy in a manuscript also containing a text of the *Heptaméron.* The oxymoronic phrase *loing près* is central to my argument: I suggest that de Navarre's work as a writer—and as a revisionary reader of her culture—rings many important changes on the notion of "far-nearness" as it pertains to the intersecting spheres of geography, religion, and writing. God himself is Loing Près, as is the female servant of God whom de Navarre names in her poem as a kind of mother-of-letters. One modern critic maintains that de Navarre is theologically "orthodox" because she changes Porete's name for God from *Loingpres* to *Loing Près,* thus avoiding a heretical identification of God's "near" and "far" aspects by means of a space between letters that the critic has observed in a text printed from a manuscript not written in de Navarre's hand.[13] This is a very dubious way of rescuing de Navarre for Catholicism. The rescue depends on imposing a modern literate notion about alphabetic signification onto a textual situation too fluid to support such an inference. Those who label de Navarre a "Lutheran," a "Protestant," or a "spiritual libertine" are also on shaky ground, in my view, unless they discuss how her social position as a royal woman inflected her statements about religion in whatever mode of publication they appeared—statements that have come down to us in forms marked by various kinds of censorship. She was a public woman by virtue of her position as sister of the king; as soon as she said or wrote something, however privately, it became subject to use, suppression, and transformation in an enormously contentious discursive field.

Studying this field, we see that the written word itself participates in various paradoxes of "far-nearness." Writing, especially in works of biblical translation, is not only a medium for bringing the far and disputed Christian God—the Logos—near(er) to the reader; writing itself, as de Navarre reflects on its ontology, emerges as a kind of far-nearness, something at once alien and kin to the historical writer whose book of tales emerges from, represents, and transforms the acts of conversation it claims as its source. Courtly speech, the "matter" of the tales of the *Heptaméron* in a game that specifically excludes "men of letters" (*gens de lettres*) from participation, turns out, however, to be no less marked by the paradoxes of far-nearness than is the domain of writing; speech, in de Navarre's view as well as Derrida's, permeates the *différance* of writing, and vice versa.

In the course of using writing to conceive of and "translate" God—as Porete had done—de Navarre also uses writing to narrow geographical spaces, such as that which separates Paris or La Rochelle from an island somewhere off the coast of Canada—or from a provincial "border" territory such as Navarre. In his *Dames galantes* (c. 1684), Brantôme reports that his grandmother, serving as de Navarre's "dame de l'honneur," held her mistress's inkwell so that she could write her tales while traveling in her palanquin [luy tenoit l'escritoyre dont elle escrivoit].[14] De Navarre evidently wrote her stories—which she herself referred to as "Les Nouvelles de la reyne de Navarre," according to

Brantôme, while she traveled around the territory claimed by her brother the king.[15] More specifically, she journeyed from one to another of the several properties she controlled either in her own right—she was the Duchess of Berry, for instance, through a gift from her brother in 1517—or through her re-lations to her first and second husbands, the Duke of Alençon and the King of Navarre respectively. Her tales themselves bear a complex relation to travel; the frame story explains the genesis of the tales as a "pastime" adopted as a compromise formation by a group of high-born men and women stranded, as if on an island, by a flooding river interrupting their journey to a geograph-ical and political center, the court, from a peripheral place, the spa town of Cauterets in the Pyrenees, in the province of Navarre. The tales themselves seem in some respects like little islands or rest-stops in a wider narrative sea. Typically, the tales of the *Heptaméron* begin with the naming of a distinct place: "In the city of Valencia" [En la cité de Valence] begins Story 64 (*Hep-taméron*, 492; Fr., 383). "In the town of Dijon" [En la ville de Dijon] begins Story 17 (210; Fr., 134). Although de Navarre's text has not often been read as belonging to an imperial discursive arena that encompasses many texts de-voted to describing "exotic places," I suggest here that the *Heptaméron*—in its individual "chapters" and also in its frame story—merits consideration as an imperial travel text no less than do such near-contemporary works as Ra-belais's *Quart Livre* (1552) and André Thevet's *Singularitez de la France antarc-tique* (1557). Thevet, who served as the royal cosmographer during the reigns of François I and Henri II, published a different version of the story told in *Heptaméron* 67 about a French woman castaway on a Canadian island. Mary Baine Campbell observes that Thevet's habit of dividing his books "into isles, wonder-nuggets—in short chapters" recalls the *Odyssey*, which produces "an island for every marvel" (*Wonder and Science*, 33). De Navarre participates in this discursive tradition; her version of the castaway island story begins by de-scribing a voyage "en l'isle de Canadas" (*Heptaméron*, 503; Fr., 392). The con-fusion between continent and island does not simply reflect early gaps in car-tographical knowledge. On the contrary, de Navarre's custom of giving precise spatial and often temporal coordinates for her stories in their first sentences, along with her more extended description of a tale-telling locale in the pro-logue, makes "continental" geography into a discontinuous set of islandlike places including large towns, small villages, regions, provincial courts, and even churches. Sometimes the places are "in" France but are owned by aristo-crats whom de Navarre marks as having come from afar to serve the French king: "In the chateau of Odos, in Bigorre, there lived an equerry of the king, one Carlo by name, an Italian" [Au chasteau d'Odoz en Bigorre, demoroit ung escuier d'escuyrie du Roy, nommé Charles, Italien] begins Story 69, for in-stance (*Heptaméron*, 510; Fr., 398). De Navarre's way of siting her stories, usually but not always extremely precise, not only anticipates Thevet's "wonder nugget" chapters but also recalls Marco Polo's habit of writing chapters that "surround and contain individual cities or provinces (sometimes called isles) of Asia" (Campbell, *Wonder and Science*, 33).[16]

De Navarre shows us a European territory—including Austria and England (see Stories 31 and 57)—in which aristocrats continually journey from one place to another and in which the "central" part of France (the "Isle de France," as it was and still is known) is divided, as are the more peripheral regions, by issues and behaviors pertaining to religion, gender, and social status. The uniting solvent which this writer at once assumes (an ideological fiction) and deploys (an imperialist action) is language—a "modern" language of the French court that all the characters are presumed to understand and that translates (and clearly in some cases traduces and transforms) the words in many tongues, and from both oral and written sources, that de Navarre takes as the matter or natural landscape, as it were, to be transformed by her art, her culture. Sainte-Beuve's derogatory remark about her ("After all, when a woman writes, one is always tempted to ask, smiling, who's standing behind her" [Et puis, quand une femme ecrit, on est tenté toujours de demander, en souriant, qui est là derrière]) proves in one sense true: many men's verbal productions stand "behind" de Navarre's text, as do some verbal productions by historical women; as Dora Polachek has argued, however, the last laugh may be on Sainte-Beuve if one looks closely at just what de Navarre does to the texts by others that she rewrites.[17] She sometimes calls attention to her verbal appropriations, but often the revisions go unmentioned. It is then up to her readers to discern the intertextual jokes, some quite serious, that she repeatedly plays on her precursors and contemporaries. Imitation and an "illustrious vernacular" become her chief instruments for appropriating lands and peoples for her reformed vision of the French nation.

Deviating from the standard modern practice of referring to this writer as "Marguerite," I use the most familiar of her surnames, which signals not her place of origin but that of her second husband, to explore her socially constructed identities as wife and queen.[18] Despite its problems, this name has the virtue of calling attention to this writer's relation to a geographical territory that was claimed by both French and Spanish monarchs during the sixteenth century and which de Navarre's daughter Jeanne would inherit, and rule as queen, after her parents' deaths.[19] The historical Marguerite Valois (the one who lived from 1492 to 1549) carried during her life various names and titles associating her with various parts of the French kingdom.[20] Navarre is the territory now most commonly named with Marguerite, though she spent little time there until the 1540s.[21] A land far from the court that became near to Marguerite through a (troubled) marriage—and that also became near to her heart because of her daughter—Navarre was, in the sixteenth century, a contested place repeatedly claimed in name and divided in fact by monarchs of France and Spain. It is from this far-near territory that de Navarre's interlocutors are journeying back "home" (or rather, to various homes linked by their owners' ties to the monarchical court) when the *Heptaméron* begins.

Story 67 presents an image of female religious self-governance in an as yet worthless territory far from the metropolis, but if we read this story within the frames provided both by other early narratives of the woman castaway and by the stories—and metastory—of the *Heptaméron*, we can see de Navarre's interest in the potential of literate women ruling islandlike territories both far from and close to the kingdom's courtly center. De Navarre herself was clearly interested in the competitions for territory among various European kingdoms of her time. As Timothy Hampton remarks in his analysis of *Heptaméron* 10's contribution to the "chorographic marking out of national territory," Navarre changed hands "at least four times between 1512 and 1521" ("On the Border," 517n. 1). And Marguerite de Navarre's second marriage "marked an important stage" in the Franco-Spanish struggle: "by arranging for [Marguerite's] marriage to Henri, Francis I secured French Navarre. At the same time he promised (in vain) to recapture the rest of Henri's kingdom from Charles V Hapsburg" (Freccero, "1527: Margaret of Angoulême," 146). The *Heptaméron's* first sentence mentions "baths," like those of Rome, visited by people of leisure (and their servants) who come "tant de France que d'Espaigne." Parlamente's first tale (Day 1, Story 10) is set not in one locale but in several Spanish and French sites that become, in their shifting and multiplicity, an emblem for the divided loyalties—erotic, familial, political—the tale explores. Political disputes for territory, both at home and in the New World, are evoked, I think, by the allegorically charged name of the heroine of Parlamente's first story; the name, "Florida," recalls the female figure at the center of the *Romance of the Rose* (de Navarre's Florida is pursued by a man named "Lover" [Amadour]) as well as the tropical New World territory that Juan Ponce de León (c. 1460–1521) briefly explored in 1513, fully convinced that he had found the island of "Bimini" believed to contain a marvelous spring or fountain that would restore old men to youth.[22] He returned to the coast of Florida—as he soon named the country—in 1521, and many other Spanish explorers and colonizers followed over the next thirty years.[23] Who would possess Florida? Who would possess Navarre? What is the relation between desired (is)lands and the female bodies so often used as counters in disputes between monarchs seeking to expand their dominion? And what happens when a woman uses the pen to reflect on such property disputes?

These questions arise and intersect when de Navarre has Parlamente announce that her (French) version of the story of Florida and Amadour is a distinct revision, an appropriation, of an "original" told by a Spanish man presumably in some version of a Spanish language. The *Heptaméron*'s tale insists, conspicuously, on its status as a translation, a bringing of something "across" a border of languages, times, cultures, and geographical sites. Parlamente performs her retelling on a tale she attributes to a Spanish man praising a Spanish soldier who attempts to rape his beloved after years of frustrated "service" to her.[24] Stories of erotic conflict, in de Navarre's book, often comment on contemporary political conflicts that she viewed both from the perspective afforded by her status as sister of the monarch and from the still socially privileged but geographically marginal perspective afforded by her status as wife of the king of Navarre. Many people spoke versions of Spanish in this place; it was one of those "internal colonies," as discussed in chapter 2. The linguistic pluralism of this territory, however, is obscured though not erased by Marguerite de Navarre's "uniform" style of writing courtly French, which makes characters from different regions and social classes sound remarkably alike (through graphic representation of voice) even when their opinions differ greatly.

Reforming the Imperial Project:
Heptaméron 67 and Some of Its Intertexts

Born in the year Columbus arrived in America, de Navarre died less than a decade after her brother François had authorized Jacques Cartier to undertake a colonizing expedition to "the lands of Canada and Hochelaga, forming one extremity of Asia on the West," in order to "do something that is pleasing to God our creator and redeemer."[25] France's belated efforts to gain a share of the New World, like those of England, were notoriously ineffective throughout the sixteenth century.[26] Perhaps for this reason, and perhaps also because de Navarre's sole explicit comment on France's colonial attempts occurs in the form of a very short tale late in her supposedly unfinished book, she has not generally been read as contributing to the literature of early European colonialism.[27] I argue, however, that she did contribute and, in so doing, also participated, though from an unusual angle, in the emergent discourses of wonder and science. Assuming that the reader's initial response, like the sailors', will be disbelief, de Navarre attempts to transform the response into wonder about an amazing human sign of God's goodness. The virtuous French subject inhabiting an island is clearly a polemical comment on the kinds of marvelous objects, natural and human, that usually preoccupy writers describing the New World for Old World readers.

Offering an allegorical entrée into de Navarre's ideological project of a "reformed" imperialism, Story 67 is evidently one of the first reworkings in writing of a set of oral materials about an island assigned different names and locations by different sixteenth-century texts that circulated both in manuscript and in print to overlapping audiences. Even within one of these texts—which exists today in the hybrid form of manuscript and print—the island in question has at least four names and three different locations in the northern sea somewhere off the coast of Canada.[28] The island was evidently best known for its voices—strange sounds heard by mariners and ascribed by early texts either to "demons" or to "spirits"—and for its first human occupant, the woman of de Navarre's story who is a *demoiselle,* or gentlewoman, in the narratives about her by two other sixteenth-century writers, André Thevet and François de Belleforest. Belleforest tells the story in his *Histoires tragiques* (2d ed., 1572).[29] Thevet gives his versions (along with multiple names and different geographical coordinates for the island in question) in his *Cosmographie universelle* (1575) and his *Grand insulaire* (1586–87); the latter text has never been printed in full.

Thevet first mentions the island (under the name "Isle des Demons") in a travel-text printed in 1557, a year before the *Heptaméron* appeared in print. Thevet seems, however, not to have known the story of the island or, at the least, not to have grasped its narrative potential, until after reading de Navarre's account, which her male storyteller claims to have received directly from the mouth of the story's "captain" and "several of his crew" (*Heptaméron,* 502; Fr., 392). When Thevet claims in his *Cosmographie* and later in his *Grand insulaire* to have "known" the castaway story in the 1540s, soon after the events related in the story occurred, we can see him continuing a struggle for narrative ownership that is already intimated in de Navarre's own text; her male storyteller, named "Simontaut," may claim to have had the story directly from Roberval's own mouth and those of the unnamed (lower-class) crew members, but the story itself, as de Navarre gives it, locates moral and narrative authority not in the male captain but rather in the story's humble wife/widow. Perhaps it was the historical woman behind that heroine who spoke to de Navarre even if Roberval—well known in the courtly circle— spoke to the nobleman figured in de Navarre's storyteller Simontaut, about whom I shall have more to say later.

There are many complexities in the historical web of property, kinship, and royal "service" from which the story of the female castaway emerges—and through which de Navarre gives it an allegorical interpretation at odds, it seems, with the meanings ascribed to it by most of her contemporaries. Thevet boasts that he heard it from the noble Roberval, "mon familier," and from the heroine, who had "come to the city of Nontron, country of Perigord, when I was there."[30] After reading various versions of the tale in question, however, one realizes that the captain's oral version almost certainly would not have corresponded to the story the female castaway would have given of her sojourn on the island. Indeed, her version of the causes, main events, and results of her exile would evidently have differed from Roberval's no less significantly than Parlamente's version of Story 10 differs from that allegedly given by the Spanish man who initially possessed the tale as Amadour sought to possess Florida's virginal body. One of the most strikingly gendered inflections of de Navarre's literacy is her repeated suggestion that the property of a woman's "fame," her reputation in and through words, is no less disputed than the property of her body.

Inferring from the incomplete evidence in the historical record, we can see that the castaway narrative, extending across oral and written modes of publication and fractured *ab ovo* across lines of gender and social class, has two main lines of genealogical development. One focuses on the strange voices—allegedly of demons or spirits—emanating from the island and evidently reported by some of Cartier's or Roberval's sailors; this is the version that fascinates Rabelais and that he adapts, from an episode in Guillaume Postel's *De orbis concordia* (1543), in the well-known chapters on "les parolles gelées" in the *Quart Livre*. This book began to appear in print in the year of de Navarre's death and was printed in full in 1552; it is this later version that contains, in chapters 55 and 56, the story of the frozen words. In the other genealogical line, the center of the listener or reader's attention is the figure of the female castaway. Her social status and the reason for her exile vary dramatically in different versions of the story. In two of these, by Belleforest and Thevet, the frightening voices are a hallmark of the island even though the castaway is the main attraction. In de Navarre's version, the voices don't appear at all. If, however, one assumes that their alleged "existence" was known via word of mouth to at least some members of de Navarre's sixteenth-century audience, one could surmise that she silences the voices. Presuming intentionality and a concern with various modalities of censorship, one could then ask, as I do here, why the island's "other" voices are absent from de Navarre's scene, and why they are replaced by the voice of a woman who is alleged—but only in de Navarre's version of the tale—to have become a teacher of reading and writing to the daughters of "ladies."

To see her story as an ideologically complex intervention in an equally complex discursive arena—filled with voices in different languages and media, and with inflections partly determined by gender as well as class differences among the various "recorders" of the story—one needs to scan, at least briefly, the arena of discourse or, in an alternative metaphor, the sea of words in which many traveling writers compete to appropriate for their own purposes a marvelous island with a changing cast of inhabitants. In his version of the story, Rabelais locates the island at "the edge of the frozen sea" [le confin de la mer glaciale], where his heroes Panurge and Pantagruel hear (or think they hear) several strange voices "both male and female" [tant d'homes comme de femmes].[31] Questions about the credibility of such voices—and of the written texts, both sacred and secular, that discuss them—arise when the captain explains that the voices they are hearing are the "melting" remnants of shouts and cries actually produced during a great battle that occurred during the previous winter. "By God," Panurge cries, "I believe you. But could we see just one of them?" (*Quart Livre*, 568; Fr., 2:206). Pantagruel answers this doubting Thomas question by throwing on the boat's deck "whole handfuls of frozen words, which looked like crystallized sweets of different colors" (569; Fr., 2:206).[32] Rabelais traces how the voices carried "on the air" to the sea voyagers gradually become accepted as "real" and nearly simultaneously acquire, if not credibility of the sort claimed by the Bible, at least that facsimile of credibility which we might describe as credit: a quality that allows the words to appeal to and be bought by readers.

Once Rabelais's characters decide that the words are not merely projections of their own minds, "a ringing in our ears," the narrative mixes religious parody with an almost anthropological interest in the birth of commerce (567; Fr., 2:203). Panurge asks Pantagruel to give him some more of the delicious frozen words that sensuously melt in one's hands, "[b]ut Pantagruel answered that only lovers gave their words." "Sell me some, then," says Panurge (569; Fr., 2:207). The words, like the New World land from which they supposedly emanate, are revealed as in the process of becoming commodities. Rabelais's story of the frozen words, which melt pleasurably but nonetheless remain "incomprehensible" or "barbarous" to the Frenchmen, is a tragicomic allegorical meditation on a scene of ontological and economic translation (ibid.). If writing is a way of "freezing" spoken words so they may communicate across time and space, such communication, Rabelais darkly suggests, comes from a scene of war among the Others on the island, the Others whom we never see. The remnants of their battle, however, may well lead to another scene of war, Rabelais suggests, via the related cultural activity of competitive buying and selling. Pantagruel refuses to let Panurge buy the foreign words and refuses also to let the narrator hoard them (he wants to "preserve a few of the gay quips in oil" and, of course, has already preserved them for the reader in letters, preempting Pantagruel's prohibition). With a searching glance at the historical wars of religion occurring in France, Pantagruel prudently expresses his preference for selling silence rather than words (569; Fr., 2:207). Concerns about political and religious censorship, as well as about the strange ontology and emerging sociology of writing, shine through Rabelais's playful words about words, including "bloody" ones that "sometimes return to the place from which they come, but with their throats cut" (569; Fr., 2:207).

De Navarre, unlike Rabelais, seems uninterested in rumors about the island's mysterious voices. Questions about oral and written media of communication, however—and about deathly punishments and about the kind of "credit" one gives to sacred and secular texts—are no less intricately woven into her account of the island than they are into Rabelais's. Both writers give early written translations of materials generated by the first official set of French colonial voyages, a set of three expeditions usually discussed, by modern historians, as led by Cartier in 1534, 1536, and 1541.[33] The final voyage, to which de Navarre's story refers more directly than Rabelais's, ended only in 1545; her tale was probably written soon after the voyagers returned home with their news.

De Navarre offers an "unofficial" perspective on the royal imperial enterprise from the beginning of the tale, the moment when she names one "captain Robertval" [sic] and several of his crew ("companie") as the oral sources for her written narrative.[34] She goes on to describe how the king himself appointed Roberval leader ("chef") of an expedition to the "island" of Canada, an expedition that carried "artisans of all types" to "populate the land with Christians" (Heptaméron, 503; Fr., 392). Among these "artisans," as she calls them (the French word is the same as the English), are a poor man and his wife. Through the character of the wife, de Navarre subtly critiques certain aspects of what was already becoming "official" imperialist rhetoric.

Two details mentioned in the story's first paragraph—that Roberval was the leader and that the colonists were artisans—carry important hints of the critique elaborated in the tale. Roberval was not the sole leader of the expedition; he was appointed to lead jointly with Cartier, and the arrangement, as one might suspect, produced tensions between the two men. Roberval outranked the now better known Cartier and was clearly brought in because Cartier alone did not seem capable of realizing the king's hopes for this third voyage, which, as one commentator remarks, was to be a voyage "d'une veritable colonisation" rather than a voyage of "exploration."[35] De Navarre's description of Roberval's orders ("to stay in Canada and establish towns and forts") offers a concise echo of the doublet-filled document of appointment drawn up by the king's chancellery for Roberval. That document directs him to "build and erect [towns, fortresses, and habitations] in the said countries and to install inhabitants in them" (Cartier, Voyages, 146). Delicately acknowledging that Roberval carried out only "the first steps" of these orders, de Navarre's text begins to probe the relation between official versions of a story and other possible renderings of it.

François's letter commissioning Cartier appoints him "captain general and master pilot," while the letter commissioning Roberval, written a few months later, describes his position as "lieutenant general, head, leader, and captain of the said enterprise" (Cartier, *Voyages*, 136, 145). It is not surprising that the written evidence shows Cartier at one point simply refusing to accept Roberval's authority.[36] Having started their joint voyage at different times, with different sets of ships, the two captains met in Canada just as Cartier was leaving to return to France with some ore that he claimed was gold (it turned out to be copper, an apt symbol for the series of "grand disillusions" associated with Cartier's three expeditions).[37] Roberval ordered Cartier to return to the "colony" that they were jointly to found, but Cartier disobeyed. According to the account published in English (and only in English, by Richard Hakluyt, although Cartier and Rabelais have both been named as authors), Cartier and his company wanted the "fame" of being first home with the news of discoveries along the St. Lawrence—and, one presumes, with the gold that Cartier suspected would greatly interest the king.[38] "[M]oved as it seemeth with ambition, because they would have all the glory of the discoverie of those partes themselves, [Cartier's company] stole privily away" from Roberval and returned to France (Cartier, *Voyages*, 108–9).

By mentioning Roberval but not Cartier—who was already famous as the leader of the two earlier expeditions—does de Navarre's story subtly support Roberval's claims for authority (and fame) over those of Cartier? We cannot know how members of her contemporary audience would have interpreted this aspect of the tale, but she does stress that the knight Roberval, Cartier's social superior, is "well known" to many of the initial privileged group of *Heptaméron* tale-tellers, and her own tale certainly engages thematically with issues of competition for the leader's role and with the problematic relation between fame—as public knowledge of one's deeds—and a mode of humble leadership that serves God's empire.

De Navarre introduces a major element in her critique of worldly imperialism when she refers in her opening paragraph to Roberval's company as "artisans" sent to populate the New World territory with "Christians": "Et, pour habituer le pays de chretiens, mena avecq luy de toutes sortes d'artisans" (*Heptaméron*, 503; Fr., 392). The clause admits of two interpretations: the French artisans are themselves Christians who will populate the New World for the Christian God; alternatively, the French artisans will serve as missionaries to the natives, converting them to Christianity and thus populating Canada with (new) Christians. Both interpretations are ironically undermined by the fact that François actually authorized Cartier to remedy a population problem nearer to home that was threatening the expedition. There were simply too few French people willing to become colonists in Canada, and therefore the king looked to stock his expedition with involuntary colonists. Cartier was specifically charged to look to the prisons and to draw his colonists from those criminals who had already been condemned to death and who had not committed crimes of heresy, lèse-majesté, or counterfeiting.[39]

De Navarre arguably plays on her contemporary audience's knowledge of the criminal element among the emigrants when, immediately after mentioning the artisans "of all types," she describes one of them as "so unhappy that he betrayed his master and put him in danger of being taken by the natives of the country" [si malheureux, qui'il trahit son maistre et le mist en danger d'estre prins des gens du pays] (my translation; Fr., 392). The line between being miserably imprisoned in France and being imprisoned in the New World—by one's leader or by the natives—becomes blurred here in a way that reminds us of de Navarre's lifelong interest in the prison as a metaphor for earthly life. The crime of betrayal of a master points to the gap between the official rhetoric of colonial legitimation, motivated by desires for wealth and for political advantage over Spain, and the historical reality concerning who actually went to New France as part of the expedition of 1540–42. Many of those people, high as well as low born, were "Christians" only in name. In the letter commissioning Roberval, the king had defined a colonizing enterprise aimed at "the augmentation of our Christian faith and the growth of our sainted mother the Catholic church" [l'augmentation de nostre foy chrestienne et l'accroissement de nostre mere saincte eglise catholique].[40] In its spare first paragraph, de Navarre's story suggests that something is rotten in the state of France and in its methods of appropriating new territory for God's empire through men of all ranks who seem inclined to serve their own ambitions rather than their master's.

God, she tells us, wishes the artisan's crime of betrayal to be quickly "uncovered" (congneue) (Heptaméron, 503; Fr., 392) before it can harm Roberval. The traitor's wife, however, intervenes at this point to plead for mercy, and with this unnamed character, de Navarre herself intervenes in a field of contested cultural knowledge. In her story, the heroine is poor, pious, eloquent, and morally unblemished. In the oral narrative de Navarre is arguably countering—the version evidently elaborated by Belleforest and Thevet—the heroine is well born, a demoiselle who is a "relative" of the expedition's captain (a sister, according to Belleforest; a niece, according to Thevet's account in the Grand insulaire, where he also reveals her name to be—coincidentally?—Marguerite). She is guilty of "betraying" her brother/uncle Roberval by her decision to take a lover on board ship. Belleforest's and Thevet's female castaway is thus not only of high social standing; she is also, in the men's versions, guilty of a typically female crime of passion. Betrayal is at the heart of all the sixteenth-century versions of the story (and many of the later ones, including modern film versions, as well), but the different versions construe the betrayer's gender differently.[41] Only de Navarre insists that the main crime is committed by the lover/husband figure and is a political crime of treason against a leader who reveals himself to be something of a tyrant. Thevet, who has much less sympathy toward the heroine than Belleforest does, also shows the crime to be political in the sense that it is an offense against patriarchal property rights. The criminal case remains as unresolved in the discursive arena as it probably was in the historical and familial nexus we can only partly discern.

In the male writers' accounts, the woman commits a crime with a lover who is never named; de Navarre gives the quality of namelessness (which saves the character's reputation) not only to the male transgressor-figure (whom she remakes as a husband) but also to the heroine, whom she recasts as a legitimate wife. Belleforest and Thevet differ in the way they judge the (alleged) illicit erotic relation; Belleforest, in line with his more romantic perspective, defines the affair as a kind of "common law" marriage, while Thevet writes indignantly of "wanton and shameless passions" in "this illegitimate and libidinous union." Still, both male writers show Roberval being much more angry with his female relative than with her seducer.[42] Her crime of passion is clearly legible, by some among de Navarre's initial audience, as a crime against aristocratic property and against the male family leader's right to dispose of his female relative's body as he sees fit. In Belleforest's and Thevet's texts, the errant lady's lover gallantly accompanies her into the exile decreed by Roberval for her, but not, it seems, for him. Along with an old female servant, the couple survive in hardship until the birth of an illegitimate child, the sign of the woman's crime.

Belleforest calls attention to the problem that encircles this narrative about a New World voyage "interrupted" by an experience of island exile that neither produces nor discovers any material wealth whatsoever. The problem has to do with the commodification of knowledge and with the question of who has the rights—or the power—to purvey it. Among the persons making the voyage to the New World with Cartier, Belleforest writes, was a gentleman "whose name I know, & which I am purposely withholding." Here the writer emphasizes the social hierarchy he is using his literacy to support; at the same time, he uses his literacy to incite desires for new (social) knowledge among readers excluded from the courtly group defined as epistemologically as well as socially privileged—and as accessible to the writer but not to most of his readers (then or now). Thevet puts less weight than Belleforest does on the (titillating) discrepancy between his insider's knowledge and that of most of his readers; Thevet instead is obsessed with the question of who has first rights to the narrative properties at issue. "I know well," he writes at the end of the *Cosmographie* account of the castaways, "that some hare-brained wags, after hearing me talk about it, as indeed happened, have added to it follies and lies, which they have stuck into their fables and tragical stories, stolen from here and there" (fol. 1020r; cited and translated in Stabler, *Legend of Marguerite de Roberval*, 18). Stabler thinks that Thevet is referring here to Belleforest, who "scooped" the story by going into print with it before Thevet did.[43] Stabler assumes that Thevet would not have "committed the lèse majesté" of referring to Marguerite de Navarre as a "hare-brained wag."[44] I contend, however, that de Navarre's writerly as well as political authority is very much an issue for both Thevet and Belleforest—and perhaps for Rabelais as well. Whose version of this story will be most widely circulated in the emergent nation—and whose will be believed? De Navarre's ambitions for her literacy, inflected both by her religious beliefs and by her desires to reform the institution of aristocratic marriage in the direction of greater justice for women, contribute, I think, to her decision to (re)make her heroine as a commoner. The implied audience for the tale is extended to a print readership that could include women like the heroine herself.

When read in relation to Belleforest's and Thevet's narratives, which despite their differences both focus the reader's attention on the heroine's noble body, de Navarre's story looks like a series of opportunities missed, narrative riches *not* developed. The tale seems ascetic, from a modern point of view, oddly repressive, in its handling of the castaway materials. What happens, however, if we (modern) readers grant a literate intentionality to de Navarre's narrative practices read in an intertextual context? Nicole Cazauran does just that when she suggests that de Navarre uses the stylistic "austerity" of this tale to effect a deliberate turn against the generic and experiential paths signaled by the French word *romanesque* (*"L'Heptaméron" de Marguerite de Navarre*, 189). I would add, however, that de Navarre's austerity—a function not only of style but of an implicitly revisionary relation to an oral archive—has political and economic dimensions interwoven with its protest against common views of women's sexual nature and verbal authority. Not exploiting the "voices" of the island that so intrigued Rabelais as signs of "barbarian" inhabitants, not exploiting the *romanesque* resources of the allegedly historical materials, de Navarre is arguably pursuing ideological ends of her own. These are interrelated and can only be sketched here. One has to do with articulating—

prudently—a critical perspective on her brother's official project of colonization; another has to do with sending a message—perhaps apologetic, perhaps
cautionary—to her recently married daughter Jeanne. This intimate reader's
second marriage—though not her mother's strenuous opposition to it—is
mentioned at the outset of Story 66.

The implicit critique of imperial expansion is limited but nonetheless interesting; it consists mainly, I suggest, of an act of rhetorical purging directed
against the religious hypocrisy of many royal narratives legitimizing New
World colonization. De Navarre's heroine saves her husband, at least temporarily, from the death he deserved for betraying the king's representative in
the New World. Although the reprieve is only temporary, the time the wife
buys for her erring husband allows her to attend to his spiritual reform, and
the time allows de Navarre to imply that the husband's crime may be less
against royal authority than against his wife's feelings and reputation. Subversively imitating descriptions of the colonizing process given in the official documents drawn up by the literate men serving the king, de Navarre's tale opens
veins of cultural irony untouched in other versions of the story. Just as poor
French prisoners were freed by order of the king to go to a colony that may
have looked to them like another cold and badly provisioned prison, so the
man in de Navarre's story is freed by Roberval, the king's representative, to go
to an "alternative" colonial site, a small island, off the coast of the main "island" of Canada. This one is inhabited not by "savages"—as Cartier repeatedly
refers to the Iroquois—but only by "savage beasts," a concept that de Navarre's
book repeatedly associates with the lusts of French men. Her tale offers, with
regard to official documents, repetition with a difference—and the key difference is not the absence of human "savages" but rather the fact that the governor's decision about appropriate punishment for the husband-criminal is influenced by a humble woman. The official documents about Cartier's and
Roberval's voyages to Canada mention no women at all in politically influential roles, though women are among the French colonizers and also among the
"gifts" that Iroquois men give Cartier at various points in his vastly troubled
encounter with native Others.[45] In de Navarre's colonial tale, however, a female
character not only shapes the main political plot but effectively co-authors it.

Acceding to the wife's plea, Roberval lightens the husband's punishment
(if life on a bare colonial site is regarded as preferable to death, a proposition
that many who have been sent to penal colonies might dispute) by allowing
both him and his wife to be left, with minimal supplies, on an island inhabited only by "des bestes sauvaiges" (Heptaméron, 503; Fr., 393). Like an improved version of Eve, the wife "labor[s] alongside her husband"; they build
a hut and succeed in killing threatening animals, he with his "arquebus," she
with the more primitive weapon of stones. Although they are able to eat the

flesh of the animals they have killed, the husband nonetheless becomes sick and dies. There is some suggestion that his death is a punishment for his sins, since he becomes ill from "the water *they* had to drink" (504; Fr., 393, my emphasis). His sinless wife, drinking the same water, lives on to pursue her "incessant" labor—the reading of the New Testament.

Her creator arguably used this story itself to perform an act of peculiarly Protestant literacy, making her story analogous to the New Testament in its work of fulfilling and implicitly reforming a passage from the Old Testament (as Christians call it). The scriptural subtext—not, to my knowledge, remarked by editors or critics of the *Heptaméron* but quite legible, I suspect, to female readers versed in the tactics of biblical dispute illustrated in the "commentary" section of this very story—comes from Num. 5:12–31. This is a passage describing just the kind of quasi-magical "test" for a wife suspected of adultery that an incipiently Protestant female reader might have found problematically superstitious as well as unjust. De Navarre's story remedies the problem of equity by ascribing an originary crime of betrayal or infidelity to the man rather than to the woman. De Navarre's tale thus uses intertextual irony—with regard to the ur-text of the Bible as well as the disputed histories of the castaway couple—to support a brief in defense of the wife. In de Navarre's tale, a husband "becomes so swollen" [devint si enflé] from the island's water that he dies; he thus undergoes just the fate prescribed for an unfaithful wife in Num. 5:20–21. There God is reported as explaining to Moses what should be done if a husband suspects his wife of being "polluted" through adultery. If he even so much as feels a "spirit of jealousy" coming over him, the wife should be brought before a priest (*sacerdos* in the Latin text of the Vulgate). He will give her bitter water to drink, mixed with dust from the temple floor, and will say to her (in Tyndale's English version of 1530): "If thou . . . art defiled and some other man hath lien with thee besides thine husband. . . . the Lord make thy thigh rot, and thy belly swell, and this bitter cursing water go into the bowels of thee, that thy belly swell and thy thigh rot, and the wife shall say Amen, Amen."[46] The biblical passage allows at the outset for the possibility that the husband rather than the wife may have gone astray (5:12); the text also allows for the possibility that the wife may be proven innocent by the water-drinking test. If she is "clean," her belly will not swell and she will be able to conceive children—and thus have the right kind of swelling—in the future (Num. 5:28). Given that a woman is the only example of a person "tried" by the bitter water test, however, and that the test is said to occur if a husband merely imagines his wife is tainted, the story is skewed against the wife so strongly that one early modern female reader felt impelled to rewrite the source text with new kinds of water in sight.

De Navarre revises the biblical test in part by naturalizing and rationalizing it; she removes the role of the priest (*sacrificateur* in the 1535 French text) as a "mixer" of the dust and bitter water. Indeed she excises the biblical priest from any position of authority in the working out of divine justice. All intermediaries between the natural and supernatural realms—the "demons" or "spirits" of other textual and presumably oral versions of the island-story—are banished from de Navarre's narrative; in this ascetic space, only the text of the New Testament (and the author's own allusively revised version of the Hebrew Scripture) mediate between the heroine and her God, on the one hand, and between the writer and her readers, on the other.

De Navarre's narrative frees the castaway woman from any taint of sexual crime; this revisionary reading of the Bible therefore counters the charges made against the (historical) castaway by the men who first told and wrote down her story. For readers of either sex and with different kinds of literacy, de Navarre makes an Old World wife removed to a bare New World setting into a figure for the salvific (and liberatory) powers of Bible reading. The wife's innocence is both proclaimed (for new readers) and refashioned (for readers who know the Old Testament) from a physical to a spiritual phenomenon. Her spiritual innocence, of course, would be invisible to men chiefly concerned with chastity as a property or commodity. Accused (and through the birth of the illegitimate child, convicted) of sexual impropriety in other versions of the tale, the wife here becomes a righteous widow who "conceives seed" through her teaching of the Word to others, not through her literal bearing of children. In de Navarre's redemptive and here quite subversive vision of the institution of marriage, the wife/widow has no child but the Word.

The socially as well as hermeneutically radical thrust of de Navarre's revision of Numbers appears when the wife is allowed (evidently by God) to assume roles usually reserved for men, once the husband's (God-given) illness-by-water makes him relinquish his worldly position as master in the stripped-down society of the New World island. Like Christine de Pizan's saintly widows, however, the heroine of de Navarre's Story 67 remains a humble servant of God even as she usurps masculine authority. While her husband is dying, for instance, she becomes his "physician and confessor" (*Heptaméron*, 504; Fr., 393). So effective is she in the priest's role that the husband—we are told—goes joyously to heaven despite his unnamed sins and the named one of "betrayal" that makes him such a prime candidate for a revised version of the biblical jealousy test.[47] After he dies, the wife heroically protects his buried remains from hungry beasts by appropriating his weapon. Depriving not only the beasts but also herself of flesh, it seems, she is described as becoming increasingly emaciated in body while her soul's sustenance takes up more and more of her time. Eventually, she spends "all her time in reading the Scriptures, in contemplation, prayer, and other devotions" (504; Fr., 393). It looks as if she is ready to follow her husband in the journey from the "desolate island"—increasingly allegorized as earthly life itself—to heaven, described as "la celeste patrie" (ibid.). That final voyage is deferred, however, when the sailors find the heroine and take her back to France, an earthly and inferior *patrie*.

Why is the heroine rescued from a symbolic New World landscape that looks like a penal colony but is also twice described as a "dessert," recalling the landscape where Christ resisted the devil's temptations (Fr. 393, 394)?[48] The story suggests that her rescue is part of a providential plan to publicize her virtue and thus to educate others; the educative mission is in turn aimed at reforming her country's imperial mission. The latter goal entails making the French "back home" rather than the Indians "out there" the primary audience for the woman's (and de Navarre's) proselytizing discourses.

The geographical shift of the imperial mission, also an ideological shift, is marked by de Navarre's gender, and by her interpretation of it as causing unjust disempowerment despite the privileges she enjoyed as a member of France's ruling family. Her critical perspective, marked by what might fairly be called a gendered *ressentiment*, appears in the paradoxical absence—or perhaps, transformed presence—of the indigenous Americans in de Navarre's version of a colonizing story. As Elaine Ancekewicz has argued, de Navarre's heroine virtuously eking out her minimalist "culture" on the hostile nature of the island stands in strange relation—part resemblance, part contrast—to the image of the "savage" Huron women often given in early Jesuit descriptions of indigenous Canadians and also in Thevet's and Belleforest's texts. There, the figure of the indigenous woman typically "represents resistance" to the "new French and Christian order."[49] Standing in, as it were, not only for the male agents of French colonization but for its usually recalcitrant female "pupils" or objects, de Navarre's woman is a complex ideological construction; the tale, for all its implied criticism of the hypocrisy of the colonizing enterprise, participates in it by appropriating the position (and cultural reputation) of the Native American Other for a European woman's purposes. De Navarre's unnamed heroine, and not the king or his colonizing captain, is shown "augmenting" the Christian faith and thus increasing the spiritual territory held by "our sainted mother, the church"—or rather by the reformed version of that institution limned in de Navarre's text.

To carry out her imperial task, she usurps the roles of teacher and preacher that St. Paul had reserved for men, and that Spanish priests had actually begun to fill in New World sites. She begins her pedagogical and evangelizing work when still on her island, but her pupils there, interestingly, are not "natives," as the official rhetoric of converting the heathen suggests they might be, nor are they the "savage beasts" who occupy the structural role of Indians on the allegorical New World island. Instead, and arguably with a polemical corrective force, the story defines the women's pupils first as Old World men—French men—and then as Old World (French) women: those who are nominally already Christian, but whom the text here and elsewhere suggests are in desperate need of spiritual renewal.

The wife's first pupil is her husband, whose confession she hears and whose soul she evidently cleanses, with God's help. Her second audience is composed of the French crew members who rescue her—but only after undergoing a brief but powerful experience of religious instruction at her hands. The instruction appropriates—or, more precisely, from a religious perspective, justly reappropriates—a type of wonder typically prompted by New World phenomena in the burgeoning genre of travel narratives to which this story alludes and which it seeks to reform: "Giving thanks to God, she led them into her humble abode, and showed them how she had been living. They would have found it beyond belief, without the knowledge that God is almighty to nourish His servants in the barren desert even as in the finest banquets in the world" [Apres avoir rendu louange à Dieu, les mena en sa pauvre maisonnette, et leur monstra de quoy elle vivoit durant sa demeure; ce que leur eust esté incroiable, sans la congnoissance qu'ils avoient que Dieu est puissant de nourrir en ung desert ses serviteurs, comme aux plus grans festins du monde] (*Heptaméron*, 504; Fr., 394).

Without specifying exactly what about her mode of life generates such wonder among the crewmen—is it that she has survived on so little, like a saint in the desert, or that she has fought off beasts with a man's "arquebus"?— the narrative makes her an exemplum of God's power and a test of religious belief. Her audience here is men; her instruments of instruction are her voice and, presumably, her body, the "evidence" of her miraculous life. When she returns to France, however, her audience is figured as upper-class and female; now, her instruments of instruction become the book and the pen rather than the voice and the body.

Back in France—but a France implicitly defined as merely a temporary substitute for the true homeland or *patrie*—the heroine of Story 67 is "received with great honour by all the ladies." And it is the ladies who provide the heroine with a means to live, for the wife newly turned into a widow has apparently returned from the New World no richer than she was when she set out—an ironic allusion, perhaps, to French colonizers' dreams of wealth, which went almost entirely unfulfilled during the sixteenth century. The ladies of La Rochelle "[were] glad to send their daughters to [the widow] to learn to read and write" [voluntiers luy baillerent leurs filles pour aprendre à lire et à escripre] (*Heptaméron*, 504; Fr., 394).

Among de Navarre's first readers was her daughter Jeanne d'Albret, who in the passage I quoted at the end of chapter 4 described her mother turning to "romans jovials" when her husband and brother berated her for meddling with matters of religious doctrine. Jeanne d'Albret also, however, "commissioned the first authorized edition of her mother's stories in 1559," as Carla Freccero points out, and shortly thereafter, converted publicly to Calvinism ("Archives in the Fiction," 87). If I am right that Story 67 was partly written for the daughter named as newly (and happily) married in Story 66, the final image of mothers sending daughters to learn to read seems pregnant with private meanings. Whether the tale carries a symbolic apology for the "crimes" of betrayal Jeanne had accused her own mother of committing (on behalf of fathers and uncles and—in general—men like Roberval), or whether it carries a warning against relying too heavily on husbands for one's material or spiritual well-being, I can only guess.[50] The tale does seem to imbue with both private and public meanings its image of a community of mothers and daughters who thrive on, and transmit to each other, a specifically religious kind of literacy that construes female "nature" differently from the way in which it was commonly construed in men's words, both spoken and written.

De Navarre's story displaces onto a traitorous husband a crime that other texts attributed to a young noblewoman. The story also offers an image of a woman undergoing a painful "trial" on an island—a trial that appears, in retrospect, a preparation for a governing position back home, insofar as the ideal governor needs powers of self-mastery and of persuasion. The materially poor but spiritually rich woman of de Navarre's fiction thus reforms—ironically, before the official "printing" of her existence—the *demoiselle* whom Belleforest and Thevet represent as refusing to obey her uncle's wishes. This gentlewoman, manipulated by men at various levels of her strange discursive existence, was named Marguerite, according to the king's cosmographer. In ignoring or censoring that allegedly historical name, Marguerite de Navarre was, I suspect, sending an ironic and coded message to her present and future readers. We can decode the message only in part, but it seems fair to say that the hero of Story 67 serves, as Parlamente does, to represent the female author herself as well as the daughters and mothers, historical and figurative, among her imagined readers.

Story 67 in Its Narrative Frame

To understand more fully what the story says about ideologies of gendered literacy and empire, we need to consider how the tale is generated and received in the metastory of the *Heptaméron*, the evolving narrative of the interrelations among the speakers, and particularly, for my purposes here, the drama with two spiritually ambitious women at its center: Oisille, the oldest woman in the group, who serves as its spiritual mother, and Parlamente, the group's highest-ranking woman, who has often been read as a figure for de Navarre herself.[51] Both characters represent aspects of female literate authority as de Navarre reflected on and practiced that phenomenon; and both characters are partly mirrored in the heroine of Story 67. The heroine's allegorical meaning is yoked to the larger narrative's reflections on Oisille and Parlamente as women who exercise verbal and political authority, sometimes covertly, in the mixed company of tale-tellers.[52] The heroine's allegorical meaning is also yoked to our assessment of the character of the man who tells the tale, Simontaut.

His very name signals that he is sexually and politically ambitious; the name could be translated "thus [or "if"] one mounts on high." From the prologue onward, we catch glimpses of him as one of two courtiers apparently seeking the favor of Parlamente. His story about Canada is introduced as a direct refutation of a point about men in general made by Ennasuite, a young woman who seems to be erotically interested in Simontaut, as he is interested in Parlamente.[53] Ennasuite is the teller of Story 66, about a comic mistake in which an old servant woman mistakes a newly married high-born woman—none other than de Navarre's daughter Jeanne—for a "young lady of the house" carrying on an illicit affair with a man who "bore the office of protonotary apostolical" (*Heptaméron*, 501; Fr., 391). The mistake leads Jeanne and her new (second) husband to laughter as well as to increased knowledge about the noble household in which they are guests. The marriage of the "princesse de Navarre" in "Vendosme," the estate of the new husband, is mentioned in the first clause of Story 66, and this is the single explicit mention of Jeanne d'Albret in the *Heptaméron*. The marriage, which occurred in 1548, less than two years before de Navarre's death, is presented by Ennasuite as an occasion not only of joy but of implied reconciliation between the daughter and the parents with whom she had fought so bitterly about both marriages.[54] Despite the comic nature of her story and its opening allusion to a time and a place—an island of sorts—of marital joy and generational harmony, Ennasuite's tone darkens in the conversation following her tale, when she remarks that men like to publicize their erotic exploits, thus endangering women's reputations. Simontaut uses his tale to disprove the generalization that all men are "slanderers" (*mesdisants*) of women—a point particularly important for him to establish, I surmise, with regard to the most significant member of his internal audience, Parlamente. His tale flatters Parlamente and carries forward his effort to woo her—to entice her out of wedlock—through allegorical discourse that constitutes a kind of gift to her: an image of a virtuous and literate heroine capable of surviving in a dangerous world (however small) without male protection and also capable of warding off a symbolic threat of bestial savagery. In the prologue, Parlamente's other cavalier, the apparently gentle and idealistic Dagoucin, is ironically described as having a heart "so inflamed by pity and by love" for a woman not his wife that he comes to resemble an "enraged bear" when his lady is threatened by "outlaws" (*bandouliers*) (62; Fr., 3). The difference between savage animals, gentlemen, and outlaws blurs in this passage and elsewhere in the *Heptaméron*.[55]

Read in light of the metastory about the complex relations among the *Heptaméron*'s tale-tellers, Story 67 looks like a courtier's clever, highly self-reflexive attempt to persuade his lady that she is strong and virtuous enough to resist any unwanted advances from men whom she might be inclined to see as "savage beasts"; at the same time, the story carries to Parlamente Simontaut's assurance that he is *not* like such men. Thus he seeks to refute Ennasuite's prefatory argument about him. She dryly offers him "her place" in the storytelling game with the caution that he restrain his "natural inclinations" [contrainder vostre naturel] (*Heptaméron*, 502; Fr., 392). The phrase leads Ancekewicz to suggest that Simontaut is a figure for the uncivilized man so many writers associated with the New World—but which de Navarre finds alive and well in the Old. The framing narrative suggests a set of interesting doublings and reversals whereby *la femme sauvage*—the woman of rampant sexuality for whom Jeanne d'Albret has just been mistaken in Story 66 and who appears in the historical figure of Marguerite de Roberval as well—will be refigured and "contained" in and by the heroine whose portrait Simontaut draws for the company: the portrait of a woman who looks like a *femme sauvage*, but who turns out to be "the mistress and mother of the culture and of the primitive man" [la femme maîtresse et mère de la culture et de l'homme sauvage] (Ancekewicz, "L'Ecriture du Nouveau Monde," 430, my translation). That latter figure, in his famous American guise, never appears on the castaway's island, but he is limned in the traitorous husband and is alluded to in the savage beasts with which the heroine fights. He lurks, moreover, at the story's edge, in Ennasuite's and perhaps Parlamente's vision of the character of Simontaut. He uses the story to alter their vision of him—to show them that he himself can "constrain" his nature, as it were, through language, but his ownership of the tale is contested, and the contest over property and propriety is dramatized in the tale's discourse as well as in the debate that follows it.

Although Simontaut appears to use his story to refute Ennasuite's slurs both on men's sexual nature and on their verbal behavior—their tendency to "publish" stories about women's honor that result in their dishonor—at the end of the prefatory exchange, Simontaut presents a thesis about female "fame" in a way that undermines the terms of Ennasuite's challenge and puts him, rhetorically at least, on top—fulfilling the ambition of his name—in the ongoing battle of the sexes dramatized in the book. Deploying a rhetorical technique highly reminiscent of the one we have seen Boccaccio using—and de Pizan countering—in tales of "famous" women, and specifically addressing the women in his audience, Simontaut insists that he will publish the news of one virtuous woman's life because it is so "exceptional," so surprising ("si nouvelle") that "it should not be concealed but rather written in letters of gold, in order to serve as an example to women and as a source of wonderment to men" [me semble ne debvoir estre celé, mais plus tost escript en letters d'or, afin de servir aux femmes d'exemple et aux hommes d'admiration] (*Heptaméron*, 502; Fr., 392).

Thus Simontaut lays down the gauntlet not only to Ennasuite, whose place he is taking in the storytelling game, but also to Parlamente and, by implication, to Marguerite de Navarre, Simontaut's female "author" whose manuscript stories publish virtuous female deeds often enough to refute the idea that such deeds are rare. Exploring how differences of gender and social status affect the social meaning of publication (and its consequences), the stories repeatedly limn a process through which an oral publication to a small audience opens the door for written, and even printed, versions of the "news" to go to socially mixed groups with varying degrees of literacy and with widely different interpretive agendas. This process of transformative publication, as we might call it, is indeed enacted in Story 67, where deeds performed by a poor woman whose only audience is savage beasts are eventually—and intentionally—made known to a group of seamen and their captain; Simontaut names these men as the authority for his story. He uses the material for his own social purposes in an oral game, which Marguerite de Navarre subsequently records—but with a different social agenda than her male character's—in a manuscript that presumably circulated among an original audience of aristocrats before it was printed for the wider, mixed-class audience that the book arguably anticipates and that is crucial to its imperialist and religious projects.

The latter project is chiefly forwarded by Oisille—the book's female spiritual authority, whose name recalls the bird that symbolizes the Holy Spirit in the New Testament and, in the Old, God's covenant with Noah.[56] Both projects (which are sometimes but not always one) are forwarded by Parlamente, who may be Oisille's daughter but who is in any case her close ally in the book's representation of quasi-Protestant religious views, reading practices, and "reformed" social practices, such as giving virtuous women some of the powers currently misused by confessors and even, the text implies, by kings.[57] The main agent of the book's self-reflexivity is Parlamente. Her name plays not only on that of the historical "Marguerite" ("loving pearl" is one way of reading Parlamente's name, "perle amante") but also, as critics have often noted, on the verb "to speak."[58] Critics have less often noted the further pun on *mentir*, "to lie," or its homophonic relation to *monter*, "to climb."[59] That bit of wordplay links Parlamente to her "serviteur," Simontaut. There is also a significant allusion in Parlamente's name to the "semi-autonomous courts of justice," the Parlements, to which, as Natalie Zemon Davis notes, de Navarre herself sometimes resorted.[60] Parlements possessed certain important juridical powers but lacked the supreme authority of the male monarch; the Parlement is to the monarchy, one might say, as some privileged wives are to some even more privileged husbands. The Parlements of France derived from the *curia regis*, the king's court, and they achieved some autonomy and even oppositional stature: the sixteenth-century political commentator Claude de Seyssel thought that the Parlements were "instituted principally . . . in order to bridle the absolute power which the kings were wishing to use"; nonetheless, the French Parlements never acquired the independence as legislative bodies held (at least intermittently) by their English cousin.[61]

As complex as her name, Parlamente's mode of leadership seems an oblique reformation of the absolutist mode embodied by de Navarre's brother, by Roberval in Story 67, and by the autocratic husband represented, many critics believe, by Parlamente's philandering husband Hircan. Although in the sixteenth-century French monarchy the ruling powers of Parlements were chiefly limited to rendering judgments on local cases, the existence of these institutions, especially the relatively powerful Parlement de Paris, seems a significant social subtext for de Navarre's meditation on "female" modes of verbal leadership such as that figured in Parlamente and also, I suggest, in the unnamed heroine of Story 67. I turn now to the ties that bind the heroine with Parlamente, considered here as a figure for women's literacy. As de Navarre understands it, literacy evidently includes both oral and written verbal production for differently educated audiences; it also includes the courtier's quintessential survival skill: the ability to read an audience and censor or tailor one's words so as to lessen, if not eradicate, the risk of offending those whose political power exceeds one's own. The successful courtier may, as Castiglione himself suggests, become an educator of the prince with the dangerous potential of taking his place.

The Woman of Letters as Governor

Parlamente plays at governing with a velvet glove. Her talents as a leader who wears the courtier's or subaltern's mask begin to show themselves in the prologue to the *Heptaméron*, which defines the storytelling game as intervening in religious, political, and educational spheres. The prologue inaugurates a sustained meditation on questions of textual property. Marks of de Navarre's authority—her claims, as it were, to the dominant if not the sole rulership of her textual territory—emerge through multiple references to her as an "absent" yet influential historical personage in the stories told by members of the aristocratic company. She is far and near, and her readers are not allowed to forget her name for long. It is repeatedly mentioned from the prologue to the final tale, and thus she becomes the striking exception, it seems, to the general rule laid down by the dauphin in the prologue—a rule banishing *gens de lettres* from the tale-telling scene. The English translation gives this prohibition, not simply erroneously but certainly incompletely, as "men of letters." The entire passage, issuing from the textual voice ascribed to Parlamente, merits scrutiny:

> If I felt myself to be as capable as the ancients, by whom the arts were discovered, then I would invent some pastime myself that would meet the requirements you have laid down for me. However, I know what lies within the scope of my own knowledge and ability—I can hardly even remember the clever things other people have invented, let alone invent new things myself. So I shall be quite content to follow closely in the footsteps of the people who have already provided for your needs. For example, I don't think there's one of us who hasn't read the hundred tales by Boccaccio, which have recently been translated from Italian into French, and which are so highly thought of by the [most Christian] King Francis I, by Monseigneur the Dauphin, Madame the Dauphine and Madame Marguerite. If Boccaccio could have heard how highly these illustrious people praised him, it would have been enough to raise him from the grave. As a matter of fact, the two ladies I've mentioned, along with other people at the court, made up their minds to do the same as Boccaccio. There was to be one difference—that they should not write any story that was not truthful [*c'est de n'escripre nulle nouvelle qui ne soit veritable histoire*]. Together with Monseigneur the Dauphin the ladies promised to produce ten stories each, and to get together a party of ten people who were qualified to contribute [*racompter*] something, excluding those who studied and were men of letters [*sauf ceulx qui avoient estudié et estoient gens de lettres*]. For Monseigneur the Dauphin didn't want their art brought in, and he was afraid that rhetorical ornament would in part falsify the truth of the account [*la beaulté de la rethoricque feit tort en quelque partye à la verité de l'histoire*]. A number of things led to the project being completely forgotten. . . . However, it can now be completed in the ten days of leisure [*loisir*] we have before us, while we wait for our bridge to be finished. . . . And if, God willing, the lords and ladies I've mentioned find our endeavours worthy of their attention, we shall make them a present of them when we get back, instead of the usual statuettes and beads [*ymages et patenostres*]. (*Heptaméron*, 68–69; Fr., 9–10)

This passage, which ends with a witty assertion of the book's superiority to objects of "superstitious" religious purchase and veneration—objects, that is, of Catholic idolatry—dramatizes Parlamente's status as an authority figure who *mediates* between various realms, among them those of oral and written modes of discourse, with their different ontologies and temporalities: she straddles the boundary between a "present" of storytelling and a future when some less ephemeral representation will memorialize that now-past "present." The French text uses the same word as the English and suggests the same pun: *present* as both gift and temporal moment. The exclusionary clause in this rich passage, like Porete's gesture of defining "Theologiens et autres clers" as persons unable to understand the rules of her textual space, clearly suggests that gender is important in the game Parlamente is devising; the English translator is not wrong to assume that *gens de lettres* refers chiefly to educated and "professional" men of letters such as Boccaccio, whose name is admitted into the textual space of the prologue even as his "kind" are being banished by de Navarre's representation of the text's highest voice of masculine authority— the voice of the prince who has, by the time of the text's "present," become king: Henri II. With Henri's replacement of François, de Navarre's power at court waned. Lurking in the dauphin's banishment of *gens de lettres* is the question of where "Madame Marguerite" is in relation to the temporal and geographical space defined in the prologue and in the book as a whole.

The dauphin's rule proscribing *gens de lettres* turns out to be no less breakable, as the interlocutors interpret it over time, than the rule prescribing that the stories be "truthful" rather than rhetorically embellished. The interlocutors often admit, for instance, to renaming their characters in order to protect the identities of the well-born folk whose "true histories" are being recounted for a variety of purposes. Moreover, in just what sense is the mixed-gender company of tale-tellers not *gens de lettres,* since they are sometimes—increasingly toward the end of the book—revealed as retiring to their rooms to prepare their stories? The oral performances ostensibly recorded in the book may, in other words, themselves be based on written notes even though the tales are supposed to have been "heard" directly from believable people. The book constantly reflects on its own hybrid ontology—and on its multiple potential audiences, aristocratic auditors and common readers both, as it defines multiple kinds of literacy but privileges one over the others. This privileged literacy is, I contend, illustrated by Parlamente and by the unnamed heroine of Story 67. It is a literacy that hides its aggressivity beneath a veil composed of feminine virtue, innocent piety, and a mode of discourse that seems to take account of the wishes of a group while in truth aiming at shaping those wishes and controlling their ends.

The "other world" or heterocosm represented as coming into existence

in the *Heptaméron* originates with an act of diplomatic leadership by Parlamente.[62] She proposes her tale-telling game as a compromise solution to a
potentially divisive disagreement between Hircan and Oisille, who represent
extreme, and gender-marked, views about the purpose of life itself. According to the prologue's frame story, ten well-born French people journeying
"home" from the Pyrenees on initially separate paths find their progress interrupted by a series of natural disasters. Forced by a flooding river to constitute themselves as a new society while they take shelter in a monastery (ruled
badly by a shady abbot), the ten people agree that they need something to occupy their time. (Manual labor is out of the question for these people: others
build the bridge and attend to the storytellers' needs, replacing the several servants whose deaths the prologue narrates even as it stresses the "miraculous"
rescue of the ten privileged travelers.) What will their pastimes be? Two answers initially emerge, one from the highest ranking, and most hedonistic
man, Hircan, and one from the oldest, most spiritually ascetic woman, Oisille.
The man wants to amuse himself with sexual gratification, possibly adulterous; Oisille counters by suggesting that the only truly satisfying way to spend
one's time is in praying and reading the Bible—without the intervening authority of (male) priests. It is at this point that Parlamente makes her first
effort at governing in a "parliamentary" rather than an "absolutist" mode. She
proposes storytelling as a way of mediating between apparently antithetical visions of what members of the group should do. Storytelling—a more inclu-
sive pastime than either the "game for two" proposed by Hircan or the solitary
prayer recommended by Oisille—has the virtue of providing some erotic
pleasures (potentially leading to others) while also allowing for the soul's education and sustenance.

Significantly, Parlamente's politic compromise is not altogether successful; it does not, for instance, prevent either Hircan or Oisille from continuing
to pursue their different goals. Storytelling gives some satisfactions to those
desiring sexual and/or religious experience, the book suggests, but storytelling is presented, above all, as a deferral of battle, a mode of buying time,
as it were, while a more truly satisfactory solution is sought. If the storytelling
game is in some sense utopian, occurring on a more even playing ground for
men and women than exists in "real" society, the game also generates desires
for yet more equality, or indeed dominance, among many of the characters.
Parlamente's inaugural act of leadership does cause her husband, deemed by
society her "natural" leader, to cede some of his power in the (he presumes
temporary) society of the game. "Where games are concerned," he says toward the end of the prologue, "everybody is equal" [Au jeu nous sommes
toutes égales] (*Heptaméron*, 70; Fr., 10). His words allow both the women and

the male *serviteurs* in the company more scope to speak, if not to act, than they would have had in their ordinary world, the constraints of which are repeatedly represented in the tales themselves. Significantly, however, no sooner has Hircan rhetorically allowed for a more republican or parliamentary social organization to be envisioned than another male character—none other than Simontaut—proclaims his desire to be an absolute ruler of others: "Would to God, sighed Simontaut, that the one thing in all the world I had were the power to order everyone in our party to comply with my wishes!" [Pleut à Dieu, dist Simontault, que je n'eusse bien en ce monde que de povoir commander à toute ceste compaignye] (70; Fr., 10). His internal "chief addressee" is Parlamente, as I have noted, and she is said to know very well what Simontaut means by his words. Her role as leader, from the prologue on, clearly involves restraining others from becoming absolutist monarchs over the new society constituted in and by the book. The storytelling enterprise, the building of a fragile new society, emerges in the prologue and in the book as a whole as an analogue for an activity described as occurring nearby and simultaneously—the building of the bridge over the flooding river. The flood has effectively placed the storytellers on an island, since their route home to the courtly center of France is blocked by water. Like the castaways of Story 67 in their solitary couple phase (before the husband drinks the water that is fatal to him), the society formed in and through the storytelling game is an ur-society, an experimental formation that allows the writer to contemplate how human nature, under pressure from nonhuman nature, may perhaps become cultured in a better way than history allowed the first time around.

The question of divine providence and possible divine punishment lurks on the margin of the prologue as it does on the margin of Story 67 about "artisans" revealed by the official records of the court to be drawn from French prisons in the absence of volunteers. The leveling perspective of de Navarre's theology—all humans are in some sense sinners, all are sick and in need of a cure—appears repeatedly in the prologue's language: the second paragraph ironically combines aristocrats and servants into a group simply called "les malades" as they prepare to depart—evidently uncured by the weeks spent at the spa. This undifferentiated group endures a fatal wound before regrouping as the storytellers; while people are preparing to leave Cauterets, such enormous rains come that the shallow Gave du Pau becomes a torrent that kills an unspecified number of the nobles and many of their servants. "[Y]ou would have thought that God had quite forgotten that once He had promised to Noah never again to destroy the world by water," remarks the narrator (*Heptaméron*, 60; Fr., 1). Whether the disaster is caused by human sin or by a nature obeying or indifferent to divine behest, or by a combination of these things, as seems to be the case for the castaway couple as well as for the *Heptaméron*'s general company, the effort of bridge-building is a complex symbol of a (possibly) redemptive labor.[63] Will an apparently forgetful God meet the human builders halfway? Or is his grace enabling the entire storytelling and bridge-building enterprise? The questions remain open, but Oisille, in particular, invites the reader not to forget them. She insists that the storytelling that parallels the bridge-building should be buttressed, as it were, by the reading of Scripture. In the New World governed by Parlamente, Oisille exercises governing powers too; she leads the company in at least "a good hour" of *leçons* every day they wait for the bridge to be finished. Oisille also sees to it that the company attends mass even if the priests officiating at the services are morally unreliable.

Recalling the Book of Genesis—especially the chapters devoted to Eden and to the Flood—the landscape of the prologue is also likened, by Oisille, to the same biblical desert or wilderness invoked in Story 67, a place reminiscent both of the Old Testament Exodus and of sojourns in the wilderness undertaken by Christ and his saintly followers. The prologue's landscape also emerges through a tissue of textual allusions to the opening scenes of two secular literary sites of mixed-gender conversation and tale-telling, Boccaccio's *Decameron* and (unmentioned but equally important, I have argued elsewhere) Castiglione's *Cortegiano*.[64] De Navarre's landscape is, however, considerably more menacing than the *locus amoenus* where Boccaccio's interlocutors finally rest, after escaping the plague-ridden city of Florence. Issues of bodily and spiritual health are important to all three secular texts; only in de Navarre's, however, does a woman lead the company toward what she defines as health through prayerful reading of Scripture.

The Protestant tenet of the "priesthood of all believers" is at the uneasy heart of the new world Parlamente and Oisille attempt, with many setbacks, to govern—or at least to sustain for a period of time defined initially as ten days but later changed to seven, in a development I take as more intentional on the writer's part than most critics allow when they see the *Heptaméron* as a "failed" or incomplete *Decameron*. As a game-playing society in a distinctly, though not uniformly, Protestant landscape, the *Heptaméron*'s company repeatedly engages with issues about textual authority and translation, issues central to the Protestant movement broadly viewed. Removing the priest and the pope as stabilizers of the Bible's meanings led some Protestant readers, to the consternation of some ostensibly Protestant authorities, to reading practices that assumed that even the non-Latin-speaking person could be a master interpreter of a (vernacular) scriptural text. Master-servant relations are indeed profoundly labile in the emergent realm of Protestant reading inhabited by women and "other unlearned persons such as merchants and artisans."[65] And this lability, as we saw in chapter 3, troubled Protestant as well as Catholic authorities. "Like the Catholic critics who had quoted Paul's dictum from 1 Corinthians that 'women keep silence in the churches' against Protestants who were reading and talking about the Bible," Natalie Zemon Davis notes, "Reformed pastors quoted it against Protestant women who wanted to preach publicly or have some special vocation in the church" (*Society and Culture*, 83). The problem of unstable master-servant relations surfaces repeatedly in the stories of the *Heptaméron* and in the metanarrative about the tale-tellers as well. Sometimes de Navarre seems to construct ideologically conservative responses to the problem; sometimes her responses are radically ambiguous, pitting theological against secular interpretations of the master-servant relation; and sometimes she envisions utopian alliances between female servants and their mistresses who unite, through wit and a shared facility with words, to foil a master's desires.[66] Such an alliance is dramatized in Story 69, which Dora Polachek has persuasively interpreted as a comic revision of a fifteenth-century tale.[67] The story reforms its unnamed precursor text while also dramatizing some kind of reformation in its teller's views of women. The teller is none other than Hircan; he approvingly describes how an aging wife and a poor girl join wits and verbal talents to prevent the master of the house from carrying through a planned act of rape. The mistress and her maid successfully expose the husband as a fool, moreover, in a French language that affords them great amusement as they play repeatedly on the word *beluter*, meaning both "to sift" and "to fuck."[68]

Some Costs and Benefits of de Navarre's Literacy

Story 67 provides an important vantage point from which to assess some of the key ideological projects of the *Heptaméron*. The artisanal heroine of that story, replacing an upper-class heroine who dominates the oral and later the printed intertexts, becomes a carrier of de Navarre's ambitions to extend her God's empire across lines of social status as well as across various geographical spaces both divided and linked, in her theological-ideological vision, by water. The writer's imperial ambitions lead her, of course, to misrepresent the social realities of the impoverished people she figures first in the castaway couple and then in the woman alone. They are shown eking out a living from nothing, with real difficulty but also with fantastic resourcefulness and help from God; the man is shown dying happily, comforted by the ministrations of his Bible-reading wife. From one perspective, this is a disturbing tissue of falsifications, no less objectionable as an allegory appropriating Native American life than as an allegory of the life experienced by poor French artisans or worse, French criminals "rescued" by the king for colonial ventures. From another perspective, however—and I believe that both are needed—Story 67 has utopian seeds in its intertextual gesture of putting a poor woman in the place of a rich one and, by so doing, querying the institution of marriage and the masculinist definitions of women's nature upon which that institution, especially in its dynastic form, rests.[69] De Navarre's use of a courtly French language to tell the castaway woman's story at once betrays that woman—if we imagine her as a historical being—and makes some kind of common cause with her. The commonality, for better or worse, is signaled in the story's gesture of giving the unnamed woman some access to the very power being deployed by the Queen of Navarre—the power to read authoritative cultural texts critically and to communicate thoughts, in however veiled a fashion, through the activity of teaching reading and writing.

Looking at (or for) the utopian dimensions of de Navarre's self-reflective exercise of literacy, one can see her building a kind of bridge from the poor (but literate) beguine Marguerite Porete to the "Marguerite" unnamed but implied in Story 67 to the Marguerite named, sometimes without her titles or family name, in many of the texts attributed to the historical Marguerite de Navarre. The blurring of master-servant distinctions implicit in the doctrine of the priesthood of all believers is an effect that carries across boundaries of time and even of the kind of official censorship visited on the writings of both Porete and de Navarre. Some of the more radical seeds in de Navarre's texts grew only after her own queenly body was dead. One of her poems, for instance, mocking "those who say it's not for women / To look at Holy Writ" and denouncing them as "evil seducers," was printed in Lyons in 1564 as part of a volume of Protestant songs; two years earlier, an anonymous pamphlet, also printed in Lyons, had used the same trope of seducers to characterize those men who sought to prevent women from reading the Bible.[70] Natalie Zemon Davis classifies de Navarre's poem along with the anonymous pamphlet as part of a printed corpus of Protestant propaganda. Most of de Navarre's written work dealing with the reformation of both secular and theological domains did not initially appear in a form likely to be read by commoners, but the women of letters she figures in the *Heptaméron*—and the martyred one she invokes in *Les Prisons,* knowing full well that the Church had ordered all copies of this woman's book destroyed—suggest repeatedly that the word spoken by a woman, even by one who appears as bereft of an audience as the castaway of Story 67, can have a life after the speaker's death through writing and eventually, perhaps, through print.

To achieve such an afterlife in words, the woman writer may need to test, even at times to break, what her society regards as the law in both secular and religious spheres. De Navarre finds in the New Testament authorization for her playful yet serious exploration of how female subjects may bend the "letter" of the law. Exhibiting a revisionary creativity similar to that which I've located in Story 67's extended allusion to the biblical test of wifely fidelity, Parlamente and Oisille discuss whether and how to deal with one of the narrative project's own foundational "laws." In a reported dialogue that occurs just before the final story of the last complete day of storytelling, Oisille proposes to censor herself from telling a story about a beautiful woman who did not censor her own carnal desires (*Heptaméron*, 512; Fr., 44). Telling the story would break a rule which the company has "sworn" in the past to obey: the rule "not to tell stories from a written source" [de ne rien mectre icy qui ayt esté escript] (512; Fr., 400). Since the story in question will entail translating into modern French prose a text of the thirteenth-century poem, *La Chastelaine de Vergi*, how can de Navarre's female characters justify this story's inclusion? They do so, I think, by inviting their near audience and far readers both to reflect on what, really, an oath of obedience means in the world of the text and in the larger social world it refracts. The interrogation of the meaning of obedience begins when we note that Oisille's formulation of the law isn't quite the same as the one given in the prologue by Parlamente, in a passage where she seems to be casually translating for the "present company" the earlier laws against *gens de lettres* and for *veritable histoire*. These laws were formulated by the dauphin—with "Madame Marguerite" helping him in some way—as part of a game imitating Boccaccio that was interrupted by history. Returning (later) to the idea of the game, but subtly altering it too, Madame Marguerite's character Parlamente translated the "original" rules into the following directive, which can be read both as a law and as a courtly suggestion: "Each of us will tell a story which he has either witnessed himself, or which he has heard from somebody worthy of belief" [Dira chascun quelque histoire, qu'il aura veue ou bien oy dire a quelque homme digne de foy] (*Heptaméron*, 69; Fr., 10). Near the end of the book, Oisille offers yet another translation of the original rules, formulated for a French courtly imitation of an Italian text. Translation itself, that "carrying across" of words and meanings, seems quite wonderfully to provide the grounds for Parlamente's ingenious way of legitimizing the bending/breaking of the rule here (re)formulated as prohibiting drawing the book's stories from "anything that has been written." Acknowledging the "truth" of Oisille's concern for the law (but whose law?), Parlamente remarks: "But if it's the story I think it is, then it's written in such antiquated language, that apart from you and me, there's no one here who will have heard it. So it can be regarded as a new one" [Il est vray, dit Parlamente, mais, me doubtant du compte que c'est, il a esté escript en si viel langaige, que je croys que, hor mis nous deux, il n'y a icy homme ne femme qui en ayt ouy parler; parquoy sera tenu pour nouveau] (*Heptaméron*, 512; Fr., 400). Translation—from an "old" language to a new one—justifies the breaking of an old law and its replacement by the formulation of a value that wasn't mentioned at all (explicitly) in the prologue's various formulations of the game's rules. This is the value of the "new"—or, more precisely, of what can be passed off as new to those who don't share these two female speakers' knowledge (claimed knowledge) of an old form of their native language. The value of the *nouveau,* carried by the genre of discourse de Navarre and others have named *la nouvelle,* has aesthetic and geographical as well as theological components.

As figures of the female translator who bring to a wider audience a knowledge previously held only by an elite few, Parlamente and Oisille join forces with the heroine of Story 67 and with the historical Marguerite Porete in dramatizing the thin and always contestable line between carrying God's word—or that of his representative the king—and remaking it. Reformation, the portraits of these women suggest, is never a politically or theologically straightforward project. How can it be, when God is *loing près,* and when some of his followers may be deemed heretical on the basis of a single word they wrote—or that someone copied long after their death? Such women may believe God to be on their side and in their hearts, but, as John Lyons remarks with regard to de Navarre's portrait of a young woman who defies her guardians' wishes in the matter of disposing of her marriageable body, the woman who speaks against the dictates of her kin and rulers has no way of making others see that God has authorized her speech. God "cannot speak for her; she must speak for Him."[71]

The truth of a speaker's or writer's claims will be sifted in the ongoing history of interpretation. De Navarre inscribes this point into her narrative through the debates that follow the stories, debates that are much longer than those in Boccaccio's *Decameron.* In the debate prompted by Simontaut's story of the castaway woman, Saffredent denigrates the tale's claims to any exemplary truth by remarking that "[i]f you've read Scripture properly . . . you will know that Saint Paul wrote that Apollos planted and that he watered, but he says nothing about women lending a hand in God's labour [*louvraige*]" (1 Cor. 3:6; *Heptaméron,* 505; Fr., 394). In a gesture important for the practitioner of a literacy of reformation that relies on translation as its chief vehicle, de Navarre here insists that the language of the Bible is not exempt from the problem of rhetorical manipulation for dubious ends. "You're as bad as all the other men who take a passage from Scripture which serves their purposes, and leave out anything that contradicts it," says Parlamente acerbically to Saffredent (505; Fr., 394).

One of the major Renaissance/Reformation arguments against giving women as a group—and poor men as well—the tools of alphabetic literacy was that such new readers would "abuse" Scripture, appropriating it for subversive ends. De Navarre repeatedly reminds her own readers that powerful men already commit this sin against (and by means of) Scripture. Hence limiting access to the Bible by limiting access to literacy will not remedy the problem that Parlamente identifies. Story 67 suggests that the only remedy for what the book as a whole defines as a kind of imperialism of scriptural interpretation, an absolutist desire to appropriate textual (and other) territories for one's own selfish desires, lies within the individual soul, the soul disciplined by "incessant reading" of the New Testament and eager to mortify the flesh while serving God. This is a very traditional and unsatisfactory answer, I think, to the problems of textual and political imperialism the story limns; the questions, here, escape the ideological container de Navarre seems to provide through the portrait of the selfless female colonist who returns—with no worldly goods at all—from the New World to teach reading, writing, and virtue to the daughters of ladies.

The questions raised by Parlamente's remark about scriptural imperialism reverberate beyond Story 67; they are not answered by any single portion, or narrative voice, of the *Heptaméron*. The two most authoritative female speakers, indeed—Oisille and Parlamente—make theoretical statements about belief and narrative that work against the ideological statement provided by Story 67's image of ascetic female religious virtue. For Parlamente and Oisille, despite their frequent advocacy of an ethics of renunciation, also succeed in challenging a "religious" solution to the workings of imperialist desire by blurring the distinction between humanly authored stories, generated in some part by fallen human wills, and the divinely authored stories of Scripture. Both kinds of text can deceive gullible readers, and both acquire authority when rightly interpreted. The blurring of an essential distinction between sacred and secular rhetoric, of course, allows the two kinds to be viewed as *competing* for attention and authority, with the interpreter, ideally strengthened by divine grace, the judge of the match. In the prologue to Day 7, Oisille is described as ministering to the whole company with "the saving nourishment" she drew from her reading of the New Testament; she tells her audience how the "tales" (*comptes*) she finds in Acts and Luke should "be sufficient" to make the audience "long to live in such an age" (presumably, the once and future age of Christ's presence on earth) and "weep for the corruption of the present" (*Heptaméron*, 476; Fr., 370). Here, at the beginning of the last full day of storytelling, the company is so excited by Oisille's apocalyptically colored renderings of biblical stories that the "enterprise" of human storytelling is almost forgotten. Nomerfide, however, whose name plays on "name" and "faith," who has a penchant for scatological tales, who is probably the object of Hircan's adulterous affections, and who often speaks, as he does, for the needs of the flesh when Oisille's spiritual exercises threaten to become too all-consuming, urges her companions to return to the present, and to the pleasures of telling their tales: let us, she says, retire to our rooms to prepare "à racompter nos nouvelles" (476; Fr., 370). Her term *racompter* underscores the link between this storytelling activity and Oisille's reading of New Testament *comptes*; her term *nouvelles* points both to the good news of the Gospel and to the fictional truths, or truth-bearing fictions, made or translated by de Navarre.

Nomerfide's mention of a time of private "preparation" of the stories, which echoes a sentence in the prologue to the previous day describing Oisille rising "earlier than usual to prepare her reading in the hall [*preparer sa leçon en la salle*]" (*Heptaméron*, 428; Fr., 328), also works to blur the boundary between sacred and secular discursive spaces, *veritables histoires* and fictions. Both distinctions, as commonly used to denigrate some textual materials and elevate others, are rendered problematic in de Navarre's book; it gives contradictory statements on reading, suggesting at times that the "spirit" of the activity transcends the "matter" being read, while also suggesting that the matter of what one reads is critical to one's salvation: Oisille prepares a *leçon* that contrasts and competes with those presented by Hircan and Nomerfide.

The contradictions of a proto-Protestant consciousness are strikingly illustrated in a passage spoken by Parlamente, a passage that insists on the distinction between sacred and secular texts but locates the power to make the distinction in the individual consciousness rather than in the authority of any priest. In the discussion after Story 44, she tells the company that ever since she heard one priest try to persuade others "that the Gospel was no more credible than Caesar's *Commentaries* or any other histories written by [pagan authors]," she has refused to believe all priests "unless what they say seems to me to conform to the word of God, which is the only true touchstone by which one can know whether one is hearing truth or falsehood" (*Heptaméron*, 400; Fr., 304). The female interpreter here becomes the judge of what "conforms" to the Gospel's truth. And even though a transcendent objectivity of that truth is urged on the company by Oisille ("Be assured [*Croyez*] that whosoever reads the Scriptures often and with humility will never be deceived by human fabrications and inventions, for whoever has his mind filled with truth can never be the victim of lies" [ibid.]), that optimistic claim for the power of one (inspired) text's truth to remain untarnished by human lies remains just that—a claim on our belief that is questioned both by other speakers and by some of the *Heptaméron*'s darker tales about humble, often "simple" and virtuous characters who are entrapped by lies, including those of male priests. The innovative images of the female interpreter as an authority (though not an un-challenged or infallible one) who seeks to discern and defend the truth of Scripture as well as the multiple, sometimes conflicting truths of human social and erotic ambitions, contributes, I suggest, to the new portrait of the female author sketched in the *Heptaméron*. That shadowy portrait of an author, real-ized only when the reader works as a co-producer of the text, encompasses var-ious functions ascribed to Parlamente (as tale-teller, daughter, wife, mediator, and object of illicit love), to Oisille (as tale-teller, mother, Bible reader, and evangelical religious leader), and to other characters, such as the heroine of Story 67. Ostensibly demonstrating the virtues of an ascetic life of religious reading, that heroine succeeds in occupying the roles of various Old World men (the priest, the colonial ruler, the teacher) even as she appears to disavow selfish imperialist desires. Like Parlamente, the unnamed New World heroine occupies a textual landscape in which an idealized and feminized version of Christianity takes on the ideological form—and force—of a "good" imper-ialism. The text, however, interrogates as well as promotes that ideological construct, showing the moral distinction between "good" and "bad" imperi-alism to be as slippery as the distinction between sacred texts and secular ones, or between "speaking" some version of French or Spanish or Italian and representing such speech—or translating, re-creating, or traducing it—in writing. Parlamente lies even as she discourses, in speech mediated by writ-ing. And like Dido, she lies because she aspires to govern present and future subjects in her world.

Allegories of Imperial Subjection
Literacy as Equivocation in Elizabeth Cary's
Tragedy of Mariam

This equivocating and lying is a kind of unchastity . . . for as it hath been said of old . . .
The law and sanction of nature hath, as it were married the heart and tongue . . . and
therefore, when there is discord between them two, the speech that proceeds from them
is said to be conceived in adultery.

> SIR EDWARD COKE, state trial of the Jesuit Henry Garnet

Tongues-othes, Harts-thoughts, disjunctives, by a Mental reservation.

> WILLIAM WARNER, *A Continuance of Albion's England*

I conceive women to be no fit solicitors of state affairs.

> HENRY CARY, Viscount Falkland and Lord Deputy of Ireland, letter of 5 April 1626

Be and seem.

> MOTTO that Cary had inscribed in her eldest daughter's wedding ring

This chapter examines a mode of female literacy that relies on several types
of equivocation to articulate (but also to disguise) a critical perspective on England as an imperial nation.[1] The critique emerges through an implied comparison between two imperial locales in which some subjects are distinctly
dissatisfied with their rulers. The first locale, the setting of Cary's *Tragedy of
Mariam,* is ancient Judea in the years before Christ's birth when it was part
of the Roman empire and ruled by Herod. The second locale, never explicitly
mentioned, is Tudor-Stuart England. This absent presence is, I argue, important to the play's address to a group of imagined readers, present and future;
the locale is also critical to the play's thematic meditation on censorship and
to the play's status as the literate product of a political situation of censorship
and persecution.[2]

The events dramatized in *Mariam* occurred around 29 B.C.E., when the
man later known as Herod the Great, having been appointed tetrarch or governor of Judea by Mark Antony, married the Maccabean princess Mariam and
thereby secured his "title" to the throne of Judea.[3] The moral legitimacy of that
title is rendered hugely doubtful, however, by Cary's Argument, which serves
to preface the play's plot and to signal that it comments on affairs of state, as

do other French and English dramas in the neo-Senecan tradition.[4] Like earlier plays by Mary Sidney and her followers, Cary's drama uses ancient Roman
materials to explore a debate important to both Catholic and Protestant
thinkers, a debate about the "duty"—incipiently a "right"—to resist "lawful
authority" if it degenerated into tyranny.[5] The Argument begins by emphasizing the ruler's illegitimacy:

> Herod, the son of Antipater (an Idumean), having crept by the favour of
> the Romans, into the Jewish monarchy, married Mariam, the [granddaughter]
> of Hircanus, the rightful king and priest, and for her (besides her high blood,
> being of singular beauty) he repudiated Doris, his former wife, by whom he
> had children.
>
> This Mariam had a brother called Aristobulus, and next him and Hirca-
> nus, his grandfather, Herod in his wife's right had the best title. Therefore to
> remove them, he charged the [second] with treason: and put him to death:
> and drowned the [first] under color of sport. (Mariam, ed. Weller and Fergu-
> son, 67)

How many obstacles to Herod's legitimacy are here evoked! He has displaced
a "rightful" male king who is also his people's priest; he has repudiated a
wife who had given him heirs (their gender is not mentioned here, but we
learn later that they are boys); he has killed his wife's brother (under cover of
"sport") as well as her grandfather (by a false charge of treason) in order to appropriate a title which, the phrasing suggests, belongs by right to his wife (the
ironic echo of "rightful" in "wife's right" yokes the question of female succession subtly to the notion, beloved of England's King James I, of a kingly "divine right").[6] A king who was also a priest who is now dead because of a false
charge of treason: this figure presides like a ghost over Cary's play and shapes
her reading of Roman history at the key moment when Augustus triumphed
over Antony to establish a "single ruled" empire. Cary's main ancient source,
Josephus's Antiquities of the Jews (c. 90 C.E.), presents Herod as a greatly flawed
ruler but not as a Satanic figure who "creeps" with bestial stealth into the "Jewish monarchy" (for Cary's stress on Herod's racial otherness, his status as an
"Idumean," see below).[7] Nor, to the best of my knowledge, do other versions
of the Herod and Mariam story suggest that at the heart of this troubled marriage lies a serious, though occluded, competition for the throne in which the
wife is accused of attempting to poison the husband to "usurp" his place.[8] The
complex political plot of the play, which is actually several plots simultaneously constructed by different characters' interpretive desires and suspicions, grows from the equivocal seeds planted in the Argument and, in particular, from that impacted clause, "Herod in his wife's right had the best title."

Both the setting and the plot of Cary's play suggest an analogical relation between Judea in the years just before Christ's birth and England in the years after its traumatic break from the Church of Rome. When Cary sets a play written in English rhyming verse in ancient Palestine, a land revered in the sixteenth century as the birthplace of Christianity and also viewed as the home of the Jewish infidels who killed the Christian god-hero, she invites her readers to consider the relation between Herod's land and an England torn by religious disputes. As Frances Dolan notes in *Whores of Babylon*, "before 1536 most English subjects were Catholics or heretics; after 1536, most were Protestants and Catholics," with the latter group being, by definition, proto-traitors.[9] The English were indeed divided into three rather than two groups, with respect to how their religion was perceived and judged by others: there were those who accepted the authority of the Church of England, those who merely pretended to accept it, and those who refused to conform and hence became *recusants.* That term does not simply denote those Catholics and dissenting Protestants who refused to attend their parish church; instead, it applies, as Dolan notes, to those whose absence was observed and prosecuted, and who, in the face of accusation or conviction, refused to conform. After June 1606, moreover, those under the rank of nobleman or noblewoman could become recusant by refusing to take the Oath of Allegiance that James's Parliament had enacted in reaction to the Gunpowder Plot.[10] Many Catholics were "church papists" who conformed outwardly and occasionally to the state religion while maintaining private observances of their Catholic faith.[11] Women, as historians have observed, played a significant and culturally debated role in both recusant and church papist households.[12] In those like Cary's, where the husband was Protestant while the wife harbored Catholic beliefs, there was clearly an opportunity for mutual distrust between husband and wife. In domestic spaces as in the imperial nation at large, then, the distinction between friend and enemy, loyalist and traitor, could be extremely labile.

During the early years of King James's reign when Cary wrote her play, both Jews and Catholics were frequently excoriated as inherently untrustworthy enemies of the English body politic; persons perceived to be Jewish or Catholic, whatever the actual state of their religious views, were feared and sometimes punished as spies and traitors, transmitters of secret and dangerous information from sources outside the body politic. Yoked through an association with illicit transmission of illicit knowledges, Jews, whether ancient or modern, and Catholics, whether professed adherents to the Church of Rome or church papists, shared with educated women a vexed relation to the activity of verbal communication and to what Cary's play refers to, in its opening line, as a "public voice."

In 1602 the Catholic Thomas Lodge printed a translation entitled *The Famous and Memorable Workes of Josephus, A Man of Much Honour and Learning Among the Jewes. Faithfully translated out of the Latine, and the French.* Lodge's work, which Cary's play sometimes echoes directly, was licensed in 1598 and had thus probably circulated in manuscript before being printed.[13] The translation of Josephus's text at this historical juncture, when Elizabeth was being succeeded by the son of an executed Catholic, may well have had political implications for English Catholic readers that modern readers have failed to appreciate.[14] Although Lodge had earlier written *An Alarum Against Usurers,* which contains many implicitly anti-Jewish statements, his decision at the turn of the century to describe an ancient Jew as a man of honor and to bring that learned Jew's writings "faithfully" into the English language certainly goes against the usual negative stereotypes of Jewish masculinity; moreover, as James Shapiro remarks, Lodge's translation explicitly refutes in an ancient context a common contemporary charge against Jews—namely, that they committed ritual murder.[15] Lodge evidently saw that, like Jews in fifteenth-century Portugal and Spain, English Catholics constituted a demographically significant group of political subjects who were required, by the state, to change (or hide) their religion. Lodge's translation, as Elaine Beilin notes, adds to Josephus's text marginal dates giving the number of years between the events in the history and the epochal moment of Christ's birth; this "countdown" suggests how an English Catholic might have read Josephus's text as a source for allegories, prophecies, and warnings to some among the contemporary audience (Beilin, *Redeeming Eve,* 165). Josephus's works were seen by a famous contemporary of Cary's, who was himself executed for treason, as too full of dangerous "fables" to be believed except with "discreet reservations." By this phrase Sir Walter Raleigh may well have aimed to link Josephus's text to current debates about the Catholic doctrine of *equivocation* as entailing a "mental reservation," a withholding, in speech, of part of a (truthful) statement voiced in the mind.[16]

The concepts and practices associated with Catholic equivocation, which will be discussed in detail below, testify to a profound sense of distance between political subjects in England and to an equally profound gap between a subject's inner landscape and the way that landscape might be perceived, mapped, or appropriated by another person who claimed superior authority and perhaps actually possessed superior power. The growing distances I have just mentioned were traversed by methods of reading (alone or in groups) and by modes of writing, in both manuscript and print media, that used techniques of allusion to create a kind of second-order literacy, a field of vernacular discourse partly designed to exclude some from fully comprehending its letters.

As a semi-public convert to Catholicism ("semi-public" because so few in the population at large could read), Lodge seems to have led Cary toward her perception of parallels between oppressed ancient Jews and oppressed modern Catholics. For those shrewd enough to interpret the veiled analogies, the message might have looked quite threatening to supporters of the English Protestant regime. Coded textual messages about possible alternative futures abounded in Elizabeth's waning years and in the first, unsettled years of James's reign, when a new queen sympathetic to Catholicism shared the king's bed and when Catholic plots to overthrow the Protestant state were allegedly occurring frequently; the infamous Gunpowder Plot supposedly master-minded by the Jesuit priest Henry Garnet, author of a treatise on equivocation, took place in 1605 and is, as I argue below, equivocally but explosively present in the text of Cary's play. Writers like Lodge and Cary, whether they were openly or secretly sympathetic to the Church of Rome, were well aware that they could look, to some of their countrymen and countrywomen, like poten-tial traitors in league with foreigners.

We don't know exactly when Cary wrote *The Tragedy of Mariam*, but it was certainly after Lodge's translation of Josephus appeared (in manuscript or in print) and also probably after the adolescent Elizabeth Tanfield was married to Henry Cary, a Protestant aristocrat who held the post of Master of the Jewel House under Elizabeth and who, according to the "Life" composed by one of Cary's Catholic daughters, married the lawyer Tanfield's daughter "only for her being an heir."[17] Sir Henry soon left his bride to fight the Spanish in the Netherlands, where he was captured and held for some three years before he was ransomed. During this time, I surmise, his wife, living unhappily with his mother, probably wrote the play. It explores a condition of alienation from the state that has psychological, ethical, and political dimensions; in this state gender plays a more prominent role than it does in most other contemporary explorations of such alienation. But Cary's culture provided ample materials for viewing both Jews and Catholics with reference to ideologies of gender, since both groups were regularly effeminized in the polemical literature of the era. And sometimes they were explicitly linked as types of the "dangerous familiar" analyzed by Frances Dolan—the wife or servant who uses under-handed means, often poison, to commit petty treason. Note that in Cary's play Mariam is accused of this crime when another woman close to the throne, the king's sister Salome, actually concocts and executes the plot, suborning a ser-vant to pretend to give Herod poison under the guise of a love potion suppos-edly ordered by Mariam. The servant is tortured for his part in the crime, and Mariam is executed. Salome, however, remains undetected and unpunished.

As a female villain who is both Jewish (albeit less "purely" so than Mariam) and a master of dissimulation, Salome embodies various elements of cultural fantasies about Jews, Catholics, and women. It is as if Cary were building, in her construction of Salome, on equivalencies circulating in her culture and dramatized in productions such as the play entitled *England's Joy*, which was presented in 1602 at the Swan Theater.[18] In this anonymously authored play, a Spanish tyrant sends forth letters, privy spies, and secret underminers who are said to signify "Lopus, and certain Jesuits."[19] The name Lopus refers here to the notorious Jewish doctor Roderigo Lopez, executed in 1594 for spying and for an alleged act of treason, an attempt to poison Queen Elizabeth.[20] Lopez, in the view of modern historians, may well have been unjustly accused of treason, but he was almost certainly guilty of spying. Cary's heroine Mariam, who is also accused of plotting to poison a monarch, her own husband to boot, resembles Lopez in being ambiguously guilty. She is clearly innocent of plotting to poison Herod; Salome engineers the appearance of Mariam's guilt as Iago engineers the appearance of Desdemona's in *Othello*. But Mariam has certainly wished for Herod's death, so she is not innocent from a moral perspective. She is, one might say, technically innocent of the poison plot as she is technically or literally innocent of the crime of unchastity for which she is also punished by Herod. But she is gradually revealed to be ambiguously guilty of various quasi-crimes, and for this reason among others, she may be read as an ancient Jew equivocally like a modern Catholic wife.

Cary's play refracts an England that is "imperial" in two rather different ways. One reveals a positive and, for English Catholics like Cary, a counterfactual, even a utopian understanding of empire; the other reveals a negative or dystopian understanding of empire, which implicitly challenges the burgeoning Protestant nationalism of men like Richard Mulcaster, with their faith that education can increase a "uniformity" desired not only in orthography but also among English subjects' religious views. Inevitably alienated from her native land by virtue of her loyalty to the Church of Rome, Cary was one of many English subjects to resist the nation-building efforts implicit in anti-Catholic legislation during the Tudor and Stuart eras. The significantly named Act of Uniformity of 1559, as we saw in chapter 3, was the first in a long series of laws that punished English subjects for failing to attend services in the English national church.[21]

The two senses of empire circulating in Cary's play interpenetrate and contribute to many of the play's representational complexities and allegorical densities, particularly those rooted in the figure of the king or tyrant, Herod, and in his wife, as a type of the "disempowered" imperial subject. Drawing on Gorden Braden's important argument that Stoicism provided a philosophical defense for aristocrats in the first centuries of the Roman empire, Marta Straznicky has argued that Mariam herself exhibits a form of Stoic heroism that "reappropriates" political power to the (female) subject.[22] My reading of Mariam's character differs from Straznicky's, but I am indebted to her and Braden's diagnosis of an imperial political problem in the play. I stress, however, that ideas about a later empire—that of the Holy Roman Church— are superimposed on Cary's representation of the early phase of the ancient Roman empire. In the utopian political vision adumbrated in the play, England is part of a spiritual empire ruled by the pope, in God's name, and centered in Rome. This, of course, is an understanding of empire denied by Henry VIII and his Protestant heirs to the English throne. Through the figure of Herod, who is being called to account for his behavior in Rome when the play opens (and whose throne in Judea is therefore temporarily empty, giving rise to hope and ambition among most of the play's characters), Cary arguably alludes to an ideal of spiritual *imperium* that suffuses the play and makes Herod, historical enemy of Christ, a potent allegorical double for the king who sought to divorce England from Rome—but who, in the eyes of Catholic English subjects, would ultimately be chastised for an apostasy which providential history would render temporary in its effects.

The situation of English Catholics during that hard time "before" the country's postulated reunion with Rome is, then, a major subtext for the play's dystopian representation of empire in a period infused with eschatological urgency. Cary offers a view of earthly polities in which Judean subjects divided by race, social status, and custom become analogues for English subjects also divided by race (in multiple senses; see below), status, and religious belief. Although some modern critics have denied that differences in religious belief are refracted in Cary's representation of a marriage in which the wife is said to be of a different race from the husband, such a critical view rests, I contend, on an anachronistic understanding of religion. In Cary's world, as those who conducted treason trials against Jesuits knew well, religious allegiances and ritual practices, especially those that Catholic and Marrano (converted Jewish) subjects were accused of hiding, were intricately bound up with the politics of the household and the state.

The experience of subjection in an imperial locale, which includes experiences of censorship, fear, mistrust, and longing for political change, receives complex articulation in Cary's play about Palestine under Herod's rule. I read Cary's play as showing us a female literacy of equivocation at work both to refract a historical experience of subjection and to articulate, for readers who share the author's beliefs and hopes, a utopian view of empire that hovers, inevitably, between fantasy and prophecy. Whether the prophecy is to be proved true by providential history the writer cannot know; she does know, however, that some members of her present readership—including, I suggest, her

Protestant husband and social superior—would judge the Catholic prophecy both delusional and treasonous. In her portrait of Herod Cary offers a brilliant example of a censorious reader who is also a husband with juridical powers. Herod loves his wife's words (and her "look") only when she aims to please him, and when another interpreter persuades him that his wife harbors treasonous ideas beneath her fair surface, he has her beheaded. After her death, he rereads her "text" and rewrites its meaning in a way that tyrants are free to do, although even Herod is not wholly a free agent in the play's world, for he is subjected to Roman authority and almost loses his own, at home, as a result.

This chapter doesn't complete the task of specifying, much less assessing, the ideological statement(s) made by Cary's play read as a response to a fractured social text. A useful first step in that task, however, is to return, with the help of several recent scholars, to the question of why the apparently innocuous term *equivocation,* from the Latin *aequus* (equal) + *vocare* (to call), should have come over time to signify not only ambiguity—an instance when something is the same in name, as the *OED* puts it, but "not in reality" (meaning 1)—but also "doubtful in character or reputation . . . suspicious" (meaning 5). The *OED* gives that latter sense as first occurring in 1790, but the word's strongly negative connotations go back much earlier, I think: to the era when English rulers were seeking some uniformity in the national language as well as in religion, as we have seen, and when equivocations of many different kinds could conjure up images of treason. Moreover, as a Latinate term frequently used in conjunction with the Greek-rooted word *amphibole* or, as George Puttenham anglicizes it, *amphibologia, equivocation* was often associated with dangerous, and, more specifically, foreign, religious discourses. Puttenham, as Steven Mullaney has shrewdly remarked, makes amphibology "the figure of treason" par excellence by associating it with pagan oracles, Greek, Roman, and pre-Christian British.[23] Puttenham, moreover, describes amphibology in terms of a religious elite's power to use language to lead a gullible populace into sedition. His denunciation of amphibology thus neatly parallels later denunciations of the equivocation allegedly practiced by Catholic priests when they crafted "false prophecies" and disseminated them in England. The "vicious" and "doubtfull" speech of "amphibologia," the "figure of sense uncertain," was, according to Puttenham, "used much in the old times" and was "devised by the religious persons . . . to abuse the superstitious people." Through such "abuse" of words (and one should recall that for Puttenham, all rhetorical figures are "in a sorte abuses or rather trespasses in speech"), an elite group of "religious persons" misled an illiterate or semiliterate multitude (*Arte of English Poesie,* 166). And though the models are ancient and pagan, the problem clearly persists into England's present time and invites us to look further into the historical context for Cary's literacy of equivocation. Through the "propheticall rymes" and verbal ambiguities that are the typical tools of religious persons whose interests deviate from those of the state, "many insurrections and rebellions have bene stirred up in this Realme," Puttenham avers, "as that of *Jacke Straw,* and *Jacke Cade* in Richard the seconds time, and, in our time by a seditious fellow in Norffolke calling himself Captaine Ket and others in other places of the Realme" (*Arte of English Poesie,* 267).

Equivocation in the Realm of England

In Cary's era, the term *equivocation* signaled a variety of verbal acts ranging from homophonic word-play (Cary puns tellingly on *prey* and *pray,* for instance; see below) to extended discourses in speech or writing that are ambiguous in syntax and/or diction. In one complex definition of equivocation, the phenomenon consists of a "mixture" of speech and/or thought and/or writing. I want to posit an ideological continuum among these notions of equivocation, which themselves occur within a larger field of naming and practicing "ambiguous" linguistic acts in an emergent national language that was notoriously prone to borrow terms from abroad and that was deeply hybrid, as Puttenham and others acknowledged, in its formation (see chapter 3). Moreover, as Margreta de Grazia has brilliantly shown, homophonic and homonymic word-play flourished, in early modern versions of English, in ways that rhetoricians and lexicographers since the eighteenth century have typically underestimated, partly because of the rise of lexicography itself as a scientific enterprise of codification or "standardization."[24]

In an innovative effort to historicize and theorize the complex of linguistic operations that modern rhetoricians call punning, de Grazia remarks that in an era when "the written word was as variable as the pronounced" and when "a given word could readily perform diverse grammatical functions," puns did not necessarily carry the eccentric or disruptive charge associated with them by theorists as different as Samuel Johnson, Freud, and Derrida ("Homonyms before and after Lexical Standardization," 147–48). It may be significant, she suggests, that the very term *pun* appears in English only around 1660, with "its origin unknown ('I know not whence this word is to be deduced,' admitted Johnson, and neither do modern lexicographers)" (ibid., 153). De Grazia notes that Renaissance handbooks of rhetoric give names for various kinds of word-play, but none of these figures "precisely covers the simple [modern] definition of a pun as a single sound possessing multiple senses"—or rather, I would suggest, a single grapheme possessing multiple senses and quite possibly a more complex relation to the spoken language(s) than modern philologists can reconstruct. While Cary's play does include examples of many of the tropes that have been cited as Renaissance equivalents to the modern pun (syllepsis and paranomasia, for instance), de Grazia points us to a very useful alternative context for understanding the pun historically, namely Renaissance manuals of logic rather than rhetoric.[25] "A single word cannot constitute a trope, figure, or scheme," she notes, but a word "appearing in different senses in the premises of a syllogism will obviously produce an invalid conclusion" (ibid., 154–55 and n. 30). In Thomas Wilson's oft-reprinted *Rule of Reason* (1551), such words are called "homonyms, ambiguous words, or equivocals."

De Grazia rightly stresses that such "equivocals" were "integral" to early modern discourse in ways hardly imaginable to those of us brought up to groan when we hear or see a pun; the examples of homonyms in the logic manuals "consist of such ordinary words as 'love,' 'common,' and 'world' as frequently as linguistic anomalies like 'bear,' 'light,' and 'lie,' suggesting that what we regard as ordinary words produce multiple senses no less than the linguistic accidents we term puns" ("Homonyms before and after Lexical Standardization," 154). I think that de Grazia slightly overstates the ordinariness and "naturalness" of punning word-play in early modern English discourse. At least by the late sixteenth century, when the Latin-derived term *equivocate* began to be associated with foreigners and traitors, word-plays that could be named "doubtful" and "equivocal" arguably appeared threatening at least to some of those in the literate, elite culture who were beginning to articulate the desires for "uniformity" in spelling that would eventually branch into Puritan calls for plain speech and Royal Society (and Hobbesian) suspicions of figurative language.[26] The tectonic shift that de Grazia associates with Samuel Johnson's famous denigration of "quibbles" in the preface to his edition of Shakespeare's works (1765) obviously began long before Johnson, as de Grazia herself intimates when she mentions the several "efforts at orthographic reform" that occurred during Elizabeth's reign (ibid., 152). It was also during that reign that the term *equivocal* began to acquire its association with traitors and, specifically, with treasonous ideas that seep into the body politic from abroad.

When he attacked Shakespeare for being a "quibbler" in 1765, Samuel Johnson was drawing on quite a long tradition in English letters of yoking equivocal language with a Siren-like temptation to deviate from a man's proper political, ethical, theological, and sexual path. The association of equivocation with deviancy is dramatized in Hobbes's *Leviathan,* in a passage that Steven Mullaney adduces as an ideological precursor to Johnson's famous attack on Shakespeare. Hobbes likens "metaphors, and senseless and ambiguous words" to "ignes fatui" among which the mental traveler wanders dangerously, with his (or her) "end" being "contention, and sedition."[27] Writing with a similar glance at the old epic tradition in which the hero's quest is threatened by a Circe figure, Johnson accuses Shakespeare of following quibbles as Antony followed Cleopatra's boats at the Battle of Actium. Mixing the language of sacrifice with the language of commerce and giving the entire dubious transaction a Roman, and pagan, context, Johnson writes that Shakespeare was "content to purchase" a quibble, "poor and barren as it is," by the "sacrifice of reason, propriety, and truth." A quibble, Johnson goes on to explain, was to Shakespeare "the fatal Cleopatra for which he lost the world, and was content to lose it."[28] Transforming Shakespeare into a version of his own character Mark Antony, Johnson in truth practices a form of the very quibbling, as equivocation, which he denounces. His formulation shows that a quibble is not quite what his name for it suggests, since the quibble is enormously valued by someone whose different conception of value is at once derided and acknowledged in Johnson's elegant sentence.

Equivocation in many of its forms, I suggest, achieves its unsettling effects through positing competing systems of value at work in one place. This is the kind of equivocation Shakespeare pursued both rhetorically and thematically in *Antony and Cleopatra*, where "Roman" values are contrasted repeatedly to foreign, Egyptian ones, and it is a kind of equivocation that Elizabeth Cary was pursuing at almost the same time in pages of a manuscript that evidently circulated for some years before its publication in 1613. Cary, like Shakespeare and Mary Sidney, was fascinated by the figure of Cleopatra and also by the kind of word-play Johnson associated with her—the kind of word-play through which one risked nothing less than losing the world. Even in the word *losing* Cary saw a chance for a pun—and in the most serious of contexts. "Tell thou my lord thou saw'st me loose my breath," Mariam says to the messenger who will report her death to Herod (5.1.73; p. 141). The spelling of "loose," as Maureen Quilligan observes, "allows the text to have it both ways: Mariam not only 'loses' her breath by dying" but also "sets her speech 'loose,' finally free from Herod's control in death" ("Staging Gender," 227). In this pun, as in many others in her text, Cary seems to create for future readers an equivocal message about freedom from tyranny. The pun's message emerges if we see word play on an ideological continuum with other modes of equivocation, and reflections thereon, in the play.

"Faith," Shakespeare's porter exclaims in *Macbeth*, "here's an equivocator, that could swear in both scales against either scale; who committed treason enough for God's sake, yet could not equivocate to heaven" (2.3.7–11). Steven Mullaney and many other scholars think that the original Jacobean audience of *Macbeth* would have heard (or seen) in these lines an allusion to the trial and subsequent hanging of Father Henry Garnet (28 March 1606) for treasonous complicity in the Gunpowder Plot.[29] While critics and editors are agreed on the existence of a topical allusion in Shakespeare's play, however, there is no critical consensus about what it means with respect to Shakespeare's attitudes toward James I (who had explicitly refuted one of Father Garnet's lines of self-justification) or toward Catholics accused of plotting against the crown.[30] The import of the lines about equivocation remains equivocal, asking for "double toil and trouble" from interpreters, and spoken, appropriately, by one who earns his living by bearing burdens. Whatever we make of the old idea that Shakespeare or at least his father was sympathetic to the "old religion" (the latter possibility, in Schoenbaum's wonderful formulation, is "supported" by a "Spiritual Last Will and Testament" and by a document of "doubtful authenticity" found in the eighteenth century and "since lost": a Catholic profession attributed to "John Shakespear"), there is no question that both professed and closet Catholics were in Shakespeare's audience (Schoenbaum, "Life of Shakespeare," 2). How many is and was a matter of polemical debate; so is, and was, the question of what their existence meant for England's nation.[31] Shakespeare's porter reminds us of the "Catholic problem" in England, the division in religious "faith" that resulted in some substantial part of the population also experiencing a conflict between their faith (as loyalty) to their monarch and their faith to God and his representative, the pope. Faith had become an equivocal phenomenon, double, with equal pulls in two directions; it was the seedbed for a type of moral discourse at once modeled and justified by men like Father Henry Garnet. This kind of discourse provides an uncanny historical illustration of Emily Dickinson's gnomic imperative to "tell all the truth but tell it slant."

Developed in the late sixteenth and early seventeenth centuries and disavowed, by the Catholic Church itself, after 1679, the so-called Jesuitical theory of equivocation consists of a public discursive act often perceived (by non-Catholics) as a dangerous lie, or false oath, that is temporally yoked to a private discursive act legitimated, at least to the equivocator's conscience and to other members of her or his belief community, by means of an ingenious set of propositions about God, language, and criteria for truth.[32] This theory of equivocation, described in more detail below, is particularly relevant to the situation of literate Catholic women in seventeenth-century England because the theory envisions an individual capable of self-censorship and self-revelation at once; it also posits the political subject's ability to split a "private" act of discourse, made either in the mind or, rather surprisingly, in writing, from a "public" act usually conceived as a speech act directed to a disapproving audience with the power to punish the body as well as the mind.

In 1584, about a year before Elizabeth Cary was born, a Spanish professor

of canon law named Martín de Azpilcueta (1493–1586) published a Latin treatise on equivocation that most modern scholars regard as historically new and
that Azpilcueta himself defined as "novus modus" even as he defended his innovation by citing ancient precedents for it.[33] Equivocation, he argued, is a
mode of discourse legitimate under certain (dire) social circumstances; it consists of one proposition made for two different audiences but uttered in full
only to one of those audiences. As an example, Azpilcueta asks the reader to
imagine himself (or herself) saying aloud, that is, to an earthly audience, "God
is not," while going on, in thought, to say "an angel."[34] The statement is true in
its entirety and hence, according to its defenders, is a legitimate mode of discourse for God's servants to employ when they find themselves in certain difficult situations of interrogation.

An English Catholic living in Rome when Azpilcueta published his treatise,
Robert Southwell, evidently used this practice (and ingenious theory) of
equivocation, though unsuccessfully, when he was tried for treason in London
in 1595; he is generally credited with, or denounced for, bringing Jesuitical
equivocation to England. Henry Garnet, superior of the English Jesuits from
1586 until his arrest in 1605, sought to explain Southwell's use of equivocation
in the large treatise on the topic that he probably wrote in the late 1590s.[35] Writing to his fellow Jesuit Robert Persons, Garnet explains that he "wrote a treatise of equivocation to defend Father Southwell's assertion, which was much
wondered at by Catholics and heretics."[36] Although some Catholics would
continue to wonder and even be distinctly uneasy about a doctrine repeatedly
tied, by state officials, to accusations of treason, Garnet, himself executed for
treason after his (ambiguous) role in the Gunpowder Plot was discovered,
made an important contribution to the evolving arena of contest around
equivocation.[37] This area dealt with the philosophy and politics of language as
much as with issues of religious doctrine. Garnet adapts Azpilcueta's formulations about equivocation in ways particularly suited to the situation of
Catholics in England. Garnet defends equivocation as a verbal practice of le-
gitimately "hiding" the (whole) truth, and insists that this practice was authorized and illustrated by Christ himself in various New Testament passages
of great hermeneutic difficulty. Such passages come to be the model for what
counts as a "literary" language of irony, indirection, and "dark conceit."[38]

For Azpilcueta, Garnet, and Robert Persons, who also wrote an important
treatise on equivocation first published in 1602 and reissued in 1607, a year
after Garnet's execution, an equivocal statement can be distinguished from a
lie because in the former type of discourse, the whole truth is present in the
discourser's mind and is indeed communicated to the primary audience of all
discourse, God. This claim rests on the notion, adapted from Aristotle, that

propositions may be "mixed," as compounds of speech, writing, and thought
(*De interpretatione,* 16a). Illustrating this point, Garnet explains that "a dying
man could say before witnesses to his heir, 'I bequeathe to you, my son,' then,
his voice failing, write with the pen thrust into his hand, '1000 florins.'"[39] This
is an interesting example, for it equates writing—classically defined as "silent
speech"—with the "mentally reserved" or thought part of the proposition.
Writing thus emerges as a domain of "internal" literacy, we might say, for
Catholics seeking to satisfy their consciences when attempting to serve God in
situations where they have been accused of political disloyalty. As Malloch observes, the doctrine of equivocation emerged at a moment when Catholics
were finding it "urgent to withhold knowledge under interrogation. It was not
enough merely to be able to identify occasions on which it was lawful to withhold knowledge, for the lawfulness of an occasion did not automatically
supply a lawful means, and as St. Augustine had unconditionally forbidden lying, the permissible means were very limited. A refusal to answer, as often as
not, disclosed information. . . . For the conscientious, the dilemma was acute"
("Father Henry Garnet's Treatise of Equivocation," 389).

The Jesuitical doctrine of equivocation provides not only an expedient
mode of discourse for those under duress, but also a powerful justification for
acts of self-censorship occurring simultaneously with (and in response to)
acts of enforced speech, required by a power that the subject regards, in her
heart and before her God, as illegitimate. Far from being merely a term for
word-play, as it has become for most modern literary critics, *equivocation* was,
for a subset of literate English people in the seventeenth century, the name for
a contested mode of "mixed" discourse arising from a social situation that demanded verbal acquiescence even as it forced "conscientious" subjects to develop a theory and practice of verbal resistance to state power. Equivocation
thus opens and explores, for Catholics, precisely that internal terrain of "personal" communication with God usually associated with Protestantism. Not
surprisingly, however, Protestant authorities were not eager to accept this particular blurring of the boundaries between licit and illicit religious domains.
In his long opening statement at Garnet's trial for treason (see the epigraph to
this chapter), Attorney General Edward Coke denounced the treatise of equivocation "seen and allowed by" Garnet (Coke isn't sure if Garnet is the author)
as an extremely dangerous educational text. In it, Coke writes, "under the pre-
text of the lawfulness of a mixt proposition to express one part of a man's
mind, and retain another, people are indeed taught, not only simple lying, but
fearful and damnable blasphemy."[40]

Although most modern critical discussions of Catholic equivocation focus
on the type of proposition in which part is spoken, part is thought (hence the
phrase "mental reservation" to describe the contested religious practice), I

want to stress the conceptual significance of writing, as well as speech, in many of the early debates about equivocation. It is the existence of *written* documents about equivocation, circulating secretly among conspirators or being printed abroad or, without license, in England that seems to fuel Coke's perception of an educational danger set loose in the land.[41] Garnet's treatise illustrates "legitimate" equivocation with an example that puts the written word precisely into the silent but critical role played by the mental or inward word in other examples. One could not be properly accused of atheism, Garnet writes, choosing an example interestingly varied from Azpilcueta's, if one said out loud "God is not" and then held up a sign on which was written "unjust."[42] The irony, of course—and Garnet, writing in manuscript to defend the already executed Robert Southwell, would have been well aware of it—is that one could most certainly be *accused* of atheism if one said or wrote something so inflammatory as "God is not." The Jesuits' argument is that one should not be convicted, by secular authorities, for such a statement. The argument was not likely to be welcome to any state authority, for it makes the determination of truth a matter between the speaker (or thinker or writer) and God, putting secular authorities into the role of spectators vouchsafed only a part of the truth. The argument seeks to shift the balance of power; but the argument only became necessary in the first place because Catholics were being persecuted for their "hidden" thoughts, including treasonous ones they heatedly—but on epistemological grounds, shakily—denied. A particularly ingenious defense, clearly a response to Protestant charges that Catholics had designs on Queen Elizabeth's life, took the form of the so-called bloody question. This is the question that Southwell had famously posed to his prosecutors, and which Persons re-posed, in his (printed) reply to an attack by the Anglican bishop Thomas Morton:

> [I]f their Princesse then living Queene Elizabeth upon a suddaine assault or insurrection against her, should be unjustly pursued by enemies . . . with intention to deprive her, both of Crowne and life, and that only Thomas Morton knowing where she were, should be demaunded therof, and this with such impetuosity and eagernesse, as if he answered not directly to their demaund, her life and state were utterly lost, what would he doe, or what might he doe, in this case of his Princesse extreame distresse? For to discover her were against justice, and duty, in that she is his leige, & innocently pursued; to deny that he knoweth where she is, must be either a lye (which we all hold to be unlawfull to be made, no not for the saving the temporall life of any, as in the next consideration more largely shall be declared) or by some Equivocation or doubtfull speech (but yet such as is no lye) she must be covered, and the persecutours deluded, which our Minister thinketh not lawfull, but holdeth it for impious, yea hellish, heathenish, and sacrilegious also, if it be with an oath.[43]

Turning the tables on the Protestants by making them potential traitors to the queen, Persons proves that equivocation is the logical "third way" between betraying the queen and simply lying about her whereabouts. The model answer, as Persons unveils it much later in the treatise, draws its moral authority from Christ's own example. One may answer "justly" by telling one's interlocutors that one knows "nothing" of a certain matter because Christ gave such an answer—not a lie, but not the full truth either—when he said, "I know it not to tell it [to] yow at this time, sicut filius hominis nescit diem iudicii ut dicat, as Christ knew not the day of Judgment to tell, or utter it to his disciples" (*Treatise tending to Mitigation,* chap. 10, 434–35, citing Mark 13:35–37). An equivocal statement of the kind Persons describes (in two languages) was divided into two parts, one articulated to a human and usually hostile audience, the other articulated within the mind and heard only by the self and by God. Such statements, which Garnet and Persons insist are not licit if the speaker is merely attempting to save his own "temporal" being (his or her life), and which they also repeatedly insist may not be used to challenge the English monarch's temporal power, clearly raise thorny epistemological, ethical, and political questions. In the convoluted casuistical style illustrated in the quotations above, Persons spends hundreds of pages expounding them, incorporating his opponent's views directly into the body of his own text. What interests me here is how Catholic equivocation, as a "mixed" proposition containing thought and spoken elements, becomes something else, ontologically and epistemologically speaking, when it is written or printed on a page. If, according to the official doctrine, part of the statement may be false if taken "on its own"—the part articulated in speech to an audience assumed to have censoring, and punishing, powers—the statement as a whole is alleged to be true, according to equivocation's defenders, because the whole is heard and approved by God. In written definitions, illustrations, and defenses of equivocation, however, the reader occupies the role of God, while, of course, lacking the crucial hermeneutic ability imputed by believers to God: the ability to see into the soul of the person who is making (in the case of writing, has made) the utterance. The earthly audience, whether hearing or reading an equivocal statement, cannot judge its truth; but when the audience reads rather than hears the *oratio mixta,* that audience has a different experience of the evidence and indeed of the phenomenon. Persons obliquely reflects on this issue, I think, when he discusses how interpreters make sense of apparently contradictory written statements consisting of "compounded" parts:

> That one sitting may walke, and one not writing may write, in which sentences the wordes being taken separatly and a part out of composition, they have but simple and plaine significations, but being compounded in this manner as they

ly [note the excellent pun], have manifest Equivocation and Amphibology in
them, by reason of composition. For if we understand that a man sitting, while
he sitteth, can walke, or while he writeth not, can write, which is, as Logitians
say, *in sensu composito,* it is not possible: but if we understand it *in sensu diviso,*
that he that sitteth now may walke afterward, or he that writeth not now, hath
power to write afterward, no man will deny it; and yet are neither of those
thinges falsities or lies, but only Equivocall or amphibologicall propositions,
that may be true in divers senses, and yet deceave the Reader or hearer if he
stand not attent. (*Treatise tending to Mitigation,* chap. 8, 310)

Persons cleverly insists that it is not the producer of an utterance but rather
the recipient, whether reader or auditor, who is ultimately responsible for
making it conform to a "truth" defined as inhering in the logical domain of
common sense, not (it is to be noticed) in the domain of the supernatural at
all. In addition to shifting the burden of proof, as it were, from producer to receiver of discourse, Persons also defines a contextualizing hermeneutic act that
consists of expanding a statement temporally: one must change the tenses of
the clauses to make it make sense. Persons offers here a suggestive hint for how
we might go about interpreting the prophetically freighted historical allegory
Elizabeth Cary practices, I contend, in *The Tragedy of Mariam.* Persons's discussion of written equivocation (which he contrasts with equivocation "in
word or speech" [ibid., 309]) also provides a useful model for Cary's complex
and arguably self-referential statements about female public utterance. These
statements often seem contradictory in precisely the way Persons's second example of a "mixed" equivocal proposition is: "one not writing may write."

In Cary's play, where the generic fiction of drama invites us to see all the
characters as speaking rather than writing their statements, the audience/
reader is asked again and again to evaluate differences between what characters "are" (which may not be fully known even to them) and what they say
both in dialogue and in soliloquy—the latter, of course, conventionally sig-
naling unspoken thoughts. In this verbal universe, hovering like Jesuitical
theories and practices of equivocation on the border between written, spoken,
and "mentally reserved" statements, nothing can be assumed to be quite as
it seems. It therefore becomes difficult to decide on questions of guilt and innocence. I suggest that the Jesuitical theory of equivocation, like the discourse
of casuistry to which this historically specific type of equivocation arguably
belongs, functions to delay or defer the kind of certainty necessary for state
judicial systems to operate effectively.[44] To do so, at least over the long run,
such systems usually need at least the appearance of legitimacy. It is the legitimacy of judgments leading to a subject's death that the Jesuitical doctrine of
equivocation challenges, as does the ethical-legal discourse of casuistry more
generally.

As Lowell Gallagher points out in *Medusa's Gaze,* modern readers tend to associate "casuistry" with the dry, hair-splitting tomes mocked by Pope in *The Rape of the Lock;* the poem locates "tomes of casuistry," rhyming with "chains to yoke a flea," in the lunar sphere of folly.[45] Between the thirteenth century when it arose, however (in conjunction with the institution of auricular confession), and the sixteenth century when it was attacked by Martin Luther as a prime symptom of "the abuse of papal and ecclesiastical power in the Christian world," casuistry, or "the discourse of conscience," played a nontrivial role in the world of European politics.[46] In a fine irony of history, a "science" developed by the Roman Catholic Church to resolve problems of moral choice "that arose from the 'equal poise' of conflicting laws, obligations, and loyalties" was appropriated by both the government and the church of Tudor England, and hence assumed a central place in the legal, political, and theological documents of a Protestant realm (Gallagher, *Medusa's Gaze,* 5–6). At the same time, however, Protestants continued to attack Catholic handbooks of casuistry, and the discursive practices themselves gradually drifted away from the production of moral certainty (guided by a priest) toward the production of "a more supple interpretation of the law in the face of the 'diversity of human temperament'" (ibid., 6). This "drift" reflects an ambiguity inherent in casuistry as an epistemological procedure. Whether it occurred in speech (the peculiar speech of the confessional where the speakers do not actually see one another) or in writing, casuistry "fostered a habit of dwelling on particularities and nuances of individual experience, a habit that resisted the putative purpose of casuistry: to reach a certain judgment of acts based on a clear definition of the boundary between culpability and innocence" (ibid.). Tenets of the later school of casuistry, which sought "probable" rather than certain resolution of cases, appear in the works of Protestant as well as Catholic theologians; casuistical heuristics, central to the workings of Tudor jurists negotiating interacting and competing court systems, have also been posited as a central element in the secular literary domain. Milton's epic effort to "justify the ways of God to men" is a deeply casuistical document; so, George Starr argued some years ago, are Defoe's novels (*Defoe and Casuistry*).

The discourses of casuistry proliferating in post- (or, depending on one's perspective, Counter-) Reformation England fostered vertiginous interpretive practices, as Gallagher shows. These discourses also promoted ways of exploiting silence and equivocation in order to indicate, allusively, the mechanisms of suppression at work within the culture. While Protestant casuists such as William Perkins developed ethical concepts such as "good deceit" (*dolus bonus*), casuistry continued to be associated, negatively, with Catholics.[47] While this group did indeed constitute an "Ideological Other within an enclosed, ostensibly homogeneous community," as Gallagher argues (*Medusa's Gaze*, 2), the Other was itself split by gender. Catholic wives posed particular problems for male casuists, both Protestant and Catholic, because such wives could and sometimes did claim their right to follow their consciences instead of their husband's or monarch's authority.[48] In the atmosphere of crisis following the Gunpowder Plot, for instance, when Parliament was debating "further measures to root out popery," the question of women's degree of responsibility for their moral and religious choices evidently proved so thorny that Parliament opted for delay rather than a clear judgment: when it "came to the question of whether a married man should pay for his wife's recusancy there was 'much dispute' and it was resolved that there should be 'further consideration.'"[49] A case deferred for "further consideration": this phrase epitomizes the ideological import I have been ascribing to the cultural discourses of equivocation and casuistry. A more focused, though necessarily oblique, argument for delay in judgment emerges from the practices of and reflections on equivocal discourses in Cary's play. Such discourses are no less hotly contested within the play's allegorical imperial space than they were in Cary's England.

To Speak, Perhaps to Write; To Publish, Perhaps to Perish: Cary's Literacy of Equivocation

Cary uses her play not only to explore the legitimacy of women's public voice—an issue analyzed in many recent critical studies of *Mariam*, including my own—but also to look critically at modes of censorship and political struggle in post-Reformation England. Cary's critical perspective on an imperial nation is enabled, as I suggested at the outset, by her familiarity with Catholic attacks on Henry VIII that allied him with the wicked and dubiously legitimate king Herod. Cary's political critique is also enabled, I think, by her awareness of the debates about the legitimacy of female rule generated, from many different ideological perspectives, by Henry's daughters Mary and Elizabeth, and by Mary Stuart as well.[50]

Avoiding any simple historical allegories in her treatment of female "public voice," Cary nonetheless explores her culture's ambivalent attitudes toward queens and women writers in her portraits both of Mariam and Salome. Each character bears some resemblance to Anne Boleyn, as I have argued elsewhere, and each recalls aspects of Queen Elizabeth's complex image as well.[51] Both challenge Herod's authority—Salome always covertly, equivocally, Mariam overtly when she refuses to sleep with him after his return from Rome. Mariam and Salome seem to illustrate antithetical styles of female speech: Salome lies to get her way but speaks the truth in her soliloquies, whereas Mariam refuses to lie or equivocate "tactfully" in her dealings with Herod but arguably deceives herself in some of her soliloquies. Are these female characters antitheses of each other or two aspects of a complex, contradictory whole? Gwynne Kennedy has recently argued that Mariam's anti-equivocation stance does not preclude some evidence of verbal self-censorship in her dialogues with Herod; perhaps the difference between the two characters is more a matter of degree than of kind (*Just Anger*, 51–74). Mariam insists, like the Hamlet of Act 1, that she "knows not seems," but Salome the liar may be speaking the truth when she argues that Mariam's surface and her interior don't perfectly match. Which is the virtuous woman here, and which the vice?

A possible answer comes from studying Cary's dramatization of various female and subordinated male characters' styles of making their opinions—and sometimes their very existence—public. Cary weaves a particularly complex web of similarities and differences—in moral and verbal styles both—between Mariam, Salome, and a character named Graphina. In her one brief appearance in Cary's text (2.1), Graphina is strongly associated with the feminine virtue of modest silence, but the language through which she is defined prevents us from conceiving of her simply as a foil either to Salome's vice or to Mariam's unruly tendency to "public speech." Graphina's name—which doesn't appear in Cary's source texts or in her contemporaries' versions of the story[52]—invites us to read her speech as somehow related to the question of female *writing* in either a private or a public context (indeed, the line between the private and the public is rendered equivocal in Graphina's scene, as it is in the play as a whole). The name makes a bilingual play on the Greek word *graphein*, "to write," and thus arguably alludes to the ancient idea of writing as "silent speech" or, in a Judeo-Christian version of the trope, writing as a "handmaid" to speech. According to this widespread cultural view—famously named and critiqued as "logocentrism" by Derrida—writing is logically and ontologically secondary to speech, just as woman is logically and ontologically secondary to man according to Judeo-Christian and Greco-Roman authorities. The Greek pun lurking in Graphina's name is, appropriately, supplemented, as Jonathan Goldberg has noted, by the addition of the diminutive, feminizing *-ina* to the graphic root (*Desiring Women Writing*, 164). This Latin or Italianate suffix, rather ambiguously sutured to a Greek "root" (do we have "graph=ina" or "graph[e]in=a"?), seems wittily and homonymically to underscore the humble, almost childlike quality of Cary's slave girl. She is loved by Herod's younger brother Pheroras, who risks the king's anger by preferring Graphina to the highborn bride—his niece!—whom Herod has chosen for him (2.1.23; p. 89). The "princess born" occupies the same social position as Mariam, but this princess seems to possess just the quality of speechlessness that Herod's own princess lacks; Pheroras de-scribes his niece as a "baby" whose "infant tongue" can "scarce her name dis-tinguish to another's ear" (2.1.16–17; p. 89). Something strange is going on in this short scene with its intertwined questions about naming, speaking, not speaking (*infans* means "speechless" in Latin), and the act of distinguishing— in one or more languages—one entity or identity from another. Compar-isons and contrasts proliferate among Graphina; the speechless "baby" she has replaced in Pheroras's affections; Mariam, to whom Pheroras "boastingly" compares his bride; and—last but never least—Salome, who is unmentioned in the scene but hovers over it nonetheless. She will later rewrite it, too, trans-forming it from a joyous exchange of words between lovers expecting soon to be wed into an ironic "mistaking," on both their parts, of the truth of their social situation.

The problem of female speech posed by this opaque scene should be ana-lyzed with more attention than most critics have paid to the play's complex representation of rivalries "between men."[53] These rivalries cross and blur all lines of gender in a highly equivocal meditation on relations of likeness and difference between speech and writing, free speech and censored speech, dis-course and silence, as well as between elder and younger brothers, princesses, wives, and "handmaids" as potential competitors for the peculiar position of "mate" and "copartner" to an allegedly all-powerful king whose power is, at present, in abeyance because he is absent from his throne.

Freed from the censorship of speech and desire imposed by Herod, Pheroras sounds, at the beginning of this scene, oddly like Mariam at the play's beginning where she asks or exclaims, "How oft have I with public voice run on." In a parallel rhetorical moment, Pheroras exclaims, "How oft have I with lifted hands implor'd / This blessed hour, till now implor'd in vain, / which hath my wished liberty restor'd" (2.1.5–8; p. 88). His echo of Mariam acquires deeper resonance when he later claims that Herod at some point in the past "did raise my head / to be his realm's copartner, kingdom's mate" while at the same time keeping "Graphina from my bed" (2.1.25–27; p. 89). In what sense could the younger brother have been a "copartner," an equal in governing power, while also being a subordinate in the domain of domestic desire? The image of a "realm's copartner" invokes, most obviously, the idea of a king and queen sharing power in the public sphere and somehow negotiating the com-plexities such power-sharing would generate for the domestic sphere. Queen Elizabeth clearly saw the problems in such a copartnering arrangement and declined to attach herself to a "consort." Pheroras's image also invokes, I sug-gest, the extremely unstable political partnership existing between ruling Roman men just before the time of the play. This is the relation between

Antony and Octavius (Lepidus having been recently disposed of) that dissolved at Actium when Antony, infamously, pursued erotic desire at the expense of political ambition. Antony's choice is recalled in Pheroras's declaration that possessing Graphina is "more wish'd by me than thrice Judea's state" (2.1.28; p. 89). His denial of ambition for state rulership is somewhat undermined, however, by his need to be socially equal or superior to Herod in order to achieve the goal envisioned in his final lines: "Come, fair Graphina, let us go in state, / This wish-endearéd time to celebrate" (2.1.85–86; p. 91). In truth, he needs Herod's death or deposition to fulfill his wish to marry Graphina "in state," publicly—and this will be underscored, ironically, later in the play, when the younger brother's private and unsanctioned marriage, now accomplished, is so endangered by Herod's return to Judea that Pheroras will have to betray other subordinated, effeminized men in order, precariously, to preserve Herod's favor. In his oddly negative and ambiguous relation to political power, Pheroras also resembles Mariam. He doesn't want to be Herod's "mate" in the public sphere (compare Mariam's later refusal of Herod's extravagant offer to crown her "empress of Arabia" in a copartnering enterprise: "For thou shalt rule, and I shall win the land" [4.3.104–5; p. 118]), but Pheroras does want a kind of self-ruling freedom that he can have only in Herod's absence. He joyfully commends "this blessed hour" that has "made my subject self my own again" (2.1.8; p. 88).

Even more striking than the parallels among Pheroras, Mariam, and Antony are the contrasts Cary's scene draws between Mariam and Graphina. The latter has the humility and the capacity to "bridle" her tongue that Mariam initially lacks. Graphina is initially so well bridled, indeed, that Pheroras begs her to speak, telling her (and the silent audience or reader she has until now resembled) that he prefers her to the "baby" bride Herod has chosen for him. Desiring her speech, Pheroras commands or begs her to "move [her] . . . tongue / For Silence is a signe of discontent" (2.1.42; p. 89). Pheroras here suggests that the meaning of silence has a great deal to do with the power relations between speakers in particular social circumstances—which is something that some modern feminist theorists have forgotten when associating female silence with oppression only. Historically, both the powerful and the less powerful have used silence as a weapon; kings (and queens) may say no by being silent in response to a petitioner, and wives, like courtiers—Thomas More, for example—may resist monarchs by refusing to speak. Gwynne Kennedy cites a passage in William Gouge's treatise *Of Domesticall Duties* (1622) that seems an apt analogue for Pheroras's perception that silence may be a "sign of discontent." Although Gouge begins by articulating the common view that silence is an asset in a wife, much preferable to "loquacitie, to

talkativenesse, to over-much tatling," he then recognizes something less doxical: "otherwise," he writes, "silence, as it is opposed to speech, would imply
stoutnesse of stomacke, and stubbornnesse of heart, which is an extreme con-
trarie to loquacite."[54]

"Complete silence is ambiguous," Kennedy remarks, "because it can signal
either disagreement or acceptance" of the husband's authority; hence the
conduct-book authors sometimes define wifely silence paradoxically, as "a
particular manner of speaking: self-effacing, acquiescent, and above all, not
angry" (*Just Anger,* 58). William Whately defines silence, for instance, as "not
an utter abstinence from speech, but using fewer words (and those mild and
low), not loud and eager."[55] Wifely "silence" is defined here as a kind of Aristotelian virtue of "moderation" including some element of self-censorship—
a golden mean between stubborn "utter abstinence from speech" and "over-
much tatling," a speech showing some kind of excessiveness of desire,
including, it seems, a desire for speech itself ("eager," "loud").

Graphina obeys Pheroras by "humbly speak[ing] about her silence for over
forty lines," as Kennedy wittily remarks (*Just Anger,* 58). Her words, like Pheroras's earlier ones about his preference for a speaking wife over a silent "infant" bride, serve to query the logic of the normative wife as "chaste, silent,
and obedient."[56] The interrogation occurs, first, in the scene's suggestion that
womanly "silence" may function just as erotically as speech in a marital (or a
premarital) relation. The conduct books never consider this possibility. Nor
do they consider that a marriage relation may be rudely disrupted, and indeed
translated into something that looks like an adulterous relation, by a monarch
who happens to be the groom's brother. Herod, upon his return to Jerusalem
in Act 4, will with Salome's prompting retroactively redefine Pheroras's love
for Graphina as a resistance to royal authority; Herod will also paint the virgin Graphina, who in Act 2 calls herself Pheroras's "handmaid," as a harlot
(4.2.56; p. 88). Insofar as Graphina is represented as telling her higher status
lover only what he wants to hear, when he wants to hear it, she seems to figure
a mode of "safe" speech, semiprivate speech that neither aims at nor produces
offense—at least to the primary audience, the husband (or, in this case, the
husband-to-be). Viewed from the domestic political perspective dramatized
in the dialogue scene, Graphina's speech could indeed be seen as an allegorical
version of the kind of proper writing allowed to some aristocratic women both
in the normative discourse of the conduct books and in the historical practice
of some households. Such writing would have satisfied the ideological requirement that wives be "private" as opposed to "public" creatures; at the same
time, however, as Marta Straznicky and Jonathan Goldberg have pointed out,
such writing, especially when it occurred in the ambiguous genre we anachro-

nistically call "closet drama," need not have lacked either the ambition or the power to comment on public affairs in a politically significant way.[57]

The boundary between public and private domains was in truth less fixed, in Cary's England, than it sometimes seems to be in the discourses about wifely conduct; the boundary is much more permeable in the world of Cary's play than I thought it was when I first attempted to interpret Graphina as a virtuous foil to the transgressive femininity embodied in both Mariam and Salome. I would now revise my earlier view, which coincided with Dympna Callaghan's sense that Graphina represents an "ideal of unsullied femininity" in a "dramatically insipid way."[58] For if one looks closely at Graphina's speech, one sees what a talented actress consigned to this twenty-seven-line part might have seen long ago, had the play been performed—namely, that Graphina's apparently modest and virtuous words offer numerous opportunities for suggesting that her words are not a transparent window to her mind. Graphina may well represent her culture's ideal of the "woman of modesty," but in doing so, she reminds the attentive reader that modest or self-censored speech may be an ambiguous discourse, and even a potentially dangerous one. The "woman of modesty," wrote Barnabe Rich in a text published, as *Mariam* was, in 1613, "seemeth in speaking to hould her peace, and in her silence . . . seemeth to speake."[59]

A treatise of 1591 entitled *A Preparative to Marriage* points to just the problem I see lurking in Graphina's characterization. The wife (or wife-to-be), writes Henry Smith, "must sometimes . . . observe the servant's lesson, not answering again [Titus 2:9] and hold her peace to keep the peace, because silence oftentimes doth keep the peace, when words would break it."[60] The woman who "observes the servant's lesson" of not answering "again"—the lesson so elaborately dramatized, with such debatable results, in Shakespeare's *Taming of the Shrew*—retains the ability not to "observe" the lesson at some future point. For while the wife may be *like* a servant, and may need to be schooled in the similitude, she is not identical to a servant. The analogical relation gives Renaissance theorists of the marriage relation, both Protestant and Catholic, considerable trouble.[61] They shift metaphors confusingly in their efforts to articulate the highly unstable relation between the wife and the servant. In one favorite metaphorical matrix, the wife is described as being neither the "head" (or ruler) nor the "foot" (or servant) in the one body made by the marriage relation; rather, as the Puritan William Perkins explains, she is the "companion" of the husband, his "yoke-fellow" but not quite his equal; she was taken from his side "to the end that man should take her as his mate."[62]

The potential for dissonances between the social roles of servant and wife is dramatized when Graphina speaks as if she had already been socially transformed by the institution of marriage: "Your hand hath lifted me from lowest state,/To highest eminency wondrous grace,/And me your handmaid have you made your mate" (2.1.60; p. 90). Graphina here makes her lover's hand the instrument that has changed a "handmaid" into a "mate"—but the attentive reader may suspect that the writer is showing the power of her pen-wielding hand in the repetition of the word *hand* and in the punning *maid/made/mate*. The modest Graphina is, it seems, capable of speaking equivocally, even if the equivocation works with dramatic irony against the character. Indeed, it is Graphina's desire for the future that evidently impels her to speak falsely, in some sense, here. She is in truth not yet Pheroras's "mate," although the scene begins with him declaring, "'Tis true, Graphina, now the time draws nigh/ Wherein the holy priest with hallowed right,/The happy long-desired knot shall tie" (2.1.1–3; p. 88). He too speaks falsely, here, or rather, he speaks equivocally, falsely with respect to the present facts, but truly with respect to his desire. The scene's concern with the many facets and modalities of truth is announced in his opening declaration, "'Tis true."

The play unfolds, in time, in ways that only deepen the ambiguity of the truth-claims made in Pheroras and Graphina's initial dialogue. In Act 3, scene 1, Pheroras again appears on stage in dialogue with a woman, but this time his interlocutor is Salome, not Graphina, and Salome calls into question the very grounds of Pheroras's love for the slave girl. "One mean of birth, but yet of meaner mind,/A woman full of natural defects—I wonder what your eye in her could find?" (3.1.12–14; p. 105). Salome then suggests that Graphina may harbor "ill" thoughts in her mind, behind the "porter" of self-censorship, who may allow evil thoughts to enter but not to exit from Graphina's head. We need not believe in Salome's negative judgment of Graphina to accept the interpretive challenge her lines pose: to reread the earlier scene with some skepticism, with some awareness that even an apparently innocent, virgin slave girl may think more than she says. Slaves of either gender, Shakespeare's Iago suggests, may be "bound to every act of duty" while being free not to "utter their thoughts" (*Othello*, 3.3.134–35).[63] Salome, herself twitted by Mariam with "base birth," invites us to pay more attention to Graphina than we might be inclined to grant a minor female character, and Salome also helps us see potential meaning in the parallels Cary's text draws between Mariam and Herod's younger brother. If we entertain Salome's suggestion that Graphina is capable of ambition, we may suspect that Graphina seeks, as Herod did, to use marriage to effect a dramatic rise to "eminency." And even if we ultimately dismiss Salome's view of Graphina as the villain's projection of her own bad qualities onto another character, we will have to engage in the casuist's quintessential activity of weighing one character's view, buttressed by a claim to represent common opinion ("but say you thought her fair, as none thinks else"), against another character's view.[64] The case, with its pun on *fair* as "beautiful" and as "good," cannot be unequivocally decided, and indeed Salome and Pheroras's debate about Graphina's character is interrupted by the arrival of the high priest announcing the news of Herod's return to Judea. Pheroras says he does not expect "ill news from holy mouth," but of course that is just what he gets, despite the priest's own irony-laden description of his utterance as "peaceful tidings" bringing "honey to your list'ning ear" (3.1.32, 3.2.1–2; p. 106).

In the allegorical imperial world Cary fashions in her play, what is "ill news" to some may be "peaceful tidings" to others; the meaning of the message depends as much on the receiver's politically conditioned point of view as it does on the intent of the speaker. In such a world, it is prudent to remain silent unless one is quite sure that one's audience will approve of one's words. This course of verbal action is what Graphina seems to illustrate, in striking contrast to Mariam's tendency throughout the play to "run on with public voice" without attending carefully to the character of her audience. Graphina's opening lines, like Pheroras's, invite us to see an equivocal relation between her and Mariam. "Mistake me not, my lord," says Graphina, "too oft have I / Desir'd this time to come with winged feet, / To be enrapt with grief when 'tis too nigh" (2.1.45–47; p. 90). Starting with the possibility that her silence may be misinterpreted, Graphina seeks to ensure a favorable reception for her words and her "wishes": "You know my wishes ever yours did meet: / If I be silent, 'tis no more but fear / That I should say too little when I speak" (2.1.48– 50; p. 90). Mariam, in contrast, begins with an admission that she has heretofore tended to say too much—and she addresses a man who is absent, indeed dead, rather than one who is living and susceptible to her physical charms. The "Roman lord" she apostrophizes in her opening soliloquy is actually Julius Caesar, but reading retrospectively, as the play teaches us to read—here, specifically, reading Mariam's opening lines with Graphina's later ones to Pheroras in mind—we see that the "Roman lord" is also a figure for Mariam's absent husband, Pheroras's brother and alleged "copartner" in the realm. Here is what Mariam says to the "Roman lord" and also to those absent judges of her words, the readers: "How oft have I with publike voice run on? / To censure Rome's last Hero for deceit: / Because he wept when Pompeis life was gone, / Yet when he liv'd, hee thought his Name too great."[65] These lines link the theme of female "public voice" immediately with the idea of temporal repetition (*oft* is the first thread in the verbal parallels between Mariam, Pheroras, and Graphina), the idea of transgressive excess ("run on"), and the idea of punishment or "censure." The question mark after the first line seems at first merely an oddity of seventeenth-century rhetorical punctuation.[66] But the question itself, voiced at the play's threshold moment by a female character whose "unbridled speech" is cited as a major cause for Herod's decision to censor her voice definitively, is not by any means simply rhetorical. It is, we might say, complexly rhetorical—for several reasons. First, to make it the kind of question that obviously requires the affirmative answer "very often," the reader must "run on" over the line's end and its punctuation. The structure of the verse creates for the reader a slight but significant tension between pausing—to respect the seemingly self-contained formal and semantic unit of the first line—and proceeding, according to the dictates of the syntactic logic, which retrospectively reveals the first line to have been part of a larger unit. The verse thereby works to fashion a counterpoint between formal and semantic strains. We pause on the theme of "running on," we run on to encounter the theme of censure—a word that signified not only punishment but also censoring and critical judgment in seventeenth-century English (*OED*). The lines not only work to anticipate the drama to come; they also mark the play, for Cary herself and perhaps for her early readers as well, with something we might call the woman author's *signature*.[67]

That signature consists not of a name but of a Chinese box set of questions about the logic of the Pauline injunction against female public speech and the cultural rule of chastity which that injunction ostensibly supported. Like a lawyer presenting ambiguous fact situations to a judge, Cary invites her readers to consider whether the play text itself is "covered" by the law: is *writing* a form of "public voice"? Is a *drama* not necessarily intended for performance on the public stage a legitimate form of female verbal production? Is a *soliloquy*—by theatrical convention, a "private" speech overheard (overread?) by an audience—legitimate? In short, the play opens in a way that seems designed to test, but not overtly to disobey, the rule proscribing "public voice" for women. Here we have a written representation of a female character soliloquizing, as if in private, about prior acts of culpable public speech. The censure that might have been attached to the woman's acts of "running on" verbally in public, however, is here preemptively defined as a woman's "rash" act of criticizing a high-ranking man without realizing that what she attacked as hypocrisy was in truth an appropriately double response to a genuinely complex event:

> But now I do recant, and, Roman lord,
> Excuse too rash a judgment in a woman:
> My sex pleads pardon, pardon then afford,
> Mistaking is with us but too too common.
> Now do I find, by self-experience taught,
> One object yields both grief and joye.
>
> (1.1.5–10; p. 69)

Mariam's emphatic phrase "now I do recant" is also, I want to suggest, part of this woman writer's signature. It alerts the contemporary reader to the play's ambiguous intervention in a dangerous discursive territory of religious dispute in the past—in Roman Judea—and in Cary's present. At stake is what one may learn—or forget—about a mode of behavior named "deceit" in the play's second line. Mariam, who will later be represented as scorning deceit and hypocrisy in her dealings with Herod, opens the play by reinterpreting her own earlier judgment of censoring a Roman "hero"—Julius Caesar, but the phrase could apply, ironically, to Herod as well—with "public voice": she had accused this man, also her addressee, of deceit. Taught by "self-experience," however—specifically, the experience of her own mixed emotions upon hearing the news of Herod's death—the heroine has changed her mind, come to appreciate complexity in a new way. We no sooner enter the play's world than we encounter a complex semiotic and ethical situation: how to judge someone who "recants"—revises or withdraws, but also, necessarily, repeats—a prior opinion publicly articulated. The "public voice" is censurable not only because of the speaker's gender but also because such a voice has legal consequences. By accusing a "Roman lord"—Caesar or Herod—of "deceit," Mariam has committed a crime that looks a lot like slander and—if it were indeed directed at Herod—like treason. The historical discursive territory into which the play brings its own equivocal words (and words about words) includes a significant area in which theories about women's sexuality overlap with theories about Catholics—and other cultural Others—who rely on deceit to endanger the body politic. "This equivocating and lying," as Sir Edward Coke wrote in the passage cited in my epigraph, "is a kind of unchastity."

Mariam's opening lines address a set of issues—transgressive speech, misinterpretation, the possibility of revising one's judgment over time (which of course requires that the initial judgment not entail a death sentence on the culpable party)—that bear allegorically on the play's own mode of material existence. That includes the question of the play's *right* to exist in the world, its legitimacy as a communication aimed at future as well as present readers. The act of writing a manuscript for possible publication would seem—like the dramatic form of the soliloquy—to occupy a shady territory between private and public verbal production. During the years before her play was printed but when it was evidently circulating in manuscript, Cary could have applied Mariam's opening question to herself—"How oft have I with publike voice run on?"—and answered it with a decorum the fictional character lacks: "Never." But that definitive answer would not have satisfied the culturally constructed censoring power that the play text ascribes chiefly to the figure of the tyrant-husband but also to the Chorus, which suggests that any desire for a "public" audience is culpable in a wife who is defined as the private property of her husband. If the Chorus is right, the proscription against female "public voice" would include any writing, in manuscript or print, that reached an audience of "more than one."

The Chorus's speech occurs at a pivotal moment in the plot: at the end of Act 3, just before Herod's first appearance on stage, and just after Mariam learns, through her servant Sohemus, that Herod is alive. Through talking with Sohemus, Mariam has discovered not only that Herod lives, but also that when he departed for Rome, he left secret orders that she should be killed if he died. Sohemus could perhaps be judged guilty of disobeying those orders, having let Mariam live after news of Herod's death reached Judea, and he could certainly be judged guilty of breaking his oath to keep silent about the orders. Like almost every other character in the play, he has done and said things during Herod's absence that can now, with the king's return, incur punishment. After a period of relative freedom, censure in all of its senses is again the law of the land—and with that law comes the need for complex casuistical judgments, as characters find themselves, as English Catholics invariably did, owing obedience to more than one authority. Sohemus, having broken vows of silence sworn to his king, now finds himself in fear for his life and hence giving highly self-interested advice to his queen—specifically, he tells her she must break some vows she has solemnly sworn to herself. She rejects the advice, in lines that intriguingly link a morally ambiguous act of sexual self-governance to the verbal act—also morally ambiguous— of breaking an oath or vow: "I will not to his love be reconcil'd, / with solemn vows I have forsworn his bed," Mariam asserts (3.3.132–33; p. 110). Having during Herod's absence found, as Pheroras did, "my subject self my own again," Mariam implicitly places loyalty to herself above loyalty to her husband and king (2.1.8; p. 88). In this choice, she ratifies Sohemus's decision to be more loyal to his mistress than to his master. Faced with the fact of Herod's return, however, Sohemus is apparently reconsidering his prior choice about whom to obey: "If your command should me to silence drive, / It were not to obey, but to betray," he warns her (3.3.141–42; p. 110). Silence, as we have seen Pheroras telling Graphina, may be a "sign of discontent"; here, we learn from Sohemus that it may be a short step from silent discontent to traitorous thoughts and, perhaps, actions. In this context Sohemus advises Mariam not simply to be silent when Herod returns but to be "mild" and "more tem'prate" in her verbal, and presumably her sexual, behavior: Herod's "heart," Sohemus remarks, "by affability is won" (3.3.131, 149, 150;

p. 110). Sohemus is recommending "the servant's lesson" discussed earlier, the lesson of not answering back.

Mariam, with more than a hint of the regal quality of pride in her scorn, re-jects any such advice. In so doing, she is perhaps not as virtuous as she has seemed to many modern readers. She certainly forgets the lesson in complex-ity of emotion that she claimed to have learned in her opening soliloquy, for she now accuses her earlier self of hypocrisy for having mourned Herod's death. The charge of hypocrisy rests, however, on a significant oversimplifica-tion: Mariam forgets that she, like Julius Caesar, felt both grief and joy at a ri-val's demise. Even as she rejects hypocrisy, she cannot avoid equivocal lan-guage: "Oh, now I see I was an hypocrite:/I did this *morning* for his death complain,/And yet do *mourn*, because he lives, ere night" (3.3.152–54; p. 110, my emphasis). Moreover, in rejecting her "morning" self as "an hypocrite," she creates a pun on "mourning" that works, I suggest, to interrogate her strong conviction of her innocence in this speech (see 3.3.171, 180; p. 111) and her per-haps foolish view of the truth as a single phenomenon. "But now that cur-tain's drawn from off my thought," she says, reinterpreting her earlier "self-experience" of mixed emotions in an almost Freudian way, as a "true" feeling (joy in Herod's death) covered temporarily by a screen or curtain of a more so-cially acceptable feeling, grief. The "curtain," however, could also be inter-preted theatrically, not as a veil covering a bedrock of truth but rather as an ar-ras or tapestry of the sort often used in Tudor and Stuart theaters (public and private both) to suggest "interior scenes."[68] This second reading of the line, which works to ironize Mariam's "scorn" for hypocrisy or acting, is supported by the following depiction of a medieval mystery play occurring in the inte-rior scene, as it were, of Mariam's heart. That implied play, in another ironic turn of the screw, is "about" a Herod much more one-dimensional and vil-lainous than the Herod of Cary's own drama, the Herod whom, after all, Mariam has confessed to having once loved despite the wrongs he has done to her family. Replacing that Herod—whom the reader knows, as yet, only from hearsay—is an older figure from a theatrical world not yet troubled by the di-visions within and among subjects engendered by the Reformation. "Hate doth appear again with visage grim," says Mariam, "And paints the face of Herod in my heart,/In horrid colours with detested look" (3.3.158–60; p. 110).

Perhaps, this scene suggests, Mariam needs such a simplified image of Herod, and such a univocal experience of hate, to sustain her in the course of action she goes on to embrace. This is a course of verbal as well as social action; in terms of the play's concern with "public voice," this course of action would entail making one's inner thoughts ("meaning") public without any concern for the reader's power over the thinker/speaker/writer. "I know I could enchain him with a smile," Mariam asserts, speaking of her powerful reader, Herod; and if she combined her smile with rhetorical guile, she could transform herself from a servant into a conqueror, for she could lead Herod "captive with a gentle word." Renouncing such power (easy to do when the claim hasn't been tested), she insists on her ability to stand above or outside the realm of equivocation I have been defining as an effect of, and contributor to, Cary's experience of living in an imperial nation. Mariam's statements against hypocrisy should not, however, be taken as simple articulations of the play's moral lesson. Cary's Mariam is arguably more ambitious, and less virtuous, less in a position to berate others for their failings, than she acknowledges when she denies the existence of any gap between her "look" (appearance), her "speech," and her "meaning." The very syntax of her denial gives the lie to what seems her intention to assert a perfectly transparent relation between an appearance (a text or a face), a speech act, and a meaning or intent or inner word: "I scorn my look should ever man beguile,/Or other speech than meaning to afford" (3.3.165–66; p. 111).

It is such words of principle—and the principle that generates such words—that Sohemus laments after Mariam leaves the stage: "Poor guiltless Queen! Oh that my wish might place/A little temper now about thy heart:/Unbridled speech is Mariam's worst disgrace,/And will endanger her without desert" (3.3.181–84; pp. 111–12). Sohemus's casuistical judgment, criticizing Mariam for something that is at once a "disgrace" and, although "worst," by implication trivial, venial, unworthy to be deemed a cause of "guilt," sets the stage for the extremely tortuous judgment of Mariam's "fault" offered by the Chorus at the close of Act 3 (3.215–50; pp. 113–14). Angeline Goreau thinks this speech shows the hegemonic status of female modesty in seventeenth-century England ("Two English Women," 105). Assuming that the Chorus speaks unequivocally for the author's opinions, Goreau concludes that Cary here ratifies a definition of chastity not only as abstinence from illegitimate sexual activity but also as a virtue that involves divesting oneself of "power as well as will." By thus reinterpreting chastity as passivity, Cary "sets up an infinitely expanding architecture of self-restraint, often more far-reaching and effective than any form of external censorship might be" (Goreau, ed., *Whole Duty of a Woman*, 13). Goreau is right to stress this feature of the Chorus's speech, but she fails to consider the ways in which both the rhetoric of the speech and its larger dramatic context render this extreme prescription of wifely self-censorship problematic. The Chorus, indeed, offers contradictory statements about the precise nature of the error Mariam has committed. According to the second stanza, the error involves indulging in, rather than refraining from, something that is characterized as "lawful" liberty. When the Chorus goes on to specify the error as a fault of *speech*, however, its lawful status seems to become more dubious. By stanza 5, the error is the distinctly illegitimate and incipiently political one of "usurping upon another's right." And there is a corresponding contradiction in the Chorus's views of the "virtue" it is advocating. In stanza 3, which stresses the duty of relinquishing desires for speech and fame, the virtue being advocated is quite distinct from the possession of physical chastity: the woman may be "most chaste" even if she does grant a "private word" to someone other than her husband. By stanza 5, however, the "redefinition" of chastity that Goreau remarks has occurred: "her mind if not peculiar [private] is not chaste," says the Chorus. Which formulation about chastity are we to take as authoritative?

Interpreting the Chorus's speech becomes even more difficult when we try to read it in its dramatic context, as an ethical prescription for this particular heroine. The final lines seem to suggest that Mariam's tragic fate could have been averted had she refrained from speaking her mind, publishing her thoughts, to anyone other than her husband. But the play's subsequent development makes this notion absurd: it is precisely because Mariam speaks her mind not only to Sohemus but also, at least to some extent, to her husband that she loses her life. Although Gwynne Kennedy has argued persuasively that Mariam actually does censor her anger in her speeches with Herod in Act 4, avoiding "the negative images of angry wives as shrewish, scolding, irrational, and voluble," Mariam nonetheless fails to model the qualities of mildness and affability that Sohemus—and many conduct-book authors—recommend for the wife who wants to win or retain a husband's love.[69] Indeed, Mariam articulates in Herod's presence a version of the same principle of noncompliance we have heard her voicing to Sohemus: "I cannot frame disguise, nor never taught / My face a look dissenting from my thought," she says, refusing to smile obediently when Herod bids her to (4.3.145–46; p. 119). Her response of nonresponsiveness "vexes" him, and the exchange seems to confirm Sohemus's view that Mariam brings on her own death by refusing to "bridle her tongue."

It is, however, too simple to conclude that she causes her fall by transgressively speaking her mind. The problem is that she both speaks too freely and refuses to give her body (or even her smile) to Herod, its rightful owner, according to the Chorus. She censors the wrong thing: his phallic ego rather than her tongue. The problem of her sexual withholding—a symptom, I suggest, of a broad set of political problems having to do with subjects' withholding of full loyalty to any one master, whether husband, feudal lord, or king—is addressed by the Chorus when it asks the apparently rhetorical question, "When to their husbands they themselves do bind, / Do they not wholly give themselves away?" By the end of its speech, the Chorus has evidently suppressed altogether the crucial issue of Mariam's denial of Herod's sexual rights in his wife's body. The Chorus concludes by asserting that Mariam would have been "free from fear, as well as innocent," if only she had been willing to forbear filling "any's ears but one" with her words. The pronoun *one* evidently refers here, as it does in the earlier phrase "none but one," to the husband. If, however, we grant that the play as a whole makes it extremely hard to read the Chorus's question about whether women should give themselves "wholly" away in marriage as requiring a simply affirmative answer, then we should ask, as Catherine Belsey does, whether the term *one* might alternatively refer to the wife herself (*Subject of Tragedy,* 173). Since Mariam is in danger because she speaks to her husband in a way that "vexes" him, denying him not only the smiling lips he desires but also the vaginal openness, perhaps Cary's point, if not the Chorus's, is that the wife who has independent thoughts would "be wiser to keep them to herself, precisely because in marriage they are no longer her own" (ibid., 173–74). In Mariam's case, however, such a course of silence or extreme self-censorship would not have had any practical efficacy unless it were accompanied by sexual surrender and its psychic corollary, the split between being and seeming that Mariam herself associates with hypocrisy. The Chorus's ethical precepts begin to look either incoherent or highly equivocal; if the wife cannot so relinquish individual subjectivity that she "bare[s] herself of power as well as will," becoming "wholly" an extension of her husband, she should at the least free her life from suspicion: she should seem to be her husband's private property no matter what she may really think herself to be.

What theory of wifely chastity is Cary's Chorus propounding? Hints may lie in two equivocations partly obscured by the modern edition of the play: the word *lord* in line 228, which is capitalized in the 1613 text ("That wife her hand against her fame doth rear,/That more than to her Lord alone will give/A private word to any second ear"); and the egregious pun that lurks in the central question about wives with any sort of conscience, or even consciousness, that is, those who have not "bared themselves of power as well as will": "Or give they but their body, not their mind,/Reserving that, though best, for others' prey?" In the 1613 text, *prey* is spelled *pray.* The wife's true interlocutor, the term *Lord* suggests, may be God. This interpretation, which would also expand the possible referents for the later phrase "none but one," comes into focus when we recall that the problem of the "unbelieving husband," and his "believing" wife's right to disobey him under certain circumstances, was a major site of casuistical reasoning in both Protestant and Catholic texts from the early seventeenth century. In certain situations of physical or spiritual danger, the wife might have to choose God over her husband. And if she were a Catholic, the wife might find herself required by conscience to obey God or his priestly representative rather than her husband or her monarch.[70] Political writers were well aware that women's pleas of conscience posed a problem for the state; as Patricia Crawford remarks, "female conscience" was thought to be less reliable than male conscience, for "women, since the time of Eve, had been led astray by wilfulness and carnal reasoning"—by the "rash judgment" Mariam mentions in her opening soliloquy as all too typical of her sex (Crawford, "Public Duty, Conscience, and Women," 70). In late Elizabethan and early Jacobean England, the Satanic role of leading Eve astray was often ascribed to Jesuits. The Protestant minister Edmund Bunny, for instance, accused the Catholic woman Margaret Clitherow "of being 'seduced by these Romish Jesuits and priests.'"[71] In Bunny's view, Clitherow was the prey of the Jesuits' false prayers, although in the opposing view of Clitherow's biographer John Mush, she was a holy woman who fell prey to Protestant persecutors. Clitherow, according to Mush, spoke to her accusers "boldly but with great modesty"; she was, as Arthur Marotti notes, "the first woman to be executed under the Elizabethan anti-recusancy laws" ("Alienating Catholics," 5). She was pressed to death in 1586, but lived on, through Mush's hagiographic biography, to serve as a case for English Catholics concerned, as Cary clearly was, with the moral complexities of martyrdom: a route to supreme glory for Christians from one perspective, but, from another, a temptation to pride entailing the premature abandonment of earthly labors. A casuistical manual written between 1581 and 1585 reminded English Catholics that "not every dangerous situation was a summons to martyrdom"; discretion, even silence, might be the better part of valor.[72] Even Robert Southwell held that one should not court martyrdom—as Mariam arguably does—by reprimanding the powerful.[73]

Although Mariam's martyrlike death suggests that she figures a morally virtuous failure to equivocate, Salome prevents such a simple reading of the case. For it is Salome who suggests that the Mariam we have seen scorning all hypocrisy is, in truth, a cunning hypocrite, an actor hiding dark thoughts beneath a "fair" surface. In Act 4, Salome tells Herod that there is more to Mariam than meets his eye; Salome thus repeats the gesture she had performed in Act 3 when, talking to Herod's younger brother, she exposed the potential for hidden vice or ambition in Graphina's "wit." Is Salome an exposer of vice or a slanderer, one who imputes to innocent others vices that really belong to her? The play withholds any clear answer, partly because it leaves open the question of whether hypocrisy—as in its Greek root sense of "acting"— should be classified as a vice. The play thus raises a version of the question Christine de Pizan raises with respect to Dido's (and the female writer's) "prudential" lying. Cary's text invites the reader to refine or even recant first judg-

ments or common opinions about the innocence and guilt of many of its characters. In so doing, the play's style of equivocation and casuistical reasoning
arguably models a habit of mind that Cary feels would be beneficial to the state
of England in the era of the Gunpowder Plot. That plot, I argue, is at the heart
of the play's meditation on the problem of publication broadly construed.
This problem affects female characters like Salome, Mariam, and Graphina; it
also affects subordinated male characters like Pheroras, Sohemus, and the
sons of Babas.

Salome leads us to the Gunpowder Plot, which is perhaps not surprising,
since she is the hidden author of several of the tragic plots in the play as well as
author of a tragicomic plot in which she plays a villain's role but lives to talk
another day. In Act 4, scene 7, Salome tells Herod that Mariam's tongue lures
"auditors to sin, / And is the instrument to do you wrong" (430–32; p. 130). To
this apparently slanderous remark about his wife, Herod replies with the
amazing lines, "She's unchaste, / Her mouth will ope to any stranger's ear." Salome focuses here on the damage Mariam's tongue can do to Herod, whereas
Herod slides toward thinking of Mariam's mouth opening to a stranger's—
perhaps a male sexual rival's—ear. His restatement of the idea Salome has
planted subtly transforms Mariam's mouth into a *receptacle,* whereas Salome
had stressed the agential aspect of the mouth: the phallic tongue as instrument
of speech.[74] Herod's puzzling image of a receptacle-like mouth opening to another bodily receptacle, the ear, positions Mariam precisely as what I want to
call an "imperial female subject." She has begun but not completed an allegorical metamorphosis from being like a poisoning Jew, or like the Jesuit priest
repeatedly described in the polemical literature as using his tongue to pour
dangerous secrets into unsuspecting people's ears, into being like the equally
stereotypical figure of the English Catholic wife seen as a major recipient of
the Jesuit's poison. But Mariam does not become the stereotypical wife who
might have been described as opening her *ear* to any stranger's tongue; instead, Herod stops Mariam halfway between an active and a passive verbal role
and leaves her there, after labeling her "unchaste." If she is obscurely both innocent and guilty of some crime of unchastity, it is arguably because she, like
other subordinated characters in Cary's imperial landscape, is implicated in
the cultural battles that were crystallized in the so-called Gunpowder Plot
of 1605.

This was the alleged attempt, on the part of Guy Fawkes and other Catholics, to blow up the Parliament when it met on 5 November, with king and
peers in the building. The plot was aborted when Fawkes was discovered
guarding thirty-six barrels of gunpowder in a vault next door to Parliament;
Fawkes (punningly dubbed "Faux" by one hostile contemporary) is usually

credited with masterminding the affair. It was his "confession," clearly compelled by torture, that investigators later used to implicate other conspirators
and, in Frances Dolan's apt phrase, "to confer meaning on the gunpowder."[75]
According to Edward Coke, however, it was the Jesuit Henry Garnet rather
than Fawkes who truly caused the "heavy and woeful Tragedie of the 'powder'
treason." In Coke's view, Garnet becomes the root of the plot through his failure to speak the "whole truth"—a failure Coke demonizes as equivocation, including that action of verbal and mental "reservation," which Coke describes
as "a kinde of unchastitie." His interpretation of the tragedy's cause is clearly
part of the Protestant view that Catholics were withholding their full loyalty to
the state. Although Garnet's own theory and practice of equivocation drew for
legitimation on the scholastic distinction between lying and concealment,
Coke and other Protestants sought to delegitimate such a distinction and the
hermeneutic complexities it allowed.[76] Coke draws on traditional associations
of Catholics with insubordinate women to figure the Jesuit priest himself as an
errant wife, a female who "breeds . . . bastard children" as the illicit fruit of an
adulterous liaison with the pope rather than with the priest's true husband,
the king.

Salome paints Mariam as just such an adulterous and scheming wife, while
not mentioning that the husband in question is a king who has killed a high
priest to gain the throne. Speaking to Herod in Act 4, scene 7, Salome tells him
that his wife "speaks a beauteous language, but within / Her heart is false as
powder" (429; p. 130). The statement is deeply equivocal. Not only does it play
on two different senses of *powder*, as explosive and cosmetic; it is also equivocal in a moral, epistemological, and, by implication, legal way, being neither
simply true nor simply false in its formulation of an accusatory statement
about Herod's wife (*Mariam*, ed. Weller and Ferguson, 130n. 59). The statement plays a significant role in Mariam's eventual execution, and in Cary's
text, in contrast to Josephus's original, Herod affords Mariam no legal trial.[77]
Salome's statement is false—indeed, false in the way the law calls slander—insofar as it furthers her design to persuade Herod that Mariam has treasonously
attempted to poison him and has also committed adultery with Sohemus. Salome's statement is not untrue, however, insofar as it points to Mariam's
private wish for Herod's death—a wish she has articulated to Sohemus but not
to Herod.

In the moment when Salome accuses Mariam of falsity like "powder," she
asks us to ponder the relation between the play's major female characters.
They have seemed to many readers to illustrate not only antithetical moral
styles but also, as I suggested earlier, utterly contrasting styles of speech. My
reading of the "powder" allusion suggests that these two characters are not

opposites, either morally or in verbal practice, but rather two aspects of a complex, indeed profoundly equivocal whole. The "black" Salome is, perhaps, the gunpowder hiding beneath Mariam's "white" soul.

In its radical ambiguity, Salome's statement likening Mariam's falsity of heart to powder arguably represents something of the "truth" of the Gunpowder Plot itself as an intelligent Catholic like Cary might understand it. The plot had, after all, not only led to the execution of Fawkes and others accused of actually designing to murder the king, his family, and members of Parliament; it had also caused the execution of Garnet, whose crime was the more ambiguous one of failing to prevent the plot, because he had heard about it under the seal of the confessional. Torn between his duty to his priestly office and an obligation the king himself insisted on, the obligation to report potentially treasonous "thoughts and words" to the state authorities, Garnet, as most historians now concede, was guilty not of devising a treasonous plot but only of not revealing what others had said to him. Read as an equivocal historical allusion to a debatable set of acts and words—spoken, written, or suppressed—the question that Salome's description of Mariam raises insistently is this: how do we tell the difference between the accuser and the accused in a political world where appearances are deceiving and the relation among verbal signs, deeds, and their jointly constructed meanings is anything but stable?

Most critics have assumed that Cary's play was written before 1605. The play was not published, however, until 1613, and it could have been written at any point between the appearance of Lodge's translation of Josephus and the birth of Cary's first child in 1609.[78] The biography of Cary by her daughter, as Meredith Skura has observed, dates Cary's "first (secret) Catholic sympathies" (a step beyond her childhood "aversion" to Calvin) to 1605–6 ("Reproduction of Mothering," 43). At that time, according to the "Life," "she was about twenty years old" (*Mariam,* ed. Weller and Ferguson, 9). I think it very likely that many of Cary's contemporary readers—not only those in her own circle who knew of her religious leanings—would have seen in Salome's statement about a heart "false as powder" a topical allusion to the Gunpowder Plot and, beyond that, to the Catholic practice of equivocation itself, so closely associated with the plot and its judicial aftermath. In this reading, powder in the sense of a cosmetic hiding something from the eye is no less relevant to Cary's implied statement than is powder in the sense of an explosive. Salome's lines anachronistically yoke a new element in early modern weapons with a cosmetic used by men as well as women but most frequently excoriated, in the anticosmetic literature of the early Jacobean period, as a feminine (or effeminizing) tool of deceit.[79] The negative associations of powder as a cosmetic were readily available to and often used by those who commented on the Gunpowder Plot itself.[80]

Historians are still debating the facts of the Gunpowder Plot; some commentators continue to believe that evidence against the conspirators was forged, manipulated, or produced through torture, as Dolan observes.[81] She also argues that while all the conspirators punished by the state were men, "female figures, abstract and particular," crop up with disproportionate frequency in Jacobean discussions of the threat Catholics and Catholicism offer to England (*Whores of Babylon*, 45, 47). Cary, I suggest, both alludes to and interrogates the tradition of construing the threat of Catholicism as a threat posed by a feminine, or effeminate, agent. Cary's play acknowledges the power of this cultural construction when she has Salome succeed in convincing Herod that Mariam has tried to poison him—which she clearly has not done. Mariam, however, contributes to Salome's plot by refusing to smile at, speak mildly to, and sleep with Herod. The play itself offers multiple and competing candidates for the "cause" of the tragedy; as Skura notes, Herod, "repentant, claims at the end, 'I am the villain that have done the deed,' and many readers have agreed with him" ("Reproduction of Mothering," 32). Mariam blames herself and also Doris's curse for her fall, and the butler suborned by Salome to accuse Mariam of a poison plot undergoes a Judas-like repentance (leading to suicide by hanging) and exclaims, "I am the cause that Mariam causeless died" (5.1.110; p. 143).[82] The only major character not explicitly named in the tragedy's discourse on its "cause" is Salome—who is, of course, arguably the chief architect manipulating all the others, including Mariam. The play draws equivocal connections between Salome and the Jesuitical schemer excoriated, as the true cause of the Gunpowder Plot, by Edward Coke, but it also revises the historical subtext by letting Salome exit alive from the stage, thereby suggesting that many others, including the heroine and monarch, bear part of the blame for the story's development. Cary's monarch figure, indeed, is made to wish that he had not displayed "rashness" of judgment (the same fault Mariam chastises in herself at the play's opening).[83] Moreover, the play shows the stereotypical Jesuit figure exercising her wiles not directly against the king but rather against a woman who is a potential rival for the throne—a rival of course to Salome as well as to her brother. Salome, Herod, Mariam, and perhaps Doris too—through the act of cursing the heroine, which we shall examine shortly—all contribute to a plot that results in an act of justice presented as injustice.[84] The play implicitly argues against "rash judgment" without solving the mystery of who caused the tragedy. By not solving the mystery, Cary makes a case for suspending judgment in a world of equivocal meanings. One message of Cary's plot, as Rosemary Kegl has argued, is "delay."[85]

In this world, it is dangerous to publish one's desires in any definitive form. This rule seems to apply even to the king, who is shown repenting a conse-

quential act of "public speech" in Act 5 in words that eerily recall Mariam's act
of "recanting" a rash judgment at the beginning. "Oh, that I could that sentence now control," Herod exclaims to the messenger who brings him the news
of Mariam's death (5.1.74; p. 141). His word *sentence*, meaning both utterance
and death decree, places Herod's dilemma after Mariam's death squarely in the
field of debate about "public voice"—and censorship thereof—explored by
many of the play's unhappily subordinated characters before the heroine is definitively silenced. If the play makes an equivocal argument for equivocation
as deferred or suspended judgment, it also argues, in theory and practice, for
a mode of discourse that allows second chances, revisions, "recantings." Such
a mode of discourse requires interpretive labor. The reader is made aware of
her or his participation in the production of meaning, and this too is a textual
effect that works against the notion of definitive punishment of a single individual. The play suggests, however, that subordinated groups as well as individuals need to consider carefully their strategies of publication. This allegorical point emerges, I think, in the story of three male friends—two orphan
youths and their protector, Constabarus—who happens also to be the husband whom Salome wishes to replace with another man. Constabarus, whom
Cary renames from the original in Josephus, Costabarus, in a way that emphasizes the character's quality of virtuous constancy, has defied the "sentence" of death Herod pronounced on the sons of his political enemy Babas.[86]
Constabarus has hidden the boys for twelve years on his farm outside the city.[87]
In Act 2, scene 2, Constabarus persuades the two boys to emerge from hiding
on the grounds that they have been prevented from achieving the fame they
deserve; they have been "quick buried" in a "living tomb" (117, 120; p. 92).
Constabarus's metaphor implies an equivocal relation between these boys deprived of public scope for "advanc[ing] their name" and the wife described by
the Chorus in Act 3—the wife who will "usurp upon another's right" if she
seeks "glory" by showing herself in "public language" (3.3.239–40; pp. 113–14).
Constabarus has hidden Babas's sons, after all, because Herod believes that
they wish to usurp his throne, as indeed they do, according to Josephus.[88]

The language used to describe their state of privacy, of being "confin'd"
(2.2.121; p. 92), effeminizes them and yokes them, I suggest, not only to the
feme covert held up by the Chorus as a model for Mariam in Act 3 but also to
the noble ladies evoked by Sir John Davies in his dedication to *The Muses' Sacrifice*, published in 1612. In that poem, addressed to three "patronesses of the
Muses" who were themselves writers (and hence potential competitors to the
male poet who invokes their aid, inspirational and financial), Davies refers to
Elizabeth Cary as his "pupill" and extravagantly praises her work.[89] He suggests, however, that she has not yet received the "fame" she deserves because

she has "press[ed] the Press with little [she] has made." By avoiding the route
to publicity provided by the press (instrument of torture as well as a site of dubious reputation in the eyes of many upper-class English writers), Cary, in
Davies' formulation, is giving her fame a stillbirth. "Times to come," he warns,
will "hardly credit" her achievements—"Limbes of Art and Straines of Wit"
beyond the capacity of "the weaker Sexe"—"if thus thou give thy Workes both
Birth and Grave." Even as he urges her to publish her writings and thereby gain
fame for a work he describes as addressing public matters (the play has "feet of
State," he punningly remarks), Davies paints the institution of the press in
rather lurid colors, reminding his readers of just the reasons why a chaste
noble wife—or her husband—would prefer that she keep her works confined
to the home or at least to the coterie of manuscript circulation.[90] "[Y]ou well
know the Presse so much is wrong'd / by abject Rimers that great Hearts doe
scorne / To have their Measures with such Nombers throng'd / as are so basely
got, conceiv'd and borne." Davies here articulates a common English view of
the press as both associated with and "wrong'd" by the lower-class "rimers"
who are said to frequent it. Davies' syntax creates a momentary ambiguity
about whether "great Hearts" are the object or subject of "Scorn" when they
approach the press; the stanza also conjures visions of sexual danger and of
bloodline contamination. The lines offer, therefore, highly equivocal advice to
the noblewoman about whether or not to publish her works to advance her
"fame," fame being, for a woman, intricately bound up with the perception of
her chastity on the part of others.

   Although Davies' poem has been credited with inspiring Cary to submit
Mariam to the press in 1613, the play was printed without the author's full
name on the title page.[91] Her gender and status were clearly announced, however, on a title page that arguably carried coded information to some potential
readers (fig. 5). Beneath the statement that the play is "Written by that learned,
vertuous, and truly noble Ladie, E. C." is an image of a naked and crowned
woman (a queen? a captive? both?) being scourged by an apparently divine
hand; between the woman's feet are the initials *TC*, for the printer Thomas
Creede, and around the image runs a Latin motto, *Veritas virescit vulnere*
("truth flourishes through wounding").[92] Cary's printer Creede used several
different emblems as trademarks of his printer's shop; and the one on
Mariam's title page was used for other theatrical quartos issued by Creede's
shop, among them *The First Part of the Contention* (1594, a quarto version of
Shakespeare's *Henry VI, Part 2*).[93] This emblem had also been used for *The
French History of Anne Dowriche*, a long poem about the afflictions of French
Protestants during the religious wars; it was printed by T. Orwin for T. Man in
1589.[94] Although there is no evidence of Catholic sympathies or activity on

THE
TRAGEDIE
OF·MARIAM,
THE FAIRE
Queene of Iewry.

Written by that learned,
vertuous, and truly noble Ladie,
E. C.

LONDON.
Printed by Thomas Creede, for Richard
Hawkins, and are to be solde at his shoppe
in Chancery Lane, neere vnto
Sargeants Inne.
1613.

Creede's part, or on that of the publisher, Richard Hawkins, who entered *Mariam* in the Stationers' Register in 1612, Creede did print a number of texts dealing with "contentions" both secular and religious. He used the "Truth Scourged" device in 1594 for a book entitled *Mirror of Popish Subtleties,* and in 1602, he used a different printer's device to advertise a translation from the French entitled *Acts of the Dispute and Conference . . . at Paris 1566* (McKerrow, *Printers' and Publishers' Devices,* 117 and pl. 339). One can perhaps infer that Creede saw the possibility of profit in texts with French connections bearing news about religious disputes in the recent past. Nothing very firm can be said about Creede's intent in selecting the "Truth Scourged" device for Cary's *Mariam,* but I do want to suggest that the emblem itself had cultural associations with Catholic dissent that were distinctive enough to be meaningful for some readers when the emblem was seen on the title page of a play written by a "learned, vertuous, and truly noble Ladie" whose initials were "E. C." Such an interpretive surmise requires us to think of coded meaning as a set of cues that can be activated in certain historical circumstances by readers with certain kinds of knowledge; the cues in this case are embedded in—and distributed across—an image, a motto, their respective visual and verbal intertexts, a play text, and a particular author's name signaled by initials and a statement about her social status, her gender, her learning, and her "truly virtuous" nature.

Truth stands in for virtue in the title page motto, which rings an interesting and evidently unusual change on a well-known classical saying: *Virescit vulnere virtus.* Derived from a line by a Roman poet, A. Furius Antias (fl. 100 B.C.E.), as quoted by Aulus Gellius ("increscunt animi, uirescit uolnere uirtus" [souls grow, virtue flourishes through wounding]), the phrase was adopted by Italian humanists and appears in Renaissance emblem books.[95] It was also adopted, more significantly for my purposes, by Mary Queen of Scots, a woman brought up in France who became a famous prisoner in Elizabethan England; with her execution in 1587, she became a martyred heroine in the eyes of many English Catholics. As Jennifer Summit has shown, the motto *Virescit Vulnere Virtus* had been adopted by Mary Stuart for an emblematic design that was published in a politically consequential way when a copy of the emblem Mary had embroidered onto a hanging was produced "as evidence of treason at the trial that resulted in [the Catholic Duke of] Norfolk's execution in 1571" (Summit, *Lost Property,* 199). Mary had evidently sent the copy to Norfolk, and his executioners suspected that a knife depicted as a gardening tool pruning a barren branch in Mary's emblem signaled a plot to wound Queen Elizabeth; in this reading, the barren branch (Elizabeth) will be replaced by the fruitful branch (Mary).[96] Another interpretation of the (polyvalent) emblem with its complex visual and verbal components—and one supported by other versions of it in sixteenth-century texts—is that Mary, as the suffering Christian soul, is the object of the envisioned wounding, and her virtue will "increase" through it, as a plant's strength increases when it is pruned (Mary's tapestry depicts fruit trees and a vine about to be cut by a curved blade).[97] Even in this second reading, the emblem contains an implied threat to the queen, but the threat is not an active treason-plot but rather an apparently passive act of martyrdom that will strengthen the resolve of those who oppose (or will later oppose) the crown's policies. If the historical Mary Queen of Scots lurks both in Cary's portrait of Mariam and in the figure of the crowned woman—Virtue renamed Truth—who solicits our interpretive attention from the title page, then the play text itself underscores the motto's argument that a certain kind of wounding may cause truth (ideologically defined, of course) to increase and multiply. As the *limen* or threshold of a text that is thematically concerned with competing queens, handmaids, writing, censorship, and acts that can be read as martyrdoms or treasons, depending on one's theo-political perspective, the title page could well have invited some of Cary's readers to consider the play itself as harking back to Catholic-Protestant contentions of the preceding century, while also looking ahead, prophetically, to a time when Truth would again flourish in an England reunited with Rome.

Authorial ambivalence about publishing dangerous ideas, when publication is seen as an opening of the writer's mind to those more likely to condemn than to learn from her words, is figured within the play, particularly though not only in the apparently minor subplot concerning Constabarus's view that the time is ripe for the sons of Babas to come out of hiding. When Babas's elder son admits that he is too doubtful about the rumor of Herod's death to wish, at present, to "be set at large," Constabarus reads the boy's equivocal skepticism as simple cowardice (2.2.151, 155–56; pp. 93–94). If Constabarus's name links him with the virtue of constancy, his words suggest a political naïveté that can produce more evil than good under difficult circumstances. His virtue is ironized, even interrogated, if we read him in conjunction with cultural documents such as the manuals of hard cases circulating among English Catholics. In one such text, masculine bravery is defined as "a sort of temerity" if it leads one to "put oneself into open danger of death" without any accompanying achievement for God's Kingdom.[98] In Cary's text, both of Babas's sons raise doubts about the wisdom of the grown man's advice; the younger boy correctly predicts that Augustus Caesar will forgive Herod rather than execute him, limning Caesar, implicitly, as a better ruler than the "rash" Herod will prove to be (2.2.173–92; pp. 94–95). Both boys, however, ultimately defer to the older man's interpretation of things, partly out of gratitude and friendship, partly out of fear of being thought cowardly. The result is that the boys publish themselves too soon and thereby become more vulnerable to Salome's murderous plotting, it seems, than they would have been had they remained in hiding.

Salome evidently knew of their secret existence before the scene dramatizing their emergence onto the public stage, but the play's own development suggests some causal as well as symbolic connection between Act 2, scene 2, where Constabarus persuades the two boys to seek their fame, and Act 3, scene 2, where three persons are again on stage (Salome, the high priest Ananell, and Pheroras) and where Salome proposes that Pheroras save his life—and that of Graphina, the young person under his "tuition" or protection (63; p. 107)—by making public, that is, telling Herod, the heretofore "secret" information about a secret act: that Constabarus allowed Babas's sons to live despite Herod's order, years earlier, that they be executed. Salome, in other words, chooses Pheroras as her instrument of making information public in a way that will have precisely the consequences she secretly desires. By blackmailing Pheroras into betraying Constabarus and the boys, Salome will be rid of the husband she now detests without Herod's realizing that he is being manipulated. Salome shows, in Act 3, scene 2, how one may control the publication of news to one's own advantage by making others the "minister" to one's ends, thus gaining a "credit" one would not have if one spoke (or wrote?) under one's own name. Salome also demonstrates an interesting ability to hold onto apparently worthless information until changing times make it valuable. In her dialogue with Constabarus in Act 1, she indicates that she has long known of his treasonous rescue of the sons of Babas.[99] The information was not a useful commodity, however, so long as she loved Constabarus and/or so long as Herod was absent from Judea. Herod's return, in conjunction with her own change of heart, makes her private knowledge of her husband's political action into something like a piece of private property that suddenly increases in value—and that the wife can choose to sell, as it were, via an act of calculated publication to an important reader or patron, the king.

The sons of Babas, by publishing their whereabouts, on Constabarus's naïve advice, without sufficient concern for their audience, lose their political ability to oppose Herod at a future, perhaps more propitious moment. Their tragic fate foreshadows Mariam's—as Salome explicitly suggests when she tells Pheroras (in the company of the apparently impotent high priest) that "Mariam shall not linger long behind" Constabarus as a victim of her efforts to "move" Herod's "ear" (3.2.84, 87; p. 108). The ironic parallels and contrasts between Constabarus's attitude toward information in Act 2, scene 2, and Salome's in Act 3, scene 2, imply a political message seemingly at odds with the play's glorification of Mariam's stoic virtue in Act 5, where, as Elaine Beilin has shown, Cary draws parallels between Mariam's apparently martyrlike death and that of Christ (*Redeeming Eve*, 171–72). But the virtue that Mariam models—the refusal to equivocate that links her to the constant but politically ineffective Constabarus—is not wholly affirmed by Cary's play. Through the parallels between Mariam's death and those of Constabarus and the sons of Babas, Cary asks her readers to weigh carefully the value of equivocation—at least as doubt and delay, and perhaps as strategic lying as well—over the courses of action adopted, perhaps out of pride rather than humility, by the victimized spouses of Herod and his sister, who are "matched" in their "decease," as Salome remarks (3.2.83; p. 108). This ironic matchmaker acquires political power through undermining the institution of marriage—her own and Mariam's as well. The play's interrogation of marriage, to which I now turn, is a key aspect of Cary's critique of the imperial state buttressed by the domestic polity in which wives were conceived as subject to husbands. Woven into the critique of existing states—and the state-household analogy so widespread in Tudor-Stuart culture—is a vision of an alternative empire in which women who don't eschew equivocation might survive and even rule.

Equivocation and the Destabilization of Marriage

The play's representation of three angry wives—Mariam, Salome, and Doris, who regards herself as still legally married to Herod—works to interrogate the logic of the household/state analogy that England's King James had famously deployed to bolster his right to succeed to the throne. Taking a dead queen's place in 1603, James declared to Parliament, "[W]hat God hath conjoined then, let no man separate. I am the Husband, and all the whole Isle is my lawfull Wife. I am the Head, and it is my Body."[100] By giving both Mariam and Salome a strong case for divorce, while also questioning, through Salome and Doris, the husband's right unilaterally to divorce the wife, Cary's play participates in a cultural debate on marriage and divorce that had profound implications for ideas about rulers and their subjects.[101]

The cultural debate about marriage had its historical roots in Henry VIII's divorce of his first wife to marry Anne Boleyn. Cary's play allegorically interrogates many controversial strands in Henry's story and in the biblical texts he sought to use—or to have scholars learned in Hebrew use—to legitimate his divorce and second marriage. The question of incest, which threatens the idea of an orderly succession in both the domestic realm and the state, is deeply linked to questions about divorce as Henry's case posed them for his subjects. Henry's clerkly servants had initially argued for an annulment of his marriage to Catherine on the grounds that she was his "sister" by virtue of her having been married to his older brother Arthur; Anne herself, later, would be accused of having committed adultery with her brother.[102]

In Cary's play, the main spokesperson for divorce, Salome, is strongly tainted by incest. As Cary's argument notes, Salome was married to her uncle before she was married to Constabarus; moreover, during the course of the play, she comes to act more like her brother's queen than his sister. She succeeds in her plot to take Mariam's place as Herod's adviser because Mariam eschews that (political) role. Mariam, too, is associated with the problem of incest; as Skura notes, Mariam marries a man old enough to be her father and in so doing displaces Doris, who becomes an angry mother figure. Yoked in conflict among themselves as well as with their husbands, the play's three main wife figures bring incest and divorce to center stage, as it were, in equivocal relation.

Salome poses a threat to marriage that is reductively interpreted by her second husband as a threat to the distinction between the sexes. "Are Hebrew women now transformed to men," exclaims Constabarus after Salome tells him that she wants the same legal channel for erotic inconstancy that men have under Hebrew law (1.6.419; p. 84). She plans, she says, to "free" her life from him by a "divorcing bill" before she sleeps this very night (1.6.420; p. 84). Her statement seems to confirm a plan she had described earlier, in the soliloquy in which she makes her well-known critique of the double standard in the Deuteronomic law of divorce. She argues her case, to herself and the audience, by comparing herself to Constabarus; the gesture of drawing the equivalence leads to the perception of a problematic difference, which leads, in turn, to the formulation of a plan to remedy what she has perceived as an unjust as well as undesirable situation:

> If he to me did bear as earnest hate,
> As I to him, for him there were an ease;
> A separating bill might free his fate
> From such a yoke that did so much displease.
> Why should such privilege to man be given?
> Or given to them, why barr'd from women then?
> Are men than we in greater grace with Heaven?
> Or cannot women hate as well as men?
> I'll be the custom-breaker: and begin
> To show my sex the way to freedom's door,
> And with an off'ring will I purge my sin;
> The law was made for none but who are poor.
> (1.4.301–12; p. 80)

Salome's obvious villainy, revealed with particular crudeness in the line that seems to yoke her most clearly to cultural stereotypes of "hateful" Catholics seeking to buy indulgences and a quick trip through Purgatory for their relatives, should not prevent us from seeing that in her opening soliloquy, she is grappling with a problem that also concerns Mariam. Both female characters come alone on stage to voice a desire to be *feme sole,* to be or be able to act as if they were free from a marriage that feels like a prison: "Oft have I wish'd that I from him were free," Mariam has admitted—and she has gone further, in a verbal gesture her society defined as "petty treason," to long for her husband's death: "Oft have I wish'd his carcass dead to see" (1.1.18; p. 69).[103] The parallels between Salome's and Mariam's words on the subject of undesired husbands provide a significant frame for an aspect of Salome's "custom-breaker" speech not often remarked by critics: that Salome has evidently decided to buy herself a divorce "with an off'ring," until the news of Herod's return prompts her to change her plan. Could she have used money to ensure that her "Will" would operate "instead of" "Law" (1.6.454; p. 85), as she claims in her dialogue with Constabarus? Some upper-class Englishmen, as Lawrence Stone demonstrates, had pursued just such a path through the thickets of English law—and in so doing, they had followed in the steps of Henry VIII (Stone, *Road to Divorce*). The return of the absolutist monarch Herod, whose will certainly operates as law, renders moot Salome's plan to "break custom" by gaining a divorcing bill for herself. This plan, as Betty Travitsky has noted, is "revolutionary but non-violent" ("*Feme Covert,*" 191). Herod's return prompts and enables Salome to opt for an easier but more violent path to marital freedom: the use of information—in this case, true—to secure an execution for treason.

The play poses a casuistical problem for the reader by showing such clear parallels between Mariam's refusal to pay her "marriage debt" and Salome's. Yes, the moralist may say, the Mariam who tells Sohemus she has vowed not to sleep with Herod does look a bit like the Salome who tells Constabarus she will get a "divorcing bill" before another night passes; but Constabarus is a good man, whereas Herod has murdered Mariam's brother and grandfather. Mariam knew of the murders when she married Herod, however—so what has changed, and how does the play evaluate change? Those critics who maintain that Cary unequivocally upholds the moral virtue of constancy need, I think, to look more closely at the play's depiction of marriage, which includes a quite severe moral interrogation of the virtuous heroine herself. Until her dialogue with Doris in Act 4, Mariam seems never to have considered the possibility that she may have broken some kind of ethical law not only by marrying a murderer (and she admits to having loved him, so the excuse of a forced marriage will not let her off the hook), but also by marrying someone who had, as his own brother Pheroras remarks, displaced his "lawful wife" in order to gratify his passion for another woman (see 2.1.32–33; p. 98). Mariam justifies her marriage by recourse to Hebrew legal codes, but Salome, as we have seen, has critiqued those codes as distinctly unfair to women—and to poor men. The play pits Mariam's view of herself as legally, and therefore ethically, justified in participating in Herod's casting off of Doris against Doris's own interesting, if equally self-serving, argument that it was Mariam who "robb'd" the pitiable, innocent, and lawful wife of her husband, as if the fault belonged only to the second wife and not to the fickle husband. In Doris's view, she is the victim, the bringer of "beauteous babes" to Herod, and Mariam is a "black" adulteress (4.7.576, 592; p. 136). Doris sees Mariam as some Catholic polemicists, most famously Nicholas Sanders, saw Anne Boleyn: as a thieving, witch-like adulteress wronging the first wife.[104] Depicting Herod's two wives' competing and mutually uncomprehending views of each other, Cary's play offers the reader an ethical conundrum that works to suggest, as Salome does more directly, that something is wrong with the institution of marriage itself.

In the one moment in their dialogue where Doris seems on the brink of making common cause with Mariam rather than just cursing her, Doris asks, "Oh, tell me, Mariam, tell me if you know,/Which fault of these made Herod Doris's foe?" (4.8.596–97; p. 136). Doris has just ironically listed as her faults a series of goods (in both senses of the word) that belong also to Mariam, who is just about to replace Doris as Herod's female foe. Doris's goods/faults, shared by Mariam, consist in the following: bearing Herod "beauteous babes," and being rich, noble, young, and without stain to her honor (4.8.593–95; p. 136). What seems a fine case for casuistical debate—what and whose is the true fault—is left unresolved as Doris backs off from recognizing her similarity to Mariam in order to engage in the ritual gesture of cursing the female rival rather than the husband or the institutional distribution of power and property that oppresses both royal wives.

Mariam's scene with Doris gives us a glimpse of Herod's two wives locked in an equivocal relation to each other; the scene also adds another layer of complexity to the relation between Mariam and Salome. Like Judaism and Christianity, indeed, these two female characters come, in Cary's play, to seem at once mirror images of each other and moral antitypes. From Doris's perspective, it is Mariam, not Salome, who is an adulteress unfit for heaven (4.7.578; p. 136). Doris asks the audience and Mariam both to see the heroine through a rival female's eyes, and this female, whom we have no reason not to think conventionally chaste, makes an argument that directly echoes a point made by Salome to her lover in an argument designed to further adulterous passion: "In this our land," Salome says to Silleus, as if explaining a peculiar custom to a foreigner (and indeed Silleus, an Arabian, is an outsider to Judea), "we have an ancient use, / Permitted first by our law-giver's head: who hates his wife, though for no just abuse, / May with a bill divorce her from his bed. But in this custom women are not free, / Yet I for once will wrest it; blame not thou / The ill I do . . ." (1.5.333–39; p. 81). Her behavior is an "ill," but it is contextualized as part of a cultural nexus of ills, including that whereby a man may divorce a wife "for no just abuse."

The debate between Mariam and Doris in Act 4, a debate about the ethics of divorce in which Salome's critique of the double standard is a ghostly presence, ends without any clear resolution to the question, one that Milton and many other writers on divorce have also failed to resolve: how can the marriage bond be ethically broken if only one partner desires the break and has the legal and economic power to effect it?[105] Salome's case raises a corollary question: if an unjust legal system binds a partner to a marriage against her will, how unethical is it for her to resort to illegal means to gain her freedom?

Religious and ethical laws—or customs, as they may be defined from a culturally "relativist" position such as the one Montaigne famously adopts in his essay on Amerindian cannibals—are often evoked in Cary's plays, with a strange, almost anthropological detachment, leaving the reader (or this reader, at least) increasingly unsure of her moral bearings. The perspective of the alienated outsider to the nation, a perspective shaped by Cary's religion, gender, and social status as a wife "raised" by marriage, informs this anthropological tendency at the heart of the play's literacy of equivocation. Consider, for example, the passage in which Constabarus, in dialogue with Salome and just before he launches into his most "absolutist" misogynist speech, upholds the Mosaic law of divorce in words that strangely insist on a parallel between the author of that law and the villainous Herod, slayer of innocents at the time of Christ's birth. "Mildest Moses," Constabarus says, with apparently unwitting irony, was a "friend unto the Lord" who "slew the first-born babes without a sword, / In sign whereof we eat the holy lamb" (1.6.445, 447–48; p. 85). He is mild because he kills babies without a sword rather than with one? Obliquely but repeatedly suggesting that injustice in the institution of marriage is tied to injustice in the state, Cary's play yokes the question of divorce to the question of who should rightly rule Judea.

As I noted earlier, Cary departs from Josephus (and from previous dramatic renderings of the Mariam story as well) when she suggests in her Argument that Herod holds his throne in his "wife's right." The suggestion that Herod has usurped Mariam's place is fleeting but it recurs, again without textual precedent, when Herod, prompted by Salome's evil machinations including slander, comes to suspect Mariam not only of adultery but of plotting

to take (back) the throne: "And with usurper's name I Mariam stain," he exclaims (4.4.230; p. 122). Herod explicitly suggests that Mariam is plotting for
the sake of her son rather than for her own sake, and she herself disclaims any
desires for more power or riches than she has (4.3.130; p. 118), but the dis-
claimer—which echoes a similar one by Salome—leaves open the question of
the royal "mate's" true ambitions, and the extent to which they may cross the
ambiguous border between private and public domains.

The king who is also a husband, and who therefore turns the state/house-
hold analogy into an unstable identity, participates rhetorically in opening the
question of his wife's desires for action or glory in a public realm. Although he
builds a fantasy of Mariam's unchastity on the dubious grounds of Salome's
slanders, Sohemus's loyalty to his queen, and Mariam's own refusal to speak
(and act) compliantly, Herod nonetheless uses his own words to instill in his
wife desires for a public role. He thus contributes to the play's examination
of the logic that equates a wife's sexual purity with her status as a husband's
private property. Herod adopts the rhetorical stance of the Petrarchan lover-
servant praising his mistress-queen. The servant's own territorial and erotic
ambitions swell, however, even as he gives his wifely property the prerogatives
of imperial rulership:

> Art thou not Jewry's queen, and Herod's too?
> Be my commandress, be my sovereign guide:
> To be by thee directed I will woo,
> For in thy pleasure lies my highest pride.
> Or if thou think Judea's narrow bound
> Too strict a limit for thy great command:
> Thou shalt be empress of Arabia crown'd
> For thou shalt rule, and I will win the land.
> (4.3.97–104; p. 118)

The historical Elizabeth Tudor might have relished—and indeed fostered—
such poetry. In it, masculine subjection to a mistress emerges as willingness to
conquer new lands for her, with Herod's words conjuring images of gallant
Elizabethan courtier-conquerors like Essex and Drake. Herod's speech evokes,
however, a striking and politically significant parallel to a speech that Salome's
adulterous lover Silleus makes to his mistress in Act 1, in which he exclaims,
"Arabia, joy, prepare thy earth with green, / Thou never happy wert indeed till
now: / Now shall thy ground be trod by beauty's queen. . . . / Thou shalt, fair
Salome, command as much, / As if the royal ornament were thine" (1.5.345–50;
pp. 81–82).

Silleus is an Arabian courtier who claims a de facto right to rule his native land: "The weakness of Arabia's king is such / The kingdom is not his so much as mine" (1.5.351–52; p. 82). He articulates a political ambition no less illicit than his erotic ambition; indeed, the two are knotted by his offer to give Salome the political power he has (in fantasy) just claimed for himself. His words erase the distinction that I discussed in chapter 3, that between imperial conqueror of "foreign" territories and a king (or a Machiavellian usurper) working to "assure ascendancy over internal competitors" on a national political stage.[106] And the parallel between his words and Herod's later ones underscores the dubious legitimacy of Herod's rule even as it opens, yet again, the question of whether women have just as much—or just as little—right to rule as men in a world where the power to "command" is so equivocally related to "the royal ornament," the name or external trappings of royal status. Salome, intriguingly, responds to Silleus's speech by denying all ambition to achieve a "glorious state"—a phrase that can be read as denoting either public rulership or public acknowledgment for some kind of achievement (1.5.363–64; p. 82). Salome sounds here astonishingly like the modest, fame-eschewing wife limned by the Chorus in Act 3. The parallel between her denial of any desire for "glory" and Mariam's rejection of the "power and riches" Herod offers in his "empress of Arabia" speech in Act 4 works, I suggest, to make us wonder whether either woman is speaking the whole truth about her political aims. The ghost of Elizabeth Tudor, who ruled her country and her Petrarchan lovers from the legal position of *feme sole,* hovers over Cary's apparently contrasting examples of women whose lovers and husbands offer a semblance of imperial rule to their women without offering them any substance of freedom. The play's scrutiny of the marital relation uses multiple techniques of equivocation, including the sketching of unexpected parallels between characters who speak in sections of the play separated by large stretches of intervening matter, to suggest that the truth of marriage may be hidden, tainted, or even nonexistent beneath the many metaphors, customs, and laws ostensibly fixing its nature. The interrogation of marriage is part of a larger inquiry into the marks of social distinction upon which the social order depends.

Equivocal Renderings of the Social Text:
Blurring the Signs of Social Distinction

Through a rhetoric of exposure and concealment epitomized in the verbal practices of equivocation, Cary offers us a look at what an empire is from the perspective of those belonging to censored groups within it. Cary's play suggests that one effect of censorship in an imperial nation such as Jacobean England is a discourse of equivocation that exposes, without neatly resolving, conflicts of interpretation among various social groups with greater and lesser degrees of (present) power; the educated members of some groups use tactics of equivocation to articulate risky fantasies about changes in the polity that would result in a redistribution of power. Because such tactics aim, with a large risk of misfire, at reaching those who may share, or be persuaded to share, the writer's desire to alter the current regime, it becomes politically as well as epistemologically important for such writers to explore the question of what constitutes social difference: how does one tell a potential enemy from a potential ally in a fragmented regime in which manuscripts as well as unlicensed printed materials and the text of one's behavior might be used as evidence against one in (for instance) recusancy trials? Laws, as Frances Dolan observes, intervened in post-Reformation England to draw boundaries between old and new, them and us, but there was a substantial gap between what the law marked as illicit and what Catholics wrote and said (*Whores of Babylon,* 19). Literacy, too, played a significant role in the shifting terrain in which definitions and prosecutions of religious difference occurred; literacy itself was a sometimes equivocal sign of problematic difference in a world where secrets abounded and publication of belief, whether through speech, writing, or print, might be more important, for one's legal status, than the exact content of belief. In this world, educated Protestants and Catholics both debated, with new urgency, old questions about the relation between the individual conscience and dictates of various groups. Cary's play is concerned with competitions among groups, and hence with political change. Members of such groups are both defensively and aggressively concerned with marks of social distinction, the signs that allow people to recognize themselves as members of a group. Cary interests herself in social categories that often overlap and also with the ways in which subjects can change their social identities—in some cases by counterfeiting or misinterpreting the signs of social distinction.

"Race," as many scholars have argued, is never a discrete category.[107] Cary uses the term in ways that suggest its connection to ideas about status differences and differences of religion in Tudor-Stuart England.[108] She thus inscribes race into a social text that is everywhere marked by a disjunction between being and seeming. The two major modern understandings of race, both of which have important medieval and early modern, as well as biblical and classical, analogues, may be fruitfully approached in terms of the problems signaled by the motto Cary chose for her eldest daughter's wedding ring, the equivocal phrase "Be and seem" (see the epigraph to this chapter). Race has been understood, since roughly the seventeenth century, as something somatically marked, something visible, readable, on the body. In a second, alternative line of cultural interpretation, however, race has been a name for some invisible quality carried by the blood in one's veins. This alternative line of racialist thinking seems historically older, bearing traces of the premodern notion of race as lineage. This ideological formation persisted and intertwined with the somatic line of racialist thinking, producing some of the potent contradictions of American notions of "passing." In Cary's play we can see some of the early complexities of racialist thinking, as ideas of race become yoked to ideas about nation and about hidden religious belief. In *Mariam,* race is something at once hidden and physically there: hard to see, but nonetheless dangerous—like the two substances yoked by Salome's accusatory use of the word *powder* in Act 4. The play's equivocal discourse of race, like its discourse of marriage, illuminates Cary's theory and practice of a mode of female literacy that destabilizes relations between signs and signifiers in the name of a hidden and unverifiable Truth. This truth seems theological in character, but it is shot through with worldliness.

Let us consider first the somatic line of racialist thinking in Cary's play, a line most visible in the text's use of the terms *black* and *white* (or *fair*) to signify aspects of physical appearance (skin color, but also hair and eye color) and moral character. The latter set of significations is highly colored by ideologies of gender. In Cary's play, as Kim Hall has argued, female characters vie for power and position by reading religious/national differences within the black/white binarism (*Things of Darkness,* 185). That binarism puts the "fair" Mariam in direct competition with the character Herod compares to a "sunburnt blackamoor": his sister Salome (4.7.462; p. 131). The binarism also makes an oft-invoked but never visible character named Cleopatra into Mariam's antagonist and Salome's dark double. Early in the play, Mariam's mother Alexandra proudly describes her ploy of seeking to win Mark Antony's favor by, in effect, selling the erotic favors of both her children, one of whom was already married to Antony's puppet ruler, Herod. Alexandra sent portraits of Mariam and her brother Aristobulus to the "warlike lover" Antony, but her stratagem failed because he was so "hungry" for both morsels that he couldn't make a choice between them. In the classic dilemma of the equivocator torn between competing "goods," Antony would have taken action, Alexandra suggests, if she had sent only Mariam's picture. In that case, he would have loved Mariam, leaving the "brown Egyptian clean forsaken" (1.2.190; p. 76). Thus Cleopatra would have lost the lover of her "wanéd face" while Mariam, conveniently unburdened of a husband her mother dislikes, would have gained an aspiring emperor for her bedmate. Alexandra's limning of a historical road not taken presents her daughter in a highly dubious moral light—as a potential adulteress, had she won Antony's favor and become his mistress, instead of Cleopatra. The fact that Mariam's image competed with that of her brother for

Antony's erotic attention reminds us that for Vergil, the sexually dangerous Cleopatra was a reincarnation of the virago Dido (whom, of course, Vergil fashioned to recall the historical Cleopatra through a sleight of the imperial imagination).

Through its many quasi-economic inventories of the physical qualities of Mariam, Salome, and the off-stage but rhetorically present Cleopatra, the play contributes to a discourse of race that is powerfully, even constitutively, linked to an emergent discourse of female beauty and sexuality as commodities in an upper-class international market. Mariam's mother, as Kim Hall notes, constructs her daughter's rivalry with Cleopatra in terms of the standard betrothal practices of seventeenth-century European aristocrats (*Things of Darkness*, 185). With such details as the sending of the potential wife's portrait, Cary evokes the merchandising rhetoric of display: Alexandra herself speaks of the "mart of beauties" available in Mariam's visage (1.2.197; p. 76). The play's construction of race, in which "fair" Maccabeans are pitted against "brown" Egyptians, cannot be dissociated from its construction of femininity as a merchandisable phenomenon. Femininity, however, is a site of debate in the play, as Callaghan and others have shown. I want to supplement recent studies of the play's nexus of gendered and racialized ideologies by arguing that the black/white dichotomy, as applied to types of feminine beauty, is rather differently construed by different characters in the play. The interpreter's gender and social position shape not only how she or he reads the social text but also what counts as a legible text at all.

Two male characters, Constabarus and Herod, provide what can fairly be called essentializing interpretations of the connection between skin color, lineage, and moral character. Constabarus, indeed, gives voice to the most racist construction of the meaning of blackness in the play, in the course of a misogynist tirade against his wife's adulterous love for the Arabian Silleus. Damning women as a group (forgetting in his passion even his earlier vision of Mariam as an exception to the faults of her sex), Constabarus anticipates Milton's Adam in wishing that women could be excluded from God's scheme for multiplying humankind. He then yokes all women with the black and naturally slavish descendants of Noah's son Ham: "Cham's servile curse to all your sex was given, / Because in Paradise you did offend" (4.6.341–42; p. 127).[109] Constabarus's view as expressed here is no less sweeping and crude, intellectually, than is Herod's view in his eulogies of Mariam in Act 5. In this play, male characters, and specifically, husbands engaging in the traditional rhetorical exercises of blaming or praising women, tend most emphatically to construe female moral essences in terms of the stereotypical dyad of black versus white.

Salome and Mariam, in contrast, interrogate their husbands' habit of equating women's appearances with what goes on in their minds or souls. In their skeptical mode of interpreting signs, Mariam and Salome are joined by Doris, the play's most miserable wife, the wife who continues to claim that title despite her husband's abrogation of their relationship. The female characters who challenge the legibility of physical appearances end up sowing doubts about the legibility of appearances in general.

Mariam, for instance, describes Cleopatra as false but not as "black" or "brown." This occurs in the soliloquy in Act 4, scene 8, where Mariam conjures up Cleopatra's face through anaphoric statements ("That face that did captive great Julius' fate, / That face that was Anthonius' bane, / That face that to be Egypt's pride was born"), recalling Marlowe's famous line, in Dr. Faustus, about Helen of Troy: "Was this the face that launched a thousand ships?"[110] Although Mariam ascribes to Cleopatra many stereotypically bad qualities—wantonness and greed as well as falseness—nowhere does she describe Cleopatra's skin color. Acknowledging both the difficulty and—as Pierre Macherey long ago argued—the importance of including the "not said" in our efforts at ideological critique,[111] I suggest that Mariam's omission of any remark about Cleopatra's skin is significant, especially given that this speech clearly recalls Alexandra's speech, mentioned earlier, deprecating the "brown Egyptian" who rivals Mariam on the international beauty market (1.2.190; p. 76). Mariam's speech also looks ahead to Herod's later contrast of his "fair" Mariam to a "black Egyptian" (5.1.239; p. 147).

In the soliloquy where Mariam does not link Cleopatra's moral qualities to any alleged quality of visible darkness, Mariam is herself learning, painfully, not to read beautiful surfaces in a conventional way, or at least not according to a *single* set of signifying conventions. "Now death will teach me: he can pale as well / A cheek of roses as a cheek less bright," Mariam says (4.8.529–30; p. 134). "Paleness" in this line signifies the cold state to which Death brings both rosy and "less bright" cheeks, and the line works to complicate and even to ironize the convention that ascribed positive market value either to pale skin or to the "other" English characteristic, rosy cheeks. Death is palely personified as a teacher who leads Mariam herself to read beneath the surface of any skin color or the social status it allegedly signifies. She thus models a more skeptical kind of cultural interpretation than Constabarus displays when he inveighs against Salome's betrayal of him by proclaiming all women marked by the curse of Cham, or than Herod practices when he laments his dead and belatedly (re)valued wife in terms of her milky white hand (5.1.150; p. 144). The hand that wrote the pun-laden play challenges the tendency of some of the male characters to equate female skin color with female moral character.

Although the skeptical strand of female characters' discourse I have identified does not go very far to question the traditional Christian association of evil with blackness, it does work to question whether Herod, or anyone in power, can see the presence of evil well enough to persecute its alleged bearer. At stake, then, is not only a distinction among modes of identifying and reading cultural signs, but also an implied argument for acknowledging their complexity and suspending the kinds of consequential judgments made by Herod on his wife, by Henry VIII on Anne Boleyn, and even by those English authorities who, acting for the crown, executed Catholics who were only ambiguously guilty of crimes.

Herod is not a skeptical reader of the social text, as we see when he discusses Mariam (and her alleged crimes) with Salome. There, he categorizes Salome herself as beautiful according to local standards of taste; he goes on, however, to denigrate both Salome and opinions about beauty held "here" by contrasting Salome with Mariam along rhetorical lines that implicitly subordinate Near Eastern concepts of female beauty to those of Europe and, more specifically, of the Petrarchan tradition of rhetorical praise:

> Yourself are held a goodly creature here,
> Yet so unlike my Mariam in your shape
> That when to her you have approachéd near,
> Myself hath often ta'en you for an ape.
> And yet you prate of beauty: go your ways,
> You are to her a sun-burnt blackamoor:
> Your paintings cannot equal Mariam's praise,
> Her nature is so rich, you are so poor.
> (4.7.457–64; pp. 131–32)

Herod devalues Salome not only by contrasting her to Mariam in terms of a ratio of relative darkness and lightness of skin, but also by denigrating her— again relatively, by contrast with Mariam—for using cosmetics; with an anachronistic glance forward from Judea to Jacobean England, Herod seems to accuse her of "painting" to "whiten" her skin.[112] He seems unaware of the irony lurking in his own comparison of cosmetic "painting" to "praise," another form of painting or artificiality in its use of rhetorical colors. As Hall has remarked, citing Dolan's study of the anticosmetic strain in early modern English lyric, "the language of 'painting' and cosmetics is the most widespread component of the rhetoric of women's fairness and value; it is also frequently linked to English discourses of blackness" (*Things of Darkness*, 87). Hall has shown these discourses to be more deeply implicated in the politics and economics of England's empire-building mission than most literary critics commenting on "fair" and "dark" ladies in English love poetry have allowed.

Moreover, as Hall also argues (discussing Ben Jonson's *Masque of Blackness*, a text written, like Cary's play, early in the reign of James I), blackness is often a "mutable and relative quality" in Jacobean texts; women are deemed "black" or "fair" in competitive scenes that presuppose a patriarchal judge of female beauty (*Things of Darkness*, 134–35). Herod's use of a racialized black/fair dichotomy illustrates just such a competitive scenario, one in which female bodies are both equated and ranked in an endless discursive cycle: Salome is like a sun-burnt blackamoor in comparison to Mariam and, the text suggests, Salome incurs the denigratory color epithet less because of her actual skin color than because she is using her verbal skills to threaten Herod's investment in his wife's fairness as a sign of her sexual virtue. He reacts with rage: "Hence from my sight, my black tormentor, hence," Herod exclaims. Then, with an obtuseness he is made unwittingly to stress, he substitutes Mariam for Salome by agreeing to execute his wife. His tendency to conflate his wife and his sister as "black" appears ironically in his final lines in the scene, which call "destruction" on Salome at the very moment when Herod's "dullness" is allowing Mariam to be destroyed—as she is during the interval between Act 4 and Act 5: "Destruction take thee: thou has made my heart/As heavy as revenge; I am so dull,/Methinks I am not sensible of smart" (4.7.519–21; p. 134).

Having been forced to act on Salome's "black" view of Mariam, Herod immediately reverts to equating Mariam's "fairness" with her (moral, or rather sexual) virtue. This commonplace idea, articulated by Othello as well as by the jealous husbands in Cary's play, seems to work best when the heroine has been silenced and all other female characters are off stage.[113] Lamenting the death of "the King of Jewry's fair and spotless wife," as if he were viewing himself and Mariam from a great distance, Herod dismembers her in remembering her hand: "Oh what a hand she had, it was so white,/It did the whiteness of the snow impair" (5.1.150–51; p. 144). Continuing his blazon to expose the logic of relentless competition that underlies the black/white dichotomy as he deploys it, Herod not only praises Mariam's hand at the expense of a substance extremely seldom seen in Judea; he goes on to inveigh against the sun for continuing to shine when Mariam's own light—later implicitly likened to the sun's when Herod describes it as "envied" by Cynthia, the moon (5.1.234; p. 147)—has been, Desdemona-like, put out. Herod tells the sun that its shining would be tolerable, if "some Egyptian blowse,/Or Aethiopian dowdy lose her life" (5.1.195–96; p. 145). He returns to the simple fair/black dichotomy in his long speech of Petrarchan lament, this time suggesting that Mariam's fairness (rather than his own jealousy and royal power to execute) has somehow caused her death: "If she had been like an Egyptian black,/And not so fair, she had been longer liv'd" (5.1.239–42; p. 147).

He speaks more truly—and hence, this play suggests, more equivocally—than he knows, since both of Mariam's black rivals, Cleopatra and, figuratively, Salome, do live longer than Mariam does. Although Cleopatra has recently died when the play begins, she was not cut off in her youth, as Mariam is; and Salome, shockingly, lives on with no punishment whatsoever at the end of the drama. Obscurely, the play confirms Herod's self-serving placement of blame: somehow, Mariam's fairness does seem to have been a major cause of her death.[114] But in what does that fairness consist?

Salome and Doris both define it as a surface that masks an inner evil. We looked earlier at the speech in which Doris describes Mariam, to her face, as an adulteress whose soul is "black and spotted, full of sin" (4.8.576–77; p. 136), contrasting this vision of Mariam's character to Mariam's own, perhaps erroneous view of herself as simply fair and chaste. It is important to notice the difference in how Doris deploys the traditional association of blackness with vice in a situation of rhetorical dispraise and how Herod deploys the association in a situation of excessive praise in the following act. Even though Salome temporarily shakes his belief in whiteness or lightness as a stable mark of moral virtue (indeed, Salome forces Herod to use the word *light* equivocally in 4.7.490: "she is deceitful, light as vanity"), his discourse in Act 5 testifies to his fundamental certainty that he can see a woman's virtue in her white hand. Both Doris and Salome, in contrast, expose the fallacies of a mode of knowing (and acting) that relies on visual evidence; they do so, however, through binary thinking that is structurally no less simple, though rather less conventional, than Herod's. Mariam's fair surface, the other two women insist, hides a black interior.

Salome ultimately goes further than Doris in complicating our understanding of the relation between visible signs, cultural conventions, and what's truly in someone's mind. In the scene that best demonstrates her verbal energy, as she "indefatigably" prompts a "lethargic Herod to kill Mariam by various means," the self-described custom-breaker who has earlier challenged the masculinist bias of the Jewish law of divorce now interrogates the logic of another mode of discourse that privileges the man's perspective over the woman's.[115] This is the discourse of the Petrarchan blazon; Salome questions it with a specific allusion, I think, to a central trope of one of England's most famous sonnet sequences, Sidney's *Astrophil and Stella*, and perhaps also with reference to the Protestant queen Elizabeth who arguably serves, along with the blond but black-eyed Lady Penelope Rich, as a historical referent for Stella: "Your thoughts do rave with doting on the queen," Salome chides Herod. "Her eyes are ebon-hued, and you'll confess:/A sable star hath been but seldom seen" (4. 7. 453–55; p. 131).

Salome, it seems, is an astute reader of cultural and somatic ambiguities; she is also a more potent bearer of historical allegories than critics have yet allowed. If her veiled attack on Petrarchan conventions includes, as I think it does, a mocking glance at the ongoing "cult of Elizabeth," her subsequent attack on Mariam takes us even further into the cultural battles of Cary's contemporary England.[116] Continuing her interrogation of perceptual and rhetorical conventions, Salome associates Mariam's beauty with dangerous verbal skills rather than with any of the somatic features, dark or fair, that so preoccupy male poets in the Petrarchan tradition. Unlike the mostly silent ladies of that tradition, the voluble Salome attributes to her "fair" sister-in-law some of Salome's own verbal energies and talents for political deceit. These qualities, imputed—or revealed—through the image of a heart "false as powder," are described in a densely equivocal formulation that deserves another look, this time with particular attention to the question of language. Recall Salome's statement to Herod that Mariam "speaks a beauteous language, but within/ Her heart is false as powder" (4.7.429; p. 130). On first reading, it seems that Mariam's alleged falseness is beneath a surface defined as "beauteous language"; language here would be conceptualized in a traditional way as a skin or husk beneath which a supralinguistic kernel of truth lies hidden. The play on *powder*, however, undermines the neat surface/depth distinction, since powder as a cosmetic would function, as the "beauteous language" does, to cover and hide an ugly truth. The outside/inside dichotomy becomes slippery, and so do the related distinctions between fair and dark and between "base" or low and "high" as descriptors of social status. Appropriately enough, it is Salome who invites us to see both the high-born Mariam and the slave girl Graphina as sharing with Salome herself a potential for dangerous plotting through language.

Although Herod's patriarchal eye seems to be blind to the problem, the fair/black dichotomy in the play keeps sliding between references to female bodies—their skin color or their hair or eye color—and conceptions of race complexly marked by questions about religious difference, both in the ancient Judean context and in the world of Tudor-Stuart England. In both historical contexts as the play invokes them, moreover, differences of religion shade into differences of blood or lineage, and from thence, inevitably, into debates about what constitutes a nation and what constitutes a "pure" as opposed to a "mongrel" social group. Cary's play refracts these debates, with their biblical (and ancient, nonbiblical) roots, as well as their proliferating, often bloody branches in early modern Europe and its American colonies. While Cary's play engages with these debates intermittently and partially (in both senses of that word), it exhibits a persistent concern with the role of language in shaping

identity, and reveals an equally persistent concern with exploring gaps between who one is—in the eyes of others, including persecuting others—and
who one says one is, to oneself or to others.

Early in the play, Mariam uses the language of race to distinguish herself
from a woman she scorns. Race here denotes lineage, not skin color, but there
is no question that Mariam deploys it in a way that marks Salome as a member of a different, and persecutable, group:

> Though I thy brother's face had never seen,
> My birth thy baser birth so far excell'd,
> I had to both of you the princess been.
> Thou parti-Jew, and parti-Edomite,
> Thou mongrel: issu'd from rejected race,
> Thy ancestors against the Heavens did fight,
> And thou like them wilt heavenly birth disgrace.
>
> (1.3.231–37; p. 77)

The definition of the addressee as worthy of persecution comes not only from
an idea of race as something passively inherited that can be "high" and "pure"
or "base," but also from the rather different idea of race that emerges toward
the end of the passage, where it seems to become a function of moral agency
and corresponding favor, or disfavor, with God. Both ideas of race coexist—
uneasily—in the play. The idea that Mariam's blood is purer than Salome's
and Herod's—an idea that Herod himself articulates, with specific reference
to his illegitimate overthrow of Judea's throne, in Act 5—is indeed a locus for
complex ideas about lineage and inherited social status; about moral purity or,
more precisely, gendered ideologies of female chastity; and about religious purity, under which rubric we find complex notions about Jews and "parti-
Jews."[117] This latter distinction relies a great deal on one's perspective and political ambitions, and has considerable allegorical resonance, I believe, for
Cary's reflections on the proliferating splits among Christians during her era.
Some of her contemporaries were working hard to devise new names for
members of these new, or newly feared, groups within (but also always potentially outside of) the Christian world. John Florio, in one striking example
from his dictionary entitled *Queen Anne's New World of Words* (1611), defines
Marrano as "A nickname for Spaniards, that is one descended of jews or infidels, and whose parents were never christened, but for to save their goods will
say they are Christians. Also as Marrana."[118] Such a definition occludes even
the possibility that a Marrano—or Marrana—could be an unequivocal, un-
hypocritical "Christian." The definition also casually renders illegal all members of England's Marrano community, who were barred from the realm if

they were Jews. In Florio's symptomatic statement, ideas of race as lineage mix promiscuously with ideas about religious identities that are counterfeited by persons wishing to "save their goods"—and, we might add, their lives. I cite Florio's definition because it shows ideas of race as foreign blood lines mixing with ideas of religion as an equivocal or hypocritical phenomenon adopted by members of an endangered group. If, as I am arguing, Cary's play illustrates a similar mixing of ideas about race and religion, it does so in a way that stresses both the problem of what counts as "foreign" in an imperial landscape and what counts, or appears, as a persecutable group.

Mariam excoriates Salome for being an Edomite and a "parti-Jew." What does this mean? The name of the people or "nation" of Edom was frequently derived, by both Jewish and Christian commentators, from Esau, son of Isaac.[119] And Esau, as Mariam's mother Alexandra remarks in the preceding scene, sold his "birthright" for a mess of pottage (1.2.102; p. 72); therefore, according to Alexandra's logic, which is based on a highly selective reading of one of the most ethically murky stories in Genesis, the story of Jacob and Esau, Esau's descendant Herod does not deserve to occupy a throne that should be occupied instead by members of Mariam's family, the Maccabeans, who claimed descent from Jacob. Alexandra indignantly asks, "Must he ere Jacob's child the crown inherit? / Must he, vile wretch, be set in David's chair?" (1.2.85–86; p. 72).

Intriguingly, both Alexandra and Mariam rationalize their arguments for the racial inferiority of the Edomites by calling on arguments that Christians had traditionally applied to Jews. Alexandra deploys a Hebrew etymology that derives "Edom" from a root meaning "red" to explain Herod's nature as deriving from "Edom's name."[120] Herod's "cruel nature" makes blood his food and drink, Alexandra says, unwittingly reminding Cary's readers of what Herod later did to try to kill the infant Christ.[121] As Dympna Callaghan remarks, there are "significant parallels between Herod and the conventional, racialized representation of the Jew as the tyrannical patriarch" ("Re-Reading Elizabeth Cary's *The Tragedie of Mariam*," 170). Among the elements of that stereotypical representation is Herod's bloodthirsty nature, pointing toward the "Jewish crime" par excellence. Also stereotypically "Jewish" is Herod's defiance of what God (or, in Mariam's phrasing, Heaven) allegedly wants. The Hebrew prophetic books repeatedly present Edom's continued conflict with Israel (and occupation of southern Judea) as an offense against the divine will.[122] Similarly, many Christian writers before and during the transitional era presented the Jews as stubborn defiers of God's will that his creatures worship his Son.[123]

Paradoxically, the people whom Mariam excoriates as "parti-Jews" seem to look more like Jews—as some later Christians saw them—than the "pure" Jews represented (at least in Mariam's and her mother's somewhat self-interested eyes) by the Maccabean family. Through her meditation on the distinction between Jew and parti-Jew—a distinction rendered problematic in many ways during the play's unfolding—Cary arguably grapples with questions that had both political and religious resonance for her contemporary readers. Callaghan doubts that "English Renaissance Christians were particularly aware of any religious difference between Edomites and Jews," but the very passage by Samuel Purchas she cites to support her doubt seems to me to support the idea of such a perception, so long as one grants that religious difference in Cary's world as in our own has a great deal to do with the politics of territorial conquest and population control ("Re-Reading Elizabeth Cary's *The Tragedie of Mariam*," 334n. 46). The Edomites' land lay, according to Purchas, "southward from Judea. . . . It was subdued by David, according to the Prophecie, *The elder shall serve the younger*. They rebelled under Ioram the sonne of Jehsophat; as Isaak had also prophecied. From that they continued bitter enemies to the people of God, till Hircanus, the sonne of Simon [and Mariam's great-great-grandfather] compelled them to accept both the Jewish Dominion and Religion: after which they were reckoned among the Jews."[124] "Reckoned among the Jews": the phrase is equivocal. Counted *as* Jews by the ruler? Or thought to be Jews when they secretly retained a sense of their own identity as a conquered people? Mariam's epithets for Salome—"parti-Jew" and its derogatory synonym "mongrel"—suggest that Mariam herself doesn't believe that the Edomites have become "real" Jews despite four generations of living as—and under—those who do consider themselves such. Since Mariam herself is married to Herod, and has two sons by him, the play examines the nature of a marriage both joined and divided along lines of blood and religion as two components of an idea of race working in a complex imperial context. Mariam's people are members of an oppressed group under Herod and the Romans, but Herod's people have also experienced oppression and the need for hiding one's views that imperial oppression typically brings. Perhaps, indeed, the Edomites as a "rejected race" share some features with English Catholics practicing equivocation under Henry VIII and his heirs?

I am not arguing for any one-to-one allegorical relation here, but rather for Cary's ability to register—though not fully to control the terms of—a problem that preoccupied English political and religious officials as it had Spanish officials in the previous century.[125] Although there are many differences between Spanish Jews and English Catholics—and between English Catholics and those Marranos or Conversos who lived in England during Cary's time, despite the common view that there were no Jews in England after their official expulsion in 1290—the groups shared the onus of neighbors' and rulers' suspicions, and were vulnerable to persecution for religious beliefs that they may—or may not—have held. Indeed, for a brief period during the late sixteenth and early seventeenth centuries, England imitated its great rival Spain in what Elizabeth Hanson has analyzed as an unprecedented resort to judicial torture in order to discover the truth about Catholics' inner beliefs.[126] "Who is the Christian here, who the Jew?" The question prompts a laugh in most productions of *The Merchant of Venice*, on the grounds that the distinction is obvious, but there was no way of answering it simply in an era when entire segments of Jewish and Christian populations were under pressure to convert and/or to leave the country of their birth if they wanted to practice their old religion openly. In such societies, is it worth torture and death to retain one's moral or theological purity, especially if one's belief in that purity may be erroneous?[127] Cary offers an extremely equivocal answer to that question. The play interrogates Mariam's purity—racial, religious, sexual—partly through others' comments on her speech acts and partly through her own soliloquies; by the end of Act 4, she is undermining the sense of singularity and distinction, whether moral or lineal, upon which she based her claim to superiority over Salome in Act 1. Salome responded to Mariam's "rejected race" speech with a powerful version of the old "leveling" argument, "When Adam delved and Eve span, who was then the gentleman?" "Still twit you with nothing but my birth?" Salome asks Mariam. "What odds betwixt your ancestors and mine?/ Both born of Adam, both were made of earth,/And both did come from holy Abraham's line" (1.3.239–42; pp. 77–78).

It seems likely that Salome puns here on the Hebrew root (*adamah*, the word for "earth") that underlies both the name "Adam" and that of "Edom," Salome's ancestral land that was once conquered by Mariam's great-great-grandfather and is at the time of the play subsumed by a larger empire, Rome. Intriguingly, Salome's Hebrew punning omits a pun adduced by Alexandra in her racializing denigration of Salome: the association of Edom with "red" and hence with blood. Moreover, Salome's speech finds a unity of descent at precisely that moment of the genealogy which Herod later cites to support (the idea of) Mariam's purer blood. He sees her royal line deriving from "her grandam Sara," Abraham's wife. Apostrophizing Judea, then sliding into a praise of Mariam, he exclaims:

> 'Tis I that have o'erthrown your royal line
> Within her purer veins the blood did run,
> That from her grandam Sara she deriv'd,
> Whose beldame age the love of kings hath won;
> Oh that her issue had as long been liv'd.
>
> (5.1.178–82; p. 145)

Whereas Salome stresses unity of lineage, while ignoring the question of any moral distinction among holy Abraham's descendants, Herod stresses a difference between his blood and Mariam's by invoking a female ancestor whom, as we know from Salome as well as other discussions of Edomites, Herod in truth shares with Mariam. Moreover, he invokes Sara, enigmatically, as a woman who was capable of attracting the sexual desire of kings even in her old age—who was, in Herod's eyes, the object of adulterous lust and the potential ancestor, therefore, of other royal lines than Abraham's. Even as he praises Mariam's purer veins, he seems, obscurely, to be brooding on adultery and miscegenation; we may surmise that he himself would have taken Sara from her people as he took Mariam from hers, creating (though it is inexpedient for him to mention it) mixed-blood heirs to the throne from his union with the Maccabean princess. Neither Herod's nor Salome's genealogical argument is presented as true, but they work together to underscore the problem of defining or maintaining a race, and they suggest that birth, far from guaranteeing social distinctions, may work, as death does, to level them. Mariam, facing her own death at the end of Act 4, is no longer as sure as she was of her difference from Salome or, the rhetoric implies, from anyone whose skin might be darker or whose eye might cast a "meaner" light. In a passage I adduced earlier for its subversion of the fair/dark skin color binarism, Mariam suggests that death levels everyone by making them "pale" (paleness losing its status as a sign of high social status); she also suggests, through a series of puns on *Ay, I,* and *eye,* that the prospect of death can change how the female speaking subject sees and evaluates herself: "Ay, I it was that thought my beauty such,/As it alone could countermand my death" (4.8.527–28; p. 134). Now, however, Mariam is changing her mind and especially her understanding of social distinction, for she sees that death can "dim an eye whose shine doth most excel/As soon as one that casts a meaner light" (4.8.531–32). Death is the final eraser of the social distinctions the play itself has been interrogating throughout, with the effect, as I have argued, of making the social text itself less legible—with respect to marriage in particular and to ideas of social hierarchy in general—than many contemporaries thought it to be.

There is thus an ironic dimension to my argument: a play written against a certain kind of "sentence" of death (recall Herod's wish that he could "control" his "sentence" after he has ordered Mariam's beheading) nonetheless ends by showing Death's heuristic power and also his enormous allure, the pull of martyrdom. Like Christine de Pizan, however, Cary obliquely calls on prudence to resist Death's imperial power. The play's ideological statement is divided, partly because it so faithfully refracts the contradictions of Cary's historical moment, when the question of martyrdom remained open in the politics of dissent articulated and practiced by English Catholics. If in Act 5 Mariam is allowed, via a messenger's report rather than represented action, to display Stoic virtues of courage and patience that come to look very like the virtues of a Christian martyr, the reader is nonetheless left without a clear ethical perspective on the heroine's death.[128] Has she chosen it from pride or humility? Has she culpably abandoned her children? The text conspicuously refuses to examine what happens in the moments of "silent prayer" the messenger reports to Herod, and so Mariam remains, like Milton's Samson Agonistes, a potential "type" of Christ but also a possible antitype. Her relation to Christ, and to his harbinger John the Baptist, whom Mariam clearly resembles as Salome's beheaded victim, remains equivocal to the end. The apparently transcendental solution to intractable political problems itself becomes a subject for casuistical (and hence incipiently political) debate. The text puts the burden of interpretation on the reader, who must ponder the degrees of similarity and difference between Christ, later Christian martyrs, and this pre-Christian Jewish woman who refuses (or says she refuses) any "look" dissenting from her "thought." Her refusal of equivocation is presented as a refusal of empire: when she rejects Herod's offer to crown her "Empress" and make her his "commandress," she is also refusing the authorial scope and ambition that Cary figures as an act of climbing—to descry and conquer new lands, perhaps—in the Chorus's speech about the "proper wife" in Act 3: "When she hath spatious ground to walk upon, / Why on the ridge should she desire to go" (3.3.221–22; p. 113). Mariam turns away from the question at the end, but Cary's play leaves it open, like the question of the relation between Salome and Mariam as two faces of Dido: one black, one white, neither quite what it seems.

Speculations

The figure of the martyr or victim, Walter Benjamin argues in *The Origin of German Tragic Drama*, is central to the way in which baroque tragedy in general, and the subset of plays concerning Herod and Mariam in particular, work ideologically to reinforce the structures of the emergent absolutist state. More precisely, he writes, such plays serve to restore "order in a state of emergency," or to "replace the unpredictability of historical accident with the iron constitution of the laws of nature" (74). Cary's play makes a more radical ideological statement than the one Benjamin derives from a corpus of male-authored plays, I argue, although in so doing I take to heart David Norbrook's recent cautionary remark that "much postmodern theorization of reading and politics too easily conflates epistemological with political positions."[129] I hope, however, that I've made a case for a radical "ideological" statement that includes both epistemological and political elements, albeit in a muted way that is itself part of the play's political statement.[130] A critical examination of the workings of state censorship is an inherently political operation. Moreover, I have argued that a major effect of the play's literacy of equivocation is to undermine the bases for secure or legitimate judgments of guilt and innocence in an imperial nation. This effect arguably contains a genuinely political aim of challenging as illegitimate the kind of death sentences the English state was visiting upon some Catholic citizens—not to mention the Jesuit priests who were, after 1585, defined as traitors if they so much as entered the realm of England. It is better, the play seems to me to be saying, to let the ambiguously guilty go free—as the play does with Salome and also, of course, with Herod himself—than to kill the ambiguously innocent—as Herod, aided by Salome (or Salome aided by Herod), kills Mariam, Constabarus, and the sons of Babas. All these last-named characters have indeed behaved in ways that can be considered treasonous, but the play explores the complexities of their crimes and partly exonerates them by showing the many illegitimate aspects of Herod's own royal authority and the authority Salome dubiously but consequentially appropriates, though without the name or "ornament" of royalty.

A final reason for arguing that Cary's play reads "against the grain" of the absolutist state lies in its atypical depiction of a prince who aspires to make his "will" into the "law" (as Salome puts it), but whose power to do so is enormously contingent on others both at home and abroad. Specifically, his version of royal executive power depends on his sister, at home, and on the distant "Roman lords" he serves; they twice call him to account for his actions in the span of history that Cary's drama selects for analysis. Although they don't punish him in the way his crimes seem to merit (one of Babas's sons insists on Caesar's tendency to mercy in a way that reflects ironically on Herod's execution of Mariam), they nonetheless have authority over him and reveal the limits of both his fantasized and his actual regal powers. In depicting a prince who aspires to absolutist status but who, in reality, must negotiate and renegotiate his power both at home and abroad, Cary casts a skeptical eye on the institution of absolutism that her own newly installed monarch, James I, was seeking to reinforce. Her play reminds us that during what is known as the "age of absolutism," European princes were in truth competing with each other for power and authority on both sides of the Atlantic. The ideology of absolutism merits more analysis than it has received, even at the hands of Perry Anderson, as a defensive reaction against the historical facts of imperialism that worked to render the absolutist monarch a highly contingent being.[131]

Ultimately, the play's ideological work is impossible to assess under labels such as "conservative" or "radical." While I want to stress the ways in which

Cary's play deviates significantly from those tragedies of tyrants upon which Benjamin based his provocative conclusions, I do not want to overstate the play's own legibility as a political intervention in an extremely complex, and still, to me, partly occluded, social nexus. The text does not so much advocate a political alternative to absolutism (a version of the republicanism recommended by some of Cary's male contemporaries, for instance) as *decline* to "restore order" in the way Benjamin sees other Herod and Mariam plays doing. Moreover, the play offers a serious inquiry into the legitimacy of any state that is supported on and with reference to the institution of patriarchal marriage. In sum, while I do not claim that Cary's play makes a fully coherent political or epistemological statement, I do suggest that the incoherence is itself significant—partly legible, if you will—with reference to discourses that call attention to the problems of political censorship and, more generally, to culturally constructed methods of ascribing meaning to signs. If I am right in stressing equivocation as something at the center of Cary's theory and practice of literacy, then it is perhaps not surprising that Cary reads and writes Mariam's story and Herod's differently than most of her contemporaries did.

That difference comes in part from her socially constructed gender and, more specifically, from her historical experience as a wife and her intense engagement with religious discourses and practices. This point leads to my second and final qualification of Benjamin's conclusions about "tragedies of tyrants": the "strange image of the martyr" in many of these dramas, he maintains, "has nothing to do with religious conceptions." This is so, Benjamin says, because "the perfect martyr is no more released from the sphere of immanence than is the ideal image of the monarch" (*Origin of German Tragic Drama*, 73). I argue, however, throughout this chapter and indeed this book, that such a view of religion, shared by many modern critics within and outside the Marxist tradition, is ahistorical and cannot take us very far toward understanding the institutionally and discursively fractured sphere of religion in the early modern era—especially but not only as that sphere was experienced and represented by female subjects with varying types of literacy. Even Fredric Jameson's important argument about religion as a "dominant ideology" or "theological master-code" in Milton's time does not, in my view, provide an adequate theoretical language for perceiving, much less analyzing, how "minority" groups generated and circulated religious beliefs in this period.[132]

In the next and final chapter of this book, I turn to another English woman writer who used allegorical language to meditate on problems of writing and interpretation in an imperial regime. Aphra Behn's *Oroonoko*, written in 1688, represents an English empire much more embroiled in the Atlantic slave trade than Cary's England was; the text is also much more insistent than Cary's that the educated woman's ability to equivocate is implicated in an economic system that privileges white-skinned writers of both genders over black-skinned people who speak with great eloquence but who do not, and perhaps cannot, use the pen. Cary's play offers a commentary on, but no political alternative to, life in an imperial regime riven by differences among subjects and within them. The latter include the differences Mariam experiences, and seems to interpret imperfectly, between her "morning" and "mourning" selves during a single day. The differences are small—sometimes no larger than a single letter—but they matter.

New World Scenes from a Female Pen
Literacy as Colonization in Aphra Behn's
Widdow Ranter and *Oroonoko*

> I ought to tell you, that the Christians never buy any Slaves but they give 'em some Name of their own, their native ones being likely very barbarous, and hard to pronounce; so that Mr *Trefry* gave *Oroonoko* that of *Caesar*, which Name will live in that Country as long as that (scarce more) glorious one of the great Roman . . . But his [Oroonoko/ Caesar's] misfortune was to fall in an obscure World, that afforded only a Female Pen to celebrate his Fame.
>
> APHRA BEHN, Oroonoko

> If your god teaches you to break
> Your word, I need not curse you.
> Let him cheat you.
>
> OROONOKO, in 'Biyi Bandele,
Aphra Behn's "Oroonoko," A New Adaptation

The differences between Elizabeth Cary and Aphra Behn, as educated women reflecting on literacy in an imperial context, have much to do with socio-economic changes in England between the early and the late seventeenth century.[1] The differences between Cary's and Behn's reflections on empires— both English and Roman ones—arise also, however, from the different social situations in and from which the two women performed their writing and reading activities. Cary was an upper-class woman uncertain about whether her play should be published through print and unable by virtue of her gender to reach a public audience through the Jacobean theater.[2] Behn, in contrast, was a woman of lower- or middling-class origin who claimed aristocratic lineage, who wrote for money, and who had the experience—for better and for worse—of seeking various audiences through various means, including London gossip, coterie circulation of manuscripts, the press, and, last but not least, the Restoration theater, an institution that had allowed women onto its stage while also allowing the circulation of discourses excoriating actresses as whores.[3] Behn's vision of England as an imperial nation was critically colored by her experience as a woman writer who had worked in the theater—exploiting the anomaly of her gender while also defending against attacks on her status as a "public" woman.[4] During the 1680s, when her access to the theater was suddenly decreased, she turned to translation, poetry, and fiction writing while continuing to hope for a return to the theater.[5] Many of the texts she produced during her final decade were concerned with "new worlds" and implicitly, I suggest, with the new world of the stage that Behn had lost. These works included the pastoral poems "The Golden Age" and "The Disappointment" (both published in 1684) and "To the Fair Clarinda" (1688); translations of Bernard de Fontenelle's *Discovery of New Worlds* (1688) and of book 6 of Abraham Cowley's "Of Plants" (1689); and two works set in America. One of these was a novella, *Oroonoko, or The Royal Slave* (1688).[6] The other was a play not performed in the author's lifetime and still not well known today, *The Widdow Ranter, Or the History of Bacon in Virginia, A Tragicomedy* (1690).[7] In these late works Behn used her pen to relay exotic "news" to a metropolitan readership eager for novelty. Her imagined worlds, spiced with borrowings from foreign tongues, are distant: in time, in space, or in both dimensions. The temporal new worlds often draw on the classical tradition of the golden age (as in Behn's poem of that name adapted without acknowledgment from a chorus in Tasso's *Aminta*); sometimes Behn refers to the Elizabethan myth of the queen as Astraea, the virgin goddess of justice whose return to earth, famously announced by Vergil in the Fourth Eclogue, signaled a renewal of the golden age in both secular and Christian visions of empire. "Astraea" was one of Behn's pennames, and Queen Elizabeth, honorifically likened in her own time both to Aeneas and to a "chaste" Dido, plays a significant role in Behn's fantasies about a new English empire that would perhaps prove more just (at least to women and maybe to some others) than the historical regime appeared to be.[8]

Along with imagined new worlds harking back at least intermittently to classical or Elizabethan golden ages are the worlds Behn imagines existing in exotic places that were important to English trade. These include West Africa (depicted, in Orientalized fashion, in the first part of *Oroonoko*), South and North America (depicted in *Oroonoko* and *Ranter* respectively), and the populated stars she brings to her English readers by translating (and slyly recasting) Fontenelle's representation of a dialogue between a learned man and a poorly educated but intellectually quick noblewoman. In both *Oroonoko* and *Ranter*, the spatial Other blends with a temporal Other that has a distinctly autobiographical dimension.

Advertising the Author

Behn looks back to the 1660s in both *Oroonoko* and *Ranter*, and in the former she explicitly employs a first-person narrator to create an "autoethnographical" discourse, as Mary Baine Campbell aptly calls it.[9] This discourse not only re-creates a past—and incipiently romantic—moment from the narrator's life but also a moment from the 1660s when England still possessed the colony of Surinam—a colony that the deputy governor, a man named William Byam, ceded to the Dutch in exchange for Manhattan.[10] He was later nearly court-martialed for this action, and Behn laments the loss in her text, while portraying Byam as a cruel, promise-breaking tyrant who occupied a political position that should, by right, have belonged to Behn's own father, had he not died at sea. There is documentary evidence that the historical Byam disliked Behn almost as much as she disliked him. His letters, referring sarcastically to "Astraea," are a major source for the current critical consensus that Behn's novella is based on an actual trip to Surinam.[11] Janet Todd, moreover, thinks that Behn may have visited Virginia during the same American voyage when she was possibly already employed by a court official as a spy (*Secret Life,* 47, 41). Although Behn does seem to have gone to America, she evidently takes many liberties with the historical truth about herself and others. There is no evidence corroborating her claim that had her father not died at sea, he would have become Byam's replacement or perhaps superior by assuming the lieutenant-governorship of the entire colony ("six and thirty Islands, besides the Continent of *Surinam*" [*Oroonoko,* 95]).[12] The fate Behn gives to her (putative) father was in fact suffered by Francis Willoughby, Lord of Parham, a politician who had changed from the parliamentary to the royalist side during the English Civil War and who brought both factional politics and greed to his complex efforts to recoup, in the 1650s, a £20,000 investment in plantations along the Surinam river (Todd, *Secret Life,* 35, 36). Willoughby was the man who would have had the power to replace Byam with Behn's alleged father, but Willoughby died in a storm at sea shortly before Behn probably arrived in the Americas. When Behn says she occupied the "best house" in the colony, she refers to a plantation very near Willoughby's and possibly owned by him in 1666 (ibid., 449n. 43). Is she imaginatively conflating her real father (critics are still not agreed on his identity) with a man of aristocratic birth, in a brilliant example of what Freud called a "family romance" narrative? In any case, in both *Ranter* and *Oroonoko,* complex romances are formed out of fact, memory, and fiction; in both works, a strong father-ruler figure is absent but eagerly awaited, while various sons and perhaps daughters compete for his place. In the novella, the arrival of the absent father-king is the event that would somehow allow the narrator and Willoughby's plantation overseer, a man named Trefry, to make good on their (as it turns out, false) promises to free the African prince.[13] The absent-father plot has both theological and (royalist) political resonances for the daughter who wields the pen.

Into the vacuum caused by the father's absence come bad substitutes—the weak and poorly served "Wellman" of *Ranter,* the malicious Byam of the novella. Remembering and revising what seems to have been a traumatic visit to America, Behn makes the settings of both of her late colonial works into powerful sites of personal and national memory, including signs of guilt and fantastic desires for a second chance at history. Surinam is initially described as an Edenic place; while it turns from utopia to dystopia in the course of the narrative, there are several hints that the narrator hopes to inspire her English readers with a desire to regain the golden age landscape despite the tragedies that have variously befallen its peoples, both natives and visitors from other worlds. Immediately after describing her own father's death—which forced her and her party "to continue on our Voyage," she conflates the loss of the colony with the loss of the king then reigning, Charles II; the elegiac quality of the passage has something to do with King James's imminent (or perhaps recently occurred) loss of the throne in 1688: "certainly had his late Majesty, of sacred Memory, but seen and known what a vast and charming World he had been Master of in that Continent, he would never have parted so Easily with it to the Dutch." The passage modulates from elegy to real-estate advertisement from an "eye-witness" who herself saw the "Eternal spring," the "groves of Oranges, Limons, Citrons," the "very Wood of all these Trees [which] have an intrinsick Value above common Timber" (*Oroonoko,* 95). And when she returns a few pages later to the same theme, she seems to be addressing an imagined reader who would have the power and interest to give the colonizing project a second chance; the "mountains of gold" Raleigh had unsuccessfully sought up the Amazon River are still there, Behn suggests, waiting to be claimed (104). The project was interrupted, but it might be resumed for those willing to fight the Dutch just when James's daughter Mary is bringing William of Orange to England's throne: "we going off for England before the Project was further prosecuted, either the Design dy'd, or the Dutch have the Advantage of it" (104).

Ambiguously melding (alleged) scientific and historical fact with fiction, elegy, and elements of nationalist and royalist propaganda, Behn's New World texts carry "news" to metropolitan readers who are described at the outset as already surfeited with "Diversions for every Minute, new and strange" (*Oroonoko,* 57). Behn acknowledges that "where there is no Novelty, there can be no Curiosity" (59).[14] She therefore seeks to pique her readers' interest with New World texts containing numerous advertisements not only for virgin land but also for the female writer, especially in her vocation of sexually provocative playwright who, like the colony of Surinam, is not virginal but is nonetheless only incompletely "known" by the English (95). In the middle of describing her African hero's betrayal and torture, she digresses to mention an

English plantation owner (and republican), George Marten, "whom I have celebrated in a Character of my New Comedy" (111). She refers here to *The Younger Brother,* a play found among Behn's manuscripts after her death and first performed in 1694 (*Works,* ed. Todd, 1:454n. 102). The "nuns' stories" she represents herself telling to her African heroine may allude to her own racy fictions about nuns. In *Ranter* the advertisements consist, as they often do in Behn's dramas, in multiple figures of the author, including the Indian Queen, the Widow Ranter of the title, and Chrisante. Each of these female characters dresses as a man at some point in the play and each alludes to the playwright through the lens of an emergent and titillating set of cultural discourses about English women in the colonies, discourses that emphasize the danger of liberating women's nature from the restraining conventions of home.[15] Stressing women's "natural" tendency toward lust, these discourses also raise the ideologically charged specter of what later ages would call miscegenation. Behn exploits her culture's fascination with and fear of exogamous romance in an imperial setting. Writing as a female traveler with an alienated subject's perspective on England, she nonetheless seeks to export and profit from views that can be fairly defined as imperialist. She offers us a complex portrait of a writer engaging—with considerable self-reflexivity—in a project of literate colonization. This may be defined as an appropriation, in and through a metropolitan English language, that benefits the writer and metropolitan readers much more than it benefits some of the Others represented in the text. As a woman writer who challenged various norms of proper feminine behavior, Behn provides a particularly interesting glimpse into that long historical process I discussed in part 1, whereby clerkly ideologies contributed to the ways in which European observers of New World and African societies interpreted what was new through lenses colored by old ideologies of gender difference. Because Behn offers partial critiques of doxical notions about women as the inferiors to, and the property of, men, she allows her readers at least intermittently to see cultural difference as something that eludes familiar hierarchical categories and even the (expanding) conceptual umbrella provided by emergent notions of vernacular literacy as a tool of empire.

For Behn, both an international linguistic field and the institution of the London theater seem to emerge, imaginatively, as colonizable but not yet fully colonized territories; these resemble both the African shore land that Dido encircled with her "purse," her strips of bull's hide, and the American landscapes Behn depicts as places where resourceful women can prosper if they know how and when to counterfeit reality, and even themselves, in English words. In the theater as Behn depicts it in many of the prologues to her plays, one can make oneself anew in ways more satisfying than those provided (in Behn's time) by the institution of the school, much less that of the church. In the theater, as in the American colonies, the advantages conferred by birth or "nature" matter less than they do in the real world of England. Shakespeare, Behn remarks in the "Epistle to the Reader" prefixed to her early play *The Dutch Lover,* achieved greater success with theater audiences than Ben Jonson did because "[p]lays have no great room for that which is mens great advantage over women, that is Learning." She goes on both to ally the female playwright with Shakespeare and to delegitimate Jonson's classical education: "We all well know that the immortal *Shakespears* Playes (who was not guilty of much more of that [i.e., learning] than often falls to womens share) have better pleas'd the World than Johnsons works, though by the way 'tis said that Benjamin was no such Rabbi neither, for I am inform'd his Learning was but Grammar high; (sufficient indeed to rob poor Salust of his best orations)" (*Works,* ed. Todd, 5:162). Wrongly but interestingly equating her own non-grammar-school education with Shakespeare's non-university schooling, Behn advertises her own wares as being like Shakespeare's, wittily yoking education with sin. Although there are many questions about just how much learning, and in what languages, Behn actually possessed, there is no doubt that she found in Shakespeare's example a way of thinking about various brave new worlds and about how, as a writer, she could increase her share in them.

Her career as a playwright, poet, translator, and writer of short fiction dramatizes some of the logical and ideological consequences of using a certain vernacular literacy (enriched by a striking ability to appropriate materials from other languages, including Latin) to remake one's defining social marks, including those of gender, birth, and religious faith (or, perhaps, its absence). Behn may have used her pen even to counterfeit her names: I have argued elsewhere that "Aphra" harks back to a fourth-century prostitute saint and that "Behn"—allegedly a married name but no husband has ever been found in the records—conveniently rhymes with "pen" and alludes as well to Ben Jonson and his own puns on the vexed relation between literary and biological types of genealogy (*ben* means "son of" in Hebrew).[16] Behn's self-fashioning project clearly contributes, in some eccentric ways, to a larger cultural project of legitimating England's imperial ambitions and colonizing activities while also intermittently criticizing aspects of her country's (and especially her countrymen's) behavior toward non-European subjects. Exploring the emergent perception that English women, especially upper-class wives, suffered injustices similar to those suffered by African slaves, Behn's works from the last decade of her life at once examine and mystify the moral ambiguities of England's early colonizing ventures.[17] Ideologies of class entitlement and an accompanying idealization of an aristocratic "gift economy," as Laura Rosenthal has persuasively argued, severely limit Behn's critique of slavery as an institution.[18] The critique is also disturbingly colored, as Mary Beth Rose observes, by the narrator's own "conflicted relation to slavery."[19]

In *Oroonoko* and *Ranter,* the "other world" texts most engaged with English colonial activity, Behn weaves a lurid strand of domestic royalist ideology into her portrait of her two heroes displaced from their native countries onto New World land. There are striking parallels between the two rebellious heroes, one white and one black, and the female narrator of the novella, but the parallels render two differences among the three New World visitors even more significant. These are differences in skin color, on the one hand, and, on the other, differences in degree and kind of literacy. Both sets of differences contribute to an emerging binary contrast between the modern and the premodern. Behn shows herself to be implicated in creating, exploiting, and legitimating this ideological contrast as she both critiques and illustrates a type of literacy she associates with the advent of modernity. This phenomenon called modernity is presented at times as inevitable, if dreadfully costly for some; at other times, however, modernity is presented as something the narrator or her non-English characters might have prevented or altered in historically significant ways. Modernity, as an ideologically fractured concept, sometimes works in Behn's colonial texts as it does in the writings of various ethnographers analyzed by Johannes Fabian in *Of Time and the Other: How Anthropology Makes Its Object.* Like Fabian's ethnographers, Behn casts Others who are actually her historical contemporaries (or who were her contemporaries twenty years earlier) into the strange role of "precursors" to modernity. They become premodern because they are portrayed as lacking literacy, which Behn defines, significantly, as a set of verbal techniques including lies in speech and writing—lies, moreover, that even written contracts cannot prevent. The heterogeneous vernacular practices of literacy that Behn defines and illustrates in her late "American" texts are techniques that belong to Europeans from various social backgrounds; Behn shows that even well-traveled and well-read women can acquire these techniques and profitably deploy them. Mystifying the actual historical situation in Europe by implying that possession of both alphabetic literacy and a "set" toward signs that we can consider cultural literacy is somehow normal in the 1680s, Behn defines literacy not as a civilizing or ethical phenomenon but rather as an amoral but crucial instrument for success, including bodily survival, in a "modern" world.

Such literacy is exhibited both by the female narrator of *Oroonoko* and by the Widow Ranter, the comic heroine whose name takes precedence over Bacon's on the printed play's title page. Ranter uses her verbal powers to fulfill her desires for life and love and, in pursuing the latter, is more successful than the narrator of *Oroonoko*. Both female characters, however, are shown operating outside the confines of marriage, and both engage in forms of cross-dressing and in the manufacture of lies that command others' belief. The widow pursues her desires for a man named Daring by forging a letter containing her "Credentials" (*Ranter*, 4.3.214; p. 339).

Behn's major male heroes lack this kind of literacy, and so do the non-English women whom they love. Oroonoko, however, is represented as acquiring some "education in skepticism" in the course of the novella, although the education proves tragically incomplete.[20] He gains some recognition of his illiteracy, and he attempts, impotently, to remedy his problem. Late in the story, he tells an English colonial governor attempting to "parlay" with him that "there was no Faith in the White Men, or the Gods they ador'd" (*Oroonoko*, 109).[21] Armed with this cruel lesson of experience, Oroonoko initially refuses to "credit" the governor's promises of clemency; eventually, however, and against his better judgment, Oroonoko is persuaded by one of his "friends" among the English to accede to the governor's terms so long as they are "ratify'd by their [the Englishmen's] Hands in Writing, because he had perceived that was the common way of Contract between Man and Man amongst the Whites" (110). "All of this is performed," as in a theater of colonial cruelty. For Oroonoko evidently lacks the ability to read the contract much less write one of his own. He has learned an empty lesson: he knows contracts are important, but he is too credulous to survive in the white people's world, for he still trusts too much in the spoken words of his "friends," who include the female narrator. Lacking what Behn defines as the critical skill of literacy, Oroonoko and his white double Bacon are vouchsafed (through the narrator's generosity and verbal potency) another kind of survival than mere bodily life. As a kind of bizarre symbolic compensation for their deaths, the narrator gives an afterlife to the heroes' names—and to at least one version of their stories, a version which, in Oroonoko's case, is said to come "directly" from him. We know, however, that he was unable to ratify this version in writing, and the text gives us ample reason to doubt the narrator's credibility.

A memorializing project defined, in its last sentence, as an effort to give her hero an afterlife, Behn's novella begins by "assuring" the metropolitan readers to whom her tale is specifically addressed that the hero is no less metropolitan than the best of London or European society: "the most Illustrious Courts," the narrator remarks, "cou'd not have produc'd a braver Man, both for Greatness of Courage and Mind" and for "solidity" of "Judgment," "quickness" of "Wit," and sweetness of "Conversation" (*Oroonoko*, 62). Conversational skills he has in abundance, along with physical and mental charms; but something is oddly lacking, since we later learn that Oroonoko has been tutored, in

Africa, by a Frenchman. The tutoring seems to have given the African prince some elements of cultural literacy but not the basic skills necessary for the "instrumental" kind of literacy Behn's novella marks, ambivalently, as valuable. "He knew almost as much as if he had read much: He had heard of, and admir'd the Romans; he had heard of the late Civil Wars in England . . . He had nothing of Barbarity in his Nature, but in all Points address'd himself, as if his Education had been in some European Court" (62). In all points but one, it seems; the narrator's balanced clauses leave us wondering about the quality of his education: he "was as sensible of Power as any Prince civiliz'd in the most refin'd Schools of Humanity and Learning" (63).

This paragraph, early in the narrative, seems to say that Oroonoko's lack of literacy, like his lack of whiteness, doesn't matter to his overall value in the admiring narrator's eyes, but she nonetheless senses that something about him will disturb her readers. Into the implied gap between her value-judgment and that which she anticipates from those to whom she is giving or selling her book comes a rhetorical quality of protesting too much. Oroonoko can speak eloquently in both French and English, and his physical appearance is so attractive to the narrator that "bating his Colour, there cou'd be nothing in Nature more beautiful agreeable, and handsome. There was no one Grace wanting, that bears the Standard of true Beauty" (63). The repetition of the negative absolutes—"nothing," "no one thing," accompanied by their qualifications— tells us that something is wrong with this picture and points to the narrator's implication in the tragic story she is about to narrate, in words that her hero, evidently, could not have read. His lack of alphabetic literacy comes in the end to cost him more than his color does, although color, as both a literal and a metaphorical phenomenon, is part of the broader legitimizing of empire her novella and play perform.

Another key element is the narrator's gendered depiction of herself, in *Oroonoko,* as being helpless to prevent the unfolding of a "history" which she suspects, in hindsight, that she might have had the "authority" to change. Her literacy is divided between her representations of herself as a weak female, even a servant or slavelike person bound to obey laws set by others, and representations of herself as a virago, even a queenlike person free to undertake bold adventures in the colonial setting and powerful enough to make her hero's "Glorious Name," along with that of his wife Imoinda, "survive to all ages" (*Oroonoko,* 119).[22] The oscillation between power and powerlessness that is an aspect of the female narrator's self-presentation in the novella appears also in *Ranter.* There, the eponymous heroine plays an authorlike role in manipulating the plot; her persona and powers are contrasted with those of the Indian Queen. In both the novella and the play, a political statement about literacy emerges in and through romantic plots that show various triangles forming and dissolving. This chapter examines those triangles, in which distinctions of skin color, nationality, and gender are constantly redrawn with reference to an emergent set of distinctions about attitudes toward, and the ability to manipulate, the English language. Those characters who lack "modern" literacy as Behn defines it come to look increasingly like Hannibal, Mark Antony, Dido, and Cleopatra—admirable but doomed enemies of the ancient Roman empire ideologically reborn in seventeenth-century England.

Anachronistic Heroism as a Form of Cultural Illiteracy

In contrast to Oroonoko, Behn's other transplanted "American" hero, the English man Nathaniel Bacon, possesses alphabetic literacy. But he resembles Oroonoko in lacking a manipulative or Machiavellian "set" toward language that would closely resemble the operations of feigned empathy and verbal mimicry we have already seen in Cary's Salome and which Stephen Greenblatt has analyzed in Shakespeare's portrait of Iago.[23] This kind of literacy entails an ability to read others' psyches and to improvise on those readings to one's own advantage, as the early European explorers, in Greenblatt's account, did with the Amerindians they encountered. Modern literacy, as Behn models and reflects on it, includes skepticism about received truths and a concern for the morally shady territory between intent, appearance, and reception of signs. Behn's theory and practice of a modern imperial literacy go hand in hand, it seems, with an idealization and drastic oversimplification of a premodern "oral" mentality as involving what David Paxman calls "an immediate and unproblematic veracity."[24] Behn thus anticipates—and reveals ideological and economic contexts for—the dichotomy between literate and oral subjectivities so important to modern theorists of the Great Divide school. In Behn's account, but not according to other narratives about Bacon, his tragedy comes about in large part because he is credulous.[25] This quality appears just at the moment when we first see him dealing with a written document. A stage direction in Act 2, scene 1, describes Bacon as reading "again" the treacherous letter that his lieutenant Daring has already read aloud to him and warned him to disbelieve.[26] This is a letter that the justices of the peace have sent him in order to kill him under the guise of "acknowledg[ing] his Services" to the colony (*Ranter*, 1.2.43; p. 304). Like a latter-day Coriolanus, Bacon is preparing to lead an "enemy force" on countrymen who have, he feels, rejected his services to the colony. Those services consisted chiefly in fighting the Indians; at the beginning of Behn's play, however, Bacon has decided that his former enemies are less hateful than his former friends among the colonial society Behn rep-

resents as full of idiots and knaves—and lacking a true ruler. Intent on joining the Indians both militarily and romantically, since he has fallen in love
with an Indian queen named Semernia, wife to King Cavarnio, Bacon receives a letter from the colonial authorities inviting him "kindly home"—that
is, to the temporary home of Jamestown (1.2.44; p. 304).[27] The letter further-
more offers to salve Bacon's wounded ego by giving him a commission for a
general's post. Having asked Daring to read the letter to him (and to the audience), Bacon refuses to listen to the reader's warnings about the text; it displays, Daring avers, a gap between the letter senders' "hearts" and their "pen"
(2.1.60; p. 310).[28] Bacon chooses instead to believe the justices' emissary, comically named "Dunce," and in so doing, Bacon becomes a bit of a dunce himself, "illiterate" according to the play's association of literacy with the ability to
master the duplicity of words. "I see no Treachery, and can fear no danger," Bacon proclaims about the words of the letter (2.1.70–71; p. 310). As if to underscore the irony at Bacon's expense, Behn gives him a second chance to read the
letter in a way that would give him the same knowledge of planned treachery
that the play's own readers already possess. Left alone on stage a few minutes
later, he "reads the Letter again"—but instead of interpreting it correctly, Bacon allows his attention to be distracted by the entrance of the Indian queen,
another representative, it seems, from the world the play is gradually defining
as "premodern," naïve about signifying practices, and hence doomed despite
its many admirable qualities. Instead of reading the letter critically and thus
gaining the knowledge he needs to save his life, Bacon pursues his romantic
and incipiently miscegenous interest in the Indian queen. She is Behn's original addition to the historical narrative of Bacon's rebellion as it has come down
to us in a somewhat confusing welter of texts.

Behn's portrait of Bacon as a leader of a rebellion in Virginia in 1675–76 significantly revises the account of a historical rebellion that was printed in 1667
by William Harris and entitled *Strange News from Virginia, A Full and True Account of the Life and Death of Nathaniel Bacon, Esquire, Who was the only Cause
and Original of all the late Troubles in that Country . . .*[29] As Margo Hendricks
notes, Behn's depiction of members of the Virginia Council "inverts the class
affiliation of the ruling oligarchy of Virginia" by transforming the rulers into
dregs of society who think they can make a new life in the New World.[30] Behn's
play also changes what other texts tell us about Bacon's brutality as a colonial
soldier: his army of "indentured English servants, African slaves, and dissatisfied soldiers" succeeded for a time in harshly suppressing Indian resistance to
the English, but in Behn's text, we see and hear much more about his failed
love for an Indian queen than about his military successes. Behn directs her
reader's attention away from a "riff-raff" army—its structural place is occu-

pied instead by the comically inept "governors" of the colony—and toward
the tragic triangular relationship between Bacon, his beloved Indian queen,
and her husband. Behn's new story adds the character of the Widow Ranter
and erases what the record tells us about Bacon's relationship with an English-
born wife, Elizabeth Duke (Hendricks, "Civility, Barbarism, and Aphra Behn's
The Widow Ranter," 227). In *Oroonoko* Behn also brushes against the grain
of history and nowhere more so, I suspect, than in her creation of a love triangle of sorts, in which she herself plays a shadowy role—and one that differs significantly from the role that her historical enemy Byam charges her
with playing when, in letters home, he describes "Astraea" ridiculously pursuing "Celedon," his code name for the English man—and republican—
William Scot.[31] Aspects of Behn's relation to Scot—especially her work as a
spy on his allegedly republican activities in the Low Countries—may be figured in her novella's portraits of the narrator enlisted (against her will?) to
keep watch on Oroonoko when he is threatening to rebel against the English.
Some critics have also seen Scot's historical figure lurking behind Behn's portrait of the politically labile Bacon.[32] If contemporaries might have decoded
some story about Scot in Behn's plots about two male heroes who conflate
elements of the opposing sides in England's Civil War (both heroes look, at
times, like martyred kings as well as like rebels against [bad] royal authority),
we should pursue further the complex relations among Behn's fiction, her
own history, and the history of England in the years when Civil War ani-
mosities were often replayed in colonial settings.[33]

There is corroboration in the historical record for Behn's claim to have voy-
aged to Surinam, and also for her having known Scot both in Surinam and
later in the Low Countries, but there is no corroboration for her claim to have
met in Surinam an African prince whose name was Oroonoko, who was renamed "Caesar" by the English who enslaved him, and who loved, lost, found
again, and lost again a black woman named Imoinda while engaging in some
kind of relation with a white woman he called "his Great Mistress." The hero's
name recalls the South American river (in modern Venezuela) mentioned by
Sir Walter Raleigh in his *Discoverie of the Large, Rich, and Beautiful Empire of
Guiana* (1595), but Oroonoko is also the Carib word for "coiling snake."[34]
Moreover, as a multilingual signifier, the hero's name may recall—to some
but not all readers—the Yoruba god called Oro.[35] The hero's two names cross
many boundaries of the old Roman empire and new European ones. Behn's
hero, like his author, is indeed a traveler in time as well as in space. There is no
consensus in the critical tradition about whether he is wholly a figment of
Behn's English royalist imagination or a historical figure of an unspeakable
slavery who is renamed and redrawn by the English author for her own com-

plex purposes. In any case, she represents him as an unwilling traveler who is fairly newly arrived in Surinam at the time when she herself arrives (newly fatherless) with her mother, brother, and sister.

Behn's revisions of history—including, evidently, her own—in both *Oroonoko* and *Ranter* reveal the self-advertising marks of her "female pen," the instrument through which she adapted emergent definitions of literacy, gender difference, and racial "otherness" to her own purposes. In both American texts, she evidently alters received materials, oral as well as written, to emphasize triangular romances that cross lines of nationality, language, and, by implication, color as well. If she did meet a real African prince in Surinam and receive his story directly from his own mouth, she immediately invites her reader to wonder how much of his oral property she has altered in the retelling that is also a transcription (*Oroonoko*, 57). Her narration of his final torture clearly doesn't come from him, nor can we credit her opening claim to have received from him "the whole Transactions of his Youth." She undercuts that claim herself when she tells us, in her second paragraph, that "I shall omit, for Brevity's sake, a thousand little Accidents of his Life"—accidents she suggests might prove "tedious and heavy" to her metropolitan reader (57). Oroonoko talks to her in English, she reports, and his knowledge of French and English sparks her "extream Curiosity to see him" (62). But her text nonetheless repeatedly insists on its problematic status as a translation across media and cultures. The translation is economic as well as linguistic. Her apparently casual acknowledgment that she has "omitted" parts of his story to accommodate the needs of her English readers (and hence her own needs as well) foreshadows the scene of grotesque cultural censoring narrated at the end of her tale. There, Oroonoko will "cut a piece of flesh from his own throat" and, in the end, will stop up his own mouth with a pipe—preventing cries of agony—while the English torturers hack his body apart piece by piece (116–18). Something dreadful happens between the time when her pen writes and the time when his mouth speaks; her text gives us part but not the whole of that "history." Woven through the part she does give us is an implied narrative of her culture's emergent sense of taboo about intercourse (verbal or sexual) between persons of different blood lines.[36] John Rolfe's famous marriage to Pocahontas (1613)—the only formal instance of intermarriage in the earlier colonial period, according to Karen Kupperman—had been tolerated, and even approved, by some English authorities, despite the disapproval of others who adduced God's warning to Abraham not to "marry nor give in marriage to the heathen, that are uncircumcized."[37] By the 1680s such tolerance was much less prevalent. Behind the tragic scenes of Oroonoko's conversations with the Behn character and Bacon's romance with the Indian queen lurks a

set of relatively new laws proscribing cross-group sexual relations in the colonies and frequently lumping "Negroes, Indians, and Mulattos" together for
purposes of legal punishment.[38]

In *White over Black,* Winthrop Jordan cites a declaration by the Virginia
Assembly of 1670 barring both Indians and Negroes, even though "baptised"
and free, from the "purchase of christians," though they were not prohibited
"from buying any of their own nation."[39] In the tortuous language of this declaration we can see the term *Christian* being reserved, but not yet with the appearance of "natural" logic, for white Englishmen alone. Indians and Africans
(including the "brown" ones among the latter group, whom Behn seems to
classify as "natural" slaves, in contrast to the noble, jet-black Oroonoko) were
also yoked together, albeit differentially so, as prohibited mates for English
persons of either sex, who, according to Jordan, began to refer to themselves
collectively as "white" as well as "English" and "Christian" around 1680 (*White
over Black,* 94). Nonwhite men, moreover, whether Indian or African, were
easily interchangeable in the minds of Englishmen, either as members of in-
surrectionary groups (African slave revolts began to be no less terrifying than
Indian raids in the Virginia of the 1670s) or as sexual threats to English women
and, hence, to the purity of English bloodlines. It is worth noting, in this regard, that castration of both Negro and Indian men became a widely deployed
method of punishment in the late seventeenth century, and that miscegenation statutes frequently betray the lawmakers' fear that English women, if left
to their own devices, would rush to satisfy their lust with bestial, nonwhite
men. Although Kupperman argues that "status, not race, was the category
which counted for English people of the early years of colonization," Cary's
Mariam suggests a more complex chronology; by the time Behn published her
stories about America, the categories of status, gender, nation, and race were
clearly overlapping, sometimes in causal narratives with significant social
consequences (*Settling with the Indians,* 122).

Social status is clearly important to Behn's hero Bacon when he nobly—if
perhaps mistakenly—undertakes to defend Jamestown, in the colony Raleigh
named after his "Virgin Queen," against angry Indians who claim the land. In
so doing, he reminds us of Othello defending Cyprus against the "general enemy Ottoman," but in contrast to Othello, Bacon is not explicitly called to his
military role by the powers of the state (*Othello,* 1.3.48). On the contrary, communication from England to the colonies being slow and the colonial government, as Behn represents it, extremely petty and inefficient, a legal commission for the hero fails to materialize. This detail, which makes him an outlaw
in the eyes of the colonial council, serves finally to deepen his resemblance to
Othello insofar as both heroes, despite their difference of color, are regarded

as potentially (and by some, actually) dangerous to society's health. In the course of his military action, after falling in love with the Indian queen, he ambivalently acknowledges her husband's historical claims to America. Bacon rejects, however, the king's *present* claims to the land with breezy pragmatic cynicism. "[W]e were Monarchs once of all this spacious World," the Indian king says, "Till you, an unknown People landing here, Distress'd and ruin'd by destructive Storms, Abusing all our Charitable Hospitality, Usurp'd our Right, and made your friends your slaves." To these cadenced lines, Bacon replies: "I will not justify the Ingratitude of my fore-fathers, but finding here my Inheritance, I am resolv'd still to maintain it so, and by my sword which first cut out my Portion, Defend each inch of Land with my last drop of Bloud" (*Ranter*, 2.1.11–18; p. 309).

This exchange allows considerably more room for interrogating the morality of the colonial enterprise than many contemporary texts do: in the prologue of John Dryden and Robert Howard's *Indian Queen* (1665), for instance, an Indian boy justifies his country's conquest as a fated necessity rather than protesting the injustice as Behn's Indian king does.[40] The ideological limits of Behn's sympathy for the Indians' point of view appear, however, quite strikingly when her figure of exotic *female* nobility softens her husband's protest by expressing admiration for a man of the conquering people. Semernia's first words in Behn's play suggest her attraction to Bacon; her adulterous passion, a hallmark of the kind of literacy Behn was developing for the London market, works to cover over, and implicitly justify, the English appropriation of the Indians' land. We later learn that she began to love Bacon when she was a girl of twelve (*Ranter*, 5.3.177; p. 345). "Ev'n his threats have charms that please the heart," she says in an aside to the audience (2.1.19; p. 309). Thus does a symbolic personification of the New World land legitimize a brutal conquest by transforming a rape of land into a romance of mutual attraction between two noble subjects, each with some degree of agency.

Bacon eventually kills the Indian king, removing that obstacle to an English man's possession of both Indian land and Indian lady. He learns that his love has long been reciprocated, but he is not permitted to enjoy the fruits of passion. The playwright, it seems, punishes him for the wayward rebelliousness she also invites us to admire through the eyes of the sympathetic Semernia—a cultural Other whose actual skin color is never mentioned in the play but whose behavior makes her dark in the same way that English prostitutes— and prostitute-playwrights—were dark: through association with illicit sexual behavior. Both Bacon and Semernia are sacrificed, in effect, to preserve English property and norms of propriety. Meeting the now-widowed Semernia during a forest battle when she is disguised in breeches, Bacon wounds her fatally with his sword. Dying, she stands in tragic and ideologically complex counterpoint to the comically lustful and wealthy, older English widow of the play's title. Her name recalls the radical sect of the Civil War era, and she, like Semernia, changes her skirts for breeches late in the play. As I have suggested, the widow seems, from several perspectives, a striking figure for Aphra Behn herself. But the female playwright also invites her readers to see a shadowy likeness between herself and Semernia, one of the many "dark ladies" who populate Behn's texts of the 1680s.[41]

Despairing at the loss of his love and what appears to be a loss of his battle with the Englishmen, Bacon takes a fatal dose of poison just before hearing the news that his men, led by his lieutenant Daring, have in truth achieved a great victory. The act is layered with irony, for in taking his own life, Bacon activates a set of classical allusions that all work to compare England's empire to Rome's while complicating the issue of Bacon's identity, including his gender. One of his men remarks, "So fell the Roman Cassius—by mistake" (*Ranter*, 5.4.310; p. 349), likening Bacon to the Roman who killed himself during the battle of Philippi (42 B.C.E.) when he erroneously thought his and Brutus's forces had lost to those of Mark Antony and Octavius Caesar. As Cassius, Bacon would be a citizen who fails in his bid for imperial power; but Bacon himself offers a different, more alienated perspective on his relation to an imaginary Rome. "Come my good Poyson, like that of Hannibal," Bacon exclaims (5.4.287; p. 348), comparing his suicide to that of Hannibal, the great Carthaginian hero whose enmity to Rome was foretold, or rather, retroactively explained as doomed to failure, when Vergil had his Dido command an "unknown avenger" to arise from her ashes and pursue Aeneas's "whole stock and race" with undying hate (*Aeneid*, 4.622–29). Bacon's own image of himself as the brave masculine opponent of Rome doesn't stand as the last word, however; Behn draws a further comparison between Bacon and a later hero who chose love for a foreigner over his own Roman wife and the Roman way, including its notion of manhood as the pursuit of military glory. Recalling Mark Antony, Bacon exclaims that he has "too long surviv'd my Queen and Glory" (5.4.288–89; p. 348).

Preferring his Indian Queen to the penetration of Jamestown that the historical Bacon achieved, Behn's hero is subtly emasculated for the sake of at least the facsimile of order and stability in the English imperium. The historical Bacon, conspicuously aided by outspoken colonial women, as Kathleen Brown has shown, defeated Governor Berkeley's superior forces and entered Jamestown in September 1676; his men burned the town while other followers discussed the possibility of war with England: "I fear the power of England no more than a broken straw," Sarah Drummond reportedly exclaimed.[42] Behn revises history by making her Bacon more like Mark Antony, in the end, than like the historical rebel whose career was cut short (in October 1676) not by love-prompted suicide but rather by a sudden death from a fever. Behn's ideological message looks less conservative, perhaps, when one notes that her Bacon resembles not only the emasculated Mark Antony but also two powerful women whose reputations as Rome's enemies and critics lived on after their deaths. In seeking through a heroic suicide to "secure" himself from "being a publick Spectacle upon the common Theater of Death," Bacon recalls Cleopatra as she is represented both by Shakespeare and by Plutarch in his *Lives of the Famous Romans*. Janet Todd remarks on this parallel ("Spectacular Death," 77) but does not mention that Bacon's fantasy of his death, spoken before he actually follows Hannibal (and Cleopatra) by taking poison, recalls the more spectacular death chosen by Dido. Furious at the loss of his beloved, Bacon commands his followers to "make of the Trophies of the War a Pile, and set it all on Fire, that I may leap into consuming Flames" (*Ranter,* 5.3.219–21; p. 346).

Bacon's own fame, as refashioned by Behn, is a form of prowess gendered both masculine and feminine; it evidently needs a woman's eyes to give it value. Once Semernia is dead, and by Bacon's own ignorant hand, he relinquishes the hatred of England that made him a military threat, as Hannibal was to Rome. Behn seems to have made him safe for empire; his dying words, to his militarily successful followers, direct them to relinquish their advantage and, by implication, their ambitions to organize and rule the colony differently. "[N]ow while you are Victors," Behn makes Bacon say with breathtaking military stupidity, "make a Peace—with the English Councel—and never let Ambition—Love—or Interest make you forget as I have done—your Duty—and Allegiance—farewel" (5.4.306–8; p. 349). Bacon has apparently been disarmed for England's sake; but the allusions to Dido and Cleopatra help explain why the play offers a mixed message, speaking in double tongues not only for empire but for its future fracturing (though not in a way that would challenge the hegemony of the English language).[43] Perhaps Behn refashions the historical Bacon not just to emasculate him but to render him more like a virago who attacks her enemies intermittently, confusingly, and with unpredictable effects; such a figure fights with words rather than the sword and bears ambiguous messages that may be interpreted differently by differently situated readers, both male and female, both colonial and metropolitan.

The allusion to Hannibal's suicide marks out an ideological site for at least some sympathy with characters like Semernia and Bacon who resist England's laws, including the newly emerging colonial statutes against miscegenation.[44] The site for sympathy has distinct limits, however, one of them signaled by a character who remarks, early in the play, that "this Country [British America] wants nothing but to be People'd with a well-born Race to make it one of the best Collonies in the World" (*Ranter*, 1.1.105–6; p. 299). Bacon's union with the Indian queen would have been seen by many Englishmen, although not perhaps by Aphra Behn, as a threat to this genetic aim. For Behn, the union of noble characters across lines of "nation" or skin color might be preferable to the historical method of "peopling" America with "perhaps transported Criminals" who use their money and their wits—as it seems the Widow Ranter does—to gain positions of new authority in the New World (see 1.1.100–105; p. 299).

Bacon's likening of himself to the black African Hannibal is one of many textual details that make this romanticized white "Outlaw" a symbolic double of Oroonoko, who is renamed Caesar by the group Behn calls the "Christians" (see the epigraph to this chapter). Behn has Oroonoko invoke Caesar's enemy Hannibal as his own military model at a late moment in the story. In the course of using his considerable powers of eloquence to persuade his fellow slaves to revolt against the English—in a speech that Thomas Southerne drastically rewrites in his later play version of Behn's novella—Oroonoko describes Hannibal as "a great captain" who "cut his way through Mountains of solid rocks" (*Oroonoko*, 106). Behn here appropriates a great masculine hero for an effeminized mode of heroism that Mary Beth Rose has analyzed in a chapter comparing Oroonoko to Milton's Samson. Exemplars of what she calls "the heroics of endurance," such figures typically endure great suffering in a "present" shot through with memories of a "lost past composed of high status and military achievement" (*Gender and Heroism*, 101). For those among Behn's readers who knew Rome's history either through reading authors like Vergil or through hearsay, Hannibal would have evoked a gallant but ultimately defeated opponent of empire. As if to underscore the point, Behn makes Oroonoko, like Bacon, a figure of Mark Antony. She describes Oroonoko as a "Caesar" who swore "he disdain'd the Empire of the World, while he cou'd behold his Imoinda" (*Oroonoko*, 92). Behn's heroes as well as her non-English heroines revive memories of threats posed to Roman political domination as well as to Roman ideas of manhood. Dido, Hannibal, and Cleopatra were closely linked, by Vergil and other mythicizing historians, as "enemies who mounted a North African challenge to Roman dominance" (Desmond, *Reading Dido*, 31). Behn creates a similar challenge for England. In her New World texts, the condition that Vergil imputes to Dido—being "ignorant of fate" (*fati nescia* [*Aeneid*, 4.625])—is at once translated for new ideological purposes and partly unveiled as a condition that consists not in being generally "ignorant" but rather in being illiterate in one culture's tools for and ways of appropriating history. It is important to this book's larger argument about cultural literacy that Behn's Oroonoko should invoke Hannibal's example just at the moment when he seeks to shore up his modern African slave followers' resolution to fight England/Rome. What Oroonoko either does not know or does not tell his audience is that Hannibal ultimately failed in his effort to resist Rome's expansion of its territory.

Behn's Ambivalent Assessment of the Imperial Project

Behn's narrator exhibits a perspective on the colonizing project that shows her to be both inside and outside the group of male English property owners. From this divided position, she at once ratifies and challenges the ideological necessity of the outsider's punishment and ultimately, of his—and her—deaths. The colonial plots suggest that both Bacon and Oroonoko must be destroyed because of the threat their outsider status, recast as premodern, poses to the dominant social group and, specifically, to the male property owners of that group. Behn's rhetoric, however, often runs counter to the main ideological effect of her plotting, which is to suggest the necessity of the deaths of those who threaten the English.

The doubleness of Behn's assessment of the costs and benefits of the colonizing project is refracted in a certain doubleness in Oroonoko's statements about the aims of his revolt against the English. On the one hand, he tells his followers that they can become rivals to (and imitators of) the English by "plant[ing]" a "New Colony" by the sea; on the other hand, he suggests that the revolt and flight will allow them simply to await an end of their exile through the (fantastic) expedient of finding a ship that could transport them back to Africa (*Oroonoko*, 106). Having crossed in his imagination the historically thin line between being a prisoner and being a colonial planter (recall de Navarre's description of those released from French prisons to emigrate to a harsh life in Canada), Oroonoko is understandably uncertain about whether his role as colonist will be temporary or permanent. He does not get a chance to find out, however, for his followers desert him and he is then tricked into surrendering by the plantation manager Trefry, his former friend. Like the narrator, Trefry, a middle-level manager, plays an ethically dubious role in the tragedy; he sympathizes with the Africans yet contributes to their betrayal, just as the narrator befriends Oroonoko and Imoinda while working to "distract" them from harming English property through revolt. Trefry speaks "very cordially" to persuade Oroonoko to "name his conditions" for surrender, and Trefry is the procurer of that "written contract" Oroonoko demands at this point in the narrative, having learned, but ironically not well enough, not to

trust Englishmen's words (110–11). Oroonoko believes Trefry, who in turn erroneously believes the governor "to mean what he said" (109). Trefry thus becomes an oral party to a travesty of the written contract, for no sooner have
Englishmen's "Hands" ratified the contract (a document to which Oroonoko,
I presume, affixes his "mark") than the same English "Hands" are described as
binding Caesar to a stake for a brutal whipping, during which "*Indian pepper*"
is rubbed in his wounds (110). The narrator is doing some rhetorical pepper-
rubbing as well. She remarks that Imoinda is "spared" the sight of the torture,
"not in kindness to her but [rather] for fear she shou'd Dye with the Sight, or
Miscarry, and then they should lose a young *Slave*" (110). The pronoun *they*
evidently distances the narrator from the group whom she is rhetorically
defining as concerned less with kindness than with property.

Oroonoko/Caesar himself is, however, like the narrator, ambiguously en-
trammeled in concerns for present and future property in bodies. After recovering from his initial set of wounds, he seems to recover some of his freedom
as a house slave, and he takes the opportunity to go on a walk with his pregnant wife, whom he has resolved to kill before he kills Byam. The narrator
reports his motives as being a fear that if his wife outlives him, she will become
a "Prey, or at best a *Slave*, to the inrag'd Multitude; his great Heart cou'd not
indure that Thought" (*Oroonoko*, 113). Sexual jealousy reinforced by a principle of patriarchal property rights in women and children intertwines with
hatred of slavery as a dehumanizing condition. The narrator reports with
apparent approval, but also, I believe, some gender-inflected irony, on Oroonoko's "Execution of his great Design" to kill his wife and unborn child. He
tells her "the necessity of Dying," and she joyfully concurs with the plan—or
so the narrator tells us that Oroonoko told her. Indeed, the narrator calls attention to the relays of information, to the possibility of alterations creeping
in when one party to a scene is no longer able to give his or her own account
of it. Some verbal property rights have been abrogated, and it is perhaps no accident that these belong to a character who is doubly enslaved, by her gender
as well as her African origins. When Oroonoko first heard of Imoinda's presence in Surinam from Trefry—but before hearing her name—he had expressed considerable surprise that her owner should be pining fruitlessly for
her favors: he asked the English man "why, being your Slave, you do not oblige
her to yield?" (90). At a much later point in the narrative, after we have seen
Oroonoko being betrayed by the duped, but also self-blinded, Trefry, the narrator obliquely asks her reader to question her own English words as well as
those she is reporting from her hero: "'tis not to be doubted," she writes after
the wife's death scene, "but the Parting . . . of two such Lovers . . . must be very
Moving, as the Relation of it was to me afterwards" (114). With Imoinda's al-

leged acceptance of a plan that seems to assume the necessary failure of the same plan's later steps, the text asks, as Milton's Edenic epic had, whether or not necessity may be just "the tyrant's plea."

Behn stresses the cutting off of speech by the Hand—a metonymy for writing in her text as it is in Elizabeth Cary's. Imoinda dies when, "with a Hand resolv'd, and a Heart breaking within," the hero gives "the Fatal Stroke, first cutting her Throat, and then severing her yet smiling Face from that delicate Body, pregnant as it was with the Fruits of tenderest Love" (*Oroonoko*, 114). The sentence stresses an act of censorship, as does the subsequent passage describing Oroonoko's reaction to Imoinda's death. For two days, he refuses to eat and lies, drained of power, by the dead body; he acts again—but only in a self-mutilating way—when he is found by a party of Englishmen. Having an audience—a symbolic prerequisite to that facsimile of action provided by the theater—Oroonoko takes up his knife, declares that he is unafraid of dying, and cuts a piece of flesh from his throat. This gesture, a symbolic self-censoring, as I noted above, effeminizes Oroonoko and, significantly, replaces the violent action he had planned to take by killing Byam. Heroic military action becomes, as it were, part of the past; effective action directed outward seems no longer available either to the hero or to the narrator whose hand is manipulating his plot and perhaps censoring his spoken words. His "heroics of endurance," as Rose aptly calls them, continue as he "rip'd up his own Belly, and took his Bowels and pull'd them out." Charlotte Sussman has brilliantly discussed this disemboweling as an uncanny repetition, on the man's body, of his earlier deed of murdering the pregnant Imoinda ("Other Problem with Women," 220). Several long paragraphs later, after his belly has been sewed up and he has had an improbable occasion to talk about his wife's death to a group the narrator describes as "us," an official of the colonial government completes the hero's (and the narrator's) work of self-mutilating emasculation: "the Executioner came, and first cut off his Members, and threw them into the Fire" (*Oroonoko*, 117, 118).

Unlike Oroonoko's black body, Bacon's white one is not tortured before his death, but he too serves as a dubiously necessary sacrifice in—and to—the plot. To understand the ideological economy of that plot and its resemblances to *Oroonoko*, we need to look briefly at the comic story Behn interweaves with the tragedy of Bacon's miscegenous romance. The story ends in multiple marriages for Englishmen and women of varying social ranks and moral complexions. In the comic plot, the Widow Ranter, like the two virtuous young English women Madam Surelove and Mrs. Chrisante, acquires a suitable mate. If, as I have suggested, the Widow Ranter is a figure for the aging Aphra Behn herself, and a comic foil to the Indian queen, it is particularly significant that Bacon's best lieutenant, a man named Daring, is chosen by the widow for the role of husband. Daring and the widow are subversive characters, Daring because he fights with and for Bacon, the widow because she is openly unchaste, smokes tobacco, has money of her own to spend as she sees fit, and uses it to acquire respectability and sexual satisfaction with a younger man who enters into the institution of matrimony with jovial cynicism. But these two characters are *less* subversive, Behn's plot suggests, than Bacon and the Indian queen, who singly and together break too many social laws to be allowed to live. One might argue that the widow and Daring acquire their license to live at the *price* of their doubles' deaths. If this interpretation of one aspect of the play's complex ideological economy is right, then it seems fair to suggest that Aphra Behn seeks to please her English audience of people of different genders and ranks by representing, with titillating sympathy, "forbidden" modes of behavior, and finally legitimating that representation by punishing her most transgressive characters with deaths presented almost as if they were fated to occur. If Bacon is like Hannibal, readers with European cultural literacy *know* he can't win in the end, and the contemporary colonial project is rendered safe for English audiences by being thus assimilated to an old imperial plot in which the (black) Carthaginian hero loses the battle. The author thus manipulates the audience's sympathy for the tragic hero and heroine in a way that interrogates but also supports the ideological economy subtending the English colonizing project. Bacon himself is made to present the theft of the Indians' land as a "past" injustice, irremediable in the present. As a Hannibal innovatively melded with Mark Antony by a female writer who knows that love is her stock in trade, Bacon sacrifices his military ambitions, and apparently his critical perspective on England as well, on the altar of his love for Semernia.

Ambiguous News and Shady Connections from the Female Pen

The presentation of Bacon and Oroonoko as lacking in a specifically modern kind of literacy goes hand in hand with the narrator's representation of (and, in *Oroonoko,* participation in) a mode of discourse she calls "news." It is made up of both oral and written elements, and it circulates in an international system of trade. Both the narrator of *Oroonoko* and the male hero facilitate trade between the English and the Indians; both participate in the slave trade as well, Oroonoko directly, in his African youth, the narrator indirectly but in ways that allow her to call Oroonoko himself "my slave" in her prefatory letter to Lord Richard Maitland—a letter in which Behn herself plays the role of Maitland's servant giving him the "gift" of the book, in the hope of some later reward. Both the narrator and Oroonoko are complexly dependent on trade, then, as are Bacon and the widow in Behn's Virginia play. Behn mystifies this dependency, at times, as an escape into a gift economy more noble than buying and selling, but she also lucidly connects different levels and kinds of "trade" as belonging to an international system that drains many individuals of agency if they exist beneath the social level of the English male property owner.[45] Oroonoko himself is described as being (like the narrator) a translator among trading partners and a facilitator of exchanges among people who might have been or might become enemies: on a trip where the narrator sees frightfully self-mutilated Indian war captains whose facial wounds anticipate those Oroonoko later gives himself, Oroonoko "begot so good an understanding between the Indians and the English, that there were no more fears . . . but we had a perfect, open, and free Trade with 'em" (103). Oroonoko, himself "like" the English in his curiosity about "how they all came by those frightful Marks," is tragically ignorant that he should be fearing the English rather than the Indians at this point in the story.

"We trade for feathers," Behn writes early in *Oroonoko* (58). The *we*, a complex shifter throughout the novella, clearly refers here to English persons of both sexes who are trading with the Carib Indians, a group designated as Other, "them," in this passage. The Indians, Behn goes on to explain, order the feathers "into all Shapes, make themselves little short Habits of 'em, and glorious Wreaths for their Heads, Necks, Arms and Legs, whose Tinctures are unconceivable. I had a Set of these presented to me, and I gave 'em to the King's Theatre; it was the Dress of the Indian Queen, infinitely admir'd by Persons of Quality" (58). Though she gives rather than sells the "inimitable" feathers to the "King's Theatre," her gift is clearly made in the hope of future authorial benefit; Behn's own plays had been produced by the King's Company in the Royal Theater, and she may well have meant this passage to advertise her own as yet unseen "Indian queen" in *Ranter*. Her heroine was inspired by Dryden's and could well have worn the feather headdress pictured on the actress Anne Bracegirdle, an English woman playing the Indian queen Semernia and attended by two African children (fig. 6).

In the absence of those "Third Night" receipts that testified to the delayed rewards of an audience's favor, Behn was forced to rely for her living in the 1680s on very intermittent patronage and on the money she could glean from those who printed her books. "I have been without getting so long that I am just on the poynt of breaking, especially since a body has no creditt at the playhouse as we used to have . . . I want extremely or I wo'd not urge this," she wrote in a letter of 1684 asking the printer Jacob Tonson to give her £25 for her collected *Poems upon Several Occasions* rather than the £5 he had actually sent.[46] Lampooned by one Whig as suffering from "poverty, poetry, and pox,"

The Indian Queen

FIGURE 6
Anne Bracegirdle as Semernia: an Englishwoman plays an Indian
attended by two African children. Engraving by W. Vincent.
(Reproduced courtesy of The Harvard Theatre Collection, The Houghton Library)

she was clearly not merely playing aesthetic games when she called attention to her own gorgeously exotic appearance in the episode of *Oroonoko* where she travels with her hero to an Indian village. There, with hair cut short in a masculine style and sporting a "taffety cap, with black feathers on my head," she arouses "surprise" in her observers, neatly inverting the usual trope whereby Indians create amazement in Europeans (100–101).[47] Feathers, which link the androgynous narrator to the colonial objects of her gaze, are not only adornments but also the material out of which pens were made (quills). Behn's "black feathers" arguably symbolize her peculiar status, and desires, as a public woman who was also a writer.

Unlike some English visitors to the colonies who brought Native Americans home with them as "curiosities," Behn brought feathers for an actress's headdress, "some rare flies, of amazing forms and colors," and, of course, material for the verbal representations of exotic bodies contained in the book she wrote many years later (*Oroonoko*, 58). She describes Imoinda's body in a way that highlights its status—and value—as an exotic artifact: as Catherine Gallagher has observed, it is a body described as if its "natural" state were artificial (*Nobody's Story*, 73). Behn tells us that all nobly born Coramantians "are so delicately cut and raised all over the Fore-part of the Trunk of their Bodies, that it looks as if it were japan'd, the Works being raised like high Point around the edges of the Flowers" (*Oroonoko*, 92). Some, she goes on to explain, are only carved "with a little Flower or bird"; this is the case with Caesar/Oroonoko. Others, however—and the example suggests yet another significant asymmetry of gender—are carved all over. Imoinda, the narrator remarks, as if it were an afterthought ("I had forgot to tell you"), has "fine Flowers and Birds all over her Body" (92).[48]

Behn aestheticizes and commodifies both her major African characters. The narrator describes the carvings on Imoinda's body as "more delicate" than those on "our ancient Picts that are figur'd in the Chronicles" (92), for instance, in an allusion to an ancient group of Britons mentioned in chronicles such as *Britanniae speculum* (1683).[49] The comparison almost certainly alludes, as well, to Thomas Hariot's comment that the markings on the ancient Picts were similar to those on "Indians" in Virginia. Hariot's comment is in his *Brief and True Account of the New Found Land of Virginia*, first published in 1588 and reprinted in 1590 in Théodore de Bry's *India Occidentalis*. This was an enormous work of geopolitical representation made by many different hands for differently located and educated readers and viewers; printed in Latin, German, French, and English under various titles, the book included engravings based (loosely) on watercolors done by John White.[50] The engravings, showing natives of a place called "Virginia" by those seeking to make it part of

Queen Elizabeth's nascent empire, were commissioned by Sir Walter Raleigh. One represents a Pict man elaborately painted and smilingly holding the head of a bearded European enemy (fig. 7, *right*). His pose recalls many European depictions of Perseus slaying Medusa with the help of Minerva's shield, and the image thus creates an interesting ambiguity about who is the barbarian here and who the representative of European civilization. Another engraving shows a fabulously decorated female Pict who looks uncannily like Behn's descriptions of Imoinda; the body art looks almost, but not quite, like a suit of armor accompanying the virago's three sharp weapons (fig. 7, *left*). Behn's African hero and heroine, like de Bry's ancient Picts, are persons fantasized by European artists as "Old World" characters transplanted to New World places and there somehow grafted onto American landscapes and peoples for the delectation and education of metropolitan readers who were becoming culturally hybrid in their tastes. Behn, like Hariot and de Bry before her, was among the cosmopolitan artists who at once responded to and helped to create those new tastes.

Behn's allusion to a famous work of travel literature with images of "premodern" Britons dramatizes her effort to establish a scale of comparative value for an emergent international market in which books, bodies, and bodily adornments all jostle as commodities. In *Oroonoko* as in *Ranter,* Behn constructs an ambiguous reflection on the role of intellectual producers and consumers in this emergent market. The author herself is both a producer and a consumer of novelty or "news" to be sold to others or given—not, however, without some hope of a future return in goods or money. In a fascinating passage about her own role in one of the novella's climactic episodes, Oroonoko's aborted slave revolt, Behn represents her identity as well as her agency as an ambiguous function of her literacy:

> You must know, that when the News was brought . . . that Caesar had betaken himself to the Woods, and carry'd with him all the Negroes, we were possess'd with extreme Fear, which no Persuasions could dissipate, that he would secure himself till night and then, that he would come down and cut all our throats. This Apprehension made all the Females of us fly down the River to be secured; and while we were away, they acted this Cruelty; for I suppose I had Authority and Interest enough there, had I suspected any such thing, to have prevented it: but we had not gone many Leagues, but the News overtook us, that Caesar was taken and whipped like a common Slave. (110–11)

Behn draws here on a stereotypical scenario of English Renaissance drama, a scenario in which sexually vulnerable (and valuable) English women are pitted against a black man imagined as a villainous rapist. The passage occurs right after the narrator has described Oroonoko's rebellion, his desertion by his followers, his betrayal into punishment by the white men's "written contract" of an honorable surrender. Behn interrupts her plot's temporal progression to return to a point in the just-recounted story when the outcome of Oroonoko's rebellion was still uncertain. That uncertainty is oddly preserved for Behn's readers by her shift from the simple past tense to a subjunctive formulation that mixes past, present, and the possibility of a different future. In this passage, the authorial *I* seems at once extraordinarily lucid and disturbingly blind about her own complicity in her hero's capture and humiliating punishment. Had she been present, she "supposes" she could have prevented the cruelty which "they" (white male property owners) wrought upon the black male slave.[51] Her claim to possess some singular social authority, however, is belied by her representation of herself as part of a group of weak females, a passive group prone to illness: as Martine Brownley has noted, Behn later rather guiltily claims sickness as an excuse for her absence from Oroonoko's final torture ("Narrator in *Oroonoko*"). In the earlier scene of female flight, the women are possessed not by men, black or white, but rather by an agent named Fear and quickly renamed Apprehension. That oddly abstract agent, however, turns out, if we look closely, to be a product of something the passage twice calls news: a mode of verbal production often defined as unreliable and belonging, as we have seen, to a semantic complex that names crucial features of Behn's own written representation of oral discourse in *Oroonoko*.

Here, as in many other parts of the book, the narrative oscillates between criticizing and profiting from a system of circulation that includes both bodies and words, among them the lies Oroonoko discovers to be characteristic of Englishmen and even, the text repeatedly suggests, of the narrator herself.[52] This disturbing oscillation has been shrewdly analyzed by some critics, but has prompted others less comfortable with ideological contradictions to (mis)represent Behn's text either as an "antislavery" document or as a royalist allegory that is not at all opposed to the institution of slavery but only to the enslavement of kings.[53] In Behn's shifting and sometimes contradictory perspectives on the slave trade, I suggest that we can see the lineaments of a more complex model of European colonization—and a more complex perspective on European modes of literacy—than most Renaissance travel literature provides. Behn construes the relation between Old World and New not only in terms of a binary opposition between self and Other, but also in terms of a highly unstable triangular model that, in its simplest version, draws relations of sameness and difference among a black African slave, a white English woman, and a group of Native Americans who are described, in the book's opening pages, as innocents "so unadorned" and beautiful that they resemble

FIGURE 7

Théodore de Bry's engravings of ancient British Picts, after John White,
in *India occidentalis* (Frankfurt, 1590). (Photos courtesy of The Newberry Library, Chicago)

T·B·J·

"our first parents before the fall" (*Oroonoko*, 59). Neither the white English woman nor the black African man shares the Indians' (imputed) quality of primeval innocence, but Behn's stress on the Indian culture's concern with artifice (body painting, ornamentation, and even self-mutilation) suggests that her representation of the Indians offers no stable "base" for the triangle in question. On the contrary, the Indians turn out to be as ethically volatile as the black African man and the white English woman: later in the story Behn describes a time when the English in Surinam occupied precisely that position of fear toward hostile Indians that she dramatizes for the English colonists in *Ranter*. "[I]n many mortal Fears" about disputes "the English had with the Indians," the narrator and her companions were unable to venture into Indian territory except in "great Numbers"; she then projects into the future a terror based on past experience or, rather, on an experience that was past when Behn wrote her novel but was still to come according to the chronology of her narrative: the Indians, she explains, had attacked the colonizers—now mainly Dutch rather than English—"immediately after my coming away." "[T]hey cut in pieces all they could take . . . and hanging up the Mother, and all her Children about her; and cut a Footman, I left behind me, all in Joints, and nail'd him to Trees" (*Oroonoko*, 100).

If dismemberment—the fate of both the footman and Oroonoko—seems ominously likely for male servants of this particular English lady, that is perhaps symptomatic of the multiple divisions, the repeated doublings, that characterize her cultural subject matter and her own subject positions. These do not include the role of mother, for reasons I discuss later. The narrator and her hero both oscillate between masculinized and feminized subject positions, and both stand in contrast, at different moments, to the exotic, sometimes innocent, sometimes dangerous Indians. Behn thus provides a perspective on the conquest of America that complicates, among other binary oppositions, the ethical one, infinitely labile in the literature of the imperial venture, between "we" as good and "them" as "evil"—or vice versa. The triangulation effects of Behn's text have, as one of their several hermeneutic horizons, the "triangular trade" analyzed by Eric Williams in *From Columbus to Castro*. Another hermeneutic horizon, however, is Behn's carefully nurtured reputation as a woman writer with special skills and interests in depicting erotic triangles; if she has more bedroom scenes in her eighteen plays than any other Restoration dramatist, that is partly because she attempted to make profit from the accident of gender that so many (but not all) of her contemporaries saw as a liability.[54]

What even this account of the complexity of Behn's novella leaves out, however, is the specific ideological modality of the "other" black slave in the story, the character who is a major, if relatively silent player in the book's shadowy plot about an erotic triangle. In striking contrast to the unmarried narrator, who plays the role of the Petrarchan mistress and lady-lord toward Oroonoko as vassal, Imoinda blends European ideals of wifely subservience with European fantasies about wives of Oriental despots. She is, in one of her guises, the perfect embodiment of an image of the ideal English wife as the property, body and soul, of her husband. The narrator describes her as being one of those wives whose "respect for their Husbands equal to what other People pay a Deity; and when a Man finds any occasion to quit his Wife, if he love her, she dyes by his Hand; if not he sells her, or suffers some other to kill her" (*Oroonoko*, 114). In another guise, however, she is fearless and capable of masculine aggression against Byam, the figure of English political authority that the narrator clearly hates.

Behn uses Imoinda's death scene to inscribe the authority and agency of the English woman writer, figured in the narrator, as a function of a set of finely calibrated differences from the female Other embodied in Imoinda and defined, as Oroonoko is, as lacking in the type of literacy the narrator possesses. Imoinda like Semernia is represented as an eloquent speaker with a complex inner life, but that life is easily appropriated by the narrator, who effectively colonizes the heroine's feelings and "fancies" in the African part of the novella. The mental colonization does not occur, however, without verbal signals reminding us of the narrator's mediation as a purveyor of problematic knowledge: " 'twas *past doubt* whether she lov'd Oroonoko entirely"; "*I believe* she was not long resisting those Arms, where she so long'd to be" (*Oroonoko*, 66, 75, my emphasis). Imoinda has no relation to written documents and—equally important—no linguistic barriers to erect against epistemological invasion by the narrator and her readers. Whereas Oroonoko is said to be multilingual and is sometimes allowed to mark his disgust with the English by using an untranslated word from his "own" language (*Backearary,* for instance, evidently signifying "lying white man" [87]), Imoinda is represented as speaking only in a highly stylized, that is, literary, English. The way the text virtually erases her linguistic otherness goes hand in hand, I suggest, with the way it uses her to signify radically contrasting styles of female behavior. Imoinda is presented as utterly passive and obedient, yet she is also violent and powerful, a creature who threatens the European civilization in ways that are allegorically dramatized in the strange scene where Oroonoko kills two property-destroying tigers, each referred to as both "she" and "he"; the confusion created by Behn's shifts in gendered pronouns was so irritating to some later editors that they emended the episodes to make the animals consistently female (*Works,* ed. Todd, 3:452n. 76). The scenes, I contend, figure the

ambiguous genderings and political agencies not only of Imoinda but also of
Oroonoko and of the English narrator. In the first scene, Oroonoko provokes
a mother tiger's rage by stealing her cub for the entertainment of a group of
four English women, including the narrator, and one "gentleman" whose allegiance to the republican side in the civil war the narrator stresses (*Oroonoko*,
97). In a locution that directly parallels the "news" passage I discussed earlier
(but which occurs later in Behn's narrative), "we Women" are described as
fleeing from the tiger, a "Dam, bearing a Buttock of a Cow, which he had torn
off with his mighty Paw" (97). Here occupying the role of protector of English
women rather than dangerous pursuer of them, Oroonoko is also made to
carry the responsibility for causing the danger: he has stolen the tiger-native's
property. At the moment when he kills the tiger, its paw, previously gendered
male, becomes female and (nearly) impotent as an instrument of destruction:
"the dying Beast stretch'd forth her Paw, and going to grasp his Thigh . . . fee-
bly wounded him, but could not grasp the Flesh to tear off any" (97). Having
achieved this triumph over the tiger, Oroonoko is described coming to lay the
spoils of battle—the cub—at the narrator's feet, and doing this act of soldierly
homage "with nothing of the Joy or Gladness of a Victory" (97). The description of his emotional emptiness, as he plays the role both of Roman soldier giving his ruler a trophy and of the slave-trophy itself, foreshadows the passage
where he is wounded by a "numb-eel" and undergoes a symbolic (proleptic)
loss of consciousness. The cub-trophy he gives the narrator foreshadows his
own unborn child, whom he sacrifices with its mother for overdetermined
reasons.

The first tiger's death is immediately followed by the story of "another
time" when Oroonoko killed a tiger, this one also bi-gendered, viragolike, but
different from the first in being explicitly cast as an enemy to English property,
for the second tiger is a thief of meat, playing the part allocated in the previous episode to Oroonoko himself. This tiger is also, like Oroonoko, Imoinda,
the Indians, and the narrator's own text, a "curiosity" offered up to the English
readers in the hope of future gain. Oroonoko's identity is split between being
"like" the tiger—his continued life similarly engenders wonder before he is
ultimately killed—and being "like" the female narrator. He asks what the
English ladies will give him if he brings them not just the tiger's body but—
significantly—its wounded heart; the ladies promise that he will be "Rewarded at all our Hands" (*Oroonoko*, 98). This promise, like so many others
made by the literate English, including the narrator herself, seems to have been
honored only in the breach. Betrayal, romanticized and made to seem in some
obscure way Oroonoko's own fault as well as the narrator's, seems to be at the
novella's heart. The tiger-killing episodes, which are immediately followed

by the allegorically charged episode of the hero's encounter with the anes-
thetizing eel, show Oroonoko himself being motivated by a "curiosity" at once
erotic, proto-scientific, and voyeuristic: "Caesar cut him [the tiger] Open with
a Knife to see where those Wounds were that had been reported to him" (98).
He then offers the tiger's heart, as he had offered the first tiger's "whelp," to the
English women who are at once his audience and his oddly passive betrayers:
"This Heart the Conqueror brought up to us, and 'twas a very great Curiosity,
which all the Country came to see; and which gave Caesar occasion of many
fine Discourses, of Accidents in War, and strange Escapes" (99). In this sentence, Behn echoes Shakespeare, whose learning we have seen her describing
as being not much more than falls to a "womans share" and whose *Othello* had
been revived, with enormous success, on the Restoration stage (it was the first
play performed when the theaters reopened in 1660).[55] Her Oroonoko here entertains his "Great Mistress" (and other English ladies) as Othello entertains
Desdemona—before they are married—with his eloquent story of his "most
disastrous chances . . . moving accidents . . . hair breadth-scapes i' th' imminent deadly breach" (1.3.134–36). With respect to the power relation between a
speaker (or playwright) and an audience, this scene offers a mirror reversal of
that in which the narrator shows herself orally entertaining her sullen, potentially mutinous hero with *her* culture's stories of "great men," Roman men
whose "lives" she presumably takes, as Shakespeare did, from Plutarch (or
North's translation of Plutarch) to use for new cultural purposes.

The echo of Shakespeare highlights significant questions not only about
the female narrator's relation to her hero, but also about her relation to his
wife, the sexual being whom he stole from his grandfather and whom he fears
the English may steal from him. As we have seen, he kills Imoinda, in part, to
prevent such a sexual theft; in terms of the novella's ideological economy, however, Imoinda is killed, as the virago tigers are, to punish her for endangering
English property. She is represented as the only character in the book with the
power actually to wound the supreme guardian of colonial property, Deputy
Governor Byam. Imoinda's act of Amazonian aggression, however, which
ironically recalls Othello's description of Desdemona as his "fair warrior," is
undone, rendered impotent, by the agency of another woman of color. Having first reported Imoinda's wounding of the governor as fact, the narrator
then revises the information as a false rumor, an action that failed in its desired
end (*Oroonoko*, 108). "The first News we heard was that the Governour was
dead of a wound Imoinda had given him; but it was not so well" (111). Byam's
life is saved—to the regret of an indeterminate group to which the narrator
belongs—by his Indian mistress, who sucks the poison from his wound (108,
111). She is never represented as speaking a word in any language. The narra-

tor's own ambivalent relation to male English authority is figured here—but also symbolically divested of its power to do any harm other than to the man's historical reputation—by the device of splitting "other" women into the extreme roles of dangerous rebel and erotically complicitous slave. Imoinda will play that role when she agrees to her death at Oroonoko's hands.

Behn implicitly associates both the submissive and the dangerous female roles with Imoinda through an anagrammatic link between the unnamed Indian woman who nurses Byam—but who belongs to a group that later dismembers Englishmen—and the African woman whose name suggests "I'm Indian" or even more punningly, "I-me [*moi*] am Indian." Using her literate powers to hint at a community of "dark" women that includes herself, Behn nonetheless reassures her readers, or some of them, that her own agency is deployed in the service of English interests. The reassurance inheres, I suggest, in the way that Behn's text both stages and preordains the outcome of an implied competition between the white female author and the nonwhite, nonliterate female slave who is also a potential mother and rebel. The competition story focuses on possession of Oroonoko's body and its richly symbolic power to engender something that will outlive it. That power remains latent, in the sense of impotent, without a female counterpart, and for this Behn offers two distinct images: Imoinda's pregnant body, holding a potential slave laborer ("for," as the text reminds us, "all the Breed is theirs to whom the Parents belong" [*Oroonoko*, 93]); and, alternatively, the author's own "Female Pen," which she deploys to describe, with an unnerving blend of relish and horror, the novella's concluding scenes of Oroonoko's bodily dismemberment, including his castration.

The narrator seems to win the competition hands down, though the production of the text, over twenty years after the events it describes, testifies to a certain intractable residue or, we might say, psychic fallout from the narrator's comportment toward her slaves. The narrative registers guilt and some chagrin at Behn's inability either to save Oroonoko ("I suppose I had authority enough") or to undermine, as she allows Imoinda briefly to do, the old Renaissance commonplace that deeds are masculine, words feminine. Nonetheless, the narrative ascribes important powers to the female pen and to the type of Machiavellian literacy, in oral as well as written discourses, to which that instrument points (*Oroonoko*, 88). The narrator assuages her guilt—represented in her suggestions that she had some opportunities to choose differently than she did—by suggesting that in the last analysis, one needs her kind of literacy to survive in the modern world. Her African hero and heroine, like Bacon, Semernia, and Cavarnio, are shown finally to be more like the Surinam tigers, on a scale running between premodern and modern, than like the Widow Ranter or the Behn character in *Oroonoko*.

Behn's literacy, as a function both of her younger (remembered) and older (writing) self, appears in all its moral ambiguity and ideological garb of necessity in a remarkable scene where the narrator uses the English language as a potent instrument of sexual and political dominion. In this scene, which precedes the slaves' rebellion, Behn explicitly pits an image of politically "dangerous" biological reproduction against an image of "safe" verbal production. And in this scene, the narrator presents herself as both a servant and a beneficiary of the eroticized socioeconomic *system* of domination she describes. When some unnamed English authority figures perceive that Oroonoko is growing sullen because of the "Thought" that his child will belong not to him but to his owners, the narrator is "obliged," she tells us—in another of those passive formulations that at once highlights and veils the question of who governs the writer's will—to use her fiction-making powers to "divert" Oroonoko and Imoinda from mutinous thoughts (*Oroonoko,* 104). Mutiny is specifically tied to a problem in population management, a problem about which Behn's text—like much colonialist discourse, including chilling debates on whether it is better to "buy or breed" one's slaves—is fundamentally ambivalent.[56] Mutiny, the narrator observes, "is very fatal sometimes in those Colonies that abound so with Slaves, that they exceed the Whites in vast numbers" (93). It is to abort the potential mutiny that the narrator is enlisted both to watch the slaves and to distract them from putting into action an alternative plot that would have resulted in an alternative history to the one she gives. She shows herself using her rhetorical skills to feed Oroonoko with false hopes that the true governor will arrive bringing freedom, and she tells us that after this very day of narrative intercourse, she "neither thought it convenient to trust him much out of Our View, nor did the Country who fear'd him" (94–95). She was not "of" the Country, but she joined its plot to "treat him Fairly, and oblige him to remain within . . . a [narrow] compass" (95). In short, she works as a spy on Oroonoko and Imoinda, an observer who adapts her words to the needs of the colony even as she comes, increasingly, to despise the cruel promise-breaking of its governor. "Obliged" by others and her own interests, economic and romantic, to "discourse with Caesar, and to give him all the Satisfaction I possibly could," Behn entertains him with stories about "the Lives of the Romans and great Men, which charmed him to my company" and delayed his decision—inspired, significantly, by Imoinda—to become a Hannibal to a new Roman empire (93).

Behn thus dramatizes a complex mode of authorial ownership of characters who are cast as enthralled—and feminized—auditors of her words and finally as impotent actors in her plot. She represents herself creating a paradoxical *facsimile* of freedom, for herself, her immediate audience, and by implication, her readers of both sexes back home. In this facsimile, servitude—

which Oroonoko himself scornfully describes as a condition of being "Sport of Women" (*Oroonoko*, 105)—is rendered (perhaps only temporarily) tolerable by being eroticized, fantasized, "diverted" from activities, either sexual or military, that might work to dislodge the English from their precarious lordship of this New World land. Just how precarious their possession was the narrator acknowledges by repeatedly lamenting their loss of the land to the Dutch, but the deeper problems of the logic of colonialism are also signaled, albeit confusedly, by the contrast between the description of slave mutiny, quoted above, and the explanation offered early in the story for why the British do *not* enslave the native Indians. Like the Africans, the Indians are essential to the colonialists' welfare; "they being on all occasions very useful to us," the narrator says, "we find it absolutely necessary to caress 'em as Friends, and not to treat 'em as Slaves, nor dare we do other, their numbers so far surpassing ours in that Continent" (60).[57] This passage sheds an ironic light on the later moment when the narrator uses stories to divert Oroonoko from thoughts of mutiny, for we see that one logical solution to the mutiny problem, a solution that her stories to Oroonoko suppress but that her larger narrative only partially represses, is the possibility of *not* enslaving a group of Others who outnumber you. Such a solution, with respect both to Africans and to Indians, had been recommended by a few early critics of the colonial enterprise, but Behn is far from joining those few who overtly critiqued the whole system of international trade based on forced labor by persons of many skin colors, including freckled Irish white.[58]

In its characteristically disturbing way, Behn's novel shows us just enough about the author's competition with Imoinda, and the enmeshment of that competition within a larger socio-sexual-economic system, to make us uneasy when we hold the book *Oroonoko* in our hands and realize that the text itself invites us to see the book as a safe-sex substitute for the potentially mutinous but also economically valuable black slave child Oroonoko might have had with Imoinda—or indeed with Aphra Behn, had she given physical rather than verbal "satisfaction." She might have played Tamora, as it were, to Oroonoko's Aaron (according to the racist paradigm supplied in Shakespeare's *Titus Andronicus*), thereby activating long-standing English anxieties about the "genetic" strength of blackness (babies born of mixed unions were thought inevitably to follow the darker and "lower" parental hue).[59] In an apparently conservative and reassuring twist of the old trope of book as child, however, Behn offers her contemporary English readers a representation of a white woman who hints at her attraction to a strong black hero but who in the end refrains—as Shakespeare's Desdemona did not—from taking her sexual "treasure" from its rightful owner and disposer, her father or his English representative, to give to an alien. Contemporary readers might well have re-marked the text's coy dramatization of an erotic "road not taken" on the narrator's part. Thomas Southerne does so, it seems, when he revises Behn's tale as a play in which Oroonoko loves a *white* Imoinda.[60] The frontispiece from a 1735 publication of Southerne's highly popular play is reproduced, intriguingly, on the cover of the 1973 Norton edition of Behn's story (the first paperback edition widely used in U.S. universities) (fig. 8).[61]

This representation, like Southerne's play as a whole, capitalizes on the cultural prestige of Shakespeare's drama of tragic miscegenous romance. Southerne's play and its frontispiece also arguably exploit Behn's posthumous notoriety, which she herself may well have helped fashion. In 1696, the same year that Southerne's play was first produced, a biography of Behn appeared as a preface and advertisement to a posthumous collection of her novels. The biography, which has been ascribed to Charles Gilden and also to Behn herself, elaborately and titillatingly *denies* a rumor that the author of *Oroonoko* had a romance with her hero: "I knew her intimately well[,]" the author affirms, "and I believe she wou'd not have conceal'd any Love-affair from me . . . which makes me assure the World, there was no Affair between that Prince and As-trea."[62] Whatever the status of this rumor (which is reproduced, again only to be denied "credit," in the introduction to the first Norton edition of Behn's text [p. x]), the rumor as a bit of feigned news forms part of the larger discursive field in which Behn's *Oroonoko* was and continues to be read. At least a part of this field is evidently governed by an ideological economy in which the European woman's book is born, quite starkly, from a self-willed (partial) censoring of her own sexual attraction to both of her African characters. The very old story of Dido's possible marriage with Iarbas, the African owner of the territory Dido appropriates with her belt, lurks here as a cultural subtext for Behn's revisionary tale of an English empire modeled on Rome's but seen, often, from the perspective of that empire's challengers (Hannibal, Dido) and victims. The book marks itself as a a gift or trade object whose value is obscurely dependent on the news it brings of the death and silencing of its black hero and heroine. Behind the scene of Oroonoko's final torture is the murder-sacrifice of the black woman and her unborn child. And the threat represented by the black woman, I suggest, is obscurely acknowledged to be even greater than the threat represented by the black man, so that the text finally has to enlist him, through enticements of European codes of masculine honor and Petrarchan romance, to suppress the one character who uses physical force rather than words to attack the highest legal representative of the colonial system, namely Byam, the man who took Behn's (putative) father's place as chief colonial representative of the English king. Imoinda performs the kind of deed that Desdemona,

FIGURE 8

Frontispiece from a 1735 copy of Thomas Southerne's dramatic version of *Oroonoko*.
(Reproduced courtesy of the Rare Books Division, The New York Public Library,
Astor, Lenox, and Tilden Foundations)

Othello's "fair warrior," was never allowed. And in so doing, Imoinda looks, for a moment, not only like the Amazons whom Sir Walter Raleigh expected to find in Guiana, but also like Dido as seen by Christine de Pizan: Dido as a wanderer, an emigrant, a potential empire-builder, a "virago" or man-woman who at once exposes and temporarily redeems the weaknesses of a hero.[63] Inheriting some fragments of Dido's personae, Imoinda competes with the narrator, who also inherits something from that cultural mother. The story finally splits Dido—as Christine de Pizan also does—into the woman who dies for love, on the one hand, and, on the other, the leader who exhibits prudence, cleverness, an interest in trade, and an ability to lie when life and property are at stake.

In *Oroonoko* as in *The Widdow Ranter,* then, Aphra Behn uses her literacy to ward off the overdetermined set of dangers she associates with or projects onto the nonwhite heroine; among these dangers, I have suggested, lurks pregnancy, the consequence and all too visible sign, for women, of one form of sexual pleasure.[64] In both texts, moreover, Behn not only kills off the Indian and/or African woman in the end, but also performs an ideologically significant gesture of cultural appropriation and justification by making the heroine voice, as if it were her own, a desire for death at the hands of a lover, a desire founded on precisely the European ideal of female "honor" as chastity that Behn mocked and interrogated in so many of her works. In thus making her nonwhite heroines participate verbally—orally, in speech she allegedly "represents" through writing—in the mystification of the complex causes of their deaths, Behn exposes some of the dire contradictions of her society's ideologies of gender and at the same time takes advantage, we might fairly say, of the particular historical condition of silence that affected the vast majority of nonwhite women who lived in England's early imperial territories.

That condition of silence, of course, affected nonwhite men too, but differently—especially, I argue, because of the different *sexual* myths attached (again differently) to the European image of both the African and the American Indian male. The condition of silence derives from lack of access to the complex of practices and institutions that Behn defines, with some guilt and anger, as a particularly "modern" kind of vernacular literacy: it includes an ability to lie that at once fosters and abrogates the written contract Oroonoko comes to see as necessary for his own dealings with "Christians." The historical women of color represented by figures such as the Indian queen and Imoinda did not, with a very few exceptions, possess the kinds of literacy Behn herself had acquired.[65] This point may seem obvious, but for that very reason it merits attention from those of us who continue to enjoy the privileges conferred by literacy in English. We should in any event not forget that literate

metropolitan women sometimes promoted and rationalized, as well as interrogated, the colonizing process figured, not infrequently, as a rape of a female,
or feminized, Other.[66] "Guiana," as Raleigh famously wrote, "hath yet her
maidenhead," and Behn arguably contributed to the English effort to deflower
that colony. But the author who was praised in her own time as belonging to
a "third" androgynous sex contributed to this ongoing project of once and
future rape in ways that perpetuated a tradition of misrepresenting nonwhite
characters on English stages and in the pages of English books.[67] She also invited us to see and ponder the fact that we are *not* seeing the "whole truth"
about her white or nonwhite characters, including herself. In thus producing
some quantity of skepticism about the believability or "credit" of her colonial
texts and their depiction of Oroonoko and Imoinda, or their shadowy doubles
the outlaw Bacon and his Indian queen, Behn uses her self-fashioned female
literacy in a complex way: she exposes and hides her country's imperial project as she exposes and hides the historical subjects—including herself—about
whom she is writing.

In her very last sentence, she asserts her hope that "the Reputation of my
Pen is considerable enough to make his Glorious Name to survive to all ages;
with that of the Brave, the Beautiful, and the Constant *Imoinda*" (*Oroonoko*,
119). The novella ends with those words, and I will end with some questions
about them. Why doesn't Behn name her hero here? Does she hide the property of the name from view because he has not one but two names, and the
narrator does not wish (overtly) to break the rule of using the Roman imperial name that she has earlier shown herself as being forced (albeit not wholly
credibly) to obey? Her obedience to the rule of renaming (see the epigraph to
this chapter) dramatizes the same problem of agency we have seen in the
"news" passage about Oroonoko's whipping, the passage in which the narrator relinquishes (masculine) agency for a feminine passivity represented as
somewhat mindless and certainly the result of fear. Behn very consistently follows the rule requiring her to name Oroonoko "Caesar" once she switches
from an African setting to an English colonial one. This is the prescribed rule,
whereby the English rename slaves because their African names are "very barbarous, and hard to pronounce"—but not, evidently, so hard to write that the
narrator can't use the name "Oroonoko" for the first third of her narrative.
Suddenly, she dramatizes her subjection to a rule she herself rationalizes in an
illogical way that raises questions about the relation between her original
"colonial" audience and her present and future readers: "For the future, therefore, I must call Oroonoko, Caesar, since by that Name only he was known in
our Western World" (89). From this point on, she refers to her hero as Caesar,
thus participating in the ironic cruelty of her fellow colonists who give the

erstwhile prince a name from Roman history derived from the Latin verb meaning "to cut" (an allusion to Julius Caesar's "Caesarian" birth) and denoting "king" in seventeenth-century English usage. The name's humiliating qualities are not lost on Oroonoko himself, as we saw in the passage where he takes Hannibal, enemy of the Roman empire, as his model during his attempted revolt against the English. In *not* giving the hero's name at the end in either its African or Latin-English versions, is Behn asking her future readers to continue the debate over who really owns his identity?

In pondering the question of what the "glorious name" actually is—the one on the title page or the one on many pages of the book—we might also note the conspicuous contrast between what Behn does with her hero's name at the end and what she does with that of her heroine. Throughout the second part of the narrative, she has only intermittently called Imoinda by her slave name, in striking contrast to her practice with Oroonoko/Caesar. Is Behn suggesting—albeit very prudently, in a way that would have what modern jurists call deniability—that English rules, and rules making English a ruling tongue, can be broken more easily by and for (mere) women than for men? The heroine, in any case, has the novella's last word, and it is a proper name that replaces or more precisely restores to visibility an African name the English replaced with a word legible both to Latin- and English-reading people: "Clemene." The virtue of clemency denoted by that name, either in ancient Roman or in modern English cultural contexts, is conspicuously absent in the American colonial worlds that Behn depicts, justifies, and retroactively questions.

The questioning did no good to the historical personages figured under such names as Semernia, Cavarnio, Oroonoko/Caesar, and Clemene/Imoinda. But Behn's questioning does performatively fashion the historical record—her pen, for instance, "wounds" Byam's reputation as Imoinda's arrow wounded his body. And her pen does invite future readers to reconsider the evidence of the cases she represents in her colonial texts. It seems clear from what she writes that Oroonoko's oral account of events would not corroborate hers in all particulars, any more than Imoinda's account of her last moments—had she made one in any language—would fully corroborate the account Behn represents Oroonoko as giving. The record is falsified in and by Behn's letters; but by the same token, the record is shown to be multiple, incomplete, and worth returning to. Non- or anti-English subjects who lack modern literacy as Behn defines it are also shown, in the end of *Oroonoko* and *Ranter,* to be still speaking, still trying to speak more, through the medium of one female pen and its roman letters.

Afterword

The phrase "the female pen" is, of course, a trope, as is my title phrase "Dido's daughters." If you analyze the former figure—which is to say, if you subject to conscious scrutiny the ways in which you function as a meaning-making reader of black marks on a white page—you will see that the trope works by personifying an ostensibly inanimate object, the pen. The wit of the trope lies in how the transferred adjective works to alter the significance of the noun it modifies. When *female* is used to modify *pen*, the analogical and homophonic relations between "pens" and "penises" come into play, for many anglophone readers, in ways unlikely to occur if the adjective modifying pen were *heavenly*, for instance, or *delicious*.

The kind of cultural literacy to which I'm calling attention here changes over time. When pens were made of quills rather than of metal or plastic (and all pens before the eighteenth century came from birds' quills), for instance, the phrase "female pen" would invite a different readerly assessment of the "animate/inanimate" conjunction than it does for most readers today.[1] Cultural literacy involves extremely complex decoding procedures, based on unconscious as well as conscious associations of a kind we can hardly specify for ourselves, much less for persons who lived in seventeenth-century England or fifteenth-century France. Cultural literacy, in short, is an extremely abstract concept. It becomes not only plural but also highly elusive as soon as one tries to think hard about what it is in our own fractured culture, much less about what it might be elsewhere nowadays or in that other "elsewhere" that is the past.

In part 2 of this book, I have focused on the complexity of the meaning-making process as it was understood, we infer, by some early modern women who illustrate women's literacy in action without ever being representative of their sex in general or even of other literate women. Insofar as the performances of literacy examined here entailed writing for a public, mixed-gender, and often multilingual audience, the woman's enactment of literacy became culturally transgressive. Persons who marked themselves as female through signs legible to at least some among their contemporary readers start to practice what their culture defines as a masculine mode of literacy when they write for a public audience about secular as well as religious matters. A small fraction of women who could write metropolitan versions of French and English in alphabetic letters; and who could, moreover, afford to inscribe such letters on paper with ink; and who could, beyond that, manage to have their letters reproduced and disseminated to some fairly small group of readers that constituted a "public," exhibited by the act of such writing desires for public influence that some influential members of society deemed illicit for women. The gendered literacy shown by such women is a joint production of writers, readers, and cultural disputes about propriety and property. The women writers studied here as "Dido's daughters"—themselves critical readers of history and certain cultural truths held, by some, to be self-evident—may help us to glimpse, though without being able analytically to control, the multiplicity of theories and practices that compete for cultural dominance under the rubric of literacy. I have argued here that ideologies of gender and empire helped to shape that rubric in consequential ways.

Aphra Behn's pen, which translated various French works into London English while also appropriating nonwritten words of non-English subjects who spoke (are represented as speaking) in American and African places, is clearly visible in my mind's eye as I sit in my study using my fingers to form alphabetic letters on a computer screen. The computer crashes, refuses to do my bidding, forgets or obliterates my words. Behn's pen probably blotted, broke, ran out of ink. The similarities in our experiences of writing, our shared material frustrations, our shared knowledge—and ambivalent awareness of ignorance—of a multilingual literary past, seem to me sometimes to outweigh the technological and other large differences between our respective experiences of using alphabetic letters to convey something we think important to an unseen audience of persons who know the English language and some other languages, or parts of others, as well. The ties that bind me to Aphra Behn and that bind Behn to historical women like Elizabeth Cary, Marguerite de Navarre, and Christine de Pizan are at once imaginary and historical, composed of many desires filtered through some learned procedures for checking and testing desires against what others have claimed about the past. Dido, that amalgam of myth and history, stands on the edge of the web this book has at once woven and sought to analyze critically.

Does this web itself make up a segment of any *grand récit*? Yes and no. Yes, insofar as I have argued that the story of modernization has a long and dark past intimately yoked to the stories of the rise of capitalism (in its recognizably modern form) and to the kind of imperialism that began to be historically visible around 1415, with the Portuguese exploration and conquest of the west coast of Africa. No, insofar as I have repeatedly argued against the idea that subtends most grand narratives, including that in the parts of Marx's writing which remain, like the "Great Divide" literacy discourses examined in chapter 1, bound to deterministic models of history, including Christian and Hegelian brands of providentialism. The governing assumption for most "grand narrative" theories of history, as David Wallace observes, is that "the only possible history is the one that in fact resulted."[2] I have repeatedly attempted to counter the idea of a linear and necessary evolution; I have sought, instead, to explore several possible histories competing within the multiple languages of the imperial nations emerging in French and English territories, on both sides of the Atlantic, during the early modern era. Starting from a concern for an "alternative" view of nationalism as imperial rule lurking in fifteenth-century discussions of territories that have a "diversity of languages," I have focused on the costs as well as the benefits, for different individuals and groups, of the historical changes that drastically increased the significance of literacy as a sign of social distinction. Theories and practices of literacy, I have argued, emerged in complex relation to competing language uses and languages, and in complex conjunction with theories about other markers of social distinction: gender, status, religion, and race.

This book has paid particular attention to the troubled historical yoking of ideologies of literacy, gender, and empire. That yoking helped to produce a consequential distinction between a female or imperfect literacy, defined as the passive and obedient reception of discourse (written or authoritatively oral), and a masculine literacy, defined as the production of socially valuable and fame-securing discourse. In part 2 of this book I have analyzed some of the ways in which relatively privileged historical women challenged this binary opposition in the cultural field of letters. This opposition was sharpened and partially enforced by various institutional practices in the domains of education and publication. Some women used their skills in reading and writing to cross-dress, as it were, and thus to assume the productive prerogatives of literate men. What were the cultural costs and benefits of such cross-dressing? Small, from one perspective, which may seem ironic, given the length of this book. There is no question that women formed a statistically insignificant proportion of the international group of intellectuals I have taken—following Antonio Gramsci and Norbert Elias among others—as key facilitators and formulators of Europe's imperial projects.[3] I hope, however, to have shown, as well, that both historical women and ideas about gender played a significant role in the modernization drama. What counts as significant, I have been arguing, must include what the written record at once implies and erases about some early modern subjects' increasing alienation from metropolitan languages and from the technologies of reading, writing, and speaking that were coming to count as "literacy." The drama of modernization, in which gendered theories and practices of literacy played a larger part than most scholarly stories have heretofore allowed, is of course not a unified or coherent phenomenon, and people in many parts of the world are still debating the question of its value. It is, moreover, still playing itself out. This book has attempted to show how much the competing written versions of the modernization drama are shadowed by other versions that exist incompletely, if at all, in those archives that we *litteratae* and *litterati* value, and sometimes overvalue, as our repository of knowledge about the past.

Given the view reiterated throughout this book, that historical eras overlap in complex ways and that change is always uneven, it is worth noting that aspects of my book's story are taken up, from different angles, in two books that begin where I end, with Aphra Behn. Catherine Gallagher explores Behn's peculiar strategies for marketing her literate wares in *Nobody's Story: The Vanishing Acts of Women Writers in the Marketplace, 1670–1820*, and Laura Brown studies Behn's rhetorical intervention in the English slave trade in *Ends of Empire: Women and Ideology in Early Eighteenth-Century Literature*. Creator of a "cipher" code that bears some resemblance to Greek characters, translator of Ovid although Dryden alleged she was ignorant of Latin, translator also of French works about new worlds and "reproached" by contemporaries (she claims) for being an "American," Behn recalls the wanderer Dido stealing the African king Iarbas's territory through her clever ruse of cutting a bull's hide into strips.[4] With them, she encircled the expanding territory of her desires at a historical moment, partly but not wholly obliterated by Vergil's story of how her desires for political power were displaced by desires for love and how both sets of desires were ultimately frustrated by those (including some of the gods) who promoted an idea of the Roman empire. Recalling Dido, Behn offers an aptly Janus-faced ending to this study, for Behn leads us into a new historical chapter.[5] In the eighteenth century the European and American historical records expand exponentially, offering us more to recover, but also more, potentially, to forget, about the crossings of literacy, gender, and empire.[6]

Notes

Prologue

1. The best known is Vergil's *Aeneid*. See my epigraph, cited from *Eclogues, Georgics, Aeneid 1–6*, ed. Fairclough. All citations of the *Aeneid* are to this edition. Except when citing others, I spell Vergil's name as he himself did—with an *e* not an *i*. For a critical discussion of ideologically charged orthographic traditions that gave Vergil's name a new symmetry (an *i* for an *i*) as well as associations with the Latin words for man (*vir*) and for a magician's wand (*virga*), see James, "Dido's Ear," 364n. 10.

2. On the naming and early conceptual definition of the Middle Ages, see Patterson, "Court Politics and the Invention of Literature." Scholars from many disciplines have subscribed to the assumption that "the 'modern age' is the age succeeding the Middle Ages and continuing through to the present," as Robert Wallace puts it in the introduction to his translation of Hans Blumenberg's *Legitimacy of the Modern Age*, xi. For a critical discussion of various theoretical notions of modernity (including Blumenberg's) and of the term *modernization*, see Habermas, *Philosophical Discourse of Modernity*, 1–22.

3. See, for the best known proponent of this view, Eisenstein, *Printing Press as an Agent of Change*; see also Cipolla, *Literacy and Development in the West*. Versions of the association of literacy with print, Protestantism, and progress are widespread in the anglophone popular press and in many English-language textbooks for secondary- and college-level students; for a discussion of the association, see Graff, *Legacies of Literacy*, chap. 1; also his "Reflections on the History of Literacy"; and his *Literacy in History*. For critical analysis of Eisenstein's thesis, see Johns, *Nature of the Book*.

4. In *The Darker Side of the Renaissance*, Walter Mignolo follows Enrique Dussel, "Eurocentrism and Modernity," in at once defining and critiquing a conception of modernity as an era inaugurated by the European (re)discovery of America in 1492. Mignolo sometimes refers to alphabetic literacy as "Western literacy."

5. See Ong, *Orality and Literacy*; Certeau, *Writing of History*; Habermas, *Structural Transformation of the Public Sphere*; and Chartier, *Cultural Origins of the French Revolution*. For Anderson's discussion of "print capitalism," see *Imagined Communities*, chap. 4.

6. See Sanders, *Gender and Literacy*, 23, 30; Chartier, *Cultural History*, 12; Chartier, *Order of Books*. Chartier's research has been crucial for the turn to investigating historical reading

practices; he has recently modified his earlier idea of a stark "demarcation" between readers and nonreaders (see Goodman, "Public Sphere and Private Life," 11) to analyze "reading communities" such as those that arose when a Bible was read aloud to an assembled family or when peasants in Spain gathered to hear chivalric romances read. See Cavallo and Chartier's introduction to *A History of Reading in the West*, 32; and Chartier's essay in that volume, "Reading Matter and 'Popular' Reading," 272. For samples of traditional but still valuable scholarship in the history of books, see Wright, *Middle-Class Culture*; Wright, "Reading of Renaissance Women"; Bennett, *English Books and Readers*; Boffey, "Women Authors and Women's Literacy"; and Hull, *Chaste, Silent, and Obedient*. For a phenomenological and historical account, see Manguel, *History of Reading*.

7. See Sanders, *Gender and Literacy*; Timmermans, *L'Accès des femmes à la culture*; Dolan, "Reading, Writing, and Other Crimes." The new subfield of research on gendered reading, writing, speaking, and publishing practices is growing and cannot be fully cited here, but for orientations see Lamb, "Constructions of Women Readers"; Goldberg, *Writing Matter*; Ezell, *Writing Women's Literary History*; Lewalski, *Writing Women in Jacobean England*; Parker, *Literary Fat Ladies*; Parker, "Virile Style"; Lucas, *Writing for Women*; Pearson, "Women Reading, Reading Women"; Grafton and Jardine, *From Humanism to the Humanities*; Hackel, "'Great Variety' of Readers and Early Modern Reading Practices"; Roberts, "Reading in Early Modern England"; Robertson, "This Living Hand"; Robertson, *Early English Devotional Prose and the Female Audience*; Hackett, *Women and Romance Fiction*; Bartlett, *Male Authors, Female Readers*; Saenger, "Books of Hours"; Saenger, *Space between Words*; and Raven, Small, and Tadmor, eds., *Practice and Representation of Reading in England*. There is also valuable work on gender and literacy by historians discussed in chapter 1, as well as by literary scholars focusing on other periods and by anthropologists focusing on modern societies.

8. See Fox, *Oral and Literate Culture*, 46. See chapter 1, below, for further discussion of Fox's claim that a definition of literacy as reading *and* writing in the vernacular became "widespread" by the end of the fourteenth century in England.

9. For a similar point, see Houston, *Literacy in Early Modern Europe*, 3.

10. Compare Williams, *Writing in Society*: "The introduction of writing, and all the subsequent stages of its development, are intrinsically new forms of social relationship." For examples of new work on literacy as a socially embedded and plural phenomenon, see Sanders and Ferguson, eds., *Literacies in Early Modern England*; see also Roberts, ed., *Reading in Early Modern England*; Burke, "The Uses of Literacy in Early Modern Italy"; and Engelsing, *Analphabetentum und Lektüre*. For important research on the relation between historical literacies and the history of the book, see the essays collected in Petrucci, *Writers and Readers in Medieval Italy*. My understanding of relations between the history of literacy and educational discourses and practices has been enriched by a forthcoming study by Jean Carr, Stephen Carr, and Lucille Schultz, *Archives of Instruction: Nineteenth-Century Readers, Rhetorics, and Composition Books in the United States*.

11. Brief source citations will be given parenthetically in the text wherever possible.

12. For valuable recent work that studies speech as a component of early modern literacy, see, e.g., Elsky, *Authorizing Words*; McKenzie, "Speech-Manuscript-Print"; and Magnussen, *Shakespeare and Social Dialogue*.

13. For an acute analysis of the sexual politics of Hebrew and Yiddish in the modern era, see Seidman, *A Marriage Made in Heaven*; see also Bonfil's discussion of a seventeenth-century woman whose literacy was complexly marked by the fact that she read and wrote Yiddish but not Hebrew (Bonfil, "Reading in the Jewish Communities," 176). On the ideological gendering of Latin as "paternal" and vernaculars as "maternal," see below, chapter 2.

14. See MacCabe, *Eloquence of the Vulgar*, 64, for a similar argument about the importance of both speech and writing in the "reproduction" of a "national standard."

15. Examples from *Cambridge History of the English Language*, 3:341.

16. See in particular Bourdieu's chapter "Symbolic Capital" in *Outline of a Theory of Practice*; see also his *Distinction*.

17. See Saunders, "Stigma of Print." The relation between Asian and European printing techniques has been the subject of cultural debate since the sixteenth century; one early Italian writer maintained that Gutenberg's typography was a unique "modern" invention, even though some version of the phenomenon was "old in China" (Guido Panciroli, cited with other opinions on the question of Eastern vs. Western "inventions" of print, in Tsien, "Paper and Printing," 317). The non-European history of printing—and the threat it poses to notions of European exceptionalism and to some accounts of print technology as an instrument of modernization—is important to my later discussion of Eurocentric theories of the superiority of alphabetic writing to ideographic writing; see below, chap. 1, and Eisenstein, *The Printing Press as an Agent of Change*, 27n. 65.

18. See Grafton and Jardine, "Studied for Action"; and, for other new work on marginal notes as an important archive for the history of reading, see Tribble, *Margins and Marginality*; Sherman, *John Dee: The Politics of Reading and Writing in the English Renaissance*; Sherman, "What Did Renaissance Readers Write in Their Books?"; Zwicker, "Reading the Margins"; Hackel, "Impressions from a 'Scribbling Age'"; Jackson, *Marginalia*; and Sharpe, *Reading Revolutions*. There is also valuable work on women's letters as an archive for literacy studies; see, e.g., Bowden, "Women as Intermediaries"; and Altman, "Women's Letters in the Public Sphere."

19. For a discussion of some "prescribed forms of female readerly silence," see Hackel, "Boasting of Silence." For a significant exception to the rule, see Stephen Orgel's comments on a recently identified set of marginal annotations written in the early 1670s in a copy of *A Mirror for Magistrates* owned by Lady Anne Clifford. These marginalia (mostly not in Clifford's own hand) give a mediated glimpse of her experience of hearing the book read aloud and of reading it to herself (Orgel, "Margins of Truth," 95–96).

20. For reflections on the problems and virtues of the case study method, see Sharpe, *Reading Revolutions*, 61–62.

21. Margaret Tyler and Mary Sidney are among the writers/readers whom I would have liked to include in this study; Mary Wroth, Marie de Gournay, and Margaret Cavendish are others who could well have been analyzed as making significant comments on the relations between literacy and ideologies of empire. My readers will, I trust, add other names (and further inquiries) to this list. For example, Caroline Bowden has called my attention to Rachel Fane, author (at age thirteen) of a masque that stars an "Empress" as well as a Duchess. The masque remains in manuscript, as do many works by early modern women.

22. For a wide-ranging study of intellectual property in early modern England, see Loewenstein, *The Author's Due*; see also Rose, *Authors and Owners*; Peters, "Currency, Credit, and Literary Property"; and Rosenthal, *Playwrights and Plagiarists*, especially 23–57. For a discussion of eighteenth-century translation practices relevant to Behn's work for Dryden's volume, see Wilson, "Classical Poetry and the Eighteenth-Century Reader."

23. Preface to Ovid's *Epistles*, cited from Dryden, *Works of John Dryden*, ed. Hooker, Swedenberg, and Dearing, 1:114; Behn's translation of Oenone's letter to Paris is in Behn, *Works of Aphra Behn*, ed. Todd, 1:12–19.

24. Behn, *Works*, ed. Todd, 1:17, line 191. Behn substitutes a dramatic, present-tense speech act for Ovid's description of a past event (see Ovid, *"Heroides" and "Amores*," ed. Gould, 62–63,

lines 73–74). For useful discussions of Ovid's influential appropriations of female voices, see Harvey, *Ventriloquized Voices*, 38–40, 124, and passim; Kauffman, *Discourses of Desire*, 44, 61; and Enterline, *The Rhetoric of the Body*, chap. 1.

25. For Behn's interest in a form of heroism in which suffering blurs distinctions between masculine and feminine personae, see below, chapter 7; and Rose, *Gender and Heroism*, especially chap. 3.

26. Behn, *Works*, ed. Todd, 1:17, line 181. Behn here deepens the already striking resemblances between Dido and Oenone in Ovid's own text; Oenone's lament for Paris, whose theft of Helen started the Trojan War, occurs in *Heroides* V, close to Dido's lament in *Heroides* VII.

27. Behn's practice—like that of other writers studied in this book—challenges the idealist view of literary property articulated in Blackstone's well-known argument for copyright: "every duplicate of a work, whether ten or ten thousand, if it conveys the same style and sentiment, is the same identical work, which was produced by the author's invention and labour" (cited in Chartier, "Afterword," 133, from Rose, *Authors and Owners*, 89).

28. Cited and discussed in Fleming, "Dictionary English," 315n. 11. See p. 300 for her discussion of Florio's dedication to noblewomen whom he had tutored in French and Italian.

29. On the peculiarity of "possessing" literature—especially the literature of one's own country, but also, I argue, the literature one may acquire from "abroad" through translation—see Guillory, "Literary Capital," 389 and passim.

30. For examples of the attacks on Ovid as inappropriate reading for females, see Wright, *Middle-Class Culture*, 112; and Hull, *Chaste, Silent, and Obedient*, chap. 1. On the popularity of the *Heroides* in sixteenth-century England and the witty use made of the abandoned-female position by Isabella Whitney, see Jones, *Currency of Eros*, 43.

31. *Mutacion de Fortune*, lines 141–46; cited and discussed in Desmond, *Reading Dido*, 195.

32. The definition of the female as a "defective" male (*mas deficiens*) comes from Aristotle, *Generation of Animals*, bk. 4, pt. 6, 775a 15f; also often cited is bk. 2, pt. 3 of the same text, where the female is (in the most usual Latin translations of the Greek), [*quasi*] *mas laesus* and *animal occasionatum*. See Maclean, *Renaissance Notion of Woman*, 8; and, on the points of agreement between Aristotelian and Galenic theories on the matter of women's imperfection with regard to a masculine norm, ibid., 30 and passim. For the cultural meaning of early modern medical theories about women's nature in relation to man's, see Adelman, "Making Defect Perfection"; she persuasively critiques Laqueur's influential but too-sweeping argument for the "one-sex" model in *Making Sex*. See also Parker, *Literary Fat Ladies*, chap. 9.

33. *Partial* may be defined, for instance, as the ability to hear written texts read but not to read them silently, or the ability to interpret the visual but not the verbal part of a printed emblem.

34. For examples of recent feminist interrogations of the category of "woman," see Riley, *"Am I That Name?"* See also Butler, *Bodies That Matter*, especially chap. 3; Spivak, "Feminism and Critical Theory," in *In Other Worlds*, 77–92; and Mohanty, "Under Western Eyes."

35. See, e.g., Barton's argument that "oral and literate are totally intertwined in Western schooling" (*Literacy*, 186, with further references).

36. The critical literature on various modes of publication and their enmeshment in ideologies of gender and social status is large and growing; for useful orientations see the classic study by Febvre and Martin, *Coming of the Book*. On the importance of not equating women's publication with printed matter, see Ezell, *Writing Women's Literary History*. See also Marotti, "Malleable and Fixed Texts"; Wall, *Imprint of Gender*; Waddington, "Meretrix Est Stampificata"; Love, *Scribal Publication*; Goldberg, *Writing Matter*; Summit, *Lost Property*, especially 179–80 and 197–202, on embroidery as a complex means of publication; and Parker, *Subversive Stitch*.

37. For an account that conceptualizes this shift in terms of a change from an old "center" (the Mediterranean basin) to "peripheries" that become a new center of economic power (the Atlantic monarchies), see Amin, *Eurocentrism.*

38. See, e.g., Anderson, *Imagined Communities,* 19.

39. I owe this point to Karen Newman.

40. See, e.g., [Maydens of London], *Letter sent by the Maydens of London, to the vertuous Matrones [and] Mistresses of the same, in the defense of their lawfull Libertie* (1567). See also Bell, "In Defense of Their Lawful Liberty." For other useful research on nonelite women, see Watt, *Cheap Print and Popular Piety;* Amussen, "Gendering of Popular Culture"; Hellwarth, "I Wyl Wright of Women Prevy Skekenes"; Brown, *Better a Shrew Than a Sheep;* Davis, *Society and Culture.*

41. For orientation to this new scholarship see Graff, *Legacies of Literacy;* for further references see chapter 1.

42. For discussions of such ideologically constructed places, see Brotton, *The Renaissance Bazaar;* Gillies, *Shakespeare and the Geography of Difference;* and Archer, *Old Worlds.*

43. On theorizing gender ideologies in relation to nationalist ideologies and formations, see Walby, "Woman and Nation"; Pateman, *Sexual Contract;* Jayawardena, *Feminism and Nationalism in the Third World;* Yuval-Davis and Anthias, eds., *Woman-Nation-State.* For recent work on gender and early modern English nationalism, see especially Mikalachki, *Legacy of Boadicea;* Matchinske, *Writing, Gender, and State in Early Modern England;* Howard and Rackin, *Engendering a Nation;* and McEachern, *Poetics of English Nationhood.*

44. Vasari, *Delle vite* (1550), cited in Panofsky, *Renaissance and Renascences,* 34.

45. Marx offers "no generic theory of transition," as Holton observes ("Transition from Feudalism to Capitalism," 484). See Halpern, *Poetics of Primitive Accumulation,* chap. 1; and for important comparative arguments about the transition, see Anderson, *Lineages of the Absolutist State;* Brenner, "Agrarian Roots of European Capitalism"; and Brenner, "Agrarian Class Structure and Economic Development in Pre-industrial Europe."

46. English citation from *Capital,* trans. Fowkes, 1:878; German from Marx and Engels, *Werke,* 23:745-46. The specific dating, which points to Marx's focus in his later writings on the "producer" and the creation of propertyless wage labor in England, does not wholly correspond with Marx's focus in earlier writings on mercantile activity within an urban sphere as "the initial dynamic towards capitalism"; see Holton, "Transition from Feudalism to Capitalism," 484.

47. On the much-debated implications of these period-terms, see Marcus, "Renaissance/Early Modern"; and Dolan, "Reply." For a theoretical inquiry into our conceptions of periods, see de Grazia, "World Pictures, Modern Periods, and the Early Stage."

48. Althusser and Balibar offer a related, albeit more technical description of the transition as a "movement subject to a structure which has to be discovered" (*Reading Capital,* 273).

49. Benjamin, "Theses on the Philosophy of History," cited in Halpern, *Poetics of Primitive Accumulation,* 64.

50. *The Rivals,* Act 1, scene 2, 157 and following. I owe this reference to Seth Lerer.

51. De Grazia, "Shakespeare and the Craft of Language," 59.

52. For a discussion of these terms, see chapter 2.

53. See Le Strange, *Merry Passages and Jests,* 38–39. I thank Pamela Brown for this reference.

54. Emerson, *From Empire to Nation,* 6.

55. See Pratt, *Imperial Eyes,* chap. 1, for a discussion of her concept of "contact zones." For Lenin's and Gramsci's discussions of "internal colonialism," in *Development of Capitalism in Russia* and in "Southern Question," respectively, see Hechter, *Internal Colonialism,* 8–9; see also Reece, "Internal Colonialism."

56. The Roman writer Justin identifies Iarbas's tribe as the Muxitani; Iarbas appears as Dido's enemy in Vergil's narrative, as well as in most of the non-Vergilian accounts. In at least two ancient versions of Dido's story, she eventually marries Iarbas in a cross-"race" union that would not have pleased those writers like St. Jerome who seek to appropriate Dido for discourses promoting female chastity. On Iarbas, see Savage, "Dido Dies Again," 4; and for Jerome's version, Desmond, *Reading Dido*, 56.

57. For further discussion of the two traditions summarized and simplified here, see Hexter, "Sidonian Dido"; Baswell, "Dido's Purse"; Desmond, *Reading Dido*; Purkiss, "The Queen on Stage"; Poinsotte, "L'Image de Didon"; and Davidson, "Domesticating Dido." The fullest description of the extant classical sources for the older tradition of the chaste Dido is in Lord, "Dido as an Example of Chastity."

58. See, e.g., Macrobius's critique of Vergil's ability to make readers believe "as true" what "all the world knows to be fiction" in *Saturnalia*, bk. 5, cited in Hexter, "Sidonian Dido," 339. For critiques of Vergil's veracity by later writers from Petrarch through Ovid's Jacobean translator George Sandys, see Purkiss, "The Queen on Stage," 153–54.

59. See Baswell, "Dido's Purse"; and chapter 4, below. On Vergil's narrative techniques for representing Dido as a dupe of the gods, see Wofford, *Choice of Achilles*, 155–56; and Suzuki, *Metamorphoses of Helen*, 111–23. On Vergil's early pedagogical institutionalization, see Baswell, *Virgil in Medieval England*, 12–13, 146–51, and passim.

60. For an incisive study of how Shakespeare saw Vergil's Dido as an exemplary figure for a sympathetic audience, see James, "Dido's Ear."

61. See Merrim, *Early Modern Women's Writing*, xviii, for a discussion of St. Paul as a "stumbling block"—a phrase used by Margaret Fell in *Women's Speaking Justified* (1667). Paul's key statements against women's assumption of public authority through preaching are in 1 Cor. 14:34–35 and 1 Tim. 2:11–12. Juan Luis Vives and other humanist educators extended the Pauline strictures to the domain of teaching—a point that I discuss in chapter 3.

62. On Dido's African name, see Davidson, "Domesticating Dido," 68. Vergil uses both the virago and the wanderer etymologies in his portrait; see Hexter, "Sidonian Dido," 348.

63. See *The "Aeneid" of Thomas Phaer and Thomas Twyne*, ed. Lally, 24, 5; cited in Parker, "Fantasies of 'Race' and 'Gender,'" 318n. 38.

64. The typological association of Dido and Cleopatra begins in Vergil's epic; see Bono, *Literary Transvaluation*, 85–86, 216–17, and passim. On Dido and Cleopatra, see also Adelman, *The Common Liar*, 71–74; and Parker, "Fantasies of 'Race' and 'Gender,'" 96–97. On Othello playing a latter-day Aeneas to Desdemona as Dido, see James, "Dido's Ear," 371–77.

65. On the iconography of hair in this woodcut, see Jones and Stallybrass, *Renaissance Clothing*, 82. For Behn's depiction of herself as a man-woman with short-cut hair, see chapter 7, below. On the two pamphlets' rhetorical strategies and cultural contexts, see Woodbridge, *Women and the English Renaissance*, chap. 6.

66. Stephen Greenblatt has done much to make the bishop of Avila and Nebrija known to anglophone students of Renaissance literature; see his *Learning to Curse*, 16–17.

Chapter One

1. See Graff, *Literacy Myth*, xv, for a survey of several phases of postwar literacy scholarship.

2. See the classic study by Kroeber and Kluckhohn, *Culture*; see also Clifford, *Predicament of Culture*, especially 230–36.

3. On literacy and hegemony, in the senses that Antonio Gramsci influentially gave that word, see Graff, *Legacies of Literacy*, 11–12, with further references.

4. See Mignolo, *Darker Side of the Renaissance*, especially 29–67. See also Padley, *Grammatical Theory in Western Europe*, 2:157–65.

5. *Gramática de la lengua castellana*, 3; cited and translated in Mignolo, *Darker Side of the Renaissance*, 38.

6. See Nebrija, *Reglas de la ortografía*, bk. 1, chap. 2; cited and translated in Mignolo, *Darker Side of the Renaissance*, 42.

7. Seeking to distinguish his theoretical approach from Derrida's, Mignolo argues unconvincingly that Nebrija's interest in the letter was "political . . . rather than philosophical" (*Darker Side of the Renaissance*, 319).

8. Derrida, "Structure, Sign, and Play," 251, emphasis in original. Published in *L'Ecriture et la différence* (1967) and presented in French at a famous symposium on structuralism held at Johns Hopkins University in 1966, Derrida's essay was published in English translation in the proceedings of the symposium (*The Structuralist Controversy* [1970]) and again in *Writing and Difference* (1978). My citations are to the *Controversy* text, ed. Macksey and Donato.

9. On this perception of literacy as a potential weapon that can be used against the social order, see Cressy, *Literacy and the Social Order*, 20–25.

10. Gelb, *Study of Writing*, 27. For a cogent critique of this line of argument, see Harris, *Origin of Writing*, 2 and passim.

11. See, e.g., Guillory, *Cultural Capital*; Goldberg, *Writing Matter*; Lerer, *Literacy and Power*; Bloch, *Etymologies and Genealogies*.

12. See, e.g., Lazere, "Stratification in the Academic Profession."

13. The 20 percent figure comes from the Adult Performance Level Project, *Adult Performance Level Study*; the citation is from Graff, *Legacies of Literacy*, 390, who discusses the circular reasoning on many statistical arguments on p. 396. For other claims of crisis, see Hirsch, *Cultural Literacy*; Judy, *ABC's of Literacy*; and Copperman, *Literacy Hoax*.

14. Kozol is well aware of the dangers of the numbers game; in chap. 2 he discusses how the census undercounts minorities—and yet he presents statistics about illiteracy as if they were facts.

15. I refer to changes in composition theory articulated and unevenly put into practice in the wake of Mina Shaughnessy's path-breaking *Errors and Expectations* (1977).

16. See Harris, *Ancient Literacy*, 6–7, for examples of Latin usages that complicate Kelley's genealogical claims.

17. See Bartholomae, "Producing Adult Readers."

18. See Schutte, "Teaching Adults to Read in Sixteenth-Century Venice," 13–14.

19. *Littérature* denotes a body of imaginative writing reflecting a national culture, for instance, in Germaine de Stael's *De la littérature* (1800). See Ferrara, *Origin and Decline of the Concept of "Literature"*; and Wellek and Warren, *Theory of Literature*, 22. In *Marxism and Literature*, Williams argues for the late eighteenth and early nineteenth centuries as the watershed moment in the history of literature as a concept closely tied to aesthetics. For an overview of debates about the term, see Patterson, "Literary History," 250–62. For discussions of the history of literature as a social phenomenon, see Guillory, *Cultural Capital*, especially 69–70, on transhistorical concepts of literature and "literary" language; and Simpson, *Academic Postmodern*.

20. See Graham, ed., *Difference in Translation*, for a conspectus of views on this question; see also Niranjana, *Siting Translation*.

21. Those working on literacy in modern educational contexts seldom attempt the comparative philological work that I consider crucial to understanding literacy as a dynamic phenomenon marked by consequential migrations across linguistic borders. For a valuable if brief example of this line of inquiry, see Barton, *Literacy*, 20–22. For an exemplary instance of inter-

rogating influential modern (academic and Western) notions of reading through an approach that is philological, historical, and ethnographic, see Boyarin, "Placing Reading: Ancient Israel and Medieval Europe."

22. See especially the discussions in Brotherston, "Towards a Grammatology of America"; Goldberg, *Writing Matter*; Lerer, *Literacy and Power*; Clifford, "On Ethnographic Allegory"; and Bloch, *Etymologies and Genealogies*.

23. Brotherston, "Towards a Grammatology of America," 196.

24. *Structural Anthropology*, 61; quoted in Brotherston, "Towards a Grammatology of America," 196. Compare *Tristes Tropiques*, trans. Weightman and Weightman, 391. All English citations of *Tristes Tropiques* are to this translation; page references to the English are given parenthetically in the text, followed by references to the French.

25. See *Preface to Plato*, especially 40–42, 226–27, 244–47. In a striking example of the non-communication typical of (international and interdisciplinary) literacy studies, Derrida writes about Plato's views on writing in the *Phaedrus* in *La Dissémination* (1972) without mentioning Havelock's earlier arguments for a consequential shift in Greek educational practices and cultural authorities, as the philosopher replaces the poet-reciter as chief educator of young male citizens.

26. See, e.g., Havelock's *Literate Revolution* (1982) and his *Muse Learns to Write* (1986).

27. See, e.g., Ong, "Writing Restructures Thought," 33–34, which draws on an argument for technological determinism most famously set forth by McLuhan in *The Gutenberg Galaxy*, especially 24–28. Some early articulators of the Great Divide theory, however, have significantly modified their views. Jack Goody, for instance, criticizes the "Western bias" of his and Ian Watt's 1963 study, *Consequences of Literacy*; see Goody, *Interface between the Oral and the Written*, xviii; and also Goody, introduction to *Literacy in Traditional Societies*. On the changes in Goody's position, see Halverson, "Goody and the Implosion of the Literacy Thesis." For an argument that the Great Divide model retains its ideological force even as it becomes less overtly Eurocentric in the 1980s and 1990s, see Walters, "Language, Logic, and Literacy," 177. See also, on the tendency of 1980s literacy work to posit a continuum not a divide between literacy and orality, but without fundamentally altering Great Divide premises, Street, *Social Literacies*, 157–58, with examples.

28. Ong's extra-academic influence is discussed in Street, *Social Literacies*, 153. My summary of Ong's views comes mainly from *Orality and Literacy*. For useful critical analyses of his theses, see Finnegan, *Literacy and Orality*; Finnegan, "Literacy versus Non-Literacy"; Heath, *Ways with Words*, especially chap. 7; and Coleman, *Public Reading and the Reading Public*, especially chap. 1, "On beyond Ong," and chap. 4, "The Social Context of Medieval Orality."

29. Street, *Social Literacies*, 153–54; on p. 156 he criticizes Ong for oscillating among different "units" of analysis: are we dealing with subcultures, eras, or individual mentalities?

30. See Ong, *Orality and Literacy*, 74.

31. For Derrida's argument that Lévi-Strauss is "Rousseau's modern disciple," see *Of Grammatology*, trans. Spivak, 105–7. In subsequent citations, I refer first to Spivak's translation, then to the original French.

32. See Walters, "Language, Logic, and Literacy," 174, for a discussion of Lévy-Bruhl's *Fonctions mentales dans les sociétés inférieures*, translated into English in 1926 with the more neutral title, *How Natives Think*.

33. See Todorov, *Conquest of America*; see also Root, "Imperial Signifier."

34. There may be more of a rift between orality and innocence in Lévi-Strauss's narrative than Derrida allows. Immediately after describing the writing lesson episode, Lévi-Strauss turns

to describe the natives and the Europeans both suffering the devastations of an eye disease, a form of blindness, that is a "secondary" (that is, belated) effect of gonorrhea (394). His own wife was the first whose eyes were infected, and she had to be evacuated. This detail complicates the portrait of the Nambikwara as a people innocent until the moment of Lévi-Strauss's visit; it suggests, instead, that they have been tainted for a long time by some kinds of European diseases and perhaps blindnesses as well. The European wife, like Milton's Eve, seems to be a liminal figure, between innocence and guilt, between an original state of nature and an (always recurring) Fall into Culture.

35. On Derrida's concept of "phonologism," see Bloch, *Etymologies and Genealogies*, 9.

36. For a fuller list of names/concepts that have occupied the "center" of a metaphysical structure Derrida critiques, see "Structure, Sign, and Play," 249.

37. See, e.g., Ong, "Writing Restructures Thought," 33-34.

38. See, for a conspectus of views, Pfhol, ed., *Das Alphabet. Enstehung und Entwicklung der griechischen Schrift*. For critical discussions of the "single origin" and evolutionary theses, which derive from Hegel and other nineteenth-century thinkers, see Davies, "Forms of Writing in the Ancient Mediterranean World," 53-54; also Driver, *Semitic Writing*; Wallace, "Origins and Development of the Latin Alphabet"; Harris, *Origin of Writing*, chap. 2 ("The Tyranny of the Alphabet").

39. See *Of Grammatology*, 10 and n. 4. Many words for writing, including the English one, suggest that acts of carving or painting marks on stone are central to a culture's understanding of what writing is. See Lerer, *Literacy and Power*, 1 (on Anglo-Saxon runes); and Boone's introduction to *Writing without Words*, ed. Boone and Mignolo, 3 (on the Nahuatl word *tlacuiloliztli* meaning both "to write" and "to paint").

40. For an excellent example (Jack Goody's reply to Kathleen Gough's irrefutable argument that literacy in early India did not lead to a "Western" type of science), see Street, *Social Literacies*, 156.

41. Derrida himself often refers to his project by means of the Heideggerean term *destruction* or the Kantian term *critique*.

42. See *Of Grammatology*, 110; and Brotherston, "Towards a Grammatology of America," 198. Brotherston supplies the Native American name for this writing.

43. See Ong, "Latin Language Study"; see also Kahn, *Rhetoric, Prudence, and Skepticism*, 20, 68-69, on the humanist notion of arguments "on both sides of the question."

44. Barnes, in a review of Weinstein and Bell, cited in Thomas, "Meaning of Literacy," 96.

45. Lévi-Strauss, *Structural Anthropology*, quoted in Brotherston, "Towards a Grammatology of America," 196.

46. See Heisenberg, *Physics and Philosophy*, especially 137 (on the interaction of a system with the "measuring apparatus") and 181-85, on the concept of "degrees of truth." See Trinh, *Woman, Native, Other*, 71, for a similar point.

47. See Boone's introduction to *Writing without Words*, ed. Boone and Mignolo, 11-12, citing *Of Grammatology*, 4; the phrase "envision[ing] information" is the title of a book by E. Tufte; for other recent efforts to think about literacy as tied neither to speech nor to the codex, see Wrolstad and Fisher, eds., *Toward a New Understanding of Literacy*; and Martin, *History and Power of Writing*, chap. 10.

48. Ong, *Orality and Literacy*, 168-69; quoted in Goldberg, *Writing Matter*, 18. For a recent attempt to assess Ong's critique of Derrida for his alleged ethno-textual-centrism, see Tyler, *Said and the Unsaid*; and Tyler, "Postmodern Anthropology."

49. Quoted in Brotherston, "Towards a Grammatology of America," 203.

50. Mignolo, *Darker Side of the Renaissance*, 318.

51. See Civrieux, *Watunna: An Orinoco Creation Cycle*, 16; quoted in Brotherston, "Towards a Grammatology of America," 202.

52. See Fishman, "Bilingualism with and without Diglossia," 32. For further elaborations of the concept as including different functions of language that are sometimes but not always correlated with differences of social class, see Hudson, "Diglossia"; and Guillory, *Cultural Capital*, especially 69–71.

53. I take the phrase from Susan Groag Bell, "Medieval Women Book Owners."

54. On the self-contradictions of the literacy "optimists," see Harris, *Ancient Literacy*, especially 8–9.

55. There is a large bibliography on the writing systems of non-Western ancient cultures. For orientation, see the introduction to Senner, ed., *Origins of Writing*, and the essays in that volume by D. N. Keightley, "The Origins of Writing in China: Scripts and Cultural Contexts," 171–202; J. A. Bellamy, "The Arabic Alphabet," 91–102; and F. G. Lounsbury, "The Ancient Writing of Middle America," 203–38. See also Hsu, *Study of Literate Civilizations*; Houston, "Literacy among the Pre-Columbian Maya"; and Safadi, *Islamic Calligraphy*.

56. On the problem of defining culture as a unified "whole," see Scribner, "Is a History of Popular Culture Possible?" 181–82; cited and discussed in Watt, *Cheap Print and Popular Piety*, 2. On the shared linguistic code necessary to the creation of messages ethnographically understood, see Hymes, "Toward Ethnographies of Communication," 26.

57. *Ancient Literacy*, 5; for reasons explained later in this chapter, I suspect that many ancient uses of *litteratus*, like early modern ones, did not connect reading and writing in the way we do; hence I denaturalize Harris's copula.

58. See on this topic McSheffrey, *Gender and Heresy*; McSheffrey, "Literacy and the Gender Gap in the Late Middle Ages"; and the essays in Biller and Hudson, eds., *Heresy and Literacy*.

59. *Libellus de vita et miraculis S. Godrici*, cited and translated in Clanchy, *From Memory to Written Record*, 190.

60. See Grundmann, "*Litteratus-illitteratus*," 4. See also Parkes, "Literacy of the Laity," 556.

61. See Clanchy, *From Memory to Written Record*, 90–99; also Galbraith, "Literacy of English Kings," especially 95: "How far the kings of the second period were able to write as well as read, I cannot say."

62. Parkes, "Literacy of the Laity," 556.

63. See Boswell, *Christianity, Social Tolerance, and Homosexuality*, 228. For opposing views— which, however, as I've noted, seem to say more about different cultural definitions of literacy than about historical "facts"—see Baüml, "Varieties and Consequences," 237–65. Baüml himself thinks it is "simplistic" to think medieval literacy was "confined to the clergy" (237n. 1), but he is less interested in literacy as an *individual's* skills in reading and/or writing Latin than in the "*function* of literacy in medieval society" (239). For this reason he stresses the dissemination of written documents—and many nonclerics' interactions with and dependence on such documents— rather than medieval assessments of literacy, which, in Clanchy's words, "concentrate on cases of maximum ability . . . whereas modern assessors [sometimes!] measure the diffusion of minimal skills among the masses" (*From Memory to Written Record*, 238).

64. The "regular" clergy are monks, friars, and nuns, as opposed to the "secular" clergy, or priests. See Shahar, *The Fourth Estate*, 2. Shahar is wrong, however, in stating that "only upper-class women took the veil." For evidence to the contrary, see Power, *Medieval English Nunneries*, chap. 1.

65. Writing required expenditures on paper or parchment, quills, and ink; it also required training in laborious processes. Much has been written on the significance of the separation

between reading and writing in medieval and early modern England and France; see Justice, *Writing and Rebellion*, 24n. 34; Sanders, *Gender and Literacy*, 197n. 3; Spufford, "Schooling of the Peasantry in Cambridgeshire," 121n. 1; and Timmermans, *L'Accès des femmes*, 57. On the social implications of the cost of teaching writing (which contributed to the gendering of the field of literacy), see Monaghan, "Literacy Instruction"; and Simon, *Education and Society in Tudor England*, 370. For a discussion of fees for reading, writing, and arithmetic instruction in French village schools, see Grosperrin, *Les Petites écoles*, 54.

66. See Spufford, *Small Books*, 34; also Furet and Ozouf, *Reading and Writing*, 72, on the "synodal regulations and episcopal ordinances" that insist that girls should learn reading and household skills, especially sewing, but not writing. See also Lougée, *Le Paradis des femmes*, 25; Ezell, *Patriarch's Wife*, 12; Chartier, "The Practical Impact of Writing," 115.

67. See my discussion of du Bellay's sense that writing involves a "derogation" of nobility, in *Trials of Desire*, 20-21. For the historical precedents for that attitude, see Clanchy's discussion of the early thirteenth-century *Dispute between a Cleric and a Knight*, in *From Memory to Written Record*, 146.

68. *2 Henry VI*, 4.2.96-97; cited from the *Norton Shakespeare* (which gives this play's title as *The First Part of the Contention*). All citations of Shakespeare's works are to the *Norton Shakespeare*, ed. Greenblatt et al. For an analysis of Shakespeare's representation of "literacy as a crucial bridge between powerlessness and empowerment" in this play, see Cartelli, "Jack Cade in the Garden," 48-67, especially 59. See also Patterson's discussion of Cade in *Shakespeare and the Popular Voice*, 38-40; and Wilson, "Mingled Yarn."

69. Hall, *Union of the Two Noble and Illustre Famelies of Lancastre and York* (1550), cited in Cartelli, "Jack Cade in the Garden," 56. Wilson suggests that Shakespeare conveys his own "negative appraisal" of Cade by rendering him illiterate ("Mingled Yarn," 167). I would go further, and suggest that Shakespeare deprives Cade of letters in order to create an ideological distance between writers and rebels against kings.

70. Susan Crane, "Writing Lesson," 204, cites Trevelyan's judgment from his *England in the Age of Wycliffe*.

71. See "Writing Lesson," 204; the passage Crane quotes from Walsingham's *Historia* seems a good candidate for a direct source for Shakespeare's representation of Cade's murder of clerks.

72. The historian Christopher Dyer, as Crane notes, "has identified 107 separate instances of destruction of documents, 'including the burning of central estate archives'" (ibid., citing Dyer, "Social and Economic Background").

73. See Dolan's discussion of the case of Anne Bodenham, who was found guilty of witchcraft, according to a male contemporary, partly because she "took Pen Ink and Paper, and wrote something, and put some yellow powder therein" (cited in "Reading, Writing, and Other Crimes," 151-52); the same commentator construes illiteracy as a cause for Bodenham's leading another woman, Anne Styles, into witchcraft (155).

74. See Herrup, *The Common Peace*, 48; see also Hackel, "Boasting of Silence," on the significance of Herrup's research. Dolan discusses the high incidence of successful benefit-of-clergy pleas in "Reading, Writing, and Other Crimes," 146.

75. On the asymmetries between the literacy and the pregnancy pleas, see Sanders, *Gender and Literacy*, 17-18; and Dolan, "Reading, Writing, and Other Crimes," 146. Dolan remarks that pleading the belly was not available to older women and did not afford a formal pardon, although in practice many women who made this plea seem to have escaped execution.

76. Cited and discussed in Herrup, *The Common Peace*, 143; see also Sanders, *Gender and Literacy*, 201n. 42.

77. For a valuable overview of the "forms and functions of writing" in Europe between

1500 and 1800, see Martin, *The History and Power of Writing,* chap. 7. See also Petrucci's discussion of Italian vernacular books in *Writers and Readers,* chap. 9; and Coleman's discussion of lay education and literacy in late medieval France and England, *Medieval Readers and Writers,* chap. 2.

78. On texts designed for and refracting information about differently educated readers, see Petrucci, *Writers and Readers,* especially 187-89; see also Doane and Pasternack, eds., *Vox Intexta;* and Plummer, ed., *Vox Feminae.* On the different levels and kinds of literacy fostered in heretical communities, such as Lollard ones in England, see McSheffrey, *Gender and Heresy;* Aston, *Lollards and Reformers;* and Biller and Hudson, eds., *Heresy and Literacy.*

79. "Varieties and Consequences," 237. Baüml formulates these two "facts" with reference only to the period between the fourth and the fifteenth centuries, but I have extended the time frame to the early modern era. No historian I have read argues that a "majority" of a European country's population was literate until the nineteenth century.

80. See, e.g., Harris, *Ancient Literacy,* 7; M. B. Parkes uses the phrase "professional literacy" to describe a similar phenomenon in "Literacy of the Laity," 555-56.

81. See Harris, *Ancient Literacy,* 8. For a description of whole societies as having reached the level of "craftsman's" literacy, see also Havelock, *Literate Revolution,* 10, 187-88; and Houston, "Literacy among the Pre-Columbian Maya," 34.

82. For Harris's and Cressy's skepticism about the "optimists'" figures, see page 62 in this volume.

83. Cited in Clanchy, "Learning to Read," 33.

84. Kastan made the point in an oral commentary on papers presented at a conference, "The Emergence of the Female Reader, 1500-1800," directed by Heidi Brayman Hackel, at the University of Oregon, Corvallis, May 2001.

85. See Burke, "Approaches to Studying Reading Interests of Earlier Civilisation[s]."

86. For recent work on marginalia and the history of reading, see my prologue, note 18.

87. Cressy, *Literacy and the Social Order,* 41; Dolan cites this passage in "Reading, Writing, and Other Crimes," 161n. 4.

88. See, for instance, the sixteenth- and seventeenth-century English examples Cressy gives to illustrate the idea that "faith was insufficient without literacy to guide it" (*Literacy and the Social Order,* 4-5). The examples support only the conclusion that *reading* was important. Some documents do single out writing as a valuable skill, but the two examples Cressy actually supplies are in texts by socially privileged fathers to their sons.

89. On the cultural significance of such images of female pedagogical authority, see Sanders, *Gender and Literacy,* chap. 1.

90. More's argument that reading the Bible (if one needs to do so in English as opposed to Latin) is not necessary for one's salvation seems typically Catholic, but many socially privileged Protestants, in England as in Germany, came to feel that vernacular translations of the Bible fomented dangerous beliefs in the poor. For a similarly problematic (and high) estimate of a population's literacy, see Villani's claim (quoted on page 79 in this volume) about the number of children reading in Florence in the late 1330s.

91. See Porter, *Rise of Statistical Thinking;* and Porter, "Objectivity as Standardization." See also Stigler, *History of Statistics;* Poovey, *History of the Modern Fact;* and, on the "mathematization of the world," Chaunu, *La Civilisation de l'Europe Classique.*

92. Cressy discusses the problems of the signature method in the chapter "The Measurement of Literacy" in *Literacy and the Social Order;* he concludes that despite the problems, "no other body of evidence is so valuable to the sociological historian of literacy, or is so susceptible to nu-

merical analysis" (54). Similar conclusions are outlined by Schofield in "Measurement of Literacy in Pre-industrial England."

93. The statistical conclusion is mentioned in Sanders, *Gender and Literacy,* 142.

94. I cite the French original, from *Lire et écrire,* because it is thus cited by Cressy (*Literacy and the Social Order,* 55) even though the translation of *alphabétisation* as "literacy" is problematic. For the English translation, see Furet and Ozouf, *Reading and Writing,* 17: "Ability to sign one's name thus does indeed refer to what we now call literacy [*alphabétisation*], which in turn means reading and writing." But see the questions raised by Dolan, "Reading, Writing, and Other Crimes"; she remarks that "census-type documents such as the Protestation Oaths of 1642 and the Test Oaths of 1723" underestimate women not only because women were not required to take these oaths, but also because a disproportionate number of women were recusants—precisely those whom the oaths were designed to root out (161–62n. 6).

95. See Thomas, "Meaning of Literacy," 97–131 (with further bibliography); Derville, "L'Alphabétisation du peuple," 761–72; Spufford, "First Steps in Literacy," especially 414; see also Spufford, *Small Books*; and Ford, "Problem of Literacy."

96. For the widow Emma's charter and use of a seal, see Clanchy, *From Memory to Written Record,* 35, and his discussion of sealing as "two-faced images" in the "formation of a literate mentality": seals "looked back to charms and memorized symbolic objects and forward to the automation of writing" (248).

97. Schofield, "Measurement of Literacy in Pre-industrial England," 323–24. This statement is approvingly cited by Furet and Ozouf, *Reading and Writing,* 11, although they go on to suggest that it is only from 1866 onward, in France, that we have the kind of data to "allow us to overcome the tricky problem of the relation between ability to read and full literacy, which includes the ability to write as well."

98. See Hull, *Chaste, Silent, and Obedient,* 1–7; and Lucas, *Writing for Women,* especially chap. 1.

99. See Justice's argument for training students in "old" disciplines (e.g., paleography and philology), which he calls "materialist" rather than "empirical," in order to pursue the task of reconstituting the object of study for historians as well as literary scholars. For valuable comments on the problem of evidence see also Petrucci, *Writers and Readers,* chap. 10 ("The Illusion of Authentic History"); and MacLean, "Literacy, Class, and Gender," especially 308–16.

100. Villani is cited and translated in Gehl, *Moral Art,* 20–22. Gehl illustrates just the scholarly gesture I am advocating; he interprets Villani's numbers as "extraordinary" (i.e., not accurate) and as signifying "the wealth and the power of the city" as well as the habit of "accounting" typical of Florentine merchants (25). I am indebted to Bianca Calabresi for this reference.

101. For the problem of "self-assessment" and the difficulty of reading marriage-register signatures, see Vincent, *Literacy and Popular Culture,* 17. For further discussion of the problems of determining literacy rates from records of occasions where the decision of whether to sign or leave one's mark was made under "public scrutiny," see Justice, *Writing and Rebellion,* 33–34, n. 64; and Lough, *Writer and Public in France,* 59–60.

102. See Thomas, "Meaning of Literacy," 99.

103. There is a large literature on this question; for a thoughtful introduction to the feminist critique of ideals of "scientific" "objectivity" (both terms are themselves the locus of debate), see Hawkesworth, "From Objectivity to Objectification," with further references.

104. See Balibar, *L'Institution du français*; and the discussion of this concept in chapter 2, below.

105. See page 101 in this volume.

106. See Spence, "Channel Island French."

Chapter Two

1. See Blank, *Broken English*, 15; also Fox, *Oral and Literate Culture*, 64.

2. *Keywords*, 105, 296–97; for useful paths into this arena of debate, see Godzich, "Culture of Illiteracy"; Certeau, *Writing of History*; Bourdieu, *Language and Symbolic Power*; MacCabe, *Eloquence of the Vulgar*; Fleming, "Dictionary English"; Crowley, *Standard English*; and Crowley, *Proper English?* For historical perspectives see also Trahern, ed., *Standardizing English*; Jones, *Triumph of the English Language*; Bailey, *Images of English*; Haas, *Standard Languages, Spoken and Written*; Furet and Ozouf, *Reading and Writing*; and Balibar, *Le Français national.*

3. For this view of Latin as a timeless, "paternal" language, and for explorations of fissures within this ideological complex, see Townsend and Taylor, introduction to *Tongue of the Fathers*, 1–2.

4. For Cicero's ideal of a pure Latin, see *De oratore*, trans. Rackham, bk. 1, sec. 144, pp. 100–101; the ideal is discussed in Scott, *Controversies over the Imitation of Cicero*, 3.

5. For exemplary formulations of the French ideal, see du Bellay, *Deffense et illustration* (1549); and Hollyband, *De pronuntiatione linguae gallicae* (1580). See Prescott, *French Poets*, 18, for Marot's status as a writer who "helped civilize the French language." For English examples of these denominations see Fox, *Oral and Literate Culture*, 53–64; Bailey, *Images of English*, 3.

6. Kings of England before William, of course, also had French—specifically Norman—kin.

7. See Smith, "Origins of Nations." I see the role of clerks and educators as more decisive than Smith does in his account of "ethnic core formations."

8. Colet, *Rudimenta grammatices* (1539), cited in Williams, *Keywords*, 184.

9. Rive, *An Heptaglottologie* (1618), 27; quoted in Jones, *Triumph of the English Language*, 277n. 11. For other instances of this "favorite argument of Latin teachers," see Grendler, *Schooling in Renaissance Italy*, 187.

10. *Il Convivio*, 20; this passage is cited and discussed in MacCabe, *Eloquence of the Vulgar*, 148.

11. See Bailey, *Images of English*, 32, for a discussion of William Bulloker's effort (in 1580) to give a social (not a geographical) "locus" for his ideal of "right" speech as that spoken "at the center of political power" but not by "secretaries, merchants, or others influenced by foreign languages."

12. Cited in Bailey, "Development of English," 151. Compare the lament by the anonymous translator of *The boke callyd the Myrroure of Oure Lady*, second prologue (1530), that "oure language is also dyverse in yt selfe / that the commen maner of spekynge in Englysshe of some contre / can skante be understondid in some other contre of the same londe" (cited in Jones, *Triumph of the English Language*, 5).

13. See Cerquiglini, *Naissance du français*, 114–24; and, for a similar critique, Wolff, *Western Languages*, 154. On the nineteenth-century origins of the term *Francien*, see also Rickard, *History of the French Language*, 49.

14. *Here begynneth a treatyse of a galuant*, perhaps by Lydgate, cited in Jones, *Triumph of the English Language*, 5n. 5.

15. For an introductory discussion of the "linguistic divisions" within these large groups, see Brunot, "Les Dialectes de l'ancien français," in *Histoire de la langue française*, vol. 1, chap. 6. Again, the issue of what is a dialect and what is a language arises: Wolff remarks that sixteen of the nineteen criteria used by the linguist Ronjat divide "the two French languages," while only four criteria separate the *langue d'oc* from Catalan (*Western Languages*, 146).

16. Latini, *Li livres dou tresor*, ed. Carmody (from an early fourteenth-century manuscript), 18.

17. For early meanings more positive than the one Bourdieu gives, see Godefroy, *Diction-naire de l'ancienne langue française*, 6:40. The methods by which lexicographers decide and then justify how written evidence for oral usage supports hypotheses of linear sequences in meaning need more discussion than I can give them here. For a sophisticated discussion of this issue, see Knapp, *Time-Bound Words*, 1–12.

18. Dedicatory Epistle (E. K. to "Mayster Gabriell Harvey"), in *Yale Edition of the Shorter Poems of Edmund Spenser*, 15.

19. A version of this joke is given in Steinberg, "The Historian and the *Questione della Lingua*," 199; on the distinction between dialects and languages, see also McDavid, *Dialects in Culture*; Milroy and Milroy, *Authority in Language*; and Joseph, *Eloquence and Power*.

20. Gill, *Logonomia anglica*, cited in Blank, *Broken English*, 19; see also Waddington, "Re-writing the World," 288, on Ben Jonson's representations of the languages ("jargons") of occupations from gambling through street vending to pickpocketing.

21. For the legal evidence, see Cockburn, "Early Modern Assize Records," 223, cited in Blank, *Broken English*, 19.

22. The passages cited are from *Dialogic Imagination*, 17, and *Rabelais*, 468; both are cited and discussed in Blank, *Broken English*, 13. Katerina Clark and Michael Holquist argue that Bakhtin's Rabelais book was his "most comprehensive critique to date of Stalinist culture" and must be read in the context of its times and Bakhtin's own experiences of state censorship (*Mikhail Bakhtin*, 306 and passim).

23. For a discussion of the association of the Tower of Babel with the Babylon of the Hebrew psalms, see Ferguson, "Saint Augustine's Region of Unlikeness," especially 86–87.

24. Quoted from Rabelais, *Oeuvres complètes*, ed. Jourda, 1:228; English from *Histories of Gargantua and Pantagruel*, trans. Cohen, 174.

25. Moryson, *An Itinerary* (1617–c. 1626), cited in Blank, *Broken English*, 126.

26. For discussion of this concept, see chapter 4.

27. Bacon is discussed later in this chapter.

28. Anglo-Saxon was not used after the 1070s "by the king's government or by the clergy as a whole," Clanchy argues (*From Memory to Written Record*, 166). William had appointed a large number of Normans and other continental clergy to bishoprics and abbacies, and for these men Latin was the only significant language of record. Nonetheless, some monks continued to copy Anglo-Saxon texts (ibid.).

29. See Lerer, *Literacy and Power*; and O'Brian, *Visible Song*.

30. See Robertson, *Early English Devotional Prose*, 16; and Casey, "Women in Norman and Plantagenet England." See also Godfrey, "Double Monastery in Early English History."

31. Cited from the introduction to Marie de France, *The Lais*, trans. Hanning and Ferrante, 6. On her language and self-namings as "de France," see also Spitzer, "Prologue to the *Lais*."

32. For a discussion of Charlemagne's importance, as Holy Roman Emperor, to the "birth" of the French language, see Cerquiglini, *Naissance du français*, 68–71.

33. See Lambley, *Teaching and Cultivation*, especially 12–18. See also Coleman, *Medieval Readers and Writers*, especially chap. 2, "Vernacular Literacy and Lay Education."

34. See Rickard, *Britain in Medieval French Literature*, especially chap. 3.

35. See chapter 4 for a discussion of this association in *Henry V*.

36. Among the treatises that contain such a lesson are one by Walter of Bibbesworth, dis-cussed below, and *The Nominale sive Verbale*, an anonymous treatise from the early fourteenth century, which, despite its Latin title, is a French "vocabulary" modeled on Bibbesworth's with an English gloss placed after the French words. See Lambley, *Teaching and Cultivation*, 17, on the vocabularies and on the later letter-writing manuals aimed at women.

37. Cited in Lambley, *Teaching and Cultivation*, 13, my translation.

38. Cited in ibid., 27 and 27n. 2, my translation.

39. Balibar, *L'Institution du français*, 14, emphasis in original, my translation.

40. See, e.g., Stock, *Implications of Literacy*, 17.

41. See Balibar, *L'Institution du français*, 15, and the summary of its argument, in English, in Balibar, "National Language, Education, Literature." For further elaboration of her arguments see Balibar, *Les Français fictifs*; and Balibar, *Le Français national*.

42. For an example of such an account, not mentioned by Balibar, see Rickard, *History of the French Language*, 29. For a more complex example, see Bloch, "842: Louis the German and Charles the Bald."

43. As P. S. Lewis observes in his "War Propaganda and Historiography in Fifteenth-Century France and England," at the very time when Henry V was claiming France as his rightful inheritance, Jean Juvenal des Ursins sought, in his *Audite celi que loquor*, to prove "on historical grounds that the true king of England was the king of France" (15).

44. John Barton, c. 1400. For a discussion of Barton's grammar and its modern critical neglect (in France), see Lusignan, *Parler vulgairement*, 111–19.

45. Abbott, "English as a Foreign Language," 1120–21.

46. See Wooldridge, "Birth of French Lexicography"; see also Brandon, *Robert Estienne et le dictionnaire français au XVIe siècle.*

47. Writers on the French side of the Channel were also occasionally reading and imitating works written in a version of English; for examples, see Rathery, *Des relations sociales*, 13, 15.

48. There is considerable disagreement about the diffusion of Anglo-French in the English population, but most scholars agree that the language was losing ground among the aristocracy by the mid-fourteenth century. At the beginning of the Hundred Years War, Edward III found it necessary, according to the chronicler Froissart, to proclaim that "tout seigneur, baron, chevalier, et honestes hommes de bonnes villes mesissent cure et dilligence de estruire et apprendre leurs enfans le langhe françoise" (quoted in Lambley, *Teaching and Cultivation*, 23n. 5). The translator Trevisa suggests that the Black Death of 1349 played a major role in the "demise" of French in England: before the plague, French was the language used in grammar schools to teach Latin, but now (i.e., in 1387), "they leave all Frensch in scholes, and use all construction in Englisch. Wherin they have advantage on way that they lerne the soner ther gramer." But the disadvantage, he notes, is that children now know "no more French than knows their lefte heele" (translation of Higden's *Polychronicon*, quoted in Lambley, *Teaching and Cultivation*, 24).

49. See Rickard, *History of the French Language*, 37, where he regrets that one "has quite frequently to seek for continental [i.e., French] forms behind insular graphies" in a copy of a "French" (Norman) poem by an Anglo-Norman scribe.

50. Fleming, "Dictionary English," 290.

51. See chapter 4; and Charlton, *Women, Religion and Education*, especially 142–53. Although precise differences between "elementary" and "grammar" school curricula are often hard to discern from the historical records, particularly when the records concern village schools in France and England that evidently combined elementary and secondary education in a single site, the primary school played a significant role in clerkly debates about who should control education. Such schools were also critical to the process whereby the field of literacy was divided, along lines of gender and social status, into full and "partial" types.

52. Quoted from Machan, "Editing, Orality," 231.

53. I borrow the term *sociality*—and the argument for its marginalization—from MacCabe, *Eloquence of the Vulgar*, 63.

54. This is a definition of history formulated by Chartier in "Texts, Symbols, and Frenchness"; cited in Hunt, introduction to *New Cultural History*, 13.

55. *The Greek Grammar of Roger Bacon*, dist. 1, cap. 1; cited in Burnley, "Sources of Standardisation," 32. I have followed Burnley in not modernizing *u/v* and *i/j*.

56. Giles de Rome, *De regimine principum* (c. 1285), 2.2.7; cited in Latin and French in Lusignan, *Parler vulgairement*, 43, my translation.

57. See Allmand, *Henry V*, 7–15; and also Harriss, ed., *Henry V: The Practice of Kingship*.

58. Burnley, "Sources of Standardisation," 26. Elizabeth Eisenstein, *Printing Press as an Agent of Change*, expresses a similar irritation with the "fluctuating, uneven and multiform texture of scribal culture" (11–12).

59. See Bacon as cited in Burnley, "Sources of Standardisation," 32.

60. Burnley, "Sources of Standardisation," 35. On the use of French in England see also Rothwell, "Stratford atte Bowe and Paris"; Lambley, *Teaching and Cultivation*; and Wilson, "English and French in England."

61. See, e.g., Machan, "Editing, Orality," 232, where he homogenizes the vernacular even as he contrasts it to Latin.

62. Quoted in Clanchy, *From Memory to Written Record*, 157, 59. For a further discussion of these language debates, see Richter, "Socio-linguistic Approach to the Latin Middle Ages," especially 76.

63. See Crowley, *Proper English?* 13–27. Aarslef, *From Locke to Saussure*, also uses Locke as his starting point. For Swift as an initiator of the history of standardization, see Milroy and Milroy, *Authority in Language*, especially 33–34.

64. Writings associated with the Lollard religious movement achieved, according to Burnley, "the basic requirements" of a "true standard": "a high degree of internal consistency in spelling and a wide dissemination outside the centres which produced them" ("Sources of Standardisation," 25). But the persecution of the Lollards after 1401 ensured that their practices were adopted only by "the ideologically committed" (26).

65. For estimates about the numbers of London clerks, see Christianson, "Chancery Standard and the Records of Old London Bridge." See also Richardson, "Henry V, the English Chancery, and Chancery English"; and Fisher, "Chancery and the Emergence of Standard Written English."

66. This is a very truncated version of a still-contested story; for more details (and variant opinions), see Fisher, "Chancery and the Emergence of Standard Written English"; and various articles in Trudgill, ed., *Language in the British Isles*, especially those of Milroy, "The History of English in the British Isles," and Trudgill, "Standard English in England."

67. See Florio, *Essayes*, 709; the passage from Cicero is cited in note 4 above. Fleming, "Dictionary English," 320n. 31, discusses this example and notes the contrast to Elyot's view of "old" women's speech as impure.

68. Burnley, "Curial Prose in England." See also his "Christine de Pizan and the So-Called Clergial Style"; and Rasmussen, *La Prose narrative française*. For bibliography on early English translations of de Pizan's works, see chapter 4.

69. See Brunot, *Histoire de la langue française*, 2:2.

70. For an extended study of the association of "corrupt" texts with female bodies in early Italian humanist discourses, see Jed, *Chaste Thinking*.

71. *Gowrie's Conspiracy* (1600), cited in Adelman, "Born of Woman," 106.

72. Mulcaster, *First Part of the Elementarie* (1582), 69, 56, 70. See chapter 3, below, for further discussion of humanist efforts to regulate a feminine sphere of influence; in discourses urging

upper-class mothers to breast-feed their children, mothers and wet-nurses are distinguished as conduits of linguistic education.

73. Quoted from *Works of Geoffrey Chaucer,* ed. Robinson, 18, lines 124–25. For a discussion of the use of derogatory phrases for versions of Anglo-French, see Woodbine, "Language of English Law," especially 143.

74. See Robinson's note to line 519, in *Works of Geoffrey Chaucer,* 694.

75. Burrow, "Maner Latyn Corrupt," citing Isidore of Seville, *Etymologiae,* bk. 9, 1, 6–7, from the edition of W. M. Lindsay. Burrow qualifies Robinson's perception of the unusualness of Chaucer's line by noting that a contemporary of Chaucer, the northern author of the alliterative *Morte Arthure,* also represents a character—the king himself, disguised—speaking a "Latyne corromppede alle" (33–34).

76. Burnley, "Sources of Standardisation," 30. See Jed, *Chaste Thinking,* for this ideological tradition in Italian humanist and mercantile writings.

77. Probably written around 1508, *The Boke of Philip Sparrow* was apparently published in 1545 (the date is not clear on the title page); the quotation is found in Jones, *Triumph of the English Language,* 11, and, in modernized spelling, in *Complete Poems of John Skelton,* ed. Henderson, 82.

78. Cited from a manuscript source in Williams, *Recovery, Reorientation, Reformation,* 464; also in Blank, *Broken English,* 134.

79. Cited in Williams, *Recovery, Reorientation, Reformation,* 465.

80. Ascham, *The Scholemaster* (1570), ed. Schoek, 46, 119.

81. See Freccero, "Fig Tree and the Laurel."

82. My reading is particularly indebted to two finely contextualized although different readings of the poem: Greenblatt, *Renaissance Self-Fashioning,* 144–50; and Foley, *Sir Thomas Wyatt,* 96–100.

83. See, e.g., two poems "by uncertain authors" dealing with linguistic/nationalist competition and acknowledging the superiority of Italian to English ("A praise of Petrarke and of Laura his ladie" and "That Petrarck cannot be passed but notwithstanding that Lawra is far surpassed"), in Rollins, ed., *Tottel's Miscellany* (1557), 1:169 (no. 218) and 1:170 (no. 219).

84. See my prologue, page 11.

85. Quoted from the version of Egerton Ms. 2711, in *Collected Poems of Sir Thomas Wyatt,* ed. Muir, 7.

86. Though Petrarch never degrades the emblematic deer as Wyatt does, a full reading of the Italian sonnet, in the context of a poetic narrative that repeatedly depicts the poet torn between an illicit love for "Laura" as a golden-haired lady and as an emblem of pagan poetic fame, through the pun on *laurel,* would excavate the ironies of Petrarch's own line about property that alludes ambiguously both to a biblical and to a secular source, leaving undecided the question of to whom belongs not only the deer but the *Canzoniere.* For the Petrarchan original and a good modern translation, see Durling, *Petrarch's Lyric Poems.*

87. Cited from the text of *Canzoniere* 190 in *Petrarch's Lyric Poems.* For the Vulgate text I use the *Biblia Sacra,* and for English translations I use David Daniell's modern-spelling edition of William Tyndale's 1534 translation of the New Testament.

88. On Anne's status both as whore and as Protestant martyr, see Foley, *Sir Thomas Wyatt,* 100.

89. See, e.g., Abrams, ed., *Norton Anthology of English Literature,* 1:441n. 1. See also Thompson, "Wyatt and the Petrarchan Commentators," especially 225.

90. Wyatt's signet ring contained a sign of (Julius) Caesar's head; Foley interprets this object as displaying a highly complex "identification of the servant with the master" (*Sir Thomas Wyatt,* 97).

91. Marguerite Waller argues that the line describes Christ's situation as ambiguous without implying that Christ is God's private property and therefore not accessible to Mary Magdalene ("Empire's New Clothes," 171 and 182n. 18); contrast Waller's view with Greenblatt's (perhaps ironic?) assertion that "we refuse to take *noli me tangere* in a religious sense" (*Renaissance Self-Fashioning*, 149).

92. See Waller, "Empire's New Clothes," 182n. 18: "Some hold that it means one should obey Caesar and obey God. Others maintain that the saying is a witty evasion." See also Bruce, "Render unto Caesar," 249–63.

93. Compare the London waterman John Taylor's "A comparison betwixt a *Whore* and a *Booke*," in Woudhuysen, ed., *Penguin Book of Renaissance Verse*, 740: "For like a *Whore* by daylight, or by Candle,/Tis ever free for every knave to handle. . . . /And as an old *whore* may be painted new/With borrowed beauty, faire unto the view,/Whereby shee for a fine fresh *whore* may passe,/Yet is shee but the rotten *whore* shee was."

94. Allison, ed., *Norton Anthology of Poetry*, 90. The poem's status as a translation is noted in Abrams, ed., *Norton Anthology of English Literature*, 1:441n. 1, but the biblical allusion is not mentioned.

95. Cited from *Yale Edition of the Shorter Poems of Edmund Spenser*, 16. For other literary examples of the trope of a mother tongue that needs protecting and improving, see Smith, "So Much English by the Mother"; see also Jones, *Triumph of the English Language*, chaps. 3 and 4, "The Inadequate Language."

96. All citations of *De vulgari eloquentia* are to the edition by Marigo and Ricci; the passage quoted in the epigraph earlier in this chapter is from pp. 6–8. Citations are henceforth given parenthetically in the text by book, chapter, and passage number followed by the page numbers of Marigo's edition. My translations are based on those of Haller, ed., *Literary Criticism of Dante Alighieri*, and Shapiro, in her edition of *De vulgari eloquentia*.

97. For the history of the few known manuscripts of the text, see Marigo's introduction to his edition of *De vulgari eloquentia*, xli–xlvi. For interpretations that have influenced mine, see Ascoli, "Neminem ante Nos"; Ascoli, "Unfinished Author"; Grayson, "Nobilior Est Vulgaris"; and Shapiro's introduction to her edition of *De vulgari eloquentia*.

98. This scribal culture could and did include women, although they were masculinized by virtue of their education and their writing activity; see discussion of de Pizan as clerk in chapter 4.

99. See Davis, "Dante and the Empire"; also Davis, *Dante and the Idea of Rome*.

100. Mauro, *Storia linguistica dell' Italia unita*; cited in Steinberg, "Historian and the *Questione della Lingua*," 198.

101. See 2.7.3, p. 228; also 1.12.1, p. 96. Dante also uses the metaphor of the sieve in *Paradiso*, Canto 26, line 22.

102. See 2.7.4, p. 228. Dante gives the name of the mother first in his examples of *puerilia*: "necque puerilia propter sui simplicitatem, ut *mamma* et *babbo*, *mate* et *pate*." See Hollander, "Babytalk in Dante's *Commedia*."

103. Quoted in Lambley, *Teaching and Cultivation*, 28.

104. See *Femina*, edited from a manuscript in Trinity College by W. Aldis Wright in 1909; the term *provincialisms* comes from Lambley, *Teaching and Cultivation*, 28.

105. For formulations of this important modification of Elias's argument, see Goldberg, *Writing Matter*, 61–62, 41–43; and Montrose, "Work of Gender."

106. See Maclean, *Renaissance Notion of Woman*; and Laqueur, *Making Sex*.

107. César (or Charles) de Rochefort, *Histoire naturelle*. I cite from the edition of 1681, chap. 10, 449.

108. Cited in Orme, *Education and Society*, 160. There was an increasing tendency for aristo-

crats to send their sons to grammar schools in sixteenth-century England and France, although only in Scotland was this course of action required by the state (ibid., 154). In many parts of Western Europe, both Catholic and Protestant, early modern authorities were increasingly concerned to segregate girls from boys in educational sites; on this trend, see Furet and Ozouf, *Reading and Writing*, 71.

109. On this opposition see Hulme, *Colonial Encounters*, chap. 2. Hulme does not discuss de Rochefort.

110. In a chapter called "Language and Sex," Trudgill mentions de Rochefort's story—without mentioning his name—in a discussion of sex differentiation in Native American languages. Noting that the reported differences are lexical rather than syntactic, Trudgill defines them as dialectal (*Sociolinguistics*, 80).

111. Anderson, *Lineages of the Absolutist State*, 48. See also Stone, *Crisis of the Aristocracy*.

112. On the emergence of the *noblesse de robe*, see Mandrou, *Introduction to Modern France*, 100–118. See also Bitten, *French Nobility*; and Huppert, *Les Bourgeois gentilshommes*. On the "crisis of the aristocracy" as a "trans-European phenomenon," see Quint, *Epic and Empire*, 174 and 193n. 76.

113. Quint, *Epic and Empire*, 174. Among the many cultural representations of Queen Elizabeth as a virago figure are some that link her both with the chaste Dido ("Elissa") and (obliquely) with the unchaste Vergilian virago; see Purkiss, "The Queen on Stage." For a fascinating discussion of iconography that links Elizabeth not only to Dido but also to Aeneas (as empire-builder) and to an alchemical tradition of a "black emperor," see Dalton, "Art for the Sake of Dynasty: The Black Emperor in the Drake Jewel and Elizabethan Imperial Imagery." This essay and others in the same collection, *Early Modern Visual Culture*, appeared too late for me to take adequate account of their arguments.

Chapter Three

1. For an overview of terminological debates, see Zernatto, "Nation"; see also Bhabha, introduction to *Nation and Narration*; Balibar, "The Nation Form"; Seton-Watson, *Nations and States*; and the essays by Renan, Weber, Geertz, Giddens, and others collected in Hutchinson and Smith, eds., *Nationalism*, part 1: "The Question of Definition." I discuss some of the dating debates later in this chapter.

2. See Anderson, *Imagined Communities*, 36–46 and passim.

3. Anderson's use of the (European) Middle Ages to signal an "older" (premodern) kind of "imagined community" becomes ambiguous when we see that he is interested both in defining a geographically and historically specific phenomenon (a medieval Christian polity) and in associating medieval Christianity with a "type" of imagined community that persists into the recent past or even into our present. "In the Islamic tradition," he notes, "until quite recently, the Qur'an was literally untranslatable . . . because Allah's truth was accessible only through the unsubstitutable true signs of written Arabic" (*Imagined Communities*, 14).

4. See, e.g., *Imagined Communities*, 42, and also 86, where Anderson contrasts the "self-conscious Machiavellism" of late nineteenth-century "cultural conquistadors" with the "unself-conscious, everyday pragmatism" of their sixteenth-century forebears. The contrast is too stark, it seems to me, if one considers that some among the early conquistadors had read Nebrija—not to mention Machiavelli!

5. I take issue with those recent historians who find it "anachronistic" to see in early modern uses of the notion of "imperium" any serious cultural concern with territorial expansion (on the Roman model), as opposed to a concern with "sovereignty."

6. This phrase, describing a phenomenon Anderson locates as developing after, and in reaction to, the popular national movements proliferating in Europe since the 1820s, occurs on p. 83 of the 1983 edition of *Imagined Communities*; the phrase is cited and discussed in Howard and Rackin, *Engendering a Nation*, 209.

7. For the term *empire-state*, see Anderson, *English Questions*, 10; for its relevance to recent historical work on England/Britain as a plural entity containing two or more "nations," see Baker, *Between Nations*, 1-25.

8. Blank's innovative research offers a counter to the nationalistic vision of language change underlying two still valuable books about the vernacular in different moments of its "rise": Jones, *The Triumph of the English Language* (1953); and Cottle, *Triumph of English 1350-1400* (1969). My understanding of theories of language intersecting with those of nationalism is especially indebted to Blank's book and also to Beaune, *Naissance de la nation France*; Helgerson, *Forms of Nationhood*; Baker, *Between Nations*; Greenblatt, *Learning to Curse*; McEachern, *Poetics of English Nationhood*; Howard, *The Stage and Social Struggle*; Howard and Rackin, *Engendering a Nation*. I am also indebted to scholars who have written specifically on the linguistic politics of Shakespeare's *Henry V*; see note 55, below.

9. Greenfeld, *Nationalism*, 3. McEachern also sees "English nationhood" as "a sixteenth-century phenomenon," but she places more weight than Greenfeld does on national unity as a problematic ideological fiction (*Poetics of English Nationhood*, 5). Jodi Mikalachki thinks Greenfeld is "premature" (I would say idealistic) in arguing that the idea of *natio* applies for the first time to "the whole people" in sixteenth-century England rather than to an elite (see Mikalachki, *Legacy of Boadicea*, 6-7). For a survey of historians' arguments for and against a sixteenth-century emergence of (some kind of) English nation—especially in relation to the early seventeenth-century (Jacobean) "union" of the British monarchies—see Baker, *Between Nations*, 2-3.

10. The word *patriot* means "fellow countryman" in Latin and retained that meaning when it came into French in the fifteenth century and into English in the sixteenth (*OED*; Huguet, *Dictionnaire*); the first recorded uses of *patriotism* in English and *patriotisme* in French are in the eighteenth century. Some vernacular interpretation of the Latin *patria*, however, was clearly emerging—as the usage by du Bellay mentioned below suggests—to denote an entity larger than one's region of birth and, in some instances, something like the common modern understanding of a "country" or "nation." See Lestocquoy, *Histoire du patriotisme*; and Armstrong, *Nations before Nationalism*, chap. 4, "Polis and Patria."

11. As Marie-Madeleine Martin remarks, *patria* is a term "inherited from the scribes of the later [Roman] Empire" and should not "be allowed to give a false impression concerning the essential anarchy of the Frankish State." Formulas emanating from the Royal Chancellory and using the word *patria* "prove that the clerks were familiar with Latin authors," but "they in no way express what was a reality for the peoples or even for the kings" (*Making of France*, 52-53).

12. See *Quintil Horace*, in du Bellay, *Deffense et illustration* (1549), ed. Chamard, 5; my translation. Chamard attributes the anonymous critique to Barthélemy Aneau; it is cited as Charles Fontaine's in Greenfeld, *Nationalism*, 103, and Martin, *Making of France*, 123.

13. Cited in Greenfeld, *Nationalism*, 98. Compare a later treatise, by Henri Estienne, written in 1579 and entitled *Project du livre intitulé De la precellence du langage françois*; in his preface Estienne equates the "heart" of France with those places where the "nayfveté et pureté" of the language is "le mieux conservée" (Sig e5v).

14. See Rita Copeland's chapter 4, "Translation and Interlingual Commentary," in her *Rhetoric, Hermeneutics, and Translation in the Middle Ages*.

15. See du Bellay, *Deffense et illustration* (1549), ed. Chamard, 168, 178-79; on this vision of the French language as inherently weak, see Ferguson, *Trials of Desire*, 34.

16. Hare, *St. Edwards Ghost* (1647), cited in Jones, *Triumph of the English Language*, 249.

17. See Blank, *Broken English*, 40 and 23 (a lower scholarly estimate, as she notes, is ten thousand new English words).

18. See ibid., 1–2 and passim, on the early modern concept of "difference of English" (a phrase coined by the first English lexicographer, Robert Cawdrey, to signify distinctions between "learned," "rude," "court," and "Country" English; for his *Table Alphabeticall*, see figure 2 in chapter 2, above).

19. For an argument that seventeenth-century "absolutist" monarchies constitute "a subtle but fundamental departure from the concept of universal empire as a supranational hierarchy of authorities," see Armstrong, *Nations before Nationalism*, 168.

20. See Cormack, *Charting an Empire*, on new curricular attention to geography at English universities between 1580 and 1620; on imperial fantasies among the educated classes, see also Knapp, *An Empire Nowhere*; and McLeod, *Geography of Empire*.

21. Cited from *OED* 5a, s.v. *empire*; the *OED* alleges that there are examples of this meaning from as early as the twelfth and thirteenth centuries. According to the *Dictionnaire historique de la langue française*, ed. Rey, *empire* is first used around 1050 "avec le sens 'd'Etat soumis à l'autorité d'un empereur'" (682).

22. See, e.g., Goldberg, *James I*, 27–54, on the king's vision of himself—elaborated by many courtier-poets—as a Roman imperial ruler.

23. Canny, "Origins of Empire," 1; for other articulations of this view see Koebner, *Empire*, 53–55; Armitage, *Ideological Origins of the British Empire*, 30–32; and Armitage, "Literature and Empire."

24. The act (24 Henry VIII, c. 12) is reproduced in Elton, ed., *Tudor Constitution*; the phrase cited is from p. 353.

25. Quoted from Greenfeld, *Nationalism*, 33, citing Elton, *England under the Tudors*. Helgerson also considers the 1530s decisive for the formation of an English nation; he remarks, following Elton, that in that decade "parliament proclaimed England 'an empire,' severed the ties that bound the English Church to the church of Rome, and established the king as 'supreme head' of both church and state" (*Forms of Nationhood*, 4).

26. Cited and discussed in Brotton, *Renaissance Bazaar*, 115.

27. For an introduction to the philological history of *nation, nationalism, empire, country*, and related terms, see Greenfeld, "Nationalism and Language."

28. Loomis, "Nationality at the Council of Constance," 508.

29. For an account of the Schism, see Crowder, *Unity, Heresy and Reform*, 1–3.

30. See ibid., 4; and also Loomis, "Nationality at the Council of Constance," 511.

31. See Oakley, "The *Propositiones utiles* of Pierre d'Ailly"; Oakley, *Council over Pope?* and Oakley, *Political Thought of Pierre d'Ailly*.

32. See Genêt, "English Nationalism," 65; and Loomis, "Nationality at the Council of Constance," 513. For both merchant and university "nations," a common language and similar habits were the prime requisites for the constitution of the group.

33. See Greenfeld, *Nationalism*, 30 and passim; an idealized notion of the American polity arguably underlies her selection of evidence about an England she sees as coming "in fact" (in the 1530s) to be a nation understood as a community of "free and equal individuals."

34. For a discussion of the manuscripts of the *Acta Concilii constanciensis* and their reproduction in sixteenth- and seventeenth-century printed and manuscript texts, such as the British Library's Cotton Cleopatra MS F VIII containing numerous materials "'touching the precedencye of England over some other kingdomes,'" see Genêt, "English Nationalism." The best version of the Anglo-French debate on "nations" is in British Library, Cotton MS Nero E V, a manuscript

evidently written by a professional scribe for Thomas Polton, one of the four official notaries of the council. See also Crowder, *Unity, Heresy and Reform*; Powers, *Nationalism at the Council of Constance*; Finke, "Die Nation in den Spätmittelalterlichen allgemeine Konzilien"; and Loomis, "Nationality at the Council of Constance."

35. See Loomis, "Nationality at the Council of Constance," 517.

36. Crowder discusses the French protest and gives translated excerpts from the texts in *Unity, Heresy and Reform*, 108–10; for the Latin texts, see Finke, ed., *Acta Concilii constanciensis*, 2:89–90; and for a lengthier English translation, see Loomis, "Council of Constance."

37. For an English translation of Polton's reply see Crowder, *Unity, Heresy and Reform*, 111–26.

38. Genêt ("English Nationalism," 74) comments on how Campan carefully distinguishes between "Gallia" and "Francia," whereas Polton's defensive rhetorical position leads him to conflate "Britannia" and "Anglia." On later French humanist efforts to bolster national expansion by referring to their country as "Gallia" rather than "France," see Guenée, *Politique et histoire au Moyen Age*, 50–64.

39. See Genêt, "English Nationalism," 74; and Gwynn, "Ireland and the English Nation."

40. Henry IV of France (r. 1589–1610), for instance, told the people of Bresse and Bugey, on the German side of what is now France, that they should be his subjects "puisque vous parlez naturellement le français" (cited in Guenée, *Politique et histoire au Moyen Age*, 83). For clerks of Henry V who disagree with Polton on the language/nation issue, see Richardson, "Henry V," 741; and Lawrence, *English Church and the Papacy*, 211.

41. See the translation by Crowder, *Unity, Heresy and Reform*, 17: "It is really remarkable that such educated men would want to write that Wales, Ireland or even Scotland are not part of the English nation, because they do not do what the king of England tells them to do."

42. Quoted from Crowder, *Unity, Heresy and Reform*, 120. The final bracketed phrase does not correspond to Crowder's translation. This is important for Allmand's misinterpretation; had he seen that "difference" could better be rendered "diversity," he would have had a harder time making the passage support a one nation–one language interpretation. I quote the original from Von der Hardt, *Magnum oecumenicum Concilium Constantiense*, 5:92. The "Anglicae nationis vindicatio," Polton's reply, covers pp. 76–101 in the same volume. Loomis ("Nationality at the Council of Constance," 525n. 55) quotes the Latin original, but translates *diversitatem linguarem* as "peculiarities of language"—a translation that leads her to share Allmand's view that Polton is defining a nation in terms of a shared or unified language (526). For Chaucer's phrase, see his *Boece*, bk. 2, Prosa 7, line 53: "to the whiche nacyons, what for difficulte of weyes and what for diversite of langages" (*Works*, ed. Robinson, 339). Compare *Troilus and Creseyde*, bk. 5, 1793–94 (in *Works*, ed. Robinson, 479).

43. Beaune, *Naissance de la nation France*, 296–97, quoting and translating from Bibliothèque Nationale, Lat 11730, containing a text by Etienne de Conti. For other examples see ibid., 295–96; and Greenfeld, *Nationalism*, 99 and 510n. 12. I am indebted to Greenfeld's research for sources of this argument in French texts. She does not mention, however, that the same argument occurs also in writings by Englishmen.

44. Blank, *Broken English*, 15; she quotes a critic who links English verbal experimentation with a spirit of adventure that "sent them exploring across half the world."

45. Lewis, "War Propaganda and Historiography," 6, citing the French translation (1460) of Blondel's *Oratio historialis* (1449).

46. For this concept, see Hechter, *Internal Colonialism*; and my prologue.

47. Cited in Lewis, "War Propaganda and Historiography," 13, my translation. For the Salic Law, see Beaune, *Naissance de la nation France*, 267–90.

48. For examples of sixteenth-century printed and manuscript copies of the fifteenth-

century "propaganda" treatises in both French and English, see Lewis, "War Propaganda and Historiography," 15, 20.

49. For a French example from 1532, see Rabelais's comic representation of Panurge engaged in a bawdy gestural debate with "un grand clerc d'Angleterre" [a great English scholar] (*Pantagruel*, in *Oeuvres complètes*, ed. Jourda, 1:312).

50. See Jonathan Baldo, "Wars of Memory in *Henry V*," for a detailed discussion of the play's "reverse or mirror image of the Norman conquest" (141); see also Hill, "Norman Yoke," 57; and Eggert, *Showing Like a Queen*, 86.

51. For evidence that Henry V's military campaigns did a great deal to create an ideology of French national unity that had not existed in the fourteenth century, see Allmand, *Henry V*, 148–50; see also Seward, *Henry V*, especially xix–xx (on the development of a French nationalism in reaction to Henry V's "scourging" of the land).

52. For discussions of the play's representation of sexual conquest, see Wilcox, "Katherine of France as Victim and Bride"; Ostovich, "Teach You Our Princess English?"; Newman, *Fashioning Femininity*, 101; Blank, *Broken English*, 166–67; Howard and Rackin, *Engendering a Nation*, 213–15; Fleming, "*French Garden*," 43–45; and Eggert, "Nostalgia and the Not Yet Late Queen," revised and expanded in *Showing Like a Queen*, chap. 3.

53. Quoted from Kastan, "Shakespeare and English History," 177–78; in what follows about Shakespeare's deviations from history, I continue to draw on Kastan's article.

54. Blank discusses Jamy's speech, and the general "paucity of representations of Scots" in the literature of early modern England in *Broken English*, 159–60. Although James did not come to the throne until four years after *Henry V* is thought to have been written (1599), he was widely seen as Elizabeth's likely successor during the last years of her reign. On the dating of *Henry V*, see Altman, "Vile Participation," especially 2n. 5; and Taylor's introduction to his edition of *Henry V*, 4–8. On the complex relation between the quarto and the Folio versions of the play, see Taylor's introduction; and also Patterson, *Shakespeare and the Popular Voice*, chap. 4.

55. The interpretive field is unusually rich in part because "many critics have staked out Shakespeare's war play as their own battlefield for contesting . . . 'how and why a culture produces and deals with challenges to its dominant ideologies'" (Eggert, *Showing Like a Queen*, quoting Howard, "The New Historicism," 39). See Rabkin, *Shakespeare and the Problem of Meaning*, chap. 2, for a metacritical discussion of the older history of (divided) interpretation; for lucid overviews of recent critical debates among new historicists, feminists, and others concerned with the play's nationalist politics as inflected by ideologies of language and gender, see Baker, *Between Nations*, 20–23; and McEachern, *Poetics of English Nationhood*, 84–86.

56. Edwards, *Threshold of a Nation*, 75–76; see also Baker, *Between Nations*, 31–36; Holderness, "What Is My Nation?" and Altman, "Vile Participation."

57. Mullaney, "Strange Things," 8, 84; see also Neill, "Broken English and Broken Irish."

58. Greenblatt, *Shakespearean Negotiations*, 37; for a similar conclusion, see Sinfield and Dollimore's chapter on *Henry V* in Sinfield, *Faultlines*, especially 121.

59. For the classic study of Fluellen's subversive substitution of *pig* for *big*, see Quint, "Alexander the Pig." See also Baker, *Between Nations*, 53–62; and Blank, *Broken English*, 136–38.

60. See Eggert, *Showing Like a Queen*, 76 and passim; see also McEachern, *Poetics of English Nationhood*, 130–34; and Howard and Rackin on "performative masculinity" (Susan Jefford's phrase) in *Henry V*, in *Engendering a Nation*, 186–215, especially 213.

61. Juliet Fleming notes that the first two words that the princess "asks her teacher to translate, *le pied et la robe*, were used in England to mean respectively one who commits buggery (from pied, meaning variegated) and a female prostitute" ("*French Garden*," 45).

62. On the significance of this renaming and Henry's wooing in general as participating in

a "long tradition, dating at least from the troubadours, that conflates courtship and pedagogy," see Newman, *Fashioning Femininity,* 97–108, especially 103. On "cates" as foods, see Howard and Rackin, *Engendering a Nation,* 192.

63. For Essex's story in relation to the Chorus of *Henry V,* see Taylor's edition, 4–8; for discussions of the ironies in the Chorus's speech, see Patterson, *Shakespeare and the Popular Voice,* 84–88.

64. I am indebted for this point to Howard, *The Stage and Social Struggle,* 150. If I had more space, I would pursue Howard and Rackin's interesting suggestions about symbolic links between Henry V's "Kate," Hotspur's and Petrucchio's wives of the name, and the tavernkeeper Mistress Quickly; see *Engendering a Nation,* 192, 210.

65. See Schleiner, "Divina Virago."

66. James I, "A Speach . . . Delivered . . . the First Day of the First Parliament," cited in Blank, *Broken English,* 156.

67. See Woodbine, "Language of English Law"; and Wilson, "English and French in England."

68. Both passages cited in Allmand, *Henry V,* 420 and nn. 76 and 77.

69. See Fleming, "*French Garden,*" 32; also Fleming, "Dictionary English," 300. See also Lambley, *Teaching and Cultivation,* 264, on women as patrons of French grammars.

70. *John Stubbes's Gaping Gulf with Letters and Other Relevant Documents,* 4. I am indebted to Linda Gregerson for this reference.

71. Kempe, *Die Sprachen des Paradieses* (1683), cited in Fleming, "*French Garden,*" 49n. 20. According to Kempe, God spoke Swedish; Adam, Danish; and the serpent, French. Eve, presumably, was bi- or perhaps trilingual.

72. See Jones and Stallybrass, "Dismantling Irena," especially 161; and Blank, *Broken English,* 167.

73. Compare this with the tale discussed earlier from Caxton's preface; here too, linguistic incomprehension impedes commerce, but the butt of the joke is not a woman but a lower-class English traveler who seeks to buy some lamb to eat. When he asks for "un anel," the French shopkeepers mistake him for a person from Auvergne or from Germany, and they hear him as asking not for "agneau" (lamb), as he intends, but rather for "anel" (ass). I cite the French text from Rathery, *Des relations sociales,* 13.

74. See the selection of Trevisa's translation of Higden's *Polychronicon* in Emerson, *Middle English Reader,* 225; a translation is in Cottle, *Triumph of English,* 22.

75. See Blake, "Standardising Shakespeare's Non-standard Language," 58; he also discusses the battle among the copyists of Chaucer's manuscripts. For the "povre scholars two" whose speech is mocked in the "Reeve's Tale," see *Works of Geoffrey Chaucer,* ed. Robinson, 56–57.

76. See Puttenham, *Arte of English Poesie,* bk. 3, chap. 4, "Of Language," 157; compare 151, where Puttenham mocks a "good old Knight" of Yorkshire for making an "unsavourie" speech, "far from all civilite." The "farness" is geographical as well as linguistic; the old man suffers from "some lack of his teeth" but also from "want of language nothing well spoken." Lynda Mugglestone argues that Puttenham defines the spoken "standard" as a "non-localized" accent based on the conjunction of breeding and place; see "*Talking Proper,*" 23.

77. Cited from Elton, ed., *Tudor Constitution,* 403; all citations from the Tudor Acts of Uniformity are from this volume.

78. The preface to the Great Bible, by the Archbishop of Canterbury, is cited in Sanders and Ferguson's introduction to *Literacies in Early Modern England,* 1. The Act of 1543, cited from *Statutes of the Realm* 3:896, is analyzed and contrasted to the 1406 Statute of Artificers, which allowed men and women of every estate to send both sons and daughters to school, in Sanders, *Gender and Literacy,* 16–17.

79. The middle category of reader is discussed in Bennett, *English Books and Readers,* 27.

80. Cited and translated in Gilmont, "Protestant Reformations," 220; see also Gawthrop and Strauss, "Protestantism and Literacy in Early Modern Germany"; and, on catechisms, Green, "For Children in Yeeres and Children in Understanding."

81. See Bailey, *Images of English,* 28-29, on the rules for English used in efforts to colonize Ireland.

82. Palsgrave, preface to *The Comedye of Acolastus,* cited in ibid., 31.

83. Moryson, *An Itinerary,* 207; discussed in Blank, *Broken English,* 126.

84. Gill, *Logonomia Anglica* (1619), pt. 2, cited in Blank, *Broken English,* 127.

85. Mulcaster, *Positions* (1581), ed. Barker, chap. 43, 262. See Barker's introduction, xv-xvii, for classical precedents for Mulcaster's stress on "uniformity" and his view of education as "a branch of politics."

86. See Goldberg, *Writing Matter,* especially 156-57.

87. Many female teachers had to work also as spinners and farmers to earn a living; see O'Day, *Education and Society,* 167.

88. *De pueris instituendis,* 511b, p. 449 in Margolin's edition; my translation modifies Woodward's, p. 214. For a discussion of this passage, see Halpern, *Poetics of Primitive Accumulation,* 27-28; see also Correll, "Politics of Civility," 638. On the general association Erasmus exemplifies, between lower-class women and dangerous modes of oral discourse, see Fox, *Oral and Literate Culture;* and Lamb, "Old Wives' Tales." For examples and analyses of the modes of popular discourse Erasmus here derides, see Brown, *Better a Shrew Than a Sheep.*

89. Erasmus associates women with those bad schoolmasters who are only teaching because they want money; see *De pueris instituendis,* 514E-516A (pp. 459-61 in Margolin's edition; pp. 220-21 in Woodward's translation).

90. See Wayne, "Advice for Women," 60-61.

91. Erasmus's *New Mother,* translated by a puritan minister named William Burton, is cited from a 1606 edition in Wayne, "Advice for Women," 61; the point about the mother's duty to educate children in Christian virtue but not in letters is made by Edith Snook, "His Open Side Our Book," 164. For other discussions of breast-feeding and its association with the imbibing of good and bad versions of a "mother tongue," see Trubowitz, "But Blood Whitened"; and Bergmann, "Language and 'Mothers' Milk.'"

92. From Spenser's letter to Gabriel Harvey, cited and discussed in Helgerson, *Forms of Nationhood,* chap. 1.

93. *The Greek Grammar of Roger Bacon,* 26, my translation. Bacon uses *loquendi* to refer to the "idiot's" speech, *sermonis* to refer to the language of others. *Sermo* means "connected speech," and early on was associated with a *learned* mode of speech—with oratory, in short, and with the classical notion of style as having various "levels" and rules of decorum to be followed both in oral and in written discourse.

94. See Anderson, *Imagined Communities,* 38, for the assumption that "bulk of mankind" has always been "monoglot"; this assumption discourages inquiry into sites and situations in which bilingualism conferred economic and/or cultural advantages. For the importance of multilingualism to persons in trade, see Lewis, *Later Medieval France,* 4.

95. Jackson, "Language Identity of the Colombian Vaupes Indians," 55. The more than twenty languages of the various exogamous patrilineal descent clans of these Indians are not "dialects" in the common modern understanding of the term; the most closely related pair of languages is, according to one linguist, "considerably more distant . . . than Jutish is from Standard Danish"; areas of differentiation "include grammar and lexicon and, to a lesser extent, phonology" (53).

Interlude

1. See Schleiner, "Margaret Tyler"; and her discussion of women's reading groups across mistress-servant lines in *Tudor and Stuart Women Writers*. Moira Ferguson also suggests that Tyler was a servant (in the Duke of Norfolk's household), but Ferguson also calls attention to evidence for Tyler being of high birth; see Ferguson, ed., *First Feminists*, 51.

2. See Lamb, "Constructions of Women Readers," 24. For a discussion of literacy as "mastery" over the processes of encoding significant cultural information, see de Castell and Luke, "Defining 'Literacy,'" 159.

3. See his *Instruction of a Christen Woman* (*De institutione Christianae feminae*), trans. Hyrde (c. 1529), Sig Hiiiv; cited from the facsimile ed. in Bornstein, ed., *Distaves and Dames*. See also Holm, "Struggling with the Letter"; Kaufman, "Juan Luis Vives"; and Wayne, "Some Sad Sentence."

4. *The Ladies Calling*, pt. 1, sec. 1 ("Of Modesty"), A7 [pp. 8–9].

5. In so doing, she risked a loss of status; see Sanders, *Gender and Literacy*, 105.

6. See Coad's introductory note to her edition of Tyler, *Mirrour of Princely Deedes and Knighthood*, ix–x; see also Trill, "Sixteenth-Century Women's Writing," on the "femininity" of translation; and Krontiris, *Oppositional Voices*, 58–61. My understanding of Tyler's translation as a transgressive cultural gesture is indebted to an unpublished essay by Deborah Uman, "Margaret Tyler's Translation of *The Mirrour of Princely Deedes and Knighthood*."

7. Cited in Schleiner, *Tudor and Stuart Women Writers*, 200. Tyler's translation, licensed in 1578, was printed again in 1580 (STC 18860) and in 1599 (STC 18861); it was popular enough to incur censure not only from Overbury (or one of his associates) but also from Francis Meres, who "condemns *The Mirrour* . . . as inappropriate reading for youth" in his *Palladis Tamia: Wits Miscellany* of 1598 (Tyler, *Mirrour*, ed. Coad, ix).

8. Under English Common Law, the wife's status as *feme covert*, one whose being was "covered" by her husband, was based on the biblical view of husband and wife as "one flesh" (Gen. 2:24), and yet, paradoxically, the wife who is not a separate person from her husband under the law is also a "free person" and not a "servant." See Maclean, *Renaissance Notion of Woman*, 76; he discusses examples of French customary law barring women from administering property, including that which they brought into the marriage, without the "authority and consent of the said husband." For a fuller discussion of the complex and much-debated question of women's legal standing in French and English territories, see Erickson, *Women and Property*; and Petot and Vandenbossche, "Statut de la femme dans les pays coutumiers français."

9. For the Freudian lineage of the "court of conscience," see Ferguson, *Trials of Desire*, 163–84.

Chapter Four

1. *Book of the City of Ladies*, trans. Richards, bk. 1, sec. 8:1, p. 16; all citations are to this translation (based on British Library, Harley 4431) unless otherwise indicated and are followed by references to the French text prepared as a dissertation by Maureen Cheney Curnow, "The *Livre de la Cité des Dames* of Christine de Pisan: A Critical Edition," which is based on the illuminated copy presented by de Pizan herself to Duke Jean de Berry (Bibliothèque Nationale, f. fr. 697). Curnow collates her text with two other manuscripts of the *Cité*, the production of which was also evidently overseen by the author (British Library, Harley 4431, and Brussels, Bibliothèque Royale, 9393). For discussions of the manuscripts and of the evidence that de Pizan herself copied portions of the early illustrated "presentation" manuscripts, see Hicks and Ouy, "Second 'Autograph' Edition"; and Schaefer, "Die Illustrationen zu den Handschriften." Curnow's French text,

abbreviated as "Fr.," is cited by volume and page number and is quoted when textual issues are critical to my argument.

2. For biographical information see Willard, *Christine de Pizan*; and McLeod, *Order of the Rose*. On the term *clergesce*, see page 216 in this volume. Many modern critics refer to this writer as "Christine," following a convention of medieval nomenclature that de Pizan herself deployed in significant ways: see Quilligan, *Allegory of Female Authority*, 14-16, on the formula "Je, Christine"; and see also Regnier-Bohler, "Imagining a Self," 389. Christine de Pizan also, however, uses her name of ancestral origin at key moments of self-definition, e.g., "Moy, Christine de Pisan, femme soubz les tenebres d'ignorance" [I, Christine de Pizan, a woman beneath the shade of ignorance] (prologue to the *Livre des fais et bonnes meurs*, ed. Solente, 5). I refer to this writer and others by (one of) their family names not because this is a perfect solution to the problem of naming female writers (it isn't, for reasons further discussed and annotated in chapter 6 n. 18), but rather because this practice has the virtue of not separating "medieval" women from the later ones discussed here. It also marks the writer as an agent embedded in a social world, which is sometimes, as in the cases of Christine de Pizan and Marguerite de Navarre, a distinctly spatialized world as well. "De Pizan" reminds us that this writer came from a family that emigrated to the French court from Pizzano. Her grandfather, like her father and husband, was a "clerc licencie," as she notes in *Lavision-Christine*, pt. 3, ed. Towner, 149.

3. On de Pizan's differently sited patrons, see Carroll, "Christine de Pizan and the Origins of Peace Theory," 25; see also Laidlaw, "Christine de Pizan, the Earl of Salisbury and Henry IV," 129-43.

4. Much has been written on her multiple writerly personae, which vary in a way that her visual images do not. I thank Lys Ann Shore for drawing my attention to this last point. On her verbal self-portraits, see especially Brownlee, "Discourses of the Self"; Brownlee, "Ovide et le moi poétique 'moderne'"; Walters, "Chivalry and the (En)gendered Poetic Self"; Quilligan, *Allegory of Female Authority*; Jacqueline Cerquiglini-Toulet, "L'Etrangère" (on de Pizan's "privileged marginality"); Blanchard, "Compilation and Legitimation"; and Zühlke, "Christine de Pizan." On medieval concepts of the author more generally, see Minnis, *Medieval Theory of Authorship*; and Chartier, *Order of Books*.

5. *Christine's Vision*, pt. 1, trans. McLeod, 15-16; the original French is in *Lavision-Christine*, ed. Towner, 77-78. The allegorical lady's name plays on two etymological traditions: the Frankish people were said to be descended from Francio, ancient son of the Trojan Hector; and their name also was said to come from the Latin for "freedmen." On de Pizan's use of female personifications for Latin abstract nouns of the female gender, see Quilligan, *Allegory of Female Authority*, 23-26; on this medieval practice more generally, see Ferrante, *Woman as Image*, 38-64.

6. See Walters, "Woman Writer and Literary History," 42. See also Zühlke, "Christine de Pizan," 233. For biblical and classical sources for medieval uses of this theory, see Goez, *Translatio Imperii*, chaps. 1 and 2; see also Gilson, *Les Idées et les lettres*, 183-85. De Pizan also yokes her own story with the *translatio imperii* theory by stressing the Trojan origins of her native city, Venice; see *"Le Livre de la mutacion de fortune,"* ed. Solente, 2:19, lines 4753-4826.

7. On this tradition, see Davis, "'Women's History' in Transition." De Pizan also draws on the tradition of the *speculum dominarum* (mirror of women); see McCash, "Cultural Patronage: An Overview," 29-30. For debates about the political valence of de Pizan's feminist discourse, see Quilligan, *Allegory of Female Authority*; Delany, "History, Politics, and Christine Studies"; and Delany, "Mothers to Think Back Through."

8. For the ban on mentioning the Great Schism or the pope, see Delany, "Mothers to Think Back Through," 93.

9. See Carroll, "Christine de Pizan," 29-30, contrasting de Pizan with male "universal

monarchists," such as Dante, Marsilius of Padua, and Pierre Dubois. See also Hindman, *Christine de Pizan's "Epistre d'Othéa,"* 169–79; Brabant's introduction to *Politics, Gender, and Genre,* and various essays in this volume, especially those by E. J. Richards and E. Hicks; Krynen, *Idéal du prince*; Wisman, "L'Eveil du sentiment national au Moyen Age"; Dulac, "Authority in the Prose Treatises of Christine de Pizan."

10. For evidence on the book's patron and dating, see Willard, *Christine de Pizan,* 176–77. Earl Jeffrey Richards, however, suggests that the *Livre du corps de policie* may not have been finished before 1407; see Richards, "Christine de Pizan, the Conventions of Courtly Diction, and Italian Humanism," 263.

11. For this idealizing view of the Roman empire, see *Le Livre du corps de policie,* ed. Lucas, bk. 1, chap. 14 ("De liberalité en prince et exemples des Rommains"), 43–44.

12. For her interest in contemporary debates about the "just war," see Willard, *Christine de Pizan,* 184. One of de Pizan's positive examples of such a war—not mentioned by Carroll—was the one that followed the Treaty of Brétigny in 1369. De Pizan praised Charles V's military activities in the *Livre du corps de policie*; her *Livre des fais d'armes et de chivalerie* (1410), containing detailed descriptions of military matters, was translated and printed by Caxton in 1489 at the request of Henry VII—who used it, ironically enough, to bolster an unpopular military campaign against France.

13. See Willard, *Christine de Pizan,* 182–83, for the Duke of Burgundy's efforts—and those made by clerks loyal to his cause—to obtain a pardon from the king for the assassination of the "tyrant" of Orléans. De Pizan argues against tyrannicide in the *Livre du corps de policie,* citing St. Paul on the Christian subject's "absolute" duty to obey God's earthly ministers.

14. Even before she began to write extended works for patrons, she had evidently begun to earn her living in clerkly ways by copying manuscripts; her cursive handwriting was similar to that used by male clerks of the French royal chancellery and probably reflects the tutelage of her father and also her husband, both highly educated men employed by the crown; see Willard, *Christine de Pizan,* 47.

15. See *Inferno,* 1:83, where Dante tells Vergil, "vagliami 'l lungo studio e 'l grande amore / che m'ha fatto cercar lo tuo volume" [May the long study and great love avail me / that have made me search out your volume]; cited from *La Divina Commedia,* ed. Grandgent, 17. On this allusion see Richards, "Christine de Pizan and Sacred History," 24; and De Rentiis, "Sequere me," 31–42.

16. See *Chemin de long estude,* ed. Püschel, lines 2253 and following. My paraphrase is indebted to that of Zühlke, "Christine de Pizan," 234.

17. Although the *Cité* was included in a copy of her works that de Pizan presented to Isabeau of Bavaria, who is complimented in the text as the reigning queen of France (see Fr., 3:967), it seems unlikely that de Pizan expected substantial patronage from this queen, who lost public esteem in 1405 (see Quilligan, *Allegory of Female Authority,* 246–47). Some of the ideological differences between the *Cité* and its apparently more conservative continuation, the *Trésor de la cité des dames,* may have to do with the status of the latter as a bid for new patronage from Marguerite de Guyenne, the new wife of the dauphin, Louis; see Willard, *Christine de Pizan,* 146; and her "Manuscript Tradition of the *Livre des Trois Vertues.*"

18. *Lavision-Christine,* pt. 3, ed. Towner, 154, my translation.

19. Ibid. See p. 153 for her comments on her father's charity and, for a discussion of documents pertaining to her support of her mother and the niece whose dowry she paid in 1406, see de Pizan, "*Les Sept Psaumes Allegorisés,*" ed. Rains, 54–55.

20. Cited from *Le Livre des fais et bonnes meurs,* ed. Solente, 2:21. For Italian humanists' theories of prudence—and its intimate association with rhetoric—see Kahn, *Rhetoric, Prudence, and Skepticism,* especially chaps. 2 and 3.

21. On de Pizan's invention of this name, perhaps from the Greek formula "O thea," used to invoke Minerva, goddess of wisdom, see Hindman, *Christine de Pizan's "Epistre Othéa,"* 23; see also Hindman's discussion of early manuscript illustrations (plates 5 and 6) that reinforce the work's extended allegorical parallel between Othea and the female writer in her self-elected role as royal adviser.

22. See *Lavision-Christine,* pt. 3, ed. Towner, 165, and *Christine's Vision,* trans. McLeod, 120. On her paradoxical role as "female clerk," see Walters, "Woman Writer and Literary History"; Walters, "Fathers and Daughters"; and McLeod and Wilson, "Clerk in Name Only."

23. See Bornstein, "French Influence," 369-86. See also Gay, "Language of Christine de Pizan," 117-33.

24. E.g., "la premiere naissance et racine des roys de France" ("the first birth and root of the French kings") in the title of chap. 5 of *Le Livre des fais et bonnes meurs,* ed. Solente, 1:12. De Pizan herself often mentions a desire to avoid *prolixité* even as she develops a highly dilatory style. See Dulac, "De l'art de la digression dans *Le Livre des fais.*"

25. Early illuminators portray de Pizan (or her muses) addressing audiences of both men and women; see, for instance, the representation of "the virtues lecturing to court women of different ages," from a manuscript of the *Trésor de la cité des dames* held in the Yale University Library and reproduced in Quilligan, *Allegory of Female Authority,* 262.

26. For these and other Vergilian uses of the verb, see Hexter, "Sidonian Dido," 359.

27. De Pizan's return to the Dido story occurs in part 2, 55.1. The division of the Dido story exemplifies a technique of narrative fragmentation central to the book's effort to revise common opinions (*doxa*) about the female sex. For studies of her version of the story—the longest exemplum in part 1—see Desmond, *Reading Dido,* chap. 6; Baswell, *Virgil in Medieval England,* 279-81; and Quilligan, *Allegory of Female Authority,* 101-3, 171-73.

28. *Christine's Vision,* pt. 3, trans. McLeod, 117; for the French see *Lavision-Christine,* ed. Towner, 161. I thank Lys Ann Shore for calling my attention to this passage.

29. Boccaccio's *De claris mulieribus* was composed and revised between 1358 and 1374. See Jeanroy, "Boccace et Christine de Pizan"; and *"Livre de la Cité des Dames,"* ed. Curnow, 1:138. Curnow thinks that de Pizan used not the original Latin but rather the 1401 translation of Boccaccio's text that has been doubtfully attributed to Laurent de Premierfait. The 1401 translation would have been available to de Pizan, for there was a copy in the library of Jean de Berry. Curnow identifies this manuscript with Bibliothèque Nationale, f. fr. 12420; for a contrary view, see Bozzolo, *Manuscrits des traductions françaises,* 24. I have examined microfilms of MS 12420, along with another copy from the same manuscript family, British Library, Royal 16 G.V. While agreeing with Curnow that there are direct verbal parallels between the 1401 *Cleres femmes* (as I shall henceforth refer to this text) and the *Cité* (see Curnow's examples, 1:142), I maintain, as does Pinet, *Christine de Pizan,* that de Pizan also draws on the Latin text. My examination of the two *Cleres femmes* MSS does not, in any case, suggest that de Pizan's deviations from Boccaccio's text were anticipated by the presumably male translator. A full study of this translation in relation to de Pizan's text remains to be done. For recent discussions of de Pizan's use of *De claris mulieribus* (which do not deal with the 1401 translation), see Quilligan, *Allegory of Female Authority;* Philippy, "Establishing Authority"; and Schibanoff, "Taking the Gold Out of Egypt," 99-100.

30. Boccaccio's "De Didone seu Elissa Cartaginensium regina" is on pp. 166-79 of *Famous Women,* ed. Brown; all my citations are from this dual-language edition. My citations of the 1401 *Cleres femmes* are from Bibliothèque Nationale, f. fr. 12420, which has no signature or folio numbers; for reference purposes I have numbered pages 1a, 1b, etc. for each separate story cited.

31. On de Pizan's unsuccessful legal battles after Etienne du Castel's death, see Willard, *Christine de Pizan,* 39-40; for a different interpretation of these historical battles and their literary

refractions, see Quilligan, *Allegory of Female Authority*, 66–67. For French legal debates about widows' property, see the essays in Mirrer, ed., *Upon My Husband's Death*.

32. De Pizan, *Cité*, 92; Fr., 2:771; de Pizan also uses the words *prudence, cautelle, scavoir*, and *scens* to describe Dido's cunning knowledge. The 1401 translation has the phrase *grant cautele et malice* on p. 3a. In *Famous Women*, Boccaccio writes of Dido's "shrewdly devised plan" [excogitata astutia] (168–69) and apostrophizes her feminine cleverness ("O mulieris astutia!" [170]), though he eventually shows her being duped.

33. Boccaccio presents the chaste Dido of the non-Vergilian tradition, although he gives an interesting cameo appearance to an Aeneas whom Dido "never saw" (*Famous Women*, 175). For Boccaccio's renderings of Dido's tale here and in other of his works, see Desmond, *Reading Dido*, 58–73. She analyzes de Pizan's various treatments of Dido in chap. 6.

34. This is my literal translation of the phrase; it has no analogue in Boccaccio's Latin text or in the 1401 *Cleres femmes*.

35. *Cité*, 92; Fr., 2:771: "elle savoit bien que son frere, aussitost que il saroit son allee, envoyeroit après; et pour ce, fist emplir secretement grosses males, bahus et grans fardiaux de choses pesans de nulle vallue, comme ce fust son tresor, adfin que en baillant ycelles malles et ses fardiaux a ceulx que son frere envoyeroit après, ilz la laissassent aler et n'empeschassent son erre."

36. See Boccaccio, *Famous Women*, 352–53, and *Cleres femmes*, Cornificia episode, 1b: "elle fu equalle en gloire et excellence."

37. For Boccaccio's technique of the "negative example," see Jordan, "Boccaccio's In-famous Women," 28.

38. *Famous Women*, 354–55; *Cleres femmes*, Cornificia episode, 2a. See Jordan, "Boccaccio's In-famous Women," 28–29.

39. I have modified Richards's translation here to render the original more literally. It goes as follows: "Et les puet on prendre par la rigle de grammaire qui se nomme antifrasis qui s'entant, si comme tu sces, si comme on diroit tel est mauvais, c'est a dire que il est bon, et aussi a l'opposite. Si te conseille que tu faces ton prouffit de leurs diz et que tu l'entendes ainsi, quel que fust leur entente, es lieux ou ilz blasment les femmes."

40. Susan Noakes observes that de Pizan compares reading to a game of chess in the *Epistre d'Othéa*; Noakes argues with respect to that text, as do I with respect to the *Cité des dames*, that de Pizan sought to teach her readers how to interpret her own allegories (*Timely Reading*, 112–13).

41. Proba's story is number 97 of Boccaccio's *Famous Women*, 410–17. For the Latin text see Proba, *Cento Virgilianus*. Schnapp, "Reading Lessons," 118–19, notes that Proba's *Cento* was used as a textbook in some medieval schools. My thinking about Proba owes much to a graduate seminar paper by Deborah Uman.

42. Richards's translation errs, I believe, precisely on this question of intention, for he renders Rayson's words as "I advise you to profit from their works and to interpret them in the manner in which they are intended in those passages where they [the poets] attack women" (7). But the French text states that the reader ought to *invert* the original intent. For the full passage, see note 39, above.

43. Quilligan makes this point in *Allegory of Female Authority*, 97. For Boccaccio's use of the Aesculapian model to describe his own (quite risky) venture of bringing "life"—in a Christian era—to fragmented stories of pagan gods, see Osgood, *Boccaccio on Poetry*, 13. Osgood's text is a translation of the preface and books 14 and 15 of the *Genealogia deorum gentilium*.

44. "Many will rise up against my work," he writes, and "will seize it with their impious jaws and tear it to pieces" (Osgood, *Boccaccio on Poetry*, 17). A fear that his own work is "impious" is here projected onto the hostile reader.

45. Quilligan, *Allegory of Female Authority*, 98.

46. See Augustine, *On Christian Doctrine*, sec. 40, trans. Robertson, 75.

47. Richards evidently interprets "resourdant" as deriving from the verb *sourdre* (from the Latin *surgere*), "to spring up"; I suggest, however, that de Pizan's participial adjective derives from *sourd*, "deaf." Compare the recent Italian translation of the *Cité* by Patrizia Caraffi, who chooses *assordante*, "deafening," to render de Pizan's "resourdant" (*La Città delle dame*, 45).

48. Matheolus, *Lamentations*, 3, 1425–30, cited in "*Livre de la Cité des Dames*," ed. Curnow, 1:231, my translations.

49. For a persuasive analysis of why Semiramis comes "first"—and is subsequently buried by other foundation stones—see Quilligan, *Allegory of Female Authority*, 69–85.

50. I owe this phrase to Quilligan, *Allegory of Female Authority*, 66; although I disagree with her conclusions about de Pizan's view of the law and of women's language, I have learned a lot from her arguments.

51. Boccaccio refers to her as "Nicaula Etyhyopum regina" in his title and later remarks that in "Sacred Scripture" she is called Saba (*Famous Women*, Story 43, 180, 183). The 1401 *Cleres femmes* refers to this figure as "Nicaule reine des ethiopies" and in the same story mentions the figure's biblical name as "Sabe." De Pizan has added the notion of "empress."

52. For the Christian iconography of Solomon and Sheba, see Watson, "Queen of Sheba in Christian Tradition," 115–45. Matheolus had described Solomon as "led astray" by women; de Pizan vigorously refutes Matheolus and others who offered negative judgments on Sheba. See "*Livre de la Cité des Dames*," ed. Curnow, 3:1080n. 137.

53. See Watson, "Queen of Sheba in Christian Tradition," 116. Prudentius is describing "an ideal programme of decoration for Christian basilicas based on the symbolical concordance of the Old and New Testaments." For an interpretive tradition hostile to the queen, see Lassner, *Demonizing the Queen of Sheba.*

54. Watson, "Queen of Sheba in Christian Tradition," 116.

55. On Hrabanus and Josephus's use of the name "Nikaulis" or "Nikaule," see Silberman, "Queen of Sheba in Jewish Tradition," 67. Silberman also notes that some Byzantine chronicles identify the Queen of Sheba with the Sibyl Sabbe; de Pizan may have known this tradition since she discusses Sheba immediately after three sections on "the ten Sybils," which open part 2.

56. Watson, "Queen of Sheba in Christian Tradition," 122.

57. In a passage Christine omits, Boccaccio has the queen "confess" that Solomon's wisdom "far surpassed his reputation and the capacity of the human intellect" (*Famous Women*, Story 43, 182–83).

58. For new evidence of de Pizan's sophistication as a theorist of allegory, see Reno, "The Preface to the *Avision-Christine*."

59. For the theme of truth eventually emerging—often by the forced confession of the man who has oppressed the woman—in some of the longer stories Droitture relates in part 2, see the stories of, e.g., Griselda, Florence of Rome, and the wife of Bernabo. These stories anticipate the "delayed revelations" of Sts. Marina and Euphrosyna in part 3.

60. See Brownlee, "Martyrdom and the Female Voice," 125.

61. Quilligan, *Allegory of Female Authority*, 242. See also Brownlee, "Martyrdom and the Female Voice," 131.

62. Quoted from the English translation of Na (Domina) Prous Boneta's confession, dictated in Provençal to a court notary and taken down in Latin, in Petroff, ed., *Medieval Women's Visionary Literature*, 285; for the original (i.e., translated) Latin text, see May, "Confession of Prous Boneta, Heretic and Heresiarch."

63. Quoted from *The Writings of Margaret of Oingt*, trans. Blumenfeld-Kosinski, 43–45.

64. D'Oingt wrote her *Meditationes* in Latin; her *Miroir* is in a form of Franco-Provençal. See *Les Oeuvres de Marguerite d'Oingt*, ed. Duraffour, Gardette, and Durdilly.

65. Porete's *Mirouer des simples ames* is quoted from the edition by Guarnieri, 588.

66. For an example of this ambiguity, compare Droitture's description of the city as a "per-petual residence for as long as the world endures" at the end of part 2 (215; Fr., 2:971) with Justice's statement, at the end of part 3, proclaiming the city virtually identical to Augustine's *Civitas Dei* but also, much more than Augustine's, an ever-expanding home for "all the holy ladies who have lived, who are living, and who will live" (254; Fr., 2:1031). For the "celestial gynaeceum," see Schulenberg, "Sexism and the Celestial Gynaeceum."

67. "The most learned, systematic, and 'scientific' of medieval inventors of prophetic sys-tems," Joachim of Flora (d. 1202) was also highly influential (Johnson, *History of Christianity*, 257). See also Bett, *Joachim of Flora*; Bloomfield and Reeves, "Penetration of Joachism into North-ern Europe."

68. Christie-Murray, *History of Heresy*, 111. Two modern scholars feel that Olivi's ideas were "distorted" by Na Prous Boneta—the battles over the line between orthodoxy and heresy con-tinue. See Wakefield and Evans, *Heresies of the High Middle Ages*, 761n. 11.

69. Petroff, ed., *Medieval Women's Visionary Literature*, 277. For a complete text of the trial record (which of course is not a complete record of what Na Prous said), see May, "Confession of Prous Boneta, Heretic and Heresiarch," 3–30.

70. Guarnieri, "Il Movimento," 359; for a general history of the movement see Lerner, *Her-esy of the Free Spirit in the Middle Ages*.

71. On the iconography of the fortified city, see Paster, *Idea of the City*, 4.

72. Na Prous Boneta, Marguerite Porete, and also Joan of Arc, whose heroism de Pizan herself would praise in her late *Ditié de Jehanne d'Arc*, led lives that correspond to the pattern repeatedly illustrated in part 3 of the *Cité*.

73. Petroff, ed., *Medieval Women's Visionary Literature*, 277.

74. Caroline Bynum has done much to bring some of these women's writings to scholarly notice; she discusses Marguerite d'Oingt among many others in *Jesus as Mother* and *Holy Feast*. Petroff credits Marguerite d'Oingt with bringing "two new perspectives to mystical writing by women. The first is the idea that the visionary is not a vessel but a text, a body in whom or on whom a text is inscribed. The second point is her emphasis on the act of writing; the text written within her is physically transferred by her to the pages of a book" (*Medieval Women's Visionary Literature*, 278).

75. See Bloomfield, "Joachim of Flora," 257; and, on his influence on female and male mys-tics, see Grundmann, *Religious Movements*, 156.

76. Guarnieri, "Il Movimento," 359, 438.

77. The report of this beguine's life and works comes from Henricus Pomerius (1382–1454); in his *Vita domini J. Rusbrochi*, Pomerius bases his account of Bloemardinne on testimony of a close companion of the spiritual leader Ruusbroec; see Guarnieri, "Il Movimento," 438 and n. 10.

78. Gerson, *Oeuvres magistrales*, in *Oeuvres complètes*, ed. Glorieux, 3:51. On the dating and (wide) manuscript distribution of this text, see the editor's introduction, x.

79. Guarnieri, "Il Movimento," 461–62; for information on Porete's life I am also indebted to Eve Rachele Sanders's unpublished paper, "*Auctor* and *Auctoritas* in Marguerite Porete's *The Mir-ror of Simple Souls*."

80. Discussing miracles that can be known to be false because of their "little utility," Gerson remarks on this woman who was convinced that she was Christ in the paragraph immediately preceding his mention of Maria de Valenciennes's book (*Oeuvres*, 3:51–52).

81. By intervening in and literally making public an early fifteenth-century debate among intellectuals about the literary merits of Jean de Meun's part of the *Romance of the Rose*, de Pizan entered a discursive domain occupied by a group of men associated with the University of Paris and with the Royal Chancellory. Among these were Gerson, and possibly his teacher Pierre d'Ailly, who participated in the Council of Constance, discussed in chapter 3. Gerson became de Pizan's ally through his concern that parts of the *Rose* would spark lascivious thoughts among male clerkly readers, distracting them from their labors for Church and monarchy. See Willard, *Christine de Pizan*, 78.

82. Gerson quotes only line 52, "An qui amant"; I have given the fuller Vergilian context, citing the Loeb edition of the *Eclogues*, 64-65 (translation modified).

83. For Porete's diction and style, see Levine's note to his translation of an excerpt from the *Mirouer* in Petroff, ed., *Medieval Women's Visionary Literature*, 295.

84. I do not have space to undertake the detailed comparison of Porete's *Mirouer* and de Pizan's *Cité* that needs to be done; see especially Porete's chapter 87, "How This Soul Is [a] Lady of Virtue and [a] Daughter of the Deity" ("Comment ceste Ame est dame des Vertuz et fille de la Deite"), and her chapter 132, where "Justice, Misericorde et Amour" come to visit the Soul as she emerges from her "enfance."

85. Discussing the 297 errors which the bishop of Paris had condemned in the curriculum of the University of Paris in 1277, David Hult remarks that Jean de Meun's poem shows his "intimate knowledge" of the university milieu ("Jean de Meun's Continuation of *Le Roman de la Rose*," 97-98).

86. The account of sending the manuscript to the three authorities is missing in the three extant French manuscripts of the *Mirouer*, one of which (the so-called Chantilly manuscript written between 1450 and 1530) is the basis for Guarnieri's edition; the passage appears in Doiron, ed., "Marguerite Porete."

87. Sanders, "*Auctor* and *Auctoritas*," quoting from a translation of the Latin text of Porete's excommunication in Frederiq, *Corpus documentorum*, 158-60.

88. *Mirouer*, ed. Guarnieri, 504.

89. See Shell, ed., *Elizabeth's Glass*, which includes a facsimile of Elizabeth's handwritten text. See also Prescott, "Pearl of the Valois and Elizabeth I."

90. See Walters, "Fathers and Daughters," 63.

91. See above, note 7, on the tradition of the *speculum dominarum*.

92. On the convention of referring to the "visionary self" in the third person, which dates back at least to St. Paul, see Blumenfeld-Kosinski's introduction to *Writings of Margaret of Oingt*, 16n. 1.

93. *Les Grandes chroniques de la France*, cited in Guarnieri, "Il Movimento," 412, my translation. The terms *beguine* and *beguin* were used from the early thirteenth century onward, mostly in pejorative contexts, to designate various individuals and religious groups "of unconventional character, both orthodox and heretical," living in both northern and southern parts of France; see Wakefield and Evans, *Heresies of the High Middle Ages*, 702n. 8.

94. For a partial English translation of de Coinci's "Life of Saint Christina," and for information on the extant manuscripts of the texts, one of which dates from the early fourteenth century, see Cazelles, *Lady as Saint*, 138-50.

95. For information about de Pizan's revisions of her main sources in part 3, I am indebted to my former student Sarah Cardelus.

96. For a discussion and translation of Vergil's lines (*Aeneid*, 1.367-68), which describe the bull's hide trick being performed not by Dido but by an undifferentiated group of future Car-

thaginians, see Baswell, "Dido's Purse," 163; he also gives an illuminating history of the Greek word *byrsa*, which goes from signifying "bull's hide" to signifying a leather bag or purse; eventually (by the twelfth century), it was also used figuratively to mean "payment" or "stipend."

97. *Boke of the Cyte of Ladyes,* Sig Aaiv-r, cited in Summit, *Lost Property,* 95; a facsimile of Ansley's translation with Pepwell's preface is in Bornstein, ed., *Distaves and Dames.*

98. On figurings and erasures of de Pizan's gendered identity as a writer in later English versions of her books, see Rooks, "*Boke of the Cyte of Ladyes* and Its Sixteenth-Century Readership"; see also Chance, "Christine de Pizan as Literary Mother"; Chance, "Gender Subversion and Linguistic Castration"; and McLeod, ed., *Reception of Christine de Pizan.*

99. Summit, *Lost Property,* 99. On Henry's concern about his potency, see also Lerer, *Courtly Letters,* 44.

100. I am indebted for this information, and for the citation of Henry's will, to Levin, "*The Heart and Stomach of a King,*" 7.

101. See Bell, "New Approach to the Influence of Christine de Pizan: The Lost Tapestries." The implications of Bell's argument are explored in Summit, *Lost Property,* 94–95; and in Malcolmson, "Christine de Pizan's *City of Ladies.*"

102. Ames argues that Anne Boleyn entered de Navarre's service when she was still Duchess of Alençon; see his introduction to *Elizabeth,* "*The Mirror of the Sinful Soul,*" 31, cited in Shell, ed., *Elizabeth's Glass,* 291n. 2.

103. On evidence for a manuscript copy of de Pizan's works in de Navarre's library, see Reynolds-Cornell, "L'Education sous le manteau," 8.

104. See Roelker, *Queen of Navarre,* 208 and passim.

105. Cited from the translation in ibid., 127. The original, partly transcribed in Roelker, is in Bibliothèque Nationale, f. fr. 17044, fol. 446, "Jeanne to the Vicomte de Gourdon."

Chapter Five

1. In the epigraphs to this chapter, the lines from Porete's *Mirouer* are from fol. 6r, lines 8–14 of Guarnieri's edition of the manuscript; the translation is mine. Although the book was condemned by the Church, it clearly circulated across various political and linguistic boundaries; for a discussion of Latin, Italian, English, and French versions, see Doiron, "Middle English Translation." The translation of de Navarre's *Prisons* is by Hilda Dale, bk. 3, 1375–80, 1403–4, 1543–44, pp. 86–90. The original text is in *Les Prisons,* ed. Glasson, 181–87. It begins as follows: "Gentil Loing Près, celle qui t'appell / Par ung tel nom à mon gré myeulx parla / Que [le] docteur qui tant a travaillé / D'estudier. Dont je m'esmerveillay / Comme ung esprit d'une vierge si basse / Fut si remply de la divine grace."

2. On her translation of Luther (*Le Pater Noster, fait en translation et dialogue par le reine de Navarre,* 1527), and on her reputation as "the most Evangelical" lady of France, see Defaux, "Evangelism," 164; on her religious views more generally, and on those of her mother, see Roelker, "Appeal of Calvinism to French Noblewomen"; Blaisdell, "Calvin's Letters to Women," especially 75–76; Heller, "Marguerite of Navarre and the Reformers"; and Lyons (on her "Protestant poetics") in "The *Heptaméron* and the Foundation of Critical Narrative."

3. See Joseph Allaire's edition of the *Miroir,* which discusses and prints the texts of the three poems in the 1531 volume; the translation of the Salve Regina is on pp. 87–88 of this edition. See also Sommers, "The Mirror and Its Reflections."

4. On Calvin's attack, see Shell, ed., *Elizabeth's Glass,* 46; on the three printings of the *Miroir* in 1533, see Jourda, *Marguerite d'Angoulême,* 1:178. Although the book was prohibited for a brief

period in 1533, no official condemnation was ever formulated and the faculty soon denied its previous actions. Modern scholars do not fully agree on the details of this story of aborted censorship; see, e.g., Ferguson, *Mirroring Belief,* 57–58; and the introduction to *"The Prisons" of Marguerite de Navarre,* ed. Dale, ix.

5. See *Miroir,* ed. Allaire, 20–21. He examined de Navarre's personal copy of Lefèvre d'Etaples's rare French Bible (1530) and found eighty-four exact citations from it in the margins of the *Miroir* (22). Scholars differ in their explanations for the prohibition; a tradition dating back to Théodore de Bèze holds that the book was condemned for theological "sins of omission," e.g., "the absence of the notion of merit and the doctrine of purgatory" (Ferguson, *Mirroring Belief,* 57). On Catholic anxieties about vernacular translations of Scripture, see Bedouelle, "Le Débat catholique sur la traduction de la Bible en langue vulgaire."

6. Lefèvre d'Etaples, *Prefatory Epistles,* cited and translated in Defaux, "Evangelism," 165; the preface by the printer, Antoine Augureau, is also cited and translated by Defaux, 166.

7. Swanson, "Literacy, Heresy, History and Orthodoxy," 291, briefly discussing the fate of Porete's book; for further information on how it was circulated and received, see above, chapter 4; and Doiron, "Middle English Translation," 133–34.

8. On the "undefined" profile of early French Protestantism, see Potter, *History of France,* 242–43; see also Molinier, "Aux origines de la Réformation Cévenole," especially 240; and Febvre, *Au coeur religieux,* 12–13.

9. There are useful discussions of the tale as one of several versions of the "Marguerite de Roberval" legend—see especially Stabler, *Legend of Marguerite de Roberval;* and Russell, "Quatre versions d'une légende canadienne"—but so far as I know only Elaine Ancekewicz, in "L'Ecriture du Nouveau Monde," has analyzed the story in relation to de Navarre's general theological concerns and narrative practices in the *Heptaméron.*

10. For suggestive connections between Defoe's novel and Thevet's (very different) version of the female castaway story told in the *Heptaméron,* see Campbell, *Wonder and Science,* 36–37.

11. According to the *OED,* the "arquebus" was an early modern and specifically French gun. De Navarre's reference to it, as Heather James has suggested to me in a personal communication, may serve to place a historically and culturally specific object in an otherwise allegorized narrative that took shape in relation to Old Testament and classical models; among the latter, Camilla and Dido seem especially pertinent. The "arquebus" replacing Camilla's bow and Dido's bull's hide device for securing territory would dramatize the way in which the moral significance of de Navarre's tale involves a staging of a "return" to France and to the present.

12. Citations to the *Heptaméron* are, first, to the English translation by Chilton, with some modifications noted when they occur, followed by the page numbers of the French text, ed. François. François's edition is based on Bibliothèque Nationale, fr. 1512, which has remarkably "uniform" orthography and was evidently copied soon after de Navarre's death. François notes the variants given in the manuscript prepared by Adrien de Thou (fr. 1524) with a preface dated August 1553. The first published edition, from 1558, was entitled *Histoires des amans fortunez.* See *L'Heptaméron,* ed. François, xi–xxix. The pages cited here are *Heptaméron,* 504; Fr., 394.

13. See Cottrell, *Grammar of Silence,* 301.

14. Pierre de Bourdeille, Seigneur de Brantôme, *Oeuvres complètes,* ed. Lalanne, 8:125–26. On this passage and on de Navarre's composition of the text in general, see Bideaux, *"L'Heptaméron": De l'enquête au débat,* 13–36.

15. Brantôme elsewhere reports her referring to her "Cent Nouvelles," a title that stresses the relationship of her work to Boccaccio's *Decameron;* for an argument about the significance of these references, see Duval, "Et puis, quelles nouvelles?"

16. See the beginning of Story 54 for an exception to the rule of precise siting that nonetheless stresses geographical coordinates: "Somewhere between the Pyrenees and the Alps there once lived a nobleman."

17. See Polachek's reading of Story 69 in "Save the Last Laugh for Me"; she cites Sainte-Beuve on p. 155.

18. The practice of calling her "Marguerite" poses its own set of problems; we don't usually call male aristocratic writers by their first names (Joachim instead of du Bellay?). On the "alienation" of women writers from their "family" names (those given, usually, by husbands and fathers), see Gilbert and Gubar, *Madwoman in the Attic*, 555; on the particular problems of naming early modern aristocratic women—in relation to their own nonstandardized signatures—see DeJean, *Tender Geographies*, 2–3.

19. From 1555 to her death in 1572, Jeanne d'Albret ruled a kingdom consisting of Béarn, Soule, and (Basse) Navarre; she called herself "Jehanne, par la grace de Dieu Reine et dame souveraine." See Roelker, *Queen of Navarre*, 254.

20. She was Countess of Angoulême—the place where she was born—and Duchess of Alençon, where her first husband ruled as duke. She became Duchess of Berry through a gift of land from her brother François in 1517; see Michaud-Fréjaville, "Marguerite d'Angoulême," 45–57; see also the biographies by Jourda, *Marguerite d'Angoulême*; and by DeJean, *Marguerite de Navarre*.

21. See Tucoo-Chala, "Pau au Temps de Marguerite de Navarre," 25–26.

22. On the significance of these characters' names, see Conley, "Graphics of Dissimulation."

23. See Barcia Carballido y Zúñiga, *Chronological History of the Continent of Florida*, 217.

24. For analyses of this novella, see Febvre, *Autour de "L'Heptaméron,"* chap. 4; Freccero, "Rape's Disfiguring Figures"; Cholakian, *Rape and Writing*, chap. 7; Kritzman, *Rhetoric of Sexuality*, especially 47–48; Hampton, "On the Border"; and Conley, "Graphics of Dissimulation."

25. Quoted from the king's letter of 17 October 1540. I cite the translation of the letter included in Cartier, *Voyages*, 136. Cartier had led two previous expeditions to Canada—which he, like the king, thought would provide a route to Asia—in 1534 and 1536. His third voyage was delayed until 1540—by which time all but one of the ten Iroquois he had brought to France on his second voyage were dead—in part because the emperor Charles V and the king of Portugal were raising complaints about the French incursion into New World territories. King Francis, moreover, was "preoccupied by a war with Spain" (*Voyages*, xxxix); see Folmer, *Franco-Spanish Rivalry*, 19.

26. See Jeanneret, "Antarctic France," 240; and Trudel, *Les Vaines tentatives*, 124–75.

27. Ancekewicz, "L'Ecriture du Nouveau Monde"; and Hampton, "On the Border," are significant exceptions. My interpretation of de Navarre's nationalist agenda gives more weight to religious and gender-inflected divisions in the court and aristocracy than Hampton's does (see especially his discussion on p. 542). See also Carla Freccero's work on nationalist dimensions of de Navarre's writing in "Unwriting Lucretia" and "Practicing Queer Philology."

28. In his *Grand insulaire*, Thevet locates the "Isle de Démons" at 342° west longitude and 58° north latitude—somewhere off the northern coast of Labrador—and equates that island with one he has previously called "Isle de Roberval"; a later chapter locates the "same" island at 59° north latitude. At yet another spot, Thevet describes the "Isle de la Demoiselle" and equates it with the Isle of "Fiche"; see Stabler, *Legend of Marguerite de Roberval*, 12–13n. 18.

29. The first edition of 1570 may have contained the story, too, but no copies of this edition survive; see Stabler, *Legend of Marguerite de Roberval*, 6 and n. 18.

30. For the relevant passages see Stabler, *Legend of Marguerite de Roberval*, 12.

31. *Quart Livre*, chap. 56. The English is cited from *Histories of Gargantua and Pantagruel*, trans. Cohen, 568, 566; the French from *Oeuvres complètes*, ed. Jourda, 2:206, 203. Rabelais is very likely to have read the *Heptaméron* in manuscript; in a complex gesture of competitive homage, he had dedicated his marriage book, the *Tiers Livre* published in 1546, to the "divine spirit" of Marguerite de Navarre.

32. The theological import of the exchange is underscored by Panurge's slightly garbled allusion to Exod. 20:18, describing how people "palpably saw the voices" when Moses received the Law from God.

33. See, e.g., Jeanneret, "Antarctic France," 240.

34. Unless directly quoting de Navarre, I use the spelling of Roberval's name adopted by modern historians. As Natalie Zemon Davis has persuasively argued, de Navarre offers in the very first story of the *Heptaméron* another counter-perspective on a story involving the king; in this case, his official pardon of a man de Navarre's story represents as truly evil and not deserving of pardon. See Davis, *Fiction in the Archives*, 139–44. I suspect that there are many such counter-perspectives in the *Heptaméron*, subtle critiques of the king's judgments or policies that a coterie audience would have recognized as critiques. Both Story 1 and Story 67 are told by Simontaut.

35. Cited from Marichal, "Compagnons de Roberval," 53.

36. The only records of the third voyage are the two English accounts—one for each captain—first published by Richard Hakluyt in *The Third and Last Volume of the Voyages, Navigations, Traffiques, and Discoveries of the English Nation, etc.* (1600); I cite from the reprint of this text in Cartier, *Voyages*.

37. See Marichal, "Compagnons de Roberval," 54.

38. See Campbell, *Wonder and Science*, 34; and Cartier, *Voyages*, 96–113.

39. For the directives about transforming "condemned and judged" prisoners into colonists, see the king's letter commissioning Cartier (*Voyages*, 137).

40. Quoted in *L'Heptaméron*, ed. François, 495n. 803; see also Biggar, *Collection of Documents Relating to Jacques Cartier*; and Marichal, "Compagnons de Roberval."

41. For later versions of the story see Stabler, *Legend of Marguerite de Roberval*; and Russell, "Quatre versions."

42. *Grand insulaire*, fol. 146r, cited and translated in Stabler, *Legend of Marguerite de Roberval*, 21.

43. Malo, "L'Ile des Demons," thinks Thevet is here referring to Rabelais; in the *Grand insulaire*, the Rabelaisian target is clear when Thevet denounces *grabelueurs panurgiques* for plagiarizing his materials.

44. See Stabler, *Legend of Marguerite de Roberval*, 18n. 22; and Campbell, *Wonder and Science*, 37–40. Campbell notes that Thevet and de Navarre were both from Angoulême (37n. 17).

45. See Cook's introduction to *The Voyages of Jacques Cartier*, xxx, on the Indian women given to Cartier as "gifts"; these included a twelve-year-old "niece" of the Iroquois chief, Donnacona, who was himself eventually kidnapped and taken to France, where he and all but one of ten native captives died. For a general discussion of women as both producers of and images in the European genres of travel writing, see Clark, introduction to *Travel Writing and Empire*, 19–24.

46. *Tyndale's Old Testament*, Num. 5, p. 207. The modern French *Bible de Jérusalem* renders the curse as "que s'enfle ton ventre et que se flétrisse ton sexe"; in the Vulgate the curse is "et inflato ventre computrescet femur"; and in the 1535 French Bible translated by the Protestant Pierre Olivetan, the curse is that "ces eaues de malediction entre en toy pour creuer [?] le ventre & fire tomber la cuisse" (from a section of the text entitled "Ceremonies iiii. De Moses/ ou Nombres. Chap.v. feuil [fol.] .xl."). "Creuer" seems to be an old form of *crôitre*, "to grow"; it survives as *crue*,

"swelling," in modern French. The verb could also, however, be *crever,* "to empty out," which is the imagistic opposite of "to swell up." In either case, the woman's sexuality is being somehow broken, through the curse, so she can no longer conceive. De Navarre seems to translate the Vulgate here, which is consonant with her being, in her daughter Jeanne's phrase, "between two religions." A full analysis of this passage, however, would need to examine Lefèvre d'Etaples's French translation of the Bible; see above, note 5.

47. The verb in French is *trahir* (p. 392).

48. See Ancekewicz, "L'Ecriture du Nouveau Monde," 427, for a discussion of the symbolic significance of the word *dessert.* See also Reyff's edition of the *Heptaméron,* 521, on the echoes of the "leçon du Magnificat" (in the Mass) in the story and also the allusion to the biblical desert, which recalls both "l'exode et la retraite des anchorètes." The "desert" landscape of the island recalls that of the prologue, too: see *L'Heptaméron,* ed. François, 3 and 8.

49. Ancekewicz, "L'Ecriture du Nouveau Monde," 433, my translation; Ancekewicz draws here on Anderson, *Chain Her by One Foot.* On French representations of Native Canadian women, see also Davis, *Women on the Margins;* and Lestringant, *Le Huguenot et le sauvage.*

50. On Jeanne de Navarre's battles with her mother, see Roelker, *Queen of Navarre,* 46–66; Freccero, "1527: Margaret of Angoulême," 146–47; and Freccero, "Archives in the Fiction," 80–82.

51. See, e.g., Gelernt, *World of Many Loves,* 126; also Tetel, *"L'Heptaméron:* Première nouvelle," 449–58; and Delajarte, "Le Prologue de l'*Heptaméron.*" See also, however, critics who caution against considering Parlamente de Navarre's only figure of the author, e.g., Losse, "Authorial and Narrative Voice," especially 223; and Stone, "Narrative Technique."

52. These female characters exercise verbal authority covertly through a strategy of address analyzed by Cathleen Bauschatz in "Voylà, mes dames. . . ." Male characters also use this formula, which yokes this collection of tales to Boccaccio's *Decameron* while also protecting de Navarre's female authorities from overtly instructing their male superiors in the natural hierarchy of being. See also Colette Winn's discussion of how de Navarre's female speakers both submit to and break "the rule of not-speaking": "'La Loi du non-parler' dans *l'Heptaméron.*"

53. For evidence from the historical subtext suggesting that Ennasuite is Simontaut's wife, see Reynolds-Cornell, *Les Devisants,* 90. Reynolds-Cornell thinks that Ennasuite's frequent allusions to wifely infidelity make it unlikely that she is married to a man in the company; internal evidence suggests, however, that she is pursuing the man who is already her husband, but whose interest has wandered, as Hircan's has from Parlamente. See the conversation about marital happiness—and sex—at the end of Day Four (*Heptaméron,* 374–75; Fr., 280–81). For evidence of Simontaut's interest in Parlamente, and her understanding of his coded messages of desire, see the conversation at the end of the prologue (*Heptaméron,* 70; Fr., 10).

54. Story 66 begins: "L'année que monsieur de Vendosme espousa la princesse de Navarre, apres avoir festoyé à Vendosme les Roy et Royne, leur pere et mere, s'en allerent en Guyenne avecq eulx . . ." (*Heptaméron,* 500; Fr., 390).

55. For just one example, see Story 4, about a gentleman who attempts to rape a noble widow; according to Brantôme, the widow represents Marguerite de Navarre herself. See *L'Heptaméron,* ed. François, 453n. 125; see also Freccero, "Archives in the Fiction," 90n. 12; and Cholakian, *Rape and Writing.*

56. See Dubois, "Fonds mythique et jeu des sens," 154. See also Sommers, "Feminine Authority in the *Heptaméron.*"

57. Many editors and critics, noting de Navarre's practice of providing anagrammatic links between her characters and historical persons in her circle, have identified Oisille with de Navarre's mother Louise de Savoie, although Régine Reynolds-Cornell rightly suggests that de

Navarre also represents aspects of herself in the old woman (Reynolds-Cornell, *Les Devisants*, 15). See also Freccero, "Patriarchy and the Maternal Text"; and "1527: Margaret of Angoulême." For other useful discussions of the historicity of the storytellers, see Davis, "Storytellers in Marguerite de Navarre's *Heptaméron*"; Palermo, "L'Historicité des Devisants"; Cazauran, *"L'Heptaméron" de Marguerite de Navarre*, 39–57; Tetel, *Marguerite de Navarre's "Heptaméron"*; Jourda, *Marguerite d'Angoulême*, 2:740–66.

58. See Chilton's introduction to his translation of the *Heptaméron*, 38.

59. On Parlamente as one who lies, see Freccero, "Rewriting the Rhetoric of Desire," 302.

60. See Davis, *Fiction in the Archives*, 107, also 203n. 72; see also Freccero, "Archives in the Fiction," 75, on de Navarre's use of an allegorical figure of the Nation (Françoise) to educate the prince in Story 42.

61. The *Dictionnaire historique*, ed. Rey, defines *parlement* as "un cour souveraine de justice formée par un groupe de spécialistes détachés de la Cour du roi"; Seyssel's comment about Parlement as a "bridle" of the king is cited and translated in Lewis, *Later Medieval France*, 98.

62. See Berger, "Renaissance Imagination."

63. G. P. Norton and Y. Delègue have argued that this passage dramatizes the difference between Boccaccio's prologue portrait of a "vengeful medieval God" and de Navarre's conception of a "divine Architect with both unlimited powers to destroy and an infinite capacity for compassion"; see Norton, "Narrative Function," 438–39; compare Delègue, "Autour des deux prologues," 29. For a darker view of the God of de Navarre's prologue, see Lyons, *"Heptaméron* and the Foundation of Critical Narrative," 150.

64. For a discussion of the changes de Navarre rings on Boccaccio's Florentine settings and Castiglione's Urbino, see Ferguson, "Recreating the Rules," 165–69.

65. Davis, *Society and Culture*, 83.

66. For an example of the second category of response, consider the passage of the prologue where members of the noble company are said to have "praised their Creator that he had been satisfied to take the servants and save their masters and mistresses" (*Heptaméron*, 64; Fr., 4). The image of Christ as a servant authorizes an ironic reading of the passage.

67. See Polachek, "Save the Last Laugh for Me."

68. See Polachek's discussion of the double-entendre in "Save the Last Laugh for Me," 169.

69. On the importance of marriage to the state in the sixteenth century see Hanley, "Monarchic State in Early Modern France," "Family and State in Early Modern France," and "Engendering the State."

70. De Navarre's poem appears in a volume entitled *Cantique des fidelles des Eglises de France qui ont vaillamment soustenu pour la parole de Dieu . . .* [Song of the Faithful of the Churches of France Who Have Valiantly Undergone Trials for the Word of God], fol. A.iv verso; this text and the anonymous pamphlet are cited in Davis, *Society and Culture*, 78.

71. Lyons, *Exemplum*, 95, discussing the defiant Rolandine in Story 21. In "Archives in the Fiction," Freccero persuasively reads Rolandine's struggles with the queen as refracting (but not resolving) de Navarre's struggles with Jeanne d'Albret over the latter's first marriage.

Chapter Six

1. The sources of the chapter epigraphs are as follows: (1) Speech by the prosecutor for the crown, Edward Coke, at the arraignment of Henry Garnet, one of England's leading Jesuits, who was tried and convicted of a treasonous role in the Gunpowder Plot of 1605. Coke's speech was printed by Robert Barker in a pamphlet entitled *A Trve and Perfect Relation of the Whole Proceed-*

ings against the Late Most Barbarous Traitors . . . (1606), Sig T3v. Reprinted in Carswell, ed., *Trial of Guy Fawkes and Others (The Gunpowder Plot)*, 131–91; the quoted passage is from 154. (2) William Warner, *A Continuance of Albion's England* (1606), bk. 15, chap. 95. I quote from a facsimile of the first edition, Sig G3, 380, included in vol. 131 of the series Anglistica and Americana. (3) Henry Cary, letter to Lord Conway, 5 April 1626, in State Paper Office, Dublin. Quoted from appendix to Simpson, ed., *Lady Falkland*, 132. (4) "Lady Falkland: Her Life," a biography of Cary written in the 1650s by one of her Catholic daughters. Quoted from Cary, *Tragedy of Mariam*, ed. Weller and Ferguson. All quotations from the biography of Cary (first published in 1861) and from *The Tragedy of Mariam* (1613) are from this edition and will henceforth be cited parenthetically in the text.

2. My argument for censorship as a midwife for literate production is indebted to Annabel Patterson, *Censorship and Interpretation*.

3. For a discussion of the historical background, see Cary, *Mariam*, ed. Weller and Ferguson, 63–64.

4. On the political implications of Cary's choice of genre, see Fischer, "Elizabeth Cary and Tyranny," 237; Raber, "Gender and the Political Subject," 325; Shannon, "*Tragedie of Mariam*," especially 145–47; Gutierrez, "Valuing *Mariam*," 233–51; Hannay, *Philip's Phoenix*, 119; and Straznicky, "Profane Stoical Paradoxes," 104–33. On the genre question more generally, see Braden, *Renaissance Tragedy*; and Bushnell, *Tragedies of Tyrants*.

5. For a conspectus of Protestant and Catholic views on the "duty" to resist "lawful authority" abusively exercised—an idea that gradually developed in discourses defending a "right" to resist or revolt against tyranny—see Skinner, *Foundations of Modern Political Thought*, 335 and passim. On resistance to tyranny in writings by members of Mary Sidney's circle, see Shannon, "*Tragedie of Mariam*," 144. For further discussion of Cary's connection with the circle of Mary Sidney, who had translated Garnier's *Marc Antoine* as *Antonius, A Tragedy* in 1592, see Straznicky, "Profane Stoical Paradoxes," 104–5.

6. In a speech to the Lords and Commons in March 1610 James stated that "kings exercise a manner or resemblance of Divine power upon earth"; cited in Smith, "Constitutional Ideas," 161. See Smith's discussion of an alternative (parliamentary) view of royal power; for further discussion of James's claims of divine right, see Goldberg, *James I*, 117–18.

7. Although Josephus's sources were mostly partisan to Herod, Josephus's own narrative portrays Herod through a complex filter of admiration and bitterness; see introduction to *Mariam*, ed. Weller and Ferguson, 19. The episodes Cary adapts from Josephus come from the moment in Roman history just after—but looking back to just before—Augustus Caesar's accession to sole imperial rule after the Battle of Actium (31 B.C.E.). At Actium, Augustus earned the title *imperator* by defeating Mark Antony in what was in truth a civil war, although it has been influentially represented as a Roman triumph over an effeminate, luxurious, and foreign "East"; see Quint, *Epic and Empire*, 21–49. In the *Antiquities* Josephus represents Herod as killing Mariam after returning from a "tributary" visit to Augustus Caesar, whereas in his *Jewish War*, Josephus has Herod killing Mariam (and a different servant accused of adultery with her) after a visit to Mark Antony. Cary generally follows the *Antiquities* account; its description of Mariam's marriage to Herod is in book 15. On the different historical figures named Herod and Salome that Cary's play at times conflates, see *Mariam*, ed. Weller and Ferguson, 20–23.

8. For a discussion of other medieval and Renaissance dramas about Mariam and Herod, see *Mariam*, ed. Weller and Ferguson, 22–26.

9. Dolan, *Whores of Babylon*, 18; see also Clancy, "Papist-Protestant-Puritan."

10. As enacted in the second session of James's first Parliament (and published 25 June

1606), the Oath of Allegiance states, in part: "I acknowledge that the Pope hath no power or Authority to depose the King . . . And I do further sweare, that I do from my heart abhor, detest and abjure, as impious or hereticall . . . That Princes which be Excommunicated or deprived by the Pope, may be deposed or murthered by their subjects . . . according to the plaine and common sense and understanding of the same wordes, without any Equivocation or mentall evasion, or secret reservation whatsoever." Cited from Hamilton, *Shakespeare and the Politics of Protestant England,* 131-32. The exemption for the nobility ended in 1610, "when the oath was revised and reissued following the assassination of Henry IV" of France.

11. In *The English Catholic Community,* John Bossy claimed that women played such an important role that the community in question was "in effect a matriarchy" (153). This way of explaining the prominence of women is critiqued by Dolan, *Whores of Babylon,* 70. For other discussions of the problems of perception and historical fact surrounding the figure of the Catholic wife, see Marotti, "Alienating Catholics"; Rowlands, "Recusant Women"; Wright, "Legal and Linguistic Coercion of Recusant Women"; and Crawford, *Women and Religion,* especially 58-68.

12. On Catholic beliefs at this time, see Dolan, *Whores of Babylon;* on Jewish beliefs, as defined by Jews as well as (polemically) by non-Jews, see Shapiro, *Shakespeare and the Jews,* 35 and passim. See also Bartels, "Malta, the Jew, and the Fictions of Difference." Cary's plot allows her to allude allegorically to the Jews who lived both outside England and within it during the early modern era; though officially expelled in 1290, Jews did live within England's borders during the centuries before their official readmission (in 1656), both as inhabitants of "Marrano" communities and as "foreigners" performing scholarly or medical tasks for the regime.

13. For verbal parallels between Cary's play and Lodge's translation, see Cary, *Tragedy of Mariam,* ed. Dunstan and Greg, xiv-xv; passages in Lodge's translation most relevant to Cary's play are reprinted in *Mariam,* ed. Weller and Ferguson, app. A.

14. Barry Weller and I surmised (*Mariam,* ed. Weller and Ferguson, 18) that Lodge converted to Catholicism fairly late in his life, around the time that he published his *Prosopopeia, Containing the Teares of the holy, blessed, and sanctified Marie, the Mother of God* (1596); he may well, however, have harbored Catholic views from his youth onward, being in effect, like Cary, a closet Catholic who only gradually made his religious leanings public—and then only to readers sympathetic to his ideas, such as the "virtuous and devout" noblewomen he addresses in the "Epistle Dedicatory" of *Prosopopeia,* in *Complete Works of Thomas Lodge,* 3:3-5.

15. On the rebuttal of an ancient charge that Jews perpetrate ritual murder, in Lodge's translation of Josephus, see Shapiro, *Shakespeare and the Jews,* 104-5.

16. Raleigh, *History of the World* (1614), 227.

17. "Life," in *Mariam,* ed. Weller and Ferguson, 188. The "Life" states that Elizabeth was fifteen when she married and gives her date of birth as 1585 or 1586, which would place the marriage in 1600 or 1601, but the *Complete Peerage* states that "he married at her age 17, about Sep. 1602" (5:239-40). Most modern scholars accept that year for the Tanfield-Cary marriage; see introduction to *Mariam,* ed. Weller and Ferguson, 4 and n. 9.

18. See Katz, *Philo-Semitism and the Readmission of the Jews to England,* 103.

19. Oldys, ed., *Harleian Miscellany,* x, 1099; cited in Katz, *Jews in the History of England,* 103.

20. See Shapiro, *Shakespeare and the Jews,* 71-73, for a discussion of the Lopez case; see also Harvey, *Lopez the Jew* (1594). Lopez was a professed Christian as well as a man who proclaimed his loyalty to the queen until the moment of his death.

21. For a discussion of this act (1 Eliz., c. 2), which levied a fine of twelve pence for recusancy, see Rowlands, "Recusant Women," 150-51; she notes that the duty of enforcing the law "lay primarily with the ecclesiastical courts," but the act also "empowered the Queen's Justices to deal with refusal to attend" church—thus "both the church authorities and the civil authorities were

associated in the attempt to secure conformity." For a summary of the legislation against recusants (not all of whom were Catholics; in 1593, as Rowlands notes, the term *popish recusant* was introduced to distinguish Catholics from other nonconformists), see Marotti, "Alienating Catholics," 2, and n. 5; see also Dolan, *Whores of Babylon,* 31–34.

22. Straznicky, "Profane Stoical Paradoxes," 124, citing Braden, *Renaissance Tragedy,* 23. Braden makes a cogent argument for Stoicism as a philosophical defense for a disempowered aristocracy during the first and second centuries of the Roman empire.

23. See Mullaney, *Place of the Stage,* especially 120; also Puttenham, *Arte of English Poesie,* 266–67.

24. See de Grazia, "Homonyms before and after Lexical Standardization," 144–55.

25. Ibid., 154 and n. 29, where she observes that Miriam Josephs and Brian Vickers both identify the pun with syllepsis, while Jonathan Culler, well aware of the "modern" origin of the pun, "finds its closest *approximation* in classical *paronomasia* or *adnominatio.*" See Culler, "Call of the Phoneme," 1–16. For an example of Cary's use of syllepsis, which consists in "the same word serving different syntactic functions," see *Mariam,* 4.3.137–38; and Quilligan's shrewd commentary on the lines in "Staging Gender," 226.

26. There is an immense literature on the history of antifigurative thinking in the West; the association of metaphor with something not "proper," something alien to the language, goes back to Greek and Roman discussions of metaphor. The seventeenth-century English association of certain tropes and word-plays with treason should be read in the light of this long history of debate about figurative language.

27. Hobbes, *Leviathan* (1651), discussed in Mullaney, *Place of the Stage,* 127.

28. Samuel Johnson, "Preface to Shakespeare," cited in Mullaney, *Place of the Stage,* 128.

29. Mullaney, *Place of the Stage,* 123. See also Muir, introduction to *Macbeth*; Wills, *Witches and Jesuits*; Barroll, *Politics, Plague, and Shakespeare's Theater,* 135–52; Wormald, "Gunpowder, Treason, and Scots," 141–68; and Kastan, *Shakespeare after Theory,* 175–77.

30. See Muir, introduction to *Macbeth,* xvii, for James's rejection of Garnet's argument that he could not mention the Gunpowder Plot to authorities because he heard it under the seal of confession.

31. On the question of the number of Catholics in England, see Dolan, *Whores of Babylon,* 79 and passim; see also Holmes, *Resistance and Compromise,* 82.

32. See Huntley, "*Macbeth* and the Background of Jesuitical Equivocation," 390 and n. 3.

33. Azpilcueta, *Opera omnia,* 22, q. 5, "de veritate responsi verbo," cited in Malloch, "Father Henry Garnet's Treatise of Equivocation," 388.

34. Cited in Malloch, "Father Henry Garnet's Treatise of Equivocation," 388.

35. On Garnet's career, see Bossy, *English Catholic Community,* 204–9; on the treatise attributed to Garnet, which circulated secretly in manuscript among early seventeenth-century Catholics but was not printed until 1851, see Malloch, "Father Henry Garnet's Treatise of Equivocation," 387–88.

36. Cited in Malloch, "Father Henry Garnet's Treatise of Equivocation," 387.

37. On the "disquiet" that English Catholics felt about equivocation, see ibid., 393n. 3.

38. See Kermode, *Genesis of Secrecy.*

39. See Huntley, "*Macbeth* and the Background of Jesuitical Equivocation," 391n. 11.

40. Coke, *True and Perfect Relation of the Whole Proceedings against the late most barbarous Traitors, Garnet a Jesuite, and his Confederats . . .* (1606), T2; I cite from the original text, modernizing *i/j* and *u/v.* The text was reprinted in Carswell, ed., *Trial of Guy Fawkes.* See also, for the Protestant perspective on equivocation, Mason, *New Art of Lying* (1624).

41. Persons's *Treatise tending to Mitigation* (1607) was printed in England without license; the

title page conspicuously notes that it comes *permissu superiorum,* and it is dedicated "to the learned Schoole-Devines, Cyvill and Canon Lawyers of the two Universities of England."

42. Cited in Huntley, "*Macbeth* and the Background to Jesuitical Equivocation," 391.

43. Persons, *Treatise tending to Mitigation,* chap. 7, 288. I have modernized *i/j* and *u/v.*

44. For a different perspective on the ideological significance of delay in Cary's *Mariam,* see Kegl, "Theaters, Households, and a 'Kind of History.' "

45. See Gallagher, *Medusa's Gaze,* 1, 4, and passim. See also Zagorin, *Ways of Lying,* especially chaps. 8 and 9.

46. For Luther and other Protestant Reformers' attacks on casuistry, see Gallagher, *Medusa's Gaze,* 5 and n. 3.

47. Gallagher cites William Perkins, *Whole Treatise of Cases of Conscience* (1642), on p. 11, noting that Perkins's language of "indeterminate qualification" is just "what was usually attributed to the casuistry of the Jesuits." See the survey of both Protestant and Catholic instances of casuistry in Thomas, "Cases of Conscience."

48. On the importance of Catholic women "in the religious and cultural drama of early modern England," as Arthur Marotti puts it, see his "Alienating Catholics." See also Dolan, *Whores of Babylon;* Crawford, "Public Duty, Conscience, and Women"; Crawford, *Women and Religion,* especially 58–65; and Rowlands, "Recusant Women." On women's role in the printing and distribution of Catholic books in England, see Rosenberg, *Minority Press and the English Crown,* 101–7 and passim.

49. Rowlands, "Recusant Women," 155, citing a manuscript description of parliamentary debates.

50. For debates about women's rule, often including discussion of Salic law, see Jordan, *Renaissance Feminism,* 116–33, 242–46 and passim. See also Eggert, *Showing Like a Queen,* chaps. 3, 4 and passim; Marcus, *Puzzling Shakespeare,* 53–61; and Erickson, *Rewriting Shakespeare,* 36–41.

51. See Ferguson, "Running On with Almost Public Voice."

52. On Graphina's name, see Cary, *Tragedy of Mariam,* ed. Dunstan and Greg, xii.

53. See Ferguson, "Running On with Almost Public Voice," 47, for a different interpretation of the scene; the present reading is indebted to Goldberg, *Desiring Women Writing,* 169–70.

54. Cited in Kennedy, *Just Anger,* 58. For another valuable critical discussion of the topos of wifely silence, see Jones, *Currency of Eros,* chap. 1.

55. *A bride-bush or a wedding sermon* (1619); cited in Kennedy, *Just Anger,* 58.

56. For texts developing this triadic ideal, see Hull, *Chaste, Silent, and Obedient.*

57. See Straznicky, "Profane Stoical Paradoxes"; and Straznicky, "Reading the Stage." See also Goldberg, *Desiring Women Writing,* 223n. 6; and Orlin, *Private Matters and Public Culture.*

58. See Ferguson, "Running On with Almost Public Voice," 47; and Callaghan, "Re-Reading Elizabeth Cary's *The Tragedie of Mariam,*" 177; see also Miller, *Changing the Subject,* 208.

59. Rich, *Excellency of Good Women* (1613); cited in Kennedy, *Just Anger,* 59.

60. Cited in Kennedy, *Just Anger,* 58.

61. Articulating the traditional Catholic view that marriage is a lesser state than virginity, Juan Luis Vives comes to the same paradoxes Protestant writers must negotiate rhetorically when he describes the wife as an inferior who is nonetheless a "companion." See his *Office of an Husband* (1529), trans. Thomas Paynell (1555); cited in Klein, *Daughters, Wives and Widows,* 127. On the complexity of the wife/servant relation in the discourse of marriage, see Amussen, *Ordered Society;* Dolan, *Dangerous Familiars;* Jordan, "Renaissance Women and the Question of Class"; and Fletcher, *Gender, Sex and Subordination in England,* especially chap. 11, "Household Order."

62. In *Christian Oeconomie* (written in Latin in the 1590s and translated into English in

1609), William Perkins gives a classic Puritan interpretation of how a man honors his wife by "making account of her as his companion, or yoke-fellow. For this cause, the woman, when she was created, was not taken out of the man's head, because she was not made to rule over him; nor out of his feet, because God did not make her subject to him as a servant, but out of his side, to the end that man should take her as his mate" (125).

63. "Wit may show / The way to ill as well as good, you know," says Salome (3.1.23-25, p. 106), and there follows a debate about whether the "porter" of Graphina's head is "wisdom" or, as Salome suggests, Machiavellian prudence. Barry Weller, who wrote the note for these strange lines in our edition of *Mariam*, suggests the parallel between Salome's lines and Iago's; Cary's figure of the porter in the context of a meditation on self-censorship suggests a further parallel to Shakespeare's porter in *Macbeth*, 2.3.

64. Salome speaks for a hermeneutics of suspicion and for the possibility of other plots in the play than those we see at first reading. In pointing to alternative plots, she points beyond the play's time to alternative presents or futures.

65. Cited from the 1613 quarto, which is available on microfilm (STC 4613) or in the facsimile editions by Dunstan and Greg (1914; rpt., 1999) and by Travitsky and Cullen (in *Works By and Attributed to Elizabeth Cary*, 1996).

66. See the editors' note on the punctuation of the first line in *Mariam*, ed. Weller and Ferguson, 152.

67. For work related to this claim, see Stanton, ed., *Female Autograph*, especially the contributions by Stanton, "Autogynography," 3-20; and Goldsmith, "Giving Weight to Words," 96-100. See also Merrim, *Early Modern Women's Writing*, chap. 5.

68. On stage curtains, see Foakes, "Playhouses and Players," 20.

69. See Kennedy, *Just Anger*, 63-66. Kennedy shrewdly observes that Mariam expresses anger with her husband to others, but not to Herod himself (and even in expressing it to others, she goes against the conduct books' express commands that the wife speak "reverently" of her husband even when she is speaking "behind his back," in his absence). I don't agree, however, with Kennedy's view that Mariam's words "conform to the desired manner but not the matter of a good wife's speech" (65-66), because the requirement for wifely "mildness" seems to me to apply both to the tone and to the content of a speech.

70. For a Protestant example, see Perkins, *Christian Oeconomie*, chap. 9, excerpted in Klein, *Daughters, Wives and Widows*, 169. For a Catholic example, see Henry Garnet's *Treatise on Christian Renunciation*, in which he advises his female readers that "your husbands over your soul have no authority and over your bodies but limited power" (cited in Rowlands, "Recusant Women," 165; and discussed in Holmes, *Resistance and Compromise*, 109-10). Patricia Crawford argues that male political thinkers became increasingly skeptical about women's "pleas of conscience" during the seventeenth century, as difficulties increasingly arose over "allowing pleas of conscience to justify female insubordination" ("Public Duty, Conscience, and Women," 70). Crawford also notes that casuists wrestled not only with the problem posed by unbelieving husbands but also with the related problem posed by the contradictory messages in Scripture about the duty of a citizen's obedience (71).

71. Cited in Marotti, "Alienating Catholics," 7.

72. For a discussion of this manual and other texts on the complexities of the "vocation" to martyrdom, see Gregory, *Salvation at Stake*, 285-86 and passim.

73. See Southwell, *Spiritual Exercises and Devotions*; cited in Gregory, *Salvation at Stake*, 286.

74. Salome's image invites analysis in the psychological and historical frame set forth by Lynda Boose in "Scolding Brides and Bridling Scolds: Taming the Woman's Unruly Member";

analyzing the common cultural association between women's verbal and sexual looseness, Boose intriguingly sees the bridle used to punish unruly early modern English women as a type of chastity belt.

75. Dolan, *Whores of Babylon*, 3-4. The pun *fawkes/faux*, which characteristically associates the conspirator with a foreigner, is in a text by William Warner dedicated to Edward Coke, *Continuance of Albion's England* (1606), bk. 15, chap. 95, p. 379.

76. See Gallagher, *Medusa's Gaze*, 65.

77. I owe this point to Meredith Skura, "Reproduction of Mothering," 48n. 53.

78. For a discussion of the possible dates of the play's composition, see introduction to *Mariam*, ed. Weller and Ferguson, 5 and n. 13.

79. See Dolan, "Taking the Pencil Out of God's Hand"; Drew-Bear, *Painted Faces on the Renaissance Stage*; and Williams, *Powder and Paint*.

80. See, e.g., John Webster's tragicomedy, *The Devil's Lawcase*, 4.2.285-89; cited in Dolan, *Whores of Babylon*, 47. Romelio exclaims that his mother's devilish lawsuit is "like to the horrid powder-treason in England," a treason that has "a most bloody unnatural revenge / Hid under it. Oh the violencies of women!"

81. There is a large literature on the Gunpowder Plot; for its seventeenth-century and modern representations, see Dolan, *Whores of Babylon*, 45-49. For the view that the conspirators were framed, see Edwards, "Still Investigating Gunpowder Plot." For discussion of opposing views, see Dolan, *Whores of Babylon*, 47n. 5.

82. See Skura, "Reproduction of Mothering," 32.

83. For Herod's "rashness," see Argument, *Mariam*, ed. Weller and Ferguson, 68; for Mariam's, see 1.1.6, p. 69. The echo supports Walter Benjamin's contention that the figure of the tyrant and the martyr may be two sides of the same absolutist construct; see his *Origin of German Tragic Drama*, 69-70.

84. For an astute analysis of Cary's critique of a political situation in which "an authority creates laws whose 'justice' operates to the detriment of those to whom the law applies," see Shannon, "*Tragedie of Mariam*," 136.

85. See Kegl, "Theaters, Households, and a 'Kind of History,'" 145-46.

86. Of the few critical discussions of Constabarus's name and virtue, see Skura, "Reproduction of Mothering," 31. On the ideal of male friendship dramatized in Constabarus's relation to the sons of Babas (Babau in Josephus), see Shannon, "*Tragedie of Mariam*," 152-53.

87. See "Historical Background," in *Mariam*, ed. Weller and Ferguson, 63; and Josephus, *Antiquities*, 15.7.10.

88. See Josephus, *Antiquities*, bk. 15, sections 260-64, p. 125 in the Loeb bilingual edition; in the 1602 edition of Lodge's *Famous and Memorable Workes of Josephus*, the passage occurs on p. 400.

89. Davies, *Complete Works of John Davies of Hereford*, 2:5. Davies' acquaintance with Cary (he may have been her writing tutor) perhaps explains why he includes her in an address to two wealthier and higher ranking ladies, Lucy, Countess of Bedford, and Mary, Countess Dowager of Pembroke.

90. Pearse, "Elizabeth Cary, Renaissance Playwright," observes that Davies was one of Cary's childhood tutors (607). Shannon argues that Davies' phrase "Feete of State" shows "the connection of closet drama with reflection upon issues of governance" ("*Tragedie of Mariam*," 147). On Mary Sidney's creation of a Stoic heroine in her translation of Garnier's *Marc Antoine*, see Lamb, *Gender and Authorship in the Sidney Circle*, 129-32.

91. On Davies' possible influence on Cary's decision to publish, see Pearse, "Elizabeth Cary, Renaissance Playwright," 607.

92. For information on Creede, see the introduction to *Mariam*, ed. Weller and Ferguson, 45; on Creede's device of "Truth Scourged," see McKerrow, *Printers' and Publishers' Devices*, 117 and pl. 299. I am grateful to R. A. Foakes for helpful questions about this device.

93. For Creede's other devices, one of which has a mailed hand upholding a burning sword with the motto *contrahit avaritia bellum*, see McKerrow, *Printers' and Publishers' Devices*, pls. 314 and 339. For an introduction to *The First Part of the Contention*, long considered a "bad quarto" of Shakespeare's play about the strife between the houses of York and Lancaster, see the *Norton Shakespeare*, 203–12. This play, like Cary's *Mariam*, features disobedient subjects, a weak king, and powerful, witchlike women.

94. On Dowriche, sometimes known from her second husband as Anne Trefusis, see McKerrow, *Printers' and Publishers' Devices*, 117; and Travitsky, *Paradise of Women*, 94–97 and 272.

95. See Aulus Gellius, *Noctium Atticarum*, 18.11.3–4, pp. 251–52; I owe this reference to Ralph Hexter. For the Petrarchan resonances of the motto, see Greene, *The Light in Troy*, 103. For the motto's appearance in Elizabethan contexts (e.g., Geoffrey Whitney's *Choice of Embleme*, where it occurs with a different picture), see Summit, *Lost Property*, 199; she discusses Cary's title page on p. 264n. 108.

96. This is the interpretation given by Susan Frye, who reproduces and analyzes the political meanings of Mary's embroideries in conjunction with a discussion of Queen Elizabeth's (lost) tapestries from de Pizan's *City of Ladies* ("Staging Women's Relations to Textiles," 233–34 and pl. 69). Mary's embroideries still exist and may be viewed in Oxburgh Hall, Norfolk.

97. For this interpretation, see Summit, *Lost Property*, 198–201; she reads Mary's emblem as a complex salvo in a battle between queens that includes Elizabeth's poem, "The Doubt of Future Foes."

98. Cited from Gregory, *Salvation at Stake*, 286.

99. Just before she tells Constabarus that she means to obtain a "divorcing bill," Salome reminds him that she has long possessed knowledge that could kill him if she were to divulge it to Herod: the knowledge that Constabarus has traitorously rescued Babas's sons (1.6.403; p. 84).

100. See Raber, "Gender and the Political Subject," 332; see also Goldberg's discussion of this speech (and of James's ideological perception of "the married state") in *James I*, 141.

101. See Kaplan, "Subjection and Subjectivity," especially 234–35, for a valuable discussion of early Protestant efforts to liberalize divorce law; she notes that the Church of England has still not introduced "a new code of law to supersede" the Catholic canon law of divorce.

102. On the importance of (contested ideas about) incest to Henry's case for divorce, see Shell, ed., *Elizabeth's Glass*, 8–9; on Anne's alleged incest, see Warnicke, *The Rise and Fall of Anne Boleyn*, 215.

103. For the legal distinction between *feme sole* and *feme coverte*, see Baker, *Introduction to English Legal History*, 258. See also Travitsky, "*Feme Covert*"; and, for a valuable overview of the topic of marriage, Neely, *Broken Nuptials in Shakespeare's Plays*. On "petty treason" see Travitsky, "Husband Murder and Petty Treason"; Thomas, "Double Standard"; and Slater, "Weightiest Business."

104. See Sanders, *De origine et progressu schismatis Anglicani* (1585), trans. Lewis (1877), 4, 25. For Sanders's "extremely popular" portrait of Anne Boleyn, see Warnicke, *Anne Boleyn*, app. A, especially 244. See also Skura, "Reproduction of Mothering," 29.

105. Kaplan discusses some Protestant writers who argued for "an equal right and power in both parties" to a divorce, but none solved the question of whose will should prevail in cases where only one party desired divorce ("Subjection and Subjectivity," 234–35).

106. The quoted phrase is from Armitage, *Ideological Origins of the British Empire*, 31; see chapter 3, above, for a critique of those who argue, as Armitage does, for a sharp distinction

between a type of *imperium* concerned only with "internal" dominance and a type that displays ambitions for dominion "beyond" the borders of a given realm such as England.

107. See Callaghan, "Re-Reading Elizabeth Cary's *The Tragedie of Mariam*," 177; also Hall, *Things of Darkness*, 3–4, 184–85; Loomba, "The Color of Patriarchy"; and Hendricks and Parker, introduction to *Women, "Race," and Writing*.

108. For an argument against correlating "racial" with religious difference in Cary's play, see Callaghan, "Re-Reading Elizabeth Cary's *The Tragedie of Mariam*." The reader should read "race" skeptically; I will not, however, put quotation marks around the word henceforth.

109. As Barry Weller notes, Cary's "servile curse" condenses the curses pronounced against Eve after the Fall (Gen. 3:16) and against Canaan (apparently conflated with his father Ham) after he "summons his brothers to witness the drunken nakedness of their father, Noah (Genesis 9:22, 25)" (*Mariam*, ed. Weller and Ferguson, 169n. 342). Ham's curse is an ideological justification for the idea that Canaan's descendants are "natural" slaves. Later biblical commentators saw in the curse the "cause" of black skin; for analysis of competing early modern theories of the causes of blackness, see Oldenburg, "Riddle of Blackness."

110. See *Mariam*, 4.8.547–50; Barry Weller suggested the idea of an echo of Marlowe's play.

111. On the importance of attending "to what the work does not say," see Macherey, *Theory of Literary Production*, 87 and passim.

112. See Dolan, "Taking the Pencil Out of God's Hand"; and Drew-Bear, *Painted Faces on the Renaissance Stage*.

113. For the ideological linkage between blackness and female vice—a linkage that Othello activates when he describes the allegedly adulterous Desdemona as being "black as ink," see Newman, *Fashioning Femininity*, 71–94. See also Loomba, *Gender, Race, Renaissance Drama*, chap. 2.

114. See also Herod's statement that "Her heav'nly beauty 'twas that made me think / That it with chastity could never dwell" (5.1.244–45; p. 148).

115. I quote from Barry Weller's discussion of Salome as a center of theatrical and verbal energy in the play: introduction to *Mariam*, ed. Weller and Ferguson, 40.

116. On the historical persistence of Elizabeth's authority in Jacobean culture and drama, see Eggert, *Showing Like a Queen*, especially chap. 5.

117. Herod laments his killing of Mariam by saying, "'Tis I that have o'erthrown your royal line. / Within her purer veins the blood did run, / That from her grandam Sara she derived" (5.1.178–80; p. 145). Self-servingly, however, Herod here forgets that Mariam's death does not, in political terms, mean the end of her "line," since she has two sons by Herod.

118. Cited in Shapiro, *Shakespeare and the Jews*, 13.

119. See, e.g., Samuel Purchas, *Purchas His Pilgrimage* (1613), 83; cited in Callaghan, "Re-Reading Elizabeth Cary's *The Tragedie of Mariam*," 334n. 46.

120. See Gen. 25:30 and Weller's note to 1.2.103; p. 155.

121. For the conflation of Herod the Great with the Herod who slaughtered the "Innocents," see the introduction to *Mariam*, ed. Weller and Ferguson, 20–23. Note that Alexandra's description of blood as both food and drink for Herod also conjures up an image of the Catholic ritual reenactment of Christ's death, the sacrament of communion. Herod himself unwittingly foretells his crime against the children when he accuses Mariam of having "complotted Herod's massacre" (4.4.207–8; p. 122).

122. See Barry Weller's note to 1.3.237; p. 157. As examples of the prophetic view of Edom, which I see subtending Mariam's speech about the "rejected race," Weller cites Ezek. 15:13, 35; Amos 1:11–12; and Jer. 49:7–22, as well as Obad. 1.

123. See Shapiro, *Shakespeare and the Jews*, 34 and passim.

124. Quoted in Callaghan, "Re-Reading Elizabeth Cary's *The Tragedie of Mariam,*" 334n. 46.

125. Shapiro, *Shakespeare and the Jews,* 17.

126. See Hanson, *Discovering the Subject,* chap. 3; see also Halley, "Equivocation and the Legal Conflict over Religious Identity"; and Wright, "Legal and Linguistic Coercion of Recusant Women."

127. Some English Christians, including the man who later tutored Cary's sons, changed religious affiliations several times, without giving observers any way of clearly distinguishing between heartfelt and expedient conversions; see "Life," in *Mariam,* ed. Weller and Ferguson, 244.

128. On the Christian allegory of Act 5, see Beilin, *Redeeming Eve,* chap. 6.

129. See Norbrook, "Safety First in Buckinghamshire" (a review of Kevin Sharpe's *Reading Revolutions*), 22.

130. In political terms, the first three acts depict a subordinated kingdom that might come to be ruled by a woman or by a hitherto subordinated man. This is a landscape of potentiality, but the political statement, like Mariam's claims to the throne, remains oddly occluded. By the final act of the play, political potentiality seems to have been translated into religious prophecy, with the main significant action being Mariam's (off-stage) execution. There is, however, another significant action, the full meaning of which is arguably hidden from the reader. This is Salome's verbal act of persuading Herod, evidently against his will, to order Mariam's beheading. Salome is clearly motivated by revenge—and her dislike of Mariam is much more comprehensible than is Iago's of Othello, for we actually see Mariam "twitting" Salome with her low birth. But Salome's political motives are obscure: does she hope to gain more of the traditionally female power behind the throne—the sort of power infamously exercised by Catherine de Medici—than she would if Herod's wife remained alive? Or does Salome perhaps harbor ambitions to rule openly, as it seems she might when Herod goes mad with Petrarchan grief after Mariam's death? The possibilities are left open at the end, with Salome bearing much of the play's potential for weaving a new plot, an alternative plot, to the one that Cary inherited from history.

131. See Anderson, *Lineages of the Absolutist State,* for an important comparative analysis of the ideologies and institutions of absolutist monarchies during the transitional era. On early modern debates about the legitimacy of absolutist regimes, see Kastan, *Shakespeare after Theory,* 169–72.

132. See Jameson, "Religion and Ideology," especially 45.

Chapter Seven

1. On England's economic development during the seventeenth century, a topic much discussed by historians, see Beckles, "Hub of Empire"; Davies, *North Atlantic World;* Bliss, *Revolution and Empire;* Williams, *Capitalism and Slavery;* all with further references.

2. For discussions of her disputed class origins and claims about her lineage, see Ferguson, "Authorial Ciphers of Aphra Behn"; Goreau, *Reconstructing Aphra;* Todd, *Secret Life;* and O'Donnell, *Aphra Behn.*

3. See Gilder, *Enter the Actress;* Pearson, *Prostituted Muse,* 26–33; and Maus, "Playhouse Flesh and Blood."

4. For a lucid account of her use of the prostitute/playwright analogy, see Gallagher, *Nobody's Story,* chap. 1.

5. Behn suffered, as did Dryden and other playwrights, from the amalgamation in 1682 of the two London theater companies, the King's Company and the Duke's Company, for which latter Behn chiefly wrote. For her efforts to make a living in the 1680s, see Todd, *Secret Life,* 370; for her

previous economic reliance on the theater's "third night" receipts, see Gallagher, *Nobody's Story,* 10–14.

6. *Oroonoko, Or the Royal Slave. A True History,* in *Works of Aphra Behn,* ed. Todd, 3:54–119. Page references to this edition are henceforth given parenthetically in the text.

7. All references are to the first edition of *Ranter,* printed posthumously, with a preface by Dryden, and reprinted in *Works of Aphra Behn,* ed. Todd, 7:285–354. I have silently added scene numbers, which are present only occasionally in the first edition. The play was first staged in the fall of 1689; on its stage history, see *Works of Aphra Behn,* ed. Summers, 4:219–20. One of Behn's early readers, Thomas Southerne, saw and exploited parallels between *Oroonoko* and *Ranter* in his dramatization of the former (see Southerne, *Oroonoko* [1695/6], ed. Novak and Rodes). Until recently, critics focused chiefly on the sources of *Ranter;* my reading is indebted to several new studies examining the play in its social context, notably Hendricks, "Civility, Barbarism, and Aphra Behn's *The Widow Ranter*"; Todd, "Spectacular Death"; Herman, "We All Smoke Here"; Bridges, "We Were Somebody in England"; and Ross, "*The Widdow Ranter:* Old World, New World." For brief but useful perspectives on the play, see Wermuth, "Bacon's Rebellion in the London Theater"; and Pearson, *Prostituted Muse,* 157–58.

8. See Yates, *Astraea.* For fascinating new work on Elizabeth's imperial iconography in relation both to the myth of Astraea and to the figures of Dido (as "Elissa") and Aeneas (as empire builder), see Dalton, "Art for the Sake of Dynasty." Dalton's discussion of the alchemical figure of the "black emperor" associated with Saturn came to my attention too late to be considered in relation to Behn's idealized view of a melancholic black prince.

9. The term is Mary Louise Pratt's (from *Imperial Eyes*); she uses it to refer to writing by non-European writers, but Campbell suggests extending it to include those Europeans, like Behn, who provide a "Story" of a cultural Other through the voice of a "narrator so projective and appropriating . . . that the work becomes a portrait of the narrator's encounter" (*Wonder and Science,* 270).

10. On the British loss of Surinam, see Williams, *From Columbus to Castro,* 81.

11. Byam's derogatory remarks about Behn, reproduced in Duffy, *Passionate Shepherdess,* 401, are in a letter of 14 March 1664; he identifies her with the heroine of a sentimental romance by Honoré d'Urfé, *L'Astrée.* When Behn takes up "Astraea" as a pen name, she gives it a broader range of reference.

12. See Rogers, "Fact and Fiction," 1–2; and, for the absence of Behn's father from the colonial records, Todd, *Secret Life,* 38–39.

13. It appears that neither Behn nor Trefry owned land or slaves in the colony, though Behn refers to Oroonoko as "my slave" in her prefatory letter to Lord Maitland; her ownership seems to be in name but not in fact; similarly, as Katherine Rogers remarks, Behn claims high social position but lacks political power ("Fact and Fiction," 1–2).

14. On the ways in which "news" and the emergent media "helped to further a sense of the integration of local and national in the period up to 1640," see Cust, "News and Politics," 69–75. See also the discussions of Behn's opening truth-claims, in the context of discourses of "news," in Davis, *Factual Fictions,* 106–10; and McKeon, *Origins of the English Novel,* 111–13.

15. For examples of this gendered cultural discourse, see Davis, *Problem of Slavery,* 277.

16. See Ferguson, "Authorial Ciphers of Aphra Behn"; and, for Behn's attitudes toward literary property, Rosenthal, *Playwrights and Plagiarists,* chap. 3.

17. The wife/slave analogy is made, for example, by Mary Chudleigh, "To the Ladies" (1703), and by the female author of *An Essay in Defence of the female sex* (1696); cited in Rogers, "Fact and Fiction," 15n. 49.

18. See Rosenthal, "Owning Oroonoko." See also Ferguson, "Seventeenth-Century Quaker Women"; and Ferguson, *Subject to Others.*

19. Rose, *Gender and Heroism*, 100.

20. There is also a significant comic subplot about lack of literacy; see, for instance, the mock trial scene in which Whiff accuses his fellow justice of the peace, Boozer, of being unable to "write nor read, nor say the Lords Prayer" (*Ranter*, 3.1.47; p. 323). Serving as a low-life foil to the gullible Bacon, Boozer insists that he "understands the Law" although his knowledge is based on hearing others read a popular legal digest. For Oroonoko's education in skepticism, see Chibka, "Oh! Do Not Fear a Woman's Invention."

21. The verb *parlay*, anglicized from the French, evidently denotes a kind of talk involving negotiations between enemies; this is a meaning the *OED* dates from 1600. Behn's usage also invokes another early sense of the (new) English word, "to speak a foreign or strange language" (*OED*, 1b, first example from 1570).

22. For a similar point about the narrator's duality as both powerful and powerless, see Pearson, "Gender and Narrative," 132.

23. See Greenblatt, *Renaissance Self-Fashioning*, chap. 6, "The Improvisation of Power."

24. See Paxman, "Oral and Literate Discourse," 88. Paxman's argument parallels mine at several points, although he takes "oral and literate mentalities" as reified phenomena while I am interested in exploring them as ideological constructions of long duration that bear some as yet undetermined relation to reality.

25. For contemporary accounts of Bacon, see Andrews, ed., *Narratives of the Insurrections*; see also the valuable discussions in Herman, "We All Smoke Here"; and in Brown, *Good Wives, Nasty Wenches*, chap. 5, on Bacon and the "dilemma of colonial masculinity."

26. The letter is first read aloud in 2.1.51-59; p. 210. Bacon reads it again at 1.2 (stage direction after line 100); p. 211.

27. To advance what I have called the "absent father" plot, Behn excises from her version of Bacon's rebellion the powerful figure of the governor William Berkeley; though briefly deposed by Bacon, he took harsh revenge on Bacon's followers. For Berkeley's leadership in Virginia, see Brown, *Good Wives, Nasty Wenches*, 153-59 and passim. Behn's Semernia bears some relation to a historical Indian queen (in contrast to the Widow Ranter, who seems invented from whole cloth); see *Works of Aphra Behn*, ed. Todd, 7:289, on the queen of the Pamunkey Indians whose husband was killed by the English and who actively sought compensation for the murder.

28. The historical Bacon, characterized in the *Strange News* pamphlets as an appealing but finally culpable example of rebellion against true royal authority, has indeed often been read as a republican hero, especially by North American scholars who see in Bacon's Rebellion a prototype of the American Revolution, and in Bacon, a forerunner of George Washington. See, e.g., Ward, "Mrs. Behn's *The Widow Ranter*," 96.

29. For a description of this six-page pamphlet and its brief sequel, *More News from Virginia*, published later in the same year, again by William Harris, see Stearns, "Literary Treatment of Bacon's Rebellion in Virginia." Both pamphlets are reprinted in Finestone, *Bacon's Rebellion*. See also Batten, "Source of Aphra Behn's *The Widow Ranter*"; and Ward, "Mrs. Behn's *The Widow Ranter*."

30. See Hendricks, "Civility, Barbarism, and Aphra Behn's *The Widow Ranter*," 226-27.

31. For Byam's letter, see note 11 above. Scholars differ substantially on the dating of Behn's Surinam visit, but most now agree that it occurred between early fall 1663 and February or March 1664. See Goreau, *Reconstructing Aphra*, 49-69. For different datings of the trip, see Mendelson, *Mental World of Stuart Women*, 118; and Campbell, "Aphra Behn's Surinam Interlude," 27. Behn spied on Scot during her trip to Holland later in the decade.

32. For the hypothesis that the revolutionary Scot is partly figured in Oroonoko, see my "Authorial Ciphers of Aphra Behn," 229-31; and see also the passage in *Oroonoko* describing how

the hero should be "accompany'd by some" (among them evidently the narrator) "who should rather in appearance be Attendants than Spys" (95). For Scot as figured in Bacon, see Witmer and Freehafer, "Aphra Behn's Strange News from Virginia," 19-20.

33. Although modern critics have almost all read Oroonoko as a royalist hero, and some have argued for a topical allegory in which the black prince represents an amalgam of the martyred Charles I and the soon-to-be-deposed James II, such readings neglect the fact that Oroonoko rebels against a royalist, Byam, whom the narrator hates. See Mendelson, *Mental World of Stuart Women*, 120, for discussion of the "unexpected" republican perspective that pervades (I wouldn't follow her in assuming it governs) the novella.

34. See Campbell, *Wonder and Science*, 268. See also *Oroonoko*, 94, where Behn imagines a "river of Amazons" as large as the Thames and leading (as Raleigh had predicted) to gold; intriguingly, Behn presents this river as a New World counterpart to the Old World river of the same name where the empire-seeking Alexander encountered "wonderful snakes."

35. See *Works of Aphra Behn*, ed. Todd, 7:448n. 24. Todd thinks, however, that a historical Oroonoko would have been Ashanti rather than Yoruba. Imoinda's name, like Oroonoko's, could have roots and allegorical meanings in seventeenth-century Africa; I am indebted for this point to Adéléké Adéèkó, who tells me that a modern Yoruba translation of "Imoinda" would be "honey mixed with wealth." The modern Nigerian writer 'Biyi Bandele, from whose 1999 stage version of Behn's *Oroonoko* my second epigraph comes, also sees her African names as rooted in the Yoruba language; see the playwright's foreword, 5. Though we know little about what Behn might have learned about African languages from oral accounts by explorers and slave traders, we do know that she collected "foreign" words, including "heathenish Names," with zest and sometimes mated them (miscegenously and comically) with English words: see, e.g., "Hayoumorecake Bantam" in her *Memoirs of the Court of the King of Bantam*, in *Works of Aphra Behn*, ed. Todd, 3:291.

36. On the history of miscegenation laws (the word *miscegenation* was not used in its modern sense to denote prohibited behavior until the nineteenth century, according to the *OED*), see Jordan, *White Man's Burden*, 70-71.

37. See Kupperman, *Settling with the Indians*, 118-19; she notes that fornication between Indians and whites was punishable in the early period of the Virginia colony, but the penalties were the same as for fornication among whites. For John Rolfe's tortuous attempt to justify his marriage, see Hamor, *True Discourse of the Present Estate of Virginia* (1615).

38. Quoted from Winthrop Jordan's discussion of the groups affected by new laws permitting castration as a punishment in the colonies (never in England); see *White over Black*, 94.

39. Ibid. Compare Kupperman, *Settling with the Indians*, 110-11, on linguistic evidence suggesting that the English "did not come to grips with the general problem of how one designates Christian Indians."

40. "By ancient Prophesies we have been told/Our World shall be subdu'd by one more old," says the Indian Boy in the prologue to Dryden and Howard's *Indian Queen*, lines 12-13, in *Works of John Dryden*, ed. Hooker, Swedenberg, and Dearing, 8:184.

41. See, e.g., "The Adventure of the Black Lady," where the heroine is both sexually fallen and non-English; and "Moorea," who, like the narrator, steals letters and engineers the plot in "The Unfortunate Bride." On the political and sexual valences of *black* in Behn's writings, see Gallagher, *Nobody's Story*, chap. 2.

42. Cited in Brown, *Good Wives, Nasty Wenches*, 166; for Bacon's victory over Berkeley, see Andrews, ed., *Narratives of the Insurrections*, 69-70.

43. My argument here follows a line of speculation more fully explored by Peter Herman; in

a forthcoming essay ("We All Smoke Here"), he argues that Behn's play participates, though ambivalently, in the invention of "America" as a culturally independent site.

44. Given the historical fact that one of the ringleaders of Bacon's rebellion, a man named Richard Lawrence (not mentioned in Behn's play), had scandalously buried his learning and abilities "in the darke imbraces of a Blackamoore, his slave," thereby offending the English women "in or about towne," it seems likely that Behn contributed deliberately to the discourse of "news" about interracial romance. The story about Lawrence does not appear in the *Strange News* pamphlets but rather in a seventeenth-century narrative entitled "The History of Bacon and Ingram's Rebellion" that wasn't published until the nineteenth century (when it was found in a unique manuscript). Though usually discounted on that ground as a possible source for Behn's play, such a narrative—or parts of it—could well have been known to Behn's contemporaries. Positivistic assumptions about transmission seem particularly inadequate to describe the world of overlapping oral and printed routes whereby information circulated in this era. For Lawrence, see "History of Bacon and Ingram's Rebellion," in Andrews, ed., *Narratives of the Insurrections*, 96.

45. For useful perspectives on the novella's reflection on international trade, see Brown, "Romance of Empire"; Rosenthal, *Playwrights and Plagiarists*; McLeod, *Geography of Empire*, chap. 4; Andrade, "White Skin, Black Masques"; and Azim, *Colonial Rise of the Novel*.

46. Letter to Tonson cited in Todd, *Secret Life of Aphra Behn*, 325. For Behn's economic situation and practices, see Gallagher, *Nobody's Story*; and also Payne, "And Poets Shall by Patron-Princes Live."

47. For a lengthier discussion of this self-description (100–101), see Ferguson, "Feathers and Flies"; see also Campbell, *Wonder and Science*, 260–61.

48. Catherine Gallagher remarks the "abrupt scoring" of Imoinda's body, so "strongly and clumsily marked in the text" (*Nobody's Story*, 72).

49. See *Works of Aphra Behn*, ed. Todd, 3:451n. 61.

50. See Knapp, *An Empire Nowhere*, 303n. 16. In the remarkable volume published as *India Occidentalis* but also as *Grands Voyages, America,* and *Great Voyages,* de Bry included texts and illustrations about voyages to North and South America; a second set of engraved works, usually referred to as the *Petits Voyages* or *India Orientalis,* dealt with voyages to the East Indies, Africa, and the Arctic. For a description of all thirteen parts of both series (the publication of which was continued by de Bry's sons after his death in 1598), see Duchet et al., eds., *L'Amérique de Théodore de Bry*, 9–46, and other essays in this well-illustrated volume.

51. The most logical syntactic antecedent of "they" would be a group of *black* men composed of Oroonoko and his band, perpetrating the rape which one might easily construe as the referent for "this cruelty." The grammatical ambiguity points, it seems, to the struggle between the narrator's original perception of danger and her "corrected" but guiltily impotent retroactive perception that the white men, not the black ones, were her true enemies.

52. See, for instance, the passage discussed below where the narrator explicitly invites her reader to reflect on her manipulative narrative powers when she tells Oroonoko stories of the lives of famous Romans to "divert" him from thoughts of mutiny. Her promise that he will eventually be freed is also an example of the ways in which her first-person narrative participates in the Cretan liar paradox that encompasses all English-born speakers in this novella.

53. On the tonal and epistemological complexities of Behn's rhetoric, see especially Chibka, "Oh! Do Not Fear a Woman's Invention"; and Campbell, *Wonder and Science*.

54. See Ferguson, "Authorial Ciphers of Aphra Behn," 244n. 8, for Behn's "preoccupation" with bedroom scenes; see n. 2 for critical discussions of her contemporary reputation.

55. On this play's Restoration popularity, see Ferguson, "Transmuting Othello," 20.

56. On the "buy or breed" debates, see Mannix in collaboration with Cowley, *Black Cargoes*, 23.

57. Since the blacks also greatly outnumbered the whites in the colony, Behn's explanation for the distinction in the English treatment of the two nonwhite groups is clearly problematic; the issue continues to be debated by modern historians. See Davis, *Problem of Slavery*, 178; and Phillips, *Slavery*, 184.

58. For discussions of early critics of slavery, such as Las Casas (who came only late in life to decry the enslavement of blacks as well as Indians) and Albornoz, see Davis, *Problem of Slavery*, 189 and passim; Williams, *From Columbus to Castro*, 43-44; and Goreau, *Reconstructing Aphra*, 289. On the legal and ideological distinctions very unevenly and gradually introduced between white and black slaves, see Phillips, *Slavery*, 183.

59. See, for instance, the passage from George Best's *Discourse* (1578) where he insists that "I my selfe have seene an Ethiopian as blacke as a cole brought into England, who taking a faire English woman to wife, begat a sonne in all respects as blacke as the father was, although England were his native countrey, and an English woman his mother" (quoted from Hakluyt, *Principal Navigations* [1600], ed. Raleigh, 7:262). I am indebted to Karen Newman's discussion of this passage in "And Wash the Ethiop White," 46. See also Shyllon's discussion of this passage, *Black People in Britain*, 93.

60. For a discussion of this "recoloring" of Behn's heroine, see MacDonald, "Race, Women, and the Sentimental," 562-63.

61. This edition was replaced, in 1997, by a new Norton paperback with a different cover picture: see *Oroonoko: An Authoritative Text, Historical Backgrounds, Criticism*, ed. Lipking.

62. *On the Life and Memoirs of Mrs. Behn*, Sig b1 recto. On this biographer and his or her account, which was expanded in the 1696 edition of Behn's *Histories and Novels*, see Day, "Aphra Behn's First Biographer."

63. On Raleigh's quest for Amazons as described in his *Discoverie*, see Montrose, "Work of Gender," 25-29; see also Lorimer, "Ralegh's First Reconnaissance of Guiana?"

64. The descriptions of Imoinda's "carved" body suggest the possibility of female homoerotic pleasure as yet another alternative to procreative heterosexuality. See Behn's poem "To the Fair Clarinda," in *Works of Aphra Behn*, ed. Todd, 1:288.

65. For a recent attempt to counter the "invisibility" of black women in Caribbean history, see Bush, *Slave Women in Caribbean Society*. For a reading that stresses Imoinda's significance as a "mute bearer of female suffering," see Ballaster, "New Hystericism," 293-94.

66. On this trope of the New World as a "penetrable" female, see Montrose, "Work of Gender." Bandele has Byam rape Imoinda; see *Aphra Behn's "Oroonoko,"* 102.

67. "Ah, more than Woman! more than man she is," as Daniel Kendrick exclaimed in a poem published with Behn's own *Lycidus* in 1688; reprinted in *Works of Aphra Behn*, ed. Summers, 6:296-98.

Afterword

1. See Michael Finlay, *Western Writing Implements in the Age of the Quill Pen*, 3. Although the Bible refers to an "iron" pen (Job 19:24) and there are some references to metal pens in sixteenth- and seventeenth-century stationers' records (about 1620, John Newgate buys a "silver penne" for his sister, for instance), such references are almost certainly to sheaths for quill tips rather than to the pen itself. I am indebted for this information to David Kastan and Elliott Trice.

2. Wallace, *Chaucerian Polity*, xvi, quoting Baechler, *Origins of Capitalism*, 115.

3. See Elias, *Civilizing Process*; and Gramsci, "Formation of Intellectuals."

4 Under the name "Astraea" in a dedicatory letter "To Philaster" prefacing her play *The Young King* (1683), Behn refers to herself in the third person as someone who "feared the reproach of being an *American*" (in *Works of Aphra Behn*, ed. Todd, 7:83).

5 For work that extends and enriches strands of the story sketched here, see McDowell, *Women of Grub Street*; Vincent, *Literacy and Popular Culture*; and Benedict, *Making the Modern Reader*.

6 As Raymond Williams suggested long ago, and as Kathryn Shevelow has argued more recently, a "new kind of middle-class reading public" emerged in the 1690s (Shevelow, *Women and Print Culture*, 7, citing Williams, *Long Revolution*, 182). In England, moreover, although not in the tax-burdened France of Louis XIV, the 1690s were a decade of innovation in economic institutions; see Poovey, *Making a Social Body*, 6. On the emergence of a literate "public sphere" in France during the late seventeenth and eighteenth centuries, see Goodman, *Republic of Letters*.

Select Bibliography

Aarslef, Hans. *From Locke to Saussure: Essays in the Study of Language and Intellectual History.* London: Athlone Press, 1983.

Abbott, Don Paul. "Rhetoric and Writing in Renaissance Europe and England." In *A Short History of Writing Instruction from Ancient Greece to Twentieth Century America.* Ed. James J. Murphy, 95–120. Davis, Calif.: Hermagoras Press, 1980.

Abbott, Gerry. "English as a Foreign Language." In *The Encyclopedia of Language and Linguistics.* Ed. R. E. Asher, 3:1120–24. New York: Pergamon Press, 1994.

Abrams, M. H., et al., eds. *The Norton Anthology of English Literature.* 6th ed. 2 vols. New York: W. W. Norton, 1993.

Adelman, Janet. "Born of Woman: Fantasies of Maternal Power in *Macbeth.*" In *Shakespearean Tragedy and Gender.* Ed. Shirley Nelson Garner and Madelon Sprengnether, 105–34. Bloomington: Indiana University Press, 1996.

———. *The Common Liar.* New Haven: Yale University Press, 1973.

———. "Making Defect Perfection: Shakespeare and the One-Sex Model." In *Enacting Gender on the English Renaissance Stage.* Ed. Viviana Comensoli and Anne Russell, 23–52. Urbana: University of Illinois Press, 1999.

Allestree, Richard. *The Ladies Calling.* Oxford: Printed at the Theater, 1673.

Allison, Alexander, et al., eds. *The Norton Anthology of Poetry.* 3d ed. New York: W. W. Norton, 1983.

Allmand, Christopher. *Henry V.* Berkeley: Universiy of California Press, 1992.

Althusser, Louis, and Etienne Balibar, eds. *Reading Capital.* Trans. Ben Brewster. London: New Left Books, 1970.

Altick, Richard D. *The English Common Reader: A Social History of the Mass Reading Public, 1800–1900.* Chicago: University of Chicago Press, 1957.

Altman, Janet Gurkin. "Women's Letters in the Public Sphere." In *Going Public: Women and Publishing in Early Modern France.* Ed. Elizabeth C. Goldsmith and Dena Goodman, 99–115. Ithaca: Cornell University Press, 1995.

Altman, Joel. "'Vile Participation': The Amplification of Violence in the Theater of *Henry V.*" *Shakespeare Quarterly* 42 (1991): 1–32.

Ames, Percy W., ed. *Elizabeth, "The Mirror of the Sinful Soul."* London: Asher, 1897.

Amin, Samir. *Eurocentrism.* Trans. Russell Moore. New York: Monthly Press, 1989.

Amussen, Susan Dwyer. "The Gendering of Popular Culture in Early Modern England." In *Popular Culture in England, c. 1500–1850.* Ed. Tim Harris, 48–68. New York: St. Martin's Press, 1995.

———. *An Ordered Society: Class and Gender in Early Modern England.* London: Basil Blackwell, 1988.

Ancekewicz, Elaine. "L'Ecriture du Nouveau Monde: L'inscription de la femme." In *Actes du colloque "Présence et influence de l'Ouest Français en Amérique du Nord: Arcadie, Louisiane, Nouvelle Angleterre, Québec, et autres aires francophones" à l'Université d'Angers (26 May 1994),* 425–36. Angers: Presses de l'Université d'Angers, 1996.

Anderson, Benedict. *Imagined Communities: Reflections on the Origins and Spread of Nationalism.* 1983; revised and expanded ed., London: Verso, 1991.

Anderson, Karen. *Chain Her by One Foot: The Subjugation of Women in Seventeenth Century New France.* New York: Routledge, 1991.

Anderson, Perry. *English Questions.* London: Verso, 1992.

———. *Lineages of the Absolutist State.* London: New Left Books, 1974.

Andrade, Susan Z. "White Skin, Black Masques: Colonialism and the Sexual Politics of *Oroonoko.*" *Cultural Critique* 27 (spring 1994): 189–214.

Andrews, Charles, ed. *Narratives of the Insurrections, 1675–1690.* New York: Charles Scribner's Sons, 1915.

Anson, M. "Lollardy and Literacy." *History* 62 (1977): 347–71.

Archer, John Michael. *Old Worlds: Egypt, Southwest Asia, India, and Russia in Early Modern English Writing.* Stanford: Stanford University Press, 2001.

Aristotle. *Generation of Animals.* Trans. A. L. Peck. Loeb Classical Library. Cambridge, Mass.: Harvard University Press, 1943.

Armitage, David. *The Ideological Origins of the British Empire.* Cambridge: Cambridge University Press, 2001.

———. "Literature and Empire." In *The Origins of Empire.* Ed. N. Canny, 99–123. Oxford: Oxford University Press, 1998.

Armstrong, John A. *Nations before Nationalism.* Chapel Hill: University of North Carolina Press, 1982.

Asad, Talal. "The Concept of Cultural Translation in British Social Anthropology." In *Writing Culture.* Ed. James Clifford and George E. Marcus, 141–64. Berkeley: University of California Press, 1986.

Ascham, Roger. *The Scholemaster.* Ed. R. J. Schoek. Ontario: J. M. Dent, 1966.

Ascoli, Albert. "'Neminem ante Nos': Historicity and Authority in the *De vulgari eloquentia.*" *Annali d'italianistica* 8 (1990): 187–231.

———. "The Unfinished Author: Dante's Rhetoric of Authority in *Convivio* and *De vulgari eloquentia.*" In *The Cambridge Companion to Dante.* Ed. Rachel Jacoff, 45–66. New York: Cambridge University Press, 1993.

Aston, Margaret. *Lollards and Reformers: Images and Literacy in Late Medieval Religion.* London: Hambledon, 1984.

Auerbach, Erich. *Literary Language and Its Public in Late Antiquity and the Middle Ages.* Trans. Ralph Manheim. New York: Pantheon Books, 1965.

Augustine, Saint. *On Christian Doctrine.* Trans. D. W. Robertson, Jr. Indianapolis: Bobbs-Merrill, 1958.

Azim, Firdous. *The Colonial Rise of the Novel.* London: Routledge, 1993.

Azpilcueta, Martín de. *Opera omnia, in quinque tomos divisa.* Venice: Dominicus Nicolinus, 1601.

Bacon, Roger. *The Greek Grammar of Roger Bacon and a Fragment of His Hebrew Grammar.* Ed. Edmond Nolan and S. A. Hirsch. Cambridge: Cambridge University Press, 1902.

Bailey, Richard. "The Development of English." In *The Mediaeval World.* Ed. David Daiches and Anthony Thorlby, 127–61. London: Aldus Books, 1973.

———. *Images of English: A Cultural History of the Language.* Ann Arbor: University of Michigan Press, 1991.

Baker, David J. *Between Nations: Shakespeare, Spenser, Marvell and the Question of Britain.* Stanford: Stanford University Press, 1997.

Baker, J. H. *An Introduction to English Legal History.* London: Butterworth, 1971.

Baldo, Jonathan. "Wars of Memory in *Henry V.*" *Shakespeare Quarterly* 47 (1996): 132–59.

Balibar, Etienne. "The Nation Form: History and Ideology." In *Race, Nation, Class: Ambiguous Identities.* Ed. Etienne Balibar and Immanuel Wallerstein, 86–106. London: Verso, 1991.

Balibar, Renée. *Les Français fictifs: Le rapport des styles littéraires au français national.* Paris: Hachette, 1974.

———. *Le Français national: Politique et pratiques de la langue nationale sous la révolution française.* Paris: Hachette, 1974.

———. *L'Institution du français: Essai sur le colinguisme des Carolingiens à la République.* Paris: Presses Universitaires de France, 1985.

———. "National Language, Education, Literature." In *Literature, Politics and Theory: Papers from the Essex Conference, 1976–84.* Ed. Francis Barker et al., 126–47. New York: Methuen, 1986.

Ballaster, Ros. "New Hystericism: Aphra Behn's *Oroonoko*: The Body, the Text and the Feminist Critic." In *New Feminist Discourses: Critical Essays on Theories and Texts.* Ed. Isobel Armstrong, 283–95. London: Routledge, 1992.

Bandele, 'Biyi. *Aphra Behn's "Oroonoko."* A New Adaptation. London: Amber Lane Press, 1999.

Barcia Carballido y Zúñiga, Andrés González de. *Chronological History of the Continent of Florida. Containing the discoveries and principal events which came to pass in this vast kingdom, touching the Spanish, French, Swedish, Danish, English, and other nations . . . from the year 1512, in which Juan Ponce de Leon discovered Florida, until the year 1722.* Trans. with introduction by Anthony Kerrigan, foreword by Herbert E. Bolton. Gainesville: University of Florida Press, 1951.

Barroll, Leeds. *Politics, Plague, and Shakespeare's Theater.* Ithaca: Cornell University Press, 1991.

Barry, Jonathan. "Literacy and Literature in Popular Culture: Reading and Writing in Historical Perspective." In *Popular Culture in England, c. 1500–1850.* Ed. Tim Harris, 69–94. New York: St. Martin's Press, 1995.

Bartels, Emily C. "Malta, the Jew, and the Fictions of Difference: Colonialist Discourse in Marlowe's *The Jew of Malta.*" *English Literary Renaissance* 20, no. 1 (winter 1990): 1–16.

Bartholomae, David. "Producing Adult Readers: 1930–1950." In *The Right to Literacy.* Ed. Andrea A. Lunsford, Helene Moglen, and James F. Slevin, 13–28. New York: Modern Language Association, 1990.

Bartlett, Anne C. *Male Authors, Female Readers: Representation and Subjectivity in Middle English Devotional Literature.* Ithaca: Cornell University Press, 1995.

Barton, David. *Literacy: An Introduction to the Ecology of Written Language.* Oxford: Blackwell, 1994.

Baswell, Christopher. "Dido's Purse." *Multilingua* 18 (1999): 159–72.

———. *Virgil in Medieval England: Figuring the "Aeneid" from the Twelfth Century to Chaucer.* Cambridge: Cambridge University Press, 1995.

Batten, Charles L., Jr. "The Source of Aphra Behn's *The Widow Ranter.*" *Restoration and Eighteenth Century Theatre Research* 13, no. 1 (May 1974): 12–18.

Baüml, Franz. "Varieties and Consequences of Medieval Literacy and Illiteracy." *Speculum* 55 (1980): 237–65.

Bauschatz, Cathleen M. "'Voylà, mes dames . . .': Inscribed Women Listeners and Readers in the *Heptaméron.*" In *Critical Tales: New Studies of the "Heptameron" and Early Modern Culture.* Ed. John D. Lyons and Mary B. McKinley, 104–22. Philadelphia: University of Pennsylvania Press, 1993.

Beaune, Colette. *Naissance de la nation France.* Paris: Gallimard, 1985.

Beckles, Hilary McD. "The 'Hub of Empire': The Caribbean and Britain in the Seventeenth Century." In *The Origins of Empire.* Ed. N. Canny, 218–63. Oxford: Oxford University Press, 1998.

Bedouelle, Guy. "Le Débat catholique sur la traducion de la Bible en langue vulgaire." In *Théorie et pratique de l'exégèse.* Ed. I. Backus and F. Higman, 39–59. Geneva: Droz, 1990.

Behn, Aphra. *Histories and Novels.* London: S. Briscoe, 1696. Contains the anonymous biography, *On the Life and Memoirs of Mrs. Behn, Written by a Gentlewoman of her Acquaintance.*

———. *Oroonoko: An Authoritative Text, Historical Backgrounds, Criticism.* Ed. Joanna Lipking. New York: W. W. Norton, 1997.

———. *Oroonoko or the Royal Slave.* Ed. Catherine Gallagher with Simon Stern. New York: Bedford/St. Martin's Press, 2000.

———. *Oroonoko or the Royal Slave.* Ed. Lore Metzger. New York: W. W. Norton, 1973.

———. *The Works of Aphra Behn.* Ed. Montague Summers. 6 vols. London: William Heinemann, 1915.

———. *The Works of Aphra Behn.* Ed. Janet Todd. 7 vols. Columbus: Ohio State University Press, 1992–96.

Beilin, Elaine V. *Redeeming Eve: Women Writers of the English Renaissance.* Princeton: Princeton University Press, 1987.

Bell, Illona. "In Defense of Their Lawful Liberty: A Letter Sent by the Maydens of London." In *Women, Writing, and the Reproduction of Culture in Tudor and Stuart Britain.* Ed. Mary E. Burke et al., 177–92. Syracuse, N.Y.: Syracuse University Press, 2000.

Bell, Susan Groag. "Medieval Women Book Owners: Arbiters of Lay Piety and Ambassadors of Culture." *Signs: Journal of Women in Culture and Society* 7, no. 4 (1982): 741–68.

———. "A New Approach to the Influence of Christine de Pizan: The Lost Tapestries of 'The City of Ladies.'" In *Sur "Le Chemin de longue étude": Actes du colloque d'Orléans, juillet 1995.* Ed. Bernard Ribémont, 7–12. Paris: Champion, 1998.

Bellamy, James A. "The Arabic Alphabet." In *The Origins of Writing.* Ed. W. Senner, 91–102. Lincoln: University of Nebraska Press, 1991.

Belsey, Catherine. *The Subject of Tragedy.* New York: Methuen, 1985.

Benedict, Barbara. *Making the Modern Reader: Cultural Mediation in Early Modern Literary Anthologies.* Princeton: Princeton University Press, 1996.

Benjamin, Walter. *The Origin of German Tragic Drama* [*Ursprung des Deutsches Trauerspiel,* 1928]. Trans. John Osborne. London: New Left Books/Verso, 1977.

———. "Theses on the Philosophy of History." In *Critical Theory and Society: A Reader.* Ed. Stephen Bronner and Douglas Kellner, 255–63. New York: Routledge, 1989.

Bennett, H. S. *English Books and Readers, 1475–1557.* Cambridge: Cambridge University Press, 1970.

Bennett, Judith. "Medieval Women, Modern Women: Across the Great Divide." In *Culture and History, 1350–1600: Essays on English Communities, Identity, and Writing.* Ed. David Aers, 147–75. London: Harvester-Wheatsheaf, 1992.

Berger, Harry, Jr. "The Renaissance Imagination: Second World and Green World." *Centennial Review* 9 (1965): 36–78.

Bergmann, Emilie L. "Language and 'Mothers' Milk': Maternal Roles and the Nurturing Body in Early Modern Spanish Texts." In *Maternal Measures: Figuring Caregiving in the Early Modern Period.* Ed. Naomi J. Miller and Naomi Yavneh, 105–20. Burlington, Vt.: Ashgate, 2000.

Bett, Henry. *Joachim of Flora.* London: Methuen, 1931.

Bhabha, Homi K., ed. *Nation and Narration.* London: Routledge, 1990.

Bible. *King James Version.* 1611; rpt., New York: Thomas Nelson, 1972.

La Bible, Qui est toute la Saincte escripture. En laquelle sont contenus le Vieil Testament and le Nouveau translatez en Francoys. Serrières/Neuchâtel: Pierre de Wingle, 1535.

Biblia Sacra, Juxta Vulgatam Clementinam. Rome: Typis Societatis S. Joannis Evang., 1956.

Bideaux, Michel. *"L'Heptaméron": De l'enquête au débat.* Paris: Editions InterUniversitaires, 1992.

Biggar, M. *A Collection of Documents Relating to Jacques Cartier and the Sieur of Roberval.* Publications of Canada, No. 14. Ottawa, 1930.

Biller, Peter. "Heresy and Literacy: Earlier History of the Theme." In *Heresy and Literacy, 1000–1530.* Ed. P. Biller and A. Hudson, 1–18. Cambridge: Cambridge University Press, 1994.

Biller, Peter, and Anne Hudson, eds. *Heresy and Literacy, 1000–1530.* Cambridge: Cambridge University Press, 1994.

Billingsley, Martin. *The pen's excellencie, or, The secretaries delight.* [London]: Sudbury and George Humble, 1618.

Bitten, Davis. *The French Nobility in Crisis, 1560–1640.* Stanford: Stanford University Press, 1969.

Blaisdell, Charmarie Jenkins. "Calvin's Letters to Women: The Courting of Ladies in High Places." *Sixteenth Century Journal* 13, no. 3 (fall 1982): 67–84.

Blake, N. F. "Standardising Shakespeare's Non-standard Language." In *Standardizing English.* Ed. J. B. Trahern, Jr., 57–81. Knoxville: University of Tennessee Press, 1989.

———. *William Caxton and English Literary Culture.* London: Hambledon Press, 1991.

Blanchard, Joel. "Compilation and Legitimation in the Fifteenth Century: *Le Livre de la Cité des Dames.*" In *Reinterpreting Christine de Pizan.* Ed. E. J. Richards, 228–49. Athens: University of Georgia Press, 1992.

Blank, Paula. *Broken English: Dialects and the Politics of Language in Renaissance Writings.* London: Routledge, 1996.

Bliss, Robert M. *Revolution and Empire: English Politics and the American Colonies in the Seventeenth Century.* Manchester, U.K.: Manchester University Press, 1990.

Bloch, R. Howard. "842: Louis the German and Charles the Bald, Grandsons of Charlemagne, Ratify the Serments de Strasbourg: The First Document and the Birth of Medieval Studies." In *A New History of French Literature.* Ed. Denis Hollier with R. Howard Bloch et al., 6–13. Cambridge, Mass.: Harvard University Press, 1989.

———. *Etymologies and Genealogies: A Literary Anthropology of the French Middle Ages.* Chicago: University of Chicago Press, 1983.

Bloomfield, M. W. "Joachim of Flora." *Traditio* 13 (1957): 249–309.

Bloomfield, M. W., and Marjorie E. Reeves. "The Penetration of Joachism into Northern Europe." *Speculum* 29 (1954): 772–93.

Blumenberg, Hans. *The Legitimacy of the Modern Age* [*Legitimität der Neuzeit,* 1966]. Trans. Robert M. Wallace. Cambridge, Mass.: MIT Press, 1985.

Blumenfeld-Kosinski, Renate. "Christine de Pizan and the Misogynistic Tradition." *Romanic Review* 91 (1990): 279–92.

Boccaccio, Giovanni. *Des cleres femmes.* Trans. anon., c. 1401. Paris, Bibliothèque Nationale, MS Fr. 12420.

————. *Famous Women [De claris mulieribus]*. Bilingual ed., ed. and trans. Virginia Brown. Cambridge, Mass.: The I Tatti Renaissance Library, Harvard University Press, 2001.

Boffey, Julia. "Women Authors and Women's Literacy in Fourteenth- and Fifteenth-Century England." In *Women and Literature in Britain, 1150–1500*. Ed. Carol M. Meale, 159–82. Cambridge: Cambridge University Press, 1993.

Bolton, Whitney French. "The Early History of English." In *The English Language: Essays by English and American Men of Letters, 1490–1839*. Ed. Whitney French Bolton, 269–95. London: Sphere, 1975.

Bonfil, Robert. "Reading in the Jewish Communities." In *A History of Reading in the West*. Ed. G. Cavallo and R. Chartier, 149–78. Amherst: University of Massachusetts Press, 1999.

Bono, Barbara. *Literary Transvaluation: From Vergilian Epic to Shakespearean Tragicomedy*. Berkeley: University of California Press, 1984.

Boone, Elizabeth Hill, and Walter D. Mignolo, eds. *Writing without Words: Alternative Literacies in Mesoamerica and the Andes*. Durham, N.C.: Duke University Press, 1994.

Boose, Lynda. "Scolding Brides and Bridling Scolds: Taming the Woman's Unruly Member." *Shakespeare Quarterly* 42, no. 2 (1991): 179–213.

Bornstein, Diane. "French Influence on Fifteenth Century English Prose as Exemplified by the Translation of Christine de Pizan's *Livre du Corps de Policie*." *Mediaeval Studies* 39 (1977): 369–86.

Bornstein, Diane, ed. *Distaves and Dames: Renaissance Treatises for and about Women*. Delmar, N.Y.: Scholars' Facsimiles, 1978.

Bossy, John. *The English Catholic Community, 1570–1850*. London: Darton, Longman and Todd, 1975.

Boswell, John. *Christianity, Social Tolerance, and Homosexuality: Gay People in Western Europe from the Beginning of the Christian Era to the Fourteenth Century*. Chicago: Chicago University Press, 1980.

Bourdeille, Pierre de, Seigneur de Brantôme. *Oeuvres complètes*. Ed. Lodovic Lalanne. 11 vols. Paris: Jules Renouard, 1864–82.

Bourdieu, Pierre. *Distinction: A Social Critique of the Judgment of Taste*. Trans. Richard Nice. London: Routledge and Kegan Paul, 1984.

————. *Language and Symbolic Power*. Ed. John B. Thompson. Trans. Gino Raymond and Matthew Adamson. Cambridge, Mass.: Harvard University Press, 1991.

————. *Outline of a Theory of Practice*. Trans. Richard Nice. Cambridge: Cambridge University Press, 1977.

Bowden, Caroline. "Women as Intermediaries: An Example of the Use of Literacy in the Late Sixteenth and Early Seventeenth Centuries." *History of Education* 22 (1993): 215–23.

Bower, Edmond. *Doctor Lamb Revived, or, Witchcraft Condemn'd in Anne Bodenham a Servant of His*. By T. W. for Richard Best and John Place, 1653.

Boyarin, Jonathan. "Placing Reading: Ancient Israel and Medieval Europe." In *The Ethnography of Reading*. Ed. J. Boyarin, 10–37. Berkeley: University of California Press, 1992.

Bozzolo, Carla. *Manuscrits des traductions françaises d'oeuvres de Boccace, XVe siècle*. Padua: Antenore, 1973.

Brabant, Margaret, ed. *Politics, Gender, and Genre: The Political Thought of Christine de Pizan*. Boulder, Colo.: Westview Press, 1992.

Braden, Gordon. *Renaissance Tragedy and the Senecan Tradition: Anger's Privilege*. New Haven: Yale University Press, 1985.

Brandon, E. *Robert Estienne et le dictionnaire français au XVIe siècle*. 1904; rpt., Geneva: Slatkine, 1967.

Brenner, Robert. "Agrarian Class Structure and Economic Development in Pre-industrial Europe." *Past and Present* 70 (1976): 30–75.

———. "The Agrarian Roots of European Capitalism." *Past and Present* 97 (1982): 16–113.

Brewer, John, and Susan Staves, eds. *Early Modern Conceptions of Property.* London: Routledge, 1996.

Bridges, Liz. "'We Were Somebody in England': Identity, Gender, and Status in *The Widdow Ranter.*" In *Aphra Behn (1640–1689): Identity, Alterity, Ambiguity.* Ed. Mary Ann O'Donnell, Bernard Dhuicq, and Guyonne Leduc, 75–80. Paris: L'Harmattan, 2000.

Brotherston, Gordon. "Towards a Grammatology of America: Lévi-Strauss, Derrida and the Native New World Text." In *Literature, Politics, and Theory: Papers from the Essex Conference, 1976–84.* Ed. Francis Barker et al., 190–209. London: Methuen, 1986.

Brotton, Jerry. *The Renaissance Bazaar: From the Silk Road to Michelangelo.* Oxford: Oxford University Press, 2002.

Brown, Cynthia J. "The Reconstruction of an Author in Print: Christine de Pizan in the Fifteenth and Sixteenth Centuries." In *Christine de Pizan and the Categories of Difference.* Ed. Marilynn Desmond, 215–35. Minneapolis: University of Minnesota Press, 1998.

Brown, Kathleen M. *Good Wives, Nasty Wenches, and Anxious Patriarchs: Gender, Race, and Power in Colonial Virginia.* Chapel Hill: University of North Carolina Press, 1997.

Brown, Laura. *Ends of Empire: Women and Ideology in Early Eighteenth-Century Literature.* Ithaca: Cornell University Press, 1993.

———. "The Romance of Empire: *Oroonoko* and the Trade in Slaves." In *The New Eighteenth Century: Theory, Politics, English Literature.* Ed. Felicity Nussbaum and Laura Brown, 41–61. New York: Methuen, 1987.

Brown, Pamela. *Better a Shrew Than a Sheep: Jesting Women in the Dramas of Early Modern Culture.* Ithaca: Cornell University Press, 2002.

Brownlee, Kevin. "Courtly Discourse and Autocitation in Christine de Pizan." In *Gender and Text in the Later Middle Ages.* Ed. Jane Chance, 172–94. Gainesville: University Press of Florida, 1994.

———. "Discourses of the Self: Christine de Pizan and the *Rose.*" *Romanic Review* 79 (1988): 199–221.

———. "Martyrdom and the Female Voice: Saint Christine in the *Cité des Dames.*" In *Images of Sainthood in Medieval Europe.* Ed. Renate Blumenfeld-Kosinski and Timea Szell, 115–35. Ithaca: Cornell University Press, 1991.

———. "Ovide et le moi poétique 'moderne' à la fin du Moyen Age: Jean Froissart et Christine de Pizan." In *Modernité au Moyen Age: Le Défi du passé.* Ed. Brigitte Cazelles and Charles Mela, 153–73. Geneva: Droz, 1990.

Brownley, Martine Watson. "The Narrator in *Oroonoko.*" *Essays in Literature* 4, no. 2 (1977): 174–81.

Bruce, F. F. "Render unto Caesar." In *Jesus and the Politics of His Day.* Ed. E. Bammel and C. F. D. Moule, 249–63. Cambridge: Cambridge University Press, 1984.

Brunot, Ferdinand. *Histoire de la langue française des origines à nos jours.* Rev. ed. 13 vols. Paris: Librairie Armand Colin, 1966–79.

Burke, Peter. "The Uses of Literacy in Early Modern Italy." In *The Social History of Language.* Ed. Peter Burke and Roy Porter, 21–42. Cambridge: Cambridge University Press, 1987.

Burke, R. A. "Approaches to Studying Reading Interests of Earlier Civilisation[s]." In *Studies in the History of Reading.* Ed. Greg Brooks and A. K. Pugh. Reading: Centre for the Teaching of Reading, University of Reading School of Education, 1984.

Burnley, J. D. "Christine de Pizan and the So-Called Clergial Style." *Modern Language Review* 81 (1986): 1–6.

———. "Curial Prose in England." *Speculum* 61 (1986): 593–614.

———. "Sources of Standardisation in Later Middle English." In *Standardizing English.* Ed. J. B. Trahern, Jr., 23–41. Knoxville: University of Tennessee Press, 1989.

Burrow, J. "A Maner Latyn Corrupt." *Medium Aevum* 30 (1961): 33–37.

Bush, Barbara. *Slave Women in Caribbean Society, 1650–1838.* Kingston: Heinemann Publishers (Caribbean); Bloomington: Indiana University Press; London: James Currey, 1990.

Bushnell, Rebecca. *A Culture of Teaching: Early Modern Humanism in Theory and Practice.* Ithaca: Cornell University Press, 1996.

———. *Tragedies of Tyrants: Political Thought and Theater in the English Renaissance.* Ithaca: Cornell University Press, 1990.

Butler, Judith P. *Bodies That Matter: On the Discursive Limits of "Sex."* New York: Routledge, 1993.

———. *Gender Trouble.* New York: Routledge, 1990.

Bynum, Caroline. *Holy Feast and Holy Fast: The Religious Significance of Food to Medieval Women.* Berkeley: University of California Press, 1987.

———. *Jesus as Mother: Studies in the Spirituality of the High Middle Ages.* Berkeley: University of California Press, 1982.

Callaghan, Dympna. "Re-Reading Elizabeth Cary's *The Tragedie of Mariam, Faire Queene of Jewry.*" In *Women, "Race," and Writing in the Early Modern Period.* Ed. M. Hendricks and P. Parker, 163–77. London: Routledge, 1994.

The Cambridge History of the English Language. Vol. 3: 1476–1776. Ed. Roger Lass. Cambridge: Cambridge University Press, 1999.

Campbell, Elaine. "Aphra Behn's Surinam Interlude." *Kunapipi* (Aarhus, Denmark) 7, nos. 2–3 (1985): 25–35.

Campbell, Mary Baine. *Wonder and Science: Imagining Worlds in Early Modern Europe.* Ithaca: Cornell University Press, 1999.

Canny, Nicholas. "The Origins of Empire: An Introduction." In *The Origins of Empire.* Ed. N. Canny, 1–33. Oxford: Oxford University Press, 1998.

Canny, Nicholas, ed. *The Origins of Empire: British Overseas Enterprise to the Close of the Seventeenth Century.* Vol. 1 of *The Oxford History of the British Empire.* Ed. Wm. Roger Louis. Oxford: Oxford University Press, 1998.

Carew, Richard. *The Excellencie of the English Tongue.* In *Remains Concerning Britain,* by William Camden. 2d ed., 1614. Ed. R. D. Dunn, 37–44. Toronto: University of Toronto Press, 1984.

Carr, Jean, Stephen Carr, and Lucille Schultz. *Archives of Instruction: Nineteenth-Century Readers, Rhetorics, and Composition Books in the United States.* Carbondale: Southern Illinois University Press, forthcoming.

Carroll, Berenice A. "Christine de Pizan and the Origins of Peace Theory." In *Women Writers and the Early Modern British Political Tradition.* Ed. Hilda Smith, 22–39. Cambridge: Cambridge University Press, 1998.

Carswell, Donald, ed. *Trial of Guy Fawkes and Others (The Gunpowder Plot).* Notable British Trials Series. London: William Hodge and Co., Ltd., 1934.

Cartelli, Thomas. "Jack Cade in the Garden: Class Consciousness and Class Conflict in *2 Henry VI.*" In *Enclosure Acts: Sexuality, Property, and Culture in Early Modern England.* Ed. Richard Burt and John Michael Archer, 48–67. Ithaca: Cornell University Press, 1994.

Cartier, Jacques. *The Voyages of Jacques Cartier; published from the originals with translations, notes and appendices.* Ed. H. P. Biggar. Ottawa: F. A. Acland, 1924. Rpt., revised and expanded, with introduction by Ramsay Cook. Toronto: University of Toronto Press, 1993.

Cary, Elizabeth. *The Tragedy of Mariam.* Facsimile of the 1613 edition, with introduction and textual variants by A. C. Dunstan and W. W. Greg (1914). Rpt. with supplementary introduction by Marta Straznicky and Richard Rowlands. Oxford: Malone Society, Oxford University Press, 1992.

———. *The Tragedy of Mariam, the Fair Queen of Jewry.* With *The Lady Falkland: Her Life,* by One of Her Daughters. Ed. Barry Weller and Margaret W. Ferguson. Berkeley: University of California Press, 1994.

———. *Works By and Attributed to Elizabeth Cary.* Introduced by Margaret Ferguson. Vol. 2 of *The Early Modern Englishwoman: A Facsimile Library of Essential Works, Part 1: Printed Writings, 1500–1640.* Ed. Betty Travitsky and Patrick Cullen. Aldershot, U.K.: Scolar Press, 1996.

Casey, Kathleen. "Women in Norman and Plantagenet England." In *The Women of England from Anglo-Saxon Times to the Present: Interpretive Bibliographical Essays.* Ed. Barbara Kanner, 83–123. Hamden, Conn.: Archon, 1979.

Cavallo, Guglielmo, and Roger Chartier, eds. *A History of Reading in the West.* Trans. Lydia G. Cochrane. Amherst: University of Massachusetts Press, 1999.

Cawdrey, Robert. *A Table Alphabeticall.* London: Edmund Wever, 1604.

Caxton, William. Preface to his translation of Virgil's *Eneydos* (1490). In *The English Language: Essays by English and American Men of Letters, 1490–1839.* Ed. W. F. Bolton, 1–4. Cambridge: Cambridge University Press, 1966.

Cazauran, Nicole. *"L'Heptaméron" de Marguerite de Navarre.* Paris: Société d'édition d'enseignement supérieur, 1976.

Cazelles, Brigitte. *The Lady as Saint: A Collection of French Hagiographic Romances of the Thirteenth Century.* Philadelphia: University of Pennsylvania Press, 1991.

Cerquiglini, Bernard. *La Naissance du français.* 2d ed. Paris: Que Sais-Je, 1993.

Cerquiglini-Toulet, Jacqueline. "L'Etrangère." *Revue des langues romanes* 92 (1988): 239–51.

Certeau, Michel de. *The Writing of History.* Trans. Tom Conley. New York: Columbia University Press, 1988.

Chance, Jane. "Christine de Pizan as Literary Mother: Woman's Authority and Subjectivity in 'The Floure and the Leafe' and 'The Assembly of Ladies.'" In *The City of Scholars.* Ed. M. Zimmermann and D. De Rentiis, 245–59. New York: Walter de Gruyter, 1994.

———. "Gender Subversion and Linguistic Castration in Fifteenth-Century English Translations of Christine de Pizan." In *Violence against Women in Medieval Texts.* Ed. Anne Roberts, 161–94. Gainesville: University Press of Florda, 1998.

Charlton, Kenneth. *Education in Renaissance England.* London: Routledge, 1965.

———. *Women, Religion and Education in Early Modern England.* London: Routledge, 1999.

Chartier, Roger. "Afterword: Reading, Writing and Literature in the Early Modern Age." In *Reading in Early Modern England.* Ed. S. Roberts. *Critical Survey* 12, no. 2 (2000): 128–42.

———. *Cultural History: Between Practices and Representations.* Ithaca: Cornell University Press, 1988.

———. *The Cultural Origins of the French Revolution.* Trans. Lydia G. Cochrane. Durham, N.C.: Duke University Press, 1991.

———. "Culture as Appropriation: Popular Cultural Uses in Early Modern France." In *Understanding Popular Cutlure: Europe from the Middle Ages to the Nineteenth Century.* Ed. Steven L. Kaplan, 229–53. New York: Moulton, 1984.

———. *The Order of Books: Readers, Authors, and Libraries in Europe between the Fourteenth and the Eighteenth Centuries.* Trans. Lydia G. Cochrane. Stanford: Stanford University Press, 1994.

———. "The Practical Impact of Writing." In *A History of Private Life.* Vol. 3: *Passions of the*

Renaissance. Ed. Roger Chartier, trans. Arthur Goldhammer, 111–59. Cambridge, Mass.: Harvard University Press, 1989.

———. "Texts, Printing, Readings." In *The New Cultural History: Essays*. Ed. L. Hunt, 154–75. Berkeley: University of California Press, 1989.

Chaucer, Geoffrey. *The Works of Geoffrey Chaucer*. Ed. F. N. Robinson. 2d ed. Cambridge: Cambridge University Press, 1957.

Chaunu, Pierre. *La Civilisation de l'Europe Classique*. Paris: Arthaud, 1966.

Chibka, Robert. "'Oh! Do Not Fear a Woman's Invention': Truth, Falsehood, and Fiction in Aphra Behn's *Oroonoko*." *Texas Studies in Literature and Language* 30, no. 4 (winter 1988): 510–37.

Cholakian, Patricia Francis. *Rape and Writing in the "Heptameron" of Marguerite de Navarre*. Carbondale: Southern Illinois University Press, 1991.

Christianson, C. Paul. "Chancery Standard and the Records of Old London Bridge." In *Standardizing English*. Ed. J. B. Trahern, Jr., 82–112. Knoxville: University of Tennessee Press, 1989.

Christie-Murray, David. *A History of Heresy*. 1976; rpt., Oxford: Oxford University Press, 1989.

Cicero. *De oratore*. Bilingual ed., trans. H. Rackham. 2 vols. Loeb Classical Library. Cambridge, Mass.: Harvard University Press, 1982.

Cipolla, Carlo. *Literacy and Development in the West*. Harmondsworth, U.K.: Penguin Books, 1969.

Civrieux, Marc de. *Watunna: An Orinoco Creation Cycle*. Trans. David M. Guss. San Francisco: North Point Press, 1980.

Clanchy, M. T. *From Memory to Written Record: England 1066–1307*. Cambridge, Mass.: Harvard University Press, 1979.

———. "Learning to Read in the Middle Ages and the Role of Mothers." In *Studies in the History of Reading*. Ed. Greg Brooks and A. K. Pugh, 33–39. Reading: University of Reading Press, 1984.

Clancy, Thomas H. "Papist-Protestant-Puritan: English Religious Taxonomy, 1565–1665." *Recusant History* 13, no. 4 (1976): 227–53.

Clark, Katerina, and Michael Holquist. *Mikhail Bakhtin*. Cambridge, Mass.: Harvard University Press, 1984.

Clark, Steve, ed. *Travel Writing and Empire: Postcolonial Theory in Transit*. London: Zed, 1999.

Clegg, Cyndia S. "Review Essay: History of the Book: An Undisciplined Discipline?" *Renaissance Quarterly* 14, no. 1 (spring 2001): 221–45.

Clifford, James. "On Ethnographic Allegory." In *Writing Culture: The Poetics and Politics of Ethnography*. Ed. James Clifford and George E. Marcus, 98–121. Berkeley: University of California Press, 1986.

———. *The Predicament of Culture: Twentieth-Century Ethnography, Literature, and Art*. Cambridge, Mass.: Harvard University Press, 1988.

Cockburn, J. S. "Early Modern Assize Records as Historical Evidence." *Journal of Society of Archivists* 5 (1975): 215–31.

Coke, Edward. *A True and Perfect Relation of the Whole Proceedings against the late most barbarous Traitors, Garnet a Jesuite, and his Confederats . . .* London: Robert Barker, 1606.

Coleman, Janet. *Medieval Readers and Writers, 1350–1400*. New York: Columbia University Press, 1981.

Coleman, Joyce. *Public Reading and the Reading Public in Late Medieval England and France*. New York: Cambridge University Press, 1996.

Conley, Tom. "The Graphics of Dissimulation: Between *Heptameron* 10 and L'Histoire Tragique."

In *Critical Tales: New Studies of the "Heptameron" and Early Modern Culture*. Ed. John D. Lyons and Mary B. McKinley, 65–82. Philadelphia: University of Pennsylvania Press, 1993.

Cook-Gumperz, Jenny, ed. *The Social Construction of Literacy*. Cambridge: Cambridge University Press, 1986.

Coote, Edmund. *The English School-Maister*. 1596. Facsimile rpt. English Linguistics, 1500–1800, no. 98. Menston, U.K.: Scolar Press, 1968.

Copeland, Rita. *Rhetoric, Hermeneutics, and Translation in the Middle Ages: Academic Traditions and Vernacular Texts*. Cambridge: Cambridge University Press, 1991.

Copperman, Paul. *The Literacy Hoax: The Decline of Reading, Writing and Learning in the Public Schools and What We Can Do about It*. New York: William Morrow, 1978.

Cormack, Lesley B. *Charting an Empire: Geography at the English University, 1580–1620*. Chicago: University of Chicago Press, 1998.

Correll, Barbara. "The Politics of Civility in Renaissance Texts: Grobiana in Grobianus." *Exemplaria* 2, no. 2 (1990): 627–58.

Corrigan, Philip, and Derek Sayer. *The Great Arch: English State Formation as Cultural Revolution*. Oxford: Basil Blackwell, 1985.

Cotgrave, Randle. *A Dictionarie of the French and English Tongues*. 1611. Menston, U.K.: Scolar Press, 1968. Facsimile of 1st ed. New York: Da Capo Press, 1971. The English Experience, No. 367.

Cottle, Basil. *The Triumph of English 1350–1400*. London: Blandford, 1969.

Cottrell, Robert D. *A Grammar of Silence: A Reading of Marguerite de Navarre's Poetry*. Washington, D.C.: Catholic University of America Press, 1986.

Coverdale, Miles. *The Coverdale Bible, 1535*. Facsimile of the Holkham copy, British Library. Introduction by S. L. Greenlade. Folkestone: Dawson, 1975.

Crane, Mary Thomas. *Framing Authority: Sayings, Self, and Society in Sixteenth-Century England*. Princeton: Princeton University Press, 1993.

Crane, Susan. "The Writing Lesson of 1381." In *Chaucer's England: Literature in Historical Context*. Ed. Barbara Hanawalt, 201–21. Minneapolis: University of Minnesota Press, 1992.

Craven, Wesley Frank. *White, Red, and Black: The Seventeenth-Century Virginian*. Charlottesville: University Press of Virginia, 1971.

Crawford, Patricia. "Public Duty, Conscience, and Women in Early Modern England." In *Public Duty and Private Conscience in Seventeenth-Century England*. Ed. John Morrill, Paul Slack, and Daniel Woolf, 57–76. New York: Oxford University Press, 1993.

———. *Women and Religion in England, 1500–1720*. London: Routledge, 1993.

Cressy, David. "Levels of Illiteracy in England, 1530–1730." 1977; rpt. in *Literacy and Social Development in the West: A Reader*. Ed. Harvey Graff, 105–24. Cambridge: Cambridge University Press, 1981.

———. *Literacy and the Social Order: Reading and Writing in Tudor and Stuart England*. Cambridge: Cambridge University Press, 1980.

———. "Literacy in Context: Meaning and Measurement in Early Modern England." In *Consumption and the World of Goods*. Ed. John Brewer and Roy Porter, 305–19. London: Routledge, 1993.

Crowder, C. M. W. *Unity, Heresy and Reform, 1378–1460: The Conciliar Response to the Great Schism*. New York: St. Martin's Press, 1977.

Crowley, Tony. *Proper English? Readings in Language, History, and Cultural Identity*. New York: Routledge, 1991.

———. *Standard English and the Politics of Language*. Urbana: University of Illinois Press, 1989.

Culler, Jonathan. "The Call of the Phoneme." In *On Puns: The Foundation of Letters*. Ed. Jonathan Culler, 1–16. Oxford: Oxford University Press, 1988.

Cunningham, Bernadette. "Women and Gaelic Literature." In *Women in Early Modern Ireland*. Ed. Margaret MacCurtain and Mary O'Dowd, 147–59. Edinburgh: Edinburgh University Press, 1991.

Cust, Richard. "News and Politics in Early Seventeenth-Century England." *Past and Present* 112 (August 1986): 60–90.

Dalarun, Jacques. "The Clerical Gaze." In *Silences of the Middle Ages*. Vol. 2: *A History of Women in the West*. Ed. Christiane Klapisch-Zuber, 15–42. Cambridge, Mass.: Belknap Press of Harvard University Press, 1992.

Dalton, Karen C. C. "Art for the Sake of Dynasty: The Black Emperor in the Drake Jewel and Elizabethan Imperial Imagery." In *Early Modern Visual Culture: Representation, Race, Empire in Renaissance England*. Ed. Peter Erickson and Clark Hulse, 178–214. Philadelphia: University of Pennsylvania Press, 2000.

Daniel, Samuel. *Musophilus*. In *Poems and a Defence of Ryme*. Ed. A. C. Sprague, 67–107. London: Routledge and Kegan Paul, 1950.

Dante Alighieri. *De vulgari eloquentia*. Ed. Aristide Marigo and P. G. Ricci. 3d ed. Florence: Le Monnier, 1968.

———. *De vulgari eloquentia: Dante's Book of Exile*. Ed. and trans. Marianne Shapiro. Lincoln: University of Nebraska Press, 1990.

———. *La Divina Commedia*. Ed. Charles Grandgent. 1909. Rev. ed. Boston: D. C. Heath, 1933.

Darnton, Robert. "What Is the History of Books?" In *Books and Society in History: Papers of the Association of College and Research Libraries Rare Books and Manuscripts Preconference, 24–28 June, 1980*. Ed. Kenneth E. Carpenter, 3–26. New York: R. R. Bowker, 1983.

Dauzat, Sam V., and JoAnn Dauzat. "Literacy: In Quest of a Definition." *Convergence: An International Journal of Adult Education* 10, no. 1 (1977): 37–41.

Davidson, James. "Domesticating Dido." In *A Woman Scorn'd: Responses to the Dido Myth*. Ed. M. Burden, 65–88. London: Faber and Faber, 1998.

Davies, Anna Morpurgo. "Forms of Writing in the Ancient Mediterranean World." In *The Written Word: Literacy in Transition*. Ed. Gerd Baumann, 51–77. Oxford: Clarendon Press, 1986.

Davies, John. *The Complete Works of John Davies of Hereford*. Ed. Alexander B. Grosart. 2 vols. n.d.; rpt., New York: AMS Press, 1967.

Davies, K. G. *The North Atlantic World in the Seventeenth Century: Europe and the World in the Age of Expansion*. Minneapolis: University of Minnesota Press, 1974.

Davis, Betty. *The Storytellers in Marguerite de Navarre's "Heptaméron."* Lexington, Ky.: French Forum Publishers, 1978.

Davis, Charles Till. "Dante and the Empire." In *The Cambridge Companion to Dante*. Ed. Rachel Jacoff, 67–79. Cambridge: Cambridge University Press, 1993.

———. *Dante and the Idea of Rome*. Oxford: Clarendon Press, 1957.

Davis, David Brion. *The Problem of Slavery in Western Culture*. Ithaca: Cornell University Press, 1966.

Davis, Lennard. *Factual Fictions: The Origins of the English Novel*. New York: Columbia University Press, 1983.

Davis, Natalie Zemon. *Fiction in the Archives: Pardon Tales and Their Tellers in Sixteenth-Century France*. Stanford: Stanford University Press, 1987.

———. *Society and Culture in Early Modern France: Eight Essays*. Stanford: Stanford University Press, 1975.

————. *Women on the Margins: Three Seventeenth-Century Lives.* Cambridge, Mass.: Harvard University Press, 1995.

————. "'Women's History' in Transition: The European Case." *Feminist Studies* 3 (1976): 83–103.

Day, Robert Adams. "Aphra Behn's First Biographer." *Studies in Bibliography* 22 (1969): 227–40.

de Castell, Suzanne, and Allan Luke. "Defining 'Literacy' in North American Schools." In *Perspectives on Literacy.* Ed. Eugene R. Kintgen, Barry M. Kroll, and Mike Rose, 159–74. Carbondale: Southern Illinois University Press, 1988.

Defaux, Gérard. "Evangelism." In *A New History of French Literature.* Ed. Denis Hollier with R. Howard Bloch et al., 162–67. Cambridge, Mass.: Harvard University Press, 1989.

de Grazia, Margreta. "Homonyms before and after Lexical Standardization." *Shakespeare Jahrbuch* (1990): 143–56.

————. "Shakespeare and the Craft of Language." In *The Cambridge Companion to Shakespeare.* Ed. M. de Grazia and S. Wells, 49–64. Cambridge: Cambridge University Press, 2001.

————. "World Pictures, Modern Periods, and the Early Stage." In *A New History of Early English Drama.* Ed. John D. Cox and David Scott Kastan, 7–21. New York: Columbia University Press, 1997.

DeJean, Jean-Luc. *Marguerite de Navarre.* Paris: Fayard, 1987.

DeJean, Joan. *Tender Geographies: Women and the Origins of the Novel in France.* New York: Columbia University Press, 1991.

Delajarte, Philippe. "Le Prologue de l'*Heptaméron* et le processus de production de l'oeuvre." In *La Nouvelle française à la Renaissance.* Ed. Lionello Sozzi, 397–423. Geneva: Slatkine, 1981.

Delany, Sheila. "History, Politics, and Christine Studies: A Polemical Reply." In *Politics, Gender, and Genre.* Ed. M. Brabant, 193–206. Boulder, Colo.: Westview Press, 1992.

————. "'Mothers to Think Back Through': Who Are They? The Ambiguous Example of Christine de Pizan." In *Medieval Texts and Contemporary Readers.* Ed. Laurie Finke and Martin Shichtman, 177–97. Ithaca: Cornell University Press, 1987.

Delègue, Y. "Autour des deux prologues: L'*Heptaméron* est-il un anti-Boccace?" *Travaux de linguistique et de littérature* 4 (1966): 23–37.

de Navarre, Marguerite. *See* Navarre, Marguerite de

de Pizan, Christine. *See* Pizan, Christine de

De Rentiis, Dina. "'Sequere me': 'Imitatio' dans la *Divine Comédie* et dans le *Livre du Chemin de long estude.*" In *The City of Scholars.* Ed. M. Zimmermann and D. De Rentiis, 31–42. New York: Walter de Gruyter, 1994.

de Rochefort, César. *Histoire naturelle et morale des Iles Antilles de l'Amerique . . . Avec un vocabulaire caribe.* 1658. 3d ed. Rotterdam: Reiner Leers, 1681.

Derrida, Jacques. *De la grammatologie.* Paris: Editions de Minuit, 1967.

————. *La Dissémination.* Paris: Editions du Seuil, 1972.

————. *Of Grammatology.* Trans. Gayatri Spivak. Baltimore: Johns Hopkins University Press, 1974.

————. "Structure, Sign, and Play." In *The Structuralist Controversy: The Languages of Criticism and the Sciences of Man.* Ed. and trans. Richard Macksey and Eugenio Donato, 247–72. Baltimore: Johns Hopkins University Press, [1970].

Derville, Alain. "L'Alphabétisation du peuple à la fin du Moyen Age." *Revue du nord* 66 (April–September 1984): 761–72.

Des Longrais, F. Jouon. "Le Statut de la femme en Angleterre dans le droit commun médiéval." In *La Femme,* 135–41. Recueils de la Société Jean Bodin pour l'Histoire Comparative des Institutions, No. 12, part 2. Brussels: Editions de la Librairie Encyclopédique, 1962.

Desmond, Marilynn. *Reading Dido: Gender, Textuality, and the Medieval "Aeneid."* Minneapolis: University of Minnesota Press, 1994.

Detienne, Marcel. "The Violence of Well Born Ladies." In *The Cuisine of Sacrifice among the Greeks.* Ed. Marcel Detienne and Jean-Pierre Vernant, trans. Paula Wissing, 129–47. Chicago: University of Chicago Press, 1989.

Dewar, Mary. *Sir Thomas Smith: A Tudor Intellectual in Office.* London: Oxford University Press, 1964.

Dictionnaire historique de la langue française. Ed. Alain Rey. 2 vols. Paris: Dictionnaire Le Robert, 1994.

Doane, Alger Nicolaus, and Carol Braun Pasternack, eds. *Vox Intexta: Orality and Textuality in the Middle Ages.* Madison: University of Wisconsin Press, 1991.

d'Oingt, Marguerite. *See* Oingt, Marguerite d'

Doiron, Marilyn. "The Middle English Translation of *Le Mirouer des Simples Ames.*" In *Dr. L. Ruypens-Album.* Ed. Albertus Ampe, 131–51. Antwerp: Ruusbroec-Genootschap, 1964.

Doiron, Marilyn, ed. "Marguerite Porete: *The Mirror of Simple Souls,* A Middle English Translation." *Archivio italiano per la storia della pietà* 5 (1968): 241–355.

Dolan, Frances E. *Dangerous Familiars: Representations of Domestic Crime in England, 1550–1700.* Ithaca: Cornell University Press, 1994.

———. "Reading, Writing, and Other Crimes." In *Feminist Readings of Early Modern Culture: Emerging Subjects.* Ed. Valerie Traub, M. Lindsay Kaplan, and Dympna Callaghan, 142–67. Cambridge: Cambridge University Press, 1996.

———. Reply to Heather Dubrow in "Forum." *PMLA* 109, no. 5 (October 1994): 1026–27.

———. "Taking the Pencil Out of God's Hand: Art, Nature, and the Face-Painting Debate in Early Modern England." *PMLA* 108, no. 2 (March 1993): 224–39.

———. *Whores of Babylon.* Ithaca: Cornell University Press, 1999.

Drew-Bear, Annette. *Painted Faces on the Renaissance Stage: The Moral Significance of Face-Painting Conventions.* Lewisburg, Pa.: Bucknell University Press, 1994.

Driver, G. R. *Semitic Writing: From Pictograph to Alphabet.* Ed. S. A. Hopkins. London: Oxford University Press for the British Academy, 1976.

Dryden, John. *The Works of John Dryden.* Ed. Edward Niles Hooker, H. T. Swedenberg, and Vinton A. Dearing. 20 vols. Berkeley: University of California Press, 1956–2000.

du Bellay, Joachim. *La Deffense et illustration de la langue françoyse.* Ed. Henri Chamard. Paris: Didier, 1948.

Dubois, Claude-Gilbert. "Fonds mythique et jeu des sens dans le 'Prologue' de *L'Heptaméron.*" In *Etudes seizièmistes: Offertes à Monsieur le Professeur V.-L. Saulnier par plusiers de ses anciens doctorants,* 151–68. Geneva: Droz, 1980.

Dubois, Elfrieda T. "The Education of Women in Sixteenth-Century France." *French Studies* 32 (January 1978): 1–19.

Duchet, Michele, et al., eds. *L'Amérique de Théodore de Bry: Une collection de voyages protestantes du XVIe siècle: Quatre études d'iconographie.* Paris: Editions du CNRS, 1987.

Duffy, Maureen. *The Passionate Shepherdess: Aphra Behn, 1640–89.* London: Methuen, 1989.

Dulac, Liliane. "Authority in the Prose Treatises of Christine de Pizan: The Writer's Discourse and the Prince's Word." In *Politics, Gender, and Genre.* Ed. M. Brabant, 129–40. Boulder, Colo.: Westview Press, 1992.

———. "De l'art de la digression dans *Le Livre des fais et bonnes moeurs du sage Roy Charles V.*" In *The City of Scholars.* Ed. M. Zimmermann and D. De Rentiis, 148–57. New York: Walter de Gruyter, 1994.

Durling, Robert M. *Petrarch's Lyric Poems*. Cambridge, Mass.: Harvard University Press, 1976.

Dussel, Enrique. "Eurocentrism and Modernity." *Boundary 2*, 20, no. 3 (1993): 65–76.

Duval, Edward. "'Et puis, quelles nouvelles?' The Project of Marguerite's Unfinished *Decameron*." In *Critical Tales: New Studies of the "Heptameron" and Early Modern Culture*. Ed. John D. Lyons and Mary B. McKinley, 241–62. Philadelphia: University of Pennsylvania Press, 1993.

Edwards, Francis, S.J. "Still Investigating Gunpowder Plot." *Recusant History* 21, no. 3 (1993): 305–46.

Edwards, Philip. *Threshold of a Nation: A Study in English and Irish Drama*. Cambridge: Cambridge University Press, 1979.

Eggert, Katherine. "Nostalgia and the Not Yet Late Queen: Refusing Female Rule in *Henry V*." *English Literary History* 61 (1994): 523–50.

———. *Showing Like a Queen: Female Authority and Literary Experiment in Spenser, Shakespeare and Milton*. Philadelphia: University of Pennsylvania Press, 2000.

Eisenstein, Elizabeth. *The Printing Press as an Agent of Change*. 1979; rpt., Cambridge: Cambridge University Press, 1982.

Elias, Norbert. *The Civilizing Process: The History of Manners*. Vol. 1: 1939. Trans. Edmund Jephcott. New York: Pantheon, 1982.

Elsky, Martin. *Authorizing Words: Speech, Writing, and Print in the English Renaissance*. Ithaca: Cornell University Press, 1989.

Elton, G. R. *England under the Tudors*. London: Methuen; New York: Barnes and Noble, 1963.

Elton, G. R., ed. *The Tudor Constitution: Documents and Commentary*. Cambridge: Cambridge University Press, 1960.

Elyot, Thomas. *The Boke Named the Governour*. 1531. Ed. Henry Herbert Stephen Croft. 2 vols. New York: Burt Franklin, 1967.

Emerson, Oliver F. *A Middle English Reader*. London: Macmillan, 1905; rev. ed., 1929.

Emerson, Rupert. *From Empire to Nation: The Rise to Self-Assertion of Asian and African Peoples*. Cambridge, Mass.: Harvard University Press, 1960.

Engelsing, Rolf. *Analphabetentum und Lektüre: Zur Sozialgeschichte des Lesens in Deutschland zwischen feudaler und industrieller Gesellschaft*. Stuttgart: Metzler, 1973.

Enterline, Lynn. *The Rhetoric of the Body from Ovid to Shakespeare*. Cambridge: Cambridge University Press, 2000.

Erasmus, Desiderius. *The Colloquies of Erasmus*. Trans. Craig R. Thompson. Chicago: University of Chicago Press, 1965.

———. *Declamatio de pueris statim ac liberaliter instituendis*. Ed. Jean-Claude Margolin. Geneva: Droz, 1966.

———. *De pueris instituendis*. In *Desiderius Erasmus concerning the Aim and Method of Education*. Trans. William Harrison Woodward, 180–222. Classics in Education Series, No. 19. New York: Teacher's College, Columbia University, 1964.

Erickson, Amy Louise. *Women and Property in Early Modern England*. London: Routledge, 1993.

Erickson, Peter. *Rewriting Shakespeare, Rewriting Ourselves*. Berkeley: University of California Press, 1991.

Estienne, Henri. *Project du livre intitulé De la precellence du langage françois*. Paris, 1579.

Ezell, Margaret. *The Patriarch's Wife: Literary Evidence and the History of the Family*. Chapel Hill: University of North Carolina Press, 1987.

———. *Writing Women's Literary History*. Baltimore: Johns Hopkins University Press, 1993.

Fabian, Johannes. "Keep Listening: Ethnography and Reading." In *The Ethnography of Reading.* Ed. J. Boyarin, 80–97. Berkeley: University of California Press, 1992.

———. *Of Time and the Other: How Anthropology Makes Its Object.* New York: Columbia University Press, 1983.

Febvre, Lucien. *Au coeur religieux au seizième siècle.* 1957; rpt., Paris: Sevpen, 1983.

———. *Autour de "L'Heptaméron": Amour sacré, amour profane.* Paris: Gallimard, 1944.

Febvre, Lucien, and Henri-Jean Martin. *The Coming of the Book: The Impact of Printing, 1450–1800* [*L'Apparition du livre,* 1958]. Trans. David Gerard, ed. Geoffrey Nowell-Smith and David Wooton. London: New Left Books, 1976.

Femina. Ed. William Aldis Wright. Cambridge: Cambridge University Press, 1909.

Ferguson, Charles. "Diglossia." In *Language in Culture and Society: A Reader in Linguistics and Anthropology.* Ed. Dell Hymes, 429–39. New York: Harper and Row, 1964.

Ferguson, Gary. *Mirroring Belief: Marguerite de Navarre's Devotional Poetry.* Edinburgh: Edinburgh University Press, 1992.

Ferguson, Margaret W. "Attending to Literacy." In *Attending to Women.* Ed. Betty Travitsky and Adele F. Seef, 265–79. Newark: University of Delaware Press, 1994.

———. "The Authorial Ciphers of Aphra Behn." In *The Cambridge Companion to English Literature, 1650–1740.* Ed. Steven Zwicker, 225–49. Cambridge: Cambridge University Press, 1998.

———. "Feathers and Flies: Aphra Behn and the Seventeenth-Century Trade in Exotica." In *Subject and Object in Renaissance Culture.* Ed. Margreta de Grazia, Maureen Quilligan, and Peter Stallybrass, 235–59. Cambridge: Cambridge University Press, 1996.

———. "Foreword." In *Menacing Virgins: Representing Virginity in the Middle Ages and Renaissance.* Ed. Kathleen Coyne Kelly and Marina Leslie, 7–14. Newark: University of Delaware Press; London: Associated University Presses, 1999.

———. "News from the New World: Miscegenous Romance in Aphra Behn's *Oroonoko* and *The Widow Ranter.*" In *The Production of English Renaissance Culture.* Ed. David Lee Miller, Sharon O'Dair, and Harold Weber, 151–89. Ithaca: Cornell University Press, 1994.

———. "Recreating the Rules of the Game: Marguerite de Navarre's *Heptaméron.*" In *Creative Imitation: New Essays on Renaissance Literature in Honor of Thomas M. Greene.* Ed. David Quint et al., 153–89. Binghamton, N.Y.: Medieval and Renaissance Texts and Studies, 1992.

———. "Running On with Almost Public Voice: The Case of 'E. C.'" In *Tradition and the Talents of Women.* Ed. Florence Howe, 37–67. Urbana: University of Illinois Press, 1991.

———. "Saint Augustine's Region of Unlikeness: The Crossing of Exile and Language." In *Innovations of Antiquity.* Ed. Daniel Selden and Ralph Hexter, 69–94. New York: Routledge, 1992.

———. "Transmuting Othello: Aphra Behn's *Oroonoko.*" In *Cross-Cultural Performances: Differences in Women's Re-Visions of Shakespeare.* Ed. Marianne Novy, 15–49. Urbana: University of Illinois Press, 1993.

———. *Trials of Desire: Renaissance Defenses of Poetry.* New Haven: Yale University Press, 1983.

Ferguson, Moira. "Seventeenth-Century Quaker Women: Displacement, Colonialism, and Anti-Slavery Discourse." In *Culture and Society in the Stuart Restoration: Literature, Drama, History.* Ed. Gerald MacLean, 221–40. Cambridge: Cambridge University Press, 1995.

———. *Subject to Others: British Women Writers and Colonial Slavery, 1670–1834.* New York: Routledge, 1992.

Ferguson, Moira, ed. *First Feminists: British Women Writers, 1578–1799.* Bloomington: Indiana University Press; Old Westbury, N.Y.: Feminist Press, 1985.

Ferrante, Joan M. *Woman as Image in Medieval Literature: From the Twelfth Century to Dante.* New York: Columbia University Press, 1975.

Ferrara, Fernando. *The Origin and Decline of the Concept of "Literature."* Naples: Istituto Universitario Orientale, 1973.

Finestone, Harry. *Bacon's Rebellion: The Contemporary News Sheets.* Charlottesville: University of Virginia Press, 1956.

Finke, Heinrich. "Die Nation in den Spätmittelalterlichen allgemeine Konzilien." *Historisches Jahrbuch* 5 (1937): 323–38.

Finke, Heinrich, ed. *Acta Concilii constanciensis.* Münster: Regensbergsche Buchhandlung, 1826–1928.

Finlay, Michael. *Western Writing Implements in the Age of the Quill Pen.* Wetheral, U.K.: Plains Books, 1990.

Finnegan, Ruth. *Literacy and Orality: Studies in the Technology of Communication.* Oxford: Oxford University Press, 1988.

———. "Literacy versus Non-Literacy: The Great Divide? Some Comments on the Significance of 'Literature' in Non-Literate Societies." In *Modes of Thought.* Ed. R. Finnegan and B. Horton, 112–44. London: Oxford University Press, 1973.

Fischer, Sandra K. "Elizabeth Cary and Tyranny, Domestic and Religious." In *Silent But for the Word: Tudor Women as Patrons, Translators and Writers of Religious Works.* Ed. Margaret Hannay, 115–237. Kent, Ohio: Kent State University Press, 1985.

Fisher, John. "Chancery and the Emergence of Standard Written English in the Fifteenth Century." *Speculum* 52 (1977): 870–99.

Fishman, Joshua. "Bilingualism with and without Diglossia; Diglossia with and without Bilingualism." *Journal of Social Issues* 12, no. 2 (1967): 29–38.

Fleming, Juliet. "Dictionary English and the Female Tongue." In *Enclosure Acts: Sexuality, Property, and Culture in Early Modern England.* Ed. Richard Burt and John Michael Archer, 290–325. Ithaca: Cornell University Press, 1994.

———. "*The French Garden*: An Introduction to Women's French." *English Literary History* 56 (spring 1989): 19–51.

Fletcher, Anthony. *Gender, Sex and Subordination in England.* New Haven: Yale University Press, 1995.

Florio, John, trans. *The Essayes of Montaigne.* 1603. New York: Modern Library, 1933.

Foakes, R. A. "Playhouses and Players." In *The Cambridge Companion to English Renaissance Drama.* Ed. A. R. Braunmuller and Michael Hattaway, 1–52. Cambridge: Cambridge University Press, 1990.

Foley, Stephen M. *Sir Thomas Wyatt.* Boston: Twayne Publishers, 1990.

Folmer, Henry. *Franco-Spanish Rivalry in North America, 1524–1763.* Glendale, Calif.: A. H. Clark Co., 1953.

Ford, Wyn. "The Problem of Literacy in Early Modern England." *History* 78, no. 252 (February 1992): 22–37.

Foucault, Michel. *The Archaeology of Knowledge.* Trans. A. M. Sheridan Smith. New York: Pantheon Books, 1972.

———. "What Is an Author?" In *Language, Counter-Memory, Practice: Selected Essays and Interviews by Michel Foucault.* Ed. Donald F. Bouchard, trans. Donald F. Bouchard and Sherry Simon, 113–38. Ithaca: Cornell University Press, 1977.

Fox, Adam. *Oral and Literate Culture in England, 1500–1700.* Oxford: Clarendon Press, 2000.

Fradenburg, Louise, and Carla Freccero, eds. *Premodern Sexualities*. New York: Routledge, 1995.

Fraser, Nancy. "Rethinking the Public Sphere." In *Habermas and the Public Sphere*. Ed. Craig Calhoun, 109–42. Cambridge, Mass.: MIT Press, 1992.

Freccero, Carla. "Archives in the Fiction: The Rhetoric of the Law in Marguerite de Navarre's *Heptaméron*." In *Rhetoric and Law in Early Modern Europe*. Ed. Victoria Kahn and Lorna Hutson, 73–94. New Haven: Yale University Press, 2001.

———. "1527: Margaret of Angoulême, Sister of King Francis I, Is Married to Henri II d'Albret, King of Navarre." In *A New History of French Literature*. Ed. Denis Hollier with R. Howard Bloch et al., 145–48. Cambridge, Mass.: Harvard University Press, 1989.

———. "Patriarchy and the Maternal Text: The Case of Marguerite de Navarre." In *Renaissance Women Writers: French Texts/American Contexts*. Ed. Anne R. Larson and Colette H. Winn, 130–40. Detroit: Wayne State University Press, 1994.

———. "Practicing Queer Philology with Marguerite de Navarre: Nationalism and the Castigation of Desire." In *Queering the Renaissance*. Ed. Johnathan Goldberg, 107–23. Durham, N.C.: Duke University Press, 1994.

———. "Rape's Disfiguring Figures." In *Rape and Representation*. Ed. Lynn A. Higgins and Brenda A. Silver, 227–41. New York: Columbia University Press, 1991.

———. "Rewriting the Rhetoric of Desire in the *Heptaméron*." In *Contending Kingdoms: Historical, Psychological, and Feminist Approaches to the Literature of Sixteenth-Century England and France*. Ed. Marie-Rose Logan and Peter L. Rudnytsky, 298–312. Detroit: Wayne State University Press, 1991.

———. "Unwriting Lucretia: 'Heroic Virtue' in the *Heptaméron*." In *Heroic Virtue, Comic Infidelity: Reassessing Marguerite de Navarre's Heptaméron*. Ed. Dora Polachek, 77–89. Amherst, Mass.: Hestia Press, 1993.

Freccero, John. "The Fig Tree and the Laurel: Petrarch's Poetics." *Diacritics* 5 (1975): 35–40.

Frederiq, Paul. *Corpus documentorum inquisitionis haereticae pravitatis Neerlandicae*. Ghent: J. Vuylesteke, 1889.

Freire, Paulo, and Donald Macedo. *Literacy: Reading the Word and the World*. South Hadley, Mass.: Bergin and Garvey Publishers, 1987.

Frye, Susan. "Staging Women's Relations to Textiles in *Othello* and *Cymbeline*." In *Early Modern Visual Culture: Representation, Race, Empire in Renaissance England*. Ed. Peter Erickson and Clark Hulse, 215–50. Philadelphia: University of Pennsylvania Press, 2000.

Furet, François, and Jacques Ozouf. *Lire et écrire: l'alphabetisation des français de Calvin à Jules Ferry*. Paris: Editions de Minuit, 1977.

———. *Reading and Writing: Literacy in France from Calvin to Jules Ferry*. Cambridge: Cambridge University Press, 1982.

Galbraith, V. H. "The Literacy of English Kings." In *Kings and Chroniclers: Essays in English Medieval History*. London: Hambledon Press, 1982.

Gallagher, Catherine. "Embracing the Absolute: The Politics of the Female Subject in Seventeenth-Century England." *Genders* 1 (spring 1988): 24–39.

———. *Nobody's Story: The Vanishing Acts of Women Writers in the Marketplace, 1670–1820*. New Historicism, No. 31. Berkeley: University of California Press, 1994.

Gallagher, Lowell. *Medusa's Gaze: Casuistry and Conscience in the Renaissance*. Stanford: Stanford University Press, 1991.

Gawthrop, Richard L., and Gerald Strauss. "Protestantism and Literacy in Early Modern Germany." *Past and Present* 104 (1984): 31–55.

Gay, Lucy M. "The Language of Christine de Pizan." *Modern Philology* 6 (1908): 16–28.

Gee, James Paul. "What Is Literacy?" In *Rewriting Literacy: Culture and the Discourse of the Other.* Ed. Candace Mitchell and Kathleen Weiler, 3–11. New York: Bergin and Garvey, 1991.

Gehl, Paul F. *A Moral Art: Grammar, Society, and Culture in Trecento Florence.* Ithaca: Cornell University Press, 1993.

Gelb, Ignace J. *A Study of Writing.* 1953; rev. ed., Chicago: University of Chicago Press, 1963.

Gelernt, Jules. *World of Many Loves: The "Heptaméron" of Marguerite de Navarre.* Chapel Hill: University of North Carolina Press, 1966.

Gellius, Aulus. *Noctium Atticarum, libri XX.* Stuttgart: Teubner, 1959.

Gellner, Ernest. *Nations and Nationalism.* Ithaca: Cornell University Press, 1983.

Genêt, Jean-Philippe. "English Nationalism: Thomas Polton at the Council of Constance." *Nottingham Medieval Studies* 28 (1984): 60–78.

Gerson, Jean. *Oeuvres complètes.* Ed. Mgr. Palémon Glorieux. 10 vols. Paris: Desclée de Brouwer, 1962.

Gilbert, Sandra, and Susan Gubar. *The Madwoman in the Attic.* New Haven: Yale University Press, 1979.

Gilder, Rosamund. *Enter the Actress: The First Women in the Theatre.* New York: Theatre Arts Books, 1931.

Gillies, John. *Shakespeare and the Geography of Difference.* Cambridge: Cambridge University Press, 1994.

Gilmont, Jean-François. "Protestant Reformations and Reading." In *A History of Reading in the West.* Ed. G. Cavallo and R. Chartier, 213–37. Amherst: University of Massachusetts Press, 1999.

Gilson, Etienne. *Les Idées et les lettres.* 2d ed. Paris: Librairie Philosophique J. Brin, 1952.

Godefroy, Frédéric. *Dictionnaire de l'ancienne langue française et tous ses dialectes du IX au XV siècle.* 10 vols. New York: Kraus Reprint Corp., 1961.

Godfrey, John. "The Double Monastery in Early English History." *Ampleforth Journal* 79 (1974): 19–32.

Godzich, Vlad. "The Culture of Illiteracy." *Enclitic* 8, nos. 1 and 2 (spring and fall 1984): 27–34.

Goez, Werner. *Translatio Imperii: Ein Beitrag zur Geschichte des Geschichtsdenkens und der politischen Theorien im Mittel Alter und in der fruhen Neuzeit.* Tübingen: J. C. B. Mohr, 1958.

Goldberg, Jonathan. *Desiring Women Writing: English Renaissance Examples.* Stanford: Stanford University Press, 1997.

———. *James I and the Politics of Literature: Jonson, Shakespeare, Donne and Their Contemporaries.* Baltimore: Johns Hopkins University Press, 1983.

———. *Writing Matter from the Hands of the English Renaissance.* Stanford: Stanford University Press, 1990.

Goodman, Dena. "Public Sphere and Private Life: Toward a Synthesis of Current Historiographical Approaches to the Old Regime." *History and Theory* 31, no. 1 (1992): 1–20.

———. *The Republic of Letters: A Cultural History of the French Enlightenment.* Ithaca: Cornell University Press, 1994.

Goody, Jack. *The Interface between the Oral and the Written.* Cambridge: Cambridge University Press, 1987.

Goody, Jack, ed. *Literacy in Traditional Societies.* Cambridge: Cambridge University Press, 1968.

Goody, Jack, and Ian Watt. *The Consequences of Literacy.* Indianapolis: Bobbs-Merrill, 1963.

Goreau, Angeline. *Reconstructing Aphra: A Social Biography of Aphra Behn.* New York: Dial Press, 1980.

————. "Two English Women in the Seventeenth Century: Notes for an Anatomy of Feminine Desire." In *Western Sexuality: Practice and Precept in Past and Present Times.* Ed. Philippe Ariès and André Bejin, trans. Anthony Forster, 103–14. Oxford: Blackwell, 1985.

Goreau, Angeline, ed. *The Whole Duty of a Woman: Female Writers in Seventeenth Century England.* Garden City, N.Y.: Dial Press, 1985.

Graff, Gerald. *Beyond the Culture Wars: How Teaching the Conflicts Can Revitalize American Education.* New York: W. W. Norton, 1992.

Graff, Harvey. "The Historical Study of Literacy." In *Literacy in History: An Interdisciplinary Research Bibliography,* 11–18. New York: Garland, 1981.

————. *The Legacies of Literacy: Continuities and Contradictions in Western Culture and Society.* Bloomington: Indiana University Press, 1987.

————. *Literacy in History: An Interdisciplinary Research Bibliography.* New York: Garland, 1981.

————. *The Literacy Myth.* New York: Academic Press, 1979.

————. "Reflections on the History of Literacy: Overview, Critique, and Proposals." In *The Labyrinths of Literacy: Reflections on Literacy Past and Present,* 15–44. London: Falmer Press, 1987.

Grafton, Anthony. *Commerce with the Classics: Ancient Books and Renaissance Readers.* Ann Arbor: University of Michigan Press, 1997.

Grafton, Anthony, and Lisa Jardine. *From Humanism to the Humanities: Education and the Liberal Arts in Fifteenth and Sixteenth Century Europe.* Cambridge, Mass.: Harvard University Press, 1986.

————. "'Studied for Action': How Gabriel Harvey Read His Livy." *Past and Present* 129 (1990): 30–78.

Graham, Joseph F., ed. *Difference in Translation.* Ithaca: Cornell University Press, 1985.

Gramsci, Antonio. "The Formation of the Intellectuals." In *The Modern Prince and Other Writings.* Trans. Louis Marks, 118–25. New York: International Publishers, 1957.

Grayson, Cecil. "'Nobilior Est Vulgaris': Latin and Vernacular in Dante's Thought." In *Centenary Essays on Dante.* Ed. Oxford Dante Society, 54–76. Oxford: Clarendon Press, 1965.

Green, Ian. "'For Children in Yeeres and Children in Understanding': The Emergence of the English Catechism under Elizabeth and the Early Stuarts." *Journal of Ecclesiastical History* 37, no. 3 (July 1996): 397–425.

Greenblatt, Stephen. *Learning to Curse: Essays in Early Modern Culture.* New York: Routledge, 1990.

————. *Marvellous Possessions: The Wonder of the New World.* Chicago: University of Chicago Press, 1991.

————. *Renaissance Self-Fashioning: From More to Shakespeare.* Chicago: University of Chicago Press, 1980.

————. *Shakespearean Negotiations: The Circulation of Social Energy in Renaissance England.* Berkeley: University of California Press, 1988.

Greene, Thomas M. *The Light in Troy: Imitation and Discovery in Renaissance Poetry.* New Haven: Yale University Press, 1982.

Greenfeld, Liah. "Nationalism and Language." In *Encyclopedia of Language and Linguistics.* Ed. R. E. Asher, 5:2708–13. New York: Pergamon Press, 1994.

————. *Nationalism: Five Roads to Modernity.* Cambridge, Mass.: Harvard University Press, 1992.

Gregerson, Linda. "Colonials Write the Nation: Spenser, Milton, and England on the Margins." In *Milton and the Imperial Vision.* Ed. Balachandra Rajan and Elizabeth Sauer, 169–90. Pittsburgh: Duquesne University Press, 1999.

————. "Native Tongues: Effeminization, Miscegenation, and the Construction of Tudor Nationalism." *Mitteilungen des Zentrums zur Erforschung der Frühen Neuzeit* 3 (June 1995): 18–38.

Gregory, Brad S. *Salvation at Stake: Christian Martyrdom in Early Modern Europe.* Cambridge, Mass.: Harvard University Press, 1999.

Grendler, Paul F. *Schooling in Renaissance Italy: Literacy and Learning, 1300–1600.* Baltimore: Johns Hopkins University Press, 1989.

Grosperrin, Bernard. *Les Petites écoles sous l'Ancien Régime.* Rennes: Ouest-France, 1984.

Grundmann, Herman. "*Litteratus-illitteratus*: Der Wandel einer Bildungsnorm vom Altertum zum Mittelalter." *Archiv für Kulturgeschichte* 40 (1958): 1–66.

————. *Religious Movements in the Middle Ages.* Trans. Steven Rowan. Notre Dame, Ind.: University of Notre Dame Press, 1995.

Guarnieri, Romana. "Il Movimento del Libero Spirito dalle origini al secolo XVI." *Archivio Italiana per la storia della pietà* 4 (1965): 353–499.

Guenée, Bernard. *Politique et histoire au Moyen Age: Recueil d'articles sur l'histoire politique et l'historiographie médiévale (1956–1981).* Paris: Publications de la Sorbonne, 1981.

Guillory, John. *Cultural Capital: The Problem of Literary Canon Formation.* Chicago: University of Chicago Press, 1993.

————. "Literary Capital: Gray's 'Elegy,' Anna Laetitia Barbauld, and the Vernacular Canon." In *Early Modern Conceptions of Property.* Ed. J. Brewer and S. Staves, 389–410. London: Routledge, 1996.

Gutierrez, Nancy. "Valuing *Mariam*: Genre Study and Feminist Analysis." *Tulsa Studies in Women's Literature* 10 (fall 1991): 223–51.

Gwynn, Aubrey. "Ireland and the English Nation at the Council of Constance." *Proceedings of the Royal Irish Academy,* ser. C (1935): 183–223.

Haas, William. *Standard Languages, Spoken and Written.* Manchester: Manchester University Press, 1982.

Habermas, Jürgen. *Legitimation Crisis.* Trans. Thomas McCarthy. Boston: Beacon Press, 1975.

————. *The Philosophical Discourse of Modernity: Twelve Lectures.* 1985. Trans. F. G. Lawrence. Cambridge, Mass.: MIT Press, 1990.

————. *The Structural Transformation of the Public Sphere: An Inquiry into a Category of Bourgeois Society.* 1962. Trans. Thomas Burger with Federick Lawrence. Cambridge, Mass.: MIT Press, 1989.

Hackel, Heidi Brayman. "Boasting of Silence: Women Readers in a Patriarchal State." In *Reading, Society, and Politics in Early Modern England.* Ed. K. Sharpe and S. Zwicker. Cambridge: Cambridge University Press, forthcoming.

————. "The Countess of Bridgewater's London Library." In *Books and Readers in Early Modern England: Material Studies.* Ed. Jennifer Andersen and Elizabeth Sauer, 138–59. Philadelphia: University of Pennsylvania Press, 2002.

————. "The 'Great Variety' of Readers and Early Modern Reading Practices." In *A Companion to Shakespeare.* Ed. David Scott Kastan, 139–57. Oxford: Blackwell, 1999.

————. "Impressions from a 'Scribbling Age': Recovering the Reading Practices of Renaissance England." Ph.D. diss., Columbia University, 1994.

Hackett, Helen. "Courtly Writing by Women." In *Women and Literature in Britain, 1500–1700.* Ed. Helen Wilcox, 169–89. Cambridge: Cambridge University Press, 1996.

————. *Women and Romance Fiction in the English Renaissance.* Cambridge: Cambridge University Press, 2000.

Hakluyt, Richard. *The Principal Navigations, Voyages, Traffiques and Discoveries of the English Nation.* Ed. Walter Raleigh. 12 vols. Glasgow: J. MacLehose and Sons, 1903–5.

Hall, Edward. *The Union of the Two Noble and Illustre Famelies of Lancastre and Yorke.* London, 1550; Menston, U.K.: Scolar Press, 1970.

Hall, Kim F. *Things of Darkness: Economies of Race and Gender in Early Modern England.* Ithaca: Cornell University Press, 1995.

Haller, Robert S., ed. and trans. *Literary Criticism of Dante Alighieri.* Lincoln: University of Nebraska Press, 1973.

Halley, Janet. "Equivocation and the Legal Conflict over Religious Identity in Early Modern England." *Yale Journal of Law and the Humanities* 3, no. 1 (1991): 33–52.

Halpern, Richard. *The Poetics of Primitive Accumulation: English Renaissance Culture and the Genealogy of Capital.* Ithaca: Cornell University Press, 1992.

Halverson, John. "Goody and the Implosion of the Literacy Thesis." *Man* 27, no. 2 (1992): 301–17.

Hamilton, Donna. *Shakespeare and the Politics of Protestant England.* Lexington: University Press of Kentucky, 1992.

Hamor, Ralph. *A True Discourse of the Present Estate of Virginia, and the Successe of the Affaires There till the 18 of June. 1614. Together with a Relation of the Severall English Townes and Forts, the Assured Hopes of that* . . . London: John Beale for William Welby, 1615.

Hampton, Timothy. "On the Border: Geography, Gender, and Narrative Form in the *Heptaméron.*" *Modern Language Quarterly* 57, no. 4 (December 1996): 517–44.

Hanley, Sarah. "Engendering the State: Family Formation and State Building in Early Modern France." *French Historical Studies* 16 (1989): 4–27.

———. "Family and State in Early Modern France: The Marriage Pact." In *Connecting Spheres: Women in the Western World, 1500 to the Present.* Ed. Marilyn J. Boxer and Jean H. Quataert, 53–63. New York: Oxford University Press, 1987.

———. "The Monarchic State in Early Modern France: Marital Regime Government and Male Right." In *Politics, Ideology and the Law in Early Modern Europe: Essays in Honor of H. H. M. Salmon.* Ed. Adrianna Bakos, 107–26. Rochester, N.Y.: University of Rochester Press, 1994.

Hannay, Margaret. *Philip's Phoenix: Mary Sidney, Countess of Pembroke.* New York: Oxford University Press, 1990.

Hanson, Elizabeth. *Discovering the Subject in Renaissance England.* Cambridge: Cambridge University Press, 1998.

Harris, Roy. *The Origin of Writing.* La Salle, Ill.: Open Court, 1986.

Harris, William. *Ancient Literacy.* Cambridge, Mass.: Harvard University Press, 1989.

Harriss, G. L., ed. *Henry V: The Practice of Kingship.* Oxford: Oxford University Press, 1985.

Harvey, Elizabeth. *Ventriloquized Voices: Feminist Theory and English Renaissance Texts.* New York: Routledge, 1992.

Harvey, Gabriel. *Lopez the Jew.* 1594. Ed. Frank Marcham. London: Waterlow and Sons, 1927.

Havelock, Eric. *The Literate Revolution in Greece and Its Cultural Consequences.* Princeton: Princeton University Press, 1982.

———. *The Muse Learns to Write: Reflections on Orality and Literacy from Antiquity to the Present.* New Haven: Yale University Press, 1986.

———. *Preface to Plato.* Oxford: Blackwell, 1963; rpt., New York: Grosset and Dunlap, 1967.

Hawkesworth, Mary E. "From Objectivity to Objectification: Feminist Objectifications." In *Rethinking Objectivity.* Ed. Allan Megill, 151–77. Durham, N.C.: Duke University Press, 1994.

Heath, Shirley Brice. *Ways with Words.* Cambridge: Cambridge University Press, 1983.

Hechter, Michael. *Internal Colonialism: The Celtic Fringe in British National Development, 1536–1966.* London: Routledge and Kegan Paul, 1975.

Heisenberg, Werner. *Physics and Philosophy: The Revolution in Modern Science.* New York: Harper and Row, 1958.

Helgerson, Richard. *Forms of Nationhood: The Elizabethan Writing of England*. Chicago: University of Chicago Press, 1992.

Heller, H. "Marguerite of Navarre and the Reformers of Meaux." *Bibliothèque d'humanisme et renaissance* 33 (1971): 271–310.

Hellwarth, Jennifer Wynne. "'I Wyl Wright of Women Prevy Skekenes': Imagining Female Literacy and Textual Communities in Medieval and Early Modern Midwifery Manuals." In *Literacies in Early Modern England*. Ed. E. R. Sanders and M. W. Ferguson. *Critical Survey* 14, no. 1 (2002): 44–63.

Hendricks, Margo. "Civility, Barbarism, and Aphra Behn's *The Widow Ranter*." In *Women, "Race," and Writing in the Early Modern Period*. Ed. M. Hendricks and P. Parker, 225–39. London: Routledge, 1994.

Hendricks, Margo, and Patricia Parker, eds. *Women, "Race," and Writing in the Early Modern Period*. London: Routledge, 1994.

Herman, Peter. "We All Smoke Here: Behn's *The Widdow Ranter* and the Invention of America." In *Envisioning an English Empire: Jamestown and the Emergence of the North Atlantic World*. Ed. Robert Appelbaum. Forthcoming.

Herrup, Cynthia B. *The Common Peace: Participation and the Criminal Law in Seventeenth-Century England*. Cambridge: Cambridge University Press, 1987.

Hexter, Ralph. "Sidonian Dido." In *Innovations of Antiquity: The New Ancient World*. Ed. Ralph Hexter and Daniel Selden, 332–84. New York: Routledge, 1992.

Hicks, Eric. "The Political Significance of Christine de Pizan." In *Politics, Gender, and Genre*. Ed. M. Brabant, 7–15. Boulder, Colo.: Westview Press, 1992.

Hicks, Eric, and Gilbert Ouy. "The Second 'Autograph' Edition of Christine de Pizan's Lesser Poetical Works." *Manuscripta* 20 (1976): 14–15.

Hildyard, Angela, David Olson, and Nancy Torrance, eds. *Literacy, Language and Learning: The Nature and Consequences of Reading and Writing*. Cambridge: Cambridge University Press, 1985.

Hill, Christopher. "The Norman Yoke." In *Puritanism and Revolution: Studies in Interpretation of the English Revolution of the 17th Century*, 50–122. 1858; rpt., New York: Schocken Books, 1964.

Hindman, Sandra. *Christine de Pizan's "Epistre Othéa": Painting and Politics at the Court of Charles VI*. Toronto: Pontifical Institute of Medieval Studies, 1986.

Hirsch, E. D. *Cultural Literacy: What Every American Needs to Know*. New York: Vintage Books, 1988.

Hogg, Richard M., ed. *The Cambridge History of the English Language*. 5 vols. Cambridge: Cambridge University Press, 1992–99.

Holderness, Graham. "'What Is My Nation?': Shakespeare and National Identities." *Textual Practice* 5 (1991): 74–93.

Hollander, Robert. "Babytalk in Dante's *Commedia*." In *On the Rise of the Vernacular Literatures in the Middle Ages*. Ed. R. G. Collins and John Wortly, 73–84. Winnipeg: University of Manitoba Press, 1975.

Hollyband, Claudius [Claude Desainliens]. *De pronuntiatione linguae gallicae*. 1580. Facsimile rpt. English Linguistics, 1500–1800, no. 212. Menston, U.K.: Scolar Press, 1970.

Holm, Janice Butler. "Struggling with the Letter: Vives's Preface to *The Instruction of a Christen Woman*." In *Contending Kingdoms: Historical, Psychological, and Feminist Approaches to the Literature of Sixteenth-Century England and France*. Ed. Marie-Rose Logan and Peter L. Rudnytsky, 265–97. Detroit: Wayne State University Press, 1991.

Holmes, Peter. *Resistance and Compromise: The Political Thought of the Elizabethan Catholics.* Cambridge: Cambridge University Press, 1982.

Holton, Robert J. "The Transition from Feudalism to Capitalism." In *A Dictionary of Marxist Thought.* Ed. Tom Bottomore, 483–85. Cambridge, Mass.: Harvard University Press, 1983.

Houston, Robert Allan. *Literacy in Early Modern Europe: Culture and Education, 1500–1800.* New York: Longman, 1988.

Houston, Stephen. "Literacy among the Pre-Columbian Maya: A Comparative Perspective." In *Writing without Words.* Ed. E. Boone and W. Mignolo, 27–43. Durham, N.C.: Duke University Press, 1994.

Howard, Jean. "The New Historicism in Renaissance Studies." *English Literary Renaissance* 16 (1986): 13–43.

———. *The Stage and Social Struggle.* New York: Routledge, 1994.

Howard, Jean, and Phyllis Rackin. *Engendering a Nation: A Feminist Account of Shakespeare's English Histories.* London: Routledge, 1997.

Hsu, Francis L. K. *The Study of Literate Civilizations.* 1969; rpt., New York: Holt, Rinehart and Winston, 1979.

Hudson, A. "Diglossia." In *Encyclopedia of Language and Linguistics.* Ed. R. E. Asher, 2:926–30. New York: Pergamon Press, 1994.

Hudson, Anne. *Lollards and Their Books.* London: Hambledon, 1985.

———. "A Lollard Sect Vocabulary?" In *So Meny People Longages and Tonges: Philological Essays in Scots and Mediaeval English Presented to Angus McIntosh.* Ed. Michael Benskin and M. L. Samuels, 15–30. Middle English Dialect Project. Edinburgh: Privately published by M. Benskin and M. L. Samuels, 1981.

Huguet, Edmond. *Dictionnaire de la langue française au seizième siècle.* 7 vols. Paris, 1925–73.

Hull, Suzanne. *Chaste, Silent, and Obedient: English Books for Women, 1475–1600.* San Marino, Calif.: Huntington Library, 1982.

Hulme, Peter. *Colonial Encounters: Europe and the Native Caribbean, 1492–1797.* London: Methuen, 1986.

Hult, David. "Jean de Meun's Continuation of *Le Roman de la Rose.*" In *A New History of French Literature.* Ed. Denis Hollier with R. Howard Bloch et al., 97–103. Cambridge, Mass.: Harvard University Press, 1989.

Hunt, Lynn, ed. *The New Cultural History: Essays.* Berkeley: University of California Press, 1989.

Hunter, Paul. *Before Novels: The Cultural Contexts of Eighteenth-Century English Fiction.* New York: W. W. Norton, 1990.

Huntley, Frank L. "*Macbeth* and the Background of Jesuitical Equivocation." *PMLA* 79 (1964): 390–400.

Huppert, George. *Les Bourgeois gentilshommes.* Chicago: University of Chicago Press, 1977.

———. *Public Schools in Renaissance France.* Urbana: University of Illinois Press, 1984.

Hutchinson, John, and Anthony D. Smith, eds. *Nationalism.* Oxford: Oxford University Press, 1994.

Hymes, Dell. "Toward Ethnographies of Communication: The Analysis of Communicative Events." In *Language and Social Context.* Ed. Pier Paolo Giglioli, 21–42. Harmondsworth, U.K.: Penguin Books, 1972.

Jackson, H. J. *Marginalia: Readers Writing in Books.* New Haven: Yale University Press, 2001.

Jackson, Jean. "Language Identity of the Colombian Vaupes Indians." In *Explorations in the Ethnography of Speaking.* Ed. Richard Bauman and Joel Sherzer, 50–64. Cambridge: Cambridge University Press, 1989.

James I. *The Political Works of James I.* Ed. Charles Howard McIlwain. New York: Russell and Russell, 1965.

James, Heather. "Dido's Ear: Tragedy and the Politics of Response." *Shakespeare Quarterly* 52 (fall 2001): 360–82.

———. *Shakespeare's Troy: Drama, Politics, and the Translation of Empire.* Cambridge: Cambridge University Press, 1997.

Jameson, Fredric. "Religion and Ideology: A Political Reading of *Paradise Lost.*" In *Literature, Politics and Theory: Papers from the Essex Conference 1976–84.* Ed. Francis Barker et al., 35–56. London: Methuen, 1986.

Jayawardena, Kumari. *Feminism and Nationalism in the Third World.* London: Zed Books and Totowa, N.J.: Biblio Distribution Center, 1986.

Jeanneret, Michel. "Antarctic France: 1578, Jean de Léry Publishes His Account of the Villegagnon Expedition to the Bay of Rio de Janeiro." In *A New History of French Literature.* Ed. Denis Hollier with R. Howard Bloch et al., 240–43. Cambridge, Mass.: Harvard University Press, 1989.

Jeanroy, Alfred. "Boccace et Christine de Pizan. Le *De claris mulieribus,* principale source du *Livre de la cité des dames.*" *Romania* 48 (1922): 92–105.

Jed, Stephanie. *Chaste Thinking: The Rape of Lucretia and the Birth of Humanism.* Bloomington: Indiana University Press, 1989.

Johns, Adrian. *The Nature of the Book: Print and Knowledge in the Making.* Chicago: University of Chicago Press, 1998.

Johnson, Paul. *The History of Christianity.* Harmondsworth, U.K.: Penguin Books, 1978.

Jones, Ann Rosalind. *The Currency of Eros: Women's Love Lyric in Europe, 1540–1620.* Bloomington: Indiana University Press, 1990.

———. "Nets and Bridles: Early Modern Conduct Books and Sixteenth-Century Women's Lyrics." In *The Ideology of Conduct: Essays on Literature and the History of Sexuality.* Ed. Nancy Armstrong and Leonard Tennenhouse, 39–72. New York: Methuen, 1987.

———. "Surprising Fame: Renaissance Gender Ideologies and Women's Lyric." In *The Poetics of Gender.* Ed. Nancy K. Miller, 74–95. New York: Columbia University Press, 1986.

Jones, Ann Rosalind, and Peter Stallybrass. "Dismantling Irena: The Sexualizing of Ireland in Early Modern England." In *Nationalisms and Sexualities.* Ed. Andrew Parker et al., 157–71. New York: Routledge, 1992.

———. *Renaissance Clothing and the Materials of Memory.* Cambridge: Cambridge University Press, 2000.

Jones, Richard Foster. *The Triumph of the English Language: A Survey of Opinions Concerning the Vernacular from the Introduction of Printing to the Restoration.* Stanford: Stanford University Press, 1953.

Jordan, Constance. "Boccaccio's In-famous Women: Gender and Civic Virtue in the *De Mulieribus Claris.*" In *Ambiguous Realities: Women in the Middle Ages and Renaissance.* Ed. Carole Levin and Jeanie Watson, 25–65. Detroit: Wayne State University Press, 1987.

———. *Renaissance Feminism: Literary Texts and Political Models.* Ithaca: Cornell University Press, 1990.

———. "Renaissance Women and the Question of Class." In *Sexuality and Gender in Early Modern Europe: Institutions, Texts, Images.* Ed. James Grantham Turner, 90–106. Cambridge: Cambridge University Press, 1993.

Jordan, Winthrop D. *The White Man's Burden: Historical Origins of Racism in the United States.* New York: Oxford University Press, 1974.

———. *White over Black: American Attitudes toward the Negro, 1550–1812.* Chapel Hill: University

of North Carolina Press for the Institute of Early American History and Culture at Williamsburg, Va., 1968.

Joseph, John Earl. *Eloquence and Power: The Rise of Language Standards and Standard Languages.*
New York: Basil Blackwell, 1987.

Josephus, Flavius. *Antiquities of the Jews.* Trans. Thomas Lodge. Published as *The Famous and
Memorable Workes of Josephus, A Man of Much Honour and Learning Among the Jewes.
Faithfully translated out of the Latine, and the French, by Tho. Lodge, Doctor in Physicke.*
London: Peter Short, 1602.

———. *Josephus.* Vols. 5–13: *Jewish Antiquities.* Bilingual ed., trans. Ralph Marcus. Ed. and completed by Allen Wikgren. Loeb Classical Library. Cambridge, Mass.: Harvard University
Press, 1963.

Jourda, Pierre. *Marguerite d'Angoulême, duchesse d'Alençon, reine de Navarre (1492–1549): Etude
biographique et littéraire.* 2 vols. Paris: Champion, 1930.

Judy, Stephen. *The ABCs of Literacy: A Guide for Parents and Educators.* New York: Oxford, 1980.

Justice, Steven. *Writing and Rebellion: England in 1381.* Berkeley: University of California Press,
1994.

Kaestle, Carl F. "The History of Literacy and the History of Readers." In *Perspectives on Literacy.*
Ed. Eugene R. Kintgen, Barry M. Kroll, and Mike Rose, 95–126. Carbondale: Southern Illinois University Press, 1988.

Kahn, Victoria. *Rhetoric, Prudence, and Skepticism in the Renaissance.* Ithaca: Cornell University
Press, 1985.

Kaplan, M. Lindsay. "Subjection and Subjectivity: Jewish Law and Female Autonomy in Reformation English Marriage." In *Feminist Readings of Early Modern Culture: Emerging Subjects.* Ed. Valerie Traub, M. Lindsay Kaplan, and Dympna Callaghan, 229–52. Cambridge:
Cambridge University Press, 1996.

Kastan, David. *Shakespeare after Theory.* London: Routledge, 1999.

———. "Shakespeare and English History." In *The Cambridge Companion to Shakespeare.* Ed.
M. de Grazia and S. Wells, 167–82. Cambridge: Cambridge University Press, 2001.

Katz, David S. *The Jews in the History of England, 1485–1850.* New York: Oxford University Press,
1994.

———. *Philo-Semitism and the Readmission of the Jews to England, 1603–1655.* Oxford: Clarendon
Press, 1982.

Kauffman, Linda. *Discourses of Desire: Gender, Genre, and Epistolary Fictions.* Ithaca: Cornell University Press, 1986.

Kaufman, Gloria. "Juan Luis Vives on the Education of Women." *Signs* 3 (summer 1978): 891–97.

Kegl, Rosemary. "Theaters, Households, and a 'Kind of History' in Elizabeth Cary's *The Tragedy
of Mariam.*" In *Enacting Gender on the English Renaissance Stage.* Ed. Viviana Comensoli and
Anne Russell, 135–53. Urbana: University of Illinois Press, 1999.

Keightley, David N. "The Origins of Writing in China: Scripts and Cultural Contexts." In *The
Origins of Writing.* Ed. W. Senner, 171–202. Lincoln: University of Nebraska Press, 1991.

Kelley, Donald R. "Writing Cultural History in Early Modern Europe: Christophe Milieu and His
Project." *Renaissance Quarterly* 52 (summer 1999): 342–65.

Kennedy, Gwynne. *Just Anger: Representing Women's Anger in Early Modern England.* Carbondale: Southern Illinois University Press, 2000.

Kermode, Frank. *The Genesis of Secrecy.* Cambridge, Mass.: Harvard University Press, 1979.

King, Margaret. "Book-Lined Cells: Women and Humanism in the Early Italian Renaissance."

In *Beyond Their Sex: Learned Women of the European Past*. Ed. Patricia Labalme, 66–90. New York: New York University Press, 1980.

———. *Women of the Renaissance*. Chicago: University of Chicago Press, 1991.

Kintgen, Eugene R. *Reading in Tudor England*. Pittsburgh: University of Pittsburgh Press, 1996.

Klein, Joan Larsen. *Daughters, Wives and Widows: Writings by Men about Women and Marriage in England, 1500–1640*. Urbana: University of Illinois Press, 1992.

Knapp, Jeffrey. *An Empire Nowhere: England, America, and Literature from "Utopia" to "The Tempest."* Berkeley: University of California Press, 1992.

Knapp, Peggy. *Time-Bound Words: Semantic and Social Economies from Chaucer's England to Shakespeare's*. London: Macmillan, 2000.

Knott, John. *Discourses of Martyrdom in English Literature, 1593–1694*. Cambridge: Cambridge University Press, 1993.

Koebner, Richard. *Empire*. Cambridge: Cambridge University Press, 1961.

Kohn, Hans. *Nationalism: Its Meaning and History*. 1965; rev. ed., New York: Van Nostrand, 1971.

Kozol, Jonathan. *Illiterate America*. Garden City, N.Y.: Anchor/Doubleday, 1985.

Kritzman, Lawrence D. *The Rhetoric of Sexuality and the Literature of the French Renaissance*. Cambridge: Cambridge University Press, 1991.

Kroeber, A. L., and Clyde Kluckhohn. *Culture: A Critical Review of Concepts and Definitions*. New York: Vintage, 1952.

Krontiris, Tina. *Oppositional Voices: Women as Writers and as Translators of Literature in the English Renaissance*. New York: Routledge, 1992.

Krynen, Jacques. *Idéal du prince et pouvoir royal en France à la fin du moyen âge (1380–1440)*. Paris: A. and J. Picard, 1981.

Kupperman, Karen Ordahl. *Settling with the Indians: The Meeting of English and Indian Cultures in America, 1580–1640*. Totowa, N.J.: Rowman and Littlefield, 1980.

Laennec, Christine Moneera. "Christine Antigrafe: Authorial Ambivalence in the Works of Christine de Pizan." In *Anxious Power: Reading, Writing and Ambivalence in Narrative by Women*. Ed. Carol J. Singley and Susan Elizabeth Sweeney, 35–49. Binghamton, N.Y.: SUNY Press, 1993.

Laidlaw, J. C. "Christine de Pizan, the Earl of Salisbury and Henry IV." *French Studies* 36, no. 2 (April 1982): 129–43.

Lamb, Mary Ellen. "Constructions of Women Readers." In *Teaching Tudor and Stuart Women Writers*. Ed. Suzanne Woods and Margaret Hannay, 23–34. New York: MLA, 2000.

———. *Gender and Authorship in the Sidney Circle*. Madison: University of Wisconsin Press, 1990.

———. "Old Wives' Tales: George Peele, and Narrative Abjection." In *Literacies in Early Modern England*. Ed. E. R. Sanders and M. W. Ferguson. *Critical Survey* 14, no. 1 (2002): 28–43.

———. "The Sociality of Margaret Hoby's Reading Practices and the Representation of Reformation Interiority." In *Reading in Early Modern England*. Ed. S. Roberts. *Critical Survey* 12, no. 2 (2000): 17–32.

———. "'Taken by the Faeries': Fairy Practices and the Production of Popular Culture in *A Midsummer Night's Dream*." *Shakespeare Quarterly* 51, no. 3 (2000): 277–312.

Lambley, Kathleen. *The Teaching and Cultivation of the French Language in England during Tudor and Stuart Times*. Manchester, U.K.: Manchester University Press, 1920.

Laqueur, Thomas. *Making Sex: The Body and Gender from the Greeks to Freud*. Cambridge, Mass.: Harvard University Press, 1990.

Laslett, Peter. *The World We Have Lost.* New York: Scribner's, 1971.

Lassner, Jacob. *Demonizing the Queen of Sheba: Boundaries of Gender and Culture in Postbiblical Judaism and Medieval Islam.* Chicago: University of Chicago Press, 1993.

Latini, Brunetto. *Li livres dou tresor.* Ed. Francis J. Carmody. Geneva: Slatkine Reprints, 1975.

Lawrence, C. H. *The English Church and the Papacy in the Middle Ages.* London: Burns and Oates, 1965; rev. ed. Stroud, Gloucestershire: Sutton, 1999.

Lazere, Donald. "Stratification in the Academic Profession and in the Teaching of Composition." *Humanities in Society* 4, no. 4 (1981): 379–94.

Leigh, William. *Great Britaines Great Deliverance from the Great Danger of Popish Powder.* London: Printed by T. Creede for Arthur Johnson, 1606.

Lerer, Seth. *Courtly Letters in the Age of Henry VIII.* Studies in Renaissance Literature and Culture, No. 18. Cambridge: Cambridge University Press, 1997.

———. *Literacy and Power in Anglo-Saxon Literature.* Lincoln: University of Nebraska Press, 1991.

Lerner, Robert. *The Heresy of the Free Spirit in the Middle Ages.* Berkeley: University of California Press, 1972.

Lestocquoy, Jean. *Histoire du patriotisme en France des origines à nos jours.* Paris: Albin Michel, 1968.

Le Strange, Nicholas. *"Merry Passages and Jeasts": A Manuscript Jestbook of Sir Nicholas Le Strange (1603–1665).* Ed. H. F. Lippincott. Elizabethan & Renaissance Studies 29. Salzburg: Institut für Englische Sprache und Litteratur, Universität Salzburg, 1974.

Lestringant, Frank. *Le Huguenot et le sauvage: L'Amérique et la controverse coloniale en France, au temps des guerres de religion (1555–1589).* Paris: Diffusion Klincksieck, 1990.

Levin, Carole. *"The Heart and Stomach of a King": Elizabeth I and the Politics of Sex and Power.* Philadelphia: University of Pennsylvania Press, 1994.

Lévi-Strauss, Claude. *The Savage Mind.* Chicago: Chicago University Press, 1966.

———. *Structural Anthropology.* Trans. Claire Jacobson and Grooke Grundfest Schoepf. New York: Basic Books, 1963.

———. *Tristes Tropiques.* Paris: Plon, 1955. Trans. John and Doreen Weightman. Harmondsworth, U.K.: Penguin Books, 1976.

Lewalski, Barbara Kiefer. *Writing Women in Jacobean England.* Cambridge, Mass.: Harvard University Press, 1993.

Lewis, P. S. *Later Medieval France: The Polity.* New York: St. Martin's Press, 1968.

———. "War Propaganda and Historiography in Fifteenth-Century France and England." *Transactions of the Royal Historical Society,* 5th ser., 15 (1965): 1–21.

Lodge, Thomas. *An Alarum Against Vserers.* 1584. In *The Complete Works of Thomas Lodge,* vol. 1. New York: Russell and Russell, 1963.

———. *Prosopopeia, Containing the Teares of the holy, blessed, and sanctified Marie, the Mother of God.* 1596. Facsimile rpt. In *The Complete Works of Thomas Lodge,* 3:1–126. New York: Russell and Russell, 1963.

Loewenstein, Joseph. *The Author's Due: Printing and the Prehistory of Copyright.* Chicago: University of Chicago Press, 2002.

Loomba, Ania. "The Color of Patriarchy: Critical Difference, Cultural Difference, and Renaissance Drama." In *Women, "Race," and Writing in the Early Modern Period.* Ed. M. Hendricks and P. Parker, 17–34. London: Routledge, 1994.

———. *Gender, Race, Renaissance Drama.* Manchester: Manchester University Press, 1989.

Loomis, Louise R. "Nationality at the Council of Constance." *American Historical Review* 44 (1939): 508–27.

Lord, Mary Louise. "Dido as an Example of Chastity: The Influence of Example Literature." *Harvard Library Bulletin* 17 (1969): 22–44, 216–32.

Lorimer, Joyce. "Ralegh's First Reconnaissance of Guiana? An English Survey of the Orinoco in 1587." *Terrae Incognitae* 9 (1977): 7–21.

Losse, Deborah N. "Authorial and Narrative Voice in the *Heptaméron*." *Renaissance and Reformation* 11, no. 3 (summer 1987): 223–42.

Lougée, Carolyn. *Le Paradis des Femmes: Women, Salons, and Social Stratification in Seventeenth-Century France.* Princeton: Princeton University Press, 1976.

Lough, John. *Writer and Public in France.* Oxford: Clarendon Press, 1978.

Lounsbury, Floyd G. "The Ancient Writing of Middle America." In *The Origins of Writing.* Ed. W. Senner, 203–38. Lincoln: University of Nebraska Press, 1991.

Love, Harold. *Scribal Publication in Seventeenth-Century England.* Oxford: Clarendon Press, 1993.

Lucas, Caroline. *Writing for Women: The Example of Woman as Reader in Elizabethan Romance.* Philadelphia: Open University Press, 1989.

Lusignan, Serge. *Parler vulgairement: Les Intellectuels et la langue française aux XIIIe et XIVe siècles.* 2d ed. Paris: Librarie Philosophique J. Vrin, 1987.

Lyons, John D. *Exemplum: The Rhetoric of Example in Early Modern France and Italy.* Princeton: Princeton University Press, 1989.

———. "The *Heptaméron* and the Foundation of Critical Narrative." *Yale French Studies* 70 (1986): 150–63.

MacCabe, Colin. *The Eloquence of the Vulgar.* London: British Film Institute, 1999.

MacDonald, Joyce Green. "Race, Women and the Sentimental in Thomas Southerne's *Oroonoko*." *Criticism* 40 (fall 1998): 555–70.

Machan, Tim William. "Editing, Orality, and Late Middle English Texts." In *Vox Intexta.* Ed. A. N. Doane and C. B. Pasternack, 229–45. Madison: University of Wisconsin Press, 1991.

Macherey, Pierre. *A Theory of Literary Production* [*Pour une théorie de la production littéraire*, 1966]. Trans. Geoffrey Wall. London: Routledge and Kegan Paul, 1978.

MacLean, Gerald. "Literacy, Class, and Gender in Restoration England." *Text* 7 (1995): 309–35.

Maclean, Ian. *The Renaissance Notion of Woman: A Study in the Fortunes of Scholasticism and Medical Science in European Intellectual Life.* Cambridge: Cambridge University Press, 1980.

Magnussen, Lynn. *Shakespeare and Social Dialogue: Dramatic Language and Elizabethan Letters.* Cambridge: Cambridge University Press, 1999.

Malcolmson, Cristina. "Christine de Pizan's *City of Ladies* in Early Modern England." In *Debating Gender in Early Modern England, 1500–1700.* Ed. Cristina Malcolmson and Mihoko Suzuki, 15–35. New York: Palgrave, 2002.

Malloch, A. E. "Father Henry Garnet's Treatise of Equivocation." *Recusant History* 15, no. 6 (1981): 387–95.

Malo, Henri. "L'Ile des Démons, la Reine de Navarre et Alcofribas." *Mercure de france* (16 August 1910): 639–45.

Mandrou, Robert. *Introduction to Modern France, 1500–1640: An Essay in Historical Psychology.* Trans. R. E. Hallmark. New York: Holmes and Meier, 1976.

Manguel, Alberto. *A History of Reading.* New York: Penguin Books, 1996.

Mannix, Daniel Pratt, in collaboration with Malcolm Cowley. *Black Cargoes: A History of the Atlantic Slave Trade, 1518–1865.* New York: Viking Press, 1962.

Marcus, George. "Contemporary Problems of Ethnography in the Modern World System." In *Writing Culture: The Poetics and Politics of Ethnography.* Ed. James Clifford and George E. Marcus, 165–93. Berkeley: University of California Press, 1986.

Marcus, Leah. *Puzzling Shakespeare: Local Reading and Its Discontents.* Berkeley: University of California Press, 1988.

———. "Renaissance/Early Modern." In *Redrawing the Boundaries: The Transformation of English and American Literary Studies.* Ed. Stephen Greenblatt and Giles Gunn, 41–63. New York: Modern Language Association of America, 1992.

Margolis, Nadia. "Christine de Pizan and the Jews: Political and Poetic Implications." In *Politics, Gender, and Genre.* Ed. M. Brabant, 53–73. Boulder, Colo.: Westview Press, 1992.

———. "Christine de Pizan: The Poetess as Historian." *Journal of the History of Ideas* 47 (1986): 361–75.

———. "Elegant Closures: The Use of the Diminutive in Christine de Pizan and Jean de Meun." In *Reinterpreting Christine de Pizan.* Ed. E. J. Richards, 111–25. Athens: University of Georgia Press, 1992.

Marichal, Robert. "Les Compagnons de Roberval." *Humanisme et Renaissance* 1 (1934): 50–122.

Marie de France. *Les Lais de Marie de France.* Ed. Jean Rychner. Paris: Champion, 1966.

———. *The Lais of Marie de France.* Trans. Robert Hanning and Joan Ferrante. New York: Dutton, 1978.

Marotti, Arthur F. "Alienating Catholics in Early Modern England: Recusant Women, Jesuits and Ideological Fantasies." In *Catholicism and Anti-Catholicism in Early Modern English Texts.* Ed. A. F. Marotti, 1–34. Houndmills, Hampshire: Macmillan; New York: St. Martin's Press, 1999.

———. "Malleable and Fixed Texts: Manuscript and Printed Miscellanies and the Transmission of Lyric Poetry in the English Renaissance." In *New Ways of Looking at Old Texts: Papers of the Renaissance English Text Society, 1985–91.* Ed. W. Speed Hill, 159–73. Binghamton, N.Y.: Medieval and Renaissance Texts and Studies, 1993.

Marquardt, Joachim. *Das Privatleben der Römer.* 1879. 3d ed. Darmstadt: Wissenschaftliche Buchgesellschaft, 1990.

Martin, Henri-Jean. *The History and Power of Writing.* 1988. Trans. Lydia Cochrane. Chicago: University of Chicago Press, 1994.

Martin, Marie-Madeleine. *The Making of France: The Origins and Development of the Idea of National Unity* [*Histoire de l'unité française,* 1948]. Trans. Barbara and Robert North. London: Eyre and Spottiswoode, 1951.

Marx, Karl. *Capital: A Critique of Political Economy.* Introduced by Ernest Mandel. Vol. 1. Trans. Ben Fowkes. New York: Vintage, 1977.

Marx, Karl, and Friedrich Engels. *Werke.* 39 vols. Berlin: Dietz Verlag, 1957–68.

Mason, Henry. *The New Art of Lying Covered by Jesuites under the Vaile of Equivocation.* London: George Purslowe for John Clarke, 1624.

Matchinske, Megan. *Writing, Gender, and State in Early Modern England: Identity Formation and the Female Subject.* Cambridge: Cambridge University Press, 1998.

Maus, Katherine Eisaman. "Playhouse Flesh and Blood: Sexual Ideology and the Restoration Actress." *English Literary History* 46 (1979): 595–617.

May, William Harold. "The Confession of Prous Boneta, Heretic and Heresiarch." In *Essays in Medieval Life and Thought.* Ed. John H. Mundy et al., 3–30. New York: Columbia University Press, 1955.

[Maydens of London]. *A Letter sent by the Maydens of London, to the vertuous Matrones [and] Mis-*

tresses of the same, in the defense of their lawfull Libertie. Answering the Mery Meeting by us Rose, Jane, Rachell, Sara, Philumias and Dorothie. London: Henriy Binneman, for Thomas Hacket, 1567.

McCash, June Hall. "Cultural Patronage: An Overview." In *The Cultural Patronage of Medieval Women.* Ed. J. H. McCash, 1–49. Athens: University of Georgia Press, 1996.

McCormick, K. M. "Gender and Language." In *The Encyclopedia of Language and Linguistics.* Ed. R. E. Asher, 3:1353–60. New York: Pergamon Press, 1994.

McDavid, Raven I., Jr. *Dialects in Culture: Essays in General Dialectology.* Ed. William A. Kretzschmar, Jr. Tuscaloosa: University of Alabama Press, 1979.

McDowell, Paula. *The Women of Grub Street: Press, Politics and Gender in the London Marketplace, 1678–1730.* Oxford: Clarendon Press, 1998.

McEachern, Claire. *The Poetics of English Nationhood, 1590–1612.* Cambridge: Cambridge University Press, 1996.

McKenzie, D. F. "Speech-Manuscript-Print." In *New Directions in Textual Studies.* Ed. Dave Oliphant and Robin Bradford, 87–109. Austin: University of Texas Press, 1990.

McKeon, Michael. *The Origins of the English Novel, 1600–1740.* Baltimore: Johns Hopkins University Press, 1987.

McKerrow, R. B. *Printers' and Publishers' Devices in England and Scotland, 1485–1640.* London: Printed for the Bibliographical Society at Chiswick Press, 1913.

McKinley, Mary B. "Telling Secrets: Sacramental Confession and Narrative Authority in the *Heptaméron.*" In *Critical Tales: New Studies of the "Heptameron" and Early Modern Culture.* Ed. John D. Lyons and Mary B. McKinley, 146–71. Philadelphia: University of Pennsylvania Press, 1993.

McKitterick, Rosamond, ed. *The Uses of Literacy in Early Medieval Europe.* Cambridge: Cambridge University Press, 1990.

McLeod, Bruce. *The Geography of Empire in English Literature, 1580–1745.* Cambridge: Cambridge University Press, 1999.

McLeod, Enid. *The Order of the Rose: The Life and Ideas of Christine de Pizan.* London: Chatto and Windus, 1976.

McLeod, Glenda, ed. *The Reception of Christine de Pizan from the Fifteenth through the Nineteenth Centuries: Visitors to the City.* Lewiston, N.Y.: Edwin Mellen Press, 1991.

McLeod, Glenda, and Katharine Wilson. "A Clerk in Name Only—A Clerk in All but Name. The Misogamous Tradition and *La Cité des Dames.*" In *The City of Scholars.* Ed. M. Zimmermann and D. De Rentiis, 67–76. New York: Walter de Gruyter, 1994.

McLuhan, Marshall. *The Gutenberg Galaxy: The Making of Typographic Man.* Toronto: University of Toronto Press, 1962.

McQuade, Donald, ed. *The Territory of Language.* Rev ed. Carbondale: Southern Illinois University Press, 1986.

McSheffrey, Shannon. *Gender and Heresy: Women and Men in Lollard Communities, 1420–1530.* Philadelphia: University of Pennsylvania Press, 1995.

———. "Literacy and the Gender Gap in the Late Middle Ages: Women and Reading in Lollard Communities." In *Women, the Book, and the Godly: Selected Proceedings of the St. Hilda's Conference, 1993,* vol. 1. Ed. Lesley Smith and Jane H. M. Taylor, 157–70. Cambridge: D. S. Brewer, 1995.

Meale, Carol M. "'. . . Alle the Bokes That I Haue of Latyn, Englisch and Frensch': Laywomen and Their Books in Late Medieval England." In *Women and Literature in Britain, 1150–1500.* Ed. Carol Meale, 128–58. Cambridge: Cambridge University Press, 1993.

Mendelson, Sara Heller. *The Mental World of Stuart Women: Three Studies.* Brighton, Sussex: Harvester; Amherst: University of Massachusetts Press, 1987.

Merrim, Stephanie. *Early Modern Women's Writing and Sor Juana Ines de la Cruz.* Nashville: Vanderbilt University Press, 1999.

Michaud-Freville, Françoise. "Marguerite d'Angoulême, reine de Navarre, duchesse de Berry." In *Marguerite de Navarre, 1492–1992.* Ed. Nicole Cazauran and James Dauphiné, 45–57. Paris: Editions Inter-Universitaires, 1995.

Mignolo, Walter. "Afterword: Writing and Recorded Knowledge in Colonial and Postcolonial Situations." In *Writing without Words.* Ed. E. Boone and W. Mignolo, 293–313. Durham, N.C.: Duke University Press, 1994.

———. *The Darker Side of the Renaissance: Literacy, Territoriality, and Colonization.* Ann Arbor: University of Michigan Press, 1995.

Mikalachki, Jodi. *The Legacy of Boadicea: Gender and Nation in Early Modern England.* New York: Routledge, 1998.

Miller, Naomi J. *Changing the Subject: Mary Wroth and Figurations of Gender in Early Modern England.* Lexington: University Press of Kentucky, 1996.

Millett, Bella. "English Recluses and the Development of Vernacular Literature in the Twelfth and Thirteenth Centuries." In *Women and Literature in Britain, 1150–1500.* Ed. Carol Meale, 86–103. Cambridge: Cambridge University Press, 1993.

Millett, Benignus. "Irish Literature in Latin, 1550–1700." In *A New History of Ireland,* vol. 3. Ed. T. W. Moody, F. X. Martin, and F. J. Byrne, 561–86. Oxford: Clarendon Press, 1986.

Milroy, James. "The History of English in the British Isles." In *Language in the British Isles.* Ed. P. Trudgill, 5–31. Cambridge: Cambridge University Press, 1984.

Milroy, James and Leslie Milroy. *Authority in Language: Investigating Language Prescription and Standardisation.* London: Routledge, 1985.

Milsom, Stroud Francis. "Rise of the Central Courts." In *Historical Foundations of the Common Law,* 20–22. London: Butterworth, 1969.

Minnis, Alastair J. *Medieval Theory of Authorship.* London: Scolar Press, 1984.

Mirrer, Louise, ed. *Upon My Husband's Death: Widows in the Literature and Histories of Medieval Europe.* Ann Arbor: University of Michigan Press, 1992.

Miskimin, Harry A. "Widows Not So Merry: Women and the Courts in Late Medieval France." In *Upon My Husband's Death.* Ed. L. Mirrer, 207–19. Ann Arbor: University of Michigan Press, 1992.

Mohanty, Chandra Talpade. "Under Western Eyes: Feminist Scholarship and Colonial Discourses." In *Third World Women and the Politics of Feminism.* Ed. Chandra Talpade Mohanty, Ann Russo, and Lourdes Torres, 51–80. Bloomington: Indiana University Press, 1991.

Molinier, Alain. "Aux origines de la Réformation Cévenole." *Annales: Economies, Sociétés, Civilisations* 39, no. 2 (1984): 240–64.

Monaghan, E. Jennifer. "Literacy Instruction and Gender in Colonial New England." In *Reading in America.* Ed. Cathy N. Davidson, 53–80. Baltimore: Johns Hopkins University Press, 1989.

Monson, Craig A., ed. *The Crannied Wall: Women, Religion, and the Arts in Early Modern Europe.* Ann Arbor: University of Michigan Press, 1992.

Montreuil, Jean de. *Le Recueil épistolaire autographe de Pierre d'Ailly et "Les Notes d'Italie" de Jean de Montreuil.* Amsterdam: North-Holland, 1966.

Montrose, Louis. "The Work of Gender in the Discourse of Discovery." *Representations* 33 (winter 1991): 1–41.

Moran, Jo Ann Hoeppner. *The Growth of English Schooling 1340–1548: Learning, Literacy and Laicization in Pre-Reformation York Diocese*. Princeton: Princeton University Press, 1985.

———. "Literacy and Education in Northern England, 1350–1550: A Methodological Inquiry." *Northern History* 17 (1981): 1–23.

More, Thomas. *The Apology*. Vol. 9 of *The Complete Works of St. Thomas More*. Ed. J. B. Trapp. New Haven: Yale University Press, 1979.

———. *St. Thomas More: Selected Letters*. Ed. Elizabeth Frances Rogers. New Haven: Yale University Press, 1961.

Moryson, Fynes. *An Itinerary (1617–26)*. In *Elizabethan Ireland: A Selection of Writings by Elizabethan Writers on Ireland*. Ed. J. P. Myers, Jr., 185–240. Hamden, Conn.: Archon Books, 1983.

Mugglestone, Lynda. *"Talking Proper": The Rise of Accent as Social Symbol*. Oxford: Clarendon Press, 1995.

Muir, Kenneth. Introduction to *Macbeth*. In the Arden Shakespeare. Ed. K. Muir. 9th ed. London: Methuen, 1962.

Mulcaster, Richard. *The First Part of the Elementarie VVhich Entreateth Chefelie of the Right Writing of Our English Tung*. 1582. Facsimile ed. Menston, U.K.: Scolar Press, 1970.

———. *Positions Concerning the Training Up of Children*. 1581. Ed. William Barker. Toronto: University of Toronto Press, 1994.

Mullaney, Steven. *The Place of the Stage: License, Play and Power in Renaissance England*. Chicago: University of Chicago Press, 1988.

———. "Strange Things, Gross Terms, Curious Customs: The Rehearsal of Cultures in the Late Renaissance." In *Representing the English Renaissance*. Ed. Stephen Greenblatt, 65–92. Berkeley: University of California Press, 1998.

The Myrroure of Oure Lady very necessary for all religious persones. London: Richard Fawkes, 4 November 1530.

Navarre, Marguerite de. *L'Heptaméron*. Ed. Michel François. Paris: Garnier, 1964.

———. *L'Heptaméron*. Ed. Simone de Reyff. Paris: Flammarion, 1982.

———. *The Heptameron*. Trans. P. A. Chilton. Harmondsworth, U.K.: Penguin Books, 1984.

———. *Le Miroir de l'âme pécheresse* [plus two other works]. Ed. Joseph L. Allaire. Humanistische Bibliothek, Reihe 2, Band 10. Munich: Wilhelm Fink, 1972.

———. *Les Prisons*. Ed. Simone Glasson. Geneva: Droz, 1978.

———. *"The Prisons" of Marguerite de Navarre*. Ed. Hilda Dale. Reading: White Knights Press, 1983.

Nebrija, Antonio de. *Gramática castellana*. 1492. *El orthografía castellano*. 1517. Menston, U.K.: Scolar Press, 1969.

Neely, Carol Thomas. *Broken Nuptials in Shakespeare's Plays*. New Haven: Yale University Press, 1985.

Neill, Michael. "Broken English and Broken Irish: Nation, Language, and the Optic of Power in Shakespeare's Histories." *Shakespeare Quarterly* 45 (spring 1994): 1–32.

Newman, Karen. "'And Wash the Ethiop White': Femininity and the Monstrous in *Othello*." In *Shakespeare Reproduced: The Text in History and Ideology*. Ed. Jean E. Howard and Marion F. O'Connor, 141–62. New York: Methuen, 1987.

———. *Fashioning Femininity and English Renaissance Drama*. Chicago: University of Chicago Press, 1991.

Niccholes, Alexander. *A Discourse of Marriage and Wiving: and of the Greatest Mystery Therein Contained: How to Chuse a Good Wife from a Bad*. London: Printed by G. Eld for Leonard Becket, 1620.

Nicholls, Mark. *Investigating Gunpowder Plot.* Manchester, U.K.: Manchester University Press, 1991.

Nichols, Stephen. "Medieval Women Writers: Aisthesis and the Powers of Marginality." *Yale French Studies* 75 (1988): 77–94.

Niranjana, Tejaswini. *Siting Translation: History, Post-Structuralism, and the Colonial Context.* Berkeley: University of California Press, 1992.

Noakes, Susan. *Timely Reading: Between Exegesis and Interpretation.* Ithaca: Cornell University Press, 1988.

Norbrook, David. "Safety First in Buckinghamshire." *Times Literary Supplement,* 28 July 2000.

Norton, Glyn P. "Narrative Function in the *Heptaméron* Frame-Story." In *La Nouvelle française à la Renaissance.* Ed. Lionello Sozzi, 436–47. Geneva: Slatkine, 1981.

Oakley, Francis. *Council over Pope? Towards a Provisional Ecclesiology.* New York: Herder and Herder, 1969.

———. *The Political Thought of Pierre d'Ailly: The Voluntarist Tradition.* New Haven: Yale University Press, 1964.

———. "The *Propositiones Utiles* of Pierre d'Ailly: An Epitome of Conciliar Theory." *Church History* 29 (1960): 398–403.

O'Day, Rosemary. *Education and Society 1500–1800: The Social Foundations of Education in Early Modern Britain.* New York: Longman, 1982.

O'Donnell, Mary Ann. *Aphra Behn: An Annotated Bibliography of Primary and Secondary Sources.* New York: Garland, 1986.

Oingt, Marguerite d'. *Les Oeuvres de Marguerite d'Oingt.* Ed. Antonin Duraffour, Pierre Gardette, and Paulette Durdilly. Paris: Société d'Edition, Les Belles Lettres, 1965.

———. *The Writings of Margaret of Oingt.* Introd. and trans. (from Latin and Franco-Provençal) Renate Blumenfeld-Kosinski. Newburyport, Mass.: Focus Information Group, 1990.

O'Keeffe, Katherine O'Brien. *Visible Song: Transitional Literacy in Old English Verse.* Cambridge: Cambridge University Press, 1990.

Oldenburg, Scott. "The Riddle of Blackness in England's National Family Romance." *Journal for Early Modern Cultural Studies* 1, no. 1 (spring–summer 2001): 46–62.

Oldham, James C. "On Pleading the Belly: A History of the Jury of Matrons." *Criminal Justice History* 6 (1985): 1–64.

Olson, David R. *The World on Paper: Conceptual and Cognitive Implications of Writing and Reading.* Cambridge: Cambridge University Press, 1994.

Ong, Walter. "Latin Language Study as a Renaissance Puberty Rite." *Studies in Philology* 56 (1959): 103–24.

———. *Orality and Literacy: The Technologizing of the Word.* New York: Methuen, 1982.

———. *The Presence of the Word.* New Haven: Yale University Press, 1967.

———. *Rhetoric, Romance, and Technology: Studies in the Interaction of Expression and Culture.* Ithaca: Cornell University Press, 1971.

———. "Writing Restructures Thought." In *The Written Word: Literacy in Transition.* Ed. Gerd Baumann, 23–50. Oxford: Clarendon Press, 1986.

Orgel, Stephen. "Margins of Truth." In *The Renaissance Text: Theory, Editing, Textuality.* Ed. Andrew Murphy, 95–99. Manchester: Manchester University Press, 2000.

———. "Nobody's Perfect, or Why Did the English Stage Take Boys for Women?" *South Atlantic Quarterly* 88 (winter 1989): 7–29.

Orlin, Lena Cowin. *Private Matters and Public Culture in Post-Reformation England.* Ithaca: Cornell University Press, 1994.

Orme, Nicholas. *Education and Society in Medieval and Renaissance England.* Ronceverte, W.V.: Hambledon Press, 1989.

Osgood, Charles G. *Boccaccio on Poetry.* Princeton: Princeton University Press, 1930.

Ostovich, Helen. "'Teach You Our Princess English?' Equivocal Translation of the French in *Henry V.*" In *Gender Rhetorics: Postures of Dominance and Submission in History.* Ed. Richard C. Trexler, 147–61. Binghamton, N.Y.: Medieval and Renaissance Texts and Studies, 1994.

Ovid. *The Art of Love and Other Poems.* Trans. J. H. Mozley. Loeb Classical Library. Rev. ed. Cambridge, Mass.: Harvard University Press, 1969.

———. *"Heroides" and "Amores."* Bilingual ed. with translation by G. Showerman (1914), revised by G. P. Gould. Loeb Classical Library. Cambridge, Mass.: Harvard University Press, 1977.

The Oxford English Dictionary. 2d ed. Prepared by J. A. Simpson and E. S. C. Weiner. 20 vols. Oxford: Clarendon Press, 1987. Cited as *OED.*

Padley, G. Arthur. *Grammatical Theory in Western Europe 1500–1700.* 2 vols. Cambridge: Cambridge University Press, 1988.

Pagden, Anthony. *The Fall of Natural Man: The American Indian and the Origins of Comparative Ethnology.* Cambridge: Cambridge University Press, 1982.

———. "The Struggle for Legitimacy and the Image of Empire in the Atlantic to c. 1700." In *The Origins of Empire.* Ed. N. Canny, 34–54. Oxford: Oxford University Press, 1998.

Palermo, Joseph. "L'Historicité des devisants de *L'Heptaméron.*" *Revue de l'histoire littéraire de la France* 69 (1969): 193–302.

Panofsky, Erwin. *Renaissance and Renascences in Western Art.* Stockholm: Almquist and Wiksell, 1960, 1965.

Parker, Patricia. "Fantasies of 'Race' and 'Gender': Africa, Othello, and Bringing to Light." In *Women, "Race," and Writing in the Early Modern Period.* Ed. M. Hendricks and P. Parker, 84–100. London: Routledge, 1994.

———. *Literary Fat Ladies: Rhetoric, Gender, Property.* London: Methuen, 1987.

———. "On the Tongue: Cross Gendering, Effeminacy, and the Art of Words." *Style* 23, no. 3 (fall 1989): 445–50.

———. "Virile Style." In *Premodern Sexualities.* Ed. Louise Fradenberg and Carla Freccero, 199–222. New York: Routledge, 1995.

Parker, Roszika. *The Subversive Stitch: Embroidery in Women's Lives 1300–1900.* London: Woman's Press, 1984.

Parkes, Malcolm Beckwith. "The Literacy of the Laity." In *The Mediaeval World.* Ed. David Daiches and Anthony Thorlby, 555–77. London: Aldus Books, 1973.

Paster, Gail Kern. *The Idea of the City in the Age of Shakespeare.* Athens: University of Georgia Press, 1985.

Pateman, Carole. *The Sexual Contract.* Stanford: Stanford University Press, 1988.

Patterson, Annabel M. *Censorship and Interpretation: The Conditions of Writing and Reading in Early Modern England.* Madison: University of Wisconsin Press, 1984.

———. *Shakespeare and the Popular Voice.* Oxford: Basil Blackwell, 1989.

Patterson, Lee. "Court Politics and the Invention of Literature: The Case of Sir John Clanvowe." In *Culture and History, 1350–1600: Essays on English Communities, Identities, and Writing.* Ed. David Aers, 7–41. New York: Harvester Wheatsheaf, 1992.

———. "Literary History." In *Critical Terms for Literary Study.* Ed. Frank Lentricchia and Thomas McLaughlin, 250–62. Chicago: University of Chicago Press, 1990.

———. "On the Margin: Postmodernism, Ironic History, and Medieval Studies." *Speculum* 65, nos. 1–2 (1990): 87–108.

Paxman, Davis. "Oral and Literate Discourse in Aphra Behn's *Oroonoko*." *Restoration: Studies in English Literary Culture 1660–1700* 18, no. 2 (fall 1994): 88–103.

Payne, Deborah C. "'And Poets Shall by Patron-Princes Live': Aphra Behn and Patronage." In *Curtain Calls: British and American Women and the Theater 1660–1820.* Ed. Cecilia Macheski, 105–19. Athens: Ohio University Press, 1991.

Pearse, Nancy Cotton. "Elizabeth Cary, Renaissance Playwright." *Texas Studies in Literature and Language* 18 (1977): 601–8.

Pearson, Jacqueline. "Gender and Narrative in the Fiction of Aphra Behn." In *Aphra Behn: Contemporary Critical Essays.* Ed. Janet Todd, 111–41. London: Macmillan, 1999.

————. *The Prostituted Muse: Images of Women and Women Dramatists, 1642–1737.* New York: St. Martin's Press, 1988.

————. "Women Reading, Reading Women." In *Women and Literature in Britain, 1500–1700.* Ed. Helen Wilcox, 80–99. Cambridge: Cambridge University Press, 1996.

Perkins, William. *Christian Oeconomie, or, A Short Survey of the Right Manner of Erecting and Ordering a Familie According to the Scriptures.* Trans. Thomas Pickering. London: Felix Kingston, 1609.

P[ersons], R[obert]. *A Treatise tending to Mitigation towards Catholicke-Subiectes in England.* 1607. Ed D. M. Rogers. English Recusant Literature, 1558–1640, vol. 340. London: Scolar Press, 1977.

Peters, J. S. "Currency, Credit, and Literary Property." In *Early Modern Conceptions of Property.* Ed. J. Brewer and S. Staves, 365–88. London: Routledge, 1996.

Petot, Pierre, and André Vandenbossche. "Le Statut de la femme dans les pays coutumiers français du XIIIe au XVIIe siècle." In *La Femme,* 243–54. Recueils de la Societé Jean Bodin pour l'Histoire Comparative des Institutions, No. 12, part 2. Brussels: Editions de la Librairie Encyclopédique, 1962.

Petrarca, Francesco. *Canzoniere.* Ed. Gianfranco Contini, with annotation by Daniele Ponchiroli. Turin: Einaudi, 1968.

Petroff, Elizabeth Alvilda, ed. *Medieval Women's Visionary Literature.* Oxford: Oxford University Press, 1986.

Petrucci, Armando. *Writers and Readers in Medieval Italy: Studies in the History of Written Culture.* Ed. and trans. Charles M. Radding. New Haven: Yale University Press, 1995.

Pfhol, G., ed. *Das Alphabet. Enstehung und Entwicklung der griechischen Schrift.* Darmstadt: Wissenschaftliche Buchgesellschaft, 1968.

Philippy, Patricia. "Establishing Authority: Boccaccio's *De Claris Mulieribus* and Christine de Pizan's *Le Livre de la Cité des Dames*." *Romanic Review* 77 (1986): 167–94.

Phillips, William D., Jr. *Slavery from Roman Times to the Early Transatlantic Trade.* Minneapolis: University of Minnesota Press, 1985.

Pico della Mirandola, Giovanni. *Oration on the Dignity of Man.* Trans. A. Robert Caponigri. Chicago: Gateway, 1956.

Pinet, Marie Josephe. *Christine de Pizan, 1364–1430: Etude biographique et littéraire.* Paris, 1927. Rpt., Geneva: Slatkine, 1974.

Pizan, Christine de. *The Boke of the Cyte of Ladyes.* Trans. Brian Ansley. London: Thomas Pepwell, 1521. In *Distaves and Dames.* Ed. D. Bornstein. Delmar, N.Y.: Scholars' Facsimiles, 1978.

————. *The Book of Deeds of Arms and of Chivalry.* Trans. Sumner Willard, ed. Charity Cannon Willard. University Park: Pennsylvania State University Press, 1999.

————. *The Book of Fayttes of Armes and of Chivalrye.* Trans. and printed by William Caxton from the French original of Christine de Pizan. Ed. A. T. P. Byles. London: Early English Text Society, Oxford University Press, 1932.

———. *The Book of the City of Ladies*. Trans. Earl Jeffrey Richards. 1982. Rev. ed., New York: Persea Books, 1998.

———. *The Book of the Duke of True Lovers*. Trans. Alice Kemp-Welch. New York: Cooper Square, 1966.

———. *Chemin de long estude*. Ed. Robert Püschel. 1881. Geneva: Slatkine, 1974.

———. *Christine de Pizan's "Letter of Othea to Hector."* Trans. Jane Chance. Newburyport, Mass.: Focus Information Group, 1990.

———. *Christine's Vision [Lavision-Christine]*. Trans. Glenda K. McLeod. New York: Garland, 1993.

———. *La Città delle dame*. Bilingual ed. (French/Italian), trans. Patrizia Caraffi, ed. Earl Jeffrey Richards. Milan: Luni Editrice, 1997.

———. *Lavision-Christine*. Ed. Sister Mary Louis Towner. Washington, D.C.: Catholic University of America Press, 1932.

———. "The *Livre de la Cité des Dames* of Christine de Pisan: A Critical Edition." Ed. Maureen Cheney Curnow. 3 vols. Ann Arbor, Mich.: University Microfilms, 1975.

———. *"Le Livre de la mutacion de fortune" par Christine de Pizan*. Ed. Suzanne Solente. 2 vols. Paris: A. and J. Picard, 1959.

———. *The "Livre de la Paix" of Christine de Pizan*. Ed. Charity Cannon Willard. The Hague: Mouton, 1958.

———. *Le Livre de la prod'hommie de l'homme*. [Later *Livre du prudence*.] Paris, Bibliothèque Nationale, fonds français 5037, fols. 182–221.

———. *Le Livre des fais et bonnes meurs du sage roy Charles V*. Ed. Suzanne Solente. 2 vols. Paris: Champion, 1940.

———. *Livre des Trois Vertus: A Medieval Woman's Mirror of Honor*. Ed. Madeleine Pelner Cosman. Trans. Charity Cannon Willard. Tenafly, N.J.: Persea Books, 1989.

———. *Le Livre du corps de policie*. Ed. Robert H. Lucas. Geneva: Droz, 1967.

———. *Oeuvres poétiques de Christine de Pizan*. Ed. Maurice Roy. 3 vols. Paris: Firmin Didot, 1885–96.

———. *"Les Sept Psaumes Allegorisés" of Christine de Pizan*. Ed. Ruth Ringland Rains. Washington, D.C.: Catholic University of America Press, 1965.

———. *The Writings of Christine de Pizan*. Ed. Charity Cannon Willard, trans. Glenda McLeod. New York: Persea Books, 1994.

Plummer, John F., ed. *Vox Feminae: Studies in Medieval Woman's Songs*. Kalamazoo, Mich.: Medieval Institute Publications, 1981.

Pocock, J. G. A. "British History: A Plea for a New Subject." *Journal of Modern History* 47 (1974): 601–28.

Poinsotte, Jean-Michel. "L'Image de Didon dans l'antiquité tardive." In *Enée et Didon: Naissance, fonctionnement et survie d'un mythe*. Ed. René Martin, 43–54. Paris: CNRS, 1990.

Polachek, Dora E. "Save the Last Laugh for Me: Revamping the Script of Infidelity in Novella 69." In *Heroic Virtue, Comic Infidelity: Reassessing Marguerite de Navarre's "Heptaméron."* Ed. D. E. Polachek, 155–69. Amherst, Mass.: Hestia Press, 1993.

Pollock, Frederic, and Frederick W. Maitland. *The History of English Law*. Vol. 2. Cambridge: Cambridge University Press, 1898.

Pollock, Linda. "'Teach Her to Live under Obedience': The Making of Women in the Upper Ranks of Early Modern England." *Continuity and Change* 4, no. 2 (1989): 231–58.

Poovey, Mary. *A History of the Modern Fact*. Chicago: University of Chicago Press, 1998.

———. *Making a Social Body: British Cultural Formation, 1830–1914*. Chicago: University of Chicago Press, 1995.

Porete, Marguerite. *Le Mirouer des simples ames anienties et qui seulement demourent en vouloir et desir d'amour.* Ed. Romana Guarnieri. *Archivio italiano per la storia della pietà* 4 (1965): 501–636.

Porter, Theodore M. "Objectivity as Standardization: The Rhetoric of Impersonality in Measurement, Statistics, and Cost-Benefit Analysis." In *Rethinking Objectivity.* Ed. Allan Megill, 197–237. Durham, N.C.: Duke University Press, 1994.

———. *The Rise of Statistical Thinking.* Princeton: Princeton University Press, 1986.

Potter, David. *A History of France, 1460–1560: The Emergence of a Nation State.* New York: St. Martin's Press, 1995.

Power, Eileen. *Medieval English Nunneries.* Cambridge: Cambridge University Press, 1922.

Powers, George C. *Nationalism at the Council of Constance, 1414–18.* Washington, D.C.: Catholic University of America Press, 1927.

Pratt, Mary Louise. *Imperial Eyes: Travel Writing and Transculturation.* New York: Routledge, 1992.

Prescott, Anne. *French Poets and the English Renaissance: Studies in Fame and Transformation.* New Haven: Yale University Press, 1978.

———. "The Pearl of the Valois and Elizabeth I: Marguerite de Navarre's *Miroir* and Tudor England." In *Silent But for the Word: Tudor Women as Patrons, Translators and Writers of Religious Works.* Ed. Margaret Hannay, 61–76. Kent, Ohio: Kent State University Press, 1985.

Price, Richard. *First-Time: The Historical Vision of an Afro-American People.* Baltimore: Johns Hopkins University Press, 1983.

Proba, Faltonia Betitia. *Cento Vergilianus* (c. 350 C.E.). In *The Golden Bough, the Oaken Cross: The Virgilian Cento of Faltonia Betitia Proba.* Ed. Elizabeth A. Clark and Diane F. Hatch. Chico, Calif.: Scholars Press, 1981.

Purchas, Samuel. *Pvrchas His Pilgrimage; or, Relations of the VVorld and the Religions Obserued in All Ages and Places Discouered, from the Creation vnto This Present. In Foure Partes. This First Containeth a Theologicall . . .* London: W[illiam] Stansby for H[enrie] Fetherstone, 1613.

Purkiss, Diane. "The Queen on Stage: Marlowe's *Dido Queen of Carthage* and the Representation of Elizabeth I." In *A Woman Scorn'd: Responses to the Dido Myth.* Ed. M. Burden, 151–68. London: Faber and Faber, 1998.

Puttenham, George. *The Arte of English Poesie.* 1589. Facsimile rpt. with introduction by B. Hathaway. Kent, Ohio: Kent State University Press, 1970.

Quilligan, Maureen. *The Allegory of Female Authority: Christine de Pizan's "Cité des Dames."* Ithaca: Cornell University Press, 1991.

———. "Staging Gender." In *Sexuality and Gender in Early Modern Europe: Institutions, Texts, Images.* Ed. James Grantham Turner, 208–32. Cambridge: Cambridge University Press, 1993.

Quint, David. "'Alexander the Pig': Shakespeare on History and Poetry." *Boundary 2,* 10, no. 3 (spring 1982): 49–68.

———. *Epic and Empire.* Princeton: Princeton University Press, 1993.

Quintilian. *Institutio oratoria.* Trans. H. E. Butler. Vol. 1. Loeb Classical Library. Cambridge, Mass.: Harvard University Press, 1980.

Rabelais, François. *The Histories of Gargantua and Pantagruel.* Trans. J. M. Cohen. Baltimore: Penguin Books, 1955.

———. *Oeuvres complètes.* Ed. Pierre Jourda. 2 vols. Paris: Garnier Freres, 1962.

Raber, Karen L. "Gender and the Political Subject in *The Tragedy of Mariam.*" *Studies in English Literature* 35 (1995): 321–43.

Rabkin, Norman. *Shakespeare and the Problem of Meaning.* Chicago: University of Chicago Press, 1981.

Raleigh, Walter, Sir. *The Discouerie of the Large, Rich, and bevvtiful Empyre of Guiana, with a*

Relation of the Great and Golden Citie of Manoa (Which the Spanyards Call El Dorado) . . . 1596. Facsimile ed. Cleveland: World Publishing, 1966.

———. *The History of the World.* London: [William Stansby] for Walter Burre, 1614.

Rasmussen, Jens. *La Prose narrative française du XVe siècle.* Copenhagen: Munksgaard, 1958.

Rathery, E.-J.-B. *Des relations sociales et intellectuelles entre la France et l'Angleterre depuis la conquête des Normands jusqu'à la révolution française.* Paris: Dubuisson, 1856.

Raven, James, Helen Small, and Naomi Tadmor, eds. *The Practice and Representation of Reading in England.* Cambridge: Cambridge University Press, 1996.

Reece, Jack E. "Internal Colonialism: The Case of Brittany." *Ethnic and Racial Studies* 2, no. 3 (July 1979): 275–92.

Regnier-Bohler, Danielle. "Imagining a Self: Exploring Literature." In *A History of Private Life.* Vol. 2: *Revelations of the Medieval World.* Ed. Philippe Ariès and Georges Duby, trans. Arthur Goldhammer, 311–93. Cambridge, Mass.: Harvard University Press, 1988.

Renan, Ernest. "Qu'est-ce qu'une nation?" In *Discours et conférences,* 277–310. Paris: Calmann-Lévy, 1887.

Reno, Christine. "The Preface to the *Avision-Christine* in ex-Phillipps 128." In *Reinterpreting Christine de Pizan.* Ed. E. J. Richards, 207–27. Athens: University of Georgia Press, 1992.

Reynolds-Cornell, Régine. *Les Devisants de "l'Heptaméron": Dix personnages en quête d'audience.* Washington, D.C.: University Press of America, 1977.

———. "L'Education sous le manteau, ou: De la nécessité de paraître ignorante." Unpublished paper.

Richards, Earl Jeffrey. "Christine de Pizan and Sacred History." In *The City of Scholars.* Ed. M. Zimmerman and D. De Rentiis, 15–30. New York: Walter de Gruyter, 1994.

———. "Christine de Pizan, the Conventions of Courtly Diction, and Italian Humanism." In *Reinterpreting Christine de Pizan.* Ed. E. J. Richards, 250–71. Athens: University of Georgia Press, 1992.

———. "French Cultural Nationalism and Christian Universalism in the Works of Christine de Pizan." In *Politics, Gender, and Genre.* Ed. M. Brabant, 74–94. Boulder, Colo.: Westview Press, 1992.

Richards, Earl Jeffrey, ed., with Joan Williamson, Nadia Margolis, and Christine Reno. *Reinterpreting Christine de Pizan.* Athens: University of Georgia Press, 1992.

Richardson, Malcolm. "Henry V, the English Chancery, and Chancery English." *Speculum* 55 (1980): 726–50.

Richter, Michael. "A Socio-linguistic Approach to the Latin Middle Ages." In *The Materials, Sources and Methods of Ecclesiastical History.* Ed. Derek Baker, 69–82. New York: Barnes and Noble, 1975.

Rickard, Peter. *Britain in Medieval French Literature, 1100–1500.* Cambridge: Cambridge University Press, 1956.

———. *A History of the French Language.* London: Hutchinson, 1974.

Riley, Denise. *"Am I That Name?" Feminism and the Category of "Woman" in History.* Minneapolis: University of Minnesota Press, 1988.

Rive, Edmund. *An Heptaglottologie.* London: W. Jones, 1618.

Roberts, Sasha. "Reading in Early Modern England: Contexts and Problems." In *Reading in Early Modern England.* Ed. S. Roberts. *Critical Survey* 12, no. 2 (2000): 1–16.

Roberts, Sasha, ed. *Reading in Early Modern England. Critical Survey* 12, no. 2 (2000).

Robertson, Elizabeth. *Early English Devotional Prose and the Female Audience.* Knoxville: University of Tennessee Press, 1990.

———. "'This Living Hand': Thirteenth-Century Female Literacy, Materialist Immanence, and the Female Reader of the *Ancrene Wisse.*" *Speculum* 78 (2003): 1–36.

Rockhill, Kathleen. "Gender, Language and the Politics of Literacy." In *Cross-Cultural Approaches to Literacy.* Ed. Brian Street, 156–75. Cambridge: Cambridge University Press, 1993.

Roelker, Nancy L. "The Appeal of Calvinism to French Noblewomen in the Sixteenh Century." *Journal of Interdisciplinary History* 2 (1972): 391–418.

———. *Queen of Navarre: Jeanne d'Albret, 1528–1572.* Cambridge, Mass.: Harvard University Press, 1968.

Rogers, Katharine M. "Fact and Fiction in Aphra Behn's *Oroonoko.*" *Studies in the Novel* 20, no. 1 (spring 1988): 1–15.

Rollins, Hyder E., ed. *Tottel's Miscellany.* 1557. Rev. ed. Cambridge, Mass.: Harvard University Press, 1966.

Rooks, John. "*The Boke of the Cyte of Ladyes* and Its Sixteenth-Century Readership." In *The Reception of Christine de Pizan from the Fifteenth through the Nineteenth Centuries.* Ed. G. McLeod, 83–100. Lewiston, N.Y.: Edwin Mellen Press, 1991.

Root, Deborah. "The Imperial Signifier: Todorov and the Conquest of Mexico." *Cultural Critique* 9 (spring 1988): 197–219.

Rose, Mark. *Authors and Owners: The Invention of Copyright.* Cambridge, Mass.: Harvard University Press, 1993.

Rose, Mary Beth. *Gender and Heroism in Early Modern English Literature.* Chicago: University of Chicago Press, 2002.

Rosenberg, Leona. *The Minority Press and the English Crown: A Study in Repression, 1558–1625.* The Hague: Nieukoop, 1971.

Rosenthal, Joel T. "Aristocratic Cultural Patronage and Book Bequests, 1350–1500." *Bulletin of the John Rylands University Library of Manchester* 64 (1982): 522–48.

Rosenthal, Laura J. "Owning Oroonoko: Behn, Southerne, and the Contingencies of Property." *Renaissance Drama,* n.s. 23 (1992): 25–58.

———. *Playwrights and Plagiarists in Early Modern England: Gender, Authorship, Literary Property.* Ithaca: Cornell University Press, 1996.

Ross, Shannon. "*The Widdow Ranter*: Old World, New World: Exploring an Era's Authority Paradigm." In *Aphra Behn (1640–1689): Identity, Alterity, Ambiguity.* Ed. Mary Ann O'Donnell, Bernard Dhuicq, and Guyonne Leduc, 81–90. Paris: L'Harmattan, 2000.

Rothwell, W. "Stratford atte Bowe and Paris." *Modern Language Review* 80 (1985): 39–54.

Rowlands, Marie B. "Recusant Women, 1560–1640." In *Women in English Society, 1500–1800.* Ed. Mary Prior, 149–210. London: Methuen, 1985.

Rubik, Margarete. "Estranging the Familiar, Familiarizing the Strange: Self and Other in *Oroonoko* and *The Widdow Ranter.*" In *Aphra Behn (1640–1689): Identity, Alterity, Ambiguity.* Ed. Mary Ann O'Donnell, Bernard Dhuicq, and Guyonne Leduc. Paris: L'Harmattan, 2000.

Russell, D. W. "Quatre versions d'une légende canadienne." In *Canadian Literature* 95 (fall 1982): 172–78.

Saenger, Paul. "Books of Hours and the Reading Habits of the Later Middle Ages." In *The Culture of Print: Power and the Uses of Print in Early Modern Europe.* Ed. Roger Chartier, 141–73.

———. *Space between Words: The Origins of Silent Reading.* Stanford: Stanford University Press, 1997.

Safadi, Yasin H. *Islamic Calligraphy.* London: Thames and Hudson, 1978.

Said, Edward W. *Orientalism.* New York: Pantheon, 1978.

Salter, Elizabeth. *English and International: Studies in the Literature, Art and Patronage of Medieval England.* Ed. Derek Pearsall and Nicolette Zeeman. Cambridge: Cambridge University Press, 1988.

Samuels, Raphael, ed. *Patriotism: The Making and Unmaking of British National Identity.* 3 vols. London: Routledge, 1989.

Sanders, Eve Rachele. "*Auctor* and *Auctoritas* in Marguerite Porete's *The Mirror of Simple Souls.*" Unpublished paper.

———. *Gender and Literacy on Stage in Early Modern England.* Cambridge: Cambridge University Press, 1998.

Sanders, Eve Rachele, and Margaret W. Ferguson, eds. *Literacies in Early Modern England. Critical Survey* 14, no. 1 (2002): 1–8.

Sander[s], Nicholas. *De origine et progressu schismatis Anglicani.* 1585. [*The Rise and Growth of the Anglican Schism*]. Trans. David Lewis. London: Burns and Oates, 1877.

Sandved, Arthur O. "Prolegomena to a Renewed Study of the Rise of Standard English." In *So Meny People Longages and Tonges: Philological Essays in Scots and Mediaeval English Presented to Angus McIntosh.* Ed. Michael Benskin and M. L. Samuels, 31–42. Middle English Dialect Project. Edinburgh: Privately published by M. Benskin and M. L. Samuels, 1981.

Saunders, J. W. *The Profession of English Letters.* London: Routledge and Kegan Paul, 1964.

———. "The Stigma of Print: A Note on the Social Bases of Tudor Poetry." *Essays in Criticism* 1–2 (1951–52): 139–64.

Savage, Roger. "Dido Dies Again." In *A Woman Scorn'd: Responses to the Dido Myth.* Ed. Michael Burden, 3–38. London: Faber and Faber, 1998.

Schaefer, Lucie. "Die Illustrationen zu den Handschriften der Christine de Pizan." *Marburger Jahrbuch fur Kunstwissenschaft* 10 (1937): 119–208.

Scheil, Katherine West. "'Rouz'd by a Woman's Pen': The Shakespeare Ladies' Club and Reading Habits of Early Modern Women." In *Reading in Early Modern England.* Ed. S. Roberts. *Critical Survey* 12, no. 2 (2000): 106–27.

Schibanoff, Susan. "Taking the Gold Out of Egypt: The Art of Reading as a Woman." In *Gender and Reading: Essays on Readers, Texts, and Contexts.* Ed. Elizabeth A. Flynn and Patrocinio P. Schweickart, 83–106. Baltimore: Johns Hopkins University Press, 1986.

Schleiner, Louise. "Margaret Tyler, Translator and Waiting Woman." *ELN* 29 (1992): 1–8.

———. *Tudor and Stuart Women Writers.* Bloomington: Indiana University Press, 1994.

Schleiner, Winfried. "Divina Virago: Queen Elizabeth as an Amazon." *Studies in Philology* 75 (1978): 163–80.

Schnapp, Jeffrey. "Reading Lessons: Augustine, Proba and the Christian Détournement of Antiquity." *Stanford Literary Review of Books* 9 (1992): 99–123.

Schoenbaum, Sam. "The Life of Shakespeare." In *The Cambridge Companion to Shakespeare Studies.* Ed. Stanley Wells, 1–16. Cambridge: Cambridge University Press, 1986.

Schofield, Roger. "The Measurement of Literacy in Pre-industrial England." In *Literacy in Traditional Societies.* Ed. Jack Goody, 311–25. Cambridge: Cambridge University Press, 1968.

Schotter, Anne. "Woman's Song in Medieval Latin." In *Vox Feminae: Studies in Medieval Woman's Songs.* Ed. John F. Plummer, 19–33. Kalamazoo, Mich.: Medieval Institute Publications, 1981.

Schulenberg, Jane Tibbetts. "Sexism and the Celestial Gynaeceum—from 500–1200." *Journal of Medieval History* 4 (1978): 117–33.

Schutte, A. J. "Teaching Adults to Read in Sixteenth-Century Venice: Giovanni Tagliente's *Libro Maistrevole.*" *Sixteenth-Century Journal* 17, no. 1 (1986): 3–16.

Scott, Izora. *Controversies over the Imitation of Cicero in the Renaissance. Reprint of Controversies over the Imitation of Cicero as a Model for Style and Some Phases of Their Influence on the Schools of the Renaissance*. 1910; rpt., Ann Arbor: Hermagoras Press, 1991.

Scott, Joan Wallach. *Gender and the Politics of History*. New York: Columbia University Press, 1988.

Scribner, Bob. "Is a History of Popular Culture Possible?" *History of European Ideas* 10 (1989): 175–91.

Scribner, Sylvia, and Michael Cole. *The Psychology of Literacy*. Cambridge, Mass.: Harvard University Press, 1981.

Seidman, Naomi. *A Marriage Made in Heaven: The Sexual Politics of Hebrew and Yiddish*. Berkeley: University of California Press, 1997.

Senner, Wayne M., ed. *The Origins of Writing*. Lincoln: University of Nebraska Press, 1991.

Seton-Watson, Hugh. *Nations and States: An Inquiry into the Origins of Nations and the Politics of Nationalism*. Boulder, Colo.: Westview Press, 1977.

Seward, Desmond. *Henry V, The Scourge of God*. New York: Viking, 1987.

Shahar, Shulamith. *The Fourth Estate: A History of Women in the Middle Ages*. Trans. Chaya Galai. London: Methuen, 1983.

Shakespeare, William. *Henry V*. Ed. Gary Taylor. Oxford: Clarendon Press, 1982.

———. *The Norton Shakespeare, Based on the Oxford Edition*. Ed. S. Greenblatt, W. Cohen, J. E. Howard, and K. E. Maus. New York: W. W. Norton, 1997. All citations of Shakespeare's plays are from this edition.

Shannon, Laurie J. "*The Tragedie of Mariam*: Cary's Critique of the Terms of Founding Social Discourses." *English Literary Renaissance* 24, no. 1 (1994): 135–53.

Shapiro, James. *Shakespeare and the Jews*. New York: Columbia University Press, 1996.

Sharpe, Kevin. *Reading Revolutions: The Politics of Reading in Early Modern England*. New Haven: Yale University Press, 2000.

Shaughnessy, Mina P. *Errors and Expectations: A Guide for the Teacher of Basic Writing*. New York: Oxford University Press, 1977.

Shell, Marc, ed. *Elizabeth's Glass*. Lincoln: University of Nebraska Press, 1993.

Sheridan, Richard Brinsley. *The Rivals*. In *The Dramatic Works of Richard Brinsley Sheridan*. Ed. Cecil Price, 1:67–148. Oxford: Clarendon Press, 1973.

Sherman, William H. *John Dee: The Politics of Reading and Writing in the English Renaissance*. Amherst: University of Massachusetts Press, 1995.

———. "What Did Renaissance Readers Write in Their Books?" In *Books and Readers in Early Modern England: Material Studies*. Ed. Jennifer Andersen and Elizabeth Sauer, 119–37. Philadelphia: University of Pennsylvania Press, 2002.

Shevelow, Kathryn. *Women and Print Culture: The Construction of Femininity in the Early Periodical*. New York: Routledge, 1989.

Shyllon, Folarin O. *Black People in Britain, 1555–1833*. London: Oxford University Press for the Institute of Race Relations, 1977.

Silberman, Lou H. "The Queen of Sheba in Jewish Tradition." In *Solomon and Sheba*. Ed. James B. Pritchard et al., 65–84. London: Phaidon, 1974.

Simon, Joan. *Education and Society in Tudor England*. Cambridge: Cambridge University Press, 1966.

Simpson, David. *The Academic Postmodern and the Rule of Literature: A Report on Half-Knowledge*. Chicago: University of Chicago Press, 1995.

Simpson, Richard, ed. *The Lady Falkland: Her Life*. London: Catholic Publishing and Bookselling Co., 1861.

Sinfield, Alan, with Jonathan Dollimore. "History and Ideology, Masculinity and Miscegenation: The Instance of *Henry V*." In *Faultlines: Cultural Materialism and the Politics of Dissident Reading*. Ed. A. Sinfield, 109–42. Berkeley: University of California Press, 1992.

Skelton, John. *The Complete Poems of John Skelton*. Ed. Philip Henderson. London: Dent, 1959.

Skinner, Quentin. *The Foundations of Modern Political Thought*. Vol. 2: *The Age of Reformation*. Cambridge: Cambridge University Press, 1978.

Skura, Meredith. "The Reproduction of Mothering in *Mariam, Queen of Jewry*: A Defense of 'Biographical' Criticism." *Tulsa Studies in Women's Literature* 16, no. 1 (1997): 27–56.

Slater, Miriam. "The Weightiest Business: Marriage in an Upper Gentry Family in Seventeenth-Century England." *Past and Present* 72 (1976): 25–54.

Smith, Alan G. R. "Constitutional Ideas and Parliamentary Developments in England, 1603–25." In *The Reign of James VI and I*. Ed. A. Smith, 160–76. New York: St. Martin's Press, 1973.

Smith, Anthony D. "The Origins of Nations." In *Nationalism*. Ed. J. Hutchinson and A. D. Smith, 147–54. Oxford: Oxford University Press, 1994.

Smith, Buckingham. *Collecion de varios documentos para la historia de la Florida y tierros adyacentes*. London, 1857.

Smith, Emma. "'So Much English by the Mother.'" In *Medieval and Renaissance Drama in England*. Ed. John Pitcher, 13:165–81. Cranbury, N.J.: Associated University Presses, 2001.

Smith, Hilda. "Humanist Education and the Renaissance Concept of Woman." In *Women and Literature in Britain, 1500–1700*. Ed. Helen Wilcox, 9–29. Cambridge: Cambridge University Press, 1996.

———. *Reason's Disciples: Seventeenth-Century English Feminists*. Urbana: University of Illinois Press, 1982.

Smollett, Tobias. *Humphrey Clinker*. Ed. James L. Thorson. New York: W. W. Norton, 1983.

Snook, Edith. "'His Open Side Our Book': Meditation and Education in Elizabeth Grymeston's *Miscelanea Meditations Memoratives*." In *Maternal Measures: Figuring Caregiving in the Early Modern Period*. Ed. Naomi J. Miller and Naomi Yavneh, 163–78. Burlington, Vt.: Ashgate, 2000.

Société Jean Bodin. *La Femme*. Vol. 11. Brussels: Editions de la Librairie Encyclopédique, 1959.

Sommers, Paula. "Feminine Authority in the *Heptaméron*: A Reading of Oysille." *Modern Language Studies* 13 (1983): 52–59.

———. "The Mirror and Its Reflections: Marguerite de Navarre's Biblical Feminism." *Tulsa Studies in Women's Literature* 5 (1986): 29–39.

Southerne, Thomas. *Oroonoko*. Ed. Maximilian E. Novak and David Stuart Rodes. Lincoln: University of Nebraska Press, 1976.

Spence, N. C. W. "Channel Island French." In *Language in the British Isles*. Ed. P. Trudgill, 345–51. Cambridge: Cambridge University Press, 1984.

Spenser, Edmund. *The Yale Edition of the Shorter Poems of Edmund Spenser*. Ed. William A. Oram, et al. New Haven: Yale University Press, 1989.

Spitzer, Leo. "The Prologue to the *Lais* of Marie de France." In *Romanische Literaturstudien 1936–56*, 96–102. Tübingen: M. Niemeyer, 1959.

Spivak, Gayatri. *In Other Worlds: Essays in Cultural Politics*. New York: Routledge, 1988.

Spufford, Margaret. "First Steps in Literacy: The Reading and Writing Experiences of the Humblest Seventeenth-Century Spiritual Autobiographers." *Social History* 4, no. 3 (1979): 407–34.

———. "The Schooling of the Peasantry in Cambridgeshire, 1575–1700." In *Land, Church and People*. Ed. Joan Thirsk, 113–47. Reading: British Agricultural History Society, 1970.

————. *Small Books and Pleasant Histories: Popular Fiction and Its Readership in Seventeenth-Century England*. Athens: University of Georgia Press, 1981.

Stabler, Arthur P. *The Legend of Marguerite de Roberval*. Pullman: Washington State University Press, 1972.

Stanton, Domna C., ed. *The Female Autograph: Theory and Practice of Autobiography from the Tenth to the Twentieth Century*. Chicago: University of Chicago Press, 1987.

Starr, George. *Defoe and Casuistry*. Princeton: Princeton University Press, 1971.

The Statutes of the Realm. Vol. 3: 1817. Buffalo, N.Y.: William S. Hein, 1993.

Stearns, Bertha Monica. "The Literary Treatment of Bacon's Rebellion in Virginia." *Virginia Magazine of History and Biography* 52, no. 3 (July 1944): 163–79.

Steinberg, Jonathan. "The Historian and the *Questione della Lingua*." In *The Social History of Language*. Ed. Peter Burke and Roy Porter, 198–209. Cambridge: Cambridge University Press, 1987.

Stigler, Stephen M. *The History of Statistics: The Measurement of Uncertainty to 1900*. Cambridge, Mass.: Harvard University Press, 1986.

Stock, Brian. *The Implications of Literacy*. Princeton: Princeton University Press, 1983.

Stone, Donald. "Narrative Technique in *L'Heptaméron*." *Studi francesi* 11 (1967): 473–76.

Stone, Lawrence. *The Crisis of the Aristocracy, 1558–1641*. Oxford: Clarendon Press, 1965.

————. *The Family, Sex and Marriage in England 1500–1800*. 1977. Abridged ed. New York: Harper and Row, 1979.

————. "Literacy and Education in England, 1640–1900." *Past and Present* 42 (1969): 69–139.

————. *The Road to Divorce: England 1530–1987*. Oxford: Oxford University Press, 1990.

Straznicky, Marta. "'Profane Stoical Paradoxes': *The Tragedie of Mariam* and Sidnean Closet Drama." *English Literary Renaissance* 24 (1904): 104–34.

————. "Reading the Stage? Margaret Cavendish and Commonwealth Closet Drama." *Criticism* 37 (1995): 335–90.

Street, Brian. *Literacy in Theory and Practice*. Cambridge: Cambridge University Press, 1984.

————. *Social Literacies: Critical Approaches to Literacy in Development, Ethnography and Education*. New York: Longman, 1995.

Stubbes, John. *John Stubbes's Gaping Gulf with Letters and Other Relevant Documents*. [1579.] Ed. Lloyd E. Berry. Charlottesville: University of Virginia Press, 1968.

Stubbs, Michael. *Language and Literacy: The Sociolinguistics of Reading and Writing*. London: Routledge and Kegan Paul, 1980.

Suggett, Helen. "The Use of French in England in the Later Middle Ages." *Transactions of the Royal Historical Society*, 4th ser., 28 (1946): 61–83. Rpt. in *Essays in Medieval History*. Ed. R. W. Southern, 213–39. London: Macmillan, 1968.

Summit, Jennifer. *Lost Property: The Woman Writer and English Literary History, 1380–1589*. Chicago: University of Chicago Press, 2000.

Sussman, Charlotte. "The Other Problem with Women: Reproduction and Slave Culture in Aphra Behn's *Oroonoko*." In *Rereading Aphra Behn: History, Theory, and Criticism*. Ed. Heidi Hutner, 212–33. Charlottesville: University Press of Virginia, 1993.

Suzuki, Mihoko. "Gender, Power and the Female Reader: Boccaccio's *Decameron* and Marguerite de Navarre's *Heptaméron*." *Comparative Literature Studies* 30, no. 3 (1993): 231–52.

————. *Metamorphoses of Helen: Authority, Difference, and the Epic*. Ithaca: Cornell University Press, 1989.

Swanson, R. N. "Literacy, Heresy, History and Orthodoxy: Perspectives and Permutations for the Later Middle Ages." In *Literacy and Heresy, 1000–1530*. Ed. P. Biller and A. Hudson, 279–93. Cambridge: Cambridge University Press, 1994.

Swearingen, C. Jan. *Rhetoric and Irony: Western Literacy and Western Lies.* New York: Oxford University Press, 1991.

Tetel, Marcel. *"L'Heptaméron:* Première nouvelle et fonction des devisants." In *La Nouvelle française à la renaissance.* Ed. Lionello Sozzi, 449–58. Geneva: Slatkine, 1981.

———. *Marguerite de Navarre's "Heptaméron": Themes, Language, and Structure.* Durham, N.C.: Duke University Press, 1973.

Thomas, Keith. "Cases of Conscience in Seventeenth-Century England." In *Public Duty and Private Conscience in Seventeenth-Century England.* Ed. John Morrill, Paul Slack, and Daniel Woolf, 29–56. Oxford: Clarendon Press, 1993.

———. "The Double Standard." *Journal of the History of Ideas* 20 (1959): 195–96.

———. "The Meaning of Literacy in Early Modern England." In *The Written Word: Literacy in Transition.* Ed. Gerd Baumann, 97–131. Oxford: Clarendon Press, 1986.

Thompson, James W. *The Literacy of the Laity in the Middle Ages.* 1939; rpt., New York: B. Franklin, 1963.

Thomson, Patricia. "Wyatt and the Petrarchan Commentators." *Review of English Studies* 10, no. 39 (August 1959): 225–33.

Timmermans, Linda. *L'Accès des femmes à la culture.* Paris: Champion, 1993.

Todd, Janet. *The Secret Life of Aphra Behn.* New Brunswick, N.J.: Rutgers University Press, 1997.

———. "A Spectacular Death: History and Story in *The Widow Ranter.*" In *Aphra Behn: Contemporary Critical Essays.* Ed J. Todd, 73–84. New York: St. Martin's Press, New Casebooks, 1999.

Todorov, Tzvetan. *The Conquest of America: The Question of the Other.* Trans. Richard Howard. New York: Harper and Row, 1984.

Townsend, David, and Andrew Taylor, eds. *The Tongue of the Fathers: Gender and Ideology in Twelfth-Century Latin.* Philadelphia: University of Pennsylvania Press, 1998.

Trahern, Joseph B., Jr., ed. *Standardizing English: Essays in the History of Language Change, in Honor of John Hurt Fletcher.* Tennessee Studies in Literature, vol. 31. Knoxville: University of Tennessee Press, 1989.

Travitsky, Betty. "The *Feme Covert* in Elizabeth Cary's *Mariam.*" In *Ambiguous Realities: Women in the Middle Ages and Renaissance.* Ed. Carole Levin and Jeanie Watson, 184–96. Detroit: Wayne State University Press, 1987.

———. "Husband Murder and Petty Treason in English Renaissance Tragedy." *Renaissance Drama,* n.s. 21 (1990): 171–98.

———. *Paradise of Women: Writings by Englishwomen of the Renaissance.* Westport, Conn.: Greenwood Press, 1981.

Tribble, Evelyn B. *Margins and Marginality: The Printed Page in Early Modern England.* Charlottesville: University Press of Virginia, 1993.

Trill, Suzanne. "Sixteenth-Century Women's Writing: Mary Sidney's *Psalmes* and the 'Femininity' of Translation." In *Writing and the English Renaissance.* Ed. William Zunder and Suzanne Trill, 140–58. London: Longman, 1996.

Trinh T. Minh-ha. *Woman, Native, Other: Writing Postcoloniality and Feminism.* Bloomington: Indiana University Press, 1989.

Trubowitz, Rachel. "'But Blood Whitened': Nursing Mothers and Others in Early Modern Britain." In *Maternal Measures: Figuring Caregiving in the Early Modern Period.* Ed. Naomi J. Miller and Naomi Yavneh, 82–104. Burlington, Vt.: Ashgate, 2000.

Trudel, Marcel. *Les Vaines tentatives, 1524–1603.* Vol. 1 of *Histoire de la Nouvelle-France.* Montreal: Fides, 1963.

Trudgill, Peter. *Sociolinguistics: An Introduction to Language and Society.* 1974; rev. ed., London: Penguin, 1983.

———. "Standard English in England." In *Language in the British Isles.* Ed. P. Trudgill, 32–44. Cambridge: Cambridge University Press, 1984.

Trudgill, Peter, ed. *Language in the British Isles.* Cambridge: Cambridge University Press, 1984.

Tsien, Tsuen-hsuin. "Paper and Printing." In *Science and Civilisation in China.* Ed. Joseph Needham. Vol. 5, pt. 1. Cambridge: Cambridge University Press, 1985.

Tucoo-Chala, Pierre. "Pau au temps de Marguerite de Navarre." In *Marguerite de Navarre, 1492–1992.* Ed. Nicole Cazauran and James Dauphiné, 25–43. Mont de Marsan: Editions Inter-Universitaires, 1995.

Tufte, Edward. *Envisioning Information.* Cheshire, Conn.: Graphics Press, 1990.

Tyler, Margaret. *The Mirrour of Princely Deedes and Knighthood.* London: T. East, 1578. Rpt. in *The Early Modern Englishwoman: A Facsimile Library of Essential Works.* Vol. 8: *Margaret Tyler.* Selected and introduced by Kathryn Coad. Greenwood, Conn.: Scolar Press, 1996.

Tyler, Stephen. "Postmodern Anthropology." In *Discourse and the Social Life of Meaning.* Ed. Phyllis Chock and June Wyman, 23–49. Washington, D.C.: Smithsonian Institution Press, 1986.

———. *The Said and the Unsaid.* New York: Academic Press, 1978.

Tyndale, William, trans. *Tyndale's New Testament: A Modern-Spelling Edition of the 1534 Translation with an Introduction by David Daniell.* New Haven: Yale University Press, 1989.

———. *Tyndale's Old Testament: A Modern-Spelling Edition of the 1534 Translation with an Introduction by David Daniell.* New Haven: Yale University Press, 1992.

Valency, Maurice Jacques. *The Tragedies of Herod and Mariamne.* New York: Columbia University Press, 1940.

Vergil. *Eclogues, Georgics, Aeneid 1–6.* Ed. H. Rushton Fairclough. Loeb Classical Library. Cambridge, Mass.: Harvard University Press, 1978.

Vincent, David. *Literacy and Popular Culture, England 1750–1914.* Cambridge Studies in Oral and Literate Culture. Cambridge: Cambridge University Press, 1989.

Vives, Juan Luis. *The Instruction of a Christen Woman.* Trans. Rycharde Hyrde. 1529. In *Distaves and Dames.* Ed. D. Bornstein, no. 4. Delmar, N.Y.: Scholars' Facsimiles, 1978.

———. *Opera omnia, distributa et ordinata in argumentorum classes praecipuas.* Ed. Gregorio Majansio and Francisco Fabian. 1782–90; rpt., London: Gregg Press, 1964.

Von der Hardt, H. *Magnum oecumenicum Concilium Constantiense.* 6 vols. Frankfurt: In Officina Christiani Genschii, 1697–1700.

Waddington, Raymond. "Meretrix Est Stampificata: Gendering the Printing Press." In *Books Have Their Own Destiny: Essays in Honor of Robert v. Schnucker.* Ed. Robin B. Barnes et al., 131–41. Kirksville, Mo.: Thomas Jefferson University Press, 1998.

———. "Rewriting the World, Rewriting the Body." In *The Cambridge Companion to English Literature, 1500–1600.* Ed. A. F. Kinney, 287–309. Cambridge: Cambridge University Press, 2000.

Wakefield, Walter L., and Austin P. Evans. *Heresies of the High Middle Ages: Selected Sources, Translated and Annotated.* 1969; rpt., New York: Columbia University Press, 1991.

Walby, Sylvia. "Woman and Nation." In *Mapping the Nation.* Ed. Gopal Balakrishnan, 235–54. London: Verso, 1996.

Walker, Jim. "The End of Dialogue: Paolo Freire on Politics and Education." In *Literacy and Revolution: The Pedagogy of Paulo Freire.* Ed. Robert Mackie, 120–50. New York: Continuum, 1981.

Wall, Wendy. *The Imprint of Gender: Authorship and Publication in the English Renaissance.* Ithaca: Cornell University Press, 1993.

Wallace, David. *Chaucerian Polity: Absolute Lineages and Associational Forms in England and Italy.* Stanford: Stanford University Press, 1997.

Wallace, Rex. "The Origins and Development of the Latin Alphabet." In *The Origins of Writing.* Ed. W. Senner, 121–36. Lincoln: University of Nebraska Press, 1991.

Waller, Marguerite. "The Empire's New Clothes." In *Seeking the Woman in Late Medieval and Renaissance Writings: Essays in Feminist Contextual Criticism.* Ed. Sheila Fisher and Janet E. Halley, 160–83. Knoxville: University of Tennessee Press, 1989.

Walters, Keith. "Language, Logic, and Literacy." In *The Right to Literacy.* Ed. Andrea A. Lunsford, Helene Moglen, and James F. Slevin, 173–88. New York: Modern Language Association, 1990.

Walters, Lori. "Chivalry and the (En)gendered Poetic Self: Petrarchan Models in the 'Cent Ballades.'" In *The City of Scholars.* Ed. M. Zimmermann and D. De Rentiis, 63–76. New York: Walter de Gruyter, 1994.

———. "Fathers and Daughters: Christine de Pizan as Reader of the Male Tradition of *Clergie* in the *Dit de la Rose.*" In *Reinterpreting Christine de Pizan.* Ed. E. J. Richards, 63–76. Athens: University of Georgia Press, 1992.

———. "The Woman Writer and Literary History: Christine de Pizan's Redefinition of the Poetic *Translatio* in the *Epistre au Dieu d'Amours.*" *French Literature Series* 16 (1989): 1–16.

Ward, Wilber Henry. "Mrs. Behn's *The Widow Ranter:* Historical Sources." *South Atlantic Bulletin* 41, no. 4 (1976): 94–98.

Warner, William. *A Continuance of Albion's England.* 1606. Facsimile rpt. Anglistica and Americana, vol. 131. Hildesheim: Georg Olms Verlag, 1971.

Warnicke, Retha. *The Rise and Fall of Anne Boleyn: Family Politics at the Court of Henry VIII.* New York: Cambridge University Press, 1989.

Washburn, Wilcomb E. "Essay on the Sources." In *The Governor and the Rebel: A History of Bacon's Rebellion in Virginia,* 167–75. Chapel Hill: University of North Carolina Press for the Institute of Early American History and Culture at Williamsburg, Va., 1957.

Watson, Paul F. "The Queen of Sheba in Christian Tradition." In *Solomon and Sheba.* Ed. James B. Pritchard et al., 115–45. London: Phaidon, 1974.

Watt, Tessa. *Cheap Print and Popular Piety, 1550–1640.* Cambridge: Cambridge University Press, 1991.

Wayne, Valerie. "Advice for Women from Mothers and Patriarchs." In *Women and Literature in Britain, 1500–1700.* Ed. Helen Wilcox, 56–79. Cambridge: Cambridge University Press, 1996.

———. "Some Sad Sentence: Vives' *Instruction of a Christian Woman.*" In *Silent But for the Word: Tudor Women as Patrons, Translators and Writers of Religious Works.* Ed. Margaret Hannay, 15–29. Kent, Ohio: Kent State University Press, 1985.

Wellek, René, and Austin Warren. *Theory of Literature.* 1949; 3d ed., London: Penguin, 1963.

Wermuth, Paul C. "Bacon's Rebellion in the London Theater." *Virginia Cavalcade* 7, no. 1 (summer 1957): 38–39.

Whalen, Molly. "The Public Currency of the Private Letter: Gender, Class, and Epistolarity in England, 1568–1671." Ph.D. diss., University of California, Santa Cruz, 1994.

Wilcox, Helen. "Private Writing and Public Function: Autobiographical Texts by Renaissance Women." In *Gloriana's Face: Women, Public and Private.* Ed. S. P. Cerasano and Marion Wynne-Davis, 47–52. London: Harvester Wheatsheaf, 1992.

Wilcox, Lance. "Katherine of France as Victim and Bride." *Shakespeare Studies* 17 (1985): 61–76.

Willard, Charity Cannon. "Christine de Pizan: From Poet to Political Commentator." In *Politics, Gender, and Genre.* Ed. M. Brabant, 17–33. Boulder, Colo.: Westview Press, 1992.

————. *Christine de Pizan: Her Life and Works.* New York: Persea Books, 1984.

————. "The Manuscript Tradition of the *Livre des Trois Vertus* and Christine de Pizan's Audience." *Journal of the History of Ideas* 27 (1966): 433–44.

Williams, Eric Eustace. *Capitalism and Slavery.* 1944; rpt., Chapel Hill: University of North Carolina Press, 1994.

————. *From Columbus to Castro: The History of the Caribbean, 1492–1969.* London: Deutsch, Ltd., 1970. Rpt., New York: Harper and Row, 1971; New York: Vintage Books, 1984.

Williams, Glanmor. *Recovery, Reorientation, and Reformation: Wales, c. 1415–1642.* Oxford: Clarendon Press, 1987.

Williams, Neville. *Powder and Paint: A History of the Englishwoman's Toilet, Elizabeth I–Elizabeth II.* New York: Longmans, Green, [1957].

Williams, Penry. "The Tudor State." *Past and Present* 25 (July 1963): 39–56.

Williams, Raymond. *Keywords: A Vocabulary of Culture and Society.* New York: Oxford University Press, 1976.

————. *Marxism and Literature.* Oxford: Oxford University Press, 1977.

————. *Writing in Society.* London: Verso, 1983.

Wills, Garry. *Witches and Jesuits: Shakespeare's "Macbeth."* New York: Oxford University Press, 1995.

Wilson, Margo, and Martin Daly. "The Man Who Mistook His Wife for a Chattel." In *The Adapted Mind: Evolutionary Psychology and the Generation of Culture.* Ed. Jerome H. Barkow, Leda Cosmides, and John Tooby, 289–322. New York: Oxford University Press, 1995.

Wilson, Penelope. "Classical Poetry and the Eighteenth-Century Reader." In *Books and Their Readers in Eighteenth-Century England.* Ed. Isabel Rivers, 69–96. New York: St. Martin's Press, 1982.

Wilson, R. M. "English and French in England." *History* 28 (1943): 37–60.

Wilson, Richard. "A Mingled Yarn: Shakespeare and the Cloth Workers." *Literature and History* 12, no. 2 (1986): 164–80.

Wilson, Thomas. *The rule of reason, conteinyng the arte of logike. Sette foorthe in English and newlie corrected by Thomas Wilson.* London: Imprinted by Ihon Kingston, 1554.

Winn, Colette H. "'La Loi du non-parler' dans l'*Heptaméron* de Marguerite de Navarre." *Romance Quarterly* 33, no. 2 (May 1986): 157–68.

Wisman, Josette. "L'Eveil du sentiment national au Moyen Age: La Pensée politique de Christine de Pizan." *Revue historique* 257 (1977): 289–97.

Witmer, Anne, and and John Freehafer. "Aphra Behn's Strange News from Virginia." *Library Chronicle* 34 (winter 1968): 7–23.

Wofford, Suzanne. *The Choice of Achilles: The Ideology of Figure in the Epic.* Stanford: Stanford University Press, 1992.

Wogan-Browne, Jocelyn, ed. *The Idea of the Vernacular: An Anthology of Middle English Literary Theory, 1280–1520.* University Park: Pennsylvania State University Press, 1999.

Wolff, Philippe. *Western Languages A.D. 100–1500.* Trans. Frances Partridge. New York: McGraw Hill, 1971.

Woodbine, George E. "The Language of English Law." *Speculum* 18 (1943): 395–436.

Woodbridge, Linda. *Women and the English Renaissance: Literature and the Nature of Womankind, 1540–1620.* Urbana: University of Illinois Press, 1984.

Wooldridge, Terence R. "The Birth of French Lexicography." In *A New History of French Literature.* Ed. Denis Hollier with R. Howard Bloch et al., 177–80. Cambridge, Mass.: Harvard University Press, 1989.

Wormald, Jenny. "Gunpowder, Treason, and Scots." *Journal of British Studies* 24 (April 1985): 141–68.

Woudhuysen, H. R., ed. *The Penguin Book of Renaissance Verse, 1509–1659.* Selected by David Norbrook. New York: Allen Lane, Penguin Books, 1992.

Wright, Louis B. *Middle-Class Culture in Elizabethan England.* Chapel Hill: University of North Carolina Press, 1935.

———. "The Reading of Renaissance Women." *Studies in Philology* 28 (1931): 139–56.

Wright, Nancy E. "Legal and Linguistic Coercion of Recusant Women in Early Modern England." *Yale Journal of Law and the Humanities* 5 (1993): 179–86.

Wright, Nancy, and Margaret Ferguson, eds. *Women, Property and the Letters of the Law in Early Modern England.* Toronto: University of Toronto Press, forthcoming.

Wright, Stephanie. "The Canonization of Elizabeth Cary." In *Voicing Women: Gender and Sexuality in Early Modern Writing.* Ed. Kate Chedgzoy, Melanie Hansen, and Suzanne Trill, 55–68. Keele: Keele University Press, 1996.

Wrolstad, Merald E., and Dennis F. Fisher, eds. *Toward a New Understanding of Literacy.* New York: Praeger, 1986.

Wyatt, Thomas. *Collected Poems of Sir Thomas Wyatt.* Ed. Kenneth Muir. Cambridge, Mass.: Harvard University Press, 1949.

Yates, Francis Amelia. *Astraea: The Imperial Theme in the Sixteenth Century.* London: Routledge, 1975.

Yuval-Davis, Nira, and Floya Anthias, eds. *Woman-Nation-State.* Houndmills, U.K.: Macmillan, 1989.

Zagorin, Perez. *Ways of Lying: Dissimulation, Persecution, and Conformity in Early Modern Europe.* Cambridge, Mass.: Harvard University Press, 1990.

Zernatto, Guido. "Nation: The History of a Word." *Review of Politics* 6 (1944): 351–66.

Zimmermann, Margarete, and Dina De Rentiis, eds. *The City of Scholars: New Approaches to Christine de Pizan.* European Cultures: Studies in Literature and the Arts, vol. 2. New York: Walter de Gruyter, 1994.

Zook, Melinda. "Contextualizing Aphra Behn: Plays, Politics, and Party, 1679–1689." In *Women Writers and the Early Modern British Political Tradition.* Ed. Hilda Smith, 75–94. Cambridge: Cambridge University Press, 1998.

Zühlke, Bärbel. "Christine de Pizan—Le 'Moi' dans le texte et l'image." In *The City of Scholars.* Ed. M. Zimmermann and D. De Rentiis, 232–41. New York: Walter de Gruyter, 1994.

Zwicker, Steven N. "Reading the Margins: Politics and the Habits of Appropriation." In *Refiguring Revolutions: Aesthetics and Politics from the English Revolution to the Romantic Revolution.* Ed. Kevin Sharpe and Steven N. Zwicker, 101–15. Berkeley: University of California Press, 1998.

Index

Note: Italicized page numbers indicate figures.

absolutism: challenge to, 146; reform of, 251,
255–57; reinforcement of, 329–30; resistance to,
330–32; Toryism and feminism under, 26–27;
tyrant/martyr in, 424n83. *See also* monarchy
(monarchies); tyrants
Acciaiuoli, Andrea, 189
acte de mariage (French), 77
Act for the Abolishment of the Contrary, 166
Act for the Advancement of True Religion, 166
Act of Appeals (1533), 141–43
Act of Uniformity (1559), 165–66, 167, 270
Adéèkó, Adélékè, 430n35
Adelman, Janet, 116–17
administrative vernaculars, 136
Aeneas: Dido's meeting with (or not), 19–20;
Elizabeth linked to, 334, 398n113; Henry V
compared with, 159; verbs used for, 186
Aeneid (Vergil): alternative versions and, 19–23,
26; bull's hide trick in, 221–22, 412–13n96; marginalia and, 220; Shakespeare's *Henry V* compared with, 159; translation of, 121. *See also*
Aeneas; Dido
Africans: avoiding mutiny of, 368; as ideal wife,
362–63; sexual myths about, 371–72. See also
Oroonoko (Behn); servants and slaves; slavery
age hierarchies, language use and, 59–60
agency: of Dido, 2; Great Divide theory and,
45–46; of women writers, 363–66
aggression: in literacy, hidden behind virtue, 253–
54; redirection of male, 130. *See also* arquebus;
barbarians and barbarism; colonial projects;
imperialism; slavery
agonistic rhetoric, 52
agrammatos (Greek), 63
Ailly, Pierre d', 146–48, 412n81

Alanus (commentator), 114
Albret, Jeanne d': marriage of, 248–49; mother's
stories and, 242, 246–47; Reformist movement
and, 226; rule of, 224, 231, 415n19; wedding ring
of, 316–17
Aldrete, Bernardo de, 33
Allestree, Richard, 175, *176*, 177
Allmand, Christopher, 110–11, 148–49, 401n42
allusions: to Castiglione, 256; to Elizabeth, 322–23;
to equivocation, 301–2; to Gunpowder Plot,
275–76, 299–302; to laws, 206–7; second-order
literacy in, 268
alphabet and alphabetic letters: inventor of, 216–17;
orality privileged over, 48–49; privileged over
images, 33–35; privileged over orality, 44–45
alphabetic literacy: arguments against women's
and poor men's, 261; concept of, 2; inside/
outside groups and, 12–13; as precursor to
objective thought, 49–50; standardization of
language and, 86; as tool of hegemony, 32–33
alphabétisation (French), 77, 391n94
Althusser, Louis, 383n48
Altick, Richard, 76
America, concept of, 430–31n43
Ames, Percy W., 413n102
amphibology concept, 272. *See also* equivocation
Ancekewicz, Elaine, 245, 249, 414n9
Anderson, Benedict: on birth of nationalism,
144–45; on imagined community, 136–37, 154,
398n3; on nations as bounded and unbounded,
137–38; on print capitalism, 2, 135–36; on self-
consciousness vs. unselfconsciousness, 137,
398n4
Anderson, Perry, 132–33, 138
Anglo-French language, 394n48